Handbook of Computational Social Choice

The rapidly growing field of computational social choice, at the intersection of computer science and economics, deals with the computational aspects of collective decision making. This handbook, written by thirty-six prominent members of the computational social choice community, covers the field comprehensively. Chapters devoted to each of the field's major themes offer detailed introductions. Topics include voting theory (such as the computational complexity of winner determination and manipulation in elections), fair allocation (such as algorithms for dividing divisible and indivisible goods), coalition formation (such as matching and hedonic games), and many more. Graduate students, researchers, and professionals in computer science, economics, mathematics, political science, and philosophy will benefit from this accessible and self-contained book.

Felix Brandt is Professor of Computer Science and Professor of Mathematics at Technische Universität München.

Vincent Conitzer is the Kimberly J. Jenkins University Professor of New Technologies and Professor of Computer Science, Professor of Economics, and Professor of Philosophy at Duke University.

Ulle Endriss is Associate Professor of Logic and Artificial Intelligence at the Institute for Logic, Language and Computation at the University of Amsterdam.

Jérôme Lang is a senior researcher in computer science at CNRS-LAMSADE, Université Paris-Dauphine.

Ariel D. Procaccia is Assistant Professor of Computer Science at Carnegie Mellon University.

Handbook of Computational Social Choice

Edited by

Felix Brandt
Technische Universität München

Vincent Conitzer
Duke University

Ulle Endriss
University of Amsterdam

Jérôme Lang
CNRS

Ariel D. Procaccia
Carnegie Mellon University

CAMBRIDGE
UNIVERSITY PRESS

CAMBRIDGE
UNIVERSITY PRESS

32 Avenue of the Americas, New York, NY 10013-2473, USA

Cambridge University Press is part of the University of Cambridge.

It furthers the University's mission by disseminating knowledge in the pursuit of
education, learning, and research at the highest international levels of excellence.

www.cambridge.org
Information on this title: www.cambridge.org/9781107060432

First published 2016

Printed in the United States of America

A catalog record for this publication is available from the British Library.

Library of Congress Cataloging in Publication Data

Handbook of computational social choice / edited by Felix Brandt, Technische Universität
München, Vincent Conitzer, Duke University, Ulle Endriss, University of Amsterdam, Jérôme
Lang, CNRS, Ariel D. Procaccia, Carnegie Mellon University.
    pages   cm
Includes bibliographical references and index.
ISBN 978-1-107-06043-2 (alk. paper)
1. Social choice.   2. Interdisciplinary research.   3. Computer science.   I. Brandt, Felix, 1973–
editor.
HB846.8.H33   2016
302′.130285 – dc23   2015030289

Contents

Part III   Coalition Formation

Part IV   Additional Topics

Foreword

Hervé Moulin

Axiomatics and algorithmics are two methodologies at the forefront of modern mathematics. The latter goes back to the very birth of mathematics, whereas the former was not developed until Hilbert's famous contributions in the late 1800s.

Yet the axiomatic approach was the first to appear in modern social sciences, through the instant success in 1951 of K. Arrow's *Social Choice and Individual Values*. Beyond the negative, discouraging message of its famous (im)possibility theorem, that book had an immensely positive influence on the development of mathematical economics. It opened the way to the critical evaluation of actual democratic institutions through the filter of "self-evident" normative principles. Conversely, it allowed us to define "optimal" rules for collective decision making and/or the allocation of scarce resources by the convergence of a collection of such principles. In short, it started the field of *mechanism design*.

Cake division is probably the first instance of an economic model with an algorithmic twist. The mathematical statement of the problem goes back to B. Knaster and H. Steinhaus in the 1940s: it combines the normative choice of fairness axioms with the algorithmic concern for a protocol made of simple "cut and choose" operations. This literature did not have noticeable influence on the exponential development of mechanism design in the last 40 years, in part because it was developed mostly by mathematicians. Computational social choice will, I believe, bring it out from its relative obscurity.

In less than two decades, the COMSOC community has generated an intense dialogue between economists working on the normative side of mechanism design and computer scientists poised to test the computational complexity of these mechanisms. A remarkable side product of this collaboration is clear from the choice of the 19 thorough chapters. Under a common axiomatic and computational umbrella, they discuss

- the social choice problem of selecting a public outcome from the conflicting opinions of the citizens
- the microeconomic problem of dividing private commodities fairly and efficiently when individual preferences differ

- the market design problem of (bilaterally) matching employees to firms, students to schools, and so on
- the design of reputation indices and ranking methods in peer-to-peer systems such as the Internet
- the formation and stability of "local public goods," that is, (hedonic) coalitions of agents with common interests

The relative weights of these problems are naturally quite unequal, but the point is their coexistence.

The book offers to noneconomists an outstanding self-contained introduction to normative themes in contemporary economics and to economists a thorough discussion of the computational limits of their art. But I also recommend it to anyone with a taste for axiomatics: it is replete with new and open questions that will be with us for some time.

Contributors

Haris Aziz NICTA and University of New South Wales, Sydney, Australia

Craig Boutilier Department of Computer Science, University of Toronto, Canada

Sylvain Bouveret Laboratoire d'Informatique de Grenoble, Université Grenoble-Alpes, France

Felix Brandt Institut für Informatik, Technische Universität München, Germany

Markus Brill Department of Computer Science, Duke University, United States of America

Ioannis Caragiannis Department of Computer Engineering and Informatics, University of Patras, Greece

Georgios Chalkiadakis School of Electronic and Computer Engineering, Technical University of Crete, Greece

Yann Chevaleyre Laboratoire d'Informatique de Paris Nord, Université Paris-Nord, France

Vincent Conitzer Department of Computer Science, Duke University, United States of America

Edith Elkind Department of Computer Science, University of Oxford, United Kingdom

Ulle Endriss Institute for Logic, Language and Computation (ILLC), University of Amsterdam, The Netherlands

Piotr Faliszewski Katedra Informatyki, AGH University of Science and Technology, Poland

Felix Fischer Statistical Laboratory, University of Cambridge, United Kingdom

Paul Harrenstein Department of Computer Science, University of Oxford, United Kingdom

Edith Hemaspaandra Department of Computer Science, Rochester Institute of Technology, United States of America

Lane A. Hemaspaandra Department of Computer Science, University of Rochester, United States of America

Olivier Hudry Institut Mines-Télécom, Télécom ParisTech and CNRS, France

Bettina Klaus Faculty of Business and Economics, University of Lausanne, Switzerland

Jérôme Lang Laboratoire d'Analyse et Modélisation de Systèmes pour l'Aide à la Decision (LAMSADE), CNRS and Université Paris-Dauphine, France

David F. Manlove School of Computing Science, University of Glasgow, United Kingdom

Nicolas Maudet Sorbonne Universités, UPMC Univ. Paris 06, CNRS, LIP6 UMR 7606, France

Rolf Niedermeier Fakultät Elektrotechnik und Informatik, Technische Universität Berlin, Germany

Ariel D. Procaccia Computer Science Department, Carnegie Mellon University, United States of America

Jeffrey S. Rosenschein School of Computer Science and Engineering, The Hebrew University of Jerusalem, Israel

Francesca Rossi Department of Mathematics, University of Padova, Italy

Jörg Rothe Institut für Informatik, Heinrich-Heine-Universität Düsseldorf, Germany

Rahul Savani Department of Computer Science, University of Liverpool, United Kingdom

Arkadii Slinko Department of Mathematics, University of Auckland, New Zealand

Moshe Tennenholtz Faculty of Industrial Engineering and Management, Technion–Israel Institute of Technology, Israel

William Thomson Department of Economics, University of Rochester, United States of America

Toby Walsh University of New South Wales and NICTA, Sydney, Australia

Virginia Vassilevska Williams Computer Science Department, Stanford University, United States of America

Michael Wooldridge Department of Computer Science, University of Oxford, United Kingdom

Lirong Xia Computer Science Department, Rensselaer Polytechnic Institute, United States of America

Aviv Zohar School of Computer Science and Engineering, The Hebrew University of Jerusalem, Israel

William S. Zwicker Department of Mathematics, Union College, United States of America

CHAPTER 1

Introduction to Computational Social Choice

Felix Brandt, Vincent Conitzer, Ulle Endriss,
Jérôme Lang, and Ariel D. Procaccia

1.1 Computational Social Choice at a Glance

Social choice theory is the field of scientific inquiry that studies the aggregation of individual preferences toward a collective choice. For example, social choice theorists—who hail from a range of different disciplines, including mathematics, economics, and political science—are interested in the design and theoretical evaluation of voting rules. Questions of social choice have stimulated intellectual thought for centuries. Over time, the topic has fascinated many a great mind, from the Marquis de Condorcet and Pierre-Simon de Laplace, through Charles Dodgson (better known as Lewis Carroll, the author of *Alice in Wonderland*), to Nobel laureates such as Kenneth Arrow, Amartya Sen, and Lloyd Shapley.

Computational social choice (COMSOC), by comparison, is a very young field that formed only in the early 2000s. There were, however, a few precursors. For instance, David Gale and Lloyd Shapley's algorithm for finding stable matchings between two groups of people with preferences over each other, dating back to 1962, truly had a computational flavor. And in the late 1980s, a series of papers by John Bartholdi, Craig Tovey, and Michael Trick showed that, on the one hand, computational complexity, as studied in theoretical computer science, can serve as a barrier against strategic manipulation in elections, but on the other hand, it can also prevent the efficient use of some voting rules altogether. Around the same time, a research group around Bernard Monjardet and Olivier Hudry also started to study the computational complexity of preference aggregation procedures.

Assessing the computational difficulty of determining the output of a voting rule, or of manipulating it, is a wonderful example of the importation of a concept from one field, theoretical computer science, to what at that time was still considered an entirely different one, social choice theory. It is this interdisciplinary view on collective decision making that defines computational social choice as a field. But, importantly, the contributions of computer science to social choice theory are not restricted to the design and analysis of algorithms for preexisting social choice problems. Rather, the arrival of computer science on the scene led researchers to revisit the old problem of

1

social choice from scratch. It offered new perspectives, and it led to many new types of questions, thereby arguably contributing significantly to a revival of social choice theory as a whole.

Today, research in computational social choice has two main thrusts. First, researchers seek to apply computational paradigms and techniques to provide a better analysis of social choice mechanisms, and to construct new ones. Leveraging the theory of computer science, we see applications of computational complexity theory and approximation algorithms to social choice. Subfields of artificial intelligence, such as machine learning, reasoning with uncertainty, knowledge representation, search, and constraint reasoning, have also been applied to the same end.

Second, researchers are studying the application of social choice theory to computational environments. For example, it has been suggested that social choice theory can provide tools for making joint decisions in multiagent system populated by heterogeneous, possibly selfish, software agents. Moreover, it is finding applications in group recommendation systems, information retrieval, and crowdsourcing. Although it is difficult to change a political voting system, such low-stake environments allow the designer to freely switch between choice mechanisms, and therefore they provide an ideal test bed for ideas coming from social choice theory.

This book aims to provide an authoritative overview of the field of computational social choice. It has been written for students and scholars from both computer science and economics, as well as for others from the mathematical and social sciences more broadly. To position the field in its wider context, in Section 1.2, we provide a brief review of the history of social choice theory. The structure of the book reflects the internal structure of the field. We provide an overview of this structure by briefly introducing each of the remaining 18 chapters of the book in Section 1.3. As computational social choice is still rapidly developing and expanding in scope every year, naturally, the coverage of the book cannot be exhaustive. Section 1.4 therefore briefly introduces a number of important active areas of research that, at the time of conceiving this book, were not yet sufficiently mature to warrant their own chapters. Section 1.5, finally, introduces some basic concepts from theoretical computer science, notably the fundamentals of computational complexity theory, with which some readers may not be familiar.

1.2 History of Social Choice Theory

Modern research in computational social choice builds on a long tradition of work on collective decision making. We can distinguish three periods in the study of collective decision making: early ideas regarding specific rules going back to antiquity; the classical period, witnessing the development of a general mathematical theory of social choice in the second half of the twentieth century; and the "computational turn" of the very recent past. We briefly review each of these three periods by providing a small selection of illustrative examples.

1.2.1 Early Ideas: Rules and Paradoxes

Collective decision-making problems come in many forms. They include the question of how to fairly divide a set of resources, how to best match people on the basis of their preferences, and how to aggregate the beliefs of several individuals. The paradigmatic example, however, is voting: how should we aggregate the individual preferences of several voters over a given set of alternatives so as to be able to choose the "best" alternative for the group? This important question has been pondered by a number of thinkers for a long time. Also the largest part of this book, Part I, is devoted to voting. We therefore start our historic review of social choice theory with a discussion of early ideas pertaining to voting.[1]

Our first example for the discussion of a problem in voting goes back to Roman times. Pliny the Younger, a Roman senator, described in A.D. 105 the following problem in a letter to an acquaintance. The Senate had to decide on the fate of a number of prisoners: acquittal (*A*), banishment (*B*), or condemnation to death (*C*). Although option *A*, favored by Pliny, had the largest number of supporters, it did not have an absolute majority. One of the proponents of harsh punishment then strategically moved to withdraw proposal *C*, leaving its former supporters to rally behind option *B*, which easily won the majority contest between *A* and *B*. Had the senators voted on all three options, using the *plurality rule* (under which the alternative ranked at the top by the highest number of voters wins), option *A* would have won. This example illustrates several interesting features of voting rules. First, it may be interpreted as demonstrating a lack of fairness of the plurality rule: even though a majority of voters believes *A* to be inferior to one of the other options (namely, *B*), *A* still wins. This and other fairness properties of voting rules are reviewed in Chapter 2. Second, Pliny's anecdote is an instance of what nowadays is called *election control by deleting candidates*. By deleting *C*, Pliny's adversary in the senate was able to ensure that *B* rather than *A* won the election. Such control problems, particularly their algorithmic aspects, are discussed in Chapter 7. Third, the example also illustrates the issue of *strategic manipulation*. Even if option *C* had not been removed, the supporters of *C* could have manipulated the election by pretending that they supported *B* rather than *C*, thereby ensuring a preferred outcome, namely, *B* rather than *A*. Manipulation is discussed in depth in Chapters 2 and 6.

In the Middle Ages, the Catalan philosopher, poet, and missionary Ramon Llull (1232–1316) discussed voting rules in several of his writings. He supported the idea that election outcomes should be based on direct majority contests between pairs of candidates. Such voting rules are discussed in detail in Chapter 3. What exact rule he had in mind cannot be unambiguously reconstructed anymore, but it may have been the rule that today is known as the *Copeland rule*, under which the candidate who wins the largest number of pairwise majority contests is elected. Whereas Pliny specifically discussed the subjective interests of the participants, Llull saw voting as a means of revealing the divine truth about who is the objectively best candidate, for example, to fill the position of abbess in a convent. The mathematical underpinnings of this *epistemic perspective* on voting are discussed in Chapter 8.

Our third example is taken from the period of the Enlightenment. The works of the French engineer Jean-Charles de Borda (1733–1799) and the French philosopher and mathematician Marie Jean Antoine Nicolas de Caritat (1743–1794), better known

---

[1] There are also instances of very early writings on other aspects of social choice. A good example is the discussion of fair division problems in the Talmud, as noted and analyzed in modern terms by game theorists Aumann and Maschler (1985).

as the Marquis de Condorcet—and particularly the lively dispute between them—are widely regarded as the most significant contributions to social choice theory in the early period of the field. In 1770, Borda proposed a method of voting, today known as the *Borda rule*, under which each voter ranks all candidates, and each candidate receives as may points from a given voter as that voter ranks other candidates below her. He argued for the superiority of his rule over the plurality rule by discussing an example similar to that of Pliny, where the plurality winner would lose in a direct majority contest to another candidate, while the Borda winner does not have that deficiency. But Condorcet argued against Borda's rule on very similar grounds. Consider the following scenario with 3 candidates and 11 voters, which is a simplified version of an example Condorcet described in 1788:

4	3	2	2
Peter	Paul	Paul	James
Paul	James	Peter	Peter
James	Peter	James	Paul

In this example, four voters prefer candidate Peter over candidate Paul, whom they prefer over candidate James, and so forth. Paul wins this election both under the plurality rule (with $3 + 2 = 5$ points) and the Borda rule (with $4 \cdot 1 + 3 \cdot 2 + 2 \cdot 2 + 2 \cdot 0 = 14$ points). However, a majority of voters (namely, 6 out of 11) prefer Peter to Paul. In fact, Peter also wins against James in a direct majority contest, so there arguably is a very strong case for rejecting voting rules that would not elect Peter in this situation. In today's terminology, we call Peter the *Condorcet winner*.

Now suppose two additional voters join the election, who both prefer James, to Peter, to Paul. Then a majority prefers Peter to Paul, and a majority prefers Paul to James, but now also a majority prefers James to Peter. This, the fact that the majority preference relation may turn out to be cyclic, is known as the *Condorcet paradox*. It shows that Condorcet's proposal, to be guided by the outcomes of pairwise majority contests, does not always lead to a clear election outcome.

In the nineteenth century, the British mathematician and story teller Charles Dodgson (1832–1898), although believed to have been unaware of Condorcet's work, suggested a voting rule designed to circumvent this difficulty. In cases where there is a single candidate who beats every other candidate in pairwise majority contests, he proposed to elect that candidate (the Condorcet winner). In all other cases, he proposed to count how many elementary changes to the preferences of the voters would be required before a given candidate would become the Condorcet winner, and to elect the candidate for which the required number of changes is minimal. In this context, he considered the swap of two candidates occurring adjacently in the preference list of a voter as such an elementary change. The *Dodgson rule* is analyzed in detail in Chapter 5.

This short review, it is hoped, gives the reader some insight into the kinds of questions discussed by the early authors. The first period in the history of social choice theory is reviewed in depth in the fascinating collection edited by McLean and Urken (1995).

1.2.2 Classical Social Choice Theory

While early work on collective decision making was limited to the design of specific rules and on finding fault with them in the context of specific examples, around the middle of the twentieth century, the focus suddenly changed. This change was due to the seminal work of Kenneth Arrow, who, in 1951, demonstrated that the problem with the majority rule highlighted by the Condorcet paradox is in fact much more general. Arrow proved that there exists no reasonable preference aggregation rule that does not violate at least one of a short list of intuitively appealing requirements (Arrow, 1951). That is, rather than proposing a new rule or pointing out a specific problem with an existing rule, Arrow developed a mathematical framework for speaking about and analyzing all possible such rules.

Around the same time, in related areas of economic theory, Nash (1950) published his seminal paper on the bargaining problem, which is relevant to the theory of fair allocation treated in Part II of this book, and Shapley (1953) published his groundbreaking paper on the solution concept for cooperative games now carrying his name, which plays an important role in coalition formation, to which Part III of this book is devoted. What all of these classical papers have in common is that they specified philosophically or economically motivated requirements in mathematically precise terms, as so-called *axioms*, and then rigorously explored the logical consequences of these axioms. As an example of this kind of axiomatic work of this classical period, let us review Arrow's result in some detail.

Let $N = \{1, \ldots, n\}$ be a finite set of *individuals* (or *voters*, or *agents*), and let A be a finite set of *alternatives* (or *candidates*). The set of all *weak orders* $\succsim$ on A, that is, the set of all binary relations on A that are complete and transitive, is denoted as $\mathcal{R}(A)$, and the set of all *linear orders* $\succsim$ on A, which in addition are antisymmetric, is denoted as $\mathcal{L}(A)$. In both cases, we use $\succ$ to denote the strict part of $\succsim$. We use weak orders to model preferences over alternatives that permit ties and linear orders to model strict preferences. A *social welfare function* (SWF) is a function of the form $f : \mathcal{L}(A)^n \to \mathcal{R}(A)$. That is, f is accepting as input a so-called *profile* $P = (\succsim_1, \ldots, \succsim_n)$ of preferences, one for each individual, and maps it to a single preference order, which we can think of as representing a suitable compromise. We allow ties in the output, but not in the individual preferences. When f is clear from the context, we write $\succsim$ for $f(\succsim_1, \ldots, \succsim_n)$, the outcome of the aggregation, and refer to it as the *social preference order*.

Arrow argued that any reasonable SWF should be *weakly Paretian* and *independent of irrelevant alternatives* (IIA). An SWF f is weakly Paretian if, for any two alternatives $a, b \in A$, it is the case that, if $a \succ_i b$ for all individuals $i \in N$, then also $a \succ b$. That is, if everyone strictly prefers a to b, then also the social preference order should rank a strictly above b. An SWF f is IIA if, for any two alternatives $a, b \in A$, the relative ranking of a and b by the social preference order $\succsim$ only depends on the relative rankings of a and b provided by the individuals—but not, for instance, on how the individuals rank some third alternative c. To understand that it is not straightforward to satisfy these two axioms, observe that, for instance, the SWF that ranks alternatives in the order of frequency with which they appear in the top position of an individual preference is not IIA, and that the SWF that simply declares all alternatives as equally preferable is not Paretian. The majority rule, while easily seen to be both Paretian and IIA, is not an SWF, because it does not always return a weak order, as the Condorcet paradox has shown.

An example of an SWF that most people would consider rather unreasonable is a *dictatorship*. We say that the SWF f is a dictatorship if there exists an individual

$i^\star \in N$ (the dictator) such that, for all alternatives $a, b \in A$, it is the case that $a \succ_{i^\star} b$ implies $a \succ b$. Thus, f simply copies the (strict) preferences of the dictator, whatever the preferences of the other individuals. Now, it is not difficult to see that every dictatorship is both Paretian and IIA. The surprising—if not outright disturbing—result due to Arrow is that the converse is true as well:

Theorem 1.1 (Arrow, 1951). *When there are three or more alternatives, then every SWF that is weakly Paretian and IIA must be a dictatorship.*

Proof. Suppose $|A| \geqslant 3$, and let f be any SWF that is weakly Paretian and IIA. For any profile P and alternatives $a, b \in A$, let $N_{a \succ b}^P \subseteq N$ denote the set of individuals who rank a strictly above b in P. We call a coalition $C \subseteq N$ of individuals a *decisive coalition* for alternative a versus alternative b if $N_{a \succ b}^P \supseteq C$ implies $a \succ b$, that is, if everyone in C ranking a strictly above b is a sufficient condition for the social preference order to do the same. Thus, to say that f is weakly Paretian is the same as to say that the grand coalition N is decisive, and to say that f is dictatorial is the same as to say that there exists a singleton that is decisive. We call C *weakly decisive* for a vs. b if we have at least that $N_{a \succ b}^P = C$ implies $a \succ b$.

We first show that C being weakly decisive for a versus b implies C being (not just weakly) decisive for *all* pairs of alternatives. This is sometimes called the *Contagion Lemma* or the *Field Expansion Lemma*. So let C be weakly decisive for a versus b. We show that C is also decisive for a' versus b'. We do so under the assumption that a, b, a', b' are mutually distinct (the other cases are similar). Consider any profile P such that $a' \succ_i a \succ_i b \succ_i b'$ for all $i \in C$, and $a' \succ_j a$, $b \succ_j b'$, and $b \succ_j a$ for all $j \notin C$. Then, from weak decisiveness of C for a versus b we get $a \succ b$; from f being weakly Paretian, we get $a' \succ a$ and $b \succ b'$, and thus from transitivity, we get $a' \succ b'$. Hence, in the specific profile P considered, the members of C ranking a' above b' was sufficient for a' getting ranked above b' also in the social preference order. But note that, first, we did not have to specify how individuals outside of C rank a' versus b', and that, second, due to f being IIA, the relative ranking of a' versus b' can only depend on the individual rankings of a' versus b'. Hence, the only part of our construction that actually mattered was that everyone in C ranked a' above b'. So C really is decisive for a' versus b' as claimed.

Consider any coalition $C \subseteq N$ with $|C| \geqslant 2$ that is decisive (for some pair of alternatives, and thus for all pairs). Next, we will show that we can always split C into two nonempty subsets C_1, C_2 with $C_1 \cup C_2 = C$ and $C_1 \cap C_2 = \emptyset$ such that one of C_1 and C_2 is decisive for all pairs as well. This is sometimes called the *Splitting Lemma* or the *Group Contraction Lemma*. Recall that $|A| \geqslant 3$. Consider a profile P in which everyone ranks alternatives a, b, c in the top three positions and, furthermore, $a \succ_i b \succ_i c$ for all $i \in C_1$, $b \succ_j c \succ_j a$ for all $j \in C_2$, and $c \succ_k a \succ_k b$ for all $k \notin C_1 \cup C_2$. As $C = C_1 \cup C_2$ is decisive, we certainly get $b \succ c$. By completeness, we must have either $a \succ c$ or $c \succsim a$. In the first case, we have a situation where exactly the individuals in C_1 rank a above c and in the social preference order a also is ranked above c. Thus, due to f being IIA, in *every* profile where exactly the individuals in C_1 rank a above c, a will come out above c. That is, C_1 is weakly decisive for a versus c. Hence, by the Contagion Lemma, C_1 is in fact decisive for all pairs. In the second case

$(c \succsim a)$, transitivity and $b \succ c$ imply that $b \succ a$. Hence, by an analogous argument as before, C_2 must be decisive for all pairs.

Recall that, due to f being weakly Paretian, N is a decisive coalition. We can now apply the Splitting Lemma again and again, to obtain smaller and smaller decisive coalitions, until we obtain a decisive coalition with just a single member. This inductive argument is admissible, because N is finite. But the existence of a decisive coalition with just one element means that f is dictatorial. $\qquad\square$

Arrow's Theorem is often interpreted as an impossibility result: it is impossible to devise an SWF for three or more alternatives that is weakly Paretian, IIA, and nondictatorial. The technique we have used to prove it is also used in Chapter 2 on voting theory and in Chapter 17 on judgment aggregation. These chapters also discuss possible approaches for dealing with such impossibilities by weakening our requirements somewhat.

The authoritative reference on classical social choice theory is the two-volume *Handbook of Social Choice and Welfare* edited by Arrow et al. (2002, 2010). There also are several excellent textbooks available, each covering a good portion of the field. These include the books by Moulin (1988a), Austen-Smith and Banks (2000, 2005), Taylor (2005), Gaertner (2006), and Nitzan (2010).

1.2.3 The Computational Turn

As indicated, Arrow's Theorem (from 1951) is generally considered the birth of modern social choice theory. The work that followed mainly consisted in *axiomatic*, or *normative*, results. Some of these are negative (Arrow's Theorem being an example). Others have a more positive flavor, such as the characterization of certain voting rules, or certain families of voting rules, by a set of properties. However, a common point is that these contributions (mostly published in economics or mathematics journals) neglected the *computational* effort required to determine the outcome of the rules they sought to characterize, and failed to notice that this computational effort could sometimes be prohibitive. Now, the practical acceptability of a voting rule or a fair allocation mechanism depends not only on its normative properties (who would accept a voting rule that is considered unfair by society?), but also on its implementability in a reasonable time frame (who would accept a voting rule that needs years for the outcome to be computed?). This is where computer science comes into play, starting in the late 1980s. For the first time, social choice became a field investigated by computer scientists from various fields (especially artificial intelligence, operations research, and theoretical computer science) who aimed at using computational concepts and algorithmic techniques for solving complex collective decision making problems.

A paradigmatic example is *Kemeny's rule*, studied in detail in Chapter 4. Kemeny's rule was not explicitly defined during the early phase of social choice, but it appears implicitly in Condorcet's works, as discussed, for instance, in Chapter 8. It played a key role in the second phase of social choice: it was defined formally by John G. Kemeny in 1959, characterized axiomatically by H. Peyton Young and Arthur B. Levenglick in 1978, and rationalized as a maximum likelihood estimator for recovering the ground truth by means of voting in a committee by Young in 1988. Finally, it was recognized as a computationally difficult rule, independently and around the same time (the "early phase of computational social choice") by John Bartholdi, Craig Tovey, and Michael Trick, as well as by Olivier Hudry and others. None of these papers, however, succeeded in determining the exact complexity of Kemeny's rule, which was done only in 2005, at the time when computational social choice was starting to expand rapidly. Next came practical algorithms for computing Kemeny's rule, polynomial-time algorithms for approximating it, parameterized complexity studies, and applications to various fields, such as databases or "web science." We took Kemeny's rule as an example, but there are similar stories to be told about other preference aggregation rules, as well as for various fair allocation and matching mechanisms.

Deciding when computational social choice first appeared is not easy. Arguably, the Gale-Shapley algorithm (1962), discussed in Chapter 14, deals both with social choice and with computation (and even with communication, since it can also be seen as an interaction protocol for determining a stable matching). Around the same time, the Dubins-Spanier Algorithm (Dubins-Spanier, 1961), discussed in Chapter 13, was one of the first important contributions in the formal study of cake cutting, that is, of fairly partitioning a divisible resource (again, this "algorithm" can also be seen as an interaction protocol). Just as for preference aggregation, the first computational studies appeared in the late 1980s. Finally, although formal computational studies of the fair allocation of indivisible goods appeared only in the early 2000s, they are heavily linked to computational issues in combinatorial auctions, the study of which dates back to the 1980s.

By the early 2000s this trend toward studying collective decision making in the tradition of classical social choice theory, yet with a specific focus on computational concerns, had reached substantial momentum. Researchers coming from different fields and working on different specific problems started to see the parallels to the work of others. The time was ripe for a new research community to form around these ideas. In 2006 the first edition of the COMSOC Workshop, the biannual International Workshop on Computational Social Choice, took place in Amsterdam. The announcement of this event was also the first time that the term *computational social choice* was used explicitly to define a specific research area.

Today, computational social choice is a booming field, carried by a large and growing community of active researchers, making use of a varied array of methodologies to tackle a broad range of questions. There is increasing interaction with representatives of classical social choice theory in economics, mathematics, and political science. There is also increasing awareness of the great potential of computational social choice for important applications of decision-making technologies, in areas as diverse as policy making (e.g., matching junior doctors to hospitals), distributed computing (e.g., allocating bandwidth to processes), and education (e.g., aggregating student evaluations gathered by means of peer assessment methods). Work on computational social choice is regularly published in major journals in artificial intelligence, theoretical computer science, operations research, and economic theory—and occasionally also in other disciplines, such as logic, philosophy, and mathematics. As is common practice in computer science, a lot of work in the field is also published in the archival proceedings of peer-reviewed conferences, particularly the major international conferences on artificial intelligence, multiagent systems, and economics and computation.

1.3 Book Outline

This book is divided into four parts, reflecting the structure of the field of computational social choice. Part I, taking up roughly half of the book, focuses on the design and analysis of voting rules (which aggregate individual preferences into a collective decision). The room given to this topic here mirrors the breadth and depth with which the problem of voting has been studied to date.

The remaining three parts consist of three chapters each. Part II covers the problem of allocating goods to individuals with heterogeneous preferences in a way that satisfies rigorous notions of fairness. We make the distinction between divisible and indivisible goods. Part III addresses questions that arise when agents can form coalitions and each have preferences over these coalitions. This includes two-sided matching problems (e.g., between junior doctors seeking an internship and hospitals), hedonic games (where agents' preferences depend purely on the members of the coalition they are part of), and weighted voting games (where coalitions emerge to achieve some goal, such as passing a bill in parliament).

Much of classical (noncomputational) social choice theory deals with voting (Part I). In contrast, fair allocation (Part II) and coalition formation (Part III) are not always seen as subfields of (classical) social choice theory, but, interestingly, their intersection with computer science has become part of the core of computational social choice, due to sociological reasons having to do with how the research community addressing these topics has evolved over the years.

Part IV, finally, covers topics that did not neatly fit into the first three thematic parts. It includes chapters on logic-based judgment aggregation, on applications of the axiomatic method to reputation and recommendation systems found on the Internet, and on knockout tournaments (as used, for instance, in sports competitions). Next, we provide a brief overview of each of the book's chapters.

1.3.1 Part I: Voting

Chapter 2: Introduction to the Theory of Voting (Zwicker). This chapter provides an introduction to the main classical themes in voting theory. This includes the definition of the most important voting rules, such as Borda's, Copeland's, and Kemeny's rule. It also includes an extensive introduction to the axiomatic method and proves several characterization and impossibility theorems, thereby complementing our brief exposition in Section 1.2.2. Special attention is paid to the topic of strategic manipulation in elections.

Chapter 2 also introduces Fishburn's classification of voting rules. Fishburn used this classification to structure the set of Condorcet extensions, the family of rules that respect the principle attributed to the Marquis de Condorcet, by which any alternative that beats all other alternatives in direct pairwise contests should be considered the winner of the election. Fishburn's classification groups these Condorcet extensions into three classes—imaginatively called C1, C2, and C3—and the following three chapters each present methods and results pertaining to one of these classes.

Chapter 3: Tournament Solutions (Brandt, Brill, and Harrenstein). This chapter deals with voting rules that only depend on pairwise majority comparisons, so-called

C1 functions. Pairwise comparisons can be conveniently represented using directed graphs. When there is an odd number of voters with linear preferences, these graphs are tournaments, that is, oriented complete graphs. Topics covered in this chapter include McGarvey's Theorem, various tournament solutions (such as Copeland's rule, the top cycle, or the bipartisan set), strategyproofness, implementation via binary agendas, and extensions of tournament solutions to weak tournaments. Particular attention is paid to the issue of whether and how tournament solutions can be computed efficiently.

Chapter 4: Weighted Tournament Solutions (Fischer, Hudry, and Niedermeier). This chapter deals with voting rules that only depend on weighted pairwise majority comparisons, so-called C2 functions. Pairwise comparisons can be conveniently represented using weighted directed graphs, where the weight of an edge from alternative x to alternative y is the number of voters who prefer x to y. Prominent voting rules of type C2 are Kemeny's rule, the maximin rule, the ranked pairs method, Schulze's method, and—anecdotally—Borda's rule. The chapter focusses on the computation, approximation, and fixed-parameter tractability of these rules, while paying particular attention to Kemeny's rule.

Chapter 5: Dodgson's Rule and Young's Rule (Caragiannis, Hemaspaandra, and Hemaspaandra). This chapter focuses on two historically significant voting rules belonging to C3, the class of voting rules requiring strictly more information than a weighted directed graph, with computationally hard winner determination problems. The complexity of this problem is analyzed in depth. Methods for circumventing this intractability—approximation algorithms, fixed-parameter tractable algorithms, and heuristic algorithms—are also discussed.

The remaining five chapters in Part I all focus on specific methodologies for the analysis of voting rules.

Chapter 6: Barriers to Manipulation in Voting (Conitzer and Walsh). This chapter concerns the manipulation problem, where a voter misreports her preferences in order to obtain a better result for herself, and how to address it. It covers the Gibbard-Satterthwaite impossibility result, which roughly states that manipulation cannot be completely avoided in sufficiently general settings, and its implications. It then covers some ways of addressing this problem, focusing primarily on erecting computational barriers to manipulation—one of the earliest lines of research in computational social choice, as alluded to before.

Chapter 7: Control and Bribery in Voting (Faliszewski and Rothe). Control and bribery are variants of manipulation, typically seen as carried out by the election organizer. Paradigmatic examples of control include adding or removing voters or alternatives. Bribery changes the structure of voters' preferences, without changing the structure of the entire election. This chapter presents results regarding the computational complexity of bribery and control problems under a variety of voting rules. Much like Chapter 6, the hope here is to obtain computational hardness in order to prevent strategic behavior.

Chapter 8: Rationalizations of Voting Rules (Elkind and Slinko). While the best-known approach in social choice to justify a particular voting rule is the axiomatic one, several other approaches have also been popular in the computational social choice community. This chapter covers the *maximum likelihood* approach, which takes it that there is an unobserved "correct" outcome and that a voting rule should be chosen to best estimate this outcome (based on the votes, which are interpreted as "noisy observations" of this correct outcome). It also covers the *distance rationalizability* approach, where, given a profile of cast votes, we find the closest "consensus" profile which has a clear winner.

Chapter 9: Voting in Combinatorial Domains (Lang and Xia). This chapter addresses voting in domains that are the Cartesian product of several finite domains, each corresponding to an issue, or a variable, or an attribute. Examples of contexts where such voting processes occur include multiple referenda, committee (and more generally multi-winner) elections, group configuration, and group planning. The chapter presents basic notions of preference relations on multiattribute domains, and it outlines several classes of solutions for addressing the problem of organizing an election in such a domain: issue-by-issue and sequential voting, multiwinner voting rules, and the use of compact representation languages.

Chapter 10: Incomplete Information and Communication in Voting (Boutilier and Rosenschein). This chapter unifies several advanced topics, which generally revolve around quantifying the amount of information about preferences that is needed to accurately decide an election. Topics covered include the complexity of determining whether a given alternative is still a possible winner after part of the voter preferences have been processed, strategies for effectively eliciting voter preferences for different voting rules, voting in the presence of uncertainty regarding the availability of alternatives, the sample complexity of learning voting rules, and the problem of "compiling" the votes of part of the electorate using as little space a possible for further processing at a later point in time.

1.3.2 Part II: Fair Allocation

Chapter 11: Introduction to the Theory of Fair Allocation (Thomson). This chapter offers an introduction to fair resource allocation problems as studied in economics. While in most models of voting the alternatives are not structured in any particular way, in resource allocation problems the space of feasible alternatives naturally comes with a lot of internal structure. The chapter motivates and defines a wide range of fairness criteria that are relevant to such problems, for different concretely specified economic environments.

While Chapter 11 is restricted to concepts classically studied in economic theory, the next two chapters zoom in on specific classes of resource allocation problems and focus on work of a computational nature.

Chapter 12: Fair Allocation of Indivisible Goods (Bouveret, Chevaleyre, and Maudet). This chapter addresses the fair allocation of indivisible goods. The main topics covered are the compact representation of preferences for fair allocation problems (typically, though not always, using utility functions rather than ordinal preference relations as in voting), the definition of appropriate fairness criteria, the algorithmic challenges of computing socially optimal allocations, complexity results for computing socially optimal allocations, and protocols for identifying such optimal allocations in an interactive manner.

Chapter 13: Cake Cutting Algorithms (Procaccia). This chapter deals with fair allocation of heterogeneous divisible goods, also known as cake cutting. This is quite different from the indivisible goods case, especially when taking the computational perspective, because utility functions may not have a finite discrete representation. The chapter discusses models for reasoning about the complexity of cake cutting. Furthermore, the chapter covers classical cake cutting methods, as well as recent work on optimization and the tension between efficiency and fairness in cake cutting.

1.3.3 Part III: Coalition Formation

Chapter 14: Matching under Preferences (Klaus, Manlove, and Rossi). This chapter covers matching theory, starting with the setting where each side has preferences over the other side, which includes the traditional example of matching men to women but also the real-world application of matching residents (junior doctors) to hospitals. It then covers the setting where only one side has preferences over the other, which includes examples such as assigning students to campus housing and assigning papers to reviewers. The chapter covers structural, algorithmic, and strategic aspects.

Chapter 15: Hedonic Games (Aziz and Savani). Matching under preferences can be seen as a special case of coalition formation which only allows for certain types of coalitions (e.g., coalitions of size two). Hedonic games are more general in the sense that any coalition structure (i.e., any partitioning of the set of agents into subsets) is feasible. The defining property of hedonic games is that an agent's appreciation of a coalition structure only depends on the coalition he is a member of and not on how the remaining players are grouped. This chapter surveys the computational aspects of various notions of coalitional stability (such as core stability, Nash stability, and individual stability) in common classes of hedonic games.

Chapter 16: Weighted Voting Games (Chalkiadakis and Wooldridge). Weighted voting games model situations where voters with variable voting weight accept or reject a proposal, and a coalition of agents is winning if and only if the sum of weights of the coalition exceeds or equals a specified quota. This chapter covers the computation of solution concepts for weighted voting games, the relation between weight and influence, and the expressive power of weighted voting games.

1.3.4 Part IV: Additional Topics

Chapter 17: Judgment Aggregation (Endriss). This chapter provides an introduction to judgment aggregation, which deals with the aggregation of judgments regarding the truth (or falsehood) of a number of possibly related statements. These statements are expressed in the language of propositional logic, which is why judgment aggregation is also referred to as logical aggregation. The origin of the field can be traced back to discussions of the so-called *doctrinal paradox* in legal theory. The chapter covers the axiomatic foundations of judgment aggregation, the discussion of specific aggregation procedures, connections to preference aggregation, the complexity of judgment aggregation, and applications in computer science.

Chapter 18: The Axiomatic Approach and the Internet (Tennenholtz and Zohar). The axiomatic approach, which is prevalent in social choice theory, gauges the desirability of decision mechanisms based on normative properties. This chapter presents applications of the axiomatic approach to a variety of systems that are prevalent on the Internet. In particular, the chapter discusses the axiomatic foundations of ranking systems, including an axiomatic characterization of the PageRank algorithm. Furthermore, the axiomatic foundations of crowdsourcing mechanisms and recommender systems are discussed in detail.

Chapter 19: Knockout Tournaments (Vassilevska Williams). A knockout tournament specifies an agenda of pairwise competitions between alternatives, in which alternatives are iteratively eliminated until only a single alternative remains. Knockout tournaments commonly arise in sports, but more generally provide a compelling model of decision making. This chapter covers a body of work on controlling the agenda of a knockout tournament with the objective of making a favored alternative win, both in terms of computational complexity and structural conditions.

1.4 Further Topics

In this section, we briefly review a number of related topics that did not fit into the book, and provide pointers for learning more about these. We have no pretense to be complete in our coverage of the terrain.

1.4.1 Mechanism Design

In *mechanism design*, the goal is to design mechanisms (e.g., auctions, voting rules, or matching mechanisms) that result in good outcomes when agents behave strategically (see, e.g., Nisan, 2007). Here, "strategic behavior" is typically taken to mean behavior according to some game-theoretic solution concept. Several of the chapters discuss some concepts from mechanism design (notably Chapters 6 and 14), but a thorough introduction to mechanism design with money (e.g., auction theory), and topics such as approximate mechanism design without money (Procaccia and Tennenholtz, 2013) or incentive compatible machine learning (Dekel et al., 2010), are all outside the scope of the book.

1.4.2 (Computational) Cooperative Game Theory

Part III of the book covers *coalition formation*, and thereby overlaps with *(computational) cooperative game theory*. Of course, it does not exhaustively cover that field, which is worthy of a book in itself—and in fact such a book is available (Chalkiadakis et al., 2011).

1.4.3 Randomized Social Choice

While a voting rule returns a winning alternative (or possibly a set of tied winners), a *social decision scheme* returns a probability distribution over alternatives. The role of randomization as a barrier to strategic behavior is discussed in Chapter 6. Depending on how preferences over probability distributions are defined, one can define various degrees of strategyproofness, economic efficiency, and participation. The trade-off between these properties has been analyzed by Aziz et al. (2013d, 2014c) and Brandl et al. (2015a). Another line of inquiry is to quantify how well strategyproof social decision schemes approximate common deterministic voting rules such as Borda's rule (Procaccia, 2010; Birrell and Pass, 2011; Service and Adams, 2012a).

Aziz et al. (2013a) and Aziz and Mestre (2014) have addressed the computational complexity of computing the probability of alternatives under the *random serial dictatorship* rule, in the context of voting as well as fair allocation. Randomization seems particularly natural in the domain of fair allocation and researchers have transferred concepts from voting to fair allocation (Kavitha et al., 2011; Aziz et al., 2013c), and vice versa (Aziz and Stursberg, 2014).

1.4.4 Iterative Voting

In *iterative voting* settings, voters cast their vote repeatedly, starting from some initial profile. In each round, the voters observe the outcome and one or more of them may change their vote. Depending on the voting rule used and some assumptions regarding the voters' behavior, we may be able (or not) to predict that the process will converge, as well as to guarantee that the outcome to which the process converges has some desirable properties. In a paper that initiated a great deal of activity in this area, Meir et al. (2010) proved for the plurality rule that, if voters update their ballots one at a time and adopt a myopic best-response strategy, then the process converges to a Nash equilibrium, whatever the initial state. Other voting rules and other assumptions on voter behavior were considered by several authors (e.g., Chopra et al., 2004; Lev and Rosenschein, 2012; Reyhani and Wilson, 2012; Grandi et al., 2013; Obraztsova et al., 2015b). Reijngoud and Endriss (2012) added the assumption of incomplete knowledge regarding the voting intentions of others and Meir et al. (2014) added the assumption of uncertainty regarding this information. Alternative notions of equilibria (with truth bias or lazy voters) were considered by Obraztsova et al. (2015a). Brânzei et al. (2013b) studied the price of anarchy of such iterated voting processes for several rules. A different iterative model was studied by Airiau and Endriss (2009), where in each step a voter is randomly selected, proposes a new alternative as a challenger to the current winning alternative, and the voters have to choose between the two.

1.4.5 Computer-Assisted Theorem Proving in Social Choice

A promising direction in computational social choice is to address open research questions using computer-aided theorem proving techniques. The role of computer science here is very different from that in mainstream computational social choice: computational techniques are not used to address the computation of existing social choice mechanisms or to identify new problems, but rather to prove and/or discover theorems in social choice theory.[2] For example, Nipkow (2009) verified an existing proof of Arrow's Theorem using a higher-order logic proof checker. Tang and Lin (2009) reduced the same theorem to a set of propositional logic formulas, which can be checked automatically by a satisfiability solver, and Geist and Endriss (2011) extended this method to a fully automated search algorithm for impossibility theorems in the context of preference relations over sets of alternatives. Brandt and Geist (2014) and Brandl et al. (2015b) applied these techniques to improve the understanding of strategyproofness and participation in the context of set-valued (or so-called irresolute) rules, and Brandt et al. (2014b) to compute the minimal number of voters required to realize a given majority graph.

1.4.6 Approximate Single-Peakedness and Related Issues

It is well-known that certain domain restrictions enable the circumvention of impossibility theorems and can make computationally difficult problems easy. Arguably the most well-known of these domain restrictions is Black's single-peakedness (see Chapter 2); another important (but somewhat less well-known) restriction is single-crossedness. It is usually computationally easy to recognize whether a profile satisfies such restrictions (Trick, 1989; Doignon and Falmagne, 1994; Escoffier et al., 2008; Bredereck et al., 2013b; Elkind and Faliszewski, 2014). However, for larger electorates, it is often unreasonable to expect profiles to satisfy these restrictions. Therefore, researchers have sought to quantify the extent to which a profile satisfies one of these domain restrictions, and also to say something informative about its structure (for instance, for single-peakedness, by identifying the most plausible axes). Several recent papers study such notions of near-single-peakedness, or more generally approximate versions of domain restrictions—especially (Conitzer, 2009; Cornaz et al., 2012; Bredereck et al., 2013a; Sui et al., 2013; Elkind and Lackner, 2014; Elkind et al., 2015b)—and their implications to computing and manipulating voting rules (Faliszewski et al., 2011c; Cornaz et al., 2012, 2013; Faliszewski et al., 2014; Brandt et al., 2015c). A related issue is the detection of components or clone structures in profiles (Brandt et al., 2011; Elkind et al., 2012a).

1.4.7 Computational Aspects of Apportionment and Districting

Apportionment is the process of allocating a number of representatives to different regions (or districts), such as states or provinces, usually according to their relative population. Apportionment comes with electoral districting—subdividing the territory into districts in which the election is performed, which in turn can give rise to *gerrymandering*, the redrawing of district borders for strategic reasons. Another case of apportionment occurs in party-list proportional representation systems, in which seats are allocated to parties in proportion to the number of votes they receive. This area of research, which is sometimes seen as being located at the borderline between social

---

[2] Automated reasoning has been very successful in some branches of discrete mathematics (e.g., in graph theory, with the famous computer-assisted proof of the Four Color Theorem).

choice theory and political science, gives rise to a variety of computational problems. Algorithms for districting are reviewed by Ricca et al. (2013) (see also the works of Pukelsheim et al. (2012), Ricca et al. (2007), and Hojati (1996) for technical contributions to this field). Algorithms for apportionment are discussed by Balinski and Demange (1989), Serafini and Simeone (2012), and Lari et al. (2014). The computational aspects of strategic candidacy in district-based elections are studied by Ricca et al. (2011) and Ding and Lin (2014). Finally, related to that, the computational aspects of vote trading (interdistrict exchange of votes) are studied by Hartvigsen (2006) and Bervoets et al. (2015).

1.4.8 New Problem Domains for Social Choice

As stressed already in the opening paragraphs of this chapter, the interaction between social choice theory and other disciplines, such as artificial intelligence, theoretical computer science, and operations research, led some researchers to work on new problem domains. Perhaps the most prominent of these new domains is the topic of Chapter 18, which discusses social choice problems that came about with the rise of the Internet. But there are others, some of which we mention next.

Collective combinatorial optimization. Collective combinatorial optimization deals with the design of methods for the collective version of some combinatorial optimization problems. An example is the *group travel problem* (Klamler and Pferschy, 2007), where one has to find a Hamiltonian path in a graph (that is, a path that goes through each vertex exactly once), given the preferences of a set of agents. Other examples are the *group knapsack problem* (Nicosia et al., 2009) and the *group minimum spanning tree problem* (Darmann et al., 2009; Darmann, 2013). Other such problems are considered, in a more systematic way, by Escoffier et al. (2013). In a similar vein, *group planning* (Ephrati and Rosenschein, 1993) is concerned with finding a joint plan, given the agents' preferences over possible goals.

Group classification. Automated classification is a well-known supervised machine learning task where the input consists of a training set of examples (e.g., a set of email messages, some of them labeled as spam by the user and some not), and the output is a classifier mapping any possible input (any future incoming message) to a class (spam or not spam). Now, in many real-life situations, the training set may consist of data labeled by several experts, who may have conflicting preferences about the learned classifier. This problem has been studied by Meir et al. (2012), who characterize strategyproof classification algorithms.[3]

Group recommendation. Recommender systems suggest interesting items for users based on their past interaction with the system. A well-known example are book recommendations issued by online book sellers based on a user's purchasing or browsing history. Group recommendation is based on the idea that we sometimes want to make such recommendations to groups of people, based on their (possibly diverse) preferences (e.g., a restaurant for a group of friends, or a holiday package for a family).

---

[3] This line of research should not be confused with the use of voting techniques in classification (see, e.g., Bauer and Kohavi, 1999).

Examples of work on this problem include the contributions of Amer-Yahia et al. (2009) and Chen et al. (2008).

Crowdsourcing. Online platforms such as Amazon's *Mechanical Turk* have become a popular method for collecting large amounts of labeled data (e.g., annotations of images with words describing them). Social choice mechanisms can be used to aggregate the information obtained through crowdsourcing. Besides a growing number of purely theoretical contributions, examples for work in this area also include experimental studies aimed at understanding how best to model the divergence between objectively correct answers and answers actually submitted by participants (Mao et al., 2013), and the design and evaluation of practical aggregation methods for concrete tasks, such as the semantic annotation of corpora used in research in linguistics (Qing et al., 2014).

Dynamic social choice. Parkes and Procaccia (2013) deal with sequences of collective decisions to be made in a population with evolving preferences, where future preferences depend on past preferences and past actions. The output of the collective decision making process then is a policy in a Markov decision process. This setting is motivated by online public policy advocacy groups. The causes advocated by the group's leadership have an impact on the preferences of members, leading to a dynamic process that should be steered in a socially desirable direction.

1.5 Basic Concepts in Theoretical Computer Science

We conclude this chapter with a brief review of some standard concepts from (theoretical) computer science that will be used in many places in the book, particularly concepts from the theory of computational complexity. Of course, it is challenging to communicate in so little space material that students usually learn over a sequence of courses. Nevertheless, we hope that this provides the reader without computational background some intuitive high-level understanding of these concepts—enough to appreciate a result's significance at a high level, as well as to know for which terms to search in order to obtain more detailed background as needed. We imagine this may also serve as a useful reference for some readers who do have computational background.

1.5.1 Computational Complexity

Computational complexity deals with evaluating the computational resources (mostly, time and space) needed to solve a given problem. We first need to make explicit what we mean by a "problem." Most computational problems considered in this book are phrased as *decision problems*. Formally, a decision problem P is defined as a pair $\langle L_P, Y_P \rangle$ where L_P is a formal language, whose elements are called *instances*, and $Y_P \subseteq L_P$ is the set of *positive instances*. For instance, the problem of *deciding whether a directed graph is acyclic* is defined by the set L_P of all directed graphs, while Y_P is the set of all directed acyclic graphs. If $I \in Y_P$, then I is said to be a *positive instance* of P. Sometimes we will also need to deal with *search problems*, also called *function problems*, whose answer is a *solution* (when there exists one): a *function problem* is a set $\langle L_P, S_P, R_P \rangle$, where S_P is another formal language (the set of possible solutions) and $R_P \subseteq L_P \times S_P$ is a relation between instances and solutions, where $(I, S) \in R_P$ means that S is a solution for I. For instance, *find a nondominated vertex in a directed graph, if any* and *find all vertices with maximum outdegree* are both search problems. Solving the function problem on instance $I \in L_P$ consists in outputting some $S \in S_P$ such that $(I, S) \in R_P$, if any, and "no solution" otherwise.

Complexity theory deals with *complexity classes* of problems that are computationally equivalent in a certain well-defined way. Typically, (decision or function) problems that can be solved by an algorithm whose running time is polynomial in the size of the problem instance are considered *tractable*, whereas problems that do not admit such an algorithm are deemed *intractable*. Formally, an algorithm is *polynomial* if there exists a $k \in \mathbb{N}$ such that its running time is in $O(n^k)$, where n is the size of the input. Here, $O(n^k)$ denotes the class of all functions that, for large values of n, grow no faster than $c \cdot n^k$ for some constant number c (this is the "Big-O notation"). For instance, when $k = 1$, the running time is *linear*, and when $k = 2$, the running time is *quadratic* in n.

The class of decision problems that can be solved in polynomial time is denoted by P, whereas NP (for "nondeterministic polynomial time") refers to the class of decision problems whose solutions can be *verified* in polynomial time. For instance, the problem of *deciding whether a directed graph is acyclic* is polynomial while *deciding whether a directed graph has a cycle that goes through all vertices exactly once* (called a *Hamiltonian cycle*) is in NP (but is not known to be in P).

The famous P $\neq$ NP conjecture states that the hardest problems in NP do not admit polynomial-time algorithms and are thus not contained in P. Although this statement remains unproven, it is widely believed to be true. *Hardness* of a problem for a particular class intuitively means that the problem is no easier than any other problem in that class. Both membership and hardness are established in terms of *reductions* that transform instances of one problem into instances of another problem using computational means appropriate for the complexity class under consideration. Most reductions in this book rely on reductions that can be computed in time polynomial in the size of the problem instances, and are called *polynomial-time reductions*. Finally, a problem is said to be *complete* for a complexity class if it is both contained in and hard for that class. For instance, *deciding whether a directed graph possesses a Hamiltonian cycle* is NP-complete.

Given the current state of complexity theory, we cannot prove the *actual* intractability of most algorithmic problems, but merely give *evidence* for their intractability. Showing NP-hardness of a problem is commonly regarded as very strong evidence for computational intractability because it relates the problem to a large class of problems for which no efficient, that is, polynomial-time, algorithm is known, despite enormous efforts to find such algorithms.

Besides P and NP, several other classes will be used in this book. Given a decision problem $P = \langle L_P, Y_P \rangle$, the *complementary problem* of P is defined as $\overline{P} = \langle L_P, L_P \setminus Y_P \rangle$. Given a complexity class C, a decision problem belongs to the class coC if $\overline{P}$ belongs to C. Notably, coNP is the class of all decision problems whose complement is in NP. For instance, *deciding that a directed graph does not possess a Hamiltonian cycle* is in coNP (and coNP-complete).

We now introduce several complexity classes which are supersets of NP and coNP (and are strongly believed to be strict supersets). Given two complexity classes C and

C', we denote by $C^{C'}$ the set of all problems that can be solved by an algorithm for C equipped with C'-*oracles*, where a C'-*oracle* solves a problem in C' (or in coC') in unit time. The class Δ_2^P, defined as P^{NP}, is thus the class of all decision problems that can be solved in polynomial time with the help of NP-oracles, which answer in unit time whether a given instance of a problem in NP is positive or not. The class Θ_2^P is the subset of Δ_2^P consisting of all decision problems that can be solved in polynomial time using "logarithmically many" NP-oracles. Equivalently, Θ_2^P may be defined as the subset of Δ_2^P for which a polynomial number of NP-oracles may be used, but these need to be queried in parallel, that is, we cannot use the answer to one oracle to determine what question to put to the next oracle. Finally, $\Sigma_2^P = NP^{NP}$ and $\Pi_2^P = co\Sigma_2^{NP}$. Thus, for instance, Σ_2^P is the class of decision problems for which the correctness of a positive solution can be verified in polynomial time by an algorithm that has access to an NP-oracle. The following inclusions hold:

$$P \subseteq NP, coNP \subseteq \Theta_2^P \subseteq \Delta_2^P \subseteq \Sigma_2^P, \Pi_2^P.$$

It is strongly believed that all these inclusions are strict, although none of them was actually *proven* to be strict. Interestingly, Θ_2^P and (to a lesser extent) Δ_2^P, Σ_2^P and Π_2^P play an important role in computational social choice (and indeed, we find them referred to in Chapters 3, 4, 5, 8, 12, and 17). We occasionally refer to other complexity classes (such as PLS or #P) in the book; they are introduced in the chapter concerned.

For a full introduction and an extensive overview of computational complexity theory, we refer the reader to Papadimitriou (1994) and Ausiello et al. (1999).

1.5.2 Linear and Integer Programming

One notable computational problem is that of solving *linear programs*. A linear program consists of a set of *variables* x_j ($1 \leqslant j \leqslant n$), a set of *constraints* indexed by i ($1 \leqslant i \leqslant m$), and an *objective*. Constraint i is defined by *parameters* a_{ij} ($1 \leqslant j \leqslant n$) and b_i, resulting in the following inequality constraint:

$$\sum_{j=1}^{n} a_{ij}x_j \leqslant b_i.$$

The objective is defined by parameters c_j, resulting in the following objective:

$$\sum_{j=1}^{n} c_j x_j.$$

The goal is to find a vector of nonnegative values for the x_j that maximizes the value of the objective while still meeting all the constraints (i.e., all the inequalities should hold). Natural variants, such as not requiring variables to take nonnegative values, allowing equality constraints, having a minimization rather than a maximization objective, and so on, are not substantively different from this basic setup. There is a rich theory of linear programming; for the purpose of this book, what is most important to know is that linear programs can be solved to optimality in polynomial time. Thus, if a computational problem can be formulated as (equivalently, reduced to) a polynomial-sized linear program, then it can be solved in polynomial time.

Linear programs allow all their variables to take fractional values. If instead, we require the variables to take integer values, we obtain an *integer linear program*. If we allow some but not all variables to take fractional values, we obtain a *mixed integer linear program*. This apparently minor modification has significant computational ramifications: solving (mixed) integer linear programs is NP-hard. Indeed, many NP-hard problems are easily formulated as (mixed) integer linear programs. One may wonder what the point of doing so is, as after all the latter are hard to solve. However, (mixed) integer linear program solvers are available that scale quite well on many (though, unsurprisingly, not all) families of instances. Moreover, (mixed) integer linear program formulations of a problem often help us develop deeper insight into the problem at hand. One particularly natural and helpful notion is that of the *linear program relaxation* of a mixed integer linear program, which simply drops the integrality requirement, taking us back to an easy-to-solve linear program. While this relaxation necessarily does not always have the same optimal solutions as the original, it nevertheless often serves as a useful starting point for analysis and computation.

A good reference for the theory and practice of both integer and linear programming is the book by Nemhauser and Wolsey (1999).

Acknowledgments

Putting together this *Handbook of Computational Social Choice* has been a major project, taking more than four years from conception to publication. We would like to thank everyone in the research community for their significant support of this project. This includes not only the authors, but also the many colleagues who volunteered to provide in-depth reviews of individual chapters: Stéphane Airiau, Haris Aziz, Yoram Bachrach, Péter Biró, Craig Boutilier, Sylvain Bouveret, Michel Le Breton, Markus Brill, Ioannis Caragiannis, Franz Dietrich, Yair Dombb, John Duggan, Edith Elkind, Piotr Faliszewski, Felix Fischer, Wulf Gaertner, Serge Gaspers, Umberto Grandi, Davide Grossi, Paul Harrenstein, Lane Hemaspaandra, Sean Horan, Olivier Hudry, Christian Klamler, Jean-François Laslier, Nicolas Maudet, Vincent Merlin, Rolf Niedermeier, Shmuel Nitzan, Eric Pacuit, Marc Pauly, Jörg Rothe, Nisarg Shah, Arkadii Slinko, John Weymark, Gerhard Woeginger, Lirong Xia, Yair Zick, and William S. Zwicker. While our own background is primarily in computer science, many of these reviewers, as well as some authors, come from other disciplines, particularly economics. This makes the book a truly interdisciplinary resource of information. Finally, we thank our editor Lauren Cowles at Cambridge University Press for her support and patience.

Online Version

An online version of the book can be found under the Resources tab at
www.cambridge.org/9781107060432
Password: cam1CSC

PART I
Voting

CHAPTER 2

Introduction to the Theory of Voting

William S. Zwicker

2.1 Introduction to an Introduction

Suppose a finite society is about to vote on a choice of one option from among finitely many. The options, called *alternatives* in voting theory, might be candidates for mayor of a town, or different amounts to spend on building a new firehouse, or several versions of an immigration reform bill. If we assume that

1. every two voters play equivalent roles in our voting rule
2. every two alternatives are treated equivalently by the rule
3. there are only two alternatives to choose from

then the situation is simple: *May's Theorem*, discussed in Section 2.4, tells us that the only reasonable voting method is *majority rule*.

Many voting contexts, however, require us to relax some of these assumptions. In these settings, the matter of choosing a voting rule can become much less straightforward. What are the principal issues that complicate matters? Contexts for voting vary too greatly to admit any unified answer, so we will have to narrow the question.

Our focus here is on the context of *multicandidate* voting, for which an appropriate metaphor is that of electing a mayor when there are three or more candidates—so we will relax the third condition, while holding out for the first two.[1,2] Even within this framework, "voting" can mean different things, depending on the specified form of a ballot and of a collective decision. Our primary concern will be with *ranked* ballots—each voter submits a linear ordering of the alternatives, specifying their most favored

---

[1] *Legislative voting*, in which a representative assembly must choose between collective approval or disapproval of some proposal or bill under consideration, provides quite a different context. While there are only two alternatives, they may be treated unequally (as when a supermajority is required to amend a constitution) and some legislators may play different roles than others (if they represent districts with different populations and economies, as happens in the EU Council of Ministers, or have veto power, as do the five permanent members of the UN Security Council).

[2] Metaphor notwithstanding, our perspective here is primarily mathematical. See Cox (1997) and Blais et al. (1997) for a look at how the world actually votes from the political science viewpoint.

candidate, their second choice, and so on—and with single winners (or several winners, in the event of a tie) as outcomes.[3] A voting rule in this setting is called a *social choice function* or *SCF* (see examples in Section 2.2).

Within multicandidate voting, three results are most prominent. The first, observed by Marie Jean Antoine Nicolas de Caritat, Marquis de Condorcet (1785) and arguably most fundamental,[4] is the existence of *majority cycles*, in which collective preference violates what we might expect from any "rational" individual: a majority of voters prefer some alternative a to b, a (different) majority prefers b to c, and a third majority prefers c to a.[5]

Kenneth Arrow's *Independence of Irrelevant Alternatives* principle (aka *IIA*) asserts that collective voter opinion as to the relative merits of two alternatives should not be influenced by individual voter opinions about an "irrelevant" third.[6] The famous *Arrow Impossibility Theorem* (Arrow, 1950) tells us that, with some mild assumptions, every voting rule for three or more alternatives either violates IIA or is a *dictatorship*, in which the election outcome depends solely on the ballot of one designated voter. This important result, establishing a basic limitation of collective decision-making methods, contributed in a major way to the broad revival of interest in the theory of voting, about 150 years after the "Golden Age" of social choice.[7] More on IIA as well as a proof of Arrow's Theorem appear in Chapter 1 of this handbook, so we will not be dealing with it here.

The *Gibbard-Satterthwaite Theorem* (aka *GST*), third member of the triad, establishes a different fundamental limitation on voting and is the principal topic of Section 2.8 here. The GST asserts that every SCF f other than a dictatorship fails to be *strategyproof*—f sometimes provides an incentive for an individual voter i to *manipulate* the outcome, that is, to misrepresent his or her true preferences over the alternatives by casting an insincere ballot. The incentive is that voter i prefers the alternative

---

[3] Some view the reliance on ranked ballots as a major error, and see the major theorems of the field (see Section 2.8, for example) more as artifacts of this mistake than as fundamental limitations on democracy. They advocate voting rules such as range voting (Smith, 2000), majority judgment (Balinski and Laraki, 2010), or approval voting (Brams and Fishburn, 2007) that use different ballot forms. For the argument in favor of ranked ballots, see Arrow (1950).

[4] Look for its appearance in proofs of Arrow's Theorem and the Gibbard-Satterthwaite Theorem.

[5] Buchanan (1954) argues that as society is not an "organic entity," the concept of *collective rationality* (or irrationality) has no meaning; it should be unsurprising, then, when a cooked-up form of collective preference behaves inconsistently.

[6] Imagine that applicants x and y are in a tight race for an open position in your department, with a third candidate z drawing little support. An initial poll would have given the position to x. Subsequent discussion leads no one to change their mind about x vs. y, but all support for z is withdrawn, and the effect of this change is that y beats x in the revote. That's a failure of IIA. The context for Arrow's Impossibility Theorem is that of a *social welfare function* (aka *SWF*) for which an outcome is a (weak) ranking of all alternatives. Thus Arrow presumes transitivity of *social* preference. Our major (but not exclusive) concern in this chapter is with social choice functions, for which the election outcome is the winning alternative(s) (with no assumption that social preference is transitive in its entirety).

[7] The McLean and Urken (1995) collection contains English translations of original works by de Borda and Condorcet from the Golden Age (late eighteenth century), as well as some much earlier work by Ramon Lull and Nicolaus Cusanus, and important nineteenth-century contributions by Nanson and Dodgson. Duncan Black's (1958) book as well as the treatise of Thomas Hare (1859) on *single transferable vote* (see Section 2.4) should also be mentioned in any brief history of pre-Arrovian social choice. Homeshaw (2001) argues that STV was invented by the Danish mathematician and politician Carl Andræ, two years before Hare's treatise.

that wins when she casts some insincere ballot to the winner that would result from a sincere one. One limitation of the GST is that it presumes every election to have a *unique* winner (no ties). This might seem problematic, but the Duggan-Schwartz Theorem (Section 2.8) provides a pretty good solution.

Most of this chapter is devoted to introducing some of the more important voting rules in the social choice function context, along with a selection of properties, or *axioms*, that distinguish among these rules. We discuss a number of theorems that characterize classes of SCFs axiomatically, or that establish fundamental limits on what is possible by showing that certain packages of axioms conflict with others. The topic of strategic manipulation, while far from being our sole concern, never lies far beneath the surface, and a detailed proof of the GST appears in Section 2.8.

The rest of the chapter is organized as follows. In Section 2.2 we provide the definitions and notation needed for a careful discussion of social choice functions, introducing the variety of ways that a voting rule can use the information in ranked ballots through two examples, Copeland and Borda voting. We contrast these rules with plurality voting, which looks only at each voter's top choice. The idea of strategic manipulation is introduced via examples for these three SCFs, in Section 2.2. Our first consideration of axioms, in Section 2.3, looks at three examples: anonymity, neutrality, and the Pareto property. We see that even these "innocuous" axioms can conflict with other desiderata; they can force all rules to admit some ties, for example.

In Section 2.4 we introduce additional SCFs from three important classes. *Condorcet extensions*, including Copeland, respect *Condorcet's principle* by choosing the alternative majority-preferred to each other alternative—the *Condorcet winner*—whenever it exists; *majority cycles* mean that it might not exist. *Scoring rules* (including Borda and plurality) have each voter award points to the alternatives according to how highly they rank them. *Scoring run-offs* eliminate lower-scoring alternatives sequentially, until a surviving alternative exceeds some threshold of acceptance (or until only one survives). Fishburn's classification, in Section 2.5, provides insight into how these rules differ in the type of information (extracted from the ballots) that they actually use.

The reinforcement (aka consistency) axiom and various monotonicity axioms of Section 2.6 are different from those in Section 2.3, in that they discriminate among these three classes of rules. Our approach to monotonicity properties is to view them as limited forms of strategyproofness. Theorems in this section illustrate several major themes:

- It is best to avoid love at first sight with some voting rule, based on an appearance of fairness in its method for calculating winners. The law of unintended consequences applies . . . so wait until you see which axioms it satisfies.
- There is a trade-off among axioms: asking for one may rule out another.
- There is a trade-off between desirable axioms and decisiveness: some rules manage to satisfy difficult criteria by having lots of ties.
- The split between Condorcet extensions and scoring rules is fundamental: the philosophical differences between Condorcet and de Borda endure.

In Section 2.7 we consider two rules initially defined using *Kendall's tau metric*. The first, suggested by John Kemeny,[8] reconciles the apparent conflict between the

---

[8] Peyton Young (1988) argues that Kemeny's rule was first proposed by Condorcet.

reinforcement axiom and respect for Condorcet's principle, though the change in ballot form weakens the implications of reinforcement. This rule shares, with Dodgson's rule, an important role in computational social choice, as seen in Chapters 4, 5, and 6.

Our detailed proof of the Gibbard-Satterthwaite Theorem is in Section 2.8. It is followed, in Section 2.9, by results of Black and Sen showing that under certain *domain restrictions* (limitations on allowable ballots) strategyproofness is possible.

Because of its different ballot form, the *approval voting* system is not generally considered to be an SCF. Its practical and theoretical interest, however, would justify making an exception and including a brief look, in Section 2.10, at this system. Moreover, if we relax the SCF notion by allowing voters to express indifference among alternatives, approval voting becomes an SCF—in fact it coincides both with Borda and with all Condorcet extensions, when these rules are suitably adapted to handle ballots with many indifferences. The chapter ends with some brief discussion, in Section 2.11, of the possible future of voting theory.

2.2 Social Choice Functions: Plurality, Copeland, and Borda

Voting takes place whenever a group of voters cast *ballots*, that are used as the basis for a collective decision reached through the application of a *voting rule*. A variety of voting contexts are possible, depending on the specified form of a ballot and of a collective decision, and also on the interpretation we choose to make of these forms; the term "voting rule" is generic, covering all possibilities. Our principal focus will be on one context—that of *social choice functions*—which uses ranked ballots:

- $N = \{1, 2, \ldots, n\}$ is a finite set (of *voters*).
- A is a finite set of m *alternatives* (e.g., candidates for mayor), with $m \geqslant 2$.
- The *ballot* cast by voter i is a linear ordering $\succsim_i$ of A: $\succsim_i$ is *transitive* (if $a \succsim_i b$ and $b \succsim_i c$ then $a \succsim_i c$, for all $a, b, c \in A$), *complete* ($a \succsim_i b$ or $b \succsim_i a$, for all $a \neq b \in A$), *reflexive* ($a \succsim_i a$ for all $a \in A$), and *antisymmetric* (if $a \succsim_i b$ and $b \succsim_i a$, then $a = b$, for all $a, b \in A$); $\mathcal{L}(A)$ denotes the set of all linear orderings for a given A. The antireflexive version $x \succ y$ means $x \succsim y$ holds and $y \succsim x$ fails.
- A *profile* $P = (\succsim_1, \succsim_2, \ldots, \succsim_n)$ specifies such a ballot for each voter $i \in N$; $\mathcal{L}(A)^n$ denotes the set of all such profiles for a given n, and $\mathcal{L}(A)^{<\infty}$ stands for $\bigcup_{n \in \mathbb{N}} \mathcal{L}(A)^n$ (where $\mathbb{N}$ denotes the set of all natural numbers).

Such ballots are called *preference rankings* because of the favored interpretation: $x \succ_i y$ expresses voter i's (strict) preference for alternative x over alternative y.[9] By imposing antisymmetry we are making the simplifying assumption that individual rankings are *strict*—no voter may express indifference to two alternatives. Alternatively, we might allow *weak* preference rankings (aka *pre-linear* orderings) as ballots, by dropping the antisymmetry requirement. We will use R to denote a *profile* of weak preference rankings, $\mathcal{R}(A)$ to denote the set of all weak rankings of A, and $\mathcal{R}(A)^n$ as the set of all profiles of weak rankings for a given A and n.

---

[9] It is common to state $x \succ_i y$ aloud as "voter i strictly prefers x to y," but keep in mind that i's sincere preferences might differ from the binary relation $\succsim_i$ expressed as i's ballot.

In practice, will often present a profile in tabular form, with each preference ranking written vertically (in descending order of preference) and the number of voters casting each ballot recorded on top. In profile P_1 that follows, $A = \{a, b, c\}$ with $m = 3$, and of the $n = 303$ voters, 102 cast the ballot $a \succ b \succ c$:

102	101	100
a	b	c
b	c	b
c	a	a

While the table shows the number of voters who cast each ballot, it does not reveal their individual identities (as a profile would); strictly speaking, P_1 is a *voting situation*—a function $s: \mathcal{L}(A) \to \mathbb{N} \cup \{0\}$ assigning to each linear ordering the number of voters with that order as ballot—rather than a profile. Each voting situation corresponds to several profiles, but many voting rules are blind to the distinction between "profile" and "voting situation," so we will use the terms interchangeably.

A *plurality ballot* names a single, most-preferred alternative, and the *plurality voting* rule then selects, as the winner(s) of an election (aka the "social choice(s)") the alternative(s) with a plurality (greatest number) of votes. Alternately, we can identify a ranking with a plurality ballot for the top-ranked alternative (while we ignore the rest of the ranking). When we do this for P_1, a is the unique plurality winner, or "social choice" (although her 102 votes fall well short of a *majority*).

Much of the interest in voting theory arises from a widespread critique of plurality voting; the winner can be enormously unpopular (because a plurality is quite different from a majority). For example, with P_1 it is difficult to see how a could win under *any* reasonable rule that seriously made use of the second versus third place information in the ballots; in fact, b wins under each one of the voting methods (that use ranked ballots) discussed in the rest of this chapter.[10]

To make fuller use of the information in the ranking, consider profile P_2:

102	101	100	1
a	b	c	c
b	c	a	b
c	a	b	a

Note that 202 P_2-voters rank a over b, while 102 rank b over a. The *net preference*

$$Net_P(a > b) = |\{j \in N \mid a \succ_j b\}| - |\{j \in N \mid b \succ_j a\}| \qquad (2.1)$$

for a over b is $202 - 102 = 100$ (for $P = P_2$) and is strictly positive. Thus a beats b in the *pairwise majority* sense, and we write $a >^\mu b$ (or $a >^\mu_{P_2} b$ to identify the profile). Here $>^\mu$ is the *strict pairwise majority* relation, which is always complete for an odd number of voters with strict preferences; $x \geq^\mu y$ denotes the weak version

---

[10] Plurality voting led to conservative Republican Alfonse D'Amato's 1980 U.S. Senate win in New York (a predominantly liberal state), with 44.88% of the vote; liberal democrat Elizabeth Holtzmann and liberal Republican incumbent Jacob Javits split the liberal vote (with 43.54% and 11.05%, respectively). This is not the only real-world example resembling P_1.

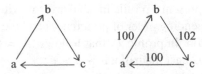

Figure 2.1. The pairwise majority tournament (left) and weighted version (right) for P_2.

$(Net_P(x > y) \geqslant 0)$, and $x =^{\mu} y$ stands for a *pairwise majority tie* $(Net_P(x > y) = 0)$. Figure 2.1 (left) depicts $>^{\mu}$ as a complete directed graph,[11] or *tournament*, using $x \to y$ to indicate $x >^{\mu} y$; the weighted version, on the right, labels $x \to y$ with $Net_P(x > y)$, to obtain a *weighted tournament*.

Our next voting rule scores candidates according to their win-loss record in this pairwise majority sense. We will define $Copeland(x)$, the *(symmetric) Copeland score* of an alternative x,[12] as the difference

$$Copeland(x) = |\{y \in A \mid x >^{\mu} y\}| - |\{y \in A \mid y >^{\mu} x\}|. \qquad (2.2)$$

For P_2 we have $a >^{\mu} b$ and $c >^{\mu} a$, so that a's Copeland score is $1 - 1 = 0$. Similarly, $Copeland(b) = 0$ and $Copeland(c) = 0$. The *Copeland rule* (Copeland, 1951) selects, as the social choice, the alternative(s) with highest Copeland score. For P_2, then, Copeland declares a three-way tie, with $\{a, b, c\}$ as the winning set.

Copeland rewards an alternative x for each pairwise victory $x >^{\mu} y$ over an opponent and punishes her for each defeat, but disregards the margins of victory or defeat. If we weight such rewards and punishments by these margins, the resulting voting rule is quite different.

Given a profile P, the *symmetric Borda score* of an alternative x is given by

$$Borda_P^{sym}(x) = \sum_{y \in A} Net_P(x > y).^{13} \qquad (2.3)$$

The *Borda* rule (also called the *Borda count*; see Borda, 1781) selects as winner the alternative(s) with the highest such score. For P_2 the symmetric Borda scores of alternatives a, b, c are $0, +2, -2$ respectively, and the set of Borda winners is $\{b\}$.

The more common *asymmetric* Borda score for 3 alternatives is defined via the *vector of scoring weights* (aka *score vector*) $\mathbf{w} = (2, 1, 0)$. Each voter awards 2 points to her top-ranked alternative, 1 point to the next, and 0 to her least preferred, and the asymmetric Borda score $Borda_P^{asym}(x)$ is obtained by summing points awarded to x by all voters. The two versions are affinely equivalent (see Footnote 12), with $Borda_P^{asym}(x) = n + \frac{1}{2}Borda_P^{sym}(x)$, so they induce the same SCF.

If we sum points awarded via the *symmetric* score vector $\mathbf{w} = (+2, 0, -2)$ we will replicate the (2.3) scores. With m alternatives the asymmetric score vector is

---

[11] That is, $>^{\mu}$ is complete as a relation, so that each edge occurs in exactly one of its two orientations (as is the case when the number of voters is odd, and ballots are linear orders).

[12] One commonly sees asymmetric forms of Copeland score, such as $C^{ass.}(x) = |\{y \in A \mid x >^{\mu} y\}|$ or $C^{ass.+}(x) = |\{y \in A \mid x >^{\mu} y\}| + \frac{1}{2}|\{y \in A \mid x =^{\mu} y\}|$. It is easy to see that $Copeland(x)$ and $C^{ass.+}(x)$ are *affinely equivalent* as scores; there is a *positive affine transform* $S \mapsto \alpha S + \beta$ (where $\alpha > 0$ and β are real number constants) that carries $Copeland(x)$ to $C^{ass.+}(x)$; it follows that they always choose the same winners. Note that $C^{ass.}$ can differ from these two, for example when there are three alternatives satisfying $a >^{\mu} b >^{\mu} c =^{\mu} a$.

[13] We will reconcile this nonstandard definition of Borda score with the standard version shortly.

$\mathbf{w} = (m - 1, m - 2, m - 3, \ldots, 0)$; the symmetric version $\mathbf{w} = (m - 1, m - 3, m - 5, \ldots, -(m - 1))$ replicates the scores from (2.3).[14] An advantage of the symmetric approach embodied by (2.1), (2.2), and (2.3) is that it is well-defined for profiles of weak preferences, yielding plausible extensions of the Borda and Copeland rules.[15]

As these examples suggest, our interest lies mainly with voting rules that take profiles of strict preferences as inputs, and return one alternative (the *winner*) or several (in the event of a tie). Let $\mathcal{C}(X)$ denote the set of all nonempty subsets of a set X. Then:

Definition 2.1. A *social choice function*, or *SCF*, is a map $f: \mathcal{L}(A)^n \to \mathcal{C}(A)$ that returns a nonempty set of alternatives for each profile of strict preferences. If $|f(P)| = 1$ then f is *single valued* on P (and we sometimes write $f(P) = x$ instead of $f(P) = \{x\}$). A *resolute* SCF is one with no ties: it is single valued on all profiles.[16]

We will also be interested in *SCFs with restricted domain*—voting rules that fit the definition, except that they are defined only on some proper subset of $\mathcal{L}(A)^n$. Definition 2.1 associates each SCF with a *single* choice of N: these are *fixed electorate* SCFs; for *variable electorate* SCFs, substitute $\mathcal{L}(A)^{<\infty}$ for $\mathcal{L}(A)^n$.[17] *The rest of this chapter presumes a fixed electorate, except where explicitly noted otherwise.*

Note that for the plurality, Copeland, and Borda SCFs the assignment of numerical scores does more than just select the socially most desirable alternative—it induces a "social ranking" in which one alternative is ranked over another when it has a higher score. Tied scores are possible, so this is a "weak" ranking in $\mathcal{R}(A)$. Many social choice functions use mechanisms that yield a weak ranking of all alternatives, and so fit the following definition:

Definition 2.2. A *social welfare function*, or *SWF*, is a map $f: \mathcal{L}(A)^n \to \mathcal{R}(A)$ that returns a weak ranking of the set of alternatives for each profile of strict preferences.[18]

A Taste of Strategic Manipulation

Do these rules give voters an incentive, on occasion, to cast insincere ballots? Consider Ali, one of the two $a \succ b \succ c \succ d \succ e$ voters of profile P_3 (see later). Under Copeland, he is about to see his least preferred alternative win: e's (symmetric) Copeland score is 2, b's is -2, and the other scores are each 0. If Ali misrepresents his sincere preferences by completely reversing his ballot ranking, the Copeland winner shifts to d—which he prefers—with a score of 4, the maximum possible.

[14] Any two scoring vectors of form $\mathbf{w} = (c, c - d, c - 2d, \ldots, c - (m - 1)d)$, $d > 0$ have affinely equivalent scoring weights, yielding affinely equivalent total scores for the alternatives. Thus, the weak ordering of alternatives induced by these scores is the same.
[15] See last part of Section 2.10, including footnotes.
[16] Some authors reserve "SCF" for the resolute case, and use *social choice correspondence* (SCC) when multiple winners are allowed.
[17] The fixed/variable distinction is often suppressed; Borda and Copeland fit both contexts, for example.
[18] Domains $\mathcal{R}(A)^n$ and $\mathcal{R}(A)^{<\infty}$ are also considered for SCFs and SWFs.

2	3	2
e	d	a
c	e	b
a	b	c
d	c	d
b	a	e

Definition 2.3. An SCF f is *single voter manipulable* if for some pair P, P' of profiles on which f is single valued, and voter i with $\succsim'_j = \succsim_j$ for all $j \neq i$, $f(P') \succ_i f(P)$; f is *single voter strategyproof* if it is not single voter manipulable.

We interpret $\succsim_i$ (in Definition 2.3) as representing voter i's sincere ranking; by switching from $\succsim_i$ to the insincere ballot $\succsim'_i$ voter i can change the winning alternative to one that, according to her sincere ballot, she strictly prefers.

Notice that for each pair of alternatives, Ali's reversed ballot of $e \succ d \succ c \succ b \succ a$ misrepresents which of the two he actually prefers. Under Borda, Ali alone can still manipulate profile P_3, but not by completely reversing his ranking.[19] Instead, by lifting d to the top (casting ballot $d \succ a \succ b \succ c \succ e$) Ali can get d to displace e, as earner of the uniquely highest Borda score.

Plurality voting is *not* single voter manipulable; any one voter preferring y to the unique plurality winner x does not top-rank x on her sincere ballot, so she cannot lower x's score. At best she can raise y's plurality score to a tie with x's. However, if the *two* $e \succ c \succ a \succ b \succ d$ voters of P_3 both switch to $a \succ \dots$ the former plurality winner d will be replaced by a, which they prefer. The example suggests that for rules with ties, single voter manipulability is an inappropriate test—we need to ban ties, or deal with them, and we touch on both routes in Section 2.3.

2.3 Axioms I: Anonymity, Neutrality, and the Pareto Property

A variety of interesting SCFs have been proposed, often based on mechanisms that seem to calculate the winner in an intuitively "fair" way. Experience suggests, however, that mechanisms may have unintended consequences that undercut their initial appeal. As a result, scholars have come to distrust arguments based solely on the intuitive appeal of an underlying mechanism[20] for calculating winners. They rely instead on *axioms*—precisely defined properties of voting rules as functions (phrased without referring to a particular mechanism). Axioms often have *normative* content, meaning that they express, in some precise way, an intuitively appealing behavior we would like our voting rules to satisfy (such as a form of fairness).

As applied to the theory of voting, the *axiomatic method* identifies interesting voting rules, formulates intuitively appealing or useful axioms, and proves theorems showing which rules satisfy which axioms. Ideally, such theorems *characterize* a class $\mathcal{S}$ of

---

[19] The example thus shows that Copeland can be manipulated via complete reversal. Borda, on the other hand, can never be manipulated in this way—see later discussion of *half-way monotonicity* in Section 2.6.

[20] As we already glimpsed in the case of the Borda SCF, a function may be computable via a variety of mechanisms, not all having the same intuitive appeal. Which of them should determine the intuitive appeal of the common function they compute? This is a second reason to be cautious when passing judgment as to the fairness of a voting rule based on its mechanism alone.

voting rules via a set $\mathcal{A}$ of axioms, by proving that $\mathcal{S}$ contains exactly those rules satisfying all axioms in $\mathcal{A}$. Such theorems may uniquely characterize one rule in terms of its properties (when $\mathcal{S}$ is a singleton), or demonstrate the impossibility of satisfying all properties of $\mathcal{A}$ (by showing $\mathcal{S}$ to be empty). In fact, impossibilities are among the most consequential results in the field, for it turns out that axioms also have unintended consequences ... as when one seemingly reasonable axiom rules out any hope of satisfying some other one.

Axioms for SCFs can be loosely sorted into three groups. The first group represent minimal demands. These axioms are absolutely required (for some contexts) and plenty of SCFs satisfy them (including plurality, Borda, and Copeland). There is little cost, then, to requiring them and they seem, as well, to offer less scope for unintended consequences, so they tend to be seen as uncontroversial.

In this section we discuss five axioms from the first group. In Section 2.6 we consider a second group of axioms, of middling strength—they are satisfied by some interesting SCFs, but requiring any one of these axioms would have a high cost: some very attractive rules, and some of the other axioms from the same group, would be ruled out. These axioms are the most controversial; your favorite voting rule may violate *some* axiom from this group, and be seen as illegitimate by anyone who finds that axiom to be compelling. A third group of axioms include strategyproofness and IIA, and these are the strongest, in that they tend to rule out *all* reasonable voting rules. Of course these axioms are associated with some controversy, in terms of how one interprets the corresponding impossibilities—does Arrow's Theorem *really* say that democracy is impossible? Or does a closer look at IIA suggest that it is less compelling than might first appear? But there is no controversy over whether or not to impose any of these axioms when choosing an SCF—the cost is too high.[21]

Definition 2.4. An SCF f is *anonymous* if each pair of voters play interchangeable roles: $f(P) = f(P^\star)$ holds whenever a profile $P^\star$ is obtained from another P by swapping the ballots cast by some two voters i and j ($\succsim_i^\star = \succsim_j$, $\succsim_j^\star = \succsim_i$, and $\succsim_k^\star = \succsim_k$ for all $k \neq i, j$);[22] f is *dictatorial* if some voter i acts as dictator, meaning $f(P)$ coincides with i's top-ranked alternative, for every profile P.

Anonymity is a very strong form of equal treatment of voters, and *nondictatoriality* serves as a particularly weak version of anonymity.

Definition 2.5. An SCF f is *neutral* if each pair of alternatives are interchangeable in the following sense: whenever a profile $P^\dagger$ is obtained from another P by swapping the positions of the two alternatives x and y in every ballot, the outcome $f(P^\dagger)$ is obtained

---

[21] We should qualify, in at least two respects, the picture painted here. First, there are important strands of research that are not axiomatic—they do not measure the success or failure of some SCF to satisfy some property in black-or-white terms. These include empirical and experimental methods in the political realm (e.g., van der Straeten et al., 2013), as well as enumerations and simulations (e.g., Kelly, 1993; Aleskerov and Kurbanov, 1999). Second, while strategyproofness may be impractical as a requirement for SCFs, it can be achieved in some collective decision-making contexts other than voting (Moulin, 1988a). Moreover, SCFs can achieve strategyproofness when their domains are limited appropriately, as we see in Section 2.9.

[22] Transpositions τ_{ij} of pairs generate the full permutation group on N, so anonymity demands that f be blind to *every* permutation of the voters; informally, "f is invariant under renaming voters." Anonymous SCFs are those that use only the information in the voting situation derived from a profile P (which represents P's equivalence class under permutations of voters).

from $f(P)$ via a similar swap;[23] f is *imposed* if some alternative x is unelectable: for no profile P does $f(P) = \{x\}$.

Neutrality is a very strong form of equal treatment of alternatives, and *nonimposition* serves as a particularly weak version of neutrality.

So far, nothing we have said rules out the following "reverse Borda" SCF: elect the alternative(s) having the *lowest* Borda score. Given a profile P we will say that alternative x *Pareto dominates* alternative y if every voter ranks x over y; y is *Pareto dominated* if such an x exists.

Definition 2.6 (Pareto Principle; Pareto, 1919). An SCF f is *Pareto* (aka *Pareto optimal*, or *Paretian*) if $f(P)$ never contains a Pareto dominated alternative.

Plurality, Copeland, and Borda are clearly anonymous, neutral, and Pareto (while reverse Borda is not Pareto). Note also that Pareto implies nonimposition.

Should a voting rule be immediately rejected if it fails anonymity, or neutrality, or Pareto optimality? Yes, in some voting contexts—but not in others. Legislative voting rules are often neither anonymous nor neutral,[24] and if our goal, for example, were to elect a committee rather than an individual, we might wish to consider the rule that adds alternatives having progressively lower Copeland scores as winners, until some minimal committee size is achieved; such a rule is not Pareto.[25]

These three axioms, while uncontroversial, do illustrate the law of unintended consequences, in the form of a (small) impossibility theorem. Consider profile P_4 for $n = 3k$ voters and $m \geqslant 3$ alternatives (with $A = \{a, b, c, x_1, \ldots, x_{m-3}\}$):

k	k	k
a	c	b
b	a	c
c	b	a
x_1	x_1	x_1
$\vdots$	$\vdots$	$\vdots$

Symmetries imply that every neutral, anonymous, and Pareto SCF f satisfies $f(P_4) = \{a, b, c\}$.[26] A similar construction forces tied outcomes whenever some factor r of n satisfies $1 < r \leqslant m$ (with $r = 3$ for P_4), establishing

---

[23] That is, $f(P^\dagger)$ is the image of $f(P)$ under τ_{xy}. As with anonymity, transpositions may be replaced with arbitrary permutations. However, neutrality is not an invariance property, so the analogy with anonymity is imperfect; we cannot directly apply f to equivalence classes of profiles under permutations of alternatives ... but for a way around this see Eğeciouglu and Giritligil (2013).

[24] In a legislative voting system, representatives vote for or against proposals (such as adding a new law) and the set of alternatives might be $A = \{yes, no\}$ (or $\{yes, no, abstain\}$, or ...). It is fairly common for the voting rule to have a deliberate bias in favor of the *status quo* ("no, do not alter the current body of law by adding a new one"), which may be quite strong when voting on constitutional change. Such rules are not neutral. In bicameral legislatures (wherein passage of a new law requires approval of both chambers) a legislator from one of the chambers is not interchangeable with one from the other, so the rule is not anonymous.

[25] While Definition 2.6 fails for this rule, arguably it is a different version of Pareto that should be applied here—one for which the *committees* are considered to be the alternatives.

[26] Suppose $f(P_4) = X$. As f is Pareto, $X \subseteq \{a, b, c\}$, so assume w.l.o.g. $a \in X$. The transposition τ_{ab}, coupled with a suitable permutation of the voters, both fixes P_4 and carries X to X's image under τ_{ab}. Thus, $b \in X$. Similarly, $c \in X$.

Proposition 2.1 (Moulin, 1983). *Let $m \geqslant 2$ be the number of alternatives and n be the number of voters. If n is divisible by any integer r with $1 < r \leqslant m$, then no neutral, anonymous, and Pareto SCF is resolute (single-valued).*[27]

Tied outcomes make life complicated in terms of real applications (we only want *one* mayor) and of theory: how can we decide whether a strategically cast ballot results in a successful manipulation, if both it and the sincere ballot yield several winning alternatives? The four main approaches taken in the literature[28] are as follows:

1. Use a fixed ordering of the alternatives (or a designated voter) to break all ties.
2. Use a randomized mechanism to break all ties.
3. Deal with set-valued outcomes directly.
4. Ignore or suppress the issue (assume no ties exist).

The first approach breaks neutrality (or anonymity, if using a designated voter). The second requires that we consider "indeterminate" voting rules, along with what it means to manipulate one. With approach 3, adapting the definitions (in Section 2.6) of monotonicity properties and strategyproofness might seem to require choosing a "set extension principle" (which extends preferences over individual alternatives to ones over sets), although alternative approaches exist.[29]

We can agree that approach 4 is quite reasonable as a preliminary, simplifying assumption when first exploring some new concept. As to the importance of (or interest in) a subsequent careful reconsideration of that concept in light of ties, opinions differ.

2.4 Voting Rules I: Condorcet Extensions, Scoring Rules, and Run-Offs

When there are only two alternatives, the distinction between a preference ranking and a plurality ballot disappears, and one SCF in particular jumps to mind. *Majority rule* declares the winner to be the alternative that gets strictly more votes, with a two-way tie when the alternatives split the vote evenly. Majority rule is neutral and anonymous, and is resolute if the number of voters is odd. A characterization, however, requires an additional element of *monotonicity* (if x is a winner and one voter switches her ballot from y to x, then x remains a winner) or of *positive responsiveness* (if x is a winner and one voter switches her ballot from y to x, then x becomes the unique winner). Monotonicity excludes certain perverse rules (e.g., elect whichever alternative gets an odd number of votes) while positive responsiveness additionally breaks all ties that are

---

[27] If every factor of n exceeds m, then a resolute SCF can be neutral, anonymous, and Pareto. See later discussion immediately after Theorem 2.7.

[28] For a fifth approach, see Footnote 66. In real world political elections with large numbers of voters, election returns may be too "noisy" to declare an exact tie with certainty, and very close elections are sometimes settled in court. However, some countries have election laws that mandate coin tosses to settle ties; in 2013 the mayoral election in San Teodoro, the Philipines, was settled this way. The French electoral code specifies that ties be broken in favor of the older candidate (consequently, parties favor older candidates in some elections).

[29] For more on these approaches—which are less different than may first appear—see Gärdenfors (1976), Gärdenfors (1979), Barberà et al. (2001), Barberà et al. (2004), Brandt and Brill (2011), Sanver and Zwicker (2012).

not "knife-edge" (excluding, for example, the rule electing all alternatives getting at least one third of the vote).

Proposition 2.2 (May's Theorem; May, 1952). *For two alternatives and an odd number of voters, majority rule is the unique resolute, anonymous, neutral, and monotonic SCF. For two alternatives and any number of voters, it is the unique anonymous, neutral, and positively responsive SCF.*

Proof. It is evident that majority rule satisfies these properties. For uniqueness, note that with any other rule we may choose a profile for which x wins with fewer votes than y. Switch enough ballots from y to x to exactly reverse these vote totals. Monotonicity implies x still wins, but neutrality + anonymity say y wins. Similarly, if x ties y, yet has fewer votes, positive responsiveness contradicts neutrality + anonymity.   □

It is not unreasonable to interpret Proposition 2.2 as saying that majority rule is the best voting rule for two alternatives (in certain contexts, anyway). So, which SCFs can claim the mantle as "majority rule for 3 or more alternatives"? On one hand, each of the SCFs we have considered so far (along with a host of others) reduces to majority rule for the case $m = 2$, and in quite a natural way. So one might argue that most rules can claim this mantle. On the other hand, for SCFs defined on the "full domain" (*all* of $\mathcal{L}(A)^n$) there is no completely satisfactory extension of May's Theorem to the case of 3 or more alternatives.[30] In this sense, then, no voting method wins the mantle. Nonetheless, one rule has long claimed a special place as most deserving:

Definition 2.7. A *Condorcet winner* for a profile P is an alternative x that defeats every other alternative in the strict pairwise majority sense: $x >^{\mu}_P y$ for all $y \neq x$.[31] *Pairwise Majority Rule*, henceforth *PMR*, declares the winning alternative to be the Condorcet winner … and is undefined when a profile *has* no Condorcet winner.

When a Condorcet winner exists, it is unique. With three or more alternatives, however, *majority cycles* can rule them out. The cycle $a >^{\mu} b$, $b >^{\mu} c$, and $c >^{\mu} a$ of profile P_2 is depicted in Figure 2.1; no PMR winner exists. Such a cycle is also known as *Condorcet's voting paradox*, and corresponds to intransitivity of the relation $>^{\mu}$. Cycles represent a disturbing type of instability. Imagine a version with 10 voters and 10 alternatives,[32] wherein *any* alternative x selected as winner would prompt 90% of the voters to agree on an alternative y they all prefer to x and to approve, by an overwhelming margin, a referendum replacing x with y. A different 90% would then replace y with z, and so on. One cannot overstate the importance of majority cycles to the theory of voting—they lie behind a number of the most important results.

A significant literature is concerned with calculating the probability that a Condorcet winner exists (or that $\geq^{\mu}$ is transitive), or the *Condorcet efficiency* of a voting rule—the conditional probability that the rule elects the Condorcet winner, given that a Condorcet

---

[30] Such extensions do exist in voting contexts other than SCFs (see Freixas and Zwicker (2009), for example) and also for SCFs on restricted domains (as we will see in a moment).

[31] Some prefer *strong Condorcet winner* for this notion; a *weak* Condorcet winner satisfies $x \geq^{\mu}_P y$ for all $y \neq x$.

[32] Voter 1 ranks a on top, with b through j following in alphabetical order; each subsequent ballot is derived from its predecessor by "vertical rotation": lift the bottom-ranked alternative to the top, and drop each of the others down by one spot.

winner exists—or with identifying the most Condorcet efficient rule (from among all scoring rules, for example).[33] The answers depend on the underlying probability distribution over profiles.[34]

PMR does not always declare a winner, so it is an *SCF with restricted domain*. Our interest here is with full SCFs that agree with PMR on its domain:

Definition 2.8. Let $\mathcal{D}_{Condorcet}$ denote the *Condorcet domain*—the set of all profiles P for which a *Condorcet winner* exists. An SCF f is a *Condorcet extension* (or is *Condorcet consistent*) if f selects the Condorcet winner alone, for each profile $P \in \mathcal{D}_{Condorcet}$.

Note that the monotonicity hypothesis in May's Theorem is equivalent to strategy-proofness (because $m = 2$). Thus if we are willing to consider SCFs whose domain is restricted to $\mathcal{D}_{Condorcet}$, the following result (see Campbell and Kelly, 2003) can plausibly claim to be "May's Theorem for three or more alternatives":

Theorem 2.3 (Campbell-Kelly Theorem).[35] *Consider SCFs with domain $\mathcal{D}_{Condorcet}$ for three or more alternatives. Pairwise Majority Rule is resolute, anonymous, neutral, and strategyproof; for an odd number of voters, it is the unique such rule.*[36]

Proof. Clearly PMR, as restricted to $\mathcal{D}_{Condorcet}$, is resolute, neutral, and anonymous. To see that it is strategyproof (Definition 2.3), assume that voter i's (sincere) ballot has $y \succ_i x$ with x being the Condorcet winner. Then replacing $\succsim_i$ with some alternative (insincere) ballot cannot reverse $x >^\mu y$, and thus cannot make y the new Condorcet winner. We postpone the proof of uniqueness to Section 2.8.   □

Some find Condorcet consistency so compelling that they view it as absolutely necessary when choosing a voting rule, but this view is not universal. We treat it here as a member of the second group—plausible axioms that cannot all be satisfied at once. Borda can fail to elect an alternative who is top-ranked by a majority of the voters, and in this sense fails rather badly to be a Condorcet extension.[37] On the other hand, the Borda score of a Condorcet winner is always strictly above the average Borda score of all alternatives.[38]

---

[33] See Gehrlein (2006), Saari (2009), Favardin et al. (2002), Cervone et al. (2005), for example.

[34] The two most prominent distributions studied are "IC" (*Impartial Culture*—voters choose linear orderings randomly and independently, with probability $\frac{1}{m!}$ for each ordering) and "IAC" (*Impartial Anonymous Culture*—each voting situation is equiprobable); see Berg (1985), Gehrlein (2002). But others have been considered, e.g., in Regenwetter et al. (2006) and Eğeciouglu and Giritligil (2013).

[35] Campbell and Kelly's result (Theorem 1 in Campbell and Kelly, 2003) is stronger; it assumes nonimposition and nondictatoriality in place of anonymity and neutrality. Another version of their theorem assumes *group* strategyproofness and does not require odd n.

[36] In applying the definition of strategyproofness to a function having this restricted domain we require that the profiles P and P' (arising respectively before, and after, voter i switches to $\succ_i'$ from her sincere ballot $\succ_i$) both lie in $\mathcal{D}_{Condorcet}$.

[37] For example, this happens if three of five voters rank $a \succ b \succ c$ while two rank $b \succ c \succ a$. For this reason, some describe Borda as a compromise that takes minority views into account, even when they are opposed by a majority who completely agree with one another.

[38] The symmetric Borda score (2.3) of a Condorcet winner is a sum of strictly positive numbers, whereas the average symmetric Borda score is always zero. Similarly, a *Condorcet loser*—an x for which $y >^\mu x$ for each alternative $y \neq x$—is assigned a negative score, which is strictly below average. In particular, a Borda winner is never a Condorcet loser.

The Copeland score of a Condorcet winner is $m - 1$, and uniquely highest, so Copeland is a Condorcet extension. Other well-known Condorcet extensions include:

- *Simpson Rule* (aka *Simpson-Kramer, minimax*): Let $\min\{Net_P(x > y) \mid y \in A \setminus \{x\}\}$ give the (symmetric) Simpson score $Simpson_P(x)$ of an alternative x. The Simpson winner is the alternative(s) with highest Simpson score.[39]
- *Top Cycle*: If there is a chain $x = x_1 \geqslant^\mu x_2 \geqslant^\mu \cdots \geqslant^\mu x_j = y$ from alternative x to y we will write $x \geqslant^\mu_T y$; $\geqslant^\mu_T$ is the transitive closure of the *weak* pairwise majority relation $\geqslant^\mu$. An alternative x is in the *top cycle* if $x \geqslant^\mu_T y$ for each alternative $y \neq x$, and the Top Cycle SCF declares each such x to be a winner. Equivalently, the top cycle is the uniquely smallest *dominant set* (where a set X of alternatives is *dominant* if $x >^\mu y$ for each $x \in X$ and $y \notin X$).[40]
- *Sequential Majority Comparison (SMC)*: Fix some enumeration $\{x_1, x_2, \ldots, x_m\}$ of the alternatives. The winner of round 1 is x_1; the winner of round $i + 1$ is the winner w of round i, if $w \geqslant^\mu x_{i+1}$, and is x_{i+1}, if $x_{i+1} >^\mu w$; and the ultimate winner is the winner of round m.[41]

To break the three-way Copeland tie of profile P_2, how many voters would need to switch their vote? As the answer suggests, Copeland is highly *indecisive* as a voting rule, yielding many ties. Simpson has an advantage over Copeland in this respect. Top Cycle is even less decisive than Copeland—in fact, the Copeland winners are always within the top cycle, and the top cycle can include Pareto-dominated alternatives. Every SMC winner is in the top cycle, and SMC can likewise elect a Pareto-dominated alternative.

Sequential Majority Comparison figures prominently in Chapter 19 and has also been called *sequential pairwise majority*. Although we use "sequential" here to refer to a linear sequence, one can also use a partial order—a tree—to dictate the order of majority comparisons between pairs of alternatives; see Horan (2013), for example. In its dependence on the enumeration, SMC may initially seem a rather odd rule, and of course its failure to be neutral argues against its use in electing the mayor of a town (for example). But legislative voting bodies are often limited by their constitutions to making binary decisions via majority rule, so if they wish to consider more than one alternative to the current body of law (such as an immigration reform bill with multiple versions arising from a number of possible amendments),[42] there is little alternative to employing something resembling SMC.

Scoring rules form a second large class of related SCFs:

---

[39] Alternately, Simpson winners *minimize* $\max\{Net_P(y > x) \mid y \in A \setminus \{x\}\}$, whence the term "minimax."

[40] A strictly weaker graph-theoretic notion has a similar name: X is a *dominating set* if for each vertex $y \notin X$ there exists an $x \in X$ with $x \to y$. A set X of alternatives that is dominating for the pairwise majority tournament need not be dominant.

[41] Banks (1985) assumes sophisticated voting (wherein voters "take into account the optimal behavior of others in solving their own optimal decisions") and characterizes the set of SMC winners arising from all possible enumerations, now known as the *Banks set*.

[42] In this case, the official with *agenda setting power* gets to choose the order in which amendments are considered, and may wield considerable influence over the final form of the legislation.

Definition 2.9. A *score vector* $\mathbf{w} = (w_1, w_2, \ldots, w_m)$ consists of real number *scoring weights*; $\mathbf{w}$ is *proper* if $w_1 \geqslant w_2 \geqslant \cdots \geqslant w_{m-1} \geqslant w_m$ and $w_1 > w_m$. Any score vector induces a *scoring rule*, in which each voter awards w_1 points to their top-ranked alternative, w_2 points to their second-ranked, and so on. All points awarded to a given alternative are summed, and the winner is the alternative(s) with greatest sum.[43] A *proper scoring rule* is one induced by a proper score vector.

In addition to the Borda count, with $\mathbf{w} = (m - 1, m - 2, \ldots, 1, 0)$, scoring rules include:

- *Plurality*: $\mathbf{w} = (1, 0, 0, \ldots, 0)$
- *Anti-plurality*: $\mathbf{w} = (1, 1, 1, \ldots, 1, 0)$
- *k-Approval*: $\mathbf{w} = (1, 1, 1, \ldots, 1, 0, 0, \ldots, 0)$ (with k 1s)
- *Formula One Championship*: $\mathbf{w} = (25, 18, 15, 12, 10, 8, 6, 4, 2, 1, 0, \ldots, 0)$[44]

A third class of multiround rules is based on the idea that less popular alternatives in one round be dropped from all ballots in the next round (with each ballot then ranking the remaining alternatives in the same relative order that they had in the initial version of that ballot); these rounds continue until some surviving alternative achieves majority support (or until only one is left standing). The best-known of these has multiple names—*Alternative Vote, Hare (Hare, 1859), Single Transferable Vote (STV), Instant Run-off Voting (IRV)*, and *Ranked Choice Voting (RCV)*—and proceeds as follows: at each stage, the alternative with lowest plurality score is dropped from all ballots, and at the first stage for which some alternative x sits atop a majority of the ballots, x is declared the winner.[45]

Related rules include the following:

- *Plurality Run-off*: If some alternative is top ranked by a majority of the voters, it wins in round 1; otherwise, round 2 consists of majority rule applied to the two alternatives with highest plurality score in round 1.
- *Baldwin*: In each round, the alternative with lowest Borda score is dropped. The final alternative eliminated is the winner (Baldwin, 1926).
- *Nanson*: In each round, drop all alternatives with below-average Borda score. The final alternative eliminated is the winner (Nanson, 1882; Niou, 1987).

---

[43] Alternately a SWF can be defined by ranking alternatives in descending order of point totals.

[44] Since 2010, a driver gets 25 points for each Formula One Grand Prix race they win, 18 points for each second place, etc., and the World Championship goes to the driver with greatest point total for that season. In effect, the races serve as voters. Related rules have been used since 1950, but in some earlier versions a driver was awarded points for his or her top j finishes only.

[45] The vexing matter of how to deal with ties for lowest plurality score is often ignored, perhaps because for large, political elections uncertainties in counting (and in classifying ballots as valid or not) leave the matter moot. One method suggested (Taylor and Pacelli, 2006) is to drop *all* alternatives sharing a lowest plurality score. If each of $k \geqslant 3$ surviving alternatives garners the same plurality score, this method eliminates all of them, with no alternative ever achieving majority support (unless one eliminates the stop-when-there-is-a-majority rule and instead declares, as winners, all alternatives eliminated in the final round). The second (Conitzer et al., 2009b) chooses at each stage *one* alternative to eliminate, among those achieving minimal plurality score, but considers all possible sequences of such choices, identifying the winning alternative for each sequence, and declaring a tie among them.

STV is perhaps the most popular rule among electoral reform societies.[46] Supporters argue that voters do not "waste" their vote when their top choice is unpopular—instead, it is transferred to the next choice on their ballot. Plurality run-off is a bit different in being limited to two rounds at most, but agrees with STV for three alternatives. Neither of these systems is a Condorcet extension.[47,48] Both Baldwin and Nanson *are* Condorcet extensions, as the elimination process never discards a Condorcet winner; for the explanation see Footnote 38, which also shows that Nanson discards any Condorcet loser in round one.

2.5 An Informational Basis for Voting Rules: Fishburn's Classification

Figure 2.1 (left) depicts the *pairwise majority tournament* for profile P_2—the complete directed graph induced by $>^\mu$ (see Footnote 11). To calculate a winner, the Copeland, Top Cycle, and Sequential Majority Comparison SCFs need only the information from this tournament. Peter Fishburn (1977) classified such SCFs as $C1$ *functions*; loosely speaking, such SCFs correspond to *tournament solutions* as studied in Chapter 3.[49]

Borda and Simpson need the additional information in the *weighted tournament*— the net preferences[50] of Figure 2.1 (right)—and are classified in $C2$. Imagine that each voter's ranking $>_i$ is represented as a set of ordered pairs in the usual way, and a union (counting multiplicity) of all rankings from the profile is taken. Ordered pairs in this multiset are sorted into bins according to which two alternatives are in the pair. Then $C2$ functions rely only on the information represented by these bins; what is lost is

<hr/>

[46] In the United Kingdom a 2011 referendum proposing a switch from plurality voting to STV lost when almost 68% voted *No*. In the United States the FairVote organization advocates STV (under the IRV name), and has been successful in some locales. For example, the city of Burlington, Vermont, adopted IRV for its 2006 mayoral election and later repealed it, when in 2009 the IRV winner (Kiss) differed from the plurality winner (Wright). One analysis argued that the Condorcet winner was a third candidate (Montroll), and that the "no show" paradox (discussed after Proposition 2.6) had applied. See http://rangevoting.org/Burlington.html and http://vermontdailybriefing.com/?p=1215.

[47] Consider any profile for 4 alternatives wherein alternative a is ranked second by all voters, with each of the other alternatives ranked first by around one third of the voters. The Condorcet winner a is eliminated in the first round.

[48] A version of plurality run-off is used for presidential elections in France, Austria , . . . indeed, in more countries than use plurality (see Blais et al., 1997); voters do not submit ranked ballots, but instead return to the ballot box if a second round is required. The method attracted international attention in the 2002 French election, when the far-right candidate Le Pen bested the Socialist Jospin in round one, and ran against the incumbent Chirac in round two (which Chirac won with over 82% of the vote, after having captured under 20% in round one). Reportedly, voters with allegiance to small left-wing parties chose to vote for these parties in round one, assuming that Jospin would survive to round two, when they would vote for him. In round one of the 2012 election Francois Bayrou came in fifth, with 11% of the vote, yet data suggests that he may have been a Condorcet winner (van der Straeten et al., 2013); there is some uncertainty because the conclusion is sensitive to the method used to control sample bias (private communication of the authors).

[49] Unlike an SCF, a tournament solution takes as input only the tournament itself (rather than an underlying profile that may have induced that tournament). Also, a tournament solution f is often assumed to satisfy the conditions corresponding to neutrality and Condorcet extension (for the $C1$ SCF f^* induced by f).

[50] Alternately, for each two alternatives draw edges in both directions, labeling the $x \to y$ edge with *gross* preference (absolute number of voters ranking x over y). In a fixed electorate context one knows the number n of voters, so the information in these labels is equivalent to the net preferences.

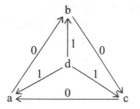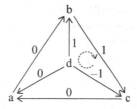

Figure 2.2. A basic cocycle (left) and a basic cycle (right). The -1 on edge $d \rightarrow c$ indicates that its pre-assigned orientation opposes the cycle's clockwise direction.

whether a given (a, b) pair came from a ranking with (b, c) or one with (c, b). Social choice functions in $C2$ correspond (speaking as loosely as in the previous paragraph) to *weighted tournament solutions*—the topic of Chapter 4.

Any SCFs not in $C1$ or $C2$ are $C3$. In a sense, $C3$ SCFs need "more" information; the bins of atomized pairs are insufficient. But plurality is in $C3$, and one should balk at a suggestion that Borda needs less information than plurality. Borda, for example, needs all the information in the *rank vector* $\rho(x) = (\rho_1(x), \rho_2(x), \ldots, \rho_m(x))$ of an alternative x (where $\rho_j(x)$ denotes the number of voters who rank x in j^{th} position), while plurality does not. Thus while Fishburn's classification is a particularly useful approach to informational bases, it is not the only such approach.

A further refinement of $C2$ is based on the orthogonal decomposition approaches of Zwicker (1991) and Saari (1995). Any weighted tournament can be viewed as a vector $\mathbf{v}$ whose scalar components are the edge weights. As such, $\mathbf{v}$ has a unique decomposition $\mathbf{v} = \mathbf{v}_{cycle} + \mathbf{v}_{cocycle}$ with $\mathbf{v}_{cycle} \perp \mathbf{v}_{cocycle}$, wherein $\mathbf{v}_{cycle}$ is a linear combination of *basic cycles* and $\mathbf{v}_{cocycle}$ is a linear combination of *basic cocycles*—see Figure 2.2 (for the case of 4 alternatives).

We may interpret $\mathbf{v}_{cycle}$ as the underlying tendency toward a majority cycle, while $\mathbf{v}_{cocycle}$ contains exactly the same information as the list of symmetric Borda scores.[51,52] Condorcet extensions use the information in both components, while the Borda count discards $\mathbf{v}_{cycle}$ and imposes a version of pairwise majority rule based on $\mathbf{v}_{cocycle}$ alone.[53] Whether the ranking according to PMR (the true version, based on both components) agrees with the ranking induced by Borda score, or differs from it, or fails to be a ranking at all, depends on the relative balance (speaking loosely) between $\mathbf{v}_{cocycle}$ and $\mathbf{v}_{cycle}$.

2.6 Axioms II: Reinforcement and Monotonicity Properties

We consider axioms that distinguish among the three classes of rules introduced in the previous section. More than two hundred years ago Condorcet and Borda disagreed

[51] This same decomposition serves as a basis for Kirchoff's laws, where the edge weights represent flow of electric current (rather than flow of net preference, as in our setting); a basic cocycle is a sink or source of current (such as a battery) while a simple cycle is a "loop current."

[52] The asymmetric scores encode one additional piece of information: the number of voters.

[53] The map that discards $\mathbf{v}_{cycle}$ is an orthogonal projection, and coincides with the boundary map of homology theory in the one-dimensional case. The version of PMR based on $\mathbf{v}_{cocycle}$ alone satisfies a strong, quantitative transitivity property.

over the best way to aggregate preferences, and the theory sketched here suggests—to a surprising degree—that their split in point-of-view is of fundamental importance.

Each axiom in this section concerns the way an SCF responds to profile changes, which can be of two kinds:

• One or more voters modify their ballots.
• One or more voters are added to a profile.

The second type requires the variable electorate context, and may be formalized in terms of voting situations: for $s, t \colon \mathcal{L}(A) \to \mathbb{Z}^+$, the pointwise sum $s + t$ represents the effect of pooling disjoint electorates corresponding to s and t while ks $(k \in \mathbb{N})$ replaces each individual voter of s with k "clones."[54]

Reinforcement (aka *Consistency*) requires that the common winning alternatives chosen by two disjoint sets of voters (assuming common winners exist) be exactly those chosen by the union of these sets; precisely, an SCF f is reinforcing if

$$f(s) \cap f(t) \neq \emptyset \Rightarrow f(s + t) = f(s) \cap f(t) \tag{2.4}$$

for all voting situations s and t. *Homogeneity*, a weak form, demands $f(ks) = f(s)$ for each $k \in \mathbb{N}$; intermediate forms include $f(s) = f(t) \Rightarrow f(s + t) = f(s) = f(t)$.

Scoring rules are reinforcing, for if some alternative x has highest score for s and t both, then x's score for $s + t$ (the sum of x's s and t scores) must also be highest. The same argument applies to the *compound* scoring rules, wherein any ties resulting from a first score vector $\mathbf{w}_1$ may be broken by score differences arising from a second such vector $\mathbf{w}_2$ (e.g., use plurality score to break ties among Borda winners), with a possible third vector used to break ties that still remain, and so on; any finite number $j \geqslant 1$ of score vectors may be used.[55] In fact, reinforcement essentially characterizes such rules:

Theorem 2.4 (Smith, 1973; Young, 1975). *The anonymous, neutral, and reinforcing SCFs are exactly the compound scoring rules.*[56]

Proposition 2.5. *All Condorcet extension SCFs for three or more alternatives violate reinforcement.*

Proof. If there are 3 alternatives,[57] consider the voting situations s and t:

2	2	2
a	c	b
b	a	c
c	b	a

2	1
b	a
a	b
c	c

[54] Formally, $(s + t)(\succsim) = s(\succsim) + t(\succsim)$ and $(ks)(\succsim) = k(s(\succsim))$.

[55] On a domain that is restricted by fixing an upper bound on the number of voters, every such compound rule is equivalent to some simple scoring rule.

[56] Moreover, the class of "simple" (non-compound) scoring rules may be characterized by adding one more axiom, *continuity* (aka the *Archimedean* property), which asserts that for all voting situations s and t with $f(t) = \{x\}$, there exist a $k \in \mathbb{N}$ such that $f(s + jt) = \{x\}$ for all $j \geqslant k$.

[57] If we additionally assume the Pareto property, extending this proof to the case of 4 or more alternatives is straightforward. Without Pareto, the proof for $m \geqslant 4$ is more complicated.

Let f be any Condorcet extension, and assume for the moment that $b \in f(s)$. As b is t's Condorcet winner, $f(t) = \{b\}$. Reinforcement would demand $f(s + t) = f(s) \cap \{b\}$ whence $b \in f(s + t)$, but $f(s + t) = \{a\}$, as a is $s + t$'s Condorcet winner. A similar contradiction results from assuming $a \in f(s)$ (or $c \in f(s)$), using a suitably permuted version of t.   □

A function f from the real numbers to the real numbers is *monotonically increasing* if $x \geqslant y \Rightarrow f(x) \geqslant f(y)$. In voting, a monotonicity property similarly asserts that a change in the input of an SCF and the corresponding output change "point in the same direction."

We first consider a particular type of change to a ballot: if one preference ranking $\succsim'$ is obtained from another $\succsim$ by moving alternative x from under one or more alternatives (in $\succsim$) to over them (in $\succsim'$), *without changing the relative order of any pair of alternatives that exclude x*, then we say that $\succsim'$ is obtained from $\succsim$ by *lifting x simply* (and $\succsim$ is obtained from $\succsim'$ by *dropping x simply*). Among various monotonicity properties considered in the literature, the earliest, most widely studied is usually known simply as *monotonicity* (Fishburn, 1982):

Definition 2.10. A resolute SCF f satisfies *monotonicity* (aka weak monotonicity) if whenever a profile P is modified to P' by having one voter i switch $\succsim_i$ to $\succsim'_i$ by lifting the winning alternative $x = f(P)$ simply, $f(P') = f(P)$.

If we apply Definition 2.10 to an irresolute f, it only "bites" for profiles lacking ties.[58]

Given an SCF f based on maximizing some form of score, suppose we know that lifting x simply never lowers x's score or raises y's score for $y \neq x$. Then f must be monotonic (and remains so if we use any fixed ordering of alternatives to break ties). It follows that Copeland, Simpson, and all proper scoring rules are monotonic.[59]

Smith (1980) shows that every scoring run-off rule violates monotonicity. We show this result for plurality run-off and STV, with the help of the following example:

6	4	5	2		6	4	5	2
a	b	c	b		a	b	c	a
b	c	a	a		b	c	a	b
c	a	b	c		c	a	b	c

When either of these rules is applied to the profile P_5 above, c is eliminated in the first round, whereupon a achieves a strict majority, and is sole winner. Let P_6 be obtained from P_5 by having one of the two $b \succ a \succ c$ voters lift a simply (over b) and P_7 be obtained from P_5 by having the remaining $b \succ a \succ c$ voter do the same. When either

---

[58] It follows that this "resolute" version of monotonicity can be satisfied vacuously by *any* SCF that has been modified by adding a tied alternative to the outcome for each profile. This suggests a need to find an appropriate "irresolute" version—one that cannot be so easily fooled. Peleg (1981) suggested the following: after any simple lift of a winning alternative x, x remains a winning alternative *and no new winning alternatives are added*. Other authors propose irresolute versions that omit the italicized part of Peleg's requirement—see Footnote 61 in this connection. Sanver and Zwicker (2012) argue for Peleg's version based on a general methodology for handling irresoluteness. Note also that by allowing the set of winners to change, Peleg's version addresses a possible critique of the resolute version—a requirement that the winning alternative not change at all seems contrary to the spirit of our generic "corresponding output change" language.

[59] Similarly, they satisfy the more stringent version due to Peleg (Footnote 58), as do SMC and Top Cycle.

procedure is now run on P_7, alternative b is eliminated first, whereupon c displaces a as the new majority winner, with 9 of the 17 ballots.

If we used an alternative definition of monotonicity allowing *several* voters to simultaneously lift the winning alternative, then monotonicity would fail as $P_5 \mapsto P_7$ (in one step). For our version we observe that no matter what set X of winners results[60] from P_6, there must be a failure of monotonicity in the first step $\{a\} \mapsto X$ (as $P_5 \mapsto P_6$) or in the second $X \mapsto \{c\}$ (as $P_6 \mapsto P_7$).[61]

Now suppose the last two voters of P_7 truly prefer $a \succ b \succ c$. They will be disappointed under STV when the winner turns out to be c. They would do better by casting $b \succ a \succ c$, and achieving a win for their most preferred alternative a. Indeed, *any* failure of monotonicity for a resolute SCF f represents an opportunity for a voter to manipulate f in a particular way: via a simple drop or simple lift.[62] Thus monotonicity is a weak form of strategyproofness. The same holds for the following monotonicity properties (except for *participation*):

Definition 2.11. A resolute SCF f satisfies:

- *Strategyproofness* if whenever a profile P is modified to P' by having one voter i switch $\succsim_i$ to $\succsim'_i$, $f(P) \succsim_i f(P')$.[63]
- *Maskin monotonicity* (aka *strong monotonicity*) if whenever a profile P is modified to P' by having one voter i switch $\succsim_i$ to a ballot $\succsim'_i$ satisfying for all y $f(P) \succsim_i y \Rightarrow f(P) \succsim'_i y$, $f(P') = f(P)$; see Maskin (1977), Maskin (1999).
- *Down monotonicity* if whenever a profile P is modified to P' by having one voter i switch $\succsim_i$ to $\succsim'_i$ by dropping a losing alternative $b \neq f(P)$ simply, $f(P') = f(P)$.
- *One-way monotonicity* if whenever a profile P is modified to P' by having one voter i switch $\succsim_i$ to $\succsim'_i$, $f(P) \succsim_i f(P')$ or $f(P') \succsim'_i f(P)$.
- *Half-way monotonicity* if whenever a profile P is modified to P' by having one voter i switch $\succsim_i$ to $\succsim_i^{rev}$, $f(P) \succsim_i f(P')$.
  (Here $\succsim^{rev}$ denotes the reverse of $\succsim$: $z \succsim w \Leftrightarrow w \succsim^{rev} z$.)
- *Participation* (the absence of no show paradoxes) if whenever a profile P is modified to P' by adding one voter i with ballot $\succsim_i$ to the electorate, $f(P') \succsim_i f(P)$.

Proposition 2.6. *For resolute social choice functions,*

1. *Strategyproofness* $\Rightarrow$ *Maskin monotonicity* $\Leftrightarrow$ *Down monotonicity* $\Rightarrow$ *Monotonicity*
2. *Strategyproofness* $\Rightarrow$ *One-way monotonicity* $\Rightarrow$ *Half-way monotonicity*
3. *Participation* $\Rightarrow$ *Half-way monotonicity*

Proof. For the first arrow of item 1 of Proposition 2.6 reason as in Footnote 62. For the second arrow in the left direction, show that repeated changes to $\succsim_i$ of the kind allowed by down monotonicity can be used to effect any change allowed by Maskin

---

[60] To resolve how STV or plurality run-off behave when handed P_6 would require addressing the issue raised in Footnote 45.

[61] This is clear if X is a singleton. If not, then either of the two "irresolute" versions of monotonicity discussed in Footnote 58 imply such a failure.

[62] Suppose $\succ_i \mapsto \succ'_i$ via a simple lift of the winning alternative a, which makes a lose and b win.
    If $b \succ_i a$, then a voter with sincere preference $\succ_i$ would gain by casting the insincere ballot $\succ'_i$; if $a \succ_i b$, then a voter with sincere preference $\succ'_i$ would gain by casting the insincere ballot $\succ_i$.

[63] In the resolute context this agrees with our earlier Definition 2.3 of single voter strategyproofness.

monotonicity. The second arrow to the right and the third arrow are straightforward, as is item 2. For item 3, see Sanver and Zwicker (2009). ☐

Down monotonicity, perhaps surprisingly, is much stronger than monotonicity—it is the form of strategyproofness used in our proof (in Section 2.8) of the Gibbard-Satterthwaite Theorem. Participation originated in the work of Brams and Fishburn (2007), who observed that some voting rules are susceptible to the *no show paradox*, wherein a voter does better by choosing to not participate in the election than by casting a sincere ballot. Such a voter can manipulate the outcome by abstaining. Speaking loosely, then, participation is a form of strategyproofness.

Speaking precisely, however, participation is a property of variable-electorate SCFs, and so cannot follow from strategyproofness, which is defined here (as is typical) for fixed-electorate SCFs.[64] Thus in the following theorem, part 1 (Moulin, 1988b) cannot be compared directly to the Gibbard-Satterthwaite Theorem. Part 2 (Sanver and Zwicker, 2009), however, is a different story; any failure of half-way monotonicity is indeed a violation of strategyproofness, of a rather drastic kind (see the earlier discussion in Section 2.2).

Theorem 2.7. *Let f be any resolute Condorcet extension for four or more alternatives. Then*

1. *f violates participation (if f is a variable-electorate SCF)[65] and*
2. *f violates half-way monotonicity (if f is a fixed-electorate SCF for sufficiently large n).*

Proper scoring rules behave quite differently—they satisfy participation and one-way monotonicity (hence half-way monotonicity) even after being rendered resolute by breaking ties via a fixed ordering of alternatives (Moulin, 1988a; Sanver and Zwicker, 2012). That tie-breaker destroys anonymity, but for values of m and n not ruled out by Proposition 2.1, an alternative method renders certain scoring rules resolute while preserving anonymity, neutrality, monotonicity, and one-way monotonicity.[66] Keep these examples in mind when interpreting the next result:

Corollary 2.8. *Let f be a resolute SCF for four or more alternatives and sufficiently large odd n. If f is neutral and anonymous on $\mathcal{D}_{Condorcet}$, then either f fails to be strategyproof on $\mathcal{D}_{Condorcet}$, or f violates half-way monotonicity.[67]*

Proof. On $\mathcal{D}_{Condorcet}$, pairwise majority rule is the unique resolute, anonymous, neutral and strategyproof SCF for odd n (Theorem 2.3). So if f *is* strategyproof on $\mathcal{D}_{Condorcet}$ then f is a Condorcet extension, and Theorem 2.7, part 2 applies. ☐

Corollary 2.8 is a version of the Gibbard-Satterthwaite Theorem, with stronger hypotheses that reveal additional information about the split between Condorcet extensions and scoring rules in terms of vulnerability to strategic manipulation.

---

[64] Any rule using different voters as dictator, depending on the number of voters, will be strategyproof yet violate participation.

[65] Some irresolute tournament solutions satisfy versions of participation (see Chapter 3).

[66] See Eğeciouglu and Giritligil (2014) and Doğan (2015).

[67] In place of anonymity and neutrality, it suffices to assume nondictatoriality and nonimposition; use the stronger version of Theorem 2.3 actually proved in Campbell and Kelly (2003)—see Footnote 35.

How seriously should we take it when a voting rule fails to satisfy one of the axioms in this section? Should STV and plurality run-off be dismissed out of hand for violating monotonicity? Some would say "yes," either because the failure itself is offensive, or because the nature of the violation demonstrates a behavior of the sequential elimination mechanism that is not at all what we expected, suggesting an unpredictable and untrustworthy process. To the extent that STV's initial appeal rested on an intuitive feeling about sequential elimination that made it *seem* fair, the monotonicity failure hits STV at its core, showing that intuition to have been poorly grounded. However, even some who agree with this critique seem willing to live with STV's flaws, if it means dethroning plurality.[68]

The failure of Condorcet extensions to be reinforcing is not commonly advanced as a critique. Some see reinforcement as a natural mathematical principle with an important role in classification theorems, but one that lacks the normative heft of monotonicity, for example.[69] Failures of participation or half-way monotonicity seem somewhat more serious, however, so what does Theorem 2.7 say about the viability of "Condorcet's Principle"? Opinions differ. The theorem only states that Condorcet extensions behave badly *after* all ties are broken by some mechanism, so one might argue that the tie-breaking mechanism, not the original rule, is guilty of the violation. Nonetheless, the Copeland and Simpson rules both violate participation (as well as half-way monotonicity), in their original, irresolute form.[70]

2.7 Voting Rules II: Kemeny and Dodgson

Although no social choice function is both reinforcing and a Condorcet extension (Proposition 2.5), John Kemeny (1959) defined a neutral, anonymous, and reinforcing Condorcet extension that escapes this limitation via a change in context: his rule is a *social preference function*—meaning that the outcome of an election is a set of one or more *rankings*—rather than a social choice function.

The *Kendall tau metric* d_K (Kendall and Smith, 1939; Kendall, 1962) measures the distance between two linear orderings $\succ$, $\succ^*$ by counting pairs of alternatives on which

---

[68] In the rump session of the 2010 VPP Workshop *Assessing Alternative Voting Procedures* (July–August 2010), 22 of the 23 participants used approval voting (see Section 2.10) to vote on "What is the best voting rule that the city council of your town should use to elect the mayor?" The 17 options included all rules discussed here (except for Baldwin) as well as others, such as range voting and majority judgement, that do not fit the SCF context. Approval voting received the most votes (68.18% approval) followed by STV(45.45%), Copeland (40.91%), and Kemeny (36.36%). Plurality received *no* approvals, inspiring the title of the article (Laslier, 2012) analyzing the poll. Although STV approvals were presumably cast by two participants from the Electoral Reform Society (which advocates for STV), without them STV would still have done no worse than a tie for fourth.

[69] Ashley Piggins has pointed out that reinforcement gains some normative force when one interprets it as a coalitional form of the *Pareto principle*, and Wulf Gaertner notes that a failure would allow strategic manipulation by splitting or merging the electorate (private communications).

[70] Top Cycle satisfies these monotonicities, but is particularly prone to ties and is not Pareto. Is there a theorem showing that all half-way monotonic Condorcet extensions are highly irresolute? If so, it might determine the correct interpretation of Theorem 2.7, much as the Duggan-Schwarz Theorem (see the "limitations" part of Section 2.8) suggests that the Gibbard-Satterthwaite Theorem is less compromised by its resoluteness hypothesis than might first appear.

they disagree:

$$d_K(\succ, \succ^\star) = |\{(a, b) \in A^2 \,|\, a \succ b \text{ and } b \succ^\star a\}|.$$

Equivalently, d_K gives the minimum number of sequential inversions (reversals of pairs of alternatives that are adjacent when a linear ordering is listed vertically) needed to convert $\succ$ to $\succ^\star$. We extend any metric d on ballots to one on profiles by summing: $d(P, P') = \sum_{i=1}^{n} d(\succ_i, \succ'_i)$, and for each $\succ$ define the *unanimous profile* $U^\succ$ by $U_i^\succ = \succ$ for all i. For any profile P, the *Kemeny Rule* returns the ranking(s) $\succ$ minimizing $d_K(P, U^\succ)$. If a were a Condorcet winner for the profile P and $\succ$ did not rank a on top, then lifting a simply to $\succ$'s top would strictly decrease $d_K(P, U^\succ)$. Thus all rankings in the Kemeny outcome place a on top and in this sense Kemeny is a Condorcet extension.[71]

Kemeny is not a scoring rule in the sense of Definition 2.9, but suppose we make a modification:

Definition 2.12. A *ranking score function* $\mathbf{W}: \mathcal{L}(A) \times \mathcal{L}(A) \to \mathbb{R}$ assigns a real number *scoring weight* $\mathbf{W}(\succ^\star, \succ)$ to each pair of rankings. Any such function induces a *ranking scoring rule*, in which a voter with ranking $\succ_i$ awards $\mathbf{W}(\succ_i, \succ)$ points to each ranking $\succ \in \mathcal{L}(A)$. All points awarded to a given ranking are summed, and the winner is the ranking(s) with greatest sum.

This expands the class of scoring rules strictly[72] to include Kemeny—set the points awarded to $\succ^\star$ by a ballot of $\succ$ equal to the number of pairs of *agreement*: $\frac{m(m-1)}{2} - d_K(\succ, \succ^\star)$. Reinforcement now follows for Kemeny (just as it did in Section 2.5 for ordinary scoring rules) but one needs to interpret the reinforcement equation $f(s) \cap f(t) \neq \emptyset \Rightarrow f(s + t) = f(s) \cap f(t)$ with care—$f(s)$, $f(t)$, and $f(s + t)$ now denote sets of *rankings*, and this substantially weakens the reinforcement requirement.[73]

The preceding paragraphs establish the easy part of the following theorem, but it is the uniqueness that impresses:

Theorem 2.9 (Young and Levenglick, 1978). *Among social preference functions Kemeny's rule is the unique neutral and reinforcing Condorcet extension.*

A second rule based on counting inversions was proposed by Charles Dodgson (1876) (aka Lewis Carroll), and is often compared to Kemeny's rule: for any profile P the Dodgson rule returns the Condorcet winner(s) for the profile(s) $P' \in \mathcal{D}_{Condorcet}$ minimizing $d_K(P, P')$ among all $P' \in \mathcal{D}_{Condorcet}$. Dodgson's rule is interesting from a

---

[71] Also, if majority preference $>^\mu$ is transitive and complete, it is the unique Kemeny outcome. The *Slater* rule chooses the linear order $\succ$ minimizing the number of pairs of alternatives for which $>^\mu$ and $\succ$ disagree; unlike Kemeny, it ignores the sizes of the majorities determining $>^\mu$.

[72] Every (standard) scoring rule is a ranking scoring rule (if interpreted as a social preference function), but not conversely: Conitzer et al. (2009b) and Zwicker (2008). Other generalizations of scoring rules can be found in Myerson (1991), Zwicker (2008), Xia (2013), and Dietrich (2014).

[73] For example, consider the profiles s, t, and $s + t$ from the proof of Proposition 2.5. Every standard scoring rule f has $f(s) = \{a, b, c\}$ and $f(t) = \{b\}$ (or $\{a, b\}$ for antiplurality) so that reinforcement applies, forcing $f(s + t) = \{a\}$ or $\{a, b\}$ (which shows f is not a Condorcet extension). But for the Kemeny rule, $f_{Kem}(s) = \{a \succ b \succ c, c \succ a \succ b, b \succ c \succ a\}$ and $f_{Kem}(t) = \{b \succ a \succ c\}$, so that $f_{Kem}(s) \cap f_{Kem}(t) = \emptyset$ and reinforcement fails to apply at all. In a political setting, an outcome similar to $f_{Kem}(s)$ might be worrisome—it is difficult to imagine the reaction of voters who have not studied voting theory.

computational point of view (see Hemaspaandra et al., 1997a; Chapter 5), differs from Kemeny (Ratliff, 2001), and has some severe drawbacks as a voting method (Brandt, 2009c), failing even to be homogeneous (Fishburn, 1977).

Both Kemeny and Dodgson may be interpreted as minimizing a distance to "consensus." They use the same metric on rankings, but different notions of consensus: unanimity for Kemeny versus membership in $\mathcal{D}_{Condorcet}$ for Dodgson.[74] It is not difficult to see that every preference function that can be defined by minimizing distance to unanimity is a ranking scoring rule,[75] hence is reinforcing in the preference function sense. We can convert a preference function into an SCF by selecting all top-ranked alternatives from winning rankings, but this may transform a reinforcing preference function into an nonreinforcing SCF—as happens for Kemeny. The conversion preserves homogeneity, however, so every distance-from-unanimity minimizer is homogeneous as a social choice function. In this light, the inhomogeneity of Dodgson argues an advantage for unanimity over $\mathcal{D}_{Condorcet}$ as a consensus notion.

In fact a large variety of voting rules are "distance rationalizable"—they fit the *minimize distance from consensus* scheme. Chapter 8 is devoted to this topic, and includes an extensive selection of references.

2.8 Strategyproofness: Impossibilities

Our immediate goal is to show that every resolute, nonimposed, and nondictatorial SCF for three or more alternatives is manipulable, by way of the following theorem, due (independently) to Allan Gibbard (1973) and Mark Satterthwaite (1975):

Theorem 2.10 (Gibbard-Satterthwaite Theorem). *Any resolute, nonimposed, and strategyproof SCF for three or more alternatives must be a dictatorship.*

Of course, a dictatorship *is* resolute, strategyproof, and nonimposed, so we could restate the theorem as an *if and only if*. Over the years, a variety of interesting and distinct proofs have emerged (e.g., see Barberà and Peleg, 1990). The version here follows Taylor (2005). It relies on the following key definition, and on a sequence of lemmas, which appear *after* the proof of Theorem 2.10 itself.

Definition 2.13. Let f be a resolute social choice function for $m \geqslant 3$ alternatives, $a, b \in A$ be two distinct alternatives and $X \subseteq N$ be a set of voters. Then we say that X *can use a to block b*, notated $X_{a>b}$, if for every profile P wherein each voter in X ranks a over b, $f(P) \neq b$; X is a *dictating set* if $X_{z>w}$ holds for every choice $z \neq w$ of distinct alternatives.

Proof (Gibbard-Satterthwaite Theorem). First, we will show that each resolute, down monotonic, and Pareto f has a dictator j in the form of a singleton dictating set $X = \{j\}$. As f is Pareto, the set N of all voters is a finite dictating set. The Splitting Lemma 2.17 shows that when a dictating set $X = Y \cup Z$ is split into disjoint subsets

---

[74] Chapter 5 discusses a rule due to Peyton Young, using membership in $\mathcal{D}_{Condorcet}$ as consensus notion, but a different metric. It shares some complexity properties with Dodgson.

[75] Assuming that some metric on rankings is extended to profiles via summation, as described earlier.

Y and Z, either Y is a dictating set, or Z is. Hence repeated application of the Splitting Lemma (first to $X = N$, then to the half of N that is a dictating set, etc.) will terminate, yielding the desired singleton dictating set.

Next, the Adjustment Lemma 2.18 establishes that the Pareto assumption can be relaxed to nonimposition (when f is resolute and down monotonic). By Proposition 2.6 the down monotonicity assumption can be strengthened to strategyproofness, and this completes the proof. $\qquad\square$

A well known variant reformulates Theorem 2.10 in terms of monotonicity:

Theorem 2.11 (Muller and Satterthwaite, 1977). *Any resolute, nonimposed, and Maskin monotonic SCF for three or more alternatives must be a dictatorship.*

Proof. By Proposition 2.6 a resolute, Maskin monotonic SCF f is down monotonic. If f is also nonimposed, then it is dictatorial by our proof of Theorem 2.10. $\qquad\square$

Lemma 2.12 (Push-Down Lemma). *Let $a, b, c_1, c_2, \ldots, c_{m-2}$ enumerate the $m \geqslant 3$ alternatives in A, f be a resolute and down monotonic SCF for A, and P be any profile with $f(P) = a$. Then there exists a profile $P^\star$ with $f(P^\star) = a$ such that:*

- *For each voter i with $a \succ_i b$, $\succ_i^\star = a \succ b \succ c_1 \succ \cdots \succ c_{m-2}$*
- *For each voter i with $b \succ_i a$, $\succ_i^\star = b \succ a \succ c_1 \succ \cdots \succ c_{m-2}$.*

Proof. Have P's voters, one-at-a-time, drop c_1 simply to the bottom of their ranking. Then have them all drop c_2 to the bottom, then $c_3, \ldots$. The final version $P^\star$ of P has exactly the ballots bulleted earlier, and by down monotonicity $f(P^\star) = a$. $\qquad\square$

Lemma 2.13. *Let f be a resolute and down monotonic SCF. If there exists a profile P for which every voter in X has a over b, every voter in $N \setminus X$ has b over a, and $f(P) = a$, then $X_{a>b}$.*

Proof. Assume we have such a profile P, yet $X_{a>b}$ fails. Choose a second profile P' for which each voter in X has a over b and $f(P') = b$. If any P' voters in $N \setminus X$ have a over b let them one-at-a-time drop a simply below b. By down monotonicity the resulting profile P'' satisfies $f(P'') = b$.

Apply the Push-Down Lemma (2.12) to P to obtain profile $P^\star$ with $f(P^\star) = a$, and apply it again to P'' to obtain profile $P''^\star$ with $f(P''^\star) = b$. But the Lemma 2.12 properties of $P^\star$ force $P^\star = P''^\star$, a contradiction. $\qquad\square$

Lemma 2.14. *Let f be a resolute, Pareto, and down monotonic SCF for three or more alternatives. Assume $X_{a>b}$, with $X = Y \cup Z$ split into disjoint subsets Y and Z. Let c be any alternative distinct from a and b. Then $Y_{a>c}$ or $Z_{c>b}$.*

Proof. Consider the profile P_8. As f is Pareto, $f(P_8) \in \{a, b, c\}$, but we know $X_{a>b}$, so $f(P_8) \neq b$. Lemma 2.13 now applies to show that if $f(P_8) = a$ then $Y_{a>c}$, and if $f(P_8) = c$ then $Z_{c>b}$. $\qquad\square$

All voters in Y	All voters in Z	All voters in $N \setminus X$
a	c	b
b	a	c
c	b	a
$\vdots$	$\vdots$	$\vdots$

Lemma 2.15. *Let f be a resolute, Pareto, and down monotonic SCF for three or more alternatives. Assume $X_{a>b}$. Let c be any alternative distinct from a and b. Then (i) $X_{a>c}$ and (ii) $X_{c>b}$.*

Proof. Nothing in the Lemma 2.14 proof rules out X or Y being empty, and Pareto implies that $\emptyset_{u>v}$ is impossible. Applying Lemma 2.14 with $Y = X$, $Z = \emptyset$ yields $X_{a>c}$, and applying it with $Y = \emptyset$, $Z = X$ yields $X_{c>b}$. $\square$

Lemma 2.16. *Let f be a resolute, Pareto, and down monotonic SCF for three or more alternatives. Assume $X_{a>b}$. Then X is a dictating set.*

Proof. Let $y \in A$. We will show $X_{y>z}$ holds for all $z \neq y$.

Case 1 Assume $y = a$. Lemma 2.15 (i) immediately implies $X_{a>z}$ for all $z \neq a$.

Case 2 Assume $y \notin \{a, b\}$. Lemma 2.15 (ii), with y replacing c, yields $X_{y>b}$. Now restate Lemma 2.15, as follows: "Assume $X_{y>b}$. Then (i) $X_{y>z}$ and $\ldots$," so $X_{y>z}$ for all $z \neq y$.

Case 3 Assume $y = b$. By Lemma 2.15 (i), $X_{a>c}$. Restate Lemma 2.15 as follows: "Assume $X_{a>c}$. Then $\ldots (ii)$ $X_{b>c}$." Restating Lemma 2.15 yet again shows $X_{b>z}$ for all $z \neq b$. $\square$

Lemma 2.17 (Splitting Lemma). *Let f be a resolute, Pareto, and down monotonic SCF for three or more alternatives. If a dictating set $X = Y \cup Z$ is split into disjoint subsets Y and Z, then either Y is a dictating set, or Z is.*

Proof. Let a, b, and c be three distinct alternatives. Split the dictating set $X = Y \cup Z$ into disjoint subsets Y and Z. As $X_{a>b}$, by Lemma 2.14 either $Y_{a>c}$ or $Z_{c>b}$. Lemma 2.16 now implies Y is a dictating set (if $Y_{a>c}$) or Z is (if $Z_{c>b}$). $\square$

Lemma 2.18 (Adjustment Lemma). *Let f be any resolute, nonimposed SCF (but no longer assume f is Pareto). If f is down monotonic then it is Pareto.*

Proof. If not, choose a profile P in which every voter ranks b over a, yet $f(P) = a$. Use nonimposition to choose a second profile P' with $f(P') = b$. Now we proceed as in the proof of Lemma 2.13. If any P' voters have a over b let them one-at-a-time drop a simply below b. By down monotonicity the resulting profile P'' satisfies $f(P'') = b$. Apply the Push-Down (Lemma 2.12) to P to obtain a profile $P^\star$ with $f(P^\star) = a$, and apply it again to P'' to obtain the profile $P''^\star$ with $f(P''^\star) = b$. But the Lemma 2.12 properties of $P^\star$ force $P^\star = P''^\star$, a contradiction. $\square$

Limitations of the Gibbard-Satterthwaite Theorem: Resoluteness

This completes our proof of the Gibbard-Satterthwaite Theorem—a central result in the theory of voting. But what is its real significance ... does the theorem tell us that voting rules are all manipulable in practice?

One issue is that several conditions seem to be required for a single voter i to be certain she can achieve such a *single voter manipulation*:

1. She needs to know the intended ballot of each of the other voters.
2. She needs to be sure that no other voter will similarly engage in strategic vote-switching.
3. She needs the computational resources to predict whether some switch in her ballot can change the outcome into one she prefers.

In many real voting settings conditions (1) and (2) are unlikely to obtain, and so there is a body of work that considers manipulation in a less restrictive context.[76] Computational barriers to manipulation are explored in Chapter 6.

Another limitation is that the theorem applies only to the social choice function context, with its associated form of ballot—ordinal rankings of the alternatives—and of election outcome. For example, there is a spirited debate as to whether certain other voting rules gain an advantage, with respect to manipulability, by using, as inputs, ballots that are quite different.[77] *Social Decision Schemes* escape the Gibbard-Satterthwaite context at the other end—the output—by declaring a probability distribution as the election outcome.

The most immediately apparent limitation of the Gibbard-Satterthwaite Theorem, however, might be that it applies only to *resolute* SCFs, while Proposition 2.1 tells us that, in the case of a neutral and anonymous SCF f, ties are often inevitable, suggesting that the theorem might say little about the rules that are of greatest interest. Of course, we can use some tie-breaking mechanism M to break all ties for f, and the resulting resolute rule is then manipulable, but the fault might then lie with M rather than with the original irresolute f.

The following question, then, would seem to be important: *How many tied outcomes must we be willing to live with, in order to achieve strategyproofness?* Several generalizations of Gibbard-Satterthwaite to irresolute SCFs suggest an answer: *a lot of ties*. This points to a certain robustness in the theorem. We state one such generalization as follows, without proof: the Duggan-Schwartz Theorem.[78] First, we need some preliminaries. For $Z \subseteq A$ let $\max_{\succ_i}[Z]$ denote i's top ranked alternative in Z, with $\min_{\succ_i}[Z]$ defined similarly.

Definition 2.14. Let f be an SCF, possibly irresolute. We say f is *manipulable by optimists* (respectively *manipulable by pessimists*) if for some pair P, P' of profiles and voter i with $\succsim'_j = \succsim_j$ for all $j \neq i$, $\max_{\succ_i}[f(P')] \succ_i \max_{\succ_i}[f(P)]$ (respectively, $\min_{\succ_i}[f(P')] \succ_i \min_{succ_i}[f(P)]$). A voter k is a *nominator* for f if for every profile

---

[76] See Peleg (1975), Dutta and Pattanaik (1978), Favardin and Lepelley (2006), and Slinko and White (2008), for example.

[77] Examples are mentioned in Footnote 3. Each context requires its own definition of *manipulation*, making cross-contextual comparisons problematic. In this regard, see Section 2.10 for the case of approval voting.

[78] Taylor (2005) proves Duggan-Schwartz using the same machinery as in his Gibbard-Satterthwaite proof (as given here).

P, k's top-ranked alternative is a member of $f(P)$. The *Omninominator* SCF returns, for each profile P, the set *OmNom*(P) of all alternatives that have been top-ranked by at least one voter.

The intuition here is that some outside agency will ultimately choose a single winning alternative from the set $f(P)$. An "optimist" assumes that the chosen x will always be his favorite alternative from $f(P)$, hence preferring one set Z of winners to another Z' when $\max_{\succ_i}[Z] \succ_i \max_{\succ_i}[Z']$. A nominator is a sort of weak dictator. It is easy to check that the Omninominator rule is not manipulable by optimists or by pessimists. This rule is notably irresolute, but it seems that every other example is even worse:

Theorem 2.19 (Duggan and Schwartz, 2000). *If a nonimposed SCF f for three or more alternatives is not manipulable by optimists and is not manipulable by pessimists, then f must have a nominator.*

Thus, if f is anonymous, *every* voter must be a nominator, whence:

Corollary 2.20 (Corollary to Theorem 2.19). *If an anonymous, nonimposed SCF f for three or more alternatives is not manipulable by optimists and is not manipulable by pessimists, then $f(P) \supseteq OmNom(P)$ for every profile P.*

Thus, for an anonymous SCF to be strategyproof (in the Theorem 2.19 sense) it must have *at least* as many ties as Omninominator. Moreover, Duggan and Schwartz also show that by requiring f to be minimally more resolute than Omninominator the conclusion of Theorem 2.19 can be strengthened to "*f must have a dictator.*"

Back to Pairwise Majority Rule on the Condorcet Domain

We return to the postponed part of our proof of Theorem 2.3, Section 2.4, showing that for functions restricted to the Condorcet domain, no SCF *other* than Pairwise Majority Rule is resolute, anonymous, neutral, and strategyproof.

Proof. Let $f: \mathcal{D}_{Condorcet} \to A$ be resolute, anonymous, neutral and strategyproof, hence down monotonic. If $f \neq$ PMR, choose a profile $P \in \mathcal{D}_{Condorcet}$ with Condorcet winner b such that $f(P) = a \neq b$. Apply the Push-Down (Lemma 2.12) (noting that the changing profile remains within $\mathcal{D}_{Condorcet}$) to obtain a profile $P^{\star}$ with $f(P^{\star}) = a$ such that

- for each voter i with $a \succ_i b$, $\succ_i^{\star} = a \succ b \succ c_1 \succ \cdots \succ c_{m-2}$, and
- for each voter i with $b \succ_i a$, $\succ_i^{\star} = b \succ a \succ c_1 \succ \cdots \succ c_{m-2}$.

We now proceed as in the May's Theorem proof. More $P^{\star}$ voters have $b \succ_i^{\star} a$ than have $a \succ_i^{\star} b$. One ballot at a time, drop b simply below a on enough ballots to reverse those numbers. As n is odd, the evolving profile remains within $\mathcal{D}_{Condorcet}$. Monotonicity implies a still wins, but neutrality + anonymity say b wins. $\square$

2.9 Strategyproofness: Possibilities

Suppose that five old friends meet annually for a hike in the country, but some are more fit than others. Each friend i has an "ideal" hike length d_i with

$$d_i \succ_i d' \succ_i d'' \text{ for all } d', d'' \text{ such that } d_i > d' > d'' \text{ or } d_i < d' < d''. \quad (2.5)$$

Such preferences are said to be *single peaked*.[79] Ali suggests using the mean (average) of the announced ideal lengths as the actual length L for the hike, but she is known to be the most ambitious hiker, and has a good idea of the others' d_is. Dieter, concerned that Ali will declare an artificially high d_i in order to raise the mean to her actual ideal, suggests the *median M* be used instead of the mean.[80]

Why consider the median? With an odd number of voters, more than half the voters prefer the median M to any value $e > M$ (namely, those voters i with $d_i \leqslant M$), and to any $e < M$ (similarly), so M is the Condorcet winner, and the hikers' profile is contained in $\mathcal{D}_{Condorcet}$.[81] It follows by Proposition 2.3 that the median rule is strategyproof (but take a moment to think about a direct argument that the median is strategyproof in this context). The argument can be iterated,[82] showing that pairwise majority preference $\geqslant^{\mu}$ is a linear ordering (in particular, it is transitive) over hike-lengths. Of course, we are not limited to taking hikes:

Definition 2.15. A ballot $\succsim_i$ is *single peaked with respect to* $>$, a linear order on the set A of alternatives, if it satisfies Condition 2.5 (with d_i denoting $\succsim_i$'s maximal alternative or *ideal point*, and for all alternatives d', d''). A profile P is *single peaked* if there exists a common linear order $>$ on A such that every ballot of P is single-peaked with respect to $>$. The *single-peaked domain* is the set of all such profiles (for a given A and N), and the *median rule* is the restricted domain SCF that selects the median of voters' ideal points, for each profile in this domain.

The ordering $>$ might represent a left-right political spectrum, with a voter's ideal point located at his own position, and more preferred candidates having positions closer to his own. Our informal reasoning about the median can easily be turned into a proof of the following theorem of Duncan Black (1958).

Theorem 2.21 (Black's Theorem). *Every single-peaked profile P yields a transitive pairwise majority preference relation $\geqslant^{\mu}$. In particular, if n is odd then $P \in \mathcal{D}_{Condorcet}$, and the median of the ideal points coincides with P's Condorcet winner. For odd n, the median rule is strategyproof on the single-peaked domain.*[83]

---

[79] Think of a graph with horizontal axis as hike-length, and vertical as i's degree-of-preference.

[80] Assume negative ballots are disallowed. Using the mean, if it is common knowledge that *all* hikers will vote strategically, and that they know each others' ideal lengths, then the Nash equilibrium will have four hikers declaring 0 as their ideal lengths, and Ali declaring five times her true d_i.

[81] With n even, there can be two medians $M_1 < M_2$, which are the two *weak Condorcet winners*: at least half the voters prefer M_i to any $e \neq M_i$.

[82] Remove the median from the set of available alternatives, assume each voter's preferences for remaining alternatives stay the same, and take the median again, etc.

[83] Strategyproofness holds for even n if one extends the strategyproofness definition to account for the particularly simple ties that arise in this context (see Footnote 81).

:

A word here on the nature of domain restrictions—single peakedness (with respect to a specified $>$) is actually a restriction on individual rankings. Voters are free to choose any ballot they wish from the set $\mathcal{P}_>$ of rankings single peaked for that $>$, without regard to other voters' choices, and the result will be a single peaked profile. Equivalently, the single peaked domain for a particular $>$ is the n-fold Cartesian product $\mathcal{P}_>{}^n$. Our earlier restriction to $\mathcal{D}_{Condorcet}$ was quite different, corresponding to no restricted set of ballots from which voters could choose freely.

The phrase "domain restriction" is sometimes used to refer exclusively to such restrictions on rankings—which sets S of ballots have the property that *every* profile built from members of S has a transitive $>^\mu$? Amartya Sen (1966) observed that:

- For preferences single-peaked with respect to $>$, and any three alternatives a, b, c, whichever of the three falls between the other two (according to $>$) will never be ranked *third* among the three.
- This condition alone guarantees transitivity of $>^\mu$, for n odd.
- Excluding any of the three relative positions (never ranked *second*, or *first*) similarly ensures transitivity, but not single peakedness.
- The excluded position need not be the same for each triple a, b, c.

Definition 2.16. A set $S \subseteq \mathcal{L}(A)$ of rankings satisfies *value restriction* if for every set $X \subseteq A$ of three alternatives there exists an $x \in X$ such that no ranking in S ranks x third among members of X, or none ranks x second, or none ranks x first.

Theorem 2.22 (Sen's Possibility Theorem). *Let $S \subseteq \mathcal{L}(A)$ be a set of rankings of A. Then S is value restricted if and only if $>^\mu$ is transitive for every profile of ballots from S having an odd number of voters.*

Proof. ($\Rightarrow$) Assume profile P has an odd number n of voters casting ballots from the value restricted set S. It suffices to show for an arbitrary set $X = \{a, b, c\}$ of three alternatives that the restriction $>^\mu|_X$ of the pairwise majority preference to X is transitive. By value restriction, one of the three—let's say a, w.l.o.g.—is excluded from one of the three positions.

Now $>^\mu|_X$ is clearly transitive if $a >^\mu b$ and $a >^\mu c$ both hold, or if $b >^\mu a$ and $c >^\mu a$ both hold. So w.l.o.g. assume $c >^\mu a >^\mu b$. If a is excluded from first among members of X, then each voter i in the majority having $a \succ_i b$ agrees that $c \succ_i a \succ_i b$ and so $>^\mu|_X$ coincides with $\succ_i|_X$, and is transitive. If a is excluded from last among members of X, then each voter i in the majority having $c \succ_i a$ agrees that $c \succ_i a \succ_i b$ and so $>^\mu|_X$ is again transitive. Finally, with $c >^\mu a >^\mu b$ it is impossible to exclude a from the middle position among X's members, because the majorities with $c \succ_i a$ and with $a \succ_i b$ must have a voter in common.

($\Leftarrow$) If S is not value restricted, choose a set $X = \{a, b, c\} \subseteq A$ such that for each $x \in X$ there are elements $\succ_x^1$, $\succ_x^2$, and $\succ_x^3$ of S whose restrictions to X rank x first, second, and third respectively. A table can be used to show that S's restrictions to X are forced to include all three from the set $C_1 = \{a \succ b \succ c,\ c \succ a \succ b,\ b \succ c \succ a\}$ or all three from $C_2 = \{a \succ c \succ b,\ b \succ a \succ c,\ c \succ b \succ a\}$. Any profile of three rankings from S having C_1 (or C_2) as their restrictions yields a majority cycle. $\qquad\square$

That single-peakedness and value restriction constitute restrictions on individual rankings is a strength, but also a weakness: if even one voter (of many) violates the restriction, Theorems 2.21 and 2.22 no longer apply; thus, the value-restricted profiles exclude many profiles with transitive $>^{\mu}$. The decomposition approach (end of Section 2.5) provides various alternative conditions guaranteeing transitivity of $>^{\mu}$.

2.10 Approval Voting

The *approval voting* rule is striking for its combination of simplicity and relatively recent discovery, its potential as a real voting reform in the political context, and its nature—it is not a social choice function . . . or is it? An *approval ballot* is a subset X of the set A of alternatives; the idea is that voter i "approves" of exactly those alternatives $x \in X_i$. Given a profile of such ballots, the *approval score* of an alternative x is the number of voters who approve of x, and *approval voting* declares the winner(s) to be the alternative(s) with highest approval score. Equivalently, a voter may vote for as many alternatives as she wishes, and whoever gets the most votes wins. In their book *Approval Voting*, Brams and Fishburn (2007) attribute the idea to five different groups, acting independently in the 1970s. The more recent edited collection by Laslier and Sanver (2010) is also a good source.

Arguments made on behalf of approval voting (primarily, as an improvement on plurality voting in a political context) include the following:

1. Simplicity: the ballot is barely more complicated than a plurality ballot, and the aggregation rule is conceptually transparent (hence an easier sell to the public).
2. It addresses the most egregious flaw of plurality voting: a single candidate at the minority end of a political spectrum can defeat several candidates at the majority end, who split that majority. For example, Holtzmann (see Footnote 10) would have won the 1980 senatorial election for New York had even a small percentage of Javits voters chosen to approve her as well as Javits.
3. It improves the odds that the winner is supported by a majority of the electorate, making it easier to claim a "mandate" that allows her or him to govern effectively.
4. It eliminates the "wasted vote" problem, allowing minor-party candidates to achieve returns that more accurately reflect the true level of support for their ideas.
5. It is likely to elect the Condorcet winner, when one exists.[84]
6. It is relatively resistant to strategic manipulation.

Criticisms of approval voting have included the following:

1. There is an ambiguity at its heart, with little agreement on or understanding of what it means to "approve" of an alternative.[85]

---

[84] See Beaujard et al. (2014), who also argue that approval voting favors "consensual" candidates located near the middle in a multidimensional issue space, generalizing advantage 2.

[85] Balinski and Laraki (2010) see this as a fatal flaw. Laslier (private communication) reports that voters see the flexibility as a solution to the dilemma they face with a plurality ballot: "Do I vote for the one I think best, or for the best among those who have a chance?"

2. It overly restricts expressivity by obligating voters to compress their ranking into two levels, forcing them to declare certain pairs of alternatives equivalent when that violates their true feelings.
3. It violates "one person, one vote."
4. It is unfair, giving more influence to voters who approve of more alternatives.
5. Some arguments on its behalf (e.g., resistance to manipulation) are rigged by the choice of methodology in comparing preference ballots with approval ballots.

We will make a few observations, without commenting on each preceding advantage. Critique 4 has no basis—one might equally claim that the voter who indicates more *nonapproved* alternatives gains the advantage[86]—and critique 3 seems more an argument of convenience than one of conviction. With regard to the meaning of "approval" there appears to be a fundamental split among points-of-view. Some presume that each voter actually has an underlying ranking (possibly weak) of the alternatives, and in choosing an approved ballot must somehow compress several distinct levels of approval into exactly two levels. Others view the dichotomous ballot as a direct reflection of a dichotomous primitive: each voter either *likes* or *dislikes* each alternative, and is indifferent among those within either group. A third view presumes that a voter has a ranking *together* with a line dividing those alternatives she likes from those she dislikes; we will refer to such a line as a *true zero*. An assignment of cardinal utilities might underlie the first view, or the third (if utilities can be negative).[87]

A strategic analysis of approval voting cannot easily be disentangled from this more philosophical matter of what it *means* to approve an alternative. If approval is a primitive, then each voter has only one sincere ballot, but lacks any incentive to vote insincerely. For a voter with an underlying ranking, it is clearly never strategically advantageous to approve an alternative without also approving all others that you like as well or better, so deciding on an approval ballot amounts to choosing "where to draw the line." If that line has no intrinsic meaning, there is no basis on which to discriminate between a sincere ballot and an insincere one; one might argue that all ballots are strategic, or that none are. If a voter has both a ranking and a line with intrinsic meaning as a true zero, then any ballot drawing the line somewhere else might be classified as insincere—and such a voter might have a strategic incentive to cast such a ballot.[88]

---

[86] It is easy to recast approval voting in terms that are symmetric in approval and nonapproval.

[87] The authors of *Approval Voting* take two views, referring sometimes to an underlying ranking and at other times speaking of the approved alternatives as those "acceptable" to the voter. The third view appears in Brams and Sanver (2009), which proposes voting rules that use a ballot consisting of a ranking and a dividing line both, and in Sanver (2010); see also the related *Bucklin voting*, *fallback voting*, and *majoritarian compromise* discussed in Hoag and Hallett (1926) and Brams (2008).

[88] Marking a voter's true zero is not the only way to ascribe intrinsic meaning to the location of "the line." For a voter who assigns a cardinal utility to each alternative, the mean utility value serves as a sort of *relative* zero (quite possibly different from that voter's "true" zero, if she has one) and arguments have been made (in Brams and Fishburn, 2007) for drawing the line there. Duddy et al. (2013) show that drawing the line at the mean maximizes a measure of total separation between the approved and unapproved groups. Laslier (2009) argues that it is strategically advantageous to draw the line near the utility (to the individual voter) of the expected winner, and that voters tend to behave this way.

Approval = Borda = Condorcet

To bridge the gap between approval voting and the SCF context we might translate each approval ballot X_i into the weak ranking $\succsim_i$ for which $a \succsim_i b$ iff $a \in X_i$ or $b \notin X_i$. This identifies approval voting with a certain SCF, for which the domain is restricted to the class $\mathcal{R}_2$ of *dichotomous preferences*; ballots in $\mathcal{R}_2$ are weak rankings having exactly two (nonempty) indifference classes, one ranked over the other. (Here, an *indifference class* is an equivalence class under the *indifference relation* $\sim_i$, defined on the set A of alternatives by $x \sim_i y$ if both $x \succsim_i y$ and $y \succsim_i x$.)

We can now ask, "Among the SCFs we have considered, which become identical to approval voting after $\mathcal{R}_2$ is imposed?" The answer depends, of course, on how these SCFs are extended to handle indifferences in the ballots. Approval voting is identical to the Borda count under the $\mathcal{R}_2$ restriction, provided that we apply, directly to profiles of weak rankings, the earlier Equations 2.1 for net preference $Net_P(a > b)$ and 2.3 for symmetric Borda score (without any modification to these equations); the result is equivalent to using the *averaging method* for modifying scoring weights in the presence of indifferences.[89],[90] Whether scoring rules other than Borda reduce to approval voting depends on the convention used to adapt their scoring weights in the presence of indifferences.[91]

The fate of Condorcet extensions under $\mathcal{R}_2$ depends on how one defines the pairwise majority relation $x >^\mu y$ in the presence of individual indifferences. Suppose we apply the earlier definition of $x >^\mu y$ as $Net_P(x > y) > 0$, directly and without modification to weak order ballots. Then $x >^\mu y$ is equivalent to "the number of voters i with $x \succ_i y$ is strictly greater than the number with $y \succ_i x$."[92] Moreover, under $\mathcal{R}_2$ this version of $x >^\mu y$ is equivalent to "more voters approve x than approve y." Thus under $\mathcal{R}_2$ every profile has a Condorcet winner (and a transitive $>^\mu$) and approval voting is identical to every Condorcet extension under $\mathcal{R}_2$.[93] One can argue, then, that approval voting reconciles de Borda and Condorcet.[94]

---

[89] This is a bit surprising, in that the total number of points awarded by a single dichotomous ballot (via Equation 2.3 for symmetric Borda score) varies depending on the number of approved alternatives. However, the *difference* between any single ballot's award to an approved and a disapproved alternative does not vary, and only these differences matter in determining the winner. That Borda reduces to approval under suitable ballot restrictions has been noted, for example, in Endriss et al. (2009)

[90] Applying Equations 2.1 and 2.3 is equivalent to applying, to any vector of scoring weights that are equally spaced—hence, serve as Borda weights—the following method for modifying scoring weights to account for indifference expressed in a weak order ballot: choose an arbitrary linear extension of the ballot, and then award, to each alternative in an indifference class of the ballot, the *average* scoring weight awarded to the members of that class by the extension.

[91] For such rules, scoring weights are unequally spaced, and applying the averaging method of Footnote 90 will typically not yield approval voting under the $\mathcal{R}_2$ restriction (because the differences discussed in Footnote 89 will vary depending on the number of approved alternatives). For each proper scoring rule there exists *some* adaptation of weights to dichotomous preferences that yields approval voting, but in some cases (k-approval, for example) the adaptation method seems artificial.

[92] However, with weak rankings this version of $x >^\mu y$ is no longer equivalent to "more than half of the voters rank x over y." This latter version seems problematic when there are many indifferences.

[93] Of course, if each approval ballot is derived by compressing a ranking, then the Condorcet winner for the uncompressed rankings might differ from that for the compressed versions.

[94] This is less surprising when one considers the fate, under the $\mathcal{R}_2$ restriction, of the orthogonal decomposition discussed at the end of Section 2.5. The difference between Borda and Condorcet resides entirely in the cyclic component of the weighted tournament, which is always 0 under $\mathcal{R}_2$.

2.11 The Future

Where is the theory of voting headed? One view holds that the results of Arrow, Gibbard, and Satterthwaite killed the field, with subsequent work amounting to picking the bones of the carcass. But such opinions were being expressed well before the birth of new, unsuspected, and vital cognate fields such as computational social choice or judgment aggregation. These opinions reflect, in our view, a naïveté as to the nature of voting. If voting is *one* thing, then perhaps one might interpret the famous impossibility results as saying, "give up—a perfect rule is impossible."

But voting for a mayor in a political context is quite different, for example, from voting on a panel of petroleum geologists ranking land tracts, to advise an oil company bidding for drilling rights. Resistance to manipulation might be irrelevant for the geologists, but quite important when deciding how to elect a mayor.

An alternative view of the future, then, is that it will bring a better understanding of the broad spectrum of contexts for voting, together with a guide to as to which, among a variety of properties and axioms, are more relevant for each context. Certainly, we are still a long way from this level of mastery today.

Under this latter view, impossibility results do not kill the subject of voting, but rather fertilize it by leading us to consider a more diverse set of axioms and voting rules appropriate to these varied contexts. Just how large, then, is the universe of interesting axioms and voting rules? On this matter, there is a similar split in point of view. Some see this universe as largely mapped. We suspect that unexplored and unsuspected regions may dwarf what is known.

Acknowledgments

This chapter benefited enormously from those who read and commented on the manuscript or otherwise gave generously of their time and knowledge, including (but not limited to) the editors, John Duggan, Wulf Gaertner, Christian Klamler, Steven J. Brams, Olivier Hudry, Jean-François Laslier, Ashley Piggins, Marcus Pivato, and Alan D. Taylor.

CHAPTER 3

Tournament Solutions

Felix Brandt, Markus Brill, and Paul Harrenstein

3.1 Introduction

Perhaps one of the most natural ways to aggregate binary preferences from individual agents to a group of agents is *simple majority rule*, which prescribes that one alternative is socially preferred to another whenever a majority of agents prefers the former to the latter. Majority rule intuitively appeals to democratic principles, is easy to understand and—most importantly—satisfies some attractive formal properties. As seen in Chapter 2, May's Theorem shows that a number of rather weak and intuitively acceptable principles completely characterize majority rule in settings with two alternatives (May, 1952). Moreover, almost all common voting rules satisfy May's axioms and thus coincide with majority rule in the two-alternative case. It would therefore seem that the existence of a majority of individuals preferring alternative a to alternative b signifies something fundamental and generic about the group's preferences over a and b. We will say that alternative a *dominates* alternative b in such a case.

As is well known from Condorcet's paradox (see Chapter 2), the dominance relation may contain cycles. This implies that the dominance relation may not admit a maximal element and the concept of maximality as such is rendered untenable. On the other hand, Arrow writes that "one of the consequences of the assumptions of rational choice is that the choice in any environment can be determined by a knowledge of the choices in two-element environments" (Arrow, 1951, p. 16). Thus, one way to get around this problem—the one pursued in this chapter—is to take the dominance relation as given and define alternative concepts to take over the role of maximality. More precisely, we will be concerned with social choice functions (SCFs) that are based on the dominance relation only, that is, those SCFs that Fishburn (1977) called $C1$ functions. Topics to be covered in this chapter include McGarvey's Theorem, various tournament solutions (such as Copeland's rule, the uncovered set, the top cycle, or the tournament equilibrium set), strategyproofness, implementation via binary agendas, and extensions of tournament solutions to weak tournaments. Particular attention will be paid to the issue of whether and how tournament solutions can be computed efficiently.

In this chapter, we will view tournament solutions as $C1$ SCFs. However, for varying interpretations of the dominance relation, tournament solutions and variants thereof can be applied to numerous other settings such as multicriteria decision analysis (Arrow and Raynaud, 1986; Bouyssou et al., 2006), zero-sum games (Fisher and Ryan, 1995; Laffond et al., 1993a; Duggan and Le Breton, 1996), and coalitional games (Brandt and Harrenstein, 2010).

3.2 Preliminaries

We first introduce and review some basic concepts and notations used in this chapter. Let $N = \{1, \ldots, n\}$ be a set of voters, A a set of m alternatives, and $R = (\succsim_1, \ldots, \succsim_n)$ a vector of linear orders over A. $\succsim_i$ is the *preference relation* of voter i and R is called a *preference profile*. The *majority relation* $\succsim$ *for* R is defined such that for all alternatives a and b,

$$a \succsim b \quad \text{if and only if} \quad |\{i \in N : a \succsim_i b\}| \geq |\{i \in N : b \succsim_i a\}|.$$

See Figure 3.1 for an example preference profile and the corresponding majority relation. A *Condorcet winner* is a (unique) alternative a such that there is no other alternative b with $b \succ a$ (or in other words, an alternative a such that $a \succ b$ for all $b \in A \setminus \{a\}$, where $\succ$ is the asymmetric part of $\succsim$). By definition, the majority relation is complete, i.e., $a \succsim b$ or $b \succsim a$ for all alternatives a and b. Apart from completeness, the majority relation has no further structural properties, that is, every complete relation over a set of alternatives can be obtained as the majority relation for some preference profile. This result is known as *McGarvey's Theorem*.

Theorem 3.1 (McGarvey, 1953). *Let A be a set of m alternatives and $\geq$ a complete relation over A. Then, there is a preference profile $R = (\succsim_1, \ldots, \succsim_n)$ over A with $n \leq m(m-1)$ such that $\geq\ =\ \succsim$.*

Proof. Denote the asymmetric part of $\geq$ by $>$. For every pair (a, b) of alternatives with $a > b$, introduce two voters, i_{ab} and j_{ab}, that is, $N = \{i_{ab}, j_{ab} : a > b\}$. Define the preference profile R such that for all $a, b \in A$,

$$a \succ_{i_{ab}} b \succ_{i_{ab}} x_1 \succ_{i_{ab}} \cdots \succ_{i_{ab}} x_{m-2} \quad \text{and}$$

$$x_{m-2} \succ_{j_{ab}} \cdots \succ_{j_{ab}} x_1 \succ_{j_{ab}} a \succ_{j_{ab}} b,$$

where $x_1, \ldots, x_{m-2}$ is an arbitrary enumeration of $A \setminus \{a, b\}$. It is easy to check that the majority relation $\succsim$ for R coincides with $\geq$. By asymmetry of $>$, moreover, we have $a > b$ for at most $\frac{1}{2}m(m-1)$ pairs (a, b) and thus $n = |N| \leq m(m-1)$. $\qquad\square$

The minimal number of voters required to obtain any majority relation has subsequently been improved by Stearns (1959) and Erdős and Moser (1964), who have eventually shown that this number is of order $\Theta(\frac{m}{\log m})$. This implies that for any fixed number of voters, there are tournaments which are not induced by any preference profile. Only little is known about the classes of majority relations that can be induced by preference profiles with small fixed numbers of voters (see Bachmeier et al., 2014).

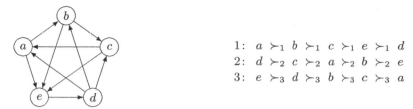

1: $a \succ_1 b \succ_1 c \succ_1 e \succ_1 d$
2: $d \succ_2 c \succ_2 a \succ_2 b \succ_2 e$
3: $e \succ_3 d \succ_3 b \succ_3 c \succ_3 a$

Figure 3.1. A tournament $T = (\{a, b, c, d, e\}, \succ)$, which depicts the asymmetric part of the majority relation of the three-voter preference profile on the right.

3.2.1 Tournaments

If the number of voters is odd, there can be no majority ties and the majority relation is antisymmetric. In this case, the asymmetric part $\succ$ of the majority relation $\succsim$ is connex and irreflexive and will be referred to as the *dominance relation*.[1] A dominance relation can be conveniently represented by an oriented complete graph, a tournament (see Figure 3.1).

Formally, a *tournament* T is a pair $(A, \succ)$ where A is a set of vertices and $\succ$ is an asymmetric and connex relation over the vertices. Tournaments have a rich mathematical theory and many results for $C1$ SCFs have a particularly nice form if the dominance relation constitutes a tournament. Moreover, many $C1$ functions have only been defined for tournaments and possess a variety of possible generalizations to majority graphs that are not tournaments. None of these generalizations can be seen as *the* unequivocal extension of the original function. We therefore assume the dominance relation to be antisymmetric and discuss generalizations of functions in Section 3.5.[2]

The dominance relation can be raised to sets of alternatives and we write $A \succ B$ to signify that $a \succ b$ for all $a \in A$ and all $b \in B$. Using this notation, a Condorcet winner can be defined as an alternative a such that $\{a\} \succ A \setminus \{a\}$. For a subset of alternatives $B \subseteq A$, we will sometimes consider the restriction $\succ_B = \{(a, b) \in B \times B : a \succ b\}$ of the dominance relation $\succ$ to B. $(B, \succ_B)$ is then called a *subtournament* of $(A, \succ)$.

For a tournament $(A, \succ)$ and an alternative $a \in A$, we denote by $D(a)$ the *dominion* of a, that is,

$$D(a) = \{ b \in A : a \succ b \},$$

and by $\overline{D}(a)$ the *dominators* of a, that is,

$$\overline{D}(a) = \{ b \in A : b \succ a \}.$$

The *order* $|T|$ of a tournament $T = (A, \succ)$ refers to the cardinality of A.

---

[1] A relation $\succ$ is *connex* if $a \succ b$ or $b \succ a$ for all *distinct* alternatives a and b. In the absence of majority ties, $\succ$ and $\succsim$ are identical except that $\succsim$ is reflexive while $\succ$ is not.

[2] The preference profile constructed in the proof of Theorem 3.1 involves an even number of voters. It is easily seen, however, that no single additional voter, no matter what his preferences are, will affect the dominance relation $\succ$ and we may assume that every tournament is also induced by a preference profile with an *odd* number of voters. Likewise, the result by Erdős and Moser (1964) also holds for tournaments (Moon, 1968, Chapter 19, Example 1 (d)).

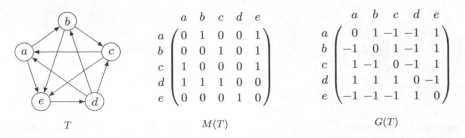

Figure 3.2. The tournament T from Figure 3.1 with its adjacency matrix $M(T)$ and its skew-adjacency matrix $G(T)$. Here, for instance, $D(a) = \{b, e\}$ and $\overline{D}(b) = \{a, d\}$.

The elements of the *adjacency matrix* $M(T) = (m_{ab})_{a,b \in A}$ of a tournament T are 1 whenever $a \succ b$ and 0 otherwise. The *skew-adjacency matrix* $G(T)$ of the corresponding tournament graph is skew-symmetric and defined as the difference of the adjacency matrix and its transpose, that is, $G(T) = M(T) - M(T)^t$ (see Figure 3.2).

An important structural notion in the context of tournaments is that of a component. A *component* is a nonempty subset of alternatives $B \subseteq A$ that bear the same relationship to any alternative not in the set, that is, for all $a \in A \setminus B$, either $B \succ \{a\}$ or $\{a\} \succ B$. A *decomposition* of T is a partition of A into components.

For a given tournament $\tilde{T}$, a new tournament T can be constructed by replacing each alternative with a component. Let $B_1, \ldots, B_k$ be pairwise disjoint sets of alternatives and consider tournaments $T_1 = (B_1, \succ_1), \ldots, T_k = (B_k, \succ_k)$, and $\tilde{T} = (\{1, \ldots, k\}, \tilde{\succ})$. The *product* of $T_1, \ldots, T_k$ with respect to $\tilde{T}$, denoted by $\Pi(\tilde{T}, T_1, \ldots, T_k)$, is the tournament $(A, \succ)$ such that $A = \bigcup_{i=1}^k B_i$ and for all $b_1 \in B_i, b_2 \in B_j$,

$$b_1 \succ b_2 \quad \text{if and only if} \quad i = j \text{ and } b_1 \succ_i b_2, \text{ or } i \neq j \text{ and } i \tilde{\succ} j.$$

Here, $\tilde{T}$ is called the *summary* of T with respect to the preceding decomposition. In the tournament depicted in Figure 3.2, for example, $\{a, b, c\}$, $\{d\}$, and $\{e\}$ are components and $\{\{a, b, c\}, \{d\}, \{e\}\}$ is a decomposition. The tournament can therefore be seen as the product of a 3-cycle and two singleton tournaments with respect to a 3-cycle summary. Importantly, every tournament admits a unique decomposition that is minimal in a well-defined sense (Laslier, 1997, pp. 15–23).

3.2.2 Tournament Solutions

A *tournament solution* is a function S that maps each tournament $T = (A, \succ)$ to a nonempty subset $S(T)$ of its alternatives A called the *choice set*. The formal definition further requires that a tournament solution does not distinguish between isomorphic tournaments, that is, if $h: A \to A'$ is an isomorphism between two tournaments $(A, \succ)$ and $(A', \succ')$, then

$$S(A', \succ') = \{h(a) : a \in S(A, \succ)\}.$$

As defined in Chapter 2, an SCF is a $C1$ function if its output only depends on the dominance relation. Because the dominance relation is invariant under renaming voters, $C1$ SCFs are anonymous by definition. Moreover, due to the invariance of tournament solutions under isomorphisms, tournament solutions are equivalent to *neutral*

*C*1 *functions.* In contrast to Laslier (1997), we do not require tournament solutions to be *Condorcet-consistent*, that is, to uniquely select a Condorcet winner whenever one exists.

For a tournament $T = (A, \succ)$ and a subset $B \subseteq A$, we write $S(B)$ for the more cumbersome $S(B, \succ_B)$. For two tournament solutions S and S', we write $S' \subseteq S$, and say that S' is a *refinement* of S and S a *coarsening* of S', if $S'(T) \subseteq S(T)$ for all tournaments T.

The literature on rational choice theory and social choice theory has identified a number of desirable properties for (social) choice functions, also referred to as *axioms*, which can be readily applied to tournament solutions. In this section, we review three of the most important properties in this context—*monotonicity, stability,* and *composition-consistency.* As we will see in Section 3.3.2, another important property of SCFs—*Pareto-optimality*—is intimately connected to a particular tournament solution, the uncovered set.

A tournament solution is monotonic if a chosen alternative remains in the choice set when its dominion is enlarged, while leaving everything else unchanged.

Definition 3.1. A tournament solution S is *monotonic* if for all $T = (A, \succ)$, $T' = (A, \succ')$, $a \in A$ such that $\succ_{A\setminus\{a\}} = \succ'_{A\setminus\{a\}}$ and for all $b \in A \setminus \{a\}$, $a \succ' b$ whenever $a \succ b$,

$$a \in S(T) \quad \text{implies} \quad a \in S(T').$$

Monotonicity of a tournament solution immediately implies monotonicity of the corresponding C1 SCF. Note that this notion of monotonicity for irresolute SCFs is one of the weakest one could think of.

While monotonicity relates choices from tournaments of the same order to each other, the next property relates choices from different subtournaments of the same tournament to each other. Informally, stability (or self-stability) requires that a set is chosen from two different sets of alternatives if and only if it is chosen from the union of these sets.

Definition 3.2. A tournament solution S is *stable* if for all tournaments $T = (A, \succ)$ and for all nonempty subsets $B, C, X \subseteq A$ with $X \subseteq B \cap C$,

$$X = S(B) = S(C) \quad \text{if and only if} \quad X = S(B \cup C).$$

In comparison to monotonicity, stability appears to be much more demanding. It can be factorized into two conditions, $\widehat{\alpha}$ and $\widehat{\gamma}$. Condition $\widehat{\gamma}$ corresponds to the implication from left to right whereas $\widehat{\alpha}$ is the implication from right to left (Brandt and Harrenstein, 2011). $\widehat{\alpha}$ is also known as Chernoff's *postulate* 5* (Chernoff, 1954), the *strong superset property* (Bordes, 1979), *outcast* (Aizerman and Aleskerov, 1995), and the *attention filter axiom* (Masatlioglu et al., 2012).[3] $\widehat{\alpha}$ implies *idempotency*,[4] that is,

$$S(S(T)) = S(T) \text{ for all } T.$$

---

[3] We refer to Monjardet (2008) for a more thorough discussion of the origins of this condition.
[4] Tournament solutions that fail to satisfy idempotency (such as the uncovered set) can be made idempotent by iteratively applying the tournament solution to the resulting choice sets until no further refinement is possible. The corresponding tournament solutions, however, often violate monotonicity.

Finally, we consider a structural invariance property that is based on components and strengthens common cloning-consistency conditions. A tournament solution is composition-consistent if it chooses the "best" alternatives from the "best" components.

Definition 3.3. A tournament solution S is *composition-consistent* if for all tournaments T, T_1, ..., T_k, and $\tilde{T}$ such that $T = \prod(\tilde{T}, T_1, \ldots, T_k)$,

$$S(T) = \bigcup_{i \in S(\tilde{T})} S(T_i).$$

Consider again the tournament given in Figure 3.2. Nonemptiness and neutrality imply that every tournament solution has to select all alternatives in a 3-cycle. It follows that every composition-consistent tournament solution has to select all five alternatives in this tournament.

Besides its normative appeal, composition-consistency can be exploited to speed up the computation of tournament solutions. Brandt et al. (2011) introduced the *decomposition degree* of a tournament as a parameter that reflects its decomposability and showed that computing any composition-consistent tournament solution is fixed-parameter tractable with respect to the decomposition degree. Because computing the minimal decomposition requires only linear time, decomposing a tournament never hurts, and often helps.[5]

A weaker notion of composition-consistency, called *weak composition-consistency*, requires that for every pair of tournaments $T = (A, \succ)$ and $T' = (A, \succ')$ that only differ with respect to the dominance relation on some component Y of T, both

(i) $S(T) \setminus Y = S(T') \setminus Y$, and
(ii) $S(T) \cap Y \neq \emptyset$ if and only if $S(T') \cap Y \neq \emptyset$.

3.3 Common Tournament Solutions

In this section we review some of the most common tournament solutions. On top of the axiomatic properties defined in the previous section, particular attention will be paid to whether and how a tournament solution can be computed efficiently. Whenever a tournament solution is computationally intractable, we state NP-hardness of the decision problem of whether a given alternative belongs to the choice set of a given tournament. This implies hardness of computing the choice set. By virtue of the construction in the proof of Theorem 3.1, it is irrelevant whether the input for this problem is a tournament or a preference profile.

Let us start with two extremely simple tournament solutions. The trivial tournament solution *TRIV* always selects all alternatives from any given tournament. While *TRIV* does not discriminate between alternatives at all and as such is unsuitable as a tournament solution, it is easily verified that it satisfies monotonicity, stability, and

---

[5] Because the representation of a tournament of order m has size $\Theta(m^2)$, the asymptotic running time of a linear time algorithm is in $O(m^2)$.

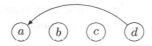

Figure 3.3. Tournament T with $MA(T) = SL(T) = \{a\}$, $CO(T) = \{a, b\}$, $UC(T) = \{a, b, d\}$, and $TRIV(T) = CNL(T) = TC(T) = \{a, b, c, d\}$. All other tournament solutions considered in this chapter coincide with UC. All omitted edges are assumed to point rightward, that is, $a \succ b$, $a \succ c$, $b \succ c$, $b \succ d$, and $c \succ d$.

composition-consistency, and, of course, can be "computed" efficiently.[6] One of the largest nontrivial tournament solutions is the set of *Condorcet non-losers (CNL)*. A *Condorcet loser* is a (unique) alternative a such that $A \setminus \{a\} \succ \{a\}$. In tournaments of order two or more, *CNL* selects all alternatives except Condorcet losers. *CNL* is barely more discriminating than *TRIV*, yet already fails to satisfy stability and composition-consistency (monotonicity is satisfied).

All tournament solutions defined in the following generalize the concept of a Condorcet winner in one way or another.

3.3.1 Solutions Based on Scores

In this section, we introduce four tournament solutions that are defined via various methods of assigning scores to alternatives: the Copeland set, the Slater set, the Markov set, and the bipartisan set.

Copeland Set

The Copeland set is perhaps the first idea that comes to mind when thinking about tournament solutions. While a Condorcet winner is an alternative that dominates *all* other alternatives, Copeland's rule selects those alternatives that dominate the *most* alternatives (see, e.g., Copeland, 1951). Formally, the *Copeland set* $CO(T)$ of a tournament T consists of all alternatives whose dominion is of maximal size, that is,

$$CO(T) = \arg\max_{a \in A} |D(a)|.$$

$|D(a)|$ is also called the *Copeland score* of a. In graph-theoretic terms, $|D(a)|$ is the outdegree of vertex a.

In the example tournament given in Figure 3.3, $CO(T) = \{a, b\}$, because both a and b have a Copeland score of 2, whereas the Copeland score of both c and d is 1.

It is straightforward to check that CO satisfies monotonicity. On the other hand, stability and composition-consistency do not hold. This can be seen by again examining the tournament in Figure 3.3. Because $CO(CO(T)) = \{a\} \neq \{a, b\} = CO(T)$, CO violates idempotency and thus stability. Moreover, as $\{\{a\}, \{b, c\}, \{d\}\}$ is a decomposition of T, composition-consistency would require that $d \in CO(T)$, which is not the case. A similar example shows that CO even violates weak composition-consistency. An axiomatic characterization of CO was provided by Henriet (1985).

---

[6] Many axiomatizations of tournament solutions only require inclusive properties (i.e., properties which demand that alternatives ought to be included in the choice set under certain circumstances) and inclusion-minimality (see, e.g., Brandt et al., 2013a, pp. 224–226).

CO can be easily computed in linear time by determining all Copeland scores and choosing the alternatives with maximum Copeland score.[7]

Theorem 3.2. *The Copeland set can be computed in linear time.*

It is possible to define "second-order" Copeland scores by adding the Copeland scores of all alternatives within the dominion of a given alternative. The process of iteratively computing these scores is guaranteed to converge (due to the Perron-Frobenius Theorem) and leads to a tournament solution, which is sometimes referred to as the *Kendall-Wei method* (see, e.g., Moon, 1968, Chapter 15; Laslier, 1997, pp. 54–56). Kendall-Wei scores can be computed in polynomial time by finding the eigenvector associated with the largest positive eigenvalue of the adjacency matrix.

Slater Set

Although the dominance relation $\succ$ of a tournament may fail to be a strict linear order, it can be linearized by inverting edges in the tournament graph. The intuition behind Slater's rule is to select from a tournament $(A, \succ)$ those alternatives that are maximal elements (i.e., Condorcet winners) in those strict linear orders that can be obtained from $\succ$ by inverting as few edges as possible, that is, in those strict linear orders that have as many edges in common with $\succ$ as possible (Slater, 1961).[8] Thus, Slater's rule can be seen as the unweighted analogue of Kemeny's social preference function (see Chapter 2 and Chapter 4).

Denote the maximal element of A according to a strict linear order $>$ by $\max(>)$. The *Slater score* of a strict linear order $>$ over the alternatives in A with respect to tournament $T = (A, \succ)$ is $|> \cap \succ|$. A strict linear order is a *Slater order* if it has maximal Slater score. Then, the Slater set SL is defined as

$$SL(T) = \{\max(>) : > \text{ is a Slater order for } T\}.$$

In the example in Figure 3.3, $SL(T) = \{a\}$ because $a > b > c > d$ is the only Slater order. *SL* satisfies monotonicity, but violates stability and composition-consistency.

Finding Slater orders is equivalent to solving an instance of the *minimum feedback arc set problem*, which is known to be NP-hard, even in tournaments.[9] Therefore, checking membership in *SL* is NP-hard as well.

Theorem 3.3 (Alon, 2006; Charbit et al., 2007; Conitzer, 2006). *Deciding whether an alternative is contained in the Slater set is NP-hard.*

It is unknown whether the membership problem is contained in NP. The best known upper bound for this problem is the complexity class Θ_2^p, and Hudry (2010)

---

[7] Brandt et al. (2009) have shown that deciding whether an alternative is contained in $CO(T)$ is TC^0-complete and therefore not expressible in first-order logic.

[8] When inverting as few edges as possible in order to obtain a *Condorcet winner* (rather than a strict linear order), we get the Copeland set.

[9] Whether the minimum feedback arc set problem is NP-hard in tournaments was a long-standing open problem that was solved independently by Alon (2006), Charbit et al. (2007), and Conitzer (2006). The minimum feedback arc set problem is APX-hard (Kann, 1992) and thus does not admit a polynomial-time approximation scheme (PTAS) unless P = NP. For tournaments, however, there exists a PTAS (Kenyon-Mathieu and Schudy, 2007).

conjectured that the problem is complete for this class. For a more detailed discussion of the computational complexity of Slater's solution, see Hudry (2010) and Charon and Hudry (2006, 2010). Bachmeier et al. (2014) have shown that deciding membership in the Slater set remains NP-hard even when there are only 13 voters.

Although *SL* is *not* composition-consistent, it satisfies weak composition-consistency. Interestingly, decompositions of the tournament can be exploited to identify a *subset* of the Slater orders (see Laslier, 1997, p. 66; Conitzer, 2006).

Markov Set

Based on ideas that date back at least to Daniels (1969) and Moon and Pullman (1970), Laslier (1997) defines a tournament solution via a Markov chain. The intuition given by Laslier is that of a table tennis tournament in which the alternatives are players who compete in a series of pairwise comparisons. If a player wins, he will stay at the table and compete in the next match. If he loses, he will be replaced with a new random player. The goal is to identify those players who, in expectation, will win most matches.

The states of the Markov chain are the alternatives and the transition probabilities are determined by the dominance relation: in every step, stay in the current state a with probability $\frac{|D(a)|}{|T|-1}$, and move to state b with probability $\frac{1}{|T|-1}$ for all $b \in \overline{D}(a)$. The *Markov set* consists of those alternatives that have maximum probability in the chain's unique stationary distribution. Formally, the transition matrix of the Markov chain is defined as

$$Q = \frac{1}{|T| - 1} \cdot (M(T) + diag(CO)),$$

where $M(T)$ is the adjacency matrix and $diag(CO)$ is the diagonal matrix of the Copeland scores. Let $\Delta(A)$ be the set of all probability distributions over A. The *Markov set MA(T)* of a tournament T is then given by

$$MA(T) = \arg\max_{a \in A} \{p(a) : p \in \Delta(A) \text{ and } Qp = p\}.$$

MA tends to select significantly smaller choice sets than most other tournament solutions. In the example in Figure 3.3, $MA(T) = \{a\}$ because the stationary distribution is $\frac{4}{10}a + \frac{3}{10}b + \frac{1}{10}c + \frac{2}{10}d$. The Markov solution is also closely related to Google's PageRank algorithm for ranking websites (see Brandt and Fischer, 2007). It satisfies monotonicity, but violates stability and weak composition-consistency.

Computing p as the eigenvector of Q associated with the eigenvalue 1 is straightforward. Accordingly, deciding whether an alternative is in *MA* can be achieved in polynomial time.

Theorem 3.4. *The Markov set can be computed in polynomial time.*

Moreover, Hudry (2009) has pointed out that computing *MA* has the same asymptotic complexity as matrix multiplication, for which the fastest known algorithm to date runs in $O(m^{2.38})$.

Bipartisan Set

The last tournament solution considered in this section generalizes the notion of a Condorcet winner to lotteries over alternatives. Laffond et al. (1993a) and Fisher and Ryan (1995) have shown independently that every tournament T admits a unique *maximal lottery*,[10] that is, a probability distribution $p \in \Delta(A)$ such that for $G(T) = (g_{ab})_{a,b \in A}$,

$$\sum_{a,b \in A} p(a)q(b)g_{ab} \geq 0 \quad \text{for all } q \in \Delta(A).$$

Let p_T denote the unique maximal lottery for a tournament T. Laffond et al. (1993a) define the *bipartisan set $BP(T)$* of T as the support of p_T, that is,

$$BP(T) = \{a \in A : p_T(a) > 0\}.$$

For the tournament in Figure 3.4, we have $p_T = \frac{1}{3}a + \frac{1}{3}b + \frac{1}{3}d$ and thus $BP(T) = \{a, b, d\}$. It is important to realize that the probabilities do not necessarily represent the strengths of alternatives and, that, in contrast to other score-based tournament solutions, just selecting those alternatives with *maximal* probabilities results in a tournament solution that violates monotonicity (see Laslier, 1997, pp. 145–146).

To appreciate this definition, it might be illustrative to interpret the skew-adjacency matrix $G(T)$ of T as a symmetric zero-sum game in which there are two players, one choosing rows and the other choosing columns, and in which the matrix entries are the payoffs of the row player. Then, if the players respectively randomize over rows and columns according to p_T this corresponds to the unique mixed Nash equilibrium of this game. An axiomatization of *BP* and an interpretation of mixed strategies in the context of electoral competition were provided by Laslier (1997, pp. 151–153) and Laslier (2000), respectively.

BP satisfies monotonicity, stability, and composition-consistency. Moreover, *BP* can be computed in polynomial time by solving a linear feasibility problem (Brandt and Fischer, 2008a).

Theorem 3.5. *The bipartisan set can be computed in polynomial time.*

In weak tournaments—that is, generalizations of tournaments where the dominance relation is not required to be antisymmetric (see Section 3.5)—deciding whether an alternative is contained in the bipartisan set is P-*complete* (Brandt and Fischer, 2008a). Whether P-hardness also holds for tournaments is open.

3.3.2 Uncovered Set and Banks Set

If dominance relations were transitive in general, every tournament (and all of its subtournaments) would admit a Condorcet winner. The *uncovered set* and the *Banks set* address the lack of transitivity in two different but equally natural ways.

The uncovered set takes into account a particular transitive subrelation of the dominance relation, called the *covering relation*, and selects the maximal alternatives thereof,

---

[10] Maximal lotteries were first considered by Kreweras (1965) and studied in detail by Fishburn (1984). The existence of maximal lotteries follows from the Minimax Theorem.

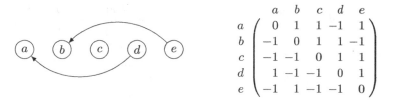

$$
G(T) = \begin{pmatrix}
 & a & b & c & d & e \\
a & 0 & 1 & 1 & -1 & 1 \\
b & -1 & 0 & 1 & 1 & -1 \\
c & -1 & -1 & 0 & 1 & 1 \\
d & 1 & -1 & -1 & 0 & 1 \\
e & -1 & 1 & -1 & -1 & 0
\end{pmatrix}
$$

Figure 3.4. Tournament T and its skew-adjacency matrix $G(T)$. $CO(T) = SL(T) = MA(T) = \{a\}$, $BP = \{a, b, d\}$, $UC(T) = BA(T) = \{a, b, c, d\}$, and $TRIV(T) = CNL(T) = TC(T) = \{a, b, c, d, e\}$. All other tournament solutions considered in this chapter coincide with BP. Omitted edges point rightward.

whereas the Banks set consists of maximal alternatives of inclusion-maximal transitive subtournaments.[11]

Uncovered Set

An alternative a is said to *cover* alternative b whenever every alternative dominated by b is also dominated by a. Formally, given a tournament $T = (A, \succ)$, the covering relation C is defined as a binary relation over A such that for all distinct $a, b \in A$,

$$a \; C \; b \quad \text{if and only if} \quad D(b) \subseteq D(a).$$

Observe that $a \; C \; b$ implies that $a \succ b$ and is equivalent to $\overline{D}(a) \subseteq \overline{D}(b)$. It is easily verified that the *covering relation* C is transitive and irreflexive, but not necessarily connex. The *uncovered set* $UC(T)$ of a tournament $T = (A, \succ)$ is then given by the set of maximal elements of the covering relation, that is,

$$UC(T) = \{a \in A : b \; C \; a \text{ for } no \; b \in A\}.$$

UC was independently proposed by Fishburn (1977) and Miller (1980) and goes back to a game-theoretic notion used by Gillies (1959).

In the example in Figure 3.4, a covers e, as $D(e) = \{b\}$ and $D(a) = \{b, c, e\}$. As this is not the case for any other two alternatives, $UC(T) = \{a, b, c, d\}$. UC satisfies monotonicity and composition-consistency, but violates stability. In fact, it does not even satisfy idempotency. An appealing axiomatic characterization of UC was given by Moulin (1986).

Interestingly, UC consists precisely of those alternatives that reach every other alternative on a domination path of length at most two (Shepsle and Weingast, 1984).[12] This equivalence can be easily seen by realizing that

$a \in UC(T)$ if and only if there is no $b \in A$ such that $b \; C \; a$

if and only if for all $b \in \overline{D}(a)$ there is some $c \in D(a)$ such that $c \succ b$

if and only if a reaches all $b \in A \setminus \{a\}$ in at most two steps.

---

[11] As Brandt (2011a) notes, the uncovered set contains exactly those alternatives that are Condorcet winners in inclusion-maximal subtournaments that admit a Condorcet winner.

[12] In graph theory, these alternatives are called the *kings* of a tournament, and they constitute the *center* of the tournament graph.

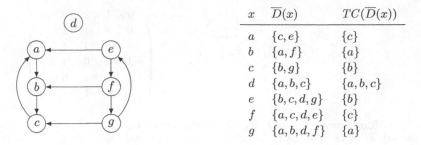

x	$\overline{D}(x)$	$TC(\overline{D}(x))$
a	$\{c, e\}$	$\{c\}$
b	$\{a, f\}$	$\{a\}$
c	$\{b, g\}$	$\{b\}$
d	$\{a, b, c\}$	$\{a, b, c\}$
e	$\{b, c, d, g\}$	$\{b\}$
f	$\{a, c, d, e\}$	$\{c\}$
g	$\{a, b, d, f\}$	$\{a\}$

Figure 3.5. Tournament T and its dominator sets. $BA(T) = \{a, b, c\}$, $UC(T) = \{a, b, c, d\}$, and $TRIV(T) = CNL(T) = TC(T) = \{a, b, c, d, e, f, g\}$. All other tournament solutions considered in this chapter coincide with BA. Omitted edges point rightward.

This characterization can be leveraged to compute UC via matrix multiplication because

$$a \in UC(T) \quad \text{if and only if} \quad (M(T)^2 + M(T) + I)_{ab} \neq 0 \text{ for all } b \in A,$$

where I is the $n \times n$ identity matrix (Hudry, 2009). Hence, the asymptotic running time is $O(n^{2.38})$.[13]

Theorem 3.6. *The uncovered set can be computed in polynomial time.*

As mentioned in Chapter 2, an alternative is Pareto-optimal if there exists no other alternative such that all voters prefer the latter to the former. A tournament solution is *Pareto-optimal* if its associated SCF only returns Pareto-optimal alternatives. Brandt et al. (2015a) have shown that UC is the coarsest Pareto-optimal tournament solution. As a consequence, a tournament solution is Pareto-optimal if and only if it is a refinement of UC.

Banks Set

The Banks set selects the maximal elements of all maximal transitive subtournaments. Formally, a transitive subtournament $(B, \succ_B)$ of tournament T is said to be *maximal* if there is no other transitive subtournament $(C, \succ_C)$ of T with $B \subset C$. The Banks set $BA(T)$ of a tournament is then defined as

$$BA(T) = \{\max(\succ_B) : (B, \succ_B) \text{ is a maximal transitive subtournament of } T\}.$$

The tournament in Figure 3.5 has six maximal transitive subtournaments, induced by the following subsets of A: $\{a, b, d, g\}$, $\{a, d, f, g\}$, $\{b, c, d, e\}$, $\{b, d, g, e\}$, $\{c, a, d, f\}$, and $\{c, d, e, f\}$. Hence, $BA(T) = \{a, b, c\}$. Like UC, BA satisfies monotonicity and composition-consistency, but violates stability. BA was originally defined as the set of sophisticated outcomes under the amendment agenda (Banks, 1985). For

---

[13] Brandt and Fischer (2008a) proved that the problem of computing UC is contained in the complexity class AC^0 by exploiting that computing the covering relation can be highly parallelized. This is interesting insofar as deciding whether an alternative lies within UC is computationally easier (in AC^0) than checking whether it is contained in CO (TC^0-complete), despite the fact that the fastest known algorithm for computing UC is asymptotically slower than the fastest algorithm for CO.

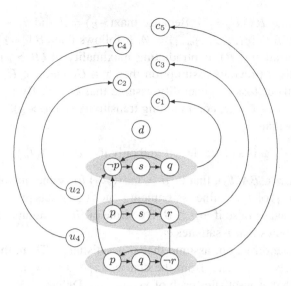

Figure 3.6. Tournament T_φ for the *3CNF* formula $\varphi = (\neg p \vee s \vee q) \wedge (p \vee s \vee r) \wedge (p \vee q \vee \neg r)$. Omitted edges point downward.

more details see Section 3.4. An alternative axiomatization of the Banks set was given by Brandt (2011a).

BA cannot be computed in polynomial time unless P equals NP.

Theorem 3.7 (Woeginger, 2003). *Deciding whether an alternative is contained in the Banks set is NP-complete.*

Proof. Membership in NP is straightforward. Given a tournament $T = (A, \succ)$ and an alternative $a \in A$, simply guess a subset B of A and verify that $(B, \succ_B)$ is a transitive subtournament of T with $a = \max(\succ_B)$. Then, check $(B, \succ_B)$ for maximality.

For NP-hardness, we give the reduction from 3SAT by Brandt et al. (2010c). Let $\varphi = (x_1^1 \vee x_1^2 \vee x_1^3) \wedge \cdots \wedge (x_m^1 \vee x_m^2 \vee x_m^3)$ be a propositional formula in 3-conjunctive normal form (3CNF). For literals x we have $\bar{x} = \neg p$ if $x = p$, and $\bar{x} = p$ if $x = \neg p$, where p is a propositional variable. We may assume that x and $\bar{x}$ do not occur in the same clause.

We now construct a tournament $T_\varphi = (A, \succ)$ with

$$A = \{c_1, \ldots, c_{2m-1}\} \cup \{d\} \cup U_1 \cup \cdots \cup U_{2m-1},$$

where for $1 \leq k \leq 2m - 1$, the set U_k is defined as follows. If k is odd, let $i = \frac{k+1}{2}$ and define $U_k = \{x_i^1, x_i^2, x_i^3\}$. If k is even, let $U_k = \{u_k\}$.

The dominance relation is defined such that $x_i^1 \succ x_i^2 \succ x_i^3 \succ x_i^1$. Moreover, for literals x_i^ℓ and $x_j^{\ell'}$ ($1 \leq \ell, \ell' \leq 3$) with $i < j$ we have $x_i^\ell \succ x_j^{\ell'}$, unless $x_i^\ell = \bar{x}_j^{\ell'}$, in which case $x_j^{\ell'} \succ x_i^\ell$. For the dominance relation on the remaining alternatives the reader is referred to Figure 3.6.

Observe that for every maximal transitive subtournament $(B, \succ_B)$ of T_φ with $\max(\succ_B) = d$ it holds that:

(i) B contains an alternative from each U_k with $1 \leq k \leq 2m - 1$, and
(ii) for no literal x, the set B contains both x and $\bar{x}$.

For (i), assume that $B \cap U_k = \emptyset$. Because $\max(\succ_B) = d$ and $c_j \succ d$ for all $1 \leq j \leq 2m - 1$, we have $B \cap \{c_1, \ldots, c_{2m-1}\} = \emptyset$. It follows that $(B \cup \{c_k\}, \succ_{B \cup \{c_k\}})$ is transitive ($c_k \succ b$ for all $b \in B$), contradicting maximality of $(B, \succ_B)$. For (ii), assume both $x, \bar{x} \in B$. By a previous assumption then $x \in U_k$ and $\bar{x} \in U_{k'}$ for odd k and k' with $k \neq k'$. Without loss of generality assume that $k < k'$. By (i), $u_{k+1} \in B$. Then, however, $x \succ u_{k+1} \succ \bar{x} \succ x$, contradicting transitivity of $(B, \succ_B)$.

We now prove that

$$\varphi \text{ is satisfiable} \quad \text{if and only if} \quad d \in BA(T_\varphi).$$

First assume that $d \in BA(T_\varphi)$, that is, $d = \max(\succ_B)$ for some maximal transitive subtournament $(B, \succ_B)$ of T_φ. Define assignment v such that it sets propositional variable p to true if $p \in B$ and to false if $\neg p \in B$. By virtue of (ii), assignment v is well-defined and with (i) it follows that v satisfies φ.

For the opposite direction, assume that φ is satisfiable. Then, there are an assignment v and literals $x_1, \ldots, x_m$ from the clauses $(x_1^1 \vee x_1^2 \vee x_1^3), \ldots, (x_m^1 \vee x_m^2 \vee x_m^3)$, respectively, such that v satisfies each of $x_1, \ldots, x_m$. Define

$$B = \{d\} \cup \{x_1, \ldots, x_m\} \cup \{u_2, u_4, \ldots, u_{2m-2}\}.$$

It is easily seen that $(B, \succ_B)$ is transitive and that $\max(\succ_B) = d$. Observe that B contains an alternative u_k from each U_k with $1 \leq k \leq 2m - 1$. Hence, for each $c_k \in C$, we have $c_k \succ d \succ u_k \succ c_k$ and, thus, $(B \cup \{c_k\}, \succ_{B \cup \{c_k\}})$ is not transitive. It follows that $d = \max(\succ_{B'})$ for some maximal transitive subtournament $(B', \succ_{B'})$ with $B \subseteq B'$, that is, $d \in BA(T_\varphi)$. $\qquad\square$

By modifying the construction only slightly and using a variant of 3SAT, Bachmeier et al. (2014) have shown that this problem remains NP-complete even when there are only 5 voters. Interestingly, finding *some* alternative in $BA(A, \succ)$ can be achieved in linear time using the following simple procedure (Hudry, 2004). Label the alternatives in A as $a_1, \ldots, a_m$ and initialize X as the empty set. Then, starting with $k = 1$, successively add alternative a_k to X if and only if a_k dominates all alternatives in X. After m steps, this process terminates and the last alternative added to X can easily be seen to be a member of the Banks set. The difficulty of computing the whole Banks set is rooted in the potentially exponential number of maximal transitive subtournaments.

3.3.3 Solutions Based on Stability

Generalizing an idea by Dutta (1988), Brandt (2011a) proposed a method for refining any tournament solution S by defining minimal sets that satisfy a natural stability criterion with respect to S. Given a tournament solution S and a tournament T, a subset of alternatives $B \subseteq A$ is called S-*stable* in T if, for all $a \in A \setminus B$,

$$a \notin S(B \cup \{a\}).$$

An S-stable set B is said to be *minimal* if there is no other S-stable set C in T such that $C \subset B$. Because the set of all alternatives is finite and trivially S-stable, minimal S-stable sets are guaranteed to exist. Now for each tournament solution S, there is a new tournament solution $\widehat{S}$, which returns the union of all minimal S-stable sets in a tournament $T = (A, \succ)$, that is,

$$\widehat{S}(T) = \bigcup \{ B \subseteq A : B \text{ is a minimal } S\text{-stable set in } T \}.$$

A crucial issue in this context is whether S admits a *unique* minimal stable set in every tournament because this is necessary for $\widehat{S}$ to satisfy stability (Brandt et al., 2014e).

In the following, we will define three tournament solutions using the notion of stable sets: the top cycle, the minimal covering set, and the minimal extending set.

Top Cycle

The top cycle TC can be defined as the unique minimal stable set with respect to CNL, the set of Condorcet nonlosers, that is,

$$TC = \widehat{CNL}.$$

Alternatively, TC can be defined via the notion of a dominant set. A nonempty subset of alternatives $B \subseteq A$ is called *dominant* in tournament $T = (A, \succ)$ if $B \succ A \setminus B$, that is, if each alternative in B dominates all alternatives not in B. Dominant sets are linearly ordered via set inclusion and TC returns the unique smallest dominant set. In yet another equivalent definition, TC is defined as the set of maximal elements of the transitive and reflexive closure of the dominance relation $\succ$. TC is a very elementary tournament solution and, in a slightly more general context (see Section 3.5), is also known as *weak closure maximality*, *GETCHA*, or the *Smith set* (Good, 1971; Smith, 1973; Schwartz, 1986). An appealing axiomatic characterization of the top cycle was given by Bordes (1976).

TC tends to select rather large choice sets and may even contain Pareto-dominated alternatives. In the example tournaments given in Figures 3.3, 3.4, and 3.5, TC selects the set of all alternatives because it is the only dominant set. TC satisfies monotonicity, stability, and weak composition-consistency, but violates the stronger notion of composition-consistency (see, e.g., Figure 3.3).

Because each alternative outside TC only dominates alternatives that are also outside TC and every alternative in TC dominates all alternatives outside TC, it can easily be appreciated that each alternative in TC has a strictly greater Copeland score than each alternative outside TC. Hence, $CO \subseteq TC$.

Exploiting this insight, $TC(T)$ can be computed in linear time by starting with $CO(T)$ and then iteratively adding alternatives that are not dominated by the current set. Alternatively, one can employ an algorithm, for example, the Kosaraju-Sharir algorithm or Tarjan's algorithm, for finding the *strongly connected components* of T and then output the unique strongly connected component that dominates all other strongly connected components.[14]

Theorem 3.8. *The top cycle can be computed in linear time.*

---

[14] Brandt et al. (2009) have shown that the problem of deciding whether an alternative is contained in the top cycle of a tournament is in the complexity class AC^0.

Minimal Covering Set

A subset B of alternatives is called a *covering set* if it is UC-stable, that is, if every $a \in A \setminus B$ is covered in the subtournament $(B \cup \{a\}, \succ_{B \cup \{a\}})$. The *minimal covering set MC* is defined as

$$MC = \widehat{UC}.$$

Dutta (1988) has shown that every tournament admits a *unique* minimal UC-stable set and that $MC \subseteq UC$. In the example in Figure 3.4, $MC(T) = \{a, b, d\}$, and hence MC is a strict refinement of UC. Observe that, for instance, $\{a, b, c\}$ is not UC-stable, as $d \in UC(\{a, b, c, d\})$. MC satisfies monotonicity, stability, and composition-consistency. Dutta also provided an axiomatic characterization of MC, which was later improved by Laslier (1997, pp. 117–120).

Laffond et al. (1993a) have shown that $BP \subseteq MC$. By virtue of Theorem 3.5, we can therefore efficiently compute a *nonempty subset* of MC. This fact can be used to compute MC by leveraging the following lemma.

Lemma 3.9. *Let $T = (A, \succ)$ be a tournament and $B \subseteq MC(A)$. Define $C = \{a \in A \setminus B : a \in UC(B \cup \{a\})\}$. Then, $MC(C) \subseteq MC(A)$.*

$MC(T)$ can then be computed by first computing the bipartisan set $BP(T)$ and then iteratively adding a specific subset of alternatives that lie outside the current set but do belong to $MC(T)$. Lemma 3.9 tells us how this subset can be found at each stage (see Algorithm 1).[15]

Algorithm 1 Minimal covering set

---
procedure $MC(A, \succ)$
  $B \leftarrow BP(A)$
  loop
    $C \leftarrow \{a \in A \setminus B : a \in UC(B \cup \{a\})\}$
    if $C = \emptyset$ **then return** B **end if**
    $B \leftarrow B \cup BP(C)$
  end loop

Theorem 3.10 (Brandt and Fischer, 2008a). *The minimal covering set can be computed in polynomial time.*

Minimal Extending Set

A subset of alternatives is called an *extending set* if it is BA-stable. Brandt (2011a) defined the *minimal extending set $ME(T)$* as the union of all minimal extending sets of a tournament T, that is,

$$ME = \widehat{BA}.$$

---

[15] Lemma 3.9 can also be used to construct a *recursive* algorithm for computing MC without making reference to BP. However, such an algorithm has exponential worst-case running time.

In the tournament in Figure 3.4, we find that $ME(T) = \{a, b, d\}$. Brandt et al. (2014c) showed that $ME \subseteq BA$ and that computing ME is computationally intractable by using a construction similar to that of the proof of Theorem 3.7.

Theorem 3.11 (Brandt et al., 2014c). *Deciding whether an alternative is contained in a minimal extending set is NP-hard.*

The best known upper bound for this decision problem is the complexity class Σ_3^p. Bachmeier et al. (2014) have shown that the problem remains NP-hard even when there are only 7 voters. A relation-algebraic specification of minimal extending sets, which can be used to compute ME on small instances, was proposed by Berghammer (2014).

Brandt (2011a) proved that ME satisfies composition-consistency, and conjectured that every tournament contains a unique minimal extending set. Even though this conjecture was later disproved, which implies that ME violates monotonicity and stability, it is unclear whether this seriously impairs the usefulness of ME (Brandt et al., 2013b, 2014c). The counterexample found by Brandt et al. consists of about 10^{136} alternatives and concrete tournaments for which ME violates any of these properties have never been encountered (even when resorting to extensive computer experiments).

3.3.4 Solutions Based on Retentiveness

Finally, we consider an operator on tournament solutions which bears some resemblance to the notion of minimal stable sets as introduced in the previous section. The underlying idea of *retentiveness* was first proposed by Schwartz (1990) and studied more generally by Brandt et al. (2014d).

For a given tournament solution S, we say that an alternative a is S-dominated by alternative b if b is chosen among a's dominators by S. Similarly, a nonempty set of alternatives is called S-retentive if none of its elements is S-dominated by some alternative outside the set. Formally, for a tournament solution S and a tournament $T = (A, \succ)$, a nonempty subset $B \subseteq A$ is S-*retentive* in T if for all $b \in B$ such that $\overline{D}(b) \neq \emptyset$,

$$S(\overline{D}(b)) \subseteq B.$$

An S-retentive set B in T is said to be *minimal* if there is no other S-retentive set C in T with $C \subset B$. As in the case of S-stable sets, minimal S-retentive sets are guaranteed to exist because the set of all alternatives is trivially S-retentive. Thus we can define $\mathring{S}$ as the tournament solution yielding the union of minimal S-retentive sets, that is, for all tournaments $T = (A, \succ)$,

$$\mathring{S}(T) = \bigcup \{B \subseteq A : B \text{ is a minimal } S\text{-retentive set in } T\}.$$

As with minimal stable sets, it is important for the axiomatic properties of $\mathring{S}$ whether S admits a *unique* minimal retentive set in every tournament. It is easily verified that there always exists a unique minimal *TRIV*-retentive set, and that in fact $\mathring{TRIV} = TC$.

The Minimal TC-Retentive Set

Brandt et al. (2014d) have shown that $\mathring{S}$ inherits several desirable properties from S—including monotonicity and stability—whenever a unique minimal S-retentive set is guaranteed to exist. They went on to show that every tournament admits a unique TC-retentive set. As a consequence, the tournament solution $\mathring{TC}$—which can also be written as $T\mathring{R}IV$—is monotonic and stable. Also, $\mathring{TC}$ inherits efficient computability from TC and satisfies weak composition-consistency.

Theorem 3.12 (Brandt et al., 2014d). *The minimal TC-retentive set can be computed in polynomial time.*

In the tournament in Figure 3.5, the set $\{a, b, c\}$ and each of its supersets is TC-retentive. Therefore, $\mathring{TC}(T) = \{a, b, c\}$.

Tournament Equilibrium Set

Schwartz (1990) defined the *tournament equilibrium set* (*TEQ*) recursively as the union of all minimal *TEQ*-retentive sets,

$$TEQ = T\mathring{E}Q.$$

This recursion is well-defined because the order of the dominator set of any alternative is strictly smaller than the order of the original tournament. In the example in Figure 3.5, $TEQ(T) = \mathring{TC}(T) = \{a, b, c\}$, because *TEQ* and *TC* coincide on all dominator sets.

TEQ is the only tournament solution defined via retentiveness that satisfies composition-consistency. Schwartz conjectured that every tournament contains a *unique* minimal *TEQ*-retentive set. As was shown by Laffond et al. (1993b) and Houy (2009b,a), *TEQ* satisfies any one of a number of important properties including monotonicity and stability *if and only if* Schwartz's conjecture holds. Brandt et al. (2013b) showed that Schwartz's conjecture does not hold by nonconstructively disproving a related weaker conjecture surrounding *ME*.[16] As a consequence, *TEQ* violates monotonicity and stability. However, counterexamples to Schwartz's conjecture appear to be extremely rare and it may be argued that *TEQ* satisfies the properties for all practical purposes.

Using a construction similar to that of the proof of Theorem 3.7, it can be shown that computing *TEQ* is intractable.[17]

Theorem 3.13 (Brandt et al., 2010c). *Deciding whether an alternative is contained in the tournament equilibrium set is NP-hard.*

There is no obvious reason why checking membership in *TEQ* should be in NP. The best known upper bound for this problem is the complexity class PSPACE. Bachmeier

---

[16] A significantly smaller counterexample for Schwartz's conjecture, consisting of only 24 alternatives, was found by Brandt and Seedig (2013). However, this smaller counterexample does not disprove the corresponding conjecture for *ME*.

[17] The proof of Theorem 3.13 actually shows that the membership decision problem for *any* tournament solution that is sandwiched between *BA* and *TEQ*, that is, computing any tournament solution S with $TEQ \subseteq S \subseteq BA$, is NP-hard.

Table 3.1. *Axiomatic and computational properties of tournament solutions*

	Monotonicity	Stability	Composition-Consistency	Computational Complexity
CO	+	−	−	in P
SL	+	−	weak	NP-hard, in Θ_2^p
MA	+	−	−	in P
BP	+	+	+	in P
UC	+	−	+	in P
BA	+	−	+	NP-complete
TC	+	+	weak	in P
MC	+	+	+	in P
ME	−	−	+	NP-hard, in Σ_3^p
TC̊	+	+	weak	in P
TEQ	−	−	+	NP-hard, in PSPACE

Note: All hardness results hold even for a constant number of voters. Computing *UC* and *TC* has been shown to be in AC^0, whereas computing *CO* is TC^0-complete.

et al. (2014) have shown that this problem remains NP-hard even when there are only 7 voters. Brandt et al. (2010c, 2011) devised practical algorithms for *TEQ* that run reasonably well on moderately sized instances, even though their worst-case complexity is, of course, still exponential.

3.3.5 Summary

Table 3.1 summarizes the axiomatic as well as computational properties of the considered tournament solutions. There are linear-time algorithms for *CO* and *TC*. Moreover, a single element of *BA* can be found in linear time. Computing *BA*, *TEQ*, and *SL* is intractable unless P equals NP. Apparently, *MC* and *BP* fare particularly well in terms of axiomatic properties as well as efficient computability.[18]

Figure 3.7 provides a graphical overview of the set-theoretic relationships between tournament solutions. It is known that *BA* and *MC* (and by the known inclusions also *UC* and *TC*) almost always select all alternatives when tournaments are drawn uniformly at random (Fey, 2008; Scott and Fey, 2012). Experimental results suggest that the same is true for *TEQ*. Interestingly, despite satisfying strong inclusive axiomatic properties such as stability and composition-consistency, *BP* is much more discriminative: For every integer $m > 1$, the average number of alternatives that *BP* selects in a labeled tournament of order m is $\frac{m}{2}$ (Fisher and Reeves, 1995; Scott and Fey, 2012).[19] Analytic results concerning the uniform distribution stand in sharp contrast to empirical observations that Condorcet winners are likely to exist in real-world settings, which

---

[18] Berghammer et al. (2013) have formalized the definitions of most of the considered tournament solutions using a computer algebra system, which can then be used to compute and visualize these functions. These general-purpose algorithms are, however, outperformed by tailor-made algorithms using matrix multiplication, linear programming, or eigenvalue decomposition (see, e.g., Seedig, 2014).

[19] Brandt et al. (2014e) have shown that there is no more discriminative stable tournament solution than *BP*. In particular, there is no stable refinement of *BP*.

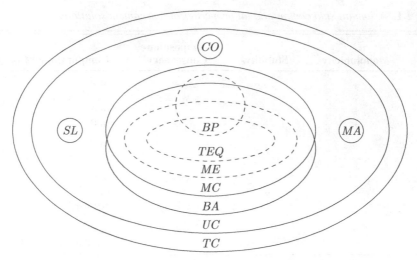

Figure 3.7. The set-theoretic relationships between tournament solutions are depicted in this Venn-like diagram. If the ellipses of two tournament solutions S and S' intersect, then $S(T) \cap S'(T) \neq \emptyset$ for all tournaments T. If the ellipses for S an S' are disjoint, however, this signifies that $S(T) \cap S'(T) = \emptyset$ for some tournament T. Thus, BA and MC are not included in each other, but they always have a nonempty intersection (see, e.g., Laslier, 1997). CO, MA, and SL are contained in UC but may be disjoint from MC and BA. The exact location of BP in this diagram is unknown, but it intersects with TEQ in all known instances and is contained in MC. TEQ and ME are contained in BA, but their inclusion in MC is uncertain. Hence, the ellipses for TEQ, ME, and BP are dashed. $\mathring{TC}$ is omitted in this figure because very little is known apart from the inclusion in TC (see Brandt et al., 2015b, for more details).

implies that tournament solutions are much more discriminative than these analytical results suggest (Brandt and Seedig, 2015).

3.4 Strategyproofness and Agenda Implementation

It is well-known from the Gibbard-Satterthwaite Theorem (see Chapter 2) that only trivial resolute SCFs are strategyproof, that is, immune against the strategic misrepresentation of preferences. Tournament solutions are irresolute by definition (think of a 3-cycle) and therefore the Gibbard-Satterthwaite Theorem does not apply directly.[20]

There are two ways to obtain weak forms of strategyproofness that are particularly well-suited for tournament solutions. The first one concerns the traditional notion of strategyproofness with respect to weakly dominant strategies, but incomplete preference relations over sets of alternatives, and the second one deals with the implementation of tournament solutions by means of sequential binary agendas and subgame-perfect Nash equilibrium. Each of these methods allows for rather positive results, but also comes at a cost: the first one requires a high degree of uncertainty

---

[20] However, the Gibbard-Satterthwaite Theorem does imply that no *resolute refinement* of any of the tournament solutions discussed in this chapter—except *TRIV*—is strategyproof. There are important extensions of the Gibbard-Satterthwaite Theorem to irresolute SCFs such as the Duggan-Schwartz Theorem (see Chapter 2). We will focus on more positive results for tournament solutions in this chapter.

among the voters as to how ties are broken, whereas the second one requires common knowledge of all preferences and may result in impractical voting procedures.

3.4.1 Strategyproofness

A proper definition of strategyproofness for *irresolute* SCFs requires the specification of preferences over *sets* of alternatives. One way to obtain such preferences is to extend the preferences that voters have over individual alternatives to (not necessarily complete) preference relations over sets. A function that yields a preference relation over subsets of alternatives when given a preference relation over single alternatives is called a *set extension*. Of course, there are various set extensions, each of which leads to a different class of strategyproof SCFs (see, e.g., Gärdenfors, 1979; Barberà et al., 2004; Taylor, 2005, Brandt, 2015; Brandt and Brill, 2011).

Here, we will concentrate on two natural and well-studied set extensions due to Kelly (1977) and Fishburn (1972), respectively.[21] Let $\succsim_i$ be the preference relation of voter i and let B and C be two nonempty sets of alternatives. Then, Kelly's extension is defined by letting

$$B \succsim_i^K C \quad \text{if and only if} \quad b \succsim_i c \text{ for all } b \in B \text{ and } c \in C.$$

One interpretation of this extension is that voters are completely unaware of the tiebreaking mechanism (e.g., a lottery) that will be used to pick the winning alternative.

Fishburn's extension is defined by letting

$$B \succsim_i^F C \quad \text{if and only if} \quad b \succsim_i c \text{ for all } b \in B \text{ and } c \in C \setminus B \text{ and}$$
$$b \succsim_i c \text{ for all } b \in B \setminus C \text{ and } c \in C.$$

One interpretation of this extension is that ties are broken according to some unknown linear order (e.g., the preferences of a chairman). It is easily seen that $B \succsim_i^K C$ implies $B \succsim_i^F C$.

Each set extension induces a corresponding notion of strategyproofness. An SCF f is *Kelly-strategyproof* if there is no voter i and no pair of preference profiles R and R' with $\succsim_j = \succsim_j'$ for all $j \neq i$ such that $f(R') \succ_i^K f(R)$. If such profiles exist, we say that voter i can *manipulate* f. *Fishburn-strategyproofness* is defined analogously. Note that in this definition of strategyproofness, set extensions are interpreted as fully specified preference relations according to which many choice sets are incomparable (and changing the outcome to an incomparable choice set does not constitute a manipulation). Clearly, because $B \succsim_i^K C$ implies $B \succsim_i^F C$, Fishburn-strategyproofness is stronger than Kelly-strategyproofness.

Kelly-strategyproofness may seem like an extremely weak notion of strategyproofness as only few pairs of sets can actually be compared. Nevertheless, almost all common SCFs fail to satisfy Kelly-strategyproofness because they can already be manipulated on profiles where these functions are resolute (Taylor, 2005, pp. 44–51).

---

[21] Gärdenfors (1979) attributed the second extension to Fishburn because it is the coarsest extension that satisfies a certain set of axioms proposed by Fishburn (1972).

Brandt (2015) has shown that stability and monotonicity are sufficient for Kelly-strategyproofness. Virtually all SCFs of interest that satisfy these conditions are tournament solutions (or weighted tournament solutions). We therefore only state the result for tournament solutions rather than for SCFs.

Theorem 3.14 (Brandt, 2015). *Every monotonic and stable tournament solution is Kelly-strategyproof. Moreover, every Condorcet-consistent coarsening of a Kelly-strategyproof tournament solution is Kelly-strategyproof.*

As a consequence, BP, each of its Condorcet-consistent coarsenings (such as MC, UC, and TC), and $\mathring{TC}$ are Kelly-strategyproof.[22] On the other hand, it can be shown that every Condorcet-consistent tournament solution that may return a single alternative in the absence of a Condorcet winner is Kelly-manipulable. It follows that CO, SL, and MA fail to be Kelly-strategyproof. More involved arguments can be used to show that ME and TEQ are not Kelly-strategyproof.

The results for Fishburn-strategyproofness are less encouraging. While it is known that TC is Fishburn-strategyproof (Brandt and Brill, 2011; Sanver and Zwicker, 2012), a computer-aided proof has shown that no refinement of UC is Fishburn-strategyproof. Because UC is the coarsest Pareto-optimal tournament solution, we have the following theorem.

Theorem 3.15 (Brandt and Geist, 2014). *There is no Pareto-optimal Fishburn-strategyproof tournament solution.*

As a consequence of this theorem, the set-theoretic relationships depicted in Figure 3.7, and other observations (Brandt and Brill, 2011), TC is the finest Fishburn-strategyproof tournament solution considered in this chapter.

3.4.2 Agenda Implementation

An important question—which has enjoyed considerable attention from social choice theorists and political scientists since the work of Black (1958) and Farquharson (1969)—is whether simple procedures exists that *implement* a particular tournament solution. This in particular concerns procedures that are based on a series of binary choices and eventually lead to the election of a single alternative. The binary choices may depend on one another and need not exclusively be between two alternatives. Such procedures are in wide use by actual committees and institutions at various levels of democratic decision making. The most prominent among these are the *simple agenda* (or *successive procedure*) and the *amendment procedure*, both of which were initially studied in their own right by political scientists. The former is prevalent in civil law or Euro-Latin legal systems, whereas the latter is more firmly entrenched in the common law or Anglo-American legal tradition (see, e.g., Apesteguia et al., 2014).

With the simple agenda, the alternatives are ordered in a sequence $a_1, \dots, a_m$ and subsequently successively being voted up or down by majority voting: First alternative a_1 is brought up for consideration; if a_1 is carried by a majority, it is accepted as

---

[22] In fact, the proof even shows that these functions are *group*-strategyproof with respect to Kelly's extension.

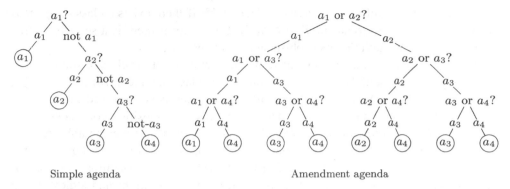

Figure 3.8. The simple agenda and the amendment agenda for four alternatives ordered as a_1, a_2, a_3, a_4.

the final decision; otherwise, a_1 is rejected and a_2 is brought up for consideration, and so on.

With the amendment agenda, the alternatives are again ordered in a sequence $a_1, \ldots, a_m$ and voting then takes place in $m - 1$ rounds. In the first round, a majority comparison is made between a_1, the status quo, and a_2, the amendment. The winner then goes through to the next round as the new status quo and is put in a majority contest with a_3, and so on. Figure 3.8 illustrates how these procedures can be depicted as binary trees, the leaves of which are associated with alternatives.

More generally, every binary tree with alternatives at its leaves could be seen as defining a multistage voting procedure. Formally, an *agenda* of order m is defined as a binary tree whose leaves are labeled by an index set I. A *seeding* of a set of alternatives A of size $|I|$ is a bijection from A to I.

For the analysis of voting procedures defined by such agendas and seedings, voters can either be *sincere* or *sophisticated*. Sincere voters myopically and nonstrategically vote "directly according to their preferences" whenever the agenda calls for a binary decision. If these choices are invariably between two alternatives, as in the amendment procedure, sincere voting simply comes down to voting for the more preferred alternative at each stage. We refer to Chapter 19 on knockout tournaments for this setting.

By contrast, sophisticated voters are forward looking and vote strategically. Hence, a more game-theoretic approach and "backward inductive" reasoning is appropriate. For the remainder of this section, we assume voters to adopt *sophisticated voting strategies*, meaning that the binary tree can be "solved" by successively propagating the majority winner among two siblings to their parent, starting at the leaves and going upward. Multistage sophisticated voting yields the same outcome as the one obtained by solving the *extensive-form game* as defined by the agenda using backward induction (McKelvey and Niemi, 1978), in an important sense leveraging the strategyproofness of majority rule in settings with more than two alternatives. Similarly, the sophisticated outcome is the alternative that survives iterated elimination of weakly dominated strategies in the *strategic form game* induced by the agenda (Farquharson, 1969; Moulin, 1979).

In order to define agenda-implementability, one defines a class of agendas (one for each order m) and considers all possible seedings for each agenda. A tournament solution S is then said to be *agenda-implementable* if there exists a class of agendas such that for every tournament T, $a \in S(T)$ if and only if there is a seeding for the agenda of size $|T|$ such that its sophisticated outcome is a.

Early results on agenda implementation demonstrated that the class of simple agendas implements *TC* and the class of amendment agendas implements *BA* (Miller, 1977, 1980; Banks, 1985; Moulin, 1986). Moulin (1986), moreover, showed that agenda-implementable tournament solutions have to be weakly composition-consistent refinements of *TC*. As a consequence, *CO* and *MA* are not agenda-implementable. A complete characterization of agenda-implementable tournament solutions, however, had long remained elusive before Horan (2013) obtained sufficient conditions for agenda-implementability that cover a wide range of tournament solutions and almost match Moulin's necessary conditions.[23]

Theorem 3.16 (Horan, 2013). *Every weakly composition-consistent tournament solutions that chooses from among the top cycle of every component is agenda-implementable.*

As a corollary to this result it follows that—besides *TC* and *BA*—also *SL*, *UC*, *MC*, *ME*, *BP*, and *TEQ* are agenda-implementable. It should be observed, however, that the agendas actually implementing these tournament solutions may be extremely large. The size of the amendment agenda, for instance, is already exponential in the number of alternatives.[24] Moreover, Horan's proof is nonconstructive and no concrete classes of agendas that implement any of the tournament solutions considered in this chapter—except the simple agenda and the amendment agenda—are known.

The fact that *CO* fails to be agenda-implementable has sparked some research on *approximating* Copeland winners via binary agendas. Fischer et al. (2011) showed that agenda-implementability is unachievable for any tournament solution that, from tournaments of order m, only chooses alternatives with a Copeland score at least as high as $\frac{3}{4} + O(\frac{1}{m})$ of the maximum Copeland score. Horan (2013) demonstrated the existence of agenda-implementable tournament solutions that only select alternatives whose Copeland score is at least $\frac{2}{3}$ of the maximum Copeland score, improving previous results by Fischer et al. (2011).

3.4.3 Summary

Table 3.2 summarizes which of the considered tournament solutions are Kelly-strategyproof, Fishburn-strategyproof, and agenda-implementable, respectively. Again, it turns out that *BP* represents a decent compromise between discriminative power and attractive axiomatic properties.

---

[23] A weaker version of Theorem 3.16 simply states that every composition-consistent refinement of *TC* is agenda-implementable.

[24] As an extreme case consider the agendas that Coughlan and Le Breton (1999) introduced to implement a refinement of the iterated Banks set (see also Laslier, 1997). The corresponding agenda of order 6 has already $2^{720!} - 1$ nodes!

Table 3.2. *Strategic properties of tournament solutions*

	Kelly- Strategyproofness	Fishburn- Strategyproofness	Agenda- Implementability
CO	−	−	−
SL	−	−	+
MA	−	−	−
BP	+	−	+
UC	+	−	+
BA	?	−	+ (amendment)
TC	+	+	+ (simple)
MC	+	−	+
ME	−	−	+
$\mathring{TC}$	+	−	?
TEQ	−	−	+

Note: It is unknown whether BA is Kelly-strategyproof and whether $\mathring{TC}$ is agenda-implementable. Interestingly, $\mathring{TC}$ falls exactly between the necessary and sufficient conditions given by Moulin (1986) and Horan (2013).

3.5 Generalizations to Weak Tournaments

So far, we assumed the majority relation to be antisymmetric, which can be justified, for instance, by assuming that there is an odd number of voters. In general, however, there may be majority ties. These can be accounted for by considering *weak tournaments* $(A, \succsim)$, that is, directed graphs that represent the complete, but not necessarily antisymmetric, majority relation.[25]

For most of the tournament solutions defined in Section 3.3, generalizations or extensions to weak tournaments have been proposed. Often, it turns out that there are several sensible ways to generalize a tournament solution and it is unclear whether there exists a unique "correct" generalization. A natural criterion for evaluating the different proposals is whether the extension satisfies (appropriate generalizations of) the axiomatic properties that the original tournament solution satisfies.

3.5.1 The Conservative Extension

A *generic* way to generalize any given tournament solution S to weak tournaments is by selecting all alternatives that are chosen by S in some orientation of the weak tournament. Formally, a tournament $T = (A, \succ)$ is an *orientation* of a weak tournament $W = (A, \succsim')$ if $a \succ b$ implies $a \succsim' b$ for all $a, b \in A$. The *conservative extension* of S, denoted $[S]$, is defined such that, for every weak tournament W,

$$[S](W) = \bigcup_{T \in [W]} S(T),$$

---

[25] Alternatively, one can consider the strict part of the majority relation $\succ$, which is asymmetric, but not necessarily connex.

where $[W]$ denotes the set of all orientations of W. Brandt et al. (2014a) have shown that $[S]$ inherits several natural properties from S, including monotonicity, stability, and composition-consistency.

An alternative interpretation of weak tournaments is in terms of a partial information setting, where the symmetric and irreflexive part of the dominance relation represents *unknown comparisons* rather than actual ties (see Chapter 10). In this setting, the set of winners according to the conservative extension exactly corresponds to the set of *possible winners* of the partially specified tournament. The computational complexity of possible and necessary winners of partially specified tournaments has been studied by Aziz et al. (2012b), who showed that for a number of tractable tournament solutions (such as CO, UC, and TC), possible winners—and thus the conservative extension—can be computed efficiently.

3.5.2 Extensions of Common Tournament Solutions

For many tournament solutions, *ad hoc* extensions have been proposed in the literature. In this section, we give an overview of these extensions and compare them to the conservative extension.

The *Copeland set CO* gives rise to a whole class of extensions that is parameterized by a number α between 0 and 1. The solution CO^α selects all alternatives that maximize the variant of the Copeland score in which each tie contributes α points to an alternative's score (see, e.g., Faliszewski et al. (2009c)). Henriet (1985) axiomatically characterized $CO^{\frac{1}{2}}$, arguably the most natural variant in this class. The conservative extension $[CO]$ does not coincide with any of these solutions. Furthermore, $[CO] \not\subseteq CO^\alpha$ for all $\alpha \in [0, 1]$ and $CO^\alpha \subseteq [CO]$ if and only if $\frac{1}{2} \leq \alpha \leq 1$.

When moving from tournaments to weak tournaments, maximal lotteries are no longer unique. Dutta and Laslier (1999) have shown that the appropriate generalization of the *bipartisan set BP* is the *essential set ES*, which is given by the set of all alternatives that are contained in the support of *some* maximal lottery. The essential set coincides with the support of any quasi-strict Nash equilibrium of the game defined by the skew-adjacency matrix. It is easy to construct tournaments where *ES* is strictly smaller than $[BP]$, and there are also weak tournaments in which $[BP]$ is strictly contained in *ES*.

Duggan (2013) surveyed several extensions of the covering relation to weak tournaments. Any such relation induces a generalization of the *uncovered set UC*. The so-called *deep covering* and *McKelvey covering* relations are particularly interesting extensions. Duggan showed that for all other generalizations of the covering relation he considered, the corresponding uncovered set is a refinement of the deep uncovered set UC_D. Another interesting property of UC_D is that it coincides with the conservative extension of *UC*. It follows that all other *UC* generalizations considered by Duggan are refinements of $[UC]$.

Banks and Bordes (1988) discussed four different generalizations of the *Banks set BA* to weak tournaments. Each of these generalizations is a refinement of the conservative extension $[BA]$.

For the *top cycle TC*, Schwartz (1972; 1986) defined two different generalizations (see also Sen, 1986). *GETCHA* (or the *Smith set*) contains the maximal elements of the transitive closure of $\succsim$, whereas *GOCHA* (or the *Schwartz set*) contains the maximal elements of the transitive closure of $\succ$. GOCHA is always contained in GETCHA, and the latter coincides with [*TC*]. A game-theoretical interpretation of *TC* gives rise to a further generalization. Duggan and Le Breton (2001) observed that the top cycle of a tournament T coincides with the unique *mixed saddle MS(T)* of the game $G(T)$, and showed that the mixed saddle is still unique for games corresponding to weak tournaments. The solution *MS* is nested between GOCHA and GETCHA. The computational complexity of GETCHA and GOCHA was analyzed by Brandt et al. (2009), and the complexity of mixed saddles was studied by Brandt and Brill (2012).

Generalizations of the *minimal covering set MC* using the McKelvey covering relation and the deep covering relation are known to satisfy stability. There exist weak tournaments in which [*MC*] is strictly contained in both the McKelvey minimal covering set MC_M and the deep minimal covering set MC_D. There are also weak tournaments in which MC_M is strictly contained in [*MC*]. Computational aspects of generalized minimal covering sets have been analyzed by Brandt and Fischer (2008a) and Baumeister et al. (2013a).

Schwartz (1990) suggested six ways to extend the *tournament equilibrium set TEQ*—and the notion of retentiveness in general—to weak tournaments. However, all of those variants can easily be shown to lead to disjoint minimal retentive sets even in very small tournaments, and none of the variants coincides with [*TEQ*].

It is noteworthy that, in contrast to the conservative extension, some of the extensions discussed earlier fail to inherit properties from their corresponding tournament solutions. For instance, GOCHA violates stability.

A further generalization of tournaments (and weak tournaments) are *weighted tournaments*, which take the size of pairwise majorities into account. Weighted tournament solutions are studied in detail in Chapter 4. Dutta and Laslier (1999) have generalized several common tournament solutions to weighted tournaments.

3.6 Further Reading

The monograph by Moon (1968) provides an excellent, but slightly outdated, overview of mathematical results about tournaments, which is nicely complemented by more recent book chapters on tournament graphs (Reid and Beineke, 1978; Reid, 2004).

The formal study of tournament solutions in the context of social choice was initiated by Moulin (1986) and sparked a large number of research papers, culminating in the definitive monograph by Laslier (1997). More recent overviews of tournament solutions, which also focus on their computational properties, were given by Brandt (2009b) and Hudry (2009). There are also comprehensive studies that exclusively deal with tournament solutions based on covering (Duggan, 2013), stability (Brandt, 2011a; Brandt and Harrenstein, 2011; Brandt et al., 2014e), and retentiveness (Brandt et al., 2014d), respectively. For some tournament solutions, continuous generalizations to the general spatial model are available (see, e.g., Banks et al., 2006; Duggan, 2013).

For a more extensive introduction to the vast literature on agenda-implementability, the reader is referred to Moulin (1988a, Chapter 9), Laslier (1997, Chapter 8), Austen-Smith and Banks (2005, Chapter 4), and Horan (2013). For an overview of the literature on and a discussion of simple and amendment procedures, see, e.g., Apesteguia et al. (2014).

This chapter focusses on *choosing* from a tournament. For the related—but different—problem of *ranking* alternatives in a tournament, finding a ranking that agrees with as many pairwise comparisons as possible (i.e., Slater's rule) has enjoyed widespread acceptance (see, e.g., Charon and Hudry, 2010). Clearly, score-based tournament solutions such as *CO* and *MA* can easily be turned into ranking functions. Bouyssou (2004) has studied ranking functions that are defined via the successive application of tournament solutions and found that monotonic and stable tournament solutions yield particularly attractive ranking functions.

Acknowledgments

We would like to thank Florian Brandl, Johannes Hofbauer, Sean Horan, Olivier Hudry, Jean-François Laslier, Michel Le Breton, Hervé Moulin, Rolf Niedermeier, Hans Georg Seedig, and the co-editors Ulle Endriss, Jérôme Lang, and Ariel Procaccia for very helpful feedback.

Felix Brandt is supported by a Heisenberg professorship of the Deutsche Forschungsgemeinschaft under grant BR 2312/7-2. Markus Brill is supported by a Feodor Lynen research fellowship of the Alexander von Humboldt Foundation. Paul Harrenstein is supported by the European Research Council under Advanced Grant 291528 ("RACE").

CHAPTER 4

Weighted Tournament Solutions

Felix Fischer, Olivier Hudry, and Rolf Niedermeier

An obvious way to move beyond tournament solutions as studied in Chapter 3 is to take into account not only the direction of the majority preference between a pair of alternatives, but also its strength in terms of the margin by which one alternative is preferred. We focus in this chapter on social choice functions that are called C2 functions by Fishburn (1977) and could also be referred to as weighted tournament solutions: social choice functions that depend only on pairwise majority margins but are not tournament solutions.

Consider a set $A = \{1, \ldots, m\}$ of alternatives and a set $N = \{1, \ldots, n\}$ of voters with preferences $\succ_i \in \mathcal{L}(A)$ for all $i \in N$. Here, we denote by $\mathcal{L}(X)$ the set of all linear orders on a finite set X, that is, the set of all binary relations on X that are complete, transitive, and asymmetric. For a given preference profile $R = (\succ_1, \ldots, \succ_n) \in \mathcal{L}(A)^n$, the *majority margin* $m_R(x, y)$ of x over y is defined as the difference between the number of voters who prefer x to y and the number of voters who prefer y to x, that is,

$$m_R(x, y) = |\{i \in N : x \succ_i y\}| - |\{i \in N : y \succ_i x\}|.$$

We will routinely omit the subscript when R is clear from the context. The pairwise majority margins arising from a preference profile R can be conveniently represented by a weighted tournament (A, M_R), where M_R is the antisymmetric $m \times m$ matrix with $(M_R)_{xx} = 0$ for $x \in A$ and $(M_R)_{xy} = m_R(x, y)$ for $x, y \in A$ with $x \neq y$.[1] An example of a weighted tournament and a corresponding preference profile is shown in Figure 4.1. Because C2 functions only depend on majority margins, they can be viewed as functions mapping weighted tournaments to sets of alternatives, or to linear orders of the alternatives.

Clearly all majority margins will be even if the number of voters is even, and odd if the number of voters is odd. The following result, similarly to McGarvey's Theorem

---

[1] Note that antisymmetry of M_R only implies asymmetry and not antisymmetry of the relation $\{(x, y) \in A \times A : m(x, y) > m(y, x)\}$. Therefore, unlike tournaments, weighted tournaments allow for ties in pairwise comparisons.

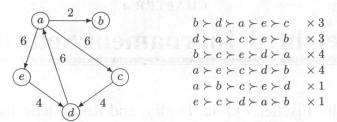

Figure 4.1. Example of a weighted tournament and a corresponding preference profile. The illustration on the left shows a weighted tournament for $A = \{a, b, c, d, e\}$, where $x \in A$ and $y \in A$ are connected by an arc with weight $m(x, y)$ if and only if $m(x, y) > 0$. The weighted tournament is induced by a preference profile for 16 voters with preferences and multiplicities as shown on the right.

for tournaments (McGarvey, 1953), establishes that this condition in fact characterizes the set of weighted tournaments induced by preference profiles.[2]

Theorem 4.1 (Debord, 1987). *Let (A, M) be a weighted tournament. Then $M = M_R$ for some profile R of preferences over A if and only if all off-diagonal elements of M have the same parity.*

For a given preference profile, the induced weighted tournament can be computed in time $O(nm^2)$. Unlike tournaments, weighted tournaments can be exponentially more succinct than the smallest preference profiles that induce them, but this turns out to be inconsequential: all computational hardness results in this chapter hold even when the input is given as a preference profile, whereas all tractable C2 functions we consider can be computed in time polynomial in the size of the weighted tournament.

We begin our investigation with Kemeny's rule. Section 4.1 introduces the rule and studies some of its properties, Section 4.2 then surveys computational hardness results and different types of algorithms. Section 4.3 provides a more general treatment of median orders and associated computational results, Section 4.4 a brief overview of applications in rank aggregation. In Section 4.5 we finally study properties and computational aspects of various other C2 functions—including Borda's rule, Black's rule, Nanson's rule, maximin rule, Schulze's method, the ranked pairs method, and the essential set.

4.1 Kemeny's Rule

Kemeny (1959) proposed to aggregate a preference profile $R = (\succ_1, \dots, \succ_n)$ into a linear order $\succ \in \mathcal{L}(A)$ that maximizes the number of agreements with the preferences in R, that is, one for which

$$\sum_{i \in N} |\succ_i \cap \succ| = \max_{\succ' \in \mathcal{L}(A)} \sum_{i \in N} |\succ_i \cap \succ'|.$$

[2] The example in Figure 4.1 provides some intuition why this result is true. We do not prove it here, but note that a short proof was given by Le Breton (2005). A proof of McGarvey's Theorem can be found in Section 3.2.

Orders with this property are an example of so-called median orders (Barthelemy and Monjardet, 1981; Charon and Hudry, 2007), which will be discussed more generally in Section 4.3. The social preference function that selects all such orders is the only neutral and consistent Condorcet extension (Young and Levenglick, 1978) and has also been characterized as the maximum likelihood estimator for a simple probabilistic model in which individual preferences are noisy estimates of an underlying "true" ranking (Young, 1988, 1995a).[3] We will see momentarily that Kemeny's rule is very interesting also from a computational perspective, and will devote a significant part of this chapter to its study.

In the literature, Kemeny's rule is often defined by minimization of disagreement rather than maximization of agreement. To this end, define the *(Kemeny) score* of a ranking $\succ$ with respect to a preference profile $R = (\succ_1, \ldots, \succ_n)$ as

$$\sum_{i \in N} \tau(\succ_i, \succ),$$

where

$$\tau(\succ_i, \succ) = \sum_{\{x,y\} \subseteq A} d_{x,y}(\succ_i, \succ)$$

with

$$d_{x,y}(\succ_i, \succ) = \begin{cases} 1 & \text{if } x \succ_i y \text{ and } y \succ x, \text{ or } y \succ_i x \text{ and } x \succ y \\ 0 & \text{otherwise} \end{cases}$$

is *Kendall's tau distance* (Kendall, 1938). In other words, the score of $\succ$ measures the sum of distances to the individual preference orders $\succ_i$ in terms of the number of inversions. Kemeny's rule then chooses rankings with minimum score.[4] Because

$$\sum_{i \in N} \tau(\succ_i, \succ) = \sum_{\substack{x,y \in A \\ x \succ y}} |\{i \in N : y \succ_i x\}| = \sum_{\substack{x,y \in A \\ x \succ y}} \frac{m_R(y, x) + n}{2},$$

Kemeny's rule is a C2 function. This characterization also emphasizes the close relationship between Kemeny's rule and Slater's rule (Chapter 3), which only takes the sign of each majority margin into account when computing scores and ignores its absolute value.

We leave it to the reader to verify that in the example of Figure 4.1 alternative a is the unique Kemeny winner, that is, the unique alternative at the top of a ranking with minimum score.

---

[3] Quite surprisingly, the alternative most likely to be the best may not simply be the alternative at the top of the ranking with the highest likelihood. In fact Borda's rule, which we discuss in Section 4.5.1, may provide a better estimate in this case (Young, 1988).

[4] There can in fact be up to $m!$ such rankings. It is also worth noting that other social choice functions can be obtained by maximizing score over a set of rankings other than linear orders, see Section 4.3 for details.

4.2 Computing Kemeny Winners and Kemeny Rankings

We consider three decision problems and one optimization problem related to Kemeny's rule.

KEMENY SCORE
Input: A preference profile R and a nonnegative integer k.
Question: Is there a linear order that has score at most k with respect to R?

KEMENY WINNER
Input: A preference profile R and an alternative $x \in A$.
Question: Is there a linear order that has minimum score with respect to R and ranks x first?

KEMENY RANKING
Input: A preference profile R and two alternatives $x, y \in A$.
Question: Is there a linear order that has minimum score with respect to R and ranks x above y?

KEMENY RANK AGGREGATION
Input: A preference profile R.
Task: Find a linear order that has minimum score with respect to R.

We will see that the first decision problem is NP-complete, whereas the other two seem computationally even harder: they are complete for the class Θ_2^P of problems solvable via parallel access to NP.[5] From a practical point of view, KEMENY RANK AGGREGATION is perhaps most interesting.

We begin with a discussion of the classical completeness results mentioned above, and then we explore two approaches that attempt to address the computational intractability these completeness results imply: exponential-time parameterized algorithms, and polynomial-time approximation algorithms for KEMENY RANK AGGREGATION. Finally we discuss additional approaches—exact, approximate, or purely heuristic—that are relevant in practice.

4.2.1 Computational Hardness

If there are only two voters, the preference order of either of them has minimum Kemeny score. By contrast, it was known since the late 1980s that KEMENY SCORE is NP-complete when the number n of voters is unbounded (Bartholdi et al., 1989a; Hudry, 1989). This result was later shown to hold already for $n = 4$, and in fact for any even $n \geqslant 4$. Quite intriguingly, the case for any odd $n \geqslant 3$ remains open.

Theorem 4.2 (Bartholdi et al., 1989b; Hudry, 1989; Dwork et al., 2001; Biedl et al., 2009). KEMENY SCORE *is NP-complete for even $n \geqslant 4$, and for odd n when n is unbounded.*

---

[5] A detailed discussion of this complexity class, and related results for Dodgson's and Young's rules, can be found in Chapter 5.

Proof sketch. The Kemeny score of a given linear order can easily be computed and compared to k in polynomial time, so KEMENY SCORE is in NP.

Hardness for the two cases can be shown by two polynomial-time reductions from the NP-complete feedback arc set problem on directed graphs (e.g., Garey and Johnson, 1979), here we sketch the reduction for even $n \geqslant 4$.

FEEDBACK ARC SET
Input: A directed graph $G = (V, E)$ and an integer $k \geqslant 0$.
Question: Is there a set $F \subseteq E$ with $|F| \leqslant k$ such that graph $G' = (V, E \setminus F)$ does not have any directed cycles?

Consider a directed graph $G = (V, E)$ with $V = \{v_1, \ldots, v_n\}$ and an integer $k \geqslant 0$, and let $m = |E|$. The goal is to find in polynomial time a preference profile R and an integer k' such that there exist a linear order that has Kemeny score at most k' with respect to R if and only if G has a feedback arc set of size at most k. To this end, let $A = V \cup E$. For each $v \in V$, let $\text{out}(v)$ and $\text{in}(v)$ respectively denote arbitrary linear orders of the incoming and outgoing arcs of v. For any linear order $\succ$, let $\overline{\succ}$ denote the reverse order. Now define R as the set of the following four linear orders, where we slightly abuse notation and compose linear orders from linear orders on subsets of the alternatives:

$$v_1 \succ_1 \text{out}(v_1) \succ_1 v_2 \succ_1 \text{out}(v_2) \succ_1 \ldots \succ_1 v_n \succ_1 \text{out}(v_n),$$

$$v_n \succ_2 \overline{\text{out}(v_n)} \succ_2 v_{n-1} \succ_2 \overline{\text{out}(v_{n-1})} \succ_2 \ldots \succ_2 v_1 \succ_2 \overline{\text{out}(v_1)},$$

$$\text{in}(v_1) \succ_3 v_1 \succ_3 \text{in}(v_2) \succ_3 v_2 \succ_3 \ldots \succ_3 \text{in}(v_n) \succ_3 v_n,$$

$$\overline{\text{in}(v_n)} \succ_4 v_n \succ_4 \overline{\text{in}(v_{n-1})} \succ_4 v_{n-1} \succ_4 \ldots \succ_4 \overline{\text{in}(v_1)} \succ_4 v_1.$$

Setting $k' = 2\binom{n}{2} + 2\binom{m}{2} + 2m(n-1) + 2k$ completes the construction.

For a rigorous proof of correctness, the reader is referred to the article of Biedl et al. (2009). It is not hard to show, however, that independently of the structure of graph G any linear order of A must have score at least $k' - 2k$ with respect to R. Given a feedback arc set F of size k, a linear order on $A \setminus F$ that has score $k' - 2k$ with respect to the restriction of R to $A \setminus F$ can be obtained by starting from a topological ordering of the acyclic graph $(V, E \setminus F)$ and inserting each arc $(u, v) \in E \setminus F$ between u and v. Inserting each arc $(u, v) \in F$ immediately after u, as in $\succ_1$ and $\succ_2$, increases the score by $2k$ due to $\succ_3$ and $\succ_4$, for an overall score of k'.

The result can easily be generalized to any even number $n \geqslant 6$ of voters by adding $(n-4)/2$ voters with an arbitrary preference order and $(n-4)/2$ voters with the reverse preference order. □

While NP-hardness of KEMENY WINNER and KEMENY RANKING follow from Theorem 4.2 and were thus known since 1989, the exact complexity of these problems remained open until they were finally shown complete for the class Θ_2^P of problems that can be decided by parallel access to an oracle for NP. Membership in Θ_2^P is straightforward. The proof of hardness follows the same general idea as the proof of Bartholdi et al. (1989b) for NP-hardness of KEMENY SCORE, but starts from a Θ_2^P-complete variant of FEEDBACK ARC SET, referred to as FEEDBACK ARC SET MEMBER, and reduces this problem in polynomial time to both KEMENY WINNER and KEMENY RANKING.

Theorem 4.3 (Hemaspaandra et al., 2005). KEMENY WINNER *and* KEMENY RANKING *are* Θ_2^p-*complete.*

The usual interpretation of the above results is that general efficient algorithms for Kemeny's rule are unlikely to exist, where efficiency is associated with running times that are polynomial in the size of the problem instance. We proceed to discuss different algorithmic approaches by which this difficulty can be and has been addressed. We focus mainly on KEMENY RANK AGGREGATION, but note that most of the techniques can easily be adapted to the three decision problems.

4.2.2 Polynomial-Time Approximation Algorithms

A common approach to computationally difficult problems sacrifices solution quality to achieve a polynomial running time, while trying to guarantee that the solution remains close to optimal. To this end, call an algorithm a polynomial-time α-approximation algorithm for KEMENY RANK AGGREGATION if it has polynomial running time and for each preference profile produces a linear order with Kemeny score at most α times the minimum Kemeny score.

Ordering the alternatives by increasing Borda score provides a 5-approximation to KEMENY RANK AGGREGATION (Coppersmith et al., 2010). Because τ is a metric and in particular satisfies the triangle inequality, the preference order of a voter selected uniformly at random in fact yields a 2-approximation in expectation, and this argument can easily be de-randomized to obtain a deterministic polynomial-time algorithm with the same approximation factor (e.g., Ailon et al., 2008). Spearman's footrule distance, that is, the sum of the absolute values of the difference between ranks, provides another polynomial-time 2-approximation algorithm (Diaconis and Graham, 1977; Dwork et al., 2001), and it turns out that the approximation factor can be improved further.

Theorem 4.4 (Ailon et al., 2008; van Zuylen and Williamson, 2009). *The following polynomial-time algorithms exist for* KEMENY RANK AGGREGATION:

- *a 4/3-approximation algorithm based on linear programming;*
- *a combinatorial 11/7-approximation algorithm.*

The 11/7-approximation algorithm selects the better of two linear orders: the preference order of a voter chosen uniformly at random and the order obtained by an algorithm similar to quicksort, which chooses a pivot alternative and recursively orders the alternatives above and below that alternative (Ailon et al., 2008). The approximation guarantee can be improved to 4/3 if the pivot element is chosen randomly based on the solution of a linear program (Ailon et al., 2008), and this algorithm can be de-randomized while preserving the approximation factor (van Zuylen and Williamson, 2009).

Whereas all of the above algorithms are reasonably efficient also in practice, the following result is of purely theoretical interest.

Theorem 4.5 (Kenyon-Mathieu and Schudy, 2007). KEMENY RANK AGGREGATION *has an efficient polynomial-time approximation scheme.*

An efficient polynomial-time approximation scheme computes an $(1 + \epsilon)$-approximation in polynomial time for any $\epsilon > 0$, where the degree of the polynomial is independent of ϵ but the running time can otherwise depend on ϵ in an arbitrary way. The running time of the algorithm underlying Theorem 4.5 is doubly exponential in $1/\epsilon$, which is too large for most practical purposes. Theorem 4.5 does imply, however, that no constant lower bound greater than one exists on possible approximation factors for KEMENY RANK AGGREGATION, so there is hope that Theorem 4.4 can be improved upon by algorithms that are efficient in practice.

4.2.3 Parameterized Algorithms

Parameterized algorithms provide a different approach to computationally difficult problems, by attempting to limit any super-polynomial growth of the running time to certain parameters of the problem at hand. If the attempt is successful the problem is fixed-parameter tractable, that is, it can be solved efficiently for small parameter values (e.g., Downey and Fellows, 2013; Niedermeier, 2006).

Perhaps the most obvious candidate parameters in our setting are the number n of voters and the number m of alternatives. Whereas a restriction of n makes little sense given the NP-completeness of KEMENY SCORE for $n = 4$, the situation looks more promising for m. Indeed, an exhaustive search through all possible linear orders for one with minimum score requires $O(m! \, nm \log m)$ time, where $O(nm \log m)$ is the time needed to compute the score of a single linear order. While this algorithm could be used to solve instances with around ten alternatives, the excessive growth of $m!$ limits its usefulness. Dynamic programming enables a reduction of this factor to 2^m.

Theorem 4.6 (Betzler et al., 2009; Raman and Saurabh, 2007). KEMENY RANK AGGREGATION *can be solved in $O(2^m m^2 n)$ time.*

Proof sketch. Consider a preference profile R on a set A of alternatives. We inductively compute a Kemeny ranking for the restriction of R to every nonempty subset of A. For subsets of size one, computation of a Kemeny ranking is trivial. For $A' \subseteq A$ with $|A'| > 1$, we exploit the fact that the exclusion of the alternative at the top of a Kemeny ranking does not change the relative ranking of the other alternatives (e.g., Young, 1988). A Kemeny ranking for A' can thus be found by considering all linear orders that begin with some alternative $a \in A'$ and continue with a Kemeny ranking for $A' \setminus \{a\}$. There are $|A'| \leqslant m$ such rankings, and the score of each such ranking can be computed from that of a Kemeny ranking for $A' \setminus \{a\}$ in $O(nm)$ time. Because the algorithm considers each nonempty subset of A, its running time is $O(2^m m^2 n)$. $\qquad \square$

Another obvious class of parameters includes the Kemeny score of the instance at hand, which we denote by k in the following, the average distance τ_{avg} between preference orders, and the average distance between the preference orders and a Kemeny ranking, which is equal to k/n. Simjour (2009) observed that $k/(n-1) \leqslant \tau_{\mathrm{avg}} \leqslant 4k/n$, which makes k/n a stronger parameter than τ_{avg} in the sense that it takes smaller values (Komusiewicz and Niedermeier, 2012). The advantage of τ_{avg} is that it can easily be computed for a given preference profile. In the following we state results in terms of k/n, but they clearly hold for τ_{avg} and any other upper bound on k/n as well.

The main theoretical result for this type of parameterization is a sub-exponential algorithm that makes use of a standard reduction from KEMENY SCORE to WEIGHTED FEEDBACK ARC SET in tournaments and a dynamic programming algorithm for the latter.

Theorem 4.7 (Karpinski and Schudy, 2010). KEMENY RANK AGGREGATION *can be solved in* $2^{O(\sqrt{k/n})} + (n+m)^{O(1)}$ *time.*

Fomin et al. (2010) gave a sub-exponential algorithm for a local search variant of KEMENY RANK AGGREGATION. Mahajan et al. (2009) showed that KEMENY SCORE remains fixed-parameter tractable if instead of k it is parameterized by the difference between k and a certain lower bound on the Kemeny score that can be shown to hold for a given preference profile.

Parameterization in terms of k and related parameters also enables a more detailed analysis of preprocessing techniques. Even when the existence of polynomial-time algorithms for a certain problem is unlikely, we may still hope for polynomial-time data reduction rules that provably reduce the size of the input instance (Guo and Niedermeier, 2007). Knowledge of k can for example be used to reduce the number of voters to at most $2k$, by distinguishing instances where at most k and more than k voters have the same preference order. In the former case, any instance with more than $2k$ voters would have Kemeny score greater than k. In the latter case, the preference order shared by more than k voters is the only one that can have score k or less and must thus be a Kemeny ranking.

Two additional data reduction rules can be obtained from an extension of the Condorcet criterion (Truchon, 1998). A linear order $\succ \in \mathcal{L}(A)$ satisfies the extended Condorcet criterion with respect to a preference profile R on A if the following holds: if there exists $A' \subseteq A$ such that $m_R(x, y) > 0$ for all $x \in A'$ and $y \in A \setminus A'$, then $x \succ y$ for all $x \in A'$ and $y \in A \setminus A'$.

Lemma 4.8 (Truchon, 1998). *Any Kemeny ranking satisfies the extended Condorcet criterion.*

This lemma implies, for example, that an alternative that is ranked in the same way by all voters relative to all other alternatives must appear in a fixed position in every Kemeny ranking. More interestingly, the lemma suggests a recursive way of computing a Kemeny ranking that can be applied whenever some set $A' \subseteq A$ satisfies the condition of the extended Condorcet criterion. In this case the elements of A' must be ranked above the elements of $A \setminus A'$, and the restrictions of the Kemeny ranking to A' and $A \setminus A'$ must be Kemeny rankings of the respective restrictions of the preference profile.

These insights can be combined with an exhaustive search for Kemeny rankings of at most $2/\epsilon$ alternatives, for some $\epsilon > 0$, and with a connection to a weighted version of FEEDBACK ARC SET, to obtain the following result.

Theorem 4.9 (Simjour, 2013). *For any $\epsilon > 0$, a given preference profile can be transformed in polynomial time into a preference profile with at most $(2 + \epsilon)k/n$ alternatives that is equivalent with regard to* KEMENY RANK AGGREGATION.

Other parameters that have been considered in the literature include the positions each alternative takes in the preferences of individual voters, and the distance to single-peaked or single-crossing preferences.

For a given preference profile, define the range of an alternative as one plus the difference between the highest and the lowest rank this alternative takes in the preference order of any voter. Let $r_{\max}$ denote the maximum range of any alternative and r_{avg} the average range of the alternatives. It is now not difficult to see that KEMENY RANK AGGREGATION remains NP-hard even for preference profiles with $r_{\text{avg}} = 2$. For this, consider an arbitrary preference profile and add m^2 new alternatives that are ranked below the original alternatives and in the same relative order in all preference orders. Then, any Kemeny ranking with respect to the new preference profile ranks the original alternatives above the new ones, and its restriction to the original alternatives is a Kemeny ranking with respect to the original preference profile. Moreover, the new profile has an average range of at most 2. By contrast, KEMENY RANK AGGREGATION can be solved in $O(32^{r_{\max}}(r_{\max}^2 + r_{\max}m^2))$ time using dynamic programming (Betzler et al., 2009).

Cornaz et al. (2013) obtained a characterization in terms of the single-peaked or single-crossing width of a preference profile, which respectively measure its distance to a single-peaked or single-crossing profile. Here, a preference profile is single-peaked if there exists a linear order of the alternatives such that each voter prefers alternatives less if they are further away in this order from its most preferred alternative. A preference profile is single-crossing if there exists a linear order of the voters such that for any two alternatives x and y the voters preferring x over y are ranked above the voters preferring y over x, or vice versa.

4.2.4 Practical Algorithms

All of the algorithms we have discussed so far come with some kind of formal guarantee regarding their running time or the quality of solutions they produce. These guarantees hold in the worst case over all preference profiles or over a restricted set of profiles with certain parameters. It is, however, not obvious that the algorithms with the strongest worst-case guarantees are the best algorithms in practice. A fair amount of work has therefore been done to validate them empirically, and potentially identify algorithms that perform better on realistic problem instances. We provide a brief overview, and refer the interested reader to the individual articles and to the survey of Charon and Hudry (2010) for details.

In discussing the empirical work, it again makes sense to distinguish two classes of algorithms: exact algorithms that are guaranteed to produce an optimal ranking, and where the goal is to reduce the running time to a reasonable level; and suboptimal algorithms that provide a trade-off between solution quality and running time and that may come with or without formal guarantees for either of these two characteristics.

Both classes of algorithms may use heuristics designed to reduce running time or improve solution quality in practice.

Members of the former class that have been evaluated include algorithms based on integer linear programming, branch and cut, and branch and bound (Davenport and Kalagnanam, 2004; Conitzer et al., 2006; Charon and Hudry, 2006; Schalekamp and van Zuylen, 2009; Ali and Meilă, 2012). In addition, effectiveness of the data reduction rules of Section 4.2.3 has been confirmed empirically (Betzler et al., 2014). While the dynamic programming algorithm underlying Theorem 4.6 is competitive only for very small numbers of alternatives, a combination of integer programming with polynomial-time data reduction and other techniques for reducing the running time leads to the fastest known algorithms in all other cases.

The second class of algorithms provides an even wider range of options. Here, Schalekamp and van Zuylen (2009) recommend a heuristic based on Borda scores when the goal is to obtain reasonably good results very quickly, and an algorithm based on Copeland's method for higher solution quality and slightly larger running time. At the cost of a further increase in running time, an initial solution may be improved further using local search. The analysis of Schalekamp and van Zuylen was extended by Ali and Meilă (2012), who investigated how the structure of preference profiles affects the complexity of finding a Kemeny ranking, and how this information can be used to select an appropriate algorithm. This approach is similar to parameterized complexity analysis in that it tries to identify certain structures in the problem input that enable faster algorithms, but at the same time abandons exactness of solutions and worst-case bounds on the running time in favor of improved practical performance.

It is finally worth mentioning that a rich set of metaheuristics has been applied to Kemeny's rule, including simulated annealing, tabu search, and genetic algorithms. The interested reader is again referred to the survey of Charon and Hudry (2010).

4.3 Further Median Orders

Kemeny's rule is defined in terms of linear orders that maximize the number of agreements with a given set of linear orders. The central role of linear orders in social choice theory notwithstanding, one may also more generally consider the problem of finding a binary relation from a set $\mathcal{M}$ that maximizes the number of agreements with a set of binary relations taken from a set $\mathcal{V}$. We focus here on sets $\mathcal{M}$ and $\mathcal{V}$ obtained by relaxing some of the properties that characterize linear orders—completeness, transitivity, and asymmetry—and refer to the literature for additional properties (Barthelemy and Monjardet, 1981; Fishburn, 1985; Bouyssou et al., 2006; Caspard et al., 2012) and complexity results (Wakabayashi, 1998; Hudry, 2008; Charon and Hudry, 2010).

For a set A of alternatives, let $\mathcal{B}(A)$ denote the set of (binary) relations, $\mathcal{T}(A)$ the set of complete and asymmetric relations, and $\mathcal{R}(A)$ the set of complete and transitive relations on A. Obviously, $\mathcal{T}(A)$ is the set of tournaments on A. Relations in $\mathcal{R}(A)$, which are also called weak orders, can model indifferences or incomparabilities among alternatives, but not both. Note also that for any A, $\mathcal{L}(A) \subseteq \mathcal{T}(A) \subseteq \mathcal{B}(A)$

and $\mathcal{L}(A) \subseteq \mathcal{R}(A) \subseteq \mathcal{B}(A)$. We now consider the following decision problem for $\mathcal{M}, \mathcal{V} \in \{\mathcal{B}, \mathcal{R}, \mathcal{T}, \mathcal{L}\}$.[6]

$(\mathcal{V}, \mathcal{M})$-SCORE
Input: An element of $\mathcal{V}(A)^n$ and a nonnegative integer k.
Question: Is there an element of $\mathcal{M}(A)$ with score at most k?

By Theorem 4.2 $(\mathcal{L}, \mathcal{L})$-SCORE, or KEMENY SCORE, is NP-complete for any even number of voters greater than or equal to four and for an unbounded odd number of voters.[7] It is easy to see that membership in NP holds for all of the preceding choices of $\mathcal{M}$ and $\mathcal{V}$. Because NP-hardness is established by identifying certain elements of $\mathcal{V}$ for which the existence of an element of $\mathcal{M}(A)$ with score at most k is hard to decide, it continues to hold if elements are added to $\mathcal{V}$. This means in particular that $(\mathcal{V}, \mathcal{L})$-SCORE is NP-complete for any $\mathcal{V} \supseteq \mathcal{L}$. Taking $\mathcal{V}$ to be a *strict* superset of $\mathcal{L}$ could of course render the problem more difficult, and indeed $(\mathcal{T}, \mathcal{L})$-SCORE is hard even for a single voter.

Theorem 4.10 (Alon, 2006; Charbit et al., 2007; Conitzer, 2006). $(\mathcal{T}, \mathcal{L})$-SCORE *is NP-complete, even when $n = 1$.*

The attentive reader may have recognized the single-voter variant as a subproblem in the computation of the Slater set of Chapter 3, and Theorem 3.3 is in fact a corollary of Theorem 4.10.

The dependence of the complexity of $(\mathcal{V}, \mathcal{M})$-SCORE on $\mathcal{M}$ is less obvious, but we will see that hardness can in many cases be attributed to transitivity. Wakabayashi (1986, 1998) studied $(\mathcal{B}, \mathcal{M})$-SCORE for various choices of $\mathcal{M}$, and identified transitivity of the relations in $\mathcal{M}$ as a source of hardness. NP-completeness for $\mathcal{M} = \mathcal{L}$ can be obtained as a corollary of Theorem 4.2, but the problem remains NP-complete when completeness, asymmetry, or both are relaxed. If we instead relax transitivity and keep completeness, asymmetry, or both, the problem can be solved in polynomial time.

Theorem 4.11 (Wakabayashi, 1986, 1998). $(\mathcal{B}, \mathcal{R})$-SCORE *is NP-complete.* $(\mathcal{B}, \mathcal{T})$-SCORE *can be solved in polynomial time.*

Theorems 4.2 and 4.10 can respectively be extended to $(\mathcal{L}, \mathcal{R})$-SCORE and $(\mathcal{T}, \mathcal{R})$-SCORE, which by earlier arguments also strengthens the first part of Theorem 4.11.

Theorem 4.12 (Hudry, 2012). $(\mathcal{L}, \mathcal{R})$-SCORE *is NP-complete for every even $n \geqslant 4$.* $(\mathcal{T}, \mathcal{R})$-SCORE *is NP-complete, even when $n = 1$.*

---

[6] In the context of this problem the term *complete preorders* has sometimes been used incorrectly for all elements of $\mathcal{R}$ and not just those that satisfy reflexivity. It is, however, easy to see that the addition of reflexivity or irreflexivity to $\mathcal{V}$ or $\mathcal{M}$ does not affect the relative sizes of scores or the complexity of $(\mathcal{V}, \mathcal{M})$-SCORE, so that all statements concerning $\mathcal{R}$ in what follows hold also for complete pre-orders. Also in what follows, statements concerning linear orders remain true, sometimes nontrivially, if linearity is replaced by acyclicity. We leave it to the interested reader to verify that this is indeed the case.

[7] Kemeny (1959) in fact followed Arrow (1951) in requiring only completeness and transitivity, and considered $(\mathcal{R}, \mathcal{R})$-SCORE. We will obtain a hardness result concerning $(\mathcal{R}, \mathcal{R})$-SCORE toward the end of this section.

Ignoring the dependence on the number of voters, and denoting by $\mathcal{A}(A)$ the set of acyclic relations on A, sufficient conditions for NP-completeness can be summarized as follows.

Theorem 4.13. $(\mathcal{V}, \mathcal{M})$-Score *is NP-complete if* $\mathcal{V} \supseteq \mathcal{L}$ *and* $\mathcal{M} \in \{\mathcal{A}, \mathcal{R}, \mathcal{L}\}$.

4.4 Applications in Rank Aggregation

The enormous interest in Kemeny's rule and other median orders across various disciplines can to a certain extent be attributed to its importance in rank aggregation, with applications that extend far beyond the realm of social choice. Rank aggregation problems arise for instance in the context of planning in multiagent systems (e.g., Ephrati and Rosenschein, 1993), in the design of metasearch engines and in spam detection (e.g., Cohen et al., 1999; Dwork et al., 2001), in collaborative filtering and recommender systems (e.g., Pennock et al., 2000a), in computational biology (e.g., Jackson et al., 2008), and in winner determination for sports competitions (e.g., Betzler et al., 2014). Here we briefly describe an application to similarity search and classification for high-dimensional data (Fagin et al., 2003).

Assume we are given a set of n data points and an additional query point, both from a Euclidean space, and are interested in finding data points that are similar to the query point. This problem can be reduced to a rank aggregation problem by associating each data point with an alternative, and each dimension with a voter who ranks alternatives in increasing distance from the query point in that dimension. What makes this approach particularly attractive in the context of databases is that it does not require complex data structures or a large amount of additional storage and mostly avoids random access to the data. It of course relies on an efficient algorithm for rank aggregation, and Fagin et al. (2003) specifically propose an approximate solution using the footrule distance.

4.5 Other C2 Functions

Whereas a large part of the computational work on C2 functions has focused on Kemeny's rule and other median orders, classical social choice theory has studied various other C2 functions, mostly with regard to their relationships and axiomatic properties.

4.5.1 Variations of Borda's Rule

The first class of functions we consider are variations of a well-known choice rule due to Borda (1781). Borda's rule is commonly defined as the scoring rule with score vector $s = (m - 1, m - 2, \ldots, 0)$. Under a scoring rule, an alternative receives score s_j whenever some voter ranks it in position j. These scores are then added up for all voters, and the alternatives with maximum cumulative score are selected (also see Section 2.4). Borda's rule in particular can be viewed as selecting the alternatives with the highest average rank in the individual preferences. Interestingly, the Borda score of alternative *x* is equal to

$$\sum_{i \in N} |\{y \in A : x \succ_i y\}| = \sum_{y \in A} |\{i \in N : x \succ_i y\}| = \sum_{y \in A} \frac{m(x, y) + n}{2}$$

and thus only depends on the majority margins. Borda's rule fails the Condorcet criterion,[8] but this is easily fixed. Black's rule selects a Condorcet winner if it exists, and the alternatives with maximum Borda score otherwise (Black, 1958). Nanson's rule successively excludes the alternatives whose Borda scores are below the average until all remaining alternatives have the same Borda score (Nanson, 1882). It is a Condorcet extension because the Borda score of a Condorcet winner is always at least the average Borda score. In the example of Figure 4.1, the unique alternative selected by each of these C2 functions is alternative *a*.

It is easy to see that the complexity of Borda's, Black's, and Nanson's rules is dominated by that of the Borda scores, which can be computed from the majority margins in time $O(m^2)$. The same is true for the choice rule obtained by successive exclusion of all alternatives with minimum Borda score, which is sometimes attributed to Nanson but differs from Nanson's rule (see Niou, 1987).

4.5.2 Maximin Rule and Schulze's Method

Maximin rule (Young, 1977), also known as Condorcet's rule or the Simpson-Kramer method, selects alternatives for which the minimum pairwise majority margin is maximized, that is, alternatives *x* for which

$$\min_{z \in A} m(x, z) = \max_{y \in A} \min_{z \in A} m(y, z).$$

Such an alternative is desirable in the sense that it minimizes the number of overruled voters, and can be computed from the majority margins in time $O(m^2)$. A drawback of maximin rule is that it violates a number of desirable properties, most notably the Condorcet loser criterion. A Condorcet loser for a given preference profile is an alternative to which every other alternative is preferred by a majority of the voters, and the Condorcet loser criterion requires that a Condorcet loser can never be selected.[9] Another C2 function, closer to Borda's rule but still violating the criterion, can be obtained by selecting alternatives that maximize the sum rather than the minimum of their majority margins with negative sign (Tideman, 2006, p. 199). This function will be discussed in a different context in Section 5.6.2.

---

[8] Borda's rule does, however, maximize the probability of selecting a Condorcet winner among all scoring rules for a preference profile chosen uniformly at random from the set of all preference profiles, in the limit as the number of voters goes to infinity (Gehrlein and Fishburn, 1978). While Borda's rule and Kemeny's rule may produce very different outcomes, both rules agree in the relative ranking of their respective best and worst alternatives (Saari and Merlin, 2000): for any Kemeny ranking, the top alternative has a higher Borda score than the bottom alternative; conversely, Kemeny's rule ranks an alternative with maximum Borda score above an alternative with minimum Borda score.

[9] In the example of Figure 4.1, maximin rule selects an alternative not preferred to any other alternative by a majority of the voters. It is easy to extend this example to a violation of the Condorcet loser criterion, showing that most other social choice functions satisfy the criterion is a more substantial exercise.

Schulze (2011) proposed a C2 function that addresses the shortcomings of maximin rule and can still be computed in polynomial time. It is currently used for internal elections by the Wikimedia Foundation, Pirate Parties in various countries, and several other organizations. The idea behind Schulze's method is to minimize opposition along paths in the weighted tournament rather than single arcs. Let $S(x, y)$ be the maximum majority margin of any path from x to y, where the majority margin of a path $(x = z_1, z_2, \ldots, z_{k-1}, z_k = y)$ is equal to the minimum majority margin of any of its arcs, that is,

$$S(x, y) = \max_{z_2, \ldots, z_{k-1} \in A, z_1 = x, z_k = y} \min_{1 \leqslant j < k} m(z_j, z_{j+1}).$$

Schulze's method then selects all alternatives $x \in A$ such that $S(x, y) \geqslant S(y, x)$ for all $y \in A \setminus \{x\}$.[10] In the example of Figure 4.1, the unique alternative with this property is alternative d.

The problem of computing $S(y, x)$ is known as the widest path problem or bottleneck shortest path problem and can for example be solved using a variant of the Floyd-Warshall algorithm. To this end, order the alternatives such that $A = \{a_1, \ldots, a_n\}$ and let $S(x, y, i)$ be the maximum majority margin of any path from x to y in which all intermediate alternatives are from $\{a_1, \ldots, a_i\}$, that is,

$$S(x, y, i) = \max_{z_2, \ldots, z_{k-1} \in \{a_1, \ldots, a_i\}, z_1 = x, z_k = y} \min_{1 \leqslant j < k} m(z_j, z_{j+1}).$$

Then $S(x, y) = S(x, y, n)$, with

$$S(x, y, 0) = m(x, y), \quad \text{and}$$

$$S(x, y, i) = \max\{S(x, y, i - 1), \min\{S(x, a_i, i - 1), S(a_i, y, i - 1)\}\} \quad \text{for } i \geqslant 1.$$

This is true because $S(x, y)$ does not change if we restrict the definition to simple paths. Now, for $i \geqslant 1$, the values $S(x, y, i)$ for all $x, y \in A$ can be computed from the values $S(x, y, i - 1)$ in time $O(m^2)$. We can thus compute $S(x, y)$ for all $x, y \in A$ in time $O(m^3)$, and it is easy to see that the overall running time of Schulze's method is $O(m^3)$ as well. Asymptotically faster algorithms can be obtained from fast algorithms for matrix multiplication.

4.5.3 The Ranked Pairs Method

The ranked pairs method, originally proposed by Tideman (1987) to achieve clone independence,[11] yields a C2 function with similar properties as Schulze's rule. The method creates a ranking $\succ$ of the alternatives by starting from the empty relation and successively adding pairs of alternatives according to a "priority" ranking unless doing so would violate transitivity of $\succ$. Priority is given to pairs with larger absolute majority margin, and a tie-breaking rule is used in cases where two or more pairs of alternatives

---

[10] Schulze actually defined a family of choice rules by allowing measures of support other than the majority margin, but this family contains only a single element when individual preferences are linear.

[11] Clone independence requires that the addition of alternatives that are very similar to an existing alternative does not harm the latter. It is violated by many social choice functions, including those of Kemeny, Borda, Black, and Nanson, but satisfied by that of Schulze.

have the same majority margin. The ranked pairs method can thus be viewed as a greedy heuristic for finding Kemeny rankings.

Consider a particular tie-breaking rule $T \in \mathcal{L}(A \times A)$, and construct a priority ordering of the set of unordered pairs of alternatives by ordering all such pairs by their majority margins and using T to break ties: $\{x, y\}$ has priority over $\{x', y'\}$ if $m(x, y) > m(x', y')$, or if $m(x, y) = m(x', y')$ and $(x, y) \, T \, (x', y')$.[12] Now let $\succ_T \in \mathcal{L}(A)$ be the ranking of alternatives obtained by means of the following iterative procedure:

1. Let $\succ = \emptyset$.
2. If all pairs of alternatives have been considered, then return $\succ$. Otherwise consider the pair $\{x, y\}$ with highest priority according to T among those not considered so far.
3. If $m(x, y) \neq 0$, then let $a, b \in \{x, y\}$ such that $m(a, b) > 0$. Otherwise let $a, b \in \{x, y\}$ such that $(a, b) \, T \, (b, a)$.
4. If the relation $\succ \cup \{(a, b)\}$ is acyclic, then add (a, b) to $\succ$. Otherwise add (b, a) to $\succ$. Go to 2.

It is easily verified that this procedure terminates and returns a complete, transitive, and asymmetric relation when it does. Now, call ranking $\succ \in \mathcal{L}(A)$ a *ranked pairs ranking* if it results from the procedure for some tie-breaking rule T, and call $x \in A$ a *ranked pairs winner* if there exists a ranked pairs ranking $\succ$ such that $x \succ y$ for all $y \in A \setminus \{x\}$. The C2 function proposed by Tideman selects all ranked pairs winners. In the example of Figure 4.1 it selects a unique alternative, alternative d.

To find some ranked pairs ranking or winner, we can simply fix a tie-breaking rule T and construct $\succ_T$ as earlier. This involves repeated checks whether $\succ$ violates transitivity and can be done efficiently (Brill and Fischer, 2012). Indeed, violation of transitivity can be recognized in constant time given the transitive closure of the current relation $\succ$, that is, a matrix $M \in \{0, 1\}^{m \times m}$ such that $m_{xy} = 1$ if and only if there exists a sequence of alternatives $z_1, \ldots, z_k$ with $z_1 = x$, $z_k = y$, and $z_i \succ z_{i+1}$ for $i = 1, \ldots, k - 1$. Upon addition of a new pair $(x, y) \in A \times A$, this matrix can be updated by setting, for every $z \in A \setminus \{y\}$ with $m_{zx} = 1$ and $m_{zy} = 0$ and every $z' \in A$, $m_{zz'} = 1$ if $m_{yz'} = 1$. Ibaraki and Katoh (1983) have shown that this requires only $O(m^3)$ operations no matter how many pairs are added, which implies that a ranked pairs ranking or winner can be found in $O(m^3)$ time.

The problem of deciding whether a given ranking $\succ$ is a ranked pairs ranking can also be solved efficiently, using an alternative characterization of ranked pairs rankings due to Zavist and Tideman (1989). Given a ranking $\succ \in \mathcal{L}(A)$ and two alternatives $x, y \in A$, we say that x attains y through $\succ$ if there exists a sequence of distinct alternatives $z_1, z_2, \ldots, z_k$, where $k \geqslant 2$, such that $z_1 = x$, $z_k = y$, and $z_i \succ z_{i+1}$ and $m(z_i, z_{i+1}) \geqslant m(y, x)$ for all i with $1 \leqslant i < k$. A ranking $\succ$ is then called a *stack* if for any pair of alternatives $x, y \in A$, $x \succ y$ implies that x attains y through $\succ$.

Lemma 4.14 (Zavist and Tideman, 1989). *A ranking is a ranked pairs ranking if and only if it is a stack.*

---

[12] Here we assume without loss of generality that the pairs (x, y) and (x', y') are ordered in such a way that $(x, y) \, T \, (y, x)$ and $(x', y') \, T \, (y', x')$.

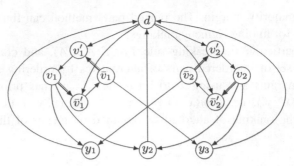

Figure 4.2. Construction used in the proof of Theorem 4.15, for the Boolean formula $\varphi = (v_1 \vee \bar{v}_2) \wedge (v_1 \vee v_2) \wedge (\bar{v}_1 \vee v_2)$. The relation $\succ^2$ is represented by arcs, the relation $\succ^4$ by double-shafted arcs. For all pairs (x, y) that are not connected by an arc, we have $m(x, y) = m(y, x) = 0$.

To decide whether a given ranking $\succ$ is a ranked pairs ranking, it therefore suffices to check whether $\succ$ is a stack. This in turn reduces to checking, for every pair of alternatives $x, y \in A$ with $x \succ y$, whether x attains y through $\succ$. The latter can be achieved in time $O(m^3)$ for all pairs by solving the widest path problem subject to the additional constraint that paths must follow the relation $\succ$.

Whether a given alternative is a ranked pairs *winner* intuitively seems harder to recognize, because this property could be witnessed by any of an exponential number of different rankings. Indeed, this problem turns out to be NP-complete.

Theorem 4.15 (Brill and Fischer, 2012). *Deciding whether a given alternative is a ranked pairs winner is NP-complete.*

Proof sketch. Membership in NP holds because ranked pairs rankings can be recognized in polynomial time.

For hardness we provide a polynomial-time reduction from SAT, the NP-complete satisfiability problem for Boolean formulae in conjunctive normal form (e.g., Garey and Johnson, 1979). Consider a formula $\varphi = C_1 \wedge \cdots \wedge C_k$, where C_j for $1 \leqslant j \leqslant k$ is a disjunction of literals, that is, of negated and nonnegated variables from a set $V = \{v_1, \ldots, v_m\}$. Our goal is to construct a preference profile R_φ over a set A_φ of alternatives such that a particular alternative $d \in A_\varphi$ is a ranked pairs winner for R_φ if and only if φ is satisfiable. Instead of constructing R_φ explicitly, we specify a majority margin $m(x, y)$ for each pair $(x, y) \in A_\varphi \times A_\varphi$, all with even parity, and then apply Theorem 4.1. In doing so, we write $x \succ^w y$ to denote that $m(x, y) = w$ and $m(y, x) = -w$.

Let us first define the set A_φ of alternatives. For each variable $v_i \in V$, $1 \leqslant i \leqslant m$, there are four alternatives v_i, $\bar{v}_i$, v_i', and $\bar{v}_i'$. For each clause C_j, $1 \leqslant j \leqslant k$, there is one alternative y_j. Finally, there is one alternative d for which we want to decide whether it is a ranked pairs winner for R_φ. Now, for each variable $v_i \in V$, $1 \leqslant i \leqslant m$, let $v_i \succ^4 \bar{v}_i' \succ^2 \bar{v}_i \succ^4 v_i' \succ^2 v_i$. For each clause C_j, $1 \leqslant j \leqslant k$, let $v_i \succ^2 y_j$ if variable $v_i \in V$ appears in clause C_j as a positive literal, and $\bar{v}_i \succ^2 y_j$ if variable v_i appears in clause C_j as a negative literal. Finally let $y_j \succ^2 d$ for $1 \leqslant j \leqslant k$ and $d \succ^2 v_i'$ and $d \succ^2 \bar{v}_i'$ for $1 \leqslant i \leqslant m$. For all pairs (x, y) for which $m(x, y)$ has not been specified so far, let $m(x, y) = m(y, x) = 0$. An example is shown in Figure 4.2.

The proof now proceeds by showing that alternative d is a ranked pairs winner for R_φ if and only if formula φ is satisfiable, and that R_φ can be constructed from the majority margins in polynomial time. The intuition for the former is that the majority relation contains cycles on the four alternatives for each variable, and that each way in which the ranked pairs method can break ties among pairs of alternatives with the same majority margin leads to an assignment of truth values to these variables.   □

The preceding results reveal an interesting trade-off: whereas Tideman's original choice rule is NP-hard to compute, tractable variants can be obtained by using a fixed tie-breaking rule. Such variants necessarily violate neutrality, which requires that permuting the alternatives in the preference profile permutes the set of chosen alternatives or rankings in the exact same way. It is worth noting that neutrality and computational tractability can be achieved simultaneously by breaking ties according to the preferences of a particular voter. However, the resulting choice rule would not be a C2 function and more specifically would violate anonymity, which requires invariance of the result when the elements of the preference profile are permuted.

4.5.4 Generalizations of C1 Functions

What distinguishes C1 functions from C2 functions is that they ignore the absolute values of the majority margins and only take their signs into account. The rules of Slater and Kemeny and those of Copeland and Borda provide obvious examples of this relationship, but it turns out that several other C1 functions discussed in Chapter 3 can be generalized in a natural way to use information about the absolute values.[13]

Laffond et al. (1993a) defined the *bipartisan set* as the support of the unique equilibrium of the tournament game (also see Section 3.3.1), which in our notation can be written as the symmetric two-player zero-sum game with action set A and payoff function $p : A \times A \to \{-1, 0, 1\}$, where

$$p(x, y) = \begin{cases} 1 & \text{if } m(x, y) > 0, \\ -1 & \text{if } m(x, y) < 0, \text{ and} \\ 0 & \text{otherwise.} \end{cases}$$

This definition can be generalized to equilibria of the *weighted tournament game*, where instead $p(x, y) = m(x, y)$. Equilibria in this more general class of games need no longer be unique, but we can define the *essential set* (Dutta and Laslier, 1999) as the union of all equilibrium supports. Because the set of equilibria of any zero-sum game is convex, the essential set is itself the support of an equilibrium, and in fact the unique support of a quasi-strict equilibrium. The latter can be found efficiently by solving a linear feasibility problem (Brandt and Fischer, 2008b).

Another notion that can be generalized to weighted tournaments is that of covering among alternatives, where now alternative $x \in A$ covers alternative $y \in A$ if $m(x, y) >$

---

[13] It is tempting to think that these generalizations should be able to discriminate better among alternatives because they have more information than the corresponding C1 functions. This is not generally the case, and the right way to generalize a C1 function is often not obvious (Laffond et al., 1994; De Donder et al., 2000). For generalizations of C1 functions to weak tournaments, that is, relations that are transitive and complete but not necessarily asymmetric, see Section 3.5.

0 and for all $z \in A$, $m(x, z) \geqslant m(y, z)$. This immediately leads to generalizations of the uncovered set and the minimal covering set (Dutta and Laslier, 1999). These generalizations can be computed efficiently using essentially the same algorithms as the corresponding C1 functions (Brandt and Brill, 2012). In the special case where all majority margins are nonzero, these generalizations and an analogous generalization of the top cycle can alternatively be understood in terms of various game-theoretic solution concepts applied to the weighted tournament game (De Donder et al., 2000).

Acknowledgments

We thank Felix Brandt, Robert Bredereck, Ioannis Caragiannis, Jérôme Lang, Michel Le Breton, and Vincent Merlin for their detailed and constructive comments on a draft of this chapter.

CHAPTER 5

Dodgson's Rule and Young's Rule

Ioannis Caragiannis, Edith Hemaspaandra, and
Lane A. Hemaspaandra

5.1 Overview

Dodgson's and Young's election systems, dating from 1876 and 1977, are beautiful, historically resonant election systems. Surprisingly, both of these systems turn out to have highly intractable winner-determination problems: The winner problems of these systems are complete for parallel access to NP. This chapter discusses both the complexity of these winner-determination problems and approaches—through heuristic algorithms, fixed-parameter algorithms, and approximation algorithms—to circumventing that complexity.

5.2 Introduction, Election-System Definitions, and Results Overview

Charles Lutwidge Dodgson, better known under his pen name of Lewis Carroll, was a mathematics tutor at Oxford. In his 1876 pamphlet, "A Method of Taking Votes on More than Two Issues" (Dodgson, 1876), printed by the Clarendon Press, Oxford and headed "not yet published," he defined an election system that is compellingly beautiful in many ways, and yet that also turned out to be so subtle and complex, also in many ways, that it has in recent decades been much studied by computational social choice researchers.

Dodgson's election system is very simply defined. An election will consist of a finite number of voters, each voting by casting a linear order over (the same) finite set of candidates. (Recall that linear orders are inherently antisymmetric, i.e., are "tie-free.") A Condorcet winner (respectively, weak Condorcet winner) is a candidate a who, for each other candidate b, is preferred to b by strictly more than half (respectively, by at least half) of the voters. It is natural to want election systems to be Condorcet-consistent, that is, to have the property that if there is a Condorcet winner, he or she is the one and only winner under the election system. Dodgson's system is Condorcet-consistent. In fact, the system is defined based on each candidate's closeness to being a Condorcet winner. Dodgson's view was that whichever candidate (or candidates if there is a tie for closest) was "closest" to being Condorcet winners should be the winner(s), and his system is a realization of that view.

In particular, the Dodgson score of a candidate, a, is the smallest number of sequential exchanges of adjacent candidates in preference orders such that after those exchanges a is a Condorcet winner. All candidates having the smallest Dodgson score among the candidates are the winner(s) in Dodgson's system.

For example, suppose our election is over the candidates a, b, and c, and there are two voters, one voting $a \succ b \succ c$ and the other also voting $a \succ b \succ c$. (Throughout this paper, when writing out a particular vote we use the strict linear order $\succ$ associated with the voter's linear order $\succsim$; as noted in Chapter 2, these are related by: $x \succ y \iff (x \succsim y \wedge \neg(y \succsim x))$.) The Dodgson score of c is four, since to make c a Condorcet winner we have to adjacently exchange c with b in the first voter, forming the vote $a \succ c \succ b$ and then, after that, we have to adjacently exchange c with a in the first vote, and then we need to do the same two exchanges in the second vote. The Dodgson scores of a and b are zero and two. In this example, there is one Dodgson winner, namely, a. However, if the votes had instead been $a \succ b \succ c$ and $b \succ a \succ c$, then the Dodgson scores of a, b, and c would be one, one, and four, and a and b would be the Dodgson winners.

The system just described is what Dodgson himself defined. (This chapter is designed to be self-contained. However, we mention that Chapter 2 provides to all interested readers an excellent treatment of the basics of voting theory, including such notions as Dodgson's election system, Condorcet winners, and so on.) However, some researchers have studied the following variant, sometimes still calling it Dodgson elections and not mentioning that it differs from Dodgson's notion. The election system WeakDodgson is defined exactly as above, except in terms of WeakDodgson scores, which are the number of sequential exchanges of adjacent candidates needed to make the given candidate become a weak Condorcet winner. The WeakDodgson scores of a, b, and c in the first example above are zero, one, and two, and in the second example above are zero, zero, and two. The WeakDodgson winners are the same as the Dodgson winners in the above examples. However, it is easy to construct examples where Dodgson and WeakDodgson produce different winner sets.

Dodgson's system is measuring each candidate's adjacent-exchange distance from being a Condorcet winner, and is electing the candidate(s) with the shortest such distance. Among the many beauties of Dodgson's system is that it is based on finding the minimum edit distance between the initial votes and a certain region in the space of all votes, under a certain basis of operations, in particular sequential adjacent-exchanges. The notion of edit distance is essential in a large number of fields, and is central in many area of algorithmics. Dodgson's use of this notion is a natural, lovely, and quite early example. The coverage of distance rationalizability in Chapter 8 will make clear that a distance-based framework can be used to capture and study a wide range of important voting systems.

H. Peyton Young (1977) defined his election system, now known as Young elections, in terms of a different type of distance. The Young score of a candidate, a, is defined to be the smallest number n such that there is a set of n voters such that a is a weak Condorcet winner when those n voters are removed from the election. All candidates having the lowest Young score in a given election are its Young winner(s). The analogous system based on the number of deletions needed to make a given candidate a Condorcet winner will be called StrongYoung, and has also been studied, sometimes in papers still calling it Young elections and not mentioning that it differs from Young's notion. If a given candidate cannot be made a Condorcet winner by any number of deletions, we will say that its StrongYoung score is infinite. So, for example, in a zero-voter election, all candidates tie under the Young system, each with Young score zero, and all candidates tie under the StrongYoung system, each with StrongYoung score infinity. StrongYoung is clearly a Condorcet-consistent system.

Let us look at an election example and find its Young scores and its Young winner(s). Consider the election in which the candidates are a, b, c, and d, and the following six votes are cast:

1. $a \succ b \succ c \succ d$,
2. $a \succ b \succ c \succ d$,
3. $a \succ b \succ d \succ c$,
4. $c \succ a \succ d \succ b$,
5. $d \succ b \succ a \succ c$, and
6. $d \succ b \succ c \succ a$.

Candidate a—who actually is already a Condorcet winner—is certainly a weak Condorcet winner, and so has Young score zero. Candidate b is losing to a four to two among the six voters, and ties or beats each of c and d. Due to b's four to two loss against a, clearly the Young score of b is at least two, since deleting one vote closes the amount by which b trails a by at most one. If one deletes the votes numbered 1 and 2 above, b will tie with a two to two, but—horrors!—now loses to d one to three. So the fact that deleting 1 and 2 removes b's weakness with regard to a does not suffice to establish that the Young score of b is at most two. However, happily, it is easy to see that deleting the votes numbered 1 and 4 above indeed makes b become a weak Condorcet winner, and so b's Young score is at most two. Thus b's Young score is exactly two. It is also easy to see that d's Young score is exactly two, and the reader may wish to verify that as practice. c is a more interesting case than d is. Initially, c ties d three to three, loses to b five to one, and loses to a four to two. Due to the five to one loss to b, clearly c's Young score is at least four. However, c also trails a, and it is possible that removing some four votes that catch c up to b might not catch c up to a, or might even leave c losing to d. This observation, and the twist we ran into above related to computing b's Young score, are related to why computing Young scores turns out to be, as further mentioned later in this chapter, computationally difficult: The number of vote collections to be considered for potential deletion can be combinatorially explosive, and deleting a given vote can affect a given candidate in some helpful and some harmful ways at the same time. However, in this particular example, deleting votes 1, 2, 3, and 5 leaves c a weak Condorcet winner, and thus c's Young score is at most four. So c's Young score in fact is exactly four. Overall, candidate a is the one and only Young winner in this example—which of course follows immediately from the fact, mentioned near the start of this paragraph, that a is a Condorcet winner here.

As noted earlier, Dodgson in effect means StrongDodgson, but Young in effect means WeakYoung. This is simply due to the history of how these notions were defined by their creators. Throughout this chapter, we will use the terms Dodgson and StrongYoung for the versions based on Condorcet winners and will use the terms WeakDodgson and Young for the versions based on weak Condorcet winners.

Dodgson's and Young's election systems have followed paths of whipsaw twists and turns in terms of their computational properties, and this chapter is mostly focused on providing an overview of those paths, with a particular stress on Dodgson's system.

Briefly summarized, in the late 1800s Dodgson defined his system, and it was natural, compelling, and lovely—so much so that it was included in McLean and Urken's (1995) collection of the key papers in the multi-thousand-year history of social choice. However, as we will discuss in Section 5.3, in the late 1900s Bartholdi et al. (1989b) proved that the winner problem of this lovely system was NP-hard, and so under current standard assumptions in computer science is computationally intractable. Hemaspaandra et al. (1997a) then obtained a tight classification of the problem's computational complexity, and it became the first truly real-world-natural problem to be "complete" for the class of problems solvable through parallel access to NP—a very high level of complexity. That result was good news for complexity theory, as it populated that complexity class with a problem that clearly was highly nonartificial, since the election system had been defined in the 1800s, long before complexity theory even existed. However, the late 1900s results were grim news indeed regarding the computational difficulty of Dodgson elections.

Yet hardness results often are not the last word on a problem. Rather, they can serve as an invitation to researchers to find ways to sidestep the problem's hardness. That is exactly what happened in the case of Dodgson elections, in work done in the 2000s. It is known that, unless the polynomial hierarchy collapses, no heuristic algorithm for any NP-hard problem can have a subexponential error rate (see Hemaspaandra and Williams, 2012). So heuristic algorithms for the Dodgson election problem are limited in what they can hope to achieve. Nonetheless, it has been shown that there are quite good heuristic algorithms for the class of instances where the number of candidates is superquadratic in the number of voters. Section 5.4 presents such heuristic results. Section 5.5 discusses another approach to bypassing hardness results—parameterized algorithms. The results covered there show, for example, that the Dodgson winner problem is fixed-parameter tractable with respect to the number of candidates. That is, there is a uniform algorithm whose running time is the product of a polynomial in the instance's size and some (admittedly very large) function of the number of candidates. Finally, Section 5.6 studies a third approach to dealing with hardness, namely, approximation algorithms. That section presents results about approximating the Dodgson score and using approximation algorithms themselves as voting rules that achieve some social-choice properties that Dodgson's system lacks.

Young elections have been less extensively studied than Dodgson elections. But as this chapter will discuss, Young's system walked a twisty results road quite similar to the one Dodgson's system walked. Like Dodgson, Young is a natural election system; like Dodgson, long after Young's system was defined it was proven that even telling who won is computationally intractable; and like Dodgson, for Young elections one can obtain fixed-parameter tractability results.

5.3 Winner-Problem Complexity

This section discusses the complexity of the winner problems of Dodgson, WeakDodgson, StrongYoung, and Young elections.

5.3.1 Basics and Background

To understand the complexity of the winner problems of Dodgson, WeakDodgson, StrongYoung, and Young elections, we will need to define and discuss an important level of the polynomial hierarchy that is far less well-known than the polynomial hierarchy's famous lowest levels, P and NP. This less well-known complexity class is the Θ_2^p level of the polynomial hierarchy, which captures the power of (polynomial-time) parallel access to NP.

Let us now define this class. We will assume that the reader is familiar with the definition of NP and has at least a general idea of what a Turing machine is. A set is in coNP exactly if its complement is in NP. We will not define the polynomial hierarchy in this chapter. However, we mention that it is widely believed that the polynomial hierarchy does not collapse. Thus any assumption that would imply that the polynomial hierarchy collapses is, in the eyes of modern computer science, viewed as highly unlikely to be true.

A Turing machine operating with parallel access to a set A is a standard Turing machine enhanced with an extra tape, called the query tape. On an arbitrary input x, the machine is allowed, after some computation, to write on the tape a sequence of binary strings (say $y_1, \ldots, y_k$), each separated by the special character #. The machine then can, at most once on each input, enter a special state, known as the query state, q_{ask_query}. After it does, the machine is by the definition of this model immediately (i.e., in one time step) placed into the state $q_{query\_answered}$, and the query tape's content is replaced with a k-bit vector containing the answers to the k questions "$y_1 \in A$?", ..., "$y_k \in A$?" After some additional computation the machine may halt and accept or halt and reject. Here, k need not be a constant; on different inputs, k might differ, and there might be no global bound on k.

For any string x, let $|x|$ denote the length of x, for example, $|01111| = 5$. A set B is said to belong to Θ_2^p exactly if there exists a Turing machine, M, and an NP set A, such that (*i*) there exists a polynomial p such that, for each input x, M operating with parallel access to A, on input x, halts and accepts or halts and rejects within time $p(|x|)$, and (*ii*) the set of all strings accepted by M operating with parallel access to A is B.

Informally put, Θ_2^p is capturing the power of what one can do with a machine that on input x can, in time polynomial in $|x|$, generate some list of queries to an NP set, and then, in light of the input and a magically delivered answer for each of those queries as to whether the queried string is in the NP set, can with at most polynomially long additional computation determine whether x is in the given set. Simply put, this class is capturing the power of (polynomial-time) parallel access to NP. Although, as mentioned above, there is no a priori limit on the number of queries that can be asked in the (one) question string, the fact that the machine has only polynomial time to write the string ensures that there are at most polynomially many queries in the question string.

Θ_2^p is sometimes alternatively denoted $P_{\parallel}^{NP}$ or P_{tt}^{NP}; the $\parallel$ denotes parallel access and the tt stands for truth-table, which is the type of reduction on which the above definition of Θ_2^p is based. For those familiar with the polynomial hierarchy and its classes, the location of Θ_2^p within the polynomial hierarchy is $\Sigma_1^p \cup \Pi_1^p \subseteq \Theta_2^p \subseteq \Delta_2^p \subseteq \Sigma_2^p \cap \Pi_2^p$, or to state that without the jargon, $NP \cup coNP \subseteq P_{\parallel}^{NP} \subseteq P^{NP} \subseteq NP^{NP} \cap coNP^{NP}$. It is well-known that unless NP is a *strict* subset of Θ_2^p, the polynomial hierarchy collapses to NP.

Let us give a brief example showing membership in Θ_2^p. Consider the set of all (undirected, nonempty) graphs in which the largest clique in the graph has an odd number of nodes, that is, the problem odd-max-clique. This problem is clearly in Θ_2^p. Why? The standard clique problem is the set of all (G, ℓ), with G a graph and ℓ a natural number, such that there is a clique in G of size at least ℓ. So our machine to show that odd-max-clique is in Θ_2^p will, given a graph G having n nodes, write on the query tape the string $(G, 1)\#(G, 2)\# \cdots \#(G, n)$ and enter the state q_{ask_query}, and then from the state $q_{query\_answered}$ will look at the answer vector, which will be, for some j, j ones followed by $n - j$ zeros, and from the number of ones will easily be able to tell whether the largest clique is odd or even. For example, if the answer vector is 111000, we know the graph has cliques of size 1, 2, and 3, but not 4, 5, or 6, so the largest clique is of size 3, which is odd, so the machine in this case will enter an accepting state and halt.

Our oracle model allowed only a single question string, although that question string itself could be encoding polynomially many different simultaneous queries to the oracle. That is why this class is said to capture parallel access to NP. However, Θ_2^p is also known to exactly capture the set of languages accepted if, in our above polynomial-time model, one can query the oracle $\mathcal{O}(\log n)$ times, except now with each question string containing a single query rather than asking many queries combined. That is, informally, polynomial-time unbounded parallel access to NP has the same power as polynomial-time logarithmic-query sequential access to NP. Indeed, the class was first studied in the sequential version (Papadimitriou and Zachos, 1983), and only later was the connection to the parallel notion established (Hemachandra, 1989).

In complexity theory, reductions provide a tool to help classify complexity. We say a set B polynomial-time many-one reduces to a set D if there is a polynomial-time computable function f such that, for each x, $x \in B$ if and only if $f(x) \in D$. Informally, there is a simple to compute, membership-preserving mapping from B to D. It certainly follows that if D is easy to compute, then so is B.

For any complexity class $\mathcal{C}$, we say a set D is $\mathcal{C}$-hard if for every set $B \in \mathcal{C}$ it holds that B polynomial-time many-one reduces to D. Since $NP \subseteq \Theta_2^p$, every Θ_2^p-hard problem is NP-hard. For any complexity class $\mathcal{C}$, we say a set D is $\mathcal{C}$-complete exactly if (a) $D \in \mathcal{C}$ and (b) D is $\mathcal{C}$-hard. The complete sets for a class are in some sense the quintessence of the class's power. They are members of the class, yet are so powerful that each other set in the class can be polynomial-time many-one reduced to them.

Θ_2^p itself has an interesting, unusual history. It is natural to worry, when one throws a party, whether anyone will come. In complexity theory, the analogous worry is that one will define a complexity class that seems intuitively natural, and yet the class will somehow not turn out to capture the complexity of important real-world problems.

The complexity of Dodgson elections helped Θ_2^p avoid being a dull party. In particular, by the mid-1990s, it was clear that Θ_2^p was important in complexity theory. For example, Kadin (1989) had proven that if NP has a "sparse Turing-complete set" then the polynomial hierarchy collapses to Θ_2^p; Θ_2^p was known to have a large number of different yet equivalent definitions (Wagner, 1990); and Θ_2^p was known to be closely connected to time-bounded Kolmogorov complexity theory (Hemachandra and Wechsung, 1991). Yet those were all results that would warm only the heart of a complexity theorist. Θ_2^p was known to have complete problems (see Wagner, 1987). But they were artificial or mathematical problems of a sort that might be interesting to theoretical computer scientists or logicians, yet that did not have the natural appeal of problems coming from compellingly important "real world" settings and challenges.

To this uneasily quiet party came the Dodgson winner problem, with party favors and noisemakers. The Dodgson winner problem turned out to be complete for Θ_2^p, and was unarguably natural, coming as it did from a question raised a hundred years earlier. And the party was soon humming, as many other problems, including such additional election-winner problems as StrongYoung elections and Kemeny elections, were shown to also be Θ_2^p-complete (Rothe et al., 2003; Hemaspaandra et al., 2005).

5.3.2 The Complexity of the Dodgson and Young Winner Problems

In 1989, Bartholdi et al. (1989b) proved that the Dodgson winner problem was NP-hard and left as an open issue whether it was NP-complete. In 1997, Hemaspaandra et al. (1997a) proved that the Dodgson winner problem was in fact Θ_2^p-complete. This implies that, unless NP = coNP, the problem is not NP-complete. Intuitively, the problem is too hard to be NP-complete.

It is natural to wonder why one should even bother to exactly classify a problem that is known to be NP-hard. After all, NP-hardness is already a powerful indicator of hardness. There are a number of answers to this question. The nerdy, technical answer that a complexity theorist might give is that improving a problem's complexity from NP-hardness to Θ_2^p-completeness tells us more about how unlikely the problem is to be solvable with certain other approaches to computation (see Hemaspaandra et al., 1997b, for a discussion of this). However, the truly compelling answer harks back to our earlier comment about complete sets capturing the core nature of their classes. By proving a set complete for a class, we learn much about the fundamental nature of the set—whether it is capturing, as NP-complete sets do, the power of polynomially bounded existential quantification connected to polynomial-time predicates, or whether it is capturing, as Θ_2^p-complete sets do, the power of parallel access to NP.

Formally, the Dodgson winner problem is a set, namely, the set of all triples (A, R, p)—where A is the set of candidates, R is the list of cast votes (each being a linear order over A), and $p \in A$—such that p is a winner of the given election, when conducted under Dodgson's election system. The following theorem pinpoints the complexity of the Dodgson winner problem.

Theorem 5.1 (Hemaspaandra et al., 1997a). *The Dodgson winner problem is Θ_2^p-complete.*

We do not have the space to give a proof of the above theorem. However, it will be important and interesting to sketch the philosophy behind and structure of the proof, as they are at first quite counterintuitive.

What is counterintuitive is that one proves the Dodgson winner problem to be Θ_2^p-hard through doing extensive work to prove that many properties of the Dodgson winner problem are computationally easy to handle. Those (three) easy properties regard trapping the potential scores of the winner to two adjacent values within the image of an NP-hardness reduction (we will refer back to this later as L1), creating in polynomial time a "double exposure" that merges two elections in a way that preserves key information from each (we will refer back to this later as L2), and providing (with some twists) a polynomial-time function that given a list of elections and a candidate of interest in each creates a single election such that the sum of the scores of each election's interesting candidate in its election is the score of a particular designated candidate in the single election. For concreteness, the last of those can be formally stated as the following "sum of the scores equals the score of the 'sum'" claim.

Lemma 5.2 (Hemaspaandra et al., 1997a). *There is a polynomial-time function, dodgsonsum, such that, for all k and for all $(A_1, R_1, p_1), \ldots (A_k, R_k, p_k)$ that are election triples (i.e., $p_i \in A_i$, and the R_i are each a collection of linear orders over the candidates in A_i), each having an odd number of voters, dodgsonsum$((A_1, R_1, p_1), \ldots, (A_k, R_k, p_k))$ is an election triple (A, R, p) having an odd number of voters and it holds that the Dodgson score of p in the election (A, R) is exactly the sum over all j of the Dodgson score of p_j in election (A_j, R_j).*

The natural question to ask is: Why on earth would one prove lots of things easy about Dodgson elections in order to prove that the Dodgson winner problem is extremely hard? The answer to this question is that, despite the "hardness" in its name, Θ_2^p-hardness is not just about hardness (and neither are other hardnesses, such as NP-hardness). Let us explain why, using NP-hardness for our example. Suppose for each string in $\{0, 1\}^*$ we independently flip an unbiased coin, and put the string in or out of a set A based on the outcome. With probability one, the obtained set A is so extraordinarily hard as to not even be computable. Yet under standard beliefs about NP (namely, that NP is not a subset of bounded probabilistic polynomial time), with probability one the set A we obtained is not NP-hard (see Ambos-Spies, 1986). Intuitively, the issue here is that NP-hardness is not just about hardness. To be NP-hard, a set indeed must have enough power to be usable to handle all NP sets. But that power must be so well-organized and accessible that polynomial-time many-one reductions can harness that power. Our random set A is simply chaos, and so provides no such organized power. Every time we prove something NP-hard, by a reduction, we are exploiting the organization of the set being mapped to. With NP, we usually do not think much about that. In contrast, Θ_2^p-hardness proofs are so demanding, and the amount of structure exploitation needed to establish Θ_2^p-hardness is so great, that this issue comes out from the shadows.

We need a lens to focus the structure provided by Lemma 5.2 and the two other "in polynomial time we can do many things regarding Dodgson elections" claims that we alluded to just before that result (though neither of those is stated formally in this chapter), and to use that structure to establish a Θ_2^p-hardness result for the Dodgson winner problem. For Θ_2^p-hardness proofs, the lens of choice is the following powerful technical lemma proven in the 1980s by the great German complexity theorist Klaus W. Wagner. χ_A denotes the characteristic function of A, that is, $\chi_A(y) = 1$ if $y \in A$ and $\chi_A(y) = 0$ if $y \notin A$.

Lemma 5.3 (Wagner, 1987). *Let A be any NP-complete set and let B be any set. Then B is Θ_2^p-hard if there is a polynomial-time function f such that, for all $k \geqslant 1$ and all $x_1, \ldots, x_{2k}$ satisfying $\chi_A(x_1) \geqslant \cdots \geqslant \chi_A(x_{2k})$, it holds that*

$$\|\{i \mid x_i \in A\}\| \equiv 1 \pmod 2 \iff f(x_1, \ldots, x_{2k}) \in B.$$

This can be used, for example, to show that odd-max-clique is Θ_2^p-hard (Wagner, 1987). Thus in light of our earlier example odd-max-clique in fact is Θ_2^p-complete.

Briefly put, the broad structure of the Θ_2^p-hardness proof for the Dodgson winner problem is as follows. The result we alluded to earlier as L1 basically seeks to show that the Dodgson winner problem is NP-hard through a reduction that achieves a number of additional properties. The original Bartholdi et al. (1989b) reduction showing NP-hardness for the Dodgson winner problem reduced from the exact cover by three-sets problem. However, that reduction does not have the properties needed to work in concert with Lemma 5.3. Nonetheless, L1 holds, because one can, by a reduction from a different NP-complete problem, three-dimensional matching, obtain the desired properties. Then using L1 and Lemma 5.2 together with Lemma 5.3, one can argue that the problem of telling whether candidate p_1's Dodgson score in an election (A_1, R_1) is less than or equal to candidate p_2's score in an election (A_2, R_2), with both $\|R_1\|$ and $\|R_2\|$ odd, is Θ_2^p-hard. Finally, using that result and the result we referred to earlier as L2 (a "merging" lemma), one can prove that Dodgson winner itself is Θ_2^p-hard. Thus rather extensive groundwork about the simplicity of many issues about Dodgson elections, used together with Wagner's Lemma, is what establishes Θ_2^p-hardness here.

Completeness for a class requires not just hardness for the class but also membership in the class. Yet we still have not argued that the Dodgson winner problem is in Θ_2^p. Happily, that is a very easy result to show. Given an election, a distinguished candidate p, and a natural number k, it clearly is an NP problem—called DodgsonScore in the literature—to determine whether the Dodgson score of p in that election is at most k. The way we see that this is in NP is that one can simply seek to guess a sequence of k sequential exchanges of adjacent candidates, making p a Condorcet winner. (In fact, this DodgsonScore is even NP-complete, as was established in the seminal paper of Bartholdi et al. (1989b).) Now, given an election instance, (A, R), and a candidate $p \in A$, we wish to determine within Θ_2^p whether p is a Dodgson winner. What we do is that we ask, in parallel, to the NP problem DodgsonScore every reasonable score question for every candidate. Note that even if a candidate p' is at the bottom of every vote, with $(\|A\| - 1)\|R\|$ sequential exchanges of adjacent candidates it can be moved to the top of every vote, at which point it easily is a Condorcet winner. So for each candidate $p' \in A$, and each natural number i, $1 \leqslant i \leqslant (\|A\| - 1)\|R\|$, we ask whether the Dodgson score of p' is at most i. That is a single parallel round of $\|A\|(\|A\| - 1)\|R\|$ queries. From the answers, we immediately know the Dodgson score of each candidate, and so we can easily tell whether p is a Dodgson winner. Since this scheme meets the definition of Θ_2^p, we have established that the Dodgson winner problem is in Θ_2^p. In light of the already discussed Θ_2^p-hardness, we may conclude that the Dodgson winner problem is Θ_2^p-complete.

Is this Θ_2^p-completeness result just a trick of the particular model of Dodgson elections, or does it hold even for natural variants? Research has shown that Θ_2^p-completeness holds even for many natural variants of the Dodgson winner problem. The WeakDodgson winner problem is Θ_2^p-complete (Brandt et al., 2010a, 2010b), asking whether p is the one and only Dodgson winner (i.e., is a so-called unique winner) is Θ_2^p-complete (Hemaspaandra et al., 2009), and asking whether p is the one and only WeakDodgson winner is Θ_2^p-complete (Brandt et al., 2010b). Even comparing two Dodgson scores in the same election is Θ_2^p-complete (Hemaspaandra et al., 1997a).

Still, there are limits to how much one can vary the problem and remain hard. For example, if one considers elections in which the electorate has so-called single-peaked preferences (Black, 1948)—an extremely important notion in political science—the complexity of the winner problem for Dodgson and WeakDodgson elections falls to polynomial time (Brandt et al., 2010a).

Although we have so far been discussing the Dodgson winner problem, the key results mentioned above also hold for the Young winner problem. In 2003, the complexity of the StrongYoung winner problem was pinpointed by Rothe et al. (2003) as being Θ_2^p-complete. Θ_2^p-completeness also holds for the Young winner problem (Brandt et al., 2010a, 2010b):

Theorem 5.4. *The Young winner problem is Θ_2^p-complete.*

Θ_2^p-completeness also holds for case of asking whether p is the one and only StrongYoung winner (Hemaspaandra et al., 2009), and for the case of asking whether p is the one and only Young winner (Brandt et al., 2010b).

Similarly to the Dodgson case, if one considers elections in which the electorate has single-peaked preferences, the complexity of the winner problem for Young and StrongYoung elections falls to polynomial time (Brandt et al., 2010a).

Dodgson and Young are not the only election systems whose winner problem turns out to be hard. For example, the lovely election system known as Kemeny elections (Kemeny, 1959; Kemeny and Snell, 1960) (see Chapters 2 and 4 for more on Kemeny elections) also has a Θ_2^p-complete winner (and unique winner) problem (Hemaspaandra et al., 2005, 2009).

Although an understandable first reaction to a Θ_2^p-hardness result might be despair and resignation, it surely is better to be positive and make the best of the situation. For example, we mentioned above that for a restricted-domain setting, called single-peaked electorates, the complexity of the Dodgson winner problem vanishes. In the coming sections, we will look at three other approaches to living with intractability results: heuristic algorithms, parameterized algorithms, and approximation algorithms.

5.4 Heuristic Algorithms

Suppose we are faced with a problem for which getting an efficient deterministic algorithm that is correct on all inputs seems unlikely, for example due to the problem being NP-hard or Θ_2^p-hard. A natural next step is to seek an algorithm that is correct a very high portion of the time.

There are severe complexity-theoretic barriers to even that goal. As mentioned earlier, it is known that, unless the polynomial hierarchy collapses, no NP-hard problem (and thus no Θ_2^p-hard problem) has (deterministic) heuristic algorithms whose asymptotic error rate is subexponential (see Hemaspaandra and Williams, 2012). Still, even a heuristic algorithm whose asymptotic error rate is not subexponential can be valuable. In fact, despite the above result, heuristic algorithms are a valuable tool when faced with complex problems.

Even better than heuristic algorithms that often are correct would be heuristic algorithms that often are self-knowingly correct. A heuristic algorithm for a total function f is said to be self-knowingly correct if, on each input x, the function (i) outputs a claim as to the value of $f(x)$, and also outputs either "definitely" or "maybe," and (ii) whenever the function outputs $(y,$ "definitely"$)$ it holds that $f(x) = y$. When the second output component is "maybe," the first output component might, or might not, equal $f(x)$. Of course, the goal is to build self-knowingly correct algorithms that very often have "definitely" as their second output component.

Since we will now often be speaking of drawing random elections, for the rest of this section we assume that in m-candidate elections the candidate names are always $1, \ldots, m$, and so in drawing a random election all that is at issue will be the votes. So in Theorem 5.5 below, the "election" will refer just to R, and both the function and the GreedyWinner algorithm we will discuss in the next paragraph will take R and p as their input.

Consider the function that on input (R, p)—where R is a list of votes (each a linear order) that for some j are all over the candidates $1, 2, \ldots, j$ and $p \in \{1, \ldots, j\}$— equals Yes if p is a Dodgson winner of that election and equals No otherwise, that is, the function in effect computes the characteristic function of the Dodgson winner problem (j is not fixed; it may differ on different inputs). It turns out that there is a frequently self-knowingly correct polynomial-time heuristic algorithm, called Greedy-Winner, for the function just described, and so, in effect, for the Dodgson winner problem.

Theorem 5.5 (Homan and Hemaspaandra, 2009).

1. *For each (election, candidate) pair it holds that if* GreedyWinner *outputs "definitely" as its second output component, then its first output component correctly answers the question, "Is the input candidate a Dodgson winner of the input election?"*

2. *For each $m \in \{1, 2, 3, \ldots\}$ and $n \in \{1, 2, 3, \ldots\}$, the probability that an election E selected uniformly at random from all elections having m candidates and n votes (i.e., all $(m!)^n$ elections having m candidates and n votes have the same likelihood of being selected) has the property that there exists at least one candidate p' such that* GreedyWinner *on input (E, p') outputs "maybe" as its second output component is less than $2(m^2 - m)e^{\frac{-n}{8m^2}}$.*

What this says is that the portion of m-candidate, n-voter elections that `Greedy-Winner` is self-knowingly correct on is at least $1 - 2(m^2 - m)e^{\frac{-n}{8m^2}}$. For example, if one looks at the asymptotics as m goes to infinity, and with n being some superquadratic polynomial of m, for example, $n = m^{2.00001}$, the error rate will go to zero exponentially fast.

How does the `GreedyWinner` algorithm work? It is almost alarmingly simple. In fact, the reason one can get such an explicit bound, rather than just being able to draw plots from experiments as so many papers do, is in large part due to the algorithm's simplicity. The simplicity of the algorithm makes it possible, in this case, to well-analyze its performance. That is why, in the `GreedyScore` algorithm below, we tie our hands by making at most one exchange per vote; it suffices to get the desired result and it simplifies the analysis.

`GreedyWinner` is built on top of a heuristic algorithm called `GreedyScore`, which given an election and a candidate p', seeks to, in a frequently self-knowingly correct way, compute the Dodgson score of p' in the election. What `GreedyScore` does is simply this: It goes through the votes one at a time, and in each it looks at what one candidate (if any), c, is immediately preferred (i.e., adjacently preferred) to p' in that vote, and if at that moment p' is not yet strictly beating c in terms of how many voters prefer one to the other, then `GreedyScore` exchanges p' and c in that vote. If at the end of this process, p' is a Condorcet winner, then the algorithm outputs as its first component the number of exchanges it made, and outputs as its second component "definitely." It does so because an obvious lower bound for the number of adjacent exchanges needed to make p' a Condorcet winner is the sum, over all candidates, of how many voters must change from preferring c to p' to instead preferring p' to c. But if we made p' become a Condorcet winner only by exchanging it with things that were initially upside-adjacent to it in the given vote, and we only did such exchanges if p' was at the moment of exchange still behind the candidate it was being exchanged with in their head-on-head contest, then our algorithm clearly uses no more exchanges than that lower bound. And so our algorithm has truly found the Dodgson score of p'.

Intuitively, if the number of voters is sufficiently large relative to the number of candidates, then it is highly likely that the above `GreedyScore` procedure will self-knowingly succeed, that is, that we can make up all the deficits that p' has simply by exchanging it with rivals that are immediately adjacent to it. (After all, for any two candidates c and d, it is easy to see that for $1/m$ of the possible vote choices c will adjacently beat d within that vote. So the expected value of the number of votes in which c will adjacently beat d is n/m.) The claim about frequent success can be made more precise. In particular, if one fixes a candidate, say candidate 1, and draws uniformly at random an m-candidate, n-voter election, the probability that `GreedyScore`'s second component is "maybe" is less than $2(m - 1)e^{\frac{-n}{8m^2}}$.

The `GreedyWinner` algorithm, on input (R, p), is simply to first run `GreedyScore` on (R, p). If "maybe" is the second component, we ourselves output "maybe" as our second component (and the first component does not matter). Otherwise, we run the `GreedyScore` algorithm on (R, p') for each candidate $p' \neq p$. If each of those runs results in a score that is not less than what we computed for p and each has a second component "definitely," then we output (as to whether p is a Dodgson winner) Yes (in fact, in this case, our algorithm self-knowingly correctly knows all the Dodgson scores and thus the complete set of Dodgson winners, and p is one of them), with second component "definitely," and otherwise if all second components were "definitely" we output No (in this case, our algorithm now self-knowingly correctly knows all the Dodgson scores and thus the complete set of Dodgson winners, and p is not one of them), with second component "definitely," and otherwise we output second component "maybe" (and the first component does not matter). By probability arguments (using the union theorem and a variant of Chernoff's Theorem), we can formally establish the claim made in the previous paragraph about GreedyScore, and Theorem 5.5's claim about the (in)frequency with which the self-knowingly correct algorithm GreedyWinner outputs "maybe."

This section has been speaking about Dodgson elections, and is based on the results of Homan and Hemaspaandra (2009). Independent work of McCabe-Dansted et al. (2008) studies essentially these issues for the case of WeakDodgson elections, and using the same general approach obtains related results for that case; see the discussion in Section 5.7.

5.5 The Parameterized Lens

Another approach that aims to cope with the inherent computational difficulty of Dodgson's and Young's election systems is the design of fixed-parameter tractable algorithms. The algorithmic challenge is the following: Is there an algorithm that computes the Dodgson (or StrongYoung) score, whose running time is polynomial for each fixed value of some important parameter of the problem, such as the number of candidates? The question falls within the research agenda of the area known as parameterized computational complexity (Downey and Fellows, 1999; Niedermeier, 2006). In general, that area's goal is to identify whether the computational explosion occurring in algorithms for NP-hard problems can be attributed solely to a certain parameter of the problem. In applications where that parameter typically takes on only small values, an algorithm with a running time that depends superpolynomially on only that parameter might be hoped to be of practical use.

In our case, attractive parameters include the number, m, of candidates; the number, n, of votes; and the number, k, of editing operations. For the Dodgson score, k denotes the number of sequential exchanges of adjacent candidates in the votes, while for the StrongYoung score, k denotes the number of votes deleted from the electorate. As a simple, initial example, fixed-parameter tractability with respect to the parameter n is clear in StrongYoung elections. Namely, one can conduct an exhaustive search over the 2^n different subsets of votes of the original profile and find (if one exists) a subset of maximum size in which the desired candidate is the Condorcet winner. The number of votes in this subset is the StrongYoung score of the preferred candidate p; if no such subset exists, we will output ∞ as p's StrongYoung score. So it is clear that the StrongYoung score is fixed-parameter tractable with respect to the number of voters.

The Dodgson score and the StrongYoung score are fixed-parameter tractable for the parameter m. This follows by a seminal result of Lenstra, Jr. (1983) that implies that a problem is fixed-parameter tractable when it can be solved by an integer linear program (ILP) in which the number of variables is upper-bounded by a function solely depending on the parameter. In particular, the seminal work of Bartholdi et al. (1989b) handles Dodgson score by integer linear programming in a way that, as has often been noted, tacitly establishes that the Dodgson score is fixed-parameter tractable with respect to the number of candidates. ILPs can also be used to compute the Young and the Strong Young scores (see Young, 1977).

Furthermore, the Dodgson score has been proved to be fixed-parameter tractable for the parameter k using dynamic programming, a standard tool for designing fixed-parameter tractable algorithms. The key idea is to solve the problem by solving sub-problems and combining overlapping solutions in order to compute the overall solution. Dynamic programming avoids multiple computation of the same (sub)solution by storing it in a so-called dynamic-programming table and by accessing its value from the table when needed.

We will now present the main ideas behind the way Betzler et al. (2010) have, using dynamic programming, upper-bounded the parameterized complexity of checking whether a candidate's Dodgson score is at most a given value. Let us be given a profile R with n votes (each specified as a linear order). We will now explore how to efficiently compute the Dodgson score of a particular candidate in that profile, say candidate a. We will denote by deficit(a, y, R) the deficit of candidate a with respect to candidate y in profile R, that is, the (minimum) number of voters who have to change their preference so that a beats y in their pairwise election. For example, if there are ten voters and eight initially prefer y to a, so a loses to y eight to two, deficit$(a, y, R) = 4$ since with the right four changed votes a will squeak past y to win by six to four. P will denote the set of candidates with respect to whom a has a positive deficit under our profile R.

The idea is to build a table whose entries store information about how candidate a can be pushed upward in the votes so that the deficit with respect to each candidate of P is eventually decreased to 0. This requires storing intermediate information concerning subsets of votes and partial decreases of the deficit in the table entries. The table for this has $n + 1$ rows. Row i will contain information about the first i votes of the profile. Each column of the table will be labeled by a vector d, and that vector will have an entry for each candidate of P, with $d(y)$ being an integer between 0 and deficit(a, y, R). Entry $T(i, d)$ of the table stores the minimum number of total upward pushes of a in the first i votes of R that will suffice to decrease a's initial deficit with respect to each $y \in P$ by at least $d(y)$. (By a "push," we mean a single exchange of adjacent candidates in a preference order.) We place ∞ in the table's $T(i, d)$ entry if even pushing a to the top of the first i votes is not enough to achieve the improvements demanded by the vector d. Using $\widetilde{d}$ to denote the vector with $\widetilde{d}(y) = $ deficit(a, y, R) for each candidate y of P, it is clear that the entry $T(n, \widetilde{d})$ will contain the Dodgson score.

The entries of the table are initialized to be $T(0, d) = 0$ if $d = (0, 0, \ldots, 0)$ and $T(0, d) = \infty$ otherwise. The entries of the ith row (doing this first for the $i = 1$ row, then the $i = 2$ row, and so on) can then be computed from the information stored in the entries of the $(i - 1)$st row. Before presenting the formal definition of this computation, let us give a small example. Let us focus on the first i votes of a profile R, for which we want to compute the Dodgson score of candidate a. Furthermore, let us suppose that the ith vote is $d \succ b \succ c \succ a$. Let us as our example seek to complete the least costly way to promote a (i.e., the minimum number of exchanges) in the first i votes in such a way (if any exists using pushes among just those votes) as to decrease the deficit of a

Table 5.1. *Profile and table example for computing the Dodgson score*

(a) A profile.			(b) The dynamic-programming table, T, for computing the Dodgson score of candidate a.					
1	2	3		$(0, 0)$	$(0, 1)$	$(0, 2)$	$(1, 0)$	$(1, 1)$	$(1, 2)$
d	d	c	0	0	∞	∞	∞	∞	∞
b	a	d							
c	b	a	1	0	3	∞	1	3	∞
a	c	b							
			2	0	1	4	1	2	4
			3	0	1	2	1	2	3

Note: The table at the right is used to compute the Dodgson score of candidate a in the profile at the left. In both the profile here and in Table 5.2, our tabular vote displays are arranged "top down," for example, the leftmost column of this profile indicates that the vote of the first voter is $d \succ b \succ c \succ a$. The "1 2 3" on the top row of profiles, both here and in Table 5.2, indicates the voters, for example, the column headed by a "3" is about voter 3. In the profile given in part (a), the deficits of a with respect to the candidates b, c, and d are 0, 1, and 2. So $P = \{c, d\}$ and each column label refers to a's deficits against c and d. The Dodgson score is the value, 3, that is computed for the entry $T(3, (1, 2))$, and it is achieved by pushing a one position upward in the second vote and two positions upward in the third vote.

with respect to candidates c and d by one and two, respectively. This can be computed by considering several different alternatives. One possibility is to use the least costly way to decrease the deficit of a with respect to d in the first $i - 1$ votes by one and then push a three positions upward in the ith vote to cut by an additional one the deficits with respect to each of c and d. Another possibility is to use the least costly way to decrease the deficit of a with respect to d by two in the first $i - 1$ votes and push a one position upward in the ith vote, to shrink by one its deficit with respect to c. A third possibility is to just use the least costly way to decrease the deficits by 1 and 2 in the first $i - 1$ votes and leave the ith vote unaltered. The entry of the table corresponding to the ith row and the column corresponding to the deficit decrease vector $(1, 2)$ will store the best among all the possibilities, including those mentioned above. This example shows how an entry in row i can be relatively easily computed if we already have in hand all the entries of row $i - 1$.

We are now ready to formally present the computation of entry $T(i, d)$ based on the entries in row $i - 1$. We use $L_i^j(d)$ for the set of all vectors of decreases of deficits such that if those decreases are satisfied over the first $i - 1$ votes of R then that will ensure that the decreases specified in d are satisfied over the first i voters of R when candidate a is pushed j positions upward in the ith vote. We use h^i to denote the number of candidates that voter i prefers to a. Then $T(i, d)$ will be assigned the value stated by the right-hand side below:

$$T(i, d) = \min_{0 \leqslant j \leqslant h^i} \ \min_{d' \in L_i^j(d)} \{T(i - 1, d') + j\}.$$

A completed table for an example with three votes and four candidates is provided as Table 5.1.

Using the approach sketched above and additional technical arguments, Betzler et al. (2010) prove that testing whether the Dodgson score of a given candidate is at most k is fixed-parameter tractable with respect to the parameter k.

It is important to mention that negative statements are also known. For example, the Dodgson score problem is not fixed-parameter tractable with respect to parameter n (the number of votes) unless a complexity-theoretic statement known as the exponential-time hypothesis is false. This follows from the fact that the problem is W[1]-hard (Fellows et al., 2010); W[1]-hardness is a central hardness notion in parameterized complexity. Young elections are also intractable with respect to the score parameter, k. In particular, Betzler et al. (2010) prove that the StrongYoung score problem is complete for the parameterized complexity class W[2].

5.6 Approximation Algorithms

We now focus specifically on Dodgson elections. Since Dodgson scores are hard to compute exactly in general, an alternative approach is to view the Dodgson score computation as a combinatorial optimization problem and exploit the rich and beautiful theory of approximation algorithms (e.g., see Vazirani, 2001) in order to approximate the Dodgson score. Briefly, the challenge is to obtain efficient (i.e., polynomial-time) algorithms that return scores that are provably close to the Dodgson score. Furthermore, such an approximation algorithm can be used as an alternative voting rule to Dodgson's rule under some circumstances. We discuss these issues below.

We consider algorithms that receive as input a candidate p from an m-candidate set A and an n-voter election profile R over A, and return a score for p. We denote the score returned by an algorithm Y when applied on such an input by $sc_Y(p, R)$. Also, $sc_D(p, R)$ will denote the Dodgson score. An algorithm Y is said to be a Dodgson approximation if $sc_Y(x, R) \geqslant sc_D(x, R)$ for every candidate $x \in A$ and every profile R. Also, Y is said to have an approximation ratio of $\rho \geqslant 1$ if $sc_Y(x, R) \leqslant \rho \cdot sc_D(x, R)$, for every candidate x and every profile R over A.

Let us give a trivial example. Again, denote by $deficit(x, y, R)$ the deficit of candidate x with respect to candidate y in profile R, that is, the minimum number of voters who have to change their preference so that x beats y in their pairwise election. Consider the algorithm Y that, given a candidate x and a preference profile R, returns a score of $sc_Y(x, R) = (m - 1) \cdot \sum_{y \in A - \{x\}} deficit(x, y, R)$. It is easy to show that this algorithm is a Dodgson approximation and, furthermore, has approximation ratio at most $m - 1$. In particular, it is possible to make x beat y in a pairwise election by pushing x to the top of the preferences of $deficit(x, y, R)$ voters, and clearly this requires at most $(m - 1) \cdot deficit(x, y, R)$ sequential exchanges of adjacent candidates. By summing over all $y \in A - \{x\}$, we obtain an upper bound of $sc_Y(x, R)$ on the Dodgson score of x. On the other hand, given $x \in A$, for every $y \in A - \{x\}$ we require $deficit(x, y, R)$ sequential adjacent-exchanges that push x above y in the preferences of some voter in order for x to beat y in a pairwise election. Moreover, these sequential adjacent-exchanges do not decrease the deficit with respect to any other candidate. Therefore, $\sum_{y \in A - \{x\}} deficit(x, y, R) \leqslant sc_D(x, R)$, and by multiplying by $m - 1$ we get that $sc_Y(x, R) \leqslant (m - 1) \cdot sc_D(x, R)$.

5.6.1 Achieving Logarithmic Approximation Ratios

In this section we present two Dodgson approximations with approximation ratios logarithmic in the number of candidates. One is a combinatorial, greedy algorithm and the other is an algorithm based on linear programming.

Table 5.2. *An example of the execution of Section 5.6.1's greedy algorithm (to compute the score of candidate p) on an election with 3 votes and 11 candidates*

(a) Initial profile.			(b) After step 1.			(c) After step 2.			(d) After step 3.		
1	2	3	1	2	3	1	2	3	1	2	3
b	b	c	b	b	c	b	p	c	b	p	c
d_1	d_4	b	d_1	d_4	b	d_1	b	b	d_1	b	p
d_2	d_5	d_6	d_2	d_5	d_6	d_2	d_4	d_6	d_2	d_4	b
c	p	d_7	p	p	d_7	p	d_5	d_7	p	d_5	d_6
d_3	c	d_8	c	c	d_8	c	c	d_8	c	c	d_7
p	d_1	p	d_3	d_1	p	d_3	d_1	p	d_3	d_1	d_8
d_4	d_2	d_1	d_4	d_2	d_1	d_4	d_2	d_1	d_4	d_2	d_1
d_5	d_3	d_2	d_5	d_3	d_2	d_5	d_3	d_2	d_5	d_3	d_2
d_6	d_6	d_3	d_6	d_6	d_3	d_6	d_6	d_3	d_6	d_6	d_3
d_7	d_7	d_4	d_7	d_7	d_4	d_7	d_7	d_4	d_7	d_7	d_4
d_8	d_8	d_5	d_8	d_8	d_5	d_8	d_8	d_5	d_8	d_8	d_5

We present the greedy algorithm first. This is a far more numerically driven greedy algorithm than the ones mentioned in Section 5.4. Given a profile R and a special candidate $p \in A$, those candidates $a \in A - \{p\}$ with deficit$(p, a, R) > 0$ are said to be alive. Candidates that are not alive, that is, those with deficit$(p, a, R) = 0$, are said to be dead. In each step, the algorithm selects an optimally cost-effective push (i.e., a least cost-ineffective push) of candidate p in the preference of some voter. The cost-ineffectiveness of pushing p in the preference of a voter i is defined as the ratio between the total number of positions p is moved upward in the preference of i compared with the original profile R, and the number of currently live candidates relative to which p gains as a result of this push. Note that the optimally cost-effective push (i.e., the push with the lowest cost-ineffectiveness) at each step may not be unique; in this case, tie-breaking has to be used in order to select one of the optimally cost-effective pushes.

After selecting an optimally cost-effective push, the algorithm decreases the deficit of p by one for each live candidate a relative to which p gains by that push. Candidates with respect to whom p has zero deficit become dead. The algorithm terminates when no live candidates remain; its output is the total number of positions that candidate p is pushed upward in the preferences of all voters.

An example of the execution of the algorithm is depicted in Table 5.2. In the initial profile R of this example, candidate p has deficits deficit$(p, b, R) = 2$, deficit$(p, c, R) = 1$, and deficit$(p, d_i, R) = 0$ for $1 \leqslant i \leqslant 8$. So candidates b and c are alive and candidates $d_1, \ldots, d_8$ are dead. At the first step of the algorithm, there are several different ways of pushing candidate p upward in order to gain relative to one or both of the live candidates b and c. Among them, the one with the smallest cost-ineffectiveness is to push p upward in the first vote. In this way, p moves two positions upward and gains relative to the live candidate c for a cost-ineffectiveness of 2. Any other push of p in the initial profile has cost-ineffectiveness at least 2.5 since p has to be pushed at least three positions upward in order to gain relative to one live candidate and at least five positions upward in order to gain relative to both b and c. After step 1, candidate c is dead. Then, in step 2, there are three ways to push candidate p upward so that it gains relative to the live candidate b: either pushing it to the top of the first vote (this has cost-ineffectiveness 5 because p would have moved five positions in total compared to the initial first vote), or pushing it to the top of the second vote (with cost-ineffectiveness 3), or pushing it four positions upward in the third vote (with cost-ineffectiveness 4). The algorithm picks the second option. Then, in step 3, the algorithm can either push candidate p to the top of the first vote or push it four positions upward in the third vote. The former has a cost-ineffectiveness of 5 (recall that cost-ineffectiveness is defined using the total number of positions p would move compared to its position at the initial profile), while the latter has a cost-ineffectiveness of 4 and is the push the algorithm picks. After step 3, all candidates are dead and the algorithm terminates by returning the total number of positions p is pushed upward, that is, 9.

Since the algorithm terminates when all candidates in $A - \{p\}$ are dead, it is clear that p becomes a Condorcet winner. The analysis of this greedy algorithm uses a linear programming relaxation of the Dodgson score. Given the profile R with a set of voters N and a set of m candidates A, denote by r^i the rank of candidate p in the preference of voter i. For every voter $i \in N$, denote by $\mathcal{S}^i$ the subcollection that consists of the sets S_k^i for $k = 1, \ldots, r^i - 1$, where the set S_k^i contains the live candidates that appear in positions $r^i - k$ to $r^i - 1$ in the preference of voter i. We denote by $\mathcal{S}$ the (multiset) union of the subcollections $\mathcal{S}^i$ for $i \in N$. The problem of computing the Dodgson score of candidate p on profile R is equivalent to selecting sets from $\mathcal{S}$ of minimum total size so that at most one set is selected among the ones in $\mathcal{S}^i$ for each voter i and each candidate $a \in A - \{p\}$ appears in at least $\text{deficit}(p, a, R)$ selected sets. This can be expressed by an integer linear program using a binary variable $x(S)$ to denote whether the set $S \in \mathcal{S}$ has been selected. We present the relaxation of this LP below, where the integrality constraint for the variables has been relaxed to fractional values between 0 and 1:

$$\text{Minimize} \quad \sum_{i \in N} \sum_{k=1}^{r^i-1} k \cdot x(S_k^i)$$

$$\text{subject to} \quad \forall a \in A - \{p\}, \sum_{i \in N} \sum_{S \in \mathcal{S}^i : a \in S} x(S) \geqslant \text{deficit}(p, a, R)$$

$$\forall i \in N, \sum_{S \in \mathcal{S}^i} x(S) \leqslant 1$$

$$\forall S \in \mathcal{S}, \ 0 \leqslant x(S) \leqslant 1.$$

Clearly, the Dodgson score of candidate p is an upper bound on the optimal objective value of this LP.

The analysis uses a technique that is known as dual fitting and is similar to the analysis of a greedy algorithm for the related constrained set multicover problem; see Rajagopalan and Vazirani (1999) and Vazirani (2001, pp. 112–116). The idea is to use the decisions taken by the algorithm and construct a feasible solution for the dual (maximization) LP that has value at most the score returned by the algorithm divided by H_{m-1}, where $H_k = 1 + \frac{1}{2} + \cdots + \frac{1}{k}$ denotes the kth harmonic number. By a simple duality argument, this implies that the score returned by the algorithm is at most H_{m-1} times the optimal objective value of the above LP and, consequently, at most H_{m-1} times the Dodgson score of p.

This suggests a different algorithm, in particular, an LP-based algorithm for approximating the Dodgson score of a candidate p without explicitly providing a way of pushing p upward in the preferences of some voters in a way making p become the Condorcet winner. This algorithm just uses the LP relaxation above, computes its optimal objective value, and returns this value multiplied by H_{m-1} as a score for candidate p. Then the approximation ratio of H_{m-1} is obvious. The algorithm is also a Dodgson approximation, since the score returned by this section's greedy algorithm (which is an upper bound for the Dodgson score of p) is not higher than the score returned by the LP-based algorithm. The following statement summarizes our discussion.

Theorem 5.6 (Caragiannis et al., 2012b). *This section's greedy algorithm and LP-based algorithm are Dodgson approximations, each with approximation ratio H_{m-1}.*

5.6.2 Approximation Algorithms as Alternative Voting Rules?

A Dodgson approximation naturally induces a voting rule by electing the candidate(s) with minimum score. Arguably, such a voting rule maintains some echo of the basic philosophy behind Dodgson's election system—more strongly so if it is a very good approximation. But can it really be used as a voting rule? Trying to support a yes answer to this question requires us to discuss an issue that we have not yet touched on. One can argue that for a voting rule to be attractive, it should not only be easy to compute, but also, ideally, should have certain properties that are considered desirable from a social-choice point of view. Several such properties are not satisfied by Dodgson's rule, and this is the main reason why the rule has been criticized in the social-choice literature, see, for example, Brandt (2009a) and the references therein.

We will see that Dodgson approximations, in return for their core disadvantage of merely being an approximation to Dodgson's rule, can satisfy desirable social-choice properties, even while also providing polynomial-time algorithms. Before going on to the three social-choice properties we will discuss, it is important to make clear just how greatly Dodgson approximations can distort Dodgson's rule, especially since we commented above that Dodgson approximations in some way echo the flavor and philosophy of Dodgson. The best Dodgson approximation we consider in this section has an approximation ratio of 2. Consider a three-candidate election for which the actual Dodgson scores of the candidates are 10, 11, and 12. A Dodgson approximation having ratio 2 could give for these candidates, respectively, scores of 18, 16, and 14. That is, the ordering of even an excellent Dodgson approximation can be a complete inversion of the actual Dodgson ordering, and the worst Dodgson loser can be named the unique winner. Clearly, the fact that even a 1.000001 approximation-ratio algorithm can completely invert the entire ranking of the candidates is a troubling (but not far from unavoidable—see the discussion at the end of Section 5.6.3) feature of using approximations as voting rules.

In the following, when we say that a Dodgson approximation satisfies a social-choice property we are referring to the voting rule induced by the algorithm. As a warm up, observe that the voting rule induced by any Dodgson approximation (regardless of its approximation ratio) is Condorcet-consistent, basically because anything times zero is zero. So every Dodgson approximation, regardless of how bad its ratio is, must assign score of 0 to any Condorcet winner. But since Dodgson approximations never underestimate scores, any candidate who is not a Condorcet winner will be assigned a score of at least 1. So any Condorcet winner will be the one and only winner under any Dodgson approximation. (Thank goodness Dodgson did not add a one in the definition of his scores. That would destroy the above claim, which is deeply dependent on the special nature of zero.) Of course, Dodgson's system itself also is Condorcet-consistent.

We will now move on to discuss two other socially desirable properties: monotonicity and homogeneity. We will see that these properties can be achieved by good Dodgson approximations that run in polynomial time.

A voting rule is said to be monotonic if a winning candidate always remains winning after it is pushed upward in the preferences of some of the voters. Dodgson's rule is known to be monotonic when there are at most three candidates and to be nonmonotonic for each number of candidates greater than or equal to four (Fishburn, 1982, p. 132). The intuition for the latter is that if a voter ranks x directly above y and y above z, exchanging x and y may not help y if it already beats x, but may help z defeat x. The two approximation algorithms presented in Section 5.6.1 are also nonmonotonic.

In contrast, the Dodgson approximation that returns $(m - 1) \cdot \sum_{y \in A - \{x\}}$ deficit(x, y, R) as the score of candidate x is monotonic as a voting rule. Indeed, consider a preference profile R and a winning candidate x. Pushing x upward in the preferences of some of the voters can neither increase its score (since its deficit with respect to each other candidate does not increase) nor decrease the score of any other candidate $y \in A - \{x\}$ (since the deficit of y with respect to each candidate in $A - \{x, y\}$ remains unchanged and its deficit with respect to x does not decrease). So we already have a monotonic Dodgson approximation with approximation ratio $m - 1$. In the following we present much stronger results.

A natural "monotonization" of Dodgson's voting rule yields a monotonic Dodgson approximation with approximation ratio of 2. The main idea is to define the winning set of candidates for a given profile first and then assign the same score to the candidates in the winning set and a higher score to the nonwinning candidates. Roughly speaking, the winning set is defined so that it contains the Dodgson winners for the given profile as well as the Dodgson winners of other profiles that are necessary so that monotonicity is satisfied. More formally put, we say that an n-vote election profile R' is a y-improvement of profile R for some candidate $y \in A$ if R' is obtained by starting from R and pushing y upward in the preferences of zero or more voters.

Monotonization proceeds as follows. Let M denote the new voting rule we are constructing. Denote by $W(R)$ the set of winners of M (or the winning set) for profile R; we will soon specify which candidates belong to $W(R)$. Let $\Delta = \max_{y \in W(R)} \text{sc}_D(y, R)$. The voting rule M assigns a score of $\text{sc}_M(y, R) = \Delta$ to each candidate $y \in W(R)$ and a score of

$$\text{sc}_M(y, R) = \max\{\Delta + 1, \text{sc}_D(y, R)\}$$

to each candidate $y \notin W(R)$. All that remains is to define the winning set $W(R)$. This is done as follows: For each profile R^* and each Dodgson winner y^* of R^*, include y^* in the winning set $W(R')$ of each profile R' that is a y^*-improvement of R^*.

Theorem 5.7 (Caragiannis et al., 2014b). *M is a monotonic Dodgson approximation with an approximation ratio of 2.*

That M is monotonic and is a Dodgson approximation follow immediately from the definitions of the winning set $W(R)$ and the scores returned by M. The proof of the approximation ratio bound is based on the following technical property: Pushing a candidate y upward does not increase his or her Dodgson score and does not decrease the Dodgson score of any other candidate by a factor larger than 2. The upper bound provided by Theorem 5.7 is the best possible: No monotonic Dodgson approximation can have an approximation ratio smaller than 2. This negative statement does not use any complexity-theoretic assumptions and actually holds for exponential-time algorithms as well. Actually, monotonization (in the rather naive approach described above) yields an exponential-time algorithm.

So from the computational point of view, the above algorithm is not at all satisfactory. Fortunately, a polynomial-time implementation of monotonization is possible, although it involves an unavoidable (see Section 5.6.3) logarithmic loss in the approximation ratio. There are two main obstacles that one has to overcome in order to implement monotonization in polynomial time. First, as discussed in Section 5.3, computing the Dodgson score and deciding whether a given candidate is a Dodgson winner are computationally hard problems. This obstacle can be overcome using the score returned by the polynomial-time LP-based Dodgson approximation that we presented in Section 5.6.1 instead of using the Dodgson score itself. Even in this case, given a profile R, we still need to be able to detect when a candidate y is the winner according to the LP-based voting rule in some profile R' of which the current one is a y-improvement; if this is the case, y has to be included in the winning set $W(R)$ of profile R. This means that exponentially many profiles may have to be checked in order to determine the winning set of the current profile. This obstacle is overcome by Caragiannis et al. (2014b) using the notion of pessimistic estimators. These are quantities defined in terms of the current profile only and are used to identify the winning set in polynomial time. The next statement follows using these two high-level ideas and additional technical arguments.

Theorem 5.8 (Caragiannis et al., 2014b). *There exists a monotonic polynomial-time Dodgson approximation with an approximation ratio of $2H_{m-1}$.*

Let us now turn to homogeneity. A voting rule is said to be homogeneous if, for every integer $k \geq 2$, its outcome does not change when replacing each vote in the preference profile with k identical copies of the vote. Fishburn (1977) observed that Dodgson's rule is not homogeneous. The intuition behind this is that if candidates x and y are tied in a pairwise election the deficit of x with respect to y does not increase by duplicating the profile, but if x strictly loses to y in a pairwise election then the deficit scales with the number of copies.

Tideman (2006, pp. 199–201) presents the following simplified version of Dodgson's rule and proves that it is both homogeneous and monotonic. A Condorcet winner—if one exists—in an election profile R is the sole winner according to Tideman's rule.

Otherwise, the rule assigns a score of

$$\mathrm{sc}_{\mathrm{Td}}(x, R) = \sum_{y \in A-\{x\}} \max\{0, n - (2 \cdot \|\{i \in N : x \succ_i y\}\|)\}$$

to each candidate x, and the candidate(s) with the minimum score win. In the above equation, the notation $x \succ_i y$ indicates that voter i prefers candidate x to candidate y. Unfortunately, this score definition does not provide a Dodgson approximation. For example, a candidate who is tied with some candidates and beats the rest has a score of 0, yet 0 is lower than its Dodgson score. However, we in fact can give a different scoring framework, Td′, that is a Dodgson approximation and that will elect exactly the same winners as does Tideman's simplified variant of Dodgson's rule (and thus will be monotonic and homogeneous). Td′ is defined as follows. If a candidate x is a Condorcet winner, then it has score $\mathrm{sc}_{\mathrm{Td}'}(x, R) = 0$. Otherwise, Td′ "scales" the score of x as follows:

$$\mathrm{sc}_{\mathrm{Td}'}(x, R) = m \cdot \mathrm{sc}_{\mathrm{Td}}(x, R) + m(1 + \log m).$$

Clearly, $\mathrm{sc}_{\mathrm{Td}'}(x, R)$ can be computed in time polynomial in n and m.

Theorem 5.9 (Caragiannis et al., 2014b). *Td′ is a monotonic, homogeneous, polynomial-time Dodgson approximation with an approximation ratio of $\mathcal{O}(m \log m)$.*

This approximation ratio is the best possible; a matching $\Omega(m \log m)$ lower bound holds for any algorithm that is homogeneous (Caragiannis et al., 2014b).

5.6.3 Hardness of Approximation

The best polynomial-time Dodgson approximations presented in Section 5.6.1 achieve—keeping in mind that $H_m = \ln n + \Theta(1)$—asymptotic approximation ratios of $\mathcal{O}(\log m)$. Under standard assumptions about NP, all polynomial-time Dodgson approximations have approximation ratios that are $\Omega(\log m)$, so the above-mentioned approximations from the previous section have ratios that are optimal within a constant, and in fact that constant can be kept down to 2. This claim is implicit in McCabe-Dansted (2006). Later, Caragiannis et al. (2012b) explicitly obtained and stated the following result, using a reduction from minimum set cover and well-known inapproximability thresholds of Feige (1998) and Raz and Safra (1997).

Theorem 5.10 (Caragiannis et al., 2012b). *There exists a constant $\beta > 0$ such that it is NP-hard to approximate the Dodgson score of a given candidate in an election with m candidates to within a factor of $\beta \ln m$. Furthermore, for any $\epsilon > 0$, there is no polynomial-time $\left(\frac{1}{2} - \epsilon\right) \ln m$-approximation for the Dodgson score of a given candidate unless all problems in NP have algorithms running in time $k^{\mathcal{O}(\log \log k)}$, where k is the input size.*

One might wonder why our particular notion of approximation has been used. For example, a natural alternative approach would be to approximate some notion of Dodgson ranking. Unfortunately, the following statement shows that this is an impossible goal: Efficient approximation algorithms for Dodgson ranking are unlikely to exist. For the purpose of the theorem below, a Dodgson ranking of an election instance is an ordering of the candidates such that if $i < j$ then the ith candidate in the ordering has Dodgson score no greater than the jth candidate in the ordering.

Theorem 5.11 (Caragiannis et al., 2012b). *Given a profile with m candidates and a special candidate p, it is NP-hard to decide whether p is a Dodgson winner or has rank at least $m - 6\sqrt{m}$ in any Dodgson ranking.*

5.7 Bibliography and Further Reading

Dodgson's election system first appeared in Dodgson's 1876 pamphlet (Dodgson, 1876). The computational complexity of the winner problem for Dodgson's system was shown NP-hard in the seminal paper of Bartholdi et al. (1989b), and was shown Θ_2^p-complete by Hemaspaandra et al. (1997a), see also Brandt et al. (2010b, p. 54). Young's election system was defined by him in 1977 (Young, 1977), and the complexity of StrongYoung was pinpointed as being Θ_2^p-complete by Rothe et al. (2003). See Brandt (2009a) and the references therein for perspectives on why Dodgson proposed his system and discussions of Dodgson's system in terms of not satisfying certain properties.

A number of other papers discuss the complexity of Dodgson and Young elections or variants of those elections (Hemaspaandra et al., 2009; Brandt et al., 2010a, 2010b, 2015b). Readers interested in the complexity of these election systems may be interested in the work showing that Kemeny's election system (Kemeny, 1959; Kemeny and Snell, 1960)—see also Chapter 4—has a Θ_2^p-complete winner problem (Hemaspaandra et al., 2005) and a Θ_2^p-complete unique winner problem (Hemaspaandra et al., 2009). Complexity has also been broadly used as a tool with which to block attacks on elections, such as manipulation (Bartholdi et al., 1989a), bribery (Faliszewski et al., 2009b), and control (Bartholdi et al., 1992); see Chapters 6 and 7, and see also the surveys by Faliszewski et al. (2009d, 2010).

Θ_2^p, in its "logarithmic number of sequential queries to NP" definition, was first studied in the early 1980s, by Papadimitriou and Zachos (1983). Hemachandra (1989) showed that that definition yields the same class of sets as the unbounded-parallel definition. Θ_2^p-completeness can also apply to a range of problems quite different from the election problems discussed in this chapter. For example, determining when greedy algorithms well-approximate maximum independent sets is known to be Θ_2^p-complete (Hemaspaandra and Rothe, 1998). The most important tool for proving Θ_2^p-completeness is Lemma 5.3, due to Wagner (1987). Readers more generally interested in complexity will find an excellent, accessible introduction in the textbook of Bovet and Crescenzi (1993), and a more advanced and technique-based tour is provided by Hemaspaandra and Ogihara (2002).

The material presented in our heuristics section (Section 5.4) is based on the work of Homan and Hemaspaandra (2009) about using greedy heuristics for Dodgson elections. The independent work of McCabe-Dansted et al. (2008) studies the use of greedy heuristics for WeakDodgson elections. The two papers are based on the same central insight and obtain related results. However, there are some nontrivial differences between the two papers and their claims; these differences are discussed in detail in Section 1 of Homan and Hemaspaandra (2009).

Readers interested in the theory of parameterized computational complexity can find a systematic treatment in textbooks such as the ones by Downey and Fellows (1999) and Niedermeier (2006). Betzler et al. (2012) survey the progress in that field in relation to voting and cover both winner determination and other problems, for several voting rules.

The first approximation algorithms for voting rules (e.g., Kemeny) are implicit in the papers of Ailon et al. (2005), Coppersmith et al. (2006), and Kenyon-Mathieu and Schudy (2007). The material presented in Section 5.6 is from Caragiannis et al. (2012b, 2014b). Several interesting results have not been covered. For example, as an alternative to Tideman's simplified Dodgson rule, the maximin voting rule yields a Dodgson approximation with approximation ratio m^2 (Faliszewski et al., 2011b). Caragiannis et al. (2014b) discuss additional social-choice properties that are more difficult than monotonicity to achieve by good Dodgson approximations. Finally, observe that Section 5.6 does not contain any results related to Young's rule. Unfortunately, such good (polynomial-time) approximations are unlikely to exist. For example, unless P = NP, the StrongYoung score is not approximable within any factor by polynomial-time algorithms (Caragiannis et al., 2012b).

Acknowledgments

We are grateful to Markus Brill, Jörg Rothe, and the editors for helpful suggestions on an earlier version. Any remaining errors are the sole responsibility of the authors. We appreciatively acknowledge the support of grants NSF-CCF-0915792, NSF-CCF-1101452, and NSF-CCF-1101479.

CHAPTER 6

Barriers to Manipulation in Voting

Vincent Conitzer and Toby Walsh

6.1 Introduction

In many situations, voters may vote strategically. That is, they may declare preferences that are not their true ones, with the aim of obtaining a better outcome for themselves. The following example illustrates this.

Example 6.1. Consider an election with three alternatives, a, b, and c, and three voters, 1, 2, and 3. Suppose the rule used is plurality—an alternative gets a point each time it is ranked first by a voter, and the alternative with the most points wins—with ties broken toward alternatives earlier in the alphabet. Suppose voter 3 knows (or strongly suspects) that voter 1 will rank a first in her vote, and that voter 2 will rank b first. Voter 3's true preferences are $c \succ b \succ a$. If she votes truthfully, this will result in a three-way tie, broken in favor of a which is 3's least preferred alternative. If, instead, voter 3 ranks b first, then b will win instead. Hence, voter 3 has an incentive to cast a vote that does not reflect her true preferences.

This is often referred to as *manipulation* or *strategic voting*; we will use "manipulation" throughout.[1] Voting rules that are never manipulable are also referred to as *strategyproof*. We start by reviewing the Gibbard-Satterthwaite impossibility result (discussed also in Chapter 2), which states that with unrestricted preferences over three or more alternatives, only very unnatural rules are strategyproof. The main focus of the chapter is on exploring whether computational complexity can be an effective barrier to manipulation. That is, we may not be concerned about manipulation of a voting rule if it is computationally hard to discover how to manipulate it.

---

[1] Of course, one may disagree, at least in some circumstances, that strategic voting is really "manipulative" in the common sense of the word. We simply use "manipulation" as a technical term equivalent to strategically reporting one's preferences incorrectly. Nevertheless, we will give some reasons why it can be undesirable in what follows.

6.2 Gibbard-Satterthwaite and Its Implications

An important axiomatic result about the properties of voting rules is the Gibbard-Satterthwaite Theorem:

Theorem 6.2 (Gibbard, 1973; Satterthwaite, 1975). *Consider a (resolute)[2] voting rule that is defined for some number m of alternatives with m $\geqslant$ 3, with no restrictions on the preference domain. Then, this rule must be at least one of the following:*

1. dictatorial*: there exists a single fixed voter whose most-preferred alternative is chosen for every profile;*
2. imposing*: there is at least one alternative that does not win under any profile;*
3. manipulable *(i.e., not strategyproof).*

Properties 1 and 2 are not acceptable in most voting settings. Hence, under the conditions of the theorem, we are stuck with property 3: there will exist profiles such that at least one of the voters has an incentive to misreport her preferences.

Before discussing how we might address this, we should first discuss why manipulability is a significant problem. It may not seem so. For example, consider a plurality election with three alternatives. If one of the candidates[3] is considered to have a poor chance of winning the election (consider, for example, a third party in the United States), then everyone might vote for one of the other two candidates, in order to avoid wasting their votes. Is this a significant problem? Will it not simply result in the same winner that plurality-with-runoff (or STV)[4] would have chosen (if everyone had voted truthfully), and is that so bad? Additionally, there are those who argue that democrats should not be worried about manipulation (Dowding and Hees, 2008). There are, however, several potential downsides to such manipulation, including the following. (Formalizing all these downsides would go beyond the scope of this chapter, so we present them informally; we hope the reader would be able to formalize these concepts if needed.)

- *Bad equilibria.* In the above example, it is not at all clear that the resulting winner will be the same as the true plurality-with-runoff winner. All that is required is that voters *expect* the third alternative to have poor chances. It is possible that this alternative is actually very much liked across the electorate, but nobody is aware of this. Even more strikingly, it is possible that everyone *is* aware of this, and yet the alternative is expected to perform poorly—for example, because nobody is aware that others are aware of the alternative's popularity. Hence, an alternative that is very much liked, and perhaps would have won under just about any reasonable rule had everyone voted truthfully, may not win.

---

[2] Recall that a voting rule is *resolute* if it returns only a single alternative for every profile.

[3] We use "alternatives" and "candidates" interchangeably.

[4] Recall that under the plurality-with-runoff rule, the alternatives with the top two plurality scores proceed to a runoff round, and the one that is preferred to the other by more voters wins. Under STV (also known as Instant Runoff Voting), only the alternative with the lowest plurality score is eliminated in each round; it is then removed from all the votes, so that votes that ranked it first now rank another alternative first. This procedure is repeated until only one alternative—the winner—remains. (For an axiomatization of this rule, see Freeman et al. (2014).)

- *Lack of information.* Even if the bad equilibria described above are in fact avoided, we cannot be sure that this is the case, because we will never know exactly how popular that third alternative really was. This also interferes with the process of identifying more desirable alternatives in the next election.
- *Disenfranchisement of unsophisticated voters.* Voters who are less well informed may end up casting less effective votes than those who are well informed (for example, votes for the third alternative). Knowledge is power—but in many elections, this is not considered desirable.
- *Wasted effort.* Even if all agents manipulate to the same extent, still much effort, whether of the computational, information gathering, or communicational variety, is expended in figuring out how to manipulate well, and presumably this effort could have been more productively spent elsewhere. This can be seen as a type of tragedy of the commons; everyone would be better off if nobody spent effort on manipulation, but individually voters are still better off manipulating.

In the theory of *mechanism design*—which applies not only to the design of voting rules but also to that of auctions, matching mechanisms, and any other setting where a decision must be made based on the preferences of multiple strategic agents—there is generally a focus on designing mechanisms in which agents have no incentive to misreport their preferences. This is justified by a result known as the *revelation principle*. Stating it formally here would take us too far afield, but roughly speaking, it says that for any mechanism that results in a good equilibrium (in a game-theoretic sense), there exists another mechanism that results in the same outcomes, but in which agents report their preferences directly and they have no incentive to misreport them.[5] That is, at some level, we should be able to get incentives to report truthfully (i.e., use a truthful mechanism) for free. The revelation principle has been criticized on the basis that it implicitly assumes agents to be computationally unbounded, and indeed it has been shown that in some cases there exist mechanisms (that are not truthful) that will perform at least as well as any truthful mechanism, and strictly better if agents are unable to compute their strategically optimal actions (Conitzer and Sandholm, 2004).

Taken together, there seem to be several arguments for attempting to erect barriers to manipulation. However, the Gibbard-Satterthwaite Theorem poses a fundamental limit to such barriers. How can we get around it? We will first discuss some avenues that are not computational in nature. Then, we devote most of the chapter to computational avenues.

6.3 Noncomputational Avenues around Gibbard-Satterthwaite

One way of sidestepping the Gibbard-Satterthwaite Theorem is to restrict the domain of preferences. Probably the best-known such restriction is that of *single-peaked*

---

[5] It should be noted that the notion of not having any incentive to misreport here is weaker than strategyproofness. Rather, it is *Bayes-Nash equilibrium*, which means that an agent is best off telling the truth *in expectation* over a prior distribution over the other agents' preferences—but the agent might be better off misreporting for a particular realization of the reports. There is a version of the revelation principle that results in a strategyproof mechanism, but this requires the original mechanism to have dominant strategies for all agents.

preferences. Here, the assumption is that there exists an ordering $<$ of the alternatives—for example, political candidates may be ordered on the left-to-right political spectrum, or the alternatives may be tax rates, locations along a single road, and so on. Moreover, the following assumption is made: if voter i's most-preferred alternative is a, and $a < b < c$ or $c < b < a$, then $b \succ_i c$ (i prefers b to c). In this case (assuming, for simplicity, an odd number of voters) consider the *median voter rule*: order the voters by their most-preferred alternatives, and choose the median voter's most-preferred alternative. (Note that this rule does not require voters to specify preferences beyond their top choice.) This rule is strategyproof and always elects a Condorcet winner[6]. Of course, the usefulness of this result is limited by the fact that we cannot simply *make* the voters' preferences single-peaked when they are not. We could declare any vote that is not single-peaked invalid, but this just comes down to forcing voters to manipulate. For more discussion of single-peaked preferences, see Chapter 2.

Another possible avenue is to use *randomized* rules, which map every profile of votes to a probability distribution over the alternatives. For example, if we break the ties of a voting rule randomly, then we have a randomized voting rule. However, there are many other ways to obtain a randomized voting rule. The Gibbard-Satterthwaite Theorem above applies to deterministic rules only, so one might hope that randomized rules are not subject to such an impossibility. Unfortunately, as it turns out, there is a subsequent result by Gibbard that generalizes the Gibbard-Satterthwaite Theorem to randomized rules. To present this result, we first need to define strategyproofness in the context of randomized rules, and for that, we need to define preferences over lotteries over alternatives. For example, if a voter's preferences are $a \succ b \succ c$, should the voter prefer b, or a 50-50 lottery over a and c? Both could be reasonable. For example, if the voter has utilities 3, 2, and 0 for the alternatives respectively, b would give higher expected utility ($2 > 1.5$), but if the voter has utilities 3, 1, and 0, then the 50-50 lottery over a and c gives higher utility ($1.5 > 1$). Therefore, in this context, a quite conservative definition of strategyproofness is often used: a randomized rule is strategyproof if and only if for *every* utility function over the alternatives that is consistent with the voter's preferences over the (pure) alternatives, the voter maximizes her utility by reporting these true preferences (regardless of how the others vote).[7] We can now present Gibbard's result:

Theorem 6.3 (Gibbard, 1977). *If there are no restrictions on the preference domain, any strategyproof randomized rule is a randomization over a collection of the following types of rules:*

- unilateral rules, *under which at most one voter's vote affects the outcome;*
- duple rules, *under which there are at most two alternatives that have a possibility of winning (i.e., that win under some profile).*

The result makes it clear that randomization is not the answer to all our problems. A coin flip results in the discarding of all but one of the votes, or in the discarding of all

---

[6] Recall that an alternative a is a *Condorcet winner* if it wins all its pairwise contests. That is, for every other alternative b, more voters prefer a to b than vice versa.

[7] For studies of other ways of extending strategyproofness to randomized voting rules, see Aziz et al. (2013d) and Aziz et al. (2014c).

but two of the alternatives. In many situations, these rules will not be acceptable. Still, the result allows for some randomized rules that are perhaps not *entirely* unreasonable. For example, we can randomly choose a dictator (the theorem implies that, with three or more alternatives, this is in fact the only way to guarantee a Pareto-optimal outcome), or randomly choose two alternatives and have a majority election between them. Barberà (1979) gives some characterizations of randomized strategyproof rules as well; these are consistent with Gibbard's result above, but seem to cast the rules in a more positive light. More recently, Procaccia (2010) studied the extent to which strategyproof randomized rules can achieve formal approximations to the scores from common voting rules.

A final possible avenue is to use *irresolute* rules, which return a *set* of alternatives (possibly larger than one) and leave it at that. Can such a rule be strategyproof (and simultaneously reasonable)? To make sense of this question, we first need to say something about what an agent's preferences over sets of alternatives can be. Building on earlier results, Brandt (2011b) and Brandt and Brill (2011) have recently provided results that show that various irresolute rules are in fact strategyproof with respect to various extensions of preferences to sets of alternatives.[8] While these positive results are encouraging, they do face a major limitation. In many voting settings, in the end, we require a single winning alternative. If we add any procedure for going from the winning set of alternatives to a single one— for example, choosing the lexicographically first alternative in the set—then the combination of the irresolute rule and the subsequent procedure is a resolute rule, and we run right back into the Gibbard-Satterthwaite impossibility result. Similarly, if we randomly choose from the winning set, we run into the impossibility results for randomized rules. Thus, for these positive results to apply, the procedure for going from the selected set of alternatives to a single alternative fundamentally needs to remain unspecified, and moreover the voters need to respond to this lack of information in a particular way. For more detail, see Chapter 3.

6.4 Computational Hardness as a Barrier to Manipulation

Another potential barrier to manipulation is computational hardness. Even if we cannot prevent a voting rule from being manipulable in principle, this may not be a significant concern as long as determining how to manipulate it is computationally prohibitive.

The argument that the complexity of computing a manipulation might be a barrier to strategic voting was first put forward in an influential paper by Bartholdi et al. (1989a). A whole subfield of social choice has since grown from this proposal, studying the computational complexity of manipulating different voting rules under several different assumptions (e.g., Conitzer et al., 2007). For two recent surveys, see Faliszewski et al. (2010) and Faliszewski and Procaccia (2010); Brandt et al. (2013a) also discuss the topic at some length. In the remainder of this section, we discuss this line of work in more detail.

---

[8] Other extensions lead to negative results (Duggan and Schwartz, 2000). For more on strategyproofness and other notions of monotonicity in this context, see Sanver and Zwicker (2012) and the references cited in that work.

6.4.1 The Basic Variant

The original paper (Bartholdi et al., 1989a) defined a basic model which has since been investigated extensively. We suppose all but one voter, the *manipulator*, have voted and that these votes and the rule to be used are known to the manipulator. We ask whether it is possible for the manipulator to ensure that a given alternative wins. More formally, we can define the following decision problem.

Manipulation Problem

> **Given.** A profile of votes Π cast by everyone but the manipulator, and a preferred alternative a.
> **Question.** Is there a vote that the manipulator can cast so that a wins?

This problem is typically in NP as a simple witness is a vote that ensures a wins. Supposing that the voting rule is polynomial to execute,[9] this witness can be checked in polynomial time. There is also a *destructive* variant of this question, where we ask if it is possible for the manipulator to cast a vote so that a given alternative does *not* win. Note that these problems correspond exactly to the predicament of voter 3 in Example 6.1, with the exception that the question is now whether she can make a particular alternative win. One may wonder if a more natural problem would be to determine the *best* (according to her own true preferences) alternative that she can make win. This problem is effectively equivalent; to answer it, it is sufficient to evaluate for each of the alternatives in turn whether she can make it win (and, conversely, it is necessary to at least evaluate whether she can make her most-preferred alternative win).

Of course, when the rule is plurality, this problem is computationally trivial: to see if you can make alternative a win, it suffices to see what would happen if you submitted a vote that ranks a first. Indeed, for many rules, the problem is in P. Bartholdi et al. (1989a) provided an algorithm that solves the problem in polynomial time for many voting rules.

Definition 6.1. Say that a voting rule satisfies the *BTT conditions* if

1. it can be run in polynomial time,
2. for every profile Π and every alternative a, the rule assigns a score $S(\Pi, a)$ to a,
3. for every profile Π, the alternative with the maximum score wins,[10] and
4. the following monotonicity condition holds: for any Π, Π', for any alternative a, if for each voter i we have that $\{b : a \succ_i b\} \subseteq \{b : a \succ'_i b\}$, then $S(\Pi, a) \leqslant S(\Pi', a)$. (That is, if we modify a vote in a way that does not rank anyone ahead of a that was previously ranked behind a, then a's score cannot have decreased.)

Theorem 6.4 (Bartholdi et al., 1989a). *The manipulation problem can be solved in polynomial time for any rule satisfying the BTT conditions.*

The algorithm for constructing a manipulator vote that successfully makes alternative a win (if any such vote exists) is quite straightforward. Rank a first. For the next

---

[9] See earlier chapters in the book for discussion of rules for which this is not the case.
[10] Assume, say, a fixed tie-breaking order.

position in the vote, find some remaining alternative b that can be ranked there so that a still wins. (To check this, complete the rest of the vote arbitrarily, and calculate b's score; by the monotonicity condition above, a and b's scores will not depend on how the rest of the vote is completed. This is because if we change the relative ordering of the remaining alternatives, this is a modification that satisfies the condition, and so cannot decrease a or b's score; it can also not increase these scores, because then the reverse modification would decrease it.) If no such alternative can be found, declare failure; if the vote is completed, declare success; otherwise, repeat for the next position. This algorithm applies not only to positional scoring rules such as plurality and Borda, but also to rules such as Copeland and maximin.[11]

Bartholdi et al. (1989a) were also the first to show that the problem is NP-hard for some rules. Specifically, they showed NP-hardness for manipulating the second-order Copeland rule, under which an alternative's score is the sum of the Copeland scores of the alternatives that it defeats. (Note that this way of scoring violates the third condition above: if in some vote, we change the relative ordering of the alternatives ranked (say) behind a only, this can affect those alternatives' Copeland scores, and thereby a's second-order Copeland score.) They also showed NP-hardness of manipulation for the (first-order) Copeland rule when ties are broken by the second-order Copeland rule; we will say more about the importance of the tie-breaking procedure later in this chapter. Shortly after, Bartholdi and Orlin (1991) proved that the better-known STV rule is NP-hard to manipulate in this sense. The problem has been shown to be NP-hard for several other rules more recently, including ranked pairs (Xia et al., 2009), and Nanson and Baldwin's rules (Narodytska et al., 2011). The ranked pairs rule orders the pairwise outcomes by the size of the victory. It then constructs a total ordering over alternatives by taking these pairs in order and fixing the order unless this contradicts previous decisions. The top of the order constructed in this way is the overall winner. Nanson and Baldwin's rules are elimination versions of Borda voting. Nanson's rule repeatedly eliminates all alternatives with less than the average Borda score. Baldwin's rule, on the other hand, successively eliminates the alternative with the lowest Borda score. Table 6.1 gives a representative sample of complexity results for this manipulation problem, as well as for some related manipulation problems discussed in the next subsections.

6.4.2 Coalitions of Manipulators

So far, we have considered the computational complexity of just *one* voter trying to manipulate the election. In practice, multiple voters may collude to manipulate the result. Indeed, it is often the case that we need a coalition of manipulators to be able to change the result.

---

[11] Recall that the Borda rule gives an alternative $m - 1$ points each time it is ranked first, $m - 2$ points each time it is ranked second, ..., and 0 points each time it is ranked last. More generally, a positional scoring rule associates a score with each rank, and the alternative with the highest score wins. Under the Copeland rule, an alternative a gets a point for each other alternative b such that more votes rank a ahead of b than vice versa (and some fraction of a point if the number of votes ranking a ahead of b is the same as vice versa). Finally, under the maximin rule, we find, for each alternative a, the alternative b that minimizes the number of votes that rank a ahead of b (the worst pairwise outcome for a); this number is a's score, and the alternative with the maximum score wins.

Table 6.1. *Computational complexity of deciding the manipulation problem with a small number of voters (unweighted votes) or a coalition of voters (weighted votes), for various voting rules*

	unweighted votes constructive manipulation		weighted votes constructive				destructive		
# alternatives			2	3	4	≥5	2	3	≥4
# manipulators	1	≥2							
plurality	P	P	P	P	P	P	P	P	P
plurality with runoff	P	P	P	NP-c	NP-c	NP-c	P	NP-c	NP-c
veto	P	P	P	NP-c	NP-c	NP-c	P	P	P
cup	P	P	P	P	P	P	P	P	P
Copeland	P	P	P	P	NP-c	NP-c	P	P	P
Borda	P	NP-c	P	NP-c	NP-c	NP-c	P	P	P
Nanson	NP-c	NP-c	P	P	NP-c	NP-c	P	P	NP-c
Baldwin	NP-c	NP-c	P	NP-c	NP-c	NP-c	P	NP-c	NP-c
Black	P	NP-c	P	NP-c	NP-c	NP-c	P	P	P
STV	NP-c	NP-c	P	NP-c	NP-c	NP-c	P	NP-c	NP-c
maximin	P	NP-c	P	P	NP-c	NP-c	P	P	P
Bucklin	P	P	P	NP-c	NP-c	NP-c	P	P	P
fallback	P	P	P	P	P	P	P	P	P
ranked pairs	NP-c	NP-c	P	P	P	NP-c	P	P	?
Schulze	P	P	P	P	P	P	P	P	P

Note: P means that the problem is polynomial, NP-c that the problem is NP-complete. For example, constructive manipulation of the veto rule is polynomial for unweighted votes or for weighted votes with a coalition of 2 manipulators, but NP-hard for 3 or more manipulators. On the other hand, destructive manipulation of the veto rule is polynomial for weighted votes with a coalition of 2 or more manipulators. We consider the variant of Copeland where an alternative gets 1 point if it defeats an opponent, 0.5 points for a draw, and 0 if it loses. "?" indicates that the computational complexity is open at the time of writing this chapter. For references, see: Faliszewski et al. (2008) and Conitzer et al. (2007) for Copeland; Davies et al. (2011), Conitzer et al. (2007), and Betzler et al. (2011) for Borda; Narodytska et al. (2011) and Davies et al. (2014) for Nanson and Baldwin; Narodytska and Walsh (2013) for Black; Xia et al. (2009) for maximin; Xia et al. (2009) and Faliszewski et al. (2014) for Bucklin; Faliszewski et al. (2014) for fallback; Xia et al. (2009) and Hemaspaandra et al. (2014c) for ranked pairs; Parkes and Xia (2012) and Gaspers et al. (2013) for Schulze; and Conitzer et al. (2007) for other results or references to them.

Coalitional Manipulation Problem

Given. A profile of votes Π cast by everyone but the manipulators, a number of manipulators, and a preferred alternative a.

Question. Is there a way for the manipulators to cast their votes so that a wins?

Again, it can be debated if this should be called "manipulation" because the manipulators might not have to vote strategically to ensure their preferred alternative wins. However, as has become common in the literature, we will refer to this problem as coalitional manipulation. Coordinating even a small coalition of voters introduces fresh computational challenges. For example, with the Borda rule, a simple greedy procedure will compute an optimal strategic vote for one voter, but it is NP-hard to compute how two voters together can manipulate the result (Davies et al., 2011; Betzler et al., 2011). Similar results hold for Copeland voting (the first rule for which it was shown that the problem is easy with one manipulator but hard with two) (Faliszewski et al., 2008), other scoring rules (Xia et al., 2010b), maximin (Xia et al., 2009), and Black's rule

(Narodytska and Walsh, 2013). Intriguingly, in all these cases, it requires only two manipulators to make manipulation hard. Black's rule is the voting rule that elects the Condorcet winner if it exists, and otherwise the Borda winner.

One criticism that can be made about the complexity results considered so far is that they require the number of alternatives to grow in an unbounded fashion. If the number of alternatives is held constant, then a single manipulator would have only a constant number ($m!$) of votes to consider. Even for a coalition of n' manipulators, if the rule is anonymous, then the total number of joint votes for the coalition is the number of ways n' indistinguishable balls (voters) can be placed into $m!$ urns (possible votes), which is $\binom{n'+m!-1}{m!-1}$, which is polynomial in n'. Hence, as long as there is a polynomial-time algorithm for executing the rule, a manipulation (if one exists) can be computed in polynomial time when the number of alternatives is constant. However, this argument fundamentally relies on the voters being indistinguishable, which is not the case when voters have weights.

6.4.3 Weighted Votes

Weighted votes occur in a number of real-world settings (e.g., shareholder elections and various parliaments). Weights are typically integers and a vote of weight k can be seen as k identical and unweighted votes. It turns out that with weighted votes, we encounter complexity in manipulation problems even with a small number of alternatives. We consider the following decision problem for weighted votes.

Coalitional Weighted Manipulation Problem

> **Given.** A profile of weighted votes Π cast by everyone but a coalition of manipulators, a weight for each of the manipulators, and a preferred alternative a.
> **Question.** Is there a way for the manipulators to cast their votes so that a wins?

There is again a destructive variant of this problem where the coalition wants a given alternative not to win.

With two alternatives, most common voting rules degenerate to majority voting. In addition, by May's Theorem, this is the only voting rule over two alternatives that is anonymous, neutral, and positively responsive. With majority voting, the manipulators' best action even when their votes are weighted is always to vote for the alternative that they wish to win. With three or more alternatives, however, computing a manipulation can be computationally hard, provided we have a coalition of manipulators (whose size is allowed to increase) and votes that are weighted. For example, computing how to manipulate the veto (aka. antiplurality) rule[12] is polynomial with unweighted votes but NP-complete with weighted votes and just 3 alternatives (Conitzer et al., 2007). Some intuition for this result is as follows. The manipulators could find themselves in the situation where, after counting the nonmanipulators' votes, two alternatives (b and c)

---

[12] Recall that under the veto rule, the winner is the alternative that is ranked last in the fewest votes. Equivalently, it is the positional scoring rule in which the bottom rank receives 0 points and all other ranks receive 1 point.

are tied for the lead (i.e., they have been vetoed the least), but the third alternative (a) is the one that the manipulators want to win. Clearly the manipulators do not want to veto a. To make a win, however, they may need to divide their total veto weight very evenly between b and c, so that a comes out just barely ahead of each of them. Thus, the manipulators face the problem of partitioning a set of integers (their weights) into two subsets (vetoing b or vetoing c) so that each subset has the same weight—and this is an NP-complete problem. This intuition can be turned into a formal NP-hardness reduction as follows.

Theorem 6.5. *The coalitional weighted manipulation problem is NP-complete under the veto rule, even with only three alternatives.*

Proof. The problem is in NP because a profile of votes for the manipulators will serve as a certificate (because the veto rule is computationally easy to execute). To prove NP-hardness, we reduce from the PARTITION problem, in which we are given a set of integers $w_1, \ldots, w_{n'}$ with $\sum_{i=1}^{n'} w_i = W$ (where W is even) and are asked whether there exists a subset $S \subseteq \{1, \ldots, n'\}$ such that $\sum_{i \in S} w_i = W/2$. We reduce this problem to the coalitional weighted manipulation problem under the veto rule with three alternatives, as follows. Let a, b, and c be the alternatives, where a is the alternative that the manipulators would like to win. Create one nonmanipulator vote with weight $W - 1$ that ranks a last. Furthermore, for each $i \in \{1, \ldots, n'\}$, create a manipulator (the ith manipulator) with weight $2w_i$.

We now show that the manipulators can succeed in this instance if and only if the original partition instance has a solution. If the partition instance has a solution S, then let the manipulators in S rank b last, and let the ones outside S rank c last. Then, a wins, appearing in last place only for $W - 1$ of the weight, whereas b and c each appear in last place for $\sum_{i \in S} 2w_i = 2W/2 = W$ of the weight.

Now suppose that the partition instance has no solution. This implies that for each subset $S \subseteq \{1, \ldots, n'\}$, either $\sum_{i \in S} w_i \leqslant W/2 - 1$ or $\sum_{i \notin S} w_i \leqslant W/2 - 1$ (due to the integrality of the w_i and $W/2$). Then, for any profile of votes for the manipulators, let S be the set of manipulators that rank b last. Then, we have either $\sum_{i \in S} 2w_i \leqslant W - 2 < W - 1$, so that b ranks ahead of a, or $\sum_{i \notin S} 2w_i \leqslant W - 2 < W - 1$, so that c ranks ahead of a. So the manipulators cannot make a win. $\square$

Note that the reduction is set up in such a way that a cannot end up tied for the win, so it does not matter how ties are handled. On the other hand, note that this is only a weak NP-hardness result because the reduction is from PARTITION. Indeed, we can compute a manipulation for a coalition of voters using dynamic programming in pseudopolynomial time—that is, in polynomial time when the weights are represented in unary (or equivalently, when the weights are small). Similar (though often more involved) reductions can be given for many other rules. In fact, a dichotomy result holds for positional scoring rules in general: every scoring rule that is not isomorphic to plurality is NP-hard to manipulate with three or more alternatives and weighted votes (Hemaspaandra and Hemaspaandra, 2007; Procaccia and Rosenschein, 2007b; Conitzer et al., 2007).

6.4.4 Tie-Breaking

For complexity-of-manipulation results like these, it is important to specify precisely how ties are broken. This perhaps should not be surprising, because a single manipulator can only change the result if the election is close to being tied. A common assumption is that we break ties in favor of the manipulator. That is, we suppose that the preferred alternative wins if it is among the set of co-winners. This is usually justified on the grounds that if ties are broken, say, at random, then this corresponds to increasing the probability that the given alternative wins. However, the choice of the tie-breaking procedure is not a minor detail. It can actually change the computational complexity of computing a manipulation. We can get different results if we break ties against the manipulator (that is, we suppose that the manipulator's preferred alternative wins only if it is the unique winner).

The importance of tie-breaking can be seen in the earliest literature on computational social choice. Recall that Bartholdi et al. (1989a) proved that a single agent can manipulate the result of a Copeland election (with "straightforward" tie-breaking schemes) in polynomial time using their greedy algorithm, but when the second-order tie-breaking rule is added manipulation becomes NP-hard.

Faliszewski et al. (2008) proved that for Copeland voting, changing the way that pairwise ties (two alternatives that are each ranked above the other equally often) are handled can change the computational complexity of manipulation. For example, with weighted votes and three alternatives, if ties result in a score of 0, then it is NP-hard for a coalition to compute a manipulation that makes a given alternative the unique winner of the election, but this problem becomes solvable in polynomial time if ties are given any other score. (Note that this is an "internal" form of tie-breaking, rather than tie-breaking between multiple winners at the end of applying an irresolute rule.) Also, if instead the manipulators seek to make that alternative just *one* of the winners, then the problem is solvable in polynomial time when a tie results in a score of 1, but NP-hard if ties are given any other score.

To study tie-breaking at random in more detail, Obraztsova et al. (2011) set up a model where the manipulators have utilities over the alternatives and the goal is to increase the expected utility of the result. *All* scoring rules, as well as Bucklin and plurality with runoff, can be manipulated in polynomial time in such a situation. On the other hand, Copeland, maximin, STV and ranked pairs are NP-hard to manipulate in this case (Obraztsova and Elkind, 2011).

Another method to deal with ties is to select a vote at random and select the highest-ranked of the tied alternatives from this vote (Tideman, 1987).[13] Aziz et al. (2013f) show that, in general, there is no connection between the complexity of computing a manipulating vote when tie-breaking with a random alternative or with a random vote. However, for common rules like k-approval, Borda, and Bucklin, the computational complexity increases from polynomial to NP-hard when tie-breaking with a random vote rather than at random among the co-winners. For other rules like plurality, veto, and plurality with runoff, it remains possible to compute a manipulating vote in polynomial

---

[13] For more on tiebreaking schemes in computational social choice, see Freeman et al. (2015).

time. Finally, for rules like STV, computing a manipulation is NP-hard irrespective of the tie-breaking method as it is possible to prove NP-hardness with a class of elections in which there are never any ties.

6.4.5 Incomplete Information

So far, we have assumed that the manipulator has complete knowledge of the other votes. This is a strong assumption that, extreme circumstances aside, is at best a rough approximation of the truth. It is often defended on the grounds that if it is NP-hard to compute a manipulation with complete information then it must remain so when we have probabilistic information about the nonmanipulators' votes (Conitzer et al., 2007). There has, however, been some work relaxing this assumption. For example, Conitzer et al. (2011a) consider the complexity of computing manipulations given only partial information about the nonmanipulators' votes. Given such partial information, they consider whether the manipulator has a *dominating* nontruthful vote that makes the winner always at least as preferable as, and sometimes more preferable than, the alternative that would win if the manipulator voted sincerely. This was further studied by Reijngoud and Endriss (2012).

6.4.6 Building in Hardness

Once we accept hardness of manipulation as a desirable property of voting rules, it becomes an interesting question whether we can engineer voting rules to be more computationally complex to manipulate. One general construction is to "hybridize" together two or more existing voting rules. For example, we might add one elimination pre-round to the election, in which alternatives are paired off and only the one preferred by more voters goes through (Conitzer and Sandholm, 2003). This generates a new voting rule that is often computationally hard to manipulate. In fact, the problem of computing a manipulation can now move to complexity classes higher than NP depending on when the schedule of the pre-round is announced. Such hybrid voting rules also inherit some (but not all) of the properties of the voting rules from which they are constructed. For example, if the initial rule is Condorcet consistent, then adding a pre-round preserves Condorcet consistency.

Other types of voting rules can be hybridized together. For example, we can construct a hybrid of the Borda and Copeland rules in which we run two rounds of Borda, eliminating the lowest-scoring alternative each time, and then apply the Copeland rule to the remaining alternatives. Such hybrids are often resistant to manipulation. For example, many hybrids of STV and of Borda are NP-hard to manipulate (Elkind and Lipmaa, 2005). More generally, voting rules that have multiple stages successively eliminating alternatives tend to be more computationally difficult to manipulate than one-stage rules (Coleman and Teague, 2007; Narodytska et al., 2011; Davies et al., 2012; Walsh and Xia, 2012).

Another way to combine together two or more voting rules is to use some aspect of the particular election (the votes, or the names of the alternatives) to pick which voting rule is used to compute the winner. For example, suppose we have a list of k different voting rules. If all the alternatives' names (viewed as natural numbers) are congruent, modulo k, to i then we use the ith voting rule, otherwise we use the default last rule. Such a form of hybridization gives elections which are often computationally difficult to manipulate (Hemaspaandra et al., 2009). Another possibility is to just leave it ambiguous which of the voting rules will be used; Elkind and Erdélyi (2012) have studied how hard it is for the manipulators to select their votes so that they succeed for any of a given set of rules. Finally, another possibility is that we have a runoff between the winners of two voting rules. This also often makes manipulations more difficult to compute (Narodytska et al., 2012).

6.5 Can Manipulation Be Hard Most of the Time?

NP-hardness is a worst-case notion. For NP-hard manipulation problems, supposing $P \neq NP$, any manipulation algorithm will face *some* families of instances on which it does not scale polynomially. But it is not at all clear that these are the instances that manipulators would need to solve in practice. They may be pathological. Hence, it is possible that these NP-hardness results lull us into a false sense of security regarding the manipulability of our voting rules. A much better type of result would be that the manipulation problem is *usually* hard. Is such a result feasible, and what exactly does "usually" mean here? To investigate this, it is helpful to first consider some actual manipulation algorithms for voting rules that are NP-hard to manipulate.

6.5.1 Some Algorithms for NP-Hard Manipulation Problems

Assuming $P \neq NP$, a manipulation algorithm for a voting rule that is NP-hard to manipulate can only hope to either (1) succeed on all instances and require more than polynomial time in the worst case, but still scale "reasonably," particularly on "typical" instances; or (2) run in polynomial time and succeed on many, but not all, instances.

For instance, under the STV rule, Coleman and Teague (2007) give a simple enumerative method for a coalition of k unweighted voters to compute a manipulation, which runs in $O(m!(n + mk))$ time (where n is the number of voters voting and m is the number of alternatives). For a single manipulator, Conitzer et al. (2007) give an $O(n1.62^m)$ time recursive algorithm to compute the set of alternatives that can win an STV election.

Such algorithms have been shown to perform well in practice. For example, Coleman and Teague (2007) showed experimentally that only a small coalition is needed to change the elimination order of the STV rule in many cases. As a second example, Walsh (2010) showed that the Conitzer et al. (2007) algorithm could often quickly compute manipulations of the STV rule even with hundreds of alternatives. Walsh (2009, 2011b) also empirically studied the computational cost of manipulating the veto rule by a coalition of weighted voters. Except in rather artificial and "hung" elections, it was easy to find manipulations or prove that none exist.

An algorithm designed for the manipulation of one specific rule, however effective it may be, may just be exploiting an idiosyncratic property of that particular rule. It may well be the case that other desirable rules do not have this property and are, in fact, "usually" hard to manipulate. One approach to addressing this criticism is to design manipulation algorithms that are not specific to one voting rule. Such algorithms, to the extent that they avoid exhaustive search, are heuristic in nature and do not always succeed. This category of algorithms includes some of the earliest work providing technical results that cast doubt on whether worst-case hardness of manipulation has any significant implications for the "typical" case. Procaccia and Rosenschein (2007b) provide a greedy algorithm for rules based on a score, in which the manipulators create their votes in sequence, at each point ranking their preferred alternative first and the remaining alternatives in increasing order of their current score. Conitzer and Sandholm (2006) provide an algorithm that attempts to find two possible winners, by first choosing an arbitrary vote profile for the manipulators to find one possible winner a_1, and then, for every remaining alternative a, choosing a vote profile for the manipulators where everyone ranks a first and a_1 last. It is argued (and supported by simulations) that usually, if the manipulators are pivotal (have a possibility of changing the outcome of the election) at all, then they can only make two alternatives win. For instances where this is so, and where the voting rule satisfies a weak monotonicity property, the algorithm can be proved to find all alternatives that the manipulators can make win.

All these empirical results suggest that we need to treat results about the NP-hardness of manipulation with some care. Voters may still be able to compute a manipulation successfully using rather simple and direct methods. The theoretically inclined reader, however, may feel dissatisfied with these types of results. Beyond getting intuition from simulations, can we actually *prove* that voting rules remain vulnerable to manipulation in the typical case? In what follows we discuss some of the approaches that researchers have taken to answer this question in the affirmative.

6.5.2 Approximation Methods

For almost all voting rules, we can easily make any alternative win provided we have enough manipulators; the hardness results are merely due to a limited supply of manipulators. With this in mind, we can consider manipulation as an optimization problem, where we try to minimize the number of manipulators required to achieve a given outcome. One option is to use approximation methods to tackle such optimization problems.[14]

For example, Zuckerman et al. (2009) consider a variant of the algorithm by Procaccia and Rosenschein (2007b) (presented above) to compute manipulations of the Borda rule. Again, the algorithm constructs the vote of each manipulator in turn. The alternative that the manipulators wish to win is put in first place, and the remaining alternatives are placed in the manipulator's vote in increasing order of their current Borda scores. The method continues constructing manipulating votes until the desired alternative wins. A rather long and intricate argument shows that this method requires at most one additional manipulator relative to the optimal solution. Based on a connection to a scheduling problem, Xia et al. (2010b) provide an algorithm that works

---

[14] Another notion of approximation in manipulation problems is to approximately maximize an alternative's increase in score, given a fixed set of manipulators (Brelsford et al., 2008). Theorem 4 in that paper relates that notion of approximability to the one discussed here.

for all positional scoring rules, though it may require as many as $m - 2$ additional manipulators.

6.5.3 Frequency of Manipulability

Again, whether the manipulators can achieve the result they want depends in large part on their number. We may then wonder whether, given an instance of the coalitional manipulation problem, we can quickly eyeball whether the manipulators are likely to be successful, purely based on the size of their coalition relative to the size of the electorate. It turns out that this is indeed the case. Building on earlier work by Procaccia and Rosenschein (2007a),[15] Xia and Conitzer (2008a) showed that for an extremely large class[16] of voting rules called *generalized scoring rules*, under some assumptions on the distribution of votes, if the number of manipulators is $O(n^p)$ for $p < 1/2$, the probability that a random profile is manipulable goes to zero; whereas if it is $\Omega(n^p)$ for $p > 1/2$, it goes to one. This leaves the knife-edge case of $p = 1/2$, which has been studied both experimentally (Walsh, 2009) and analytically (Mossel et al., 2013).

Another line of research along these lines proves *quantitative* versions of the Gibbard-Satterthwaite impossibility result. Here, the idea is not to be satisfied with a statement that says that somewhere in the space of all possible profiles, there exists a manipulable one; rather, these results state that, under Gibbard-Satterthwaite-like conditions, a randomly chosen profile has a significant probability of being manipulable. After a sequence of earlier partial results along this line (Friedgut et al., 2008; Dobzinski and Procaccia, 2008; Xia and Conitzer, 2008b; Isaksson et al., 2012), Mossel and Rácz (2012) seem to have achieved the gold standard. They prove that under a voting rule with 3 or more alternatives that is ϵ-far away from the set of nonmanipulable rules,[17] a randomly chosen profile has a probability of being manipulable that is at least inverse polynomial in n, m, and $1/\epsilon$.

6.5.4 Restricted Preferences

Finally, it is important to realize that it is unrealistic to assume that profiles of votes are drawn uniformly at random; generally, the voters' preferences over the alternatives are quite structured. For example, the profile may be single-peaked. How does this affect the complexity of the manipulation problem? Several papers have addressed this question, showing that this restriction often, but not always, makes the manipulation problem easier (Walsh, 2007; Faliszewski et al., 2009e; Brandt et al., 2010a). While it may seem odd in this context to focus on single-peaked preferences—for which, after all, a desirable strategyproof voting rule is available in the form of the median voter rule[18]—these results nevertheless provide important insight into how restricting the space of profiles can cause complexity barriers to manipulation to fall apart.

---

[15] See also Slinko (2004) and Pritchard and Wilson (2009).

[16] Xia and Conitzer (2009) characterize this class as those rules that are anonymous and *finitely locally consistent*.

[17] Here, the distance between two rules is the fraction of inputs on which they differ.

[18] Moreover, under some assumptions on strategic behavior by the voters and/or candidates, even rules such as plurality and STV end up returning the same winner as the median voter rule when preferences are single-peaked (Brill and Conitzer, 2015).

6.6 Fully Game-Theoretic Models

The computational problems studied in this chapter so far all make some major simplifying assumptions. In most cases it is assumed that the votes of the other voters are known exactly; even when this is not assumed, the other voters are not modeled as strategic agents. If we do model them this way, this leads us into fully game-theoretic models, and indeed these have received some attention in the computational social choice community.

To make sense of this, a first issue that needs to be addressed is the staggering multiplicity of equilibria in most voting scenarios.[19] Often, most profiles will not allow any single individual to change the outcome, and all of these profiles are Nash equilibria as an immediate consequence. Many of these profiles will have voters vote in ways that make no sense with respect to their true preferences. Based on this observation, we may be able to rule out many of these equilibria—for example, we might require voters not to play weakly dominated strategies.[20] However, other issues are more difficult to address. For example, in a plurality election, any two of the alternatives might be cast in a "front-runner" role, resulting in an equilibrium where everyone votes for one of these two, because to do otherwise would be to waste one's vote. This also illustrates that there will be many alternatives that win in *some* equilibrium.[21]

As it turns out, these issues are avoided when the voters, instead of voting simultaneously, vote in sequence, so that each voter has full knowledge of all the previous votes. If we additionally assume that all the preferences are common knowledge (as well as the order in which the voters vote, and the voting rule used), and all preferences are strict, then there is a unique alternative that wins in subgame-perfect Nash equilibrium.[22] This can be proved by induction on the number of voters, roughly as follows. Suppose it is true for $n - 1$ voters. Then, in the case of n voters, consider the first voter. For every vote that she might cast, she can, by the induction assumption, determine the alternative that will win in equilibrium from that point on. From all these options, she will then choose the one that ranks highest in her own preferences. (There may be multiple votes for the first voter that achieve this, so the equilibrium *votes* are not unique.) This raises several interesting questions. First of all, will this result in good outcomes? Of course, it is tricky to give a general definition of what "good" means in this context. As it turns out, though, for many rules, there exist profiles of preferences that, in equilibrium, result in outcomes that are quite unambiguously bad. Specifically, Xia and Conitzer (2010c) show that this is the case for rules with a low *domination index*, which indicates how many more than half of the voters are needed

---

[19] Recall that, given the voters' true preferences, a *Nash equilibrium* consists of a profile of votes such that no individual voter can obtain an outcome she prefers to the current one by unilaterally changing her vote.

[20] Recall that one strategy *weakly dominates* another if the former always delivers at least as good a result for the agent, and in some cases a strictly better one.

[21] A recent article investigates what game structures can emerge when multiple voters are considering strategically changing their votes (Elkind et al., 2014b).

[22] Recall that in a *subgame-perfect* Nash equilibrium, the strategies constitute a Nash equilibrium in every subgame. In our case, when a subset of the voters has cast specific votes, the remainder of the voting game constitutes a subgame.

to force the outcome.[23] Some counterintuitive examples for the plurality rule are also given by Desmedt and Elkind (2010).

Another question is whether these equilibria can be efficiently computed. A natural approach is to use a dynamic programming algorithm corresponding to the backward induction process in game theory, as follows. First compute what the last voter would do for every situation in which she might be placed; then compute what the second-to-last voter would do for every situation in which she might be placed (which is now possible because it is known at this point how the last voter would respond to any vote that the second-to-last voter might cast); and so on. This algorithm is correct, but its runtime depends on the number of possible "situations." What is a "situation," anyway? One might interpret this as the entire partial profile of votes cast so far (i.e., the node in the extensive form of the game), but this will scale very poorly. It is also overkill: for example, for a positional scoring rule, all that is needed is the total scores of the alternatives so far, not the precise votes that led to this score. More generally, the amount of information necessary to summarize the votes of a subelectorate is known as the *compilation complexity* of a voting rule (Chevaleyre et al., 2009; Xia and Conitzer, 2010b). Xia and Conitzer (2010c) exploit the connection to this concept to obtain algorithms for solving the game that, while still exponential, scale much better than the naïve approach. (Desmedt and Elkind (2010) give a similar algorithm for plurality.) Intriguingly, from simulations performed by Xia and Conitzer (2010c), the game-theoretic outcomes on random profiles do not look as bad as the worst-case results above might suggest. The exact complexity of the computational problem is not known; it may be PSPACE-complete.

Still, is there nothing substantial that we can say about the equilibria of voting games in which voters vote simultaneously? In fact, we can, if we are willing to make some further assumptions about voters' preferences in voting. One natural assumption is that voters are *truth-biased* (Meir et al., 2010). This can be interpreted as follows: voters derive most of their utility from the outcome of the election, but they also derive a small amount of utility from voting truthfully. Hence, if it makes no difference to the outcome, voters slightly prefer to tell the truth. Thompson et al. (2013) show experimentally that for the plurality rule this dramatically reduces the set of equilibria. (They also study Bayes-Nash equilibria of games in which voters are not sure about each other's preferences.) Obraztsova et al. (2013) study this model from a theoretical perspective, again under the plurality rule.[24] Another direction is to substitute the slight preference for voting truthfully with a slight preference for *abstaining* (Desmedt and Elkind, 2010). Yet another direction is to add *dynamics* where voters start at some initial profile and iteratively update their vote to make themselves better off, until this process converges (Meir et al., 2010; Lev and Rosenschein, 2012; Reyhani and Wilson, 2012; Rabinovich et al., 2014).

---

[23] A similar negative result is given by Xia et al. (2011a) in a different context, where multiple related binary decisions must be made and these issues are voted on in sequence (but with all the voters voting at the same time on each issue). For more on voting in such combinatorial domains, please see Chapter 9.

[24] They also consider *strong* Nash equilibria, in which no *subset* of the agents can deviate in a way that makes them all better off, and draw a connection to Condorcet winners. More about the relationship between strong equilibrium and Condorcet winners can be found in papers by Sertel and Sanver (2004), Messner and Polborn (2007), and Brill and Conitzer (2015).

The above approaches all rely on *noncooperative* game theory. However, as we have already seen, it is natural to think about *coalitions* of voters coordinating their actions. Doing so in a game-theoretic framework is tricky, because the voters in a coalition may not all have the same preferences. This leads us to *cooperative* (or *coalitional*) game theory. A common solution concept there is that of the *core*, which is the set of all outcomes such that no coalition of agents could break off in a way that would make all of its members happier. In the context of elections, when a group of agents deviates, how happy this makes them depends on how the agents outside of the coalition end up voting. For example, will the agents outside the coalition be able to react to the votes of the coalition, or vice versa? These modeling choices correspond to the notions of the α-core and the β-core. The computational complexity of these concepts in the context of elections is studied by Zuckerman et al. (2011). Bachrach et al. (2011) study the complexity of problems in cooperative game theory models of manipulation where payments are possible.

6.6.1 Other Topics

So far, we have supposed that the manipulating coalition can communicate and coordinate perfectly. In practice, this may be optimistic. For example, if the coalition is large, then it may be difficult for the coalition to communicate, as well as to ensure everyone votes appropriately. To address this, Slinko and White (2008) propose a more restricted model of strategic voting in which a single coalition member broadcasts a strategic vote and every member of the coalition either casts this vote or votes sincerely. In such a situation, a *safe strategic vote* is a broadcast vote that never results in an undesirable outcome, however many or few of the coalition follow it. The Gibbard-Satterthwaite Theorem extends to this notion of manipulation. Polynomial-time algorithms for computing a safe strategic vote have been given for k-approval, Bucklin, and Borda (Hazon and Elkind, 2010; Ianovski et al., 2011).

Another type of manipulation is for a single agent to vote more than once. This is often a concern in elections run in highly anonymous environments, such as Internet voting. A rule is said to be *false-name-proof* (Yokoo et al., 2004) if there is never an incentive for a voter to cast more than one vote. Conitzer (2008) gives a characterization of false-name-proof rules similar in spirit to the characterization of strategyproof rules by Gibbard (1977) that, perhaps unsurprisingly, is even more negative. Unlike in the case of strategyproofness, under the constraint of false-name-proofness, even the restriction of single-peaked preferences does not allow very appealing rules (Todo et al., 2011).

6.7 Conclusions

Besides being of interest in their own right, the computational manipulation problems discussed in this chapter are also important because of their implications for other, closely related problems in computational social choice. For example, the constructive manipulation problem is a special case of the *possible winner problem*, which asks, given a profile of partial votes and a given alternative, whether it is possible to complete the profile in such a way that that alternative wins. Similarly, the destructive manipulation problem is a special case of the *necessary winner problem*. For detailed analysis of the complexity of these problems, see, for example, Konczak and Lang (2005), Walsh (2007), Betzler and Dorn (2010), Xia and Conitzer (2011a), and Baumeister and Rothe (2012). The necessary winner problem, in turn, is important in settings in which we incrementally *elicit* voters' rankings rather than collecting them all at once. In this problem, we would like to be able to compute when we have elicited enough information to announce the winner (Conitzer and Sandholm, 2002). For further discussion of all of this, see also Chapter 10. There are also relations to *control* and *bribery* problems, which will be discussed in Chapter 7.

Acknowledgments

We thank Felix Brandt, Piotr Faliszewski, Jérôme Lang, Ariel Procaccia, Arkadii Slinko, and Bill Zwicker for very detailed and helpful comments on earlier versions of this chapter. Conitzer thanks NSF and ARO for support under grants CCF-1101659, IIS-0953756, CCF-1337215, W911NF-12-1-0550, and W911NF-11-1-0332. Walsh is supported by the Department of Communications and the Australian Research Council through the ICT Centre of Excellence Program, AOARD grant FA2386-12-1-4056, and the Federal Ministry for Education and Research through the Alexander von Humboldt Foundation.

CHAPTER 7

Control and Bribery in Voting

Piotr Faliszewski and Jörg Rothe

7.1 Introduction

In this chapter we study control and bribery, two families of problems modeling various ways of manipulating elections. Briefly put, control problems model situations where some entity, usually referred to as the chair or the election organizer, has some ability to affect the election structure. For example, the chair might be able to encourage new candidates to join the election, or might be able to prevent some voters from casting their votes. On the other hand, bribery models situations where the structure of the election stays intact (we have the same candidates and the same voters), but some outside agent pays the voters to change their votes. Naturally, such manipulative actions, dishonestly skewing election results, are undesirable. Thus it is interesting to know if there are so-called *complexity shields* against these attacks (see also Chapter 6 on manipulation and, relatedly, Section 4.3.3 in the book chapter by Baumeister and Rothe (2015)). That is, it is interesting to know the computational complexity of recognizing whether various forms of such attacks are possible or not. However, there are also other interpretations of control and bribery, many of them quite positive.

In this chapter we survey results on the complexity of control and bribery in elections, providing an overview of the specific problems studied, sketching sample proofs, and reviewing some approaches to dealing with the computational hardness of these control and bribery problems (see also Sections 4.3.4 and 4.3.5 in the book chapter by Baumeister and Rothe (2015)). Seeking ways of dealing with the computational hardness of control and bribery may seem surprising at first. However, on one hand, if we interpret control and bribery as modeling attacks on elections, then we would like to know the limitations of our complexity shields. On the other hand, if we take other interpretations of control and bribery, then we simply would like to know how to solve these problems. We survey some classical results on control in Section 7.3, on bribery in Section 7.4, and then briefly discuss their various applications in Section 7.5.

Table 7.1. *Three types of preference profiles required by different voting rules*

(a) A Borda election						(b) An approval election						(c) A fallback election			
points: 5 4 3 2 1 0							*a*	*b*	*c*	*d*	*e*	*f*	level: 1 2 3 4			
voter 1:	*a*	*c*	*b*	*f*	*e*	*d*	voter 1:	(1,	0,	0,	0,	0,	0)	voter 1:	*a*			
voter 2:	*b*	*a*	*f*	*c*	*e*	*d*	voter 2:	(1,	1,	0,	0,	0,	0)	voter 2:	*b*	*a*		
voter 3:	*c*	*d*	*b*	*a*	*f*	*e*	voter 3:	(1,	1,	1,	1,	0,	0)	voter 3:	*c*	*d*	*b*	*a*
voter 4:	*e*	*d*	*b*	*f*	*c*	*a*	voter 4:	(0,	0,	0,	1,	1,	0)	voter 4:	*e*	*d*		
voter 5:	*e*	*d*	*c*	*b*	*f*	*a*	voter 5:	(0,	0,	0,	0,	1,	0)	voter 5:	*e*			
winner: *b* with score 16							AV score:	3	2	1	2	2	0	winner: *a* on level 4			

7.2 Preliminaries

We start by recalling various voting rules, including preference-based voting rules and (variants of) approval voting. For the former, an *election* (A, R) is given by a set A of m *alternatives* (or *candidates*) and a *preference profile* $R = (\succ_1, \ldots, \succ_n)$ over A that collects n votes, each expressing a linear preference order over A. That is, letting $N = \{1, \ldots, n\}$ be the set of voters, $\succ_i$ gives voter i's preference order of the alternatives. For example, the ranking $a \succ_1 b \succ_1 c$ says that voter 1 (strictly) prefers alternative a to alternative b, and b to c. From now on we omit stating "$\succ_i$" explicitly and simply rank the alternatives in a vote from left (most preferred) to right (least preferred). That is, instead of, say, $a \succ_1 b \succ_1 c$ we simply write $a\,b\,c$. Also, for (A, R) an election and $A' \subseteq A$, we write (A', R) to denote the election with alternatives A' and the votes in R restricted to A'. For example, if (A, R) is the election from Table 7.1(a) consisting of five voters who rank six alternatives and $A' = \{b, c, d\}$, then $(A', R) = (\{b, c, d\}, (c\,b\,d,\ b\,c\,d,\ c\,d\,b,\ d\,b\,c,\ d\,c\,b))$.

We briefly recall some voting rules, see Chapter 2 for more details. *Positional scoring rules* are defined by an m-alternative *scoring vector* $\vec{\sigma} = (\sigma_1, \sigma_2, \ldots, \sigma_m)$, where the σ_i are nonnegative integers with $\sigma_1 \geqslant \sigma_2 \geqslant \cdots \geqslant \sigma_m$. Each alternative scores σ_i points for each vote where it is ranked in the ith position, and whoever scores the most points wins. Examples are *plurality voting* with scoring vector $(1, 0, \ldots, 0)$, *veto* (aka *antiplurality*) with $(1, \ldots, 1, 0)$, *k-approval* with $(1, \ldots, 1, 0, \ldots, 0)$ having a 1 in each of the first $k \leqslant m$ positions (note that 1-approval is plurality), *k-veto*, which is the same as $(m - k)$-approval (note that 1-veto is veto), and *Borda count* with $(m - 1, m - 2, \ldots, 0)$. For example, in the election given in Table 7.1(a), e wins under plurality; d under 2-approval; b under 3-approval; b, c, and f under veto; and b under Borda (with a Borda score of 16, whereas a, c, d, e, and f score, respectively, 11, 15, 12, 12, and 9 points).

Under *approval voting* (or *AV*), proposed by Brams and Fishburn (1978, 2007), instead of using preference orders the voters specify sets of alternatives they approve of. Typically, such votes are represented as m-dimensional 0/1-vectors, where each position corresponds to an alternative and 1-entries mean approval of respective alternatives. All alternatives with the most approvals win. For example, for the approval vectors given in Table 7.1(b), a is the approval winner with a score of 3. A version of approval voting (dubbed *sincere-strategy preference-based approval voting* (or *SP-AV*) by Erdélyi et al. (2009)) combines approval information with preference-order information (the voters rank the candidates that they approve of). The rule was introduced by Brams and Sanver (2006) and, in essence, is the same as approval, but the additional preference-order information is used to deduce voter behavior when the candidate set changes (we omit detailed discussion and point the reader to the original papers and to the survey of Baumeister et al. (2010)).

Range voting (or *RV*) works just as approval voting, except that entries of the vectors under k-range voting come from the set $\{0, 1, \ldots, k\}$ rather than from the set $\{0, 1\}$. *Normalized range voting* (or *NRV*) is a variant of RV that alters the votes so that the potential impact of each vote is maximized (see, e.g., the work of Menton, 2013).

Let us now move back to rules based on preference orders and, in particular, to those rules that are based on pairwise comparisons of alternatives. A *Condorcet winner* is an alternative that is preferred to every other alternative by a strict majority of votes. For example, in the election from Table 7.1(a), c is preferred to every other alternative by three of the five voters and thus is the Condorcet winner. It is easy to see that there is at most one Condorcet winner in an election, but it is possible that there is none.[1] A voting rule is *Condorcet-consistent* if it elects the Condorcet winner whenever there is one. If there is no Condorcet winner in a given preference profile, many of the known Condorcet-consistent rules elect those candidates that are closest to being Condorcet winners, one way or another. For example, under *Copeland$^\alpha$ voting*, $\alpha \in [0, 1]$, we organize a tournament among the candidates in the following way: Each pair of candidates "plays" against each other and the one that is preferred by more voters wins and receives a point (in case of a tie, both get α points). In the end, the candidates with the highest number of points win. If we omit voter 1 from the election in Table 7.1(a) then d is the unique Copeland$^\alpha$ winner for $\alpha = 0$ and $\alpha = 1/2$ (with a Copeland$^\alpha$ score of 3 if $\alpha = 0$, and of 3.5 if $\alpha = 1/2$), but both c and e are Copeland$^\alpha$ winners with a score of 5 for $\alpha = 1$. Other Condorcet-consistent rules are, for example, the *maximin rule* (aka *Simpson's rule*), *ranked pairs* due to Tideman (1987), or *Schulze's rule* (a rule proposed by Schulze (2011), which satisfies many normative properties).

Other voting rules follow yet other principles, e.g., *single transferable vote* (*STV*) proceeds in stages and eliminates the "weakest" candidates until only the winner remains. We omit the details and point the reader to Chapter 2 instead. Under *Bucklin voting* we first seek the smallest value ℓ such that there is candidate ranked among top ℓ positions by a strict majority of the voters, and then declare as winners those candidates that have highest ℓ-approval scores (or, under *simplified Bucklin voting*, those candidates that are ranked among top ℓ positions by some majority of the voters). *Fallback voting*, introduced by Brams and Sanver (2009), is a rule that combines Bucklin voting with approval voting (the voters rank only the candidates they approve of and Bucklin is used; if there are no Bucklin winners—due to the fact that voters do not have to rank all the candidates—fallback outputs the approval winners). For example, in the partial rankings given in Table 7.1(c), a alone reaches a strict majority

---

[1] If one requires voting rules to always have at least one winner, Condorcet voting (which elects the Condorcet winner whenever there is one, and otherwise no one wins) would not be a voting rule. However, we take the point of view that voting rules may have empty winner sets. Note that it has become a tradition to study (at least) plurality, Condorcet, and approval on each new approach and each new idea regarding election control (see, e.g., the papers of Bartholdi et al., 1992; Hemaspaandra et al., 2007; Faliszewski et al., 2011c).

of $\lfloor 5/2 \rfloor + 1 = 3$ votes (namely, on the fourth level) and thus is the fallback winner. However, if the first voter approved only of f instead of only of a, then no candidate would reach a majority and fallback would output a, b, d, and e, the approval winners of the election.

In Sections 7.3 and 7.4, we will define a large variety of decision problems, each related to some specific control or bribery scenario. All these problems are members of NP, the class of problems that can be solved in nondeterministic polynomial time, and they will be classified to be either in P or NP-complete.[2] Unlike, for instance, in the case of Kemeny, Dodgson, and Young elections (which we do not consider here, as their winner problems are not in P—see Chapters 4 and 5), the winner(s) can be determined efficiently for all voting systems described earlier.

7.3 Control

Every election needs to be organized, and whoever is responsible for doing so can have some influence on the outcome of the election by changing its structure. We will refer to this person, or authority, as the *chair* of the election, and to the way the election structure is changed by the chair as *control type* or *control action*. Many types of control that the chair might exert are conceivable. We present those that have been studied in the literature, starting with the four most important ones.

7.3.1 Constructive Control by Adding/Deleting Candidates/Voters

Bartholdi et al. (1992) were the first to introduce electoral control and to study it in various scenarios from a computational perspective. In particular, they defined *constructive* control types, where the chair's goal in exerting some control action is to make a given candidate p the unique winner of the resulting election.[3] It is common to assume that the chair has complete knowledge of all votes.

One control action the chair might exert is to change the candidate set, either by adding some new candidates from a given set of spoiler candidates (hoping to make p's most competitive rivals weaker relative to p), or to delete up to k candidates from the given election (to get rid of p's worst rivals). For the former, Bartholdi et al. (1992) originally defined a variant that allows adding an unlimited number of spoiler candidates. To be in sync with the other control problems (e.g., control by deleting candidates), Hemaspaandra et al. (2009) defined a variant of this problem where a bound k on the number of spoiler candidates that may be added is given. We will see later that the complexity of the resulting problems can sharply differ.

---

[2] A problem B is NP-*hard* if every NP problem A reduces to B, where "reduction" always refers to a *polynomial-time many-one reduction*, that is, a polynomial-time function r mapping instances of A to instances of B such that for each x, $x \in A \iff r(x) \in B$. B is NP-*complete* if it is NP-hard and in NP.

[3] As we do here, control problems have commonly, most especially in the earlier papers on control, been studied in their *unique-winner* variant. Alternatively, many papers on control consider the *nonunique-winner* (or *co-winner*, or simply *winner*) variant where the chair's goal is merely to make the designated candidate a winner. The complexity of control problems is usually the same in both models, requiring only minor adjustments to the proofs.

Definition 7.1. Let f be a voting rule. In the CONSTRUCTIVE-CONTROL-BY-ADDING-AN-UNLIMITED-NUMBER-OF-CANDIDATES problem for f (f-CCAUC), we are given (a) a set A of qualified candidates, a set B of spoiler candidates, where $A \cap B = \emptyset$, and an election $(A \cup B, R)$ and (b) a preferred candidate $p \in A$. We ask if we can choose a subset $B' \subseteq B$ of the spoiler candidates such that p is the unique f-winner of the election $(A \cup B', R)$. The CONSTRUCTIVE-CONTROL-BY-ADDING-CANDIDATES problem for f (f-CCAC) is defined similarly: In addition to (a) and (b) we are also given (c) a bound $k \in \mathbb{N}$, and we ask if there is a subset $B' \subseteq B$ of spoiler candidates such that $|B'| \leqslant k$ and p is the unique f-winner of $(A \cup B', R)$. In the CONSTRUCTIVE-CONTROL-BY-DELETING-CANDIDATES problem for f (f-CCDC), we are given (a) an election (A, R), (b) a preferred candidate $p \in A$, and (c) a bound $k \in \mathbb{N}$. We ask if p can be made a unique f-winner of the election resulting from (A, R) by deleting at most k candidates.

The issue of control by changing the candidate set is very natural and, indeed, happens in real-life political elections. For example, it is widely speculated that "adding" Nader to the 2000 U.S. presidential election had the effect of ensuring Bush's victory (otherwise, Gore would have won). Similarly, there are known cases where "spoiler" candidates were added to political elections to confuse the voters (see, e.g., the *New York Times* article of Lacey (2010) for a reported example). It is also easy to imagine control by deleting candidates: Some of the candidates who perform poorly in pre-election polls may be forced (or persuaded) to withdraw.

Example 7.1. For a Borda-CCAUC instance, let $(A \cup B, R)$ be the election from Table 7.1(a), where $A = \{a, b, c, d\}$ is the set of qualified candidates and $B = \{e, f\}$ is the set of spoiler candidates. Table 7.2(a) shows the restriction (A, R) of this election to the qualified candidates, which has the Borda winner c scoring 9 points, while the Borda scores of a, b, and d, respectively, are 4, 6, and 8. Supposing that b is the chair's favorite candidate, we have a yes-instance of Borda-CCAUC, since adding both spoiler candidates makes b the unique Borda winner (see Table 7.1(a)).

To turn this into a Borda-CCAC instance, we in addition need to specify an addition limit, k. If $k = 1$, we have a yes-instance of the problem: Though the chair will not succeed by adding e (which gives the election in Table 7.2(c), still won by c), adding f (giving the election in Table 7.2(b)) will make b the unique Borda winner with a score of 13, while a, c, d, and e score 8, 12, 11, and 6 points.

Finally, consider again the Borda election in Table 7.1(a) with winner b, and suppose the chair, who now wants to make c win, is allowed to delete one candidate. Deleting the current champion, b, will reach this goal. Alternatively, the chair can delete f (see Table 7.2(c)) to turn c into the unique winner with a Borda score of 12, while the Borda scores of a, b, d, and e, respectively, are reduced to 8, 11, 9, and 10. Thus this is a yes-instance of the problem Borda-CCDC.

The chair might also change the voter set, either by encouraging further voters to participate (knowing that their votes will be beneficial for p), or by excluding certain voters from the election (knowing that deleting their votes will help p). In real life, political parties often try to influence the outcome of elections by such actions (e.g.,

Table 7.2. CCAUC, CCAC, and CCDC for the Borda election in Table 7.1(a)

(a) Without spoilers e and f					(b) Deleting e						(c) Deleting f					
points:	3	2	1	0	points:	4	3	2	1	0	points:	4	3	2	1	0
voter 1:	a	c	b	d	voter 1:	a	c	b	f	d	voter 1:	a	c	b	e	d
voter 2:	b	a	c	d	voter 2:	b	a	f	c	d	voter 2:	b	a	c	e	d
voter 3:	c	d	b	a	voter 3:	c	d	b	a	f	voter 3:	c	d	b	a	e
voter 4:	d	b	c	a	voter 4:	d	b	f	c	a	voter 4:	e	d	b	c	a
voter 5:	d	c	b	a	voter 5:	d	c	b	f	a	voter 5:	e	d	c	b	a
winner:	c (score 9)				winner:	b (score 13)					winner:	c (score 12)				

think of targeted "get-out-the-vote" drives on one hand, and of voter suppression efforts or even disenfranchisement of voters, on the other).

Definition 7.2. Let f be a voting rule. In the CONSTRUCTIVE-CONTROL-BY-ADDING-VOTERS problem for f (f-CCAV), we are given (a) a list R of already registered votes, a list S of as yet unregistered votes, and an election $(A, R + S)$, where "profile addition" means concatenation of profiles, (b) a preferred candidate $p \in A$, and (c) a bound $k \in \mathbb{N}$. We ask if we can choose a sublist $S' \subseteq S$ of size at most k such that p is the unique f-winner of $(A, R + S')$. In the CONSTRUCTIVE-CONTROL-BY-DELETING-VOTERS problem for f (f-CCDV), we are given (a) an election (A, R), (b) a preferred candidate $p \in A$, and (c) a bound $k \in \mathbb{N}$, and we ask if we can make p a unique f-winner of the election resulting from (A, R) by deleting no more than k votes.

Example 7.2. Look again at the Borda election in Table 7.1(a) and assume that the chair wants to make c win. If one voter may be deleted, the chair's goal can be reached by deleting voter 2: c then is the unique Borda winner with a score of 13, while a, b, d, e, and f score only 7, 11, 12, 11, and 6 points, so this is a yes-instance of the problem Borda-CCDV. On the other hand, if a were the chair's favorite choice, the chair would not succeed even if two votes may be deleted, giving rise to a no-instance of Borda-CCDV. As an example of a Borda-CCAV instance, suppose voters 1 and 2 from the election in Table 7.1(a) are registered already, but 3, 4, and 5 are not. The current winner is a. Suppose the chair wants to make c win and is allowed to add two voters. Adding any single one of the as yet unregistered voters is not enough (the best c can reach, by adding voter 3, is to tie with a and b for first place, each having 11 points). Adding either $\{3, 4\}$ or $\{4, 5\}$ is not successful either. However, adding $\{3, 5\}$ makes c the unique Borda winner with a score of 14, while a, b, d, e, and f score only 11, 13, 8, 7, and 7 points.

Depending on the voting rule, it may never (for no preference profile at all) be possible for the chair to successfully exert some control action (e.g., constructive control by deleting voters) in the sense that p can be turned (by deleting voters) from not being a unique winner into being one. If that is the case, we say this voting rule is *immune* to this type of control. Otherwise (i.e., if there is at least one preference profile where the chair can successfully exert this control action), we say this voting rule is *susceptible* to this type of control. For a voting rule f that is susceptible to some type of control (e.g., to constructive control by adding voters), f is said to be *vulnerable* (respectively, *resistant*) to this control type if the corresponding problem (e.g., f-CCAV) is in P (respectively, NP-hard).

Immunity results appear to be very desirable. Indeed, if a voting rule is immune to a given type of control, then it is impossible to compromise its result by a corresponding type of malicious action. Nonetheless, as we will soon see, immunity can also bring some undesired side effects. First, however, let us argue that immunity for candidate control is rare. This is so due to the study of *strategic candidacy* of Dutta et al. (2001) (see also recent work on strategic candidacy of Lang et al. (2013) and Brill and Conitzer (2015)). They have considered a setting where the candidates have preferences regarding election outcomes, and can strategically choose to join the race or not. Dutta et al. (2001) have shown that for most typical election rules there are settings where some candidates would prefer not to participate in the election. In effect, such rules cannot be immune to candidate control. Nonetheless, in some rare cases (e.g., for Condorcet and approval voting) immunity results for candidate control hold (see Table 7.3).

For the case of voter control, immunity is not only rare, but also is utterly undesirable. Indeed, it is natural to expect that if we add sufficiently many voters with the same preference order, then their most preferred candidate becomes a winner. Formally, this is known as *voting rule continuity* (or, as the *Archimedean property*). Continuity says that if some candidate c is a winner in some election (A, R), then for every election (A, R'), there is a natural number t such that c is a winner in an election of the form $(A, R' + tR)$, where tR refers to a profile of t copies of profile R. See, for example, the work of Smith (1973).

The first voting rules studied with respect to control were plurality, Condorcet, and approval voting. The following theorem summarizes some of the results obtained for them by Bartholdi et al. (1992) and Hemaspaandra et al. (2007).

Theorem 7.3 (Bartholdi et al., 1992; Hemaspaandra et al., 2007).

1. *Condorcet and approval voting are immune and plurality is resistant to constructive control by adding (respectively, adding an unlimited number of) candidates.*
2. *Condorcet and approval voting are vulnerable and plurality is resistant to constructive control by deleting candidates.*
3. *Condorcet and approval voting are resistant and plurality is vulnerable to constructive control by both adding and deleting voters.*

These immunity claims generally follow from the fact that Condorcet and approval voting satisfy the ("unique" version of the) Weak Axiom of Revealed Preference, which states that a unique winner p in a set A of alternatives always is also a unique winner among each subset $A' \subseteq A$ including p. Hemaspaandra et al. (2007) identify many links (i.e., implications and equivalences) among the susceptibility/immunity statements for the control types defined previously and to be defined in Section 7.3.2. We refrain from repeating them here but point the reader to Figure 4.16 in the book by Rothe et al. (2011) for an overview.

The vulnerability claims in Theorem 7.3 follow by simple P algorithms. For example, that approval-CCDC is in P follows from this algorithm: On input $((A, R), p, k)$, if p

already is the unique winner in (A, R) (which is easy to test), output "yes"; otherwise, if no more than k candidates have at least as many approvals as p, output "yes" (as p can be made a unique winner by deleting them all), and else output "no." By contrast, vulnerability proofs for the partitioning cases to be defined in Section 7.3.2 are often much more involved (and are omitted here).

The resistance claims in Theorem 7.3 typically follow by reductions from NP-complete problems such as EXACT-COVER-BY-3-SETS (X3C), which given a base set $B = \{b_1, \ldots, b_{3k}\}$, $k > 0$, and a sequence $\mathcal{S} = (S_1, \ldots, S_n)$ of 3-element subsets of B, asks whether B can be exactly covered by k sets chosen from $\mathcal{S}$. For example, to show that approval-CCDV is NP-hard, let $(B, \mathcal{S})$ be an instance of X3C. Let $\ell_j = |\{S_i \in \mathcal{S} \mid b_j \in S_i\}|$ for each j, $1 \leqslant j \leqslant 3k$. Construct from $(B, \mathcal{S})$ the election (A, R) with $A = B \cup \{p\}$ and R consisting of the following $2n$ voters: (1) For each i, $1 \leqslant i \leqslant n$, one voter in R approves of all candidates in S_i and disapproves of all other candidates; (2) there are n voters $v_1, \ldots, v_n$ in R such that, for each i, $1 \leqslant i \leqslant n$, v_i (a) approves of p, and (b) approves of b_j if and only if $i \leqslant n - \ell_j$. Thus, every candidate in (A, R) has exactly n approvals. If there is an exact cover for B, then deleting the k votes from R corresponding to the exact cover turns p into the unique winner. Conversely, suppose that p can be turned into a unique approval winner by deleting at most k votes from R (where we may assume that none of them approves of p, so only votes from group (1) have been deleted). For p to become the unique approval winner, every $b_j \in B$ must have lost at least one approval. Thus, the deleted votes correspond to an exact cover for B.

The next system to be comprehensively studied regarding control was Copeland$^\alpha$.

Theorem 7.4 (Faliszewski et al., 2009c). *For each rational number α, $0 \leqslant \alpha \leqslant 1$, Copeland$^\alpha$ is resistant to all types of control from Definitions 7.1 and 7.2, except for $\alpha \in \{0, 1\}$ where Copeland$^\alpha$ is vulnerable to constructive control by adding an unlimited number of candidates.*

The most interesting point to note in Theorem 7.4 is that Copeland$^\alpha$-CCAUC is in P for $\alpha = 0$ and $\alpha = 1$, but is NP-complete for all other values of α. The vulnerability results are proven by the following simple P algorithm: On input $((A \cup B, R), p)$, set D_1 to be the set of all $b \in B$ such that the Copeland$^\alpha$ score of p in $(\{b, p\}, R)$ is 1; initialize D to be D_1; and then successively delete every b from D such that the Copeland$^\alpha$ score of p in $(A \cup D, R)$ is no greater than that of b. Correctness of the algorithm follows from (1) the observation that for each $D \subseteq B$, whenever p is the unique Copeland$^\alpha$ winner in $(A \cup D, R)$, then so is p in $(A \cup (D_1 \cap D), R)$, and (2) a more involved argument showing that if p is the unique winner in $(A \cup D, R)$ for some $D \subseteq D_1$, yet the above algorithm computes a set D' such that p is *not* a unique winner in $(A \cup D', R)$, then this leads to a contradiction. On the other hand, NP-hardness of Copeland$^\alpha$-CCAUC for $0 < \alpha < 1$ follows by a reduction from the NP-complete problem VERTEX-COVER (and is omitted here).

Unlike Copeland$^\alpha$-CCAUC, Copeland$^\alpha$-CCAC is NP-complete for *all* (rational) values of $\alpha \in [0, 1]$. In fact, Copeland$^\alpha$ with $0 < \alpha < 1$ (including the original system by Copeland (1951)) is the first family of voting rules known to be fully resistant to all types of constructive control, including those to be defined in Section 7.3.2. Other voting rules having this property have followed: SP-AV (Erdélyi et al., 2009),

Table 7.3. *The complexity of control problems for various voting rules*

Voting Rule	CAUC		CAC		CDC		CPC-TE		CPC-TP		CRPC-TE		CRPC-TP		CAV		CDV		CPV-TE		CPV-TP	
	C	D	C	D	C	D	C	D	C	D	C	D	C	D	C	D	C	D	C	D	C	D
plurality (Bartholdi et al., 1992; Hemaspaandra et al., 2007)	R	R	R	R	R	R	R	R	R	R	R	R	R	R	V	V	V	V	V	V	R	R
Condorcet (Bartholdi et al., 1992; Hemaspaandra et al., 2007)	I	V	I	V	V	V	I	V	I	V	I	V	I	V	I	R	V	R	V	R	V	R
approval (Hemaspaandra et al., 2007)	I	V	I	V	V	V	I	V	I	I	I	I	V	I	I	I	R	V	R	V	R	V
Copeland$^{\alpha}$ for $\alpha = 0$	V	V	R	V	R	V	R	V	R	V	R	V	R	V	R	R	R	R	R	R	R	R
$0 < \alpha < 1$	R	V	R	V	R	V	R	V	R	V	R	V	R	V	R	R	R	R	R	R	R	R
$\alpha = 1$ (Faliszewski et al., 2009c)	V	V	R	V	R	V	R	V	R	V	R	V	R	V	R	R	R	R	R	R	R	R
maximin (Faliszewski et al., 2011b)	V	V	R	V	V	V	–	–	–	–	–	–	–	–	R	R	R	R	–	–	–	–
Borda (Russel, 2007; Elkind et al., 2011a; Loreggia et al., 2014; Chen et al., 2015)	–	–	R	V	R	V	–	–	–	–	–	–	–	–	R	V	–	V	–	V	–	–
SP-AV (Erdélyi et al., 2009)	R	R	R	R	R	R	R	R	R	R	R	R	R	R	R	V	R	V	R	V	R	R
fallback (Erdélyi and Rothe, 2010; Erdélyi et al., 2011; see also Erdélyi et al., 2015a)	R	R	R	R	R	R	R	R	R	R	R	R	R	R	R	R	R	V	R	V	R	R
Bucklin (Erdélyi et al., 2011; see also Erdélyi et al., 2015a)	R	R	R	R	R	R	R	R	R	R	R	R	R	R	R	R	R	V	R	V	R	S
RV (Menton, 2013)	I	V	I	V	V	V	I	V	I	I	I	I	V	I	I	I	R	V	R	V	R	V
NRV (Menton, 2013)	R	R	R	R	R	R	R	R	R	R	R	R	R	R	R	R	R	V	R	V	R	R
Schulze (Parkes and Xia, 2012; Menton and Singh, 2013)	R	S	R	S	R	S	R	V	R	V	R	V	R	V	R	V	R	V	R	R	R	R

Key: "I" means immunity, "S" susceptibility, "V" vulnerability, and "R" resistance. We write "–" if a given result is not directly available in the literature.

fallback and Bucklin voting (Erdélyi and Rothe, 2010; Erdélyi et al., 2011, 2015a), NRV (Menton, 2013), and Schulze voting (Parkes and Xia, 2012; Menton and Singh, 2013), as shown in Table 7.3.

7.3.2 The Partitioning Cases and Destructive Control

In addition to control by adding/deleting candidates/voters, Bartholdi et al. (1992) also introduced various types of control by partitioning either candidates or voters, modeled by elections proceeding in two stages. While their original definitions were a bit unclear about what happens when more than one candidate wins some first-stage pre-election, Hemaspaandra et al. (2007) defined two rules for how to handle such pre-election ties: TE ("ties eliminate") says that whenever at least two candidates are tied for winner in a pre-election, no candidate proceeds to the final stage from it (i.e., only unique pre-election winners move forward); TP ("ties promote") says that all pre-election winners, no matter how many, proceed forward.

Definition 7.3. Let f be a voting rule. In the CONSTRUCTIVE-CONTROL-BY-RUNOFF-PARTITION-OF-CANDIDATES problem for f under TE or TP (f-CCRPC-TE or f-CCRPC-TP), we are given (a) an election (A, R), and (b) a preferred candidate $p \in A$. We ask if we can partition A into A_1 and A_2 such that p is the unique f-winner of the election $(W_1 \cup W_2, R)$, where $W_i, i \in \{1, 2\}$, is the set of those pre-election (A_i, R) winners that are promoted to the final stage according to the tie-handling rule (TE or TP). The CONSTRUCTIVE-CONTROL-BY-PARTITION-OF-CANDIDATES problem for f under TE or TP (f-CCPC-TE or f-CCPC-TP) is defined similarly, except that we ask if p can be made a unique f-winner of the election $(W_1 \cup A_2, R)$ by partitioning A into A_1 and A_2, i.e., there is only one pre-election (A_1, R) whose winners proceed (according to the tie-handling rule, TE or TP) to the final stage to face all of A_2.

Example 7.5. Let (A, R) be the Borda election in Table 7.1(a) again, and let c be the distinguished candidate the chair wants to win. This is a yes-instance in all four cases, for both CCRPC and CCPC, each in TE and TP, as witnessed by the partition of A into $A_1 = \{a, f\}$ and $A_2 = \{b, c, d, e\}$. It does not matter whether we are in the TE or TP model,[4] since both subelections have a unique winner: a alone wins (A_1, R), and c alone wins (A_2, R) (with a score of 9, while b, d, and e score only 7, 6, and 8 points). For CCRPC, both subelection winners, c and a, proceed to the final stage, which c wins. For CCPC, the winner of the first subelection, a, faces all candidates of A_2 in the final stage, and as we have seen in Table 7.2(c), the unique Borda winner of $(\{a, b, c, d, e\}, R)$ is c, again as desired by the chair.

The analogues of f-CCRPC-TE/TP where not the candidates but the voters are partitioned model a very basic kind of *gerrymandering*. (Note that it would not make sense to define voter-partition analogues of f-CCPC-TE/TP, at least not for natural voting systems f.[5])

Definition 7.4. Let f be a voting rule. In the CONSTRUCTIVE-CONTROL-BY-PARTITION-OF-VOTERS problem for f under TE or TP (f-CCPV-TE or f-CCPV-TP), we are given (a) an election (A, R), and (b) a preferred candidate $p \in A$. We ask if R can be partitioned into R_1 and R_2 such that p is the unique f-winner of $(W_1 \cup W_2, R)$,

---

[4] By contrast, partitioning A into $A_1' = \{a, b, c\}$ and $A_2' = \{d, e, f\}$ would reveal a difference between the two tie-handling models: Since b and c tie for winning (A_1', R), they both proceed to the final stage in model TP (where they face e, the winner of (A_2', R), and c wins the final stage), but b and c eliminate each other in model TE (so e alone proceeds to the final stage and wins).

[5] In such an analogue, given an election (A, R) and $p \in A$, we would partition R into R_1 and R_2 just as in Definition 7.4, but there is only one pre-election, say (A, R_1), whose TE/TP-winners W_1 would then face *all* candidates in the final stage, yet $(W_1 \cup A, R) = (A, R)$ is just the original election.

where W_i, $i \in \{1, 2\}$, is the set of those pre-election (A, R_i) winners that are promoted to the final stage according to the tie-handling rule (TE or TP).

Example 7.6. Again looking at the Borda election (A, R) in Table 7.1(a) with preferred candidate c, the chair will succeed (in both TE and TP) by partitioning R into $R_1 = \{1, 2, 4, 5\}$ and $R_2 = \{3\}$: b alone wins (A, R_1) (with a score of 13, while a, c, d, e, and f score only 9, 10, 8, 12, and 8 points), and c alone wins (A, R_2). Thus they both proceed to the final stage where c beats b by 3 to 2.

The proofs that show the complexity of control by partitioning candidates or voters are often based on similar constructions as analogous proofs for the case of deleting candidates or voters, but usually are more involved technically.

For each constructive control problem, there is also a destructive variant, introduced by Hemaspaandra et al. (2007), where the chair's goal is to preclude a given candidate from being the unique winner of the election resulting from the chair's control action. We denote the destructive control problems analogously, replacing the initial "C" by a "D," as, for example, in DCDC for "destructive control by deleting candidates." (In this problem, it is forbidden to delete the designated candidate p; otherwise, the problem would be trivial.)

7.3.3 Overview and Some Other Approaches to Control

Table 7.3 summarizes the control complexity results for some prominent voting rules. In most cases we have full knowledge of the complexity of all the basic types of control, but for Borda and maximin some types of control were never studied, and for Bucklin and Schulze for some types of control there are only susceptibility results in the literature.

We already mentioned that besides Copeland$^\alpha$ voting, $0 < \alpha < 1$, also SP-AV (Erdélyi et al., 2009), fallback and Bucklin voting (Erdélyi and Rothe, 2010; Erdélyi et al., 2011, 2015a), NRV (Menton, 2013), and Schulze voting (Parkes and Xia, 2012; Menton and Singh, 2013) are resistant to all constructive control types. Among those, Schulze has many vulnerabilities to destructive control types, but SP-AV is vulnerable to only three of them (DCAV, DCDV, and DCPV-TE), and fallback, Bucklin, and NRV even to only two (DCAV and DCDV), where the case of Bucklin-DCPV-TP is still open. Note that SP-AV is a somewhat unnatural system (as has been discussed by Baumeister et al. (2010) in detail), due to a rule introduced by Erdélyi et al. (2009) that, to cope with certain control actions, can move the voters' approval lines *after they have cast their votes*. It may be argued that NRV has a similar issue (though perhaps to a lesser extent), since after the voters have cast their votes (namely, their range voting vectors), the normalization process can change the points the alternatives will score from the votes. Fallback's drawback, on the other hand, is that it is a hybrid of two "pure" voting rules, Bucklin and approval, and requires the voters to report both approval vectors and rankings. All three voting systems have the disadvantage that it is rather complicated (even though far less complicated than in Schulze voting) to determine the winners; for example, it is hardly conceivable that many of the voters in a real-world political election would be fully aware of the effect of normalization in NRV. But this is the price to pay if we wish to have a (relatively) natural voting rule with P-time winner determination that is resistant to as many control actions as these voting rules are resistant to. On the other hand, if one is willing to accept an artificial voting rule, Hemaspaandra et al. (2009) have shown how to combine well-known rules to obtain ones that are resistant to all types of control. While their method produces rules that are not attractive in practice (even though they satisfy some natural normative properties), it suggests that indeed there might exist natural voting rules with P-time winner determination that are resistant to all types of control considered here.

Now, let us quickly point to some related work and to other approaches to control. Meir et al. (2008) study control for multiwinner voting rules. In the multiwinner setting, we are given an election (A, R) and an integer k, and the goal is to pick a "committee" of k winners. Multiwinner voting rules can be used to choose parliaments (or other collective bodies), to choose finalists in competitions, or even within recommendation systems (see, e.g., the work of Lu and Boutilier (2011a) for the application in recommendation systems and the work of Elkind et al. (2014a) for a recent general discussion of multiwinner voting). To study control in the multiwinner setting (and analogous approaches apply to other manipulative scenarios), Meir et al. (2008) assume that the election chair associates some utility value with each candidate and his or her goal is to ensure that the sum of the utilities of the candidates in the elected committee is as high as possible. As a side effect, this approach creates a natural unification of the constructive and destructive cases: In the constructive case the chair would have positive utility only for the most preferred candidate, whereas in the destructive setting the chair would have positive, equal utilities for all the candidates except the despised one.

Faliszewski et al. (2011b) provide a unified framework to capture "multimode control attacks" that simultaneously combine various of the control actions considered here. Specifically, in their setting the chair can, for example, simultaneously add some candidates and remove some voters. One of the conclusions of this work is that, typically, the complexity of such a multimode control attack is the same as that of the hardest basic control type involved. In particular, if a voting rule is vulnerable to several basic types of control, it is also vulnerable if the chair can perform these control types simultaneously (i.e., coordinating the attacks is easy). However, this conclusion is based on studying a number of natural voting rules and is not a general theorem (indeed, such a general theorem does not hold).

Fitzsimmons et al. (2013) study the complexity of control in the presence of manipulators, both in the case where the chair and the manipulators coordinate their actions and in the case where they compete with each other. While all the related cooperative problems are in NP, they show that the competitive problems can be complete for the second and the third level of the polynomial hierarchy for suitably designed artificial voting systems (though their complexity is much lower for many natural voting systems). Another approach to unifying different types of strategic behavior is due to Xia (2012b), who proposes a general framework that is based on so-called vote operations and can be used to express, for example, bribery and control by adding or deleting voters. Xia (2012b) shows that if the votes are generated i.i.d. with respect to some distribution, then, on the average, the number of vote operations (e.g., the number of voters that need to be added) necessary to achieve a particular effect (e.g., ensuring that some candidate is a winner) is either zero (the effect is already achieved), or is proportional to the square root of the number of original voters, or is linear with respect to the number of original voters, or the effect is impossible to achieve.

Going in a somewhat different direction, Chen et al. (2014) consider control by adding candidates in a combinatorial setting, where one can add whole groups of voters at unit cost. They show that even for the plurality rule, for which standard voter control is very easy, the combinatorial setting is challenging (indeed, combinatorial control by adding voters is NP-hard for plurality even in the settings where the groups of voters to add contain at most two voters each).

Hemaspaandra et al. (2014b) established the first control-related dichotomy result, showing for which pure scoring rules CCAV is easy to solve and for which this problem is NP-complete (however, Faliszewski et al. (2013) study voter control in weighted elections and in the technical report version of their paper show a dichotomy result as well). This complements similar dichotomy results of Hemaspaandra and Hemaspaandra (2007) on manipulation and of Betzler and Dorn (2010) and Baumeister and Rothe (2012) on the possible winner problem.

Some researchers investigate not only the classical complexity, but also the parameterized complexity of control problems, with respect to such parameters as the solution size (e.g., "number of added voters") or the election size (e.g., "number of candidates"); for example, see the work of Liu et al. (2009) for a discussion of plurality, Condorcet, and approval; Liu and Zhu (2010, 2013) for maximin, Copeland, Borda, Bucklin, and approval; Betzler and Uhlmann (2009) and Faliszewski et al. (2009c) for Copeland$^\alpha$; Erdélyi et al. (2015a) for Bucklin and fallback; and Hemaspaandra et al. (2013b) for Schulze and ranked-pairs voting. On the other hand, Brelsford et al. (2008) study the approximability of control, manipulation, and bribery. Faliszewski et al. (2013) discuss approximation algorithms for voter control under k-approval.

Faliszewski et al. (2011b, 2011a) and Brandt et al. (2010a) study to what extent complexity shields for manipulation and control disappear in elections with domain restrictions, such as in single-peaked or nearly single-peaked electorates (see also the book chapter by Hemaspaandra et al., 2015). Magiera and Faliszewski (2014) show similar results for single-crossing electorates.

Hemaspaandra et al. (2013a) compare the decision problems for manipulation, bribery, and control with their search versions and study conditions under which search reduces to decision. They also notice that two destructive control types that previously have been viewed as distinct are in fact identical (in both the unique-winner and the nonunique-winner model): DCRPC-TE = DCPC-TE (and, in only the nonunique-winner model, they additionally show equality of another pair of control types: DCRPC-TP = DCPC-TP).

So far, almost all the research on the complexity of control has been theoretical, establishing NP-hardness of various problems. Recently, Rothe and Schend (2012) have initiated the experimental study of control (see also the survey by Rothe and Schend (2013) and the work of Erdélyi et al. (2015b)), showing that NP-hard control problems can, sometimes, be solved efficiently in practice (cf. the work of Walsh (2011a) for such studies on manipulation).

Finally, there are a number of problems that are very closely related to control, but that, nonetheless, are usually not classified as "standard control types." These problems include, for example, candidate cloning (see the brief discussion in Section 7.5), fixing knockout tournaments (see Chapter 19 for more details), the problem of controlling sequential elections by choosing the order of voting on related issues (see the work of Conitzer et al., 2009a), and online control in sequential elections (see the work of Hemaspaandra et al., 2012a, 2012b), which is inspired by online manipulation in sequential elections due to Hemaspaandra et al. (2014a). Ideas originating from election control have also found applications in other settings. For example, Baumeister et al. (2012b, 2013b) have studied control for the case of judgment aggregation (for more details on judgment aggregation, see Chapter 17 and the book chapter by Baumeister et al. (2015)).

7.4 Bribery

Let us now move on to the study of bribery in elections. As opposed to the case of control, this time it is not possible to affect the structure of the election at hand (that is, the sets of candidates or voters cannot be changed), but it is possible to change some of the votes instead. Election bribery problems, introduced by Faliszewski et al. (2009b), model situations where an outside agent wants a particular alternative to win and pays some of the voters to vote as the agent likes. The problem name, bribery, suggests settings where an outside agent is dishonestly affecting election results, but there are other interpretations of these problems as well. For example, the formal framework of bribery can capture scenarios such as political campaign management and election fraud detection. We discuss such aspects of bribery (and control) in Section 7.5; for now we focus on the algorithmic properties of bribery problems without making judgments as to their morality.

The briber's task has two main components. First, the briber needs to decide *who* to bribe. Second, the briber has to decide *how* to change the chosen votes. In that sense, election bribery combines a control-like action (picking which voters to affect) with a manipulation-like action (deciding how to change the selected votes; see Chapter 6 and Section 4.3.3 in the book chapter by Baumeister and Rothe (2015) for more details on manipulation). Furthermore, it might be the case that while a voter agrees to change her vote in some ways, she may refuse to change it in some other ways (e.g., the voter might agree to swap the two least preferred alternatives, but not to swap the two most preferred ones). The following definition, based on the ones given by Faliszewski et al. (2009b) and—later—by Elkind et al. (2009c),[6] tries to capture these intuitions. (A careful reader should see that this definition is not sufficient for algorithmic applications; however, it will be a convenient base for further refinements.)

Definition 7.5. Let f be a voting rule. In the priced bribery problem for f, we are given (a) an election (A, R), where the set of voters is $N = \{1, \ldots, n\}$ and R contains a preference order $\succ_i$ for each $i \in N$, (b) a preferred alternative $p \in A$, (c) a budget $B \in \mathbb{N}$, and (d) a collection of price functions $\Pi = (\pi_1, \ldots, \pi_n)$. For each i, $1 \leqslant i \leqslant n$, and each preference order $\succ$ over A, $\pi_i(\succ)$ is the cost of convincing the ith voter to

---

[6] To provide historical perspective, let us mention that the paper of Faliszewski et al. (2009b) was presented in 2006 at the 21st National Conference on Artificial Intelligence (AAAI).

cast vote $\succ$ (we require that for each i, $1 \leqslant i \leqslant n$, $\pi_i(\succ_i) = 0$). We ask if there exists a preference profile $R' = (\succ_1', \ldots, \succ_n')$ such that (i) p is an f-winner of election (A, R'), and (ii) $\sum_{i=1}^{n} \pi_i(\succ_i') \leqslant B$.[7]

Informally speaking, in condition (i) we require that the bribery is successful (p becomes a winner) and in condition (ii) we require that it is cheap enough (i.e., within our budget B). However, it is impossible to use this definition directly in our algorithmic analysis. The problem is that given an election (A, R), each price function should be defined for $|A|!$ different arguments. If we represented each price function by listing all the $|A|!$ argument-value pairs, the encoding of the problem would grow exponentially and for most natural voting rules the problem could be solved by brute force (yet without giving any real insight into the nature of election bribery). In other words, to make the problem interesting (and practical), we have to limit our attention to families of price functions that can be described succinctly. To this end, researchers have mostly focused on the following families of functions (in the following description we use the notation from Definition 7.5; we use the terms *discrete* and *$discrete* to unify the discussion of bribery problems even though these terms did not appear in the original papers):

1. We say that the price functions are *discrete* if for each π_i, $1 \leqslant i \leqslant n$, and for each preference order $\succ$, it holds that $\pi_i(\succ) = 0$ if $\succ = \succ_i$, and $\pi_i(\succ) = 1$ otherwise.
2. We say that the price functions are *$discrete* if for each π_i, $1 \leqslant i \leqslant n$, there is an integer c_i such that for each preference order $\succ$, it holds that $\pi_i(\succ) = 0$ if $\succ = \succ_i$, and $\pi_i(\succ) = c_i$ otherwise. (Each voter can have a different value c_i.)
3. We say that the price functions are *swap-bribery price functions* if for each π_i, $1 \leqslant i \leqslant n$, and for each two alternatives $x, y \in A$, there is a value $c_i^{\{x,y\}}$ such that for each preference order $\succ$, $\pi_i(\succ)$ is the sum of the values $c_i^{\{x,y\}}$ such that $\succ$ ranks x and y in the opposite order than $\succ_i$ does.

That is, discrete functions give cost one for changing a vote (irrespective of which vote it is or how it is changed), $discrete functions give a (possibly different) cost for changing each vote (irrespective of the nature of the change), and swap-bribery price functions define a cost for swapping each two alternatives and, then, sum up these costs. Clearly, functions in each of these families can be described succinctly.

From the historical perspective, the first paper on the complexity of bribery in elections (due to Faliszewski et al., 2009b) focused largely on discrete and $discrete functions. Swap-bribery functions were introduced first by Faliszewski et al. (2009c) in the context of so-called irrational votes, and were later carefully studied by Elkind et al. (2009c) in the standard setting of linear preference orders. Naturally, one can also define other families of cost functions (and some researchers—including the ones just cited—have done so) but in this chapter we will focus on these three.

Definition 7.5 can be applied to weighted elections as well. In such a case, it is tempting to introduce some explicit relation between the voters' weights and the costs

---

[7] As opposed to the case of control, research on bribery typically focuses on the nonunique-winner model; the unique-winner model has been considered in addition in some papers on bribery (see, e.g., Faliszewski et al., 2015).

of changing their votes. However, doing so is not necessary and we assume that such dependencies, if needed, are embedded in the price functions.

7.4.1 Bribery, Weighted-Bribery, $Bribery, Weighted-$Bribery, and Swap-Bribery

We focus on the bribery problems that can be derived using discrete, $discrete, and swap-bribery price functions. For the former two, consider the following definition.

Definition 7.6 (Faliszewski et al., 2009b). Let f be a voting rule. By f-BRIBERY we denote the priced bribery problem with discrete price functions and by f-$BRIBERY we denote the priced bribery problem with $discrete price functions. The problems f-WEIGHTED-BRIBERY and f-WEIGHTED-$BRIBERY are defined in the same way, but for weighted elections.

Example 7.7. Consider the Borda election in Table 7.1(a) and suppose that each voter has the same unit price, and that the goal is to ensure the victory of f through bribery. Prior to the bribery, b has 16 points and f has 9. It suffices to bribe voter 3 to cast vote $f\ d\ a\ c\ e\ b$. (Afterward, b, e, and f have score 13 each, and a, c, and d have score 12 each.) This means that there is a successful bribery with cost one. On the other hand, if voters 1 and 5 had cost one and the remaining voters had cost three each, then it would be better to bribe voters 1 and 5 to shift f to the top positions in their votes.

For swap-bribery price functions, Elkind et al. (2009c) have defined the following problem (they have not studied swap bribery for weighted elections).

Definition 7.7 (Elkind et al., 2009c). Let f be a voting rule. By f-SWAP-BRIBERY we denote the priced bribery problem with swap-bribery price functions.

Example 7.8. Consider the Borda election in Table 7.1(a) once again. This time, by applying swap bribery, we want to ensure victory of candidate d. We assume that swapping each two adjacent candidates has unit cost. Prior to the bribery, b has 16 points, c has 15 points, d and e have 12 points, a has 11 points, and f has 9 points. We perform the bribery as follows: We swap b in the preference order of voter 1 first with f, then with e, and finally with d. This way b loses three points and d, e, and f gain one point each. Thus b, d, and e have score 13 each, a and f score less than 13 points, but c still has 15 points. So, next we swap c and d in the preference order of voter 3. This way both c and d have score 14 and they both tie as winners. This is a successful swap bribery of cost four (and, indeed, it is the cheapest successful swap bribery for d in this scenario).

To familiarize ourselves with bribery problems further, let us consider their complexity for the plurality rule.

Theorem 7.9. *For plurality voting it holds that:*

1. BRIBERY, WEIGHTED-BRIBERY, *and* $BRIBERY *are each in* P, *but* WEIGHTED-$BRIBERY *is* NP-*complete (Faliszewski et al., 2009b), and*
2. SWAP-BRIBERY *is in* P *(Elkind et al., 2009c).*

It is easy to see that plurality-BRIBERY can be solved by (repeating in a loop) the following greedy algorithm: If the preferred alternative is not a winner already, then pick one of the current winners and bribe one of her voters to vote for the preferred alternative. Unfortunately, such greedy approaches do not work for plurality-WEIGHTED-BRIBERY. For example, consider an algorithm that works in iterations and in each iteration bribes the heaviest voter among those that vote for one of the current winners. Let (A, R) be an election where $A = \{p, a, b, c\}$ and where we have 9 weight-1 voters voting for a, a single weight-5 voter voting for b, and a single weight-5 voter voting for c. Clearly, it suffices to bribe the two weight-5 voters, but the heuristic would bribe five voters with weight 1 each. On the other hand, bribing the heaviest voter first does not always work either (Faliszewski et al. (2009d) give a counterexample with $A = \{p, a, b\}$, p receiving no votes at first, a receiving three weight-2 votes and one weight-1 vote, and b receiving two weight-3 votes; to make p a winner it suffices to bribe one weight-2 vote and one weight-3 vote, but the heuristic bribes three votes). Nonetheless, a combination of these two heuristics does yield a polynomial-time algorithm for plurality-WEIGHTED-BRIBERY.

Let us consider some weighted plurality election and let us say that somehow we know that after an optimal bribery, our preferred alternative p has at least T points. Naturally, all the other alternatives have to end up with at most T points (and we can assume that at least one of them will get exactly T points). Thus for each alternative a that has more than T points, we should keep bribing its heaviest voters until its score decreases to at most T (this corresponds to running the *bribe the current winner's heaviest voter* heuristic). If, after bringing each alternative to at most T points, the preferred alternative still does not have T points, we bribe the globally heaviest voters to vote for the preferred alternative. We do so until the preferred alternative reaches at least T points (this corresponds to running the *bribe the heaviest voter* heuristic). If we chose the value of T correctly, by this point we would have found an optimal bribery strategy. But how do we choose T? If the weights were encoded in unary, we could try all possible values, but doing so for binary-encoded weights would give an exponential-time algorithm. Fortunately, we can make the following observation: For each alternative a, we bribe a's voters in the order of their nonincreasing weights. Thus, after executing the above-described strategy for some optimal value T, a's score is in the set $\{a$'s original score, a's score without its heaviest voter, a's score without its two heaviest voters, ...$\}$. Thus it suffices to consider values T of this form only (for each candidate) and to pick one that leads to a cheapest bribery.

It is an easy exercise for the reader to adapt the plurality-WEIGHTED-BRIBERY algorithm to the case of plurality-$BRIBERY. On the other hand, solving plurality-SWAP-BRIBERY requires a somewhat different approach. The reason is that under SWAP-BRIBERY it might not always be optimal to push our preferred candidate to the top of the votes, but sometimes it may be cheaper and more effective to replace some high-scoring alternatives with other, low-scoring ones. To account for such strategies, Elkind et al. (2009c) compute, for each vote v, the lowest cost of replacing v's current top-alternative with each other one, and then run a flow-based algorithm of Faliszewski (2008) to find the bribing strategy. We omit the details here.

For plurality-WEIGHTED-$BRIBERY, it is easy to see that the problem is in NP and so we only show NP-hardness. We give a reduction from the PARTITION problem to plurality-WEIGHTED-$BRIBERY. Recall that in the PARTITION problem the input consists of a sequence of positive integers that sum up to some value S, and we ask

Table 7.4. *The complexity of f-BRIBERY for various voting rules*

f	f-BRIBERY	reference
plurality	P	Faliszewski et al. (2009b)
veto	P	Faliszewski et al. (2009b)
2-approval	P	Lin (2012)
k-veto, $k \in \{2, 3\}$	P	Lin (2012)
k-approval, $k \geqslant 3$	NP-complete	Lin (2012)
k-veto, $k \geqslant 4$	NP-complete	Lin (2012)
Borda	NP-complete	Brelsford et al. (2008)
STV	NP-complete	Xia (2012a)
Bucklin	NP-complete	Faliszewski et al. (2015)
fallback	NP-complete	Faliszewski et al. (2015)
maximin	NP-complete	Faliszewski et al. (2011b)
Copeland	NP-complete	Faliszewski et al. (2009c)
Schulze	NP-complete	Parkes and Xia (2012)
ranked pairs	NP-complete	Xia (2012a)
approval	NP-complete	Faliszewski et al. (2009b)
range voting	NP-complete	follows from the approval result

if it is possible to partition this sequence into two subsequences that both sum up to $S/2$ (naturally, for that S needs to be even). Let $(s_1, \ldots, s_n)$ be the input sequence and let $S = \sum_{i=1}^{n} s_i$. We form an election (A, R), with $A = \{p, d\}$ and with R containing n voters voting for d; for each i, $1 \leqslant i \leqslant n$, the ith voter has weight s_i and her price function is *"it costs s_i to change the vote."* The budget B is $S/2$. In effect, any bribery of cost at most B can give p a score of at most $S/2$. The only such briberies that would ensure that p is among the winners must give p score exactly $S/2$, by solving the original PARTITION instance. This result is particularly useful because its proof easily adapts to most other typical voting rules, showing that WEIGHTED-$BRIBERY is NP-complete for them as well.

Theorem 7.9 suggests that, perhaps, for various voting rules f, not only is f-BRIBERY easy but so are even its more involved variants, f-$BRIBERY and f-WEIGHTED-BRIBERY. However, in-depth study of f-BRIBERY has shown that the problem is NP-complete for most natural voting rules f. We survey these results in Table 7.4. Naturally, the hardness results for BRIBERY immediately transfer to $BRIBERY and WEIGHTED-BRIBERY.

Theorem 7.10 (Faliszewski et al., 2009b). *For each voting rule f, f-BRIBERY reduces to f-$BRIBERY and to f-WEIGHTED-BRIBERY.*

Furthermore, for the case of $BRIBERY we can inherit multiple hardness results from the coalitional manipulation problem, through a simple reduction.

Definition 7.8 (Conitzer et al., 2007). Let f be a voting rule. In the (constructive, coalitional) f-MANIPULATION problem we are given (a) an election (A, R), (b) a preferred alternative $p \in A$, and (c) a collection R' of voters with unspecified preference orders. We ask if it is possible to ensure that p is an f-winner of election $(A, R + R')$

by setting the preference orders of the voters in R'. The (constructive, coalitional) f-Weighted-Manipulation problem is defined analogously, but for weighted elections, where the manipulators' weights are given.

Theorem 7.11 (Faliszewski et al., 2009b). *For each voting rule f, f-Manipulation reduces to f-$Bribery, and f-Weighted-Manipulation reduces to f-Weighted-$Bribery.*

For the case of Swap-Bribery, hardness results are even more abundant. Elkind et al. (2009c) have shown that the problem is NP-complete for k-approval (for $k \geqslant 2$)[8] and for Borda, Copeland, and maximin (for the latter three systems, NP-hardness holds even for Shift-Bribery, a special case of Swap-Bribery where the swaps have to involve the preferred candidate). Furthermore, the Swap-Bribery problem generalizes the Possible-Winner problem, which itself generalizes the Manipulation problem.

Definition 7.9 (Konczak and Lang, 2005). Let f be a voting rule. In the f-Possible-Winner problem we are given (a) an election (A, R), where the voters in R are represented through (possibly) partial orders, and (b) an alternative $p \in A$. We ask if it is possible to extend the partial orders in R to linear orders in such a way that p is an f-winner of the resulting election.

Theorem 7.12 (Elkind et al., 2009c). *For each voting rule f, f-Possible-Winner reduces to f-Swap-Bribery.*

Xia and Conitzer (2011a) have shown hardness of Possible-Winner for a number of voting rules (including STV, ranked pairs, Borda, Copeland, maximin, and many other rules); Betzler and Dorn (2010) together with Baumeister and Rothe (2012) show a dichotomy result regarding the complexity of Possible-Winner for pure scoring rules, obtaining hardness for almost all of them (see Chapter 10 and Section 4.3.2 in the book chapter by Baumeister and Rothe (2015) for more details on the Possible-Winner problem and on related issues). By Theorem 7.12, these hardness results immediately translate to hardness results for Swap-Bribery and the same voting rules.

Such an overwhelming number of hardness results (either shown directly or implied by Theorems 7.11 and 7.12) suggests that, perhaps, Swap-Bribery is too general a problem. That is why Elkind et al. (2009c) defined Shift-Bribery, a variant of Swap-Bribery where, as mentioned earlier, the only legal briberies shift the preferred candidate up in the voters' preference orders. While this problem turned out to typically be NP-complete as well, Elkind et al. (2009c), Elkind and Faliszewski (2010), and Schlotter et al. (2011) have found some interesting polynomial-time algorithms, exact and approximate, and Bredereck et al. (2014b) have studied the parameterized complexity of Shift-Bribery (see Section 7.5 for more motivating discussions regarding Shift-Bribery).

We now show that (the optimization variant of) Borda-Shift-Bribery can be efficiently approximated within a factor of 2.

Theorem 7.13 (Elkind et al., 2009c). *There is a polynomial-time 2-approximation algorithm for the cost of a cheapest shift bribery under Borda voting.*

---

[8] The result for $k = 2$ follows from the work of Betzler and Dorn (2010); for $k = 1$ the problem is in P; for $k = m/2$, where m is the number of alternatives, Elkind et al. (2009c) have shown hardness even for the case of a single voter.

Proof sketch. Consider an instance of our problem where the goal is to ensure candidate p's victory. By definition, the only possible actions are shifting p forward in (some of) the votes (costs are specified through swap-bribery price functions where swaps that do not involve p have infinite cost and we can think of shifting p forward in terms of its swaps with other candidates).

We start with two observations. First, there is a polynomial-time algorithm that given an instance of the optimization variant of Borda-SHIFT-BRIBERY computes the cost of a cheapest shift bribery that gives p a given number of points (the algorithm uses standard dynamic programming). Second, if there is a successful shift bribery that increases the score of p by K points, then every shift bribery that increases p's score by $2K$ points is successful (the best imaginable shift bribery gets K points for p in such a way that in each swap it increases the score of p and decreases the score of its strongest competitor; we achieve the same—or better—effect by getting $2K$ points for p).

Now the algorithm proceeds as follows: First, we guess the number K of points that p gets in the optimal solution. Then, we guess a number K', $K' \leqslant K$. (Because we are dealing with Borda elections, both guesses boil down to trying polynomially many computation paths.) We compute a cheapest shift bribery S_1 that gives K points to p. Then, we compute a cheapest shift bribery S_2 that gives K' additional points to p (we apply S_2 after we have applied S_1). We claim that $S_1 + S_2$ (that is, the two shift briberies taken together) form a 2-approximate solution.

Why is this so? Consider some optimal shift bribery O that ensures that p wins. By assumption, this shift bribery obtains K points for p. Now imagine the following situation: We start with the original election and perform only those swaps that are included in both O and S_1. In effect, p gains some K'' points. If we continued with the optimal solution, p would obtain additional $K - K''$ points and would become a winner of the election. By our second observation, this means that if after performing the swaps that occur both in O and in S_1 we obtain additional $2(K - K'')$ points for p, p certainly wins. We obtain the first of these $K - K''$ points by simply performing the remaining swaps from S_1. For the second $K - K''$ points, we can assume that we guessed $K' = K - K''$. In effect, performing the swaps from S_2 ensures p's victory. Furthermore, by definition of S_1 we know that its cost is no higher than that of O. On the other hand, the cost of S_2 also has to be at most as high as that of O because, by definition, the cost of S_2 cannot be higher than the cost of the shift bribery that contains exactly the swaps that are in O but not in S_1. □

So far, there has been relatively little research on how to cope with the hardness of bribery problems (except for results regarding special cases such as SHIFT-BRIBERY, as seen in the preceding theorem). For example, many parameterized-complexity results boil down to polynomial-time algorithms for the case where the number of candidates is constant. In this case, bribery problems can either be solved by an appropriate brute-force search, or by solving a linear integer program using the algorithm of Lenstra, Jr. (1983); see the papers of Faliszewski et al. (2009b, 2011b), Elkind et al. (2009c), Dorn and Schlotter (2012), and Hemaspaandra et al. (2013b) for examples. These approaches, however, do not work for weighted elections and, indeed, for weighted elections bribery problems are typically NP-hard (see, e.g., the dichotomy results of Faliszewski et al. (2009b)). On the other hand, there are several detailed studies of parameterized complexity of SWAP-BRIBERY (due to Dorn and Schlotter, 2012), SUPPORT-BRIBERY (Schlotter et al. (2011); we omit the discussion of SUPPORT-BRIBERY), and SHIFT-BRIBERY (Bredereck et al., 2014b).

Another natural way of coping with the hardness of bribery problems would be to design approximation algorithms. Brelsford et al. (2008) have made some attempts in this direction (though, using a rather involved goal function instead of approximating the cost of a successful bribery), Faliszewski (2008) gave a fully polynomial-time approximation scheme for plurality-WEIGHTED-$BRIBERY, and Xia (2012a) gave several approximation algorithms for destructive bribery problems (where the goal is to ensure, through buying votes, that some candidate does *not* win the election). There are also approximation results regarding SHIFT-BRIBERY (due to Elkind and Faliszewski, 2010; Bredereck et al., 2014b). While surprising at first, this limited enthusiasm for studying approximation algorithms for bribery problems can, to some extent, be understood. Theorems 7.11 and 7.12 show how to reduce the MANIPULATION and POSSIBLE-WINNER problems to appropriate $BRIBERY and SWAP-BRIBERY problems, and they do so via showing that a given MANIPULATION (POSSIBLE-WINNER) instance is a "yes" instance if and only if there is a zero-cost bribery. This means that, unless P = NP, those $BRIBERY and SWAP-BRIBERY problems whose hardness can be shown via Theorems 7.11 and 7.12 do not have constant-factor polynomial-time approximation algorithms (for finding the cheapest successful bribery). Nonetheless, it is interesting to study the approximability of f-BRIBERY for various voting rules f.

It would also be interesting to study the complexity of bribery in elections with restricted domains, for example, in single-peaked elections. While this direction has been pursued successfully for the case of control, we are aware of only a single paper that attempted it for bribery (Brandt et al., 2010a), showing that, indeed, for single-peaked elections bribery problems often become easy (see also Section 5.4 in the book chapter by Hemaspaandra et al. (2015)).

7.4.2 Other Bribery Problems

So far, we have focused on the most standard election model, where voter preferences are represented by total orders over the set of alternatives. Naturally, there are numerous other settings in which bribery was studied, and in what follows we give several (though certainly not all) examples of such settings.

Mattei et al. (2012a) have considered bribery in combinatorial domains, where the voters express their preferences over bundles of alternatives in a certain compact way. This compact representation can lead to quite interesting results. The particular language used to express preferences in the work of Mattei et al. (2012a) (CP-nets) does not allow one to express certain preference orders and, as a result, BRIBERY for k-approval becomes easy in this model (see Chapter 9 for more details on voting in combinatorial domains). If there are no direct interrelations between the bundles of items, it may be more reasonable to model bribery as the *lobbying problem* (studied by Christian et al. (2007) and later on by Bredereck et al. (2014a) and Binkele-Raible et al. (2014)): We are given a collection of yes/no votes over all items independently, where an item is accepted with a simple majority of yes votes, and is rejected otherwise. The lobby's goal is to change the outcome to its liking by bribing certain voters without exceeding its budget.

Examples of bribery problems in other settings include, for example, the work of Baumeister et al. (2011) on bribery in judgment aggregation (see Chapter 17 and the book chapter by Baumeister et al. (2015) for more details on judgment aggregation), the work of Rey and Rothe (2011) and Marple et al. (2014) on bribery in path-disruption games, and the work of Mattei et al. (2012b) on bribery in tournaments.

7.5 A Positive Look

There are a number of settings where control and bribery (and similar problems) have positive interpretations (from particular points of view). In the following we very briefly list a few examples of such settings.

Election control problems deal with affecting their structure in order to change the winner. Instead of viewing this as someone manipulating the result, we can think of it as predicting the winners given how the election's structure may change. For example, this research direction was pursued by Chevaleyre et al. (2012) and Baumeister et al. (2012c). Specifically, Chevaleyre et al. (2012) have studied a situation where we have already elicited voters' preferences regarding some set of candidates, but afterward some new candidates appeared, of whom we have no knowledge whatsoever. Naturally, possibly each new candidate can be better than each old one, so each of them, possibly, might win the election. However, can we decide which of the original candidates still have chances of winning? This problem of predicting possible winners is very close in spirit to control by adding candidates (and to cloning; see later), though—formally—it is a special case of the POSSIBLE-WINNER problem (and, as such, it is a special case of the SWAP-BRIBERY problem).

Another way of predicting election winners was suggested by Wojtas and Faliszewski (2012), who have used counting variants of election control problems. In particular, they considered the following setting: We know the preference orders of the voters, but we do not know which of them will eventually cast votes. Having some prior distribution on the number of voters that do cast votes (and assuming that if k voters participate in the election, then each size-k subset of voters is equally likely to vote), what is the probability that a given candidate wins? Formally, this problem reduces to counting the number of ways of adding (deleting) voters to (from) an election to ensure a given candidate's victory.

Quite interestingly, many of the problems that model attacks on elections have direct applications in protecting them. For example, in the margin-of-victory problem (see, e.g., the work of Cary (2011), Magrino et al. (2011), Xia (2012a), and Reisch et al. (2014)) we ask how many voters need to cast different votes to change the result of an election. If this number is high then it is unlikely that the election was tampered with. However, if this number is low, it means that it would have been easy to manipulate the result in some way and thus we should carefully check the election. The margin-of-victory problem is, in some sense, simply a destructive bribery problem. Similarly, Birrell and Pass (2011) have used bribery-related problems in the context of approximate strategyproofness of voting rules. Yet another application of a control-like problem to protect elections was given by Elkind et al. (2012a). They have considered the problem of candidate cloning, where some candidate c is replaced by a number of clones, $c_1, \ldots, c_t$, that—from the point of view of the voters—are indistinguishable (consider, for example, a party submitting several candidates for a given position and the voters forming their preference orders based on party membership only). If an election is single-peaked and we clone a candidate, it is likely that this election ceases to be single-peaked. Motivated by this observation, Elkind et al. (2012a) have given an algorithm that finds an optimal "decloning" of the candidates, so that the resulting election is single-peaked (similar results, though in a different context, were later given by Cornaz et al. (2012, 2013); we also mention that cloning, originally defined by Tideman (1987) and by Zavist and Tideman (1989), resembles control by adding candidates; its computational analysis is due to Elkind et al. (2011a)).

Finally, let us mention some positive interpretations of bribery problems. In political elections, prior to casting the votes, the candidates run their campaigns and wish to convince the voters to rank them as highly as possible. Naturally, running a campaign has cost (both in terms of money and in terms of invested time) and it is important for the candidates to decide which voters they should try to convince. However, deciding how much effort to spend on each voter (or, group of voters) is just the bribery problem (see the work of Hazon et al. (2013) for a different twist on this idea). With the campaign management interpretation in mind, it is natural to study various special cases of the bribery problems. Indeed, SHIFT-BRIBERY of Elkind et al. (2009c), where we can only convince the voters to rank the preferred candidate higher and we cannot affect the relative order of the other candidates, models campaign management in a natural way. While the SHIFT-BRIBERY problem is NP-hard for many voting rules, Elkind et al. (2009c) have given a 2-approximation algorithm for this problem with Borda's rule (see Theorem 7.13 here), Elkind and Faliszewski (2010) have extended this result to all scoring rules (and provided weaker approximations for Copeland and maximin), and Schlotter et al. (2011) have shown that SHIFT-BRIBERY is in P for Bucklin and fallback voting. These results for Bucklin and fallback voting were recently complemented by Faliszewski et al. (2015) who studied various bribery problems for these rules, including so-called EXTENSION-BRIBERY, introduced by Baumeister et al. (2012a) in the context of campaign management in the presence of truncated ballots.

7.6 Summary

We surveyed the known results on control and bribery. While often studied in the context of attacking elections, these problems also have many other applications and interpretations, often very positive ones. Many NP-hardness results have been obtained, yet recent work focuses on solving these problems effectively, either by approximation or fixed-parameter tractable algorithms, or efficient heuristics. We strongly encourage the readers to study control and bribery and to add their own contributions to the field.

CHAPTER 8

Rationalizations of Voting Rules

Edith Elkind and Arkadii Slinko

8.1 Introduction

From antiquity to these days, voting has been an important tool for making collective decisions that accommodate the preferences of all participants. Historically, a remarkably diverse set of voting rules have been used (see, e.g., Brams and Fishburn, 2002), with several new voting rules proposed in the last three decades (Tideman, 1987; Schulze, 2003; Balinski and Laraki, 2010). Thus, when decision-makers need to select a voting rule, they have plenty of choice: should they aggregate their opinions using something as basic as Plurality voting or something as sophisticated as Ranked Pairs? Or should they perhaps design a new voting rule to capture the specific features of their setting?

Perhaps the best known way to answer this question is to use the axiomatic approach, that is, identify desirable properties of a voting rule and then choose (or construct) a rule that has all of these properties. This line of work was initiated by Arrow (1951) and led to a great number of impossibility theorems, as it turned out that some desirable properties of voting systems are incompatible. By relaxing these properties, researchers obtained axiomatic characterizations of a number of classical voting rules, such as Majority (May, 1952), Borda (Young, 1975), and Kemeny (Young and Levenglick, 1978); see the survey by Chebotarev and Shamis (1998) as well as Chapter 2.

However, early applications of voting suggest a different perspective on this question. It is fair to say that in the Middle Ages voting was most often used by religious organizations (Uckelman and Uckelman, 2010). The predominant view in ecclesiastical elections was that God's cause needed the most consecrated talent that could be found for leadership in the church. Moreover, it was believed that God knew who the best candidate was, so the purpose of elections was to reveal God's will. It is therefore not surprising that when the Marquis de Condorcet (1785) undertook the first attempt at systematization of voting rules, he was influenced by the philosophy of church elections. His view was that the aim of voting is to determine the "best" decision for the society when voters are prone to making mistakes. This approach assumes that there is an objectively correct choice, but voters have different opinions due to errors of judgment;

absent these errors, they would all agree on the most suitable alternative. Thus, one should aim to design a voting rule that maximizes the probability of identifying the best choice. Depending on the model of "noise" or "mistakes" in voters' judgment, we get different voting rules. In statistics, this approach is known as *maximum likelihood estimation (MLE)*: it tries to estimate the state of the world (which is hidden) that is most likely to produce the observed noisy data.

A somewhat different, but related approach, which takes its roots in ideas of Charles Dodgson (1876), can be called consensus-based. The society agrees on a notion of a consensus (for example, we could say that there is a consensus if all voters agree which alternative is the best, or if there exists a Condorcet winner), and the result of each election is viewed as an imperfect approximation to a consensus. Specifically, if a preference profile R is a consensus, then we pick the consensus winner, and otherwise we output the winners of consensus profiles R' that are as close to R as possible. Alternatively, we may say that the society looks for a minimal change to the given preference profile that turns it into a profile with an indisputable winner. At the heart of this approach is the agreement as to (1) which preference profiles should be viewed as consensual and (2) what is the appropriate notion of closeness among preference profiles. It turns out that many common voting rules can be explained and classified by different choices of these parameters.

In this chapter we will survey the MLE framework and the consensus-based framework, starting with the latter. We demonstrate that both frameworks can be used to rationalize many common voting rules, with the consensus-based framework being somewhat more versatile. We also establish some connections between the two frameworks. We remark that these two frameworks are not the only alternatives to the axiomatic analysis. For instance, Camps et al. (2014) put forward an approach that is based on propositional logic. Furthermore, in economic literature the term "rationalization" usually refers to explaining the behavior of an agent or a group of agents via an acyclic (or transitive) preference relation, and there is a large body of literature that investigates which voting rules are rationalizable in this sense (see Bossert and Suzumura, 2010, for a survey). In this chapter, we focus on the MLE framework and the consensus-based framework because these two methods for rationalizing voting rules are interesting from a computational perspective: as we will see, explaining a voting rule via a consensus and a "good" measure of closeness implies upper bounds on its algorithmic complexity, whereas MLE-based voting rules are desirable for many applications, such as crowdsourcing, and therefore implementing them efficiently is of paramount importance.

In what follows, we assume that the set of alternatives is A and $|A| = m$; we use the terms *alternatives* and *candidates* interchangeably. Also, unless specified otherwise, voters' preferences and ballots are assumed to be linear orders over A.

8.2 Consensus-Based Rules

The goal of the consensus-based approach is to reach a compromise among all voters, that is, to arrive at a situation where there is agreement in society as to which outcome is the best. This may require persuading some voters to modify their opinions in minor ways, and, as a result, to make small changes to their ballots. Obviously it is desirable to minimize the number and magnitude of these changes. Thus, the best alternatives are the ones for which the agreement can be reached at the smallest cost (measured by the total amount of changes). In other words, given an arbitrary preference profile, we proceed by identifying the consensual profiles that are most similar to it and outputting their winners. The result then depends on how we define consensual profiles and how we measure the magnitude of change in votes. The latter question is usually addressed by using a distance over the space of profiles; this is why voting rules that can be obtained in this manner are called *distance rationalizable*. Often, this distance is obtained by computing the number of "unit changes" needed to transform one profile into the other, where the notion of "unit change" may vary from one voting rule to another.

This method of constructing voting rules can be traced back to Dodgson (1876), who was the first to define a voting rule in this manner (for a specific notion of consensus and a specific distance between profiles, see Section 8.2.1). More recently, it was formalized and studied by Nitzan (1981), Lerer and Nitzan (1985), Campbell and Nitzan (1986), and Baigent (1987), and subsequently by Meskanen and Nurmi (2008) and Elkind et al. (2010a, 2010b, 2011b, 2012b); we also point the reader to the survey of Eckert and Klamler (2011). It turns out that many classic voting rules can be obtained in this manner; Meskanen and Nurmi (2008) put together an extensive catalogue of distance rationalizations of common voting rules, with additional examples provided by Elkind et al. (2010b, 2012b). Furthermore, many properties of voting rules can be derived from their distance rationalizations: a voting rule can be shown to have "nice" properties if it can be rationalized via a "nice" consensus class and a "nice" distance. This makes the distance rationalizability approach eminently suitable for constructing new voting rules: it allows us to combine known distances and consensus classes, and derive conclusions about the resulting rules based on the properties of their components.

We start by presenting a few examples that illustrate the concepts of consensus and distance to consensus, followed by a formal definition and a discussion of properties of distance rationalizable voting rules.

8.2.1 Examples

The examples in this section are taken from the work of Meskanen and Nurmi (2008) and Elkind et al. (2012b); see these papers for additional references. We provide brief descriptions of the voting rules we consider; for formal definitions the reader is referred to Chapter 2.

Dodgson. Perhaps the most canonical example of the consensus-based approach is the Dodgson rule. Recall that winner determination under this rule proceeds as follows. If the given preference profile has a Condorcet winner, that is, a candidate that beats every other candidate in a pairwise election, then this candidate is declared the unique Dodgson winner. Otherwise, for every candidate c we compute her *Dodgson score*, that is, the number of swaps of adjacent candidates in voters' ballots that need to be performed in order to make c a Condorcet winner. We then output all candidates with the smallest Dodgson score. This definition follows the principles of the distance rationalizability framework: the underlying notion of agreement is the existence of a Condorcet winner, and the unit changes are swaps of adjacent candidates. This notion of unit change corresponds to a distance on rankings known as the *swap distance*, which is the number of swaps of adjacent candidates needed to transform one ranking into the other. We refer the reader to Chapter 5 for a complexity-theoretic analysis of the Dodgson rule.

Kemeny. The Kemeny rule is also defined in terms of the swap distance. While it is more common to view this rule as a *social preference function*, that is, a mapping that, given a preference profile, outputs a set of rankings, in this section we will be interested in the interpretation of this rule as a social choice function. Under the Kemeny rule, we identify all rankings that minimize the total swap distance to the voters' ballots. The associated social preference function then outputs all such rankings, whereas the Kemeny social choice function (which we will refer to as the Kemeny rule) outputs all candidates that are ranked first in at least one of these rankings. This rule can be viewed as another example of the distance rationalizability approach: the consensual profiles are ones where all votes are identical, and the unit changes are the same as for the Dodgson rule, that is, swaps of adjacent candidates.

Plurality. Under Plurality rule, each candidate gets one point from each voter who ranks her first; the winners are the candidates with the largest number of points. Because Plurality considers voters' top candidates only, it is natural to use a notion of consensus that also has this property: we say that there is an agreement in the society if all voters rank the same candidate first. Now, consider an n-voter preference profile. If some candidate a receives $n_a \leq n$ Plurality votes, there are $n - n_a$ voters who *do not* rank her first. Thus, if we want to turn this profile into a consensus where everyone ranks a first, and we are allowed to change the ballots in any way we like (at a unit cost per ballot), we have to modify $n - n_a$ ballots. In other words, if our notion of a unit change is an arbitrary modification of an entire ballot, then the number of unit changes required to make a candidate a consensus winner is inversely related to her Plurality score. In particular, the candidates for whom the number of required unit changes is minimal are the Plurality winners. Alternatively, we can define a unit change as a swap of two (not necessarily adjacent) candidates; the preceding argument still applies, thereby showing that this construction also leads to the Plurality rule.

Borda. Recall that the Borda score of a candidate a in an n-voter, m-candidate profile is given by $(m - r_1) + \cdots + (m - r_n) = nm - \sum_i r_i$, where $r_i, i = 1, \ldots, n$, is the rank of a in the ith ballot. To distance rationalize this rule, we use the same notion of consensus as for the Plurality rule (i.e., all voters agree on who is the best candidate) and the same notion of unit change as for the Dodgson rule and the Kemeny rule, namely, a swap of adjacent candidates. Indeed, to ensure that a is ranked first by voter i, we need to perform $r_i - 1$ swaps of adjacent candidates. Consequently, making a the unanimous winner requires $\sum_i r_i - n$ swaps. That is, the number of swaps required to make a candidate a consensus winner is inversely related to her Borda score. This construction, which dates back to Farkas and Nitzan (1979), can be extended to scoring rules other than Borda, by assigning appropriate weights to the swaps (Lerer and Nitzan, 1985).

Copeland. The Copeland score of a candidate a can be defined as the number of pairwise elections that a wins (a may also get additional points for the pairwise elections that end in a tie; in what follows we focus on elections with an odd number of voters to avoid dealing with ties). The Copeland winners are the candidates with the highest Copeland score. For this rule, an appropriate notion of consensus is the existence of a Condorcet winner. As for the notion of unit change, it is convenient to formulate it in terms of the pairwise majority graph. Recall that the pairwise majority graph $\mathcal{G}(R)$ of a profile R over a candidate set A is the directed graph whose vertex set is A and there is a directed edge from candidate a to candidate b if a strict majority of voters in R prefer a to b. Consider two n-voter profiles R^1 and R^2 over a candidate set A; assume that n is odd. A natural notion of a unit change in this setting is an edge reversal, that is, a pair $(a, b) \in A \times A$ such that in $\mathcal{G}(R^1)$ there is an edge from a to b, whereas in $\mathcal{G}(R^2)$ there is an edge from b to a. The distance between R^1 and R^2 is then defined as the number of edge reversals. To see that this distance combined with the Condorcet consensus rationalizes the Copeland rule, note that if a candidate's Copeland score is s, she can be made the Condorcet winner by reversing $m - 1 - s$ edges, so the number of edge reversals and the candidate's Copeland score are inversely related.

Maximin. The Maximin score of a candidate a in an n-voter profile R over a candidate set A is the number of votes that a gets in her most difficult pairwise election (i.e., $\min_{b \in A} n_{ab}$, where n_{ab} is the number of voters in R who prefer a to b); the winners are the candidates with the highest score. Suppose that R has no Condorcet winner, and consider a candidate $a \in A$. Let b be a's most difficult opponent, that is, a's Maximin score is $s_a = n_{ab}$; note that $s_a \leq \frac{n}{2} < \frac{n+1}{2}$, because a is not a Condorcet winner. Then if we add $n + 1 - 2s_a$ ballots where a is ranked first, a will be the Condorcet winner in the resulting profile (which has $2n + 1 - 2s_a$ voters, with $n + 1 - s_a$ of these voters ranking a above c for every $c \in A$). On the other hand, if we add $k < n + 1 - 2s_a$ ballots, we obtain a profile where at least $n - s_a$ voters out of $n + k$ prefer b to a; as $2(n - s_a) \geq n + k$, this means that at least half of the voters in this profile prefer b to a, so a is not a Condorcet winner. Thus, a candidate's Maximin score is inversely related to the number of ballots that need to be added in order to obtain a profile where this candidate is the Condorcet winner.

This argument explains the Maximin rule in the language of agreement and changes. However, this explanation does not quite fit our framework, because it uses a notion of unit change (adding a single ballot) that does not directly correspond to a distance. The problem here is that a distance is supposed to be symmetric (see Section 8.2.2), whereas adding ballots is an inherently asymmetric operation: if we can turn R into R' by adding s ballots, we cannot turn R' into R by adding s ballots. It turns out, however, that the Maximin rule can be rationalized via the distance that measures the number of ballots that need to be *added or deleted* to turn one profile into another (see Elkind et al., 2012b, for details). Intuitively, this is because for the purpose of reaching a Condorcet consensus adding a ballot is always at least as useful as deleting a ballot.

We remark that there is another voting rule that is defined in terms of deleting ballots so as to obtain a Condorcet consensus, namely, the Young rule, which is discussed in Chapter 5. While the Young rule, too, can be distance-rationalized, the construction is quite a bit more complicated than for Maximin (Elkind et al., 2012b).

These examples raise a number of questions. First, is it the case that all voting rules can be explained within the consensus-based framework? Second, what are the appropriate notions of consensus and distance to consensus? Third, can we derive any conclusions about a voting rule based on the notion of consensus and distance that explain it? To answer these questions, we need to define our framework formally.

8.2.2 Formal Model

The consensus-based framework that has been introduced informally so far has two essential components: the definition of what it means to have an agreement in the society and the notion of distance between preference profiles. We will now discuss both of these components in detail. Our presentation mostly follows Elkind et al. (2010b).

Consensus Classes

Informally, we say that a preference profile R is a consensus if it has an undisputed winner reflecting a certain concept of agreement in the society. Formally, a *consensus class for a set of candidates A* is a pair $\mathcal{K} = (\mathcal{X}, w)$ where $\mathcal{X}$ is a nonempty set of profiles over A and $w \colon \mathcal{X} \to A$ is a mapping that assigns a unique candidate to each profile in $\mathcal{X}$; this candidate is called the *consensus choice (winner)*.[1] We require $\mathcal{K}$ to be anonymous and neutral, in the following sense: For every profile $R \in \mathcal{X}$ a profile R' obtained from R by permuting voters satisfies $R' \in \mathcal{X}$ and $w(R') = w(R)$, and the profile R'' obtained from R by renaming candidates according to a permutation $\pi \colon A \to A$ satisfies $R'' \in \mathcal{X}$ and $w(R'') = \pi(w(R))$ (i.e., the winner under R'' is obtained by renaming the winner under R according to π).

The following classes of preference profiles have been historically viewed as situations of consensus:

Strong unanimity. This class, denoted $\mathcal{S}$, consists of profiles where all voters report the same preference order. The consensus choice is the candidate ranked first by all voters. The reader may note that we have used this notion of consensus in Section 8.2.1 to rationalize the Kemeny rule. Interestingly, it can also be used to provide an alternative rationalization of the Plurality rule (Elkind et al., 2010a).

Unanimity. This class, denoted $\mathcal{U}$, consists of profiles where all voters rank some candidate c first (but may disagree on the ranking of the remaining candidates). The consensus choice is this candidate c. This consensus class appears in our

---

[1] One can also consider situations in which the voters reach a consensus that several candidates are equally well qualified to be elected; this may happen, for example, under Approval voting when all voters approve the same set of candidates. However, in what follows we limit ourselves to consensus classes with unique winners.

rationalizations of Plurality and Borda. It is also used to rationalize other scoring rules (Lerer and Nitzan, 1985; Elkind et al., 2009a).

Majority. This class, denoted $\mathcal{M}$, consists of profiles where more than half of the voters rank some candidate c first. The consensus choice is this candidate c. This notion of consensus can be used to rationalize Plurality and a simplified version of the Bucklin rule (Elkind et al., 2010b).

Condorcet. This class, denoted $\mathcal{C}$, consists of profiles with a Condorcet winner. The consensus choice is the Condorcet winner. This notion of consensus appears in our rationalizations of the Dodgson rule, the Copeland rule, and Maximin.

Transitivity. This class, denoted $\mathcal{T}$, consists of profiles whose majority relation is transitive, that is, for every triple of candidates $a, b, c \in A$ it holds that if a majority of voters prefer a to b and a majority of voters prefer b to c, then a majority of voters prefer a to c. Such profiles always have a Condorcet winner, so we define the consensus choice to be the Condorcet winner. This consensus class can be used to rationalize the Slater rule (Meskanen and Nurmi, 2008).

It is easy to see that we have the following containment relations among the consensus classes: $\mathcal{S} \subset \mathcal{U} \subset \mathcal{M} \subset \mathcal{C}$ and $\mathcal{S} \subset \mathcal{T} \subset \mathcal{C}$. However, $\mathcal{U}$ and $\mathcal{T}$ are incomparable, that is, $\mathcal{U} \not\subseteq \mathcal{T}$ and $\mathcal{T} \not\subseteq \mathcal{U}$. Similarly, we have $\mathcal{M} \not\subseteq \mathcal{T}$ and $\mathcal{T} \not\subseteq \mathcal{M}$.

Remark 8.1. A consensus class $(\mathcal{X}, w)$ can be viewed as a voting rule with domain $\mathcal{X}$ that always outputs a unique candidate. Conversely, every anonymous and neutral voting rule f such that $|f(R)| = 1$ for at least one profile R defines a consensus class: if f is defined on the set of all profiles over a candidate set A, we can define a consensus class $\mathcal{K}_f = (\mathcal{X}_f, w_f)$ by setting $\mathcal{X}_f = \{R \mid |f(R)| = 1\}$ and for each $R \in \mathcal{X}_f$ defining $w_f(R)$ to be the unique candidate in $f(R)$. That is, this consensus class consists of all profiles on which f makes a definitive choice. The condition that $|f(R)| = 1$ for some profile R is necessary to ensure that $\mathcal{X}_f \neq \emptyset$.

There are other consensus classes one could consider: for example, one could study a 2/3-variant of the majority consensus $\mathcal{M}$, where more than 2/3 of the voters rank the same candidate first (this choice of threshold stems from the observation that in many countries changes to the constitution require the support of two thirds of the eligible voters). However, these five classes appear to be representative enough to rationalize many interesting voting rules.

Distances

To capture the idea of measuring the magnitude of changes in a preference profile, we use distances on profiles. Recall that a *distance* on a set X is a mapping $d : X \times X \to \mathbb{R} \cup \{+\infty\}$ such that for every $x, y, z \in X$ the following four conditions are satisfied:

(a) $d(x, y) \geqslant 0$ (nonnegativity);
(b) $d(x, y) = 0$ if and only if $x = y$ (identity of indiscernibles);
(c) $d(x, y) = d(y, x)$ (symmetry);
(d) $d(x, y) \leqslant d(x, z) + d(z, y)$ (triangle inequality).

A mapping that satisfies (a), (c), and (d), but not (b), is called a *pseudodistance*.

For distance rationalizability constructions, we need distances that are defined on pairs of profiles. Usually, it is enough to only consider pairs of profiles with the same set of candidates (this will be the case for all distances considered in this chapter), and in many cases it suffices to only consider pairs of profiles with the same number of voters. In particular, to construct a distance on the space of all n-voter profiles over a fixed set of candidates A, we can take a suitable distance d on the space $\mathcal{L}(A)$ of all linear orders over A and extend it to a distance $\widehat{d}$ over the space of all n-voter preference profiles $\mathcal{L}^n(A)$ by setting

$$\widehat{d}((u_1, \ldots, u_n), (v_1, \ldots, v_n)) = d(u_1, v_1) + \ldots + d(u_n, v_n). \tag{8.1}$$

It can be shown that $\widehat{d}$ satisfies all distance axioms whenever d does. This method of building distances over profiles from distances over votes will play an important role in our analysis (see Section 8.2.4).

We will now present several examples of distances on the space of preference profiles. Some of these distances should look familiar to the reader, as they were used to rationalize voting rules in Section 8.2.1.

Discrete distance. The *discrete distance* is defined on pairs of profiles with the same set of candidates A and the same number of voters n using formula (8.1); the underlying distance on $\mathcal{L}(A)$ is given by

$$d_{\text{discr}}(u, v) = \begin{cases} 0 & \text{if } u = v, \\ 1 & \text{if } u \neq v. \end{cases}$$

This distance was used in our rationalization of the Plurality rule.

Swap distance. The *swap distance*, which is also known as the Kendall tau distance, the Kemeny distance, the Dodgson distance, and the bubble-sort distance (Kendall and Gibbons, 1990), is also defined using formula (8.1). The underlying distance on $\mathcal{L}(A)$ is the swap distance between individual votes: $d_{\text{swap}}(u, v)$ is the number of pairs $(c, c') \in A \times A$ such that u ranks c above c', but v ranks c' above c.

(Weighted) footrule distance. This distance is also known as Spearman distance, or Spearman footrule (Kendall and Gibbons, 1990). Let $\text{pos}(u, c)$ denote the position of candidate c in vote u (the top candidate in u has position 1, and the bottom candidate in u has position m). Then the footrule distance on $\mathcal{L}(A)$ is given by

$$d_{\text{fr}}(u, v) = \sum_{c \in A} |\text{pos}(u, c) - \text{pos}(v, c)|.$$

That is, we measure the displacement of each candidate as we move from u to v, and then we take the sum over all candidates. This distance is extended to preference profiles using formula (8.1). The reader can verify that we can use the footrule distance $\widehat{d}_{\text{fr}}$ instead of the swap distance in our rationalization of the Borda rule.

Furthermore, let $\alpha = (\alpha_1, \ldots, \alpha_m)$ be a vector of m nonnegative rationals (weights). We define a (pseudo)distance $d_{\text{fr-}\alpha}(u, v)$ on $\mathcal{L}(A)$ by setting

$$d_{\text{fr-}\alpha}(u, v) = \sum_{c \in A} |\alpha_{\text{pos}(u,c)} - \alpha_{\text{pos}(v,c)}|. \tag{8.2}$$

When all weights are distinct, $d_{\text{fr-}\alpha}$ is a distance. However, when some of the weights coincide, $d_{\text{fr-}\alpha}$ is a pseudodistance, but not a distance. The reader can verify that for $\alpha = (m-1, \ldots, 1, 0)$ the distance $d_{\text{fr-}\alpha}$ coincides with d_{fr}. It can be shown that by using $\widehat{d_{\text{fr-}\alpha}}$ we can rationalize the scoring rule with the score vector α (Elkind et al., 2009a), that is, the rule that, given a profile $R = (v_1, \ldots, v_n)$, outputs the set $\operatorname{argmax}_{a \in A}(\alpha_{\text{pos}(v_1,a)} + \cdots + \alpha_{\text{pos}(v_n,a)})$.

ℓ_∞**-Sertel distance.** This distance, denoted by $\widehat{d_{\text{sert}}}^\infty$, is also obtained by extending a distance on rankings to n-voter profiles; however, in contrast with all distances considered so far, it is not defined via formula (8.1). Let $u(i)$ denote the candidate ranked in position i in vote u. We define the distance $d_{\text{sert}} : \mathcal{L}(A) \times \mathcal{L}(A) \to \mathbb{R}$ by setting

$$d_{\text{sert}}(u, v) = \max\{i \mid u(i) \neq v(i)\},$$

with the convention that $d_{\text{sert}}(u, v) = 0$ if $u = v$. The ℓ_∞-Sertel distance on n-voter preference profiles is then defined by setting

$$\widehat{d_{\text{sert}}}^\infty((u_1, \ldots, u_n), (v_1, \ldots, v_n)) = \max_{i=1,\ldots,n} d_{\text{sert}}(u_i, v_i).$$

The reason for having the symbol ℓ_∞ in the name of this distance and the notation $\widehat{d_{\text{sert}}}^\infty$ will become clear in Section 8.2.4. This distance, together with the majority consensus, can be used to provide a rationalization of a simplified version of the Bucklin rule (Elkind et al., 2010b).

Edge reversal (pseudo)distance. This distance is defined over the set of all profiles with an odd number of voters. Given two profiles R^1, R^2 over A, we set

$$d_{\text{rev}}(R^1, R^2) = |\{(a, b) \in A \times A \mid a >_{R^1} b, b >_{R^2} a\}|,$$

where we write $a >_R b$ to denote that a majority of voters in the profile R prefer a to b. This distance counts the number of edges in the pairwise majority graph of R^1 that need to be reversed to obtain the pairwise majority graph of R^2. The edge reversal distance was used in our rationalization of the Copeland rule; it can also be used to rationalize the Slater rule (Meskanen and Nurmi, 2008).

Note that, technically speaking, d_{rev} is a pseudodistance rather than a distance: we have $d_{\text{rev}}(R^1, R^2) = 0$ whenever R^1 and R^2 have the same pairwise majority graph. It is perhaps more natural to think of the domain of d_{rev} as the space of all tournaments over A, in which case d_{rev} satisfies all distance axioms.

Vote insertion (pseudo)distance. This distance is also defined over the set of all profiles with a given candidate set. Consider two profiles R^1 and R^2 over a candidate set A whose multisets of votes are given by V^1 and V^2 respectively. The vote insertion distance d_{ins} between R^1 and R^2 is the size of the symmetric difference between V^1 and V^2. This distance computes the cost of transforming R^1 into R^2 (or vice versa) if we are allowed to add or delete votes at a unit cost.

Elkind et al. (2012b) show that by combining this distance with the Condorcet consensus we obtain the Maximin rule. Again, d_{ins} is a pseudodistance rather than a distance: $d_{ins}(R^1, R^2) = 0$ if R^1 and R^2 have the same multiset of votes. It can be viewed as a distance on the space of *voting situations*, that is, multisets of votes over A.

We are now ready to put together the two components of our framework.

Definition 8.1. Let d be a (pseudo)distance on the space of preference profiles over a candidate set A, and let $\mathcal{K} = (\mathcal{X}, w)$ be a consensus class for A. We define the $(\mathcal{K}, d)$-*score* of a candidate a in a profile R to be the distance (according to d) between R and a closest profile $R' \in \mathcal{X}$ such that a is the consensus winner of R'. The set of $(\mathcal{K}, d)$-*winners* in a profile R consists of all candidates in A whose $(\mathcal{K}, d)$-score is the smallest.

Definition 8.2. A voting rule f is *distance rationalizable* via a consensus class $\mathcal{K}$ and a distance d over profiles (or, $(\mathcal{K}, d)$-*rationalizable*) if for every profile R a candidate is an f-winner in R if and only if she is a $(\mathcal{K}, d)$-winner in R.

We can now formalize our analysis of the six examples in Section 8.2.1: our arguments show that the Dodgson rule is $(\mathcal{C}, \widehat{d}_{swap})$-rationalizable, the Kemeny rule is $(\mathcal{S}, \widehat{d}_{swap})$-rationalizable, Plurality is $(\mathcal{U}, \widehat{d}_{discr})$-rationalizable, the Borda rule is $(\mathcal{U}, \widehat{d}_{swap})$-rationalizable, the Copeland rule is $(\mathcal{C}, d_{rev})$-rationalizable, and Maximin is $(\mathcal{C}, d_{ins})$-rationalizable. Observe that three of these well-known voting rules can be rationalized using the same distance (but different consensus classes). Further examples can be found in the work of Nitzan (2010): Chapter 6 of his book provides a summary of rules that are rationalizable with respect to the unanimity consensus. Meskanen and Nurmi (2008) describe distance rationalizations for several other voting rules; while some of these rationalizations are very appealing, others appear less intuitive. Motivated by this observation, we will now try to formalize what it means to have a "good" distance rationalization.

8.2.3 Universal Distance Rationalizability

It turns out that the unrestricted distance rationalizability framework defined in Section 8.2.2 is too powerful: Lerer and Nitzan (1985) show that if we do not impose any restrictions on the distance used, then essentially *any* voting rule is rationalizable with respect to all the standard consensus classes. This result was subsequently rediscovered by Elkind et al. (2010b), and our presentation follows their work.

To formally state this universal distance rationalizability result, we need a notion of compatibility between a voting rule and a consensus class.

Definition 8.3. A voting rule f is said to be *compatible* with a consensus class $\mathcal{K} = (\mathcal{X}, w)$, or $\mathcal{K}$-*compatible*, if $f(R) = \{w(R)\}$ for every profile R in $\mathcal{X}$.[2]

---

[2] One might think that the term "$\mathcal{K}$-consistent" would be more appropriate than "$\mathcal{K}$-compatible." Indeed, a voting rule that elects the Condorcet winner whenever one exists is usually referred to as Condorcet-consistent. We chose to use the term "$\mathcal{K}$-compatible" to avoid confusion with the normative axiom of consistency.

We will now show that every voting rule is distance rationalizable with respect to every consensus class that it is compatible with.

Theorem 8.2. *Let A be a set of candidates, let f be a voting rule over A, and let $\mathcal{K} = (\mathcal{X}, w)$ be a consensus class for A. Then f is $(\mathcal{K}, d)$-rationalizable for some distance d if and only if it is $\mathcal{K}$-compatible.*

Proof. Let f be a voting rule that is $(\mathcal{K}, d)$-rationalizable for some consensus class $\mathcal{K} = (\mathcal{X}, w)$ and distance d. Let R be some profile in $\mathcal{X}$. There is only one profile at distance 0 from R—namely, R itself. Hence, the unique $(\mathcal{K}, d)$-winner in R is $w(R)$. Thus, f is $\mathcal{K}$-compatible.

Conversely, suppose that f is $\mathcal{K}$-compatible. We will now define a distance d over the set of all profiles over the candidate set A as follows. We set $d(R, R') = 0$ if $R = R'$. We set $d(R, R') = 1$ if (a) $R \in \mathcal{X}$ and $w(R) \in f(R')$ or (b) $R' \in \mathcal{X}$ and $w(R') \in f(R)$. In all other cases, we set $d(R, R') = 2$. It is easy to check that d satisfies all distance axioms. It remains to argue that f is $(\mathcal{K}, d)$-rationalizable.

Consider a profile $R \in \mathcal{X}$. Because f is $\mathcal{K}$-compatible, we have $f(R) = \{w(R)\}$. Furthermore, we have $d(R, R) = 0$ and there is no profile R', $R' \neq R$, such that $d(R, R') = 0$. Thus, the unique $(\mathcal{K}, d)$-winner in R is $w(R)$, too.

On the other hand, consider a profile $R \notin \mathcal{X}$. Note that $d(R, R') \geq 1$ for every profile $R' \in \mathcal{X}$. Because $\mathcal{K}$ is neutral and $\mathcal{X} \neq \emptyset$, for each $a \in f(R)$ there exists a consensus profile R^a in which a is the consensus winner. By construction, we have $d(R, R^a) = 1$. Furthermore, we have $d(R, R') = 2$ for every profile $R' \in \mathcal{X}$ such that $w(R') \notin f(R)$. Thus, the set $f(R)$ is exactly the set of $(\mathcal{K}, d)$-winners in R, and the proof is complete. $\square$

Theorem 8.2 implies that being compatible with any of our five standard consensus classes suffices for distance rationalizability. Now, almost all common voting rules are compatible with the strong unanimity consensus $\mathcal{S}$, and hence distance rationalizable. This argument does not apply to voting rules that do not have unique winners on strongly unanimous profiles, such as Veto and k-Approval for $k > 1$ (recall that k-Approval is the scoring rule with the score vector $(\underbrace{1, \ldots, 1}_{k}, \underbrace{0, \ldots, 0}_{m-k})$, and Veto is simply the $(m-1)$-Approval rule). However, both Veto and k-Approval can be shown to be distance rationalizable by a slightly different argument.

Corollary 8.3. *For every anonymous neutral voting rule f over a set of candidates A such that $|f(R)| = 1$ for some profile R there exist a consensus class $\mathcal{K} = (\mathcal{X}, w)$ and a distance d such that f is $(\mathcal{K}, d)$-rationalizable.*

Proof. We can use the consensus class $\mathcal{K}_f = (\mathcal{X}_f, w_f)$ defined in Remark 8.1: by definition, f is $\mathcal{K}_f$-compatible, so Theorem 8.2 implies that f is $(\mathcal{K}_f, d)$-rationalizable for some distance d. $\square$

Clearly, both Veto and k-Approval satisfy the conditions of Corollary 8.3, so they are distance rationalizable as well.

Yet, intuitively, the distance used in the proof of Theorem 8.2 is utterly unnatural. For instance, we have seen that the Dodgson rule and the Kemeny rule can be rationalized via the swap distance, which is polynomial-time computable. In contrast, Elkind et al.

(2010b) show that applying Theorem 8.2 to either of these rules results in a rationalization via a distance that is not polynomial-time computable (assuming $P \neq NP$)—this follows from the fact that winner determination for these rules is computationally hard, as discussed in Chapter 5.

Thus, knowing that a rule is distance rationalizable—even with respect to a standard notion of consensus—by itself provides no further insight into the properties of this rule; for a rationalization to be informative, the distance used must be natural. Consequently, we will now shift our focus from distance rationalizability *per se* to quality of rationalizations, and seek an appropriate subclass of distances that would be expressive enough to capture many interesting rules while allowing us to draw nontrivial conclusions about rules that they rationalize.

8.2.4 Votewise Distances

In this section, we focus on distances that are obtained by first defining a distance on preference orders and then extending it to profiles. The reader may observe that the distances $\widehat{d}_{\text{discr}}, \widehat{d}_{\text{swap}}, \widehat{d}_{\text{fr}}$, and $\widehat{d_{\text{sert}}}^{\infty}$ defined in Section 8.2.2 are constructed in this way. This class of distances was identified by Elkind et al. (2010b), and our presentation in this section is based on their work.

Definition 8.4. A *norm* on $\mathbb{R}^n$ is a mapping $N \colon \mathbb{R}^n \to \mathbb{R}$ that has the following properties:

(a) positive scalability: $N(\alpha u) = |\alpha| N(u)$ for all $u \in \mathbb{R}^n$ and all $\alpha \in \mathbb{R}$;
(b) positive semidefiniteness: $N(u) \geq 0$ for all $u \in \mathbb{R}^n$, and $N(u) = 0$ if and only if $u = (0, 0, \ldots, 0)$;
(c) triangle inequality: $N(u + v) \leq N(u) + N(v)$ for all $u, v \in \mathbb{R}^n$.

A well-known class of norms on $\mathbb{R}^n$ is that of *p-norms* ℓ_p, $p \in \mathbb{Z}^+ \cup \{\infty\}$, given by

$$\ell_p(x_1, \ldots, x_n) = \left(\sum_{i=1}^{n} |x_i|^p \right)^{\frac{1}{p}} \text{ for } p \in \mathbb{Z}^+, \quad \ell_\infty(x_1, \ldots, x_n) = \max\{|x_1|, \ldots, |x_n|\}.$$

In particular, $\ell_1(x_1, \ldots, x_n) = |x_1| + \cdots + |x_n|$.

Definition 8.5. Let A be a fixed set of candidates, fix $n > 0$, let d be a distance on $\mathcal{L}(A)$, and let N be a norm on $\mathbb{R}^n$. We say that a distance D on the space of n-voter profiles over the candidate set A is *N-votewise* if for every pair of profiles R and R' over A with $R = (u_1, \ldots, u_n)$ and $R' = (v_1, \ldots, v_n)$ we have

$$D(R, R') = N(d(u_1, v_1), \ldots, d(u_n, v_n)). \tag{8.3}$$

It is easy to check that for every distance d on $\mathcal{L}(A)$ and every norm N on $\mathbb{R}^n$ the function defined by (8.3) is a (pseudo)distance. We will denote this (pseudo)distance by $\widehat{d^N}$. If $N = \ell_p$ for some $p \in \mathbb{Z}^+ \cup \{\infty\}$, we will write $\widehat{d^p}$ instead of $\widehat{d^{\ell_p}}$. Furthermore, because many distance rationalizations use ℓ_1 as the underlying norm, we will write $\widehat{d}$ instead of $\widehat{d^1}$ (note that this notation is consistent with the one used earlier in this chapter for $\widehat{d}_{\text{swap}}, \widehat{d}_{\text{discr}}, \widehat{d}_{\text{fr}}$, and $\widehat{d_{\text{sert}}}^{\infty}$).

Given a norm N, we say that a rule is N-*votewise* if it can be distance rationalized via an N-votewise distance; we say that a rule is *votewise* if it is N-votewise for some norm N.

Votewise distances are expressive enough to rationalize many classic voting rules. For instance, the rationalizations of the Dodgson rule, the Kemeny rule, Plurality, and the Borda rule described in Section 8.2.1 demonstrate that all these rules are ℓ_1-votewise, and the results of Lerer and Nitzan (1985) and Elkind et al. (2009a, 2010b) imply that the class of votewise rules includes essentially all scoring rules,[3] a simplified version of the Bucklin rule, and several other less common voting rules.

We will now demonstrate that votewise rules have a number of desirable properties, both from a normative and from a computational perspective.

Normative Properties of Votewise Rules

An important feature of the votewise distance rationalizability framework is that one can derive properties of votewise rules from the properties of their components, that is, the underlying distance on votes, the norm, and the consensus class. Elkind et al. (2010b, 2011b) consider such classic normative properties of voting rules as anonymity, neutrality, continuity, consistency, homogeneity and monotonicity, and, for each of them, derive sufficient conditions on the components of a votewise rationalization for the resulting rule to have the respective property. We present a sample of these results in the following.

Anonymity. Recall that a voting rule is said to be *anonymous* if its result does not change when the ballots are permuted. It turns out that anonymity of a votewise rule is inherited from the corresponding norm. Specifically, a norm N on $\mathbb{R}^n$ is said to be *symmetric* if it satisfies $N(x_1, \ldots, x_n) = N(x_{\sigma(1)}, \ldots, x_{\sigma(n)})$ for every permutation σ of $\{1, \ldots, n\}$; note that all p-norms are symmetric. Elkind et al. (2010b) show the following easy result.

Proposition 8.4. *Suppose that a voting rule f is $(\mathcal{K}, \widehat{d^N})$-rationalizable for some pseudodistance d over $\mathcal{L}(A)$, a consensus class $\mathcal{K}$, and a symmetric norm N. Then f is anonymous.*

Neutrality. A voting rule is said to be *neutral* if its result does not depend on the candidates' names. Neutrality of a votewise rule is a property of the underlying distance on votes. Namely, a distance d on $\mathcal{L}(A)$ is said to be *neutral* if for every permutation $\pi : A \to A$ and every pair of votes $u, v \in \mathcal{L}(A)$ it holds that $d(u, v) = d(u', v')$ where u' and v' are obtained from, respectively, u and v by renaming the candidates according to π. The following proposition is due to Elkind et al. (2010b).

Proposition 8.5. *Suppose that a voting rule f is $(\mathcal{K}, \widehat{d^N})$-rationalizable for some norm N, a consensus class $\mathcal{K}$, and a neutral pseudodistance d over $\mathcal{L}(A)$. Then f is neutral.*

Consistency. A voting rule f is said to be *consistent* if for every pair of profiles R^1, R^2 such that $f(R^1) \cap f(R^2) \neq \emptyset$, the preference profile $R^1 + R^2$ obtained by

---

[3] The exceptions are rules like Veto, which are not compatible with any standard consensus class; however, even such rules are votewise rationalizable via a pseudodistance.

concatenating R^1 and R^2 satisfies $f(R^1 + R^2) = f(R^1) \cap f(R^2)$. Consistency is a very demanding property: while all common voting rules are anonymous and neutral, the class of voting rules that are anonymous, neutral and consistent consists of compositions of scoring rules (Young, 1975). Nevertheless, Elkind et al. (2010b) obtain a sufficient condition for a distance rationalizable voting rule to be consistent.

Proposition 8.6. *Suppose that a voting rule f is $(\mathcal{U}, \widehat{d^p})$-rationalizable for some $p \in \mathbb{Z}^+$ and some pseudodistance d over $\mathcal{L}(A)$. Then f is consistent.*

Homogeneity. A voting rule f is said to be *homogeneous* if for every profile R and every positive integer k it holds that $f(R) = f(kR)$, where kR is the preference profile obtained by concatenating k copies of R. This notion can be seen as a relaxation of the notion of consistency. Elkind et al. (2011b) present several sufficient conditions for homogeneity of a votewise rule. For instance, they show that many of the voting rules that can be rationalized via the ℓ_∞ norm are homogeneous.

Proposition 8.7. *Suppose that a voting rule f is $(\mathcal{K}, \widehat{d^\infty})$-rationalizable for some pseudodistance d over $\mathcal{L}(A)$ and a consensus class $\mathcal{K} \in \{\mathcal{S}, \mathcal{U}, \mathcal{M}\}$. Then f is homogeneous.*

Monotonicity. A voting rule f is said to be *monotone* if moving a winning candidate upward in some voters' preference orders (without changing the relative order of other candidates) does not make him a loser. To identify sufficient conditions for monotonicity of a votewise rule, Elkind et al. (2011b) introduce several notions of monotonicity for distances over votes. In particular, they define *relatively monotone* distances. These are the distances over $\mathcal{L}(A)$ such that for every candidate $a \in A$ the following condition holds. Suppose that we have:

(i) two votes $y, y' \in \mathcal{L}(A)$ such that y and y' rank all candidates in $A \setminus \{a\}$ in the same order, but y' ranks a higher than y does, and
(ii) two votes $x, z \in \mathcal{L}(A)$ such that x ranks a first and z does not.

Then

$$d(x, y) - d(x, y') \geqslant d(z, y) - d(z, y'). \tag{8.4}$$

Elkind et al. (2011b) show that the relative monotonicity condition is satisfied by the swap distance. Moreover, they prove the following result.

Proposition 8.8. *Suppose that a voting rule f is $(\mathcal{K}, \widehat{d})$-rationalizable for some relatively monotone distance d over $\mathcal{L}(A)$ and a consensus class $\mathcal{K} \in \{\mathcal{S}, \mathcal{U}\}$. Then f is monotone.*

Algorithmic Properties of Votewise Rules

Votewise rules are also appealing from a complexity-theoretic perspective: it turns out that we can show tractability results for them under a mild condition on the underlying distance. For the definitions of the complexity classes mentioned in this section, we refer the reader to the book of Hemaspaandra and Ogihara (2002).

Definition 8.6. We say that a distance D on the space of profiles over a candidate set A is *normal* if:

(a) D is polynomial-time computable;
(b) D takes values in the set $\mathbb{Z}^+ \cup \{+\infty\}$;
(c) if R^1 and R^2 have a different number of votes, then $D(R^1, R^2) = +\infty$.

Given a voting rule f, we consider the problem of determining whether a given candidate is one of the winners in a given profile under f; we refer to this problem as f-WINNER. Elkind et al. (2010b) show the following set of results for this problem. Suppose that a voting rule f is $(\mathcal{K}, D)$-rationalizable for some normal distance D and a consensus class $\mathcal{K} \in \{\mathcal{S}, \mathcal{U}, \mathcal{M}, \mathcal{C}\}$. Then:

(i) f-WINNER is in P^{NP};
(ii) if there exists a polynomial p such that for every pair of n-voter m-candidate profiles R^1, R^2 it holds that $D(R_1, R_2) \leq p(m+n)$, then f-WINNER is in Θ_2^p;
(iii) if there exists a distance on votes d such that $D = \widehat{d}$, then f-WINNER is fixed-parameter tractable with respect to the number of candidates;
(iv) if there exists a distance on votes d such that $D = \widehat{d}$ or $D = \widehat{d^\infty}$, $\mathcal{K} \in \{\mathcal{U}, \mathcal{M}\}$, and D is neutral, then f-WINNER is in P/poly.

The first two results extend to the transitivity consensus $\mathcal{T}$ (which was not considered by Elkind et al. (2010b)); note also that for these results the distance D is not required to be votewise. However, it is not clear if the FPT algorithm in (iii) can be extended to $\mathcal{T}$ as well.

We emphasize that it is not the case that for every votewise rule the winner determination problem is in P (unless P = NP). In fact f-WINNER may be intractable even if f is ℓ_1-votewise rationalizable with respect to a standard consensus class via an easy-to-compute distance on votes: examples are provided by the Dodgson rule and the Kemeny rule, which are known to be computationally hard (Hemaspaandra et al., 1997a, 2005).

Votewise Distances: Discussion

We have seen that many common voting rules admit votewise distance rationalizations, and that distance rationalizable voting rules have several desirable properties. On the other hand, the "trivial" distance rationalization presented in Theorem 8.2 is clearly not votewise. Furthermore, some voting rules (most notably, STV) can be shown not to admit a votewise distance rationalization with respect to the standard consensus classes (Elkind et al., 2010a); we remark that the known distance rationalization for STV (Meskanen and Nurmi, 2008) is rather complex. Thus, the concept of a votewise distance appears to be useful for distinguishing between "good" and "bad" rationalizations.

Note, however, that the rationalizations of the Copeland rule and Maximin given in Section 8.2.1 are not votewise, despite being quite simple and intuitive. In fact, it is not known whether these rules are votewise distance rationalizable. It remains a challenge to come up with a definition of a "good" distance rationalization that covers all intuitively appealing rationalizations, but excludes the rationalization described in Theorem 8.2.

8.3 Rules as Maximum Likelihood Estimators

We will now turn our attention to voting rules that can be represented as maximum likelihood estimators. We start by revisiting the probabilistic model put forward by Condorcet (1785), and its interpretation by Young (1988).

Briefly, the basic assumption of Condorcet's model is that there always exists a correct ranking of the alternatives, which, however, cannot be observed directly. Voters derive their preferences over the alternatives from this ranking: when comparing two alternatives, each voter is more likely to make the correct judgment than the incorrect one. Moreover, voters make their decisions independently from each other, and a priori each ranking is equally likely to be correct.

Formalizing Condorcet's ideas turned out to be a challenging task; in what follows, we discuss some of the reasons for this. However, from a historical perspective, his ideas are very important, as they represent one of the earliest applications of what is now known as the *maximum likelihood estimation* approach. Under this approach, one computes the likelihood of the given preference profile for each possible "state of the world," that is, the true ranking of the alternatives. The best ranking(s) of the alternatives are then the one(s) that have the highest likelihood of producing the given profile. If we assume a uniform prior over the space of all possible rankings, this procedure can be interpreted as estimating the most likely state of the world given the preference data (the equivalence of the two interpretations follows immediately from the Bayes rule).

Condorcet's approach can be extended in two different directions: First, we can consider different *noise models*, that is, ways in which voters' preferences may arise from the true state of the world. Second, instead of associating a state of the world with a ranking of the alternatives, we can associate it with the identity of the best alternative (or, more generally, a set of pairwise comparisons between the alternatives); this approach is particularly attractive if the goal is to determine a single election winner rather than a full ranking of the alternatives (and in particular if there is indeed a unique "correct solution" to the decision problem at hand). In what follows, we survey recent research that explores these directions.

8.3.1 Two Alternatives: Condorcet Jury Theorem

When there are only two alternatives to choose from, it is natural to use *majority voting*, that is, select an alternative that is supported by at least half of the voters (breaking ties arbitrarily). It turns out that this is also the right strategy in Condorcet's model; in fact, as the number of voters grows, the probability that majority voting identifies the better alternative approaches 1. This result is known as the *Condorcet Jury Theorem*, and dates back to the original paper of Condorcet (1785).

Theorem 8.9. *Suppose that* $|A| = 2$, *and a priori each of the alternatives in A is equally likely to be the better choice. Suppose also that there are n voters, and each voter* *correctly identifies the better alternative with probability p, $1/2 < p \leq 1$; further, each voter makes her judgment independently from the other voters. Then the probability that the group makes the correct decision using the simple majority rule approaches 1 as $n \rightarrow +\infty$.*

Theorem 8.9 follows immediately from the Chernoff bound (see, e.g., Alon and Spencer, 2008); Condorcet's proof was based on a direct combinatorial argument.

Theorem 8.9 can be extended in a variety of ways. For instance, it can be generalized to the case where voters are a priori not identical, that is, voter i's probability to make the correct choice is p_i and not all p_is are equal: Nitzan and Paroush (1982) and Shapley and Grofman (1984) show that in this case it is optimal to use weighted voting, assigning a weight of $\log \frac{p_i}{1-p_i}$ to voter i. However, in practice the probabilities p_i are often not known; to mitigate this, Baharad et al. (2011, 2012) propose a procedure for estimating them. Other extensions deal with settings where voters are not independent (see, e.g., Shapley and Grofman, 1984; Berg, 1993a, 1993b; Ladha, 1992, 1993, 1995; Dietrich and List, 2004) or strategic (Austen-Banks and Smith, 1994; McLennan, 1998; Peleg and Zamir, 2012), or a priori the alternatives are not symmetric and the voters' probabilities of making the correct choice depend on the state of nature (Ben-Yashar and Nitzan, 1997).

When $|A| > 2$, the analysis becomes more complicated. In particular, it depends on whether the goal is to identify the most likely ranking of alternatives or the alternative that is most likely to be ranked first. We will now consider both of these options, starting with the former.

8.3.2 Condorcet's Model and Its Refinements

In his original paper, Condorcet made the following assumptions.

(1) In every pairwise comparison each voter chooses the better alternative with some fixed probability p, where $1/2 < p \leq 1$.
(2) Each voter's judgment on every pair of alternatives is independent of her judgment on every other pair.
(3) Each voter's judgment is independent of the other voters' judgments.
(4) Each voter's judgment produces a ranking of the alternatives.

However, assumptions (2) and (4) are incompatible. Indeed, if a voter ranks every pair of alternatives correctly with some fixed probability, then she may end up with a nontransitive judgment, which is prohibited by (4). In other words, if we insist that voters always produce a linear order as their judgment, then their judgments on different pairs of alternatives are no longer independent.

There are two differing opinions on how exactly Condorcet's model should be understood. Some believe that we should allow intransitive preferences, arguing that the vote is not really a preference, but rather the voter's best approximation to the correct ranking as she perceives it. It may happen that the best approximation is in fact intransitive (see, e.g., Truchon, 2008); however, it cannot be ignored, as it provides useful information.

Another interpretation of Condorcet's proposal is as follows: a voter forms her opinion by considering pairs of alternatives independently, but if the result happens to be intransitive, she discards it and tries to form her opinion again until a valid (acyclic) preference order is obtained. In statistics, the resulting probabilistic model is known as the *Mallows noise model* (Mallows, 1957). Note, however, that this model violates condition (2) (see, e.g., Gordon and Truchon, 2008).

Commenting on Condorcet's writings, Young (1988) wrote: "One must admit that the specific probabilistic model by which Condorcet reached his conclusions is almost certainly not correct in its details." He went further to say that the plausibility of any solution based on Condorcet's ideas must therefore be subjected to other tests. However, he went on and developed Condorcet's framework to see what Condorcet would have obtained if he possessed the necessary technical skills to perform his analysis to the end. We will now present Young's analysis, together with some refinements and extensions.

8.3.3 MLE for Choosing a Ranking

In this section, we describe an MLE approach to selecting the best ranking(s) of the alternatives. Recall that a *social preference function* is a mapping that given a list of rankings of the alternatives outputs a nonempty set of aggregate rankings; thus, in this section we focus on representing social preference functions within the MLE framework.

We start by presenting Young's analysis of Condorcet's proposal (see Young, 1988), followed by a discussion of a more general approach put forward by Conitzer and Sandholm (2005a) and Conitzer et al. (2009b).

Let $u \in \mathcal{L}(A)$ be the true state of the world, and let $v \in \mathcal{L}(A)$ be some ranking that agrees with u on k pairs of alternatives. Note that we have $d_{\text{swap}}(v, u) = \binom{m}{2} - k$. Then under both interpretations of Condorcet's model discussed in Section 8.3.2 the probability that a voter forms opinion v is proportional to

$$p^k(1 - p)^{\binom{m}{2}-k} = p^{\binom{m}{2}-d_{\text{swap}}(v,u)}(1 - p)^{d_{\text{swap}}(v,u)}.$$

If each voter forms her opinion independently from other voters, the probability of a profile $(v_1, \ldots, v_n)$ given that u is the true state of the world is proportional to

$$\prod_{i=1}^{n} \left(\frac{p}{1 - p}\right)^{-d_{\text{swap}}(v_i,u)} = \left(\frac{p}{1 - p}\right)^{-\sum_{i=1}^{n} d_{\text{swap}}(v_i,u)}.$$

If each state of the world is a priori considered equally likely, the rankings that are most likely to be correct are the ones that maximize the probability of the observed data, or, equivalently, minimize $\sum_{i=1}^{n} d_{\text{swap}}(v_i, u)$ (note that $p > 1/2$ and hence $\frac{p}{1-p} > 1$). Thus, Condorcet's approach results in a social preference function f_{Cond} that given a profile $R = (v_1, \ldots, v_n)$ over a candidate set A, outputs the set $\text{argmin}_{u \in \mathcal{L}(A)} \sum_{i=1}^{n} d_{\text{swap}}(v_i, u)$. This is exactly the social preference function associated with the Kemeny rule (see Section 8.2.1).

General r-Noise Models

Young's analysis is based on a specific *noise model*, that is, a way voters' judgments are formed given an underlying state of the world. By considering other noise models, we can obtain other social preference functions. To pursue this agenda, we need a formal definition of a noise model.

Definition 8.7. A *noise model for rankings*, or an *r-noise model*, over a candidate set A is a family of probability distributions $\mathcal{P}(\cdot \mid u)_{u \in \mathcal{L}(A)}$ on $\mathcal{L}(A)$. For a given $u \in \mathcal{L}(A)$, $\mathcal{P}(v \mid u)$ is the probability that a voter forms a preference order v when the correct ranking is u.

We emphasize that the parameters of a noise model are assumed to be the same for all voters and do not depend on the number of voters. That is, we think of voters as independent agents that are influenced by the same factors in the same way.

Example 8.10. The *Mallows model* (Mallows, 1957) is a family of r-noise models $\left(\mathcal{P}_{d_{\text{swap}}, p}\right)_{1/2 < p < 1}$ given by

$$\mathcal{P}_{d_{\text{swap}}, p}(v \mid u) = \frac{1}{\mu_p} \varphi^{-d_{\text{swap}}(v, u)}, \quad \text{where } \varphi = \frac{p}{1-p} \text{ and } \mu_p = \sum_{v \in \mathcal{L}(A)} \varphi^{-d_{\text{swap}}(v, u)}.$$

Here, μ_p is the normalization constant; because d_{swap} is a neutral distance, the value of μ_p does not depend on the choice of u (Mallows, 1957).

Under the MLE approach, every r-noise model leads to a social preference function.

Definition 8.8. A social preference function f over A is the *maximum likelihood estimator (MLE) for an r-noise model* $\mathcal{P}$ over A if for every positive integer n and every n-voter profile $R = (v_1, \ldots, v_n)$ it holds that

$$f(R) = \underset{u \in \mathcal{L}(A)}{\operatorname{argmax}} \prod_{i=1}^{n} \mathcal{P}(v_i \mid u).$$

A very general method of constructing r-noise models was proposed by Conitzer et al. (2009b), who introduced the notion of a *simple ranking scoring function*.

Definition 8.9. A social preference function f over A is said to be a *simple ranking scoring function (SRSF)* if there exists a mapping $\rho : \mathcal{L}(A) \times \mathcal{L}(A) \to \mathbb{R}$ such that for every positive integer n and every n-voter profile $R = (v_1, \ldots, v_n)$ it holds that

$$f(R) = \underset{u \in \mathcal{L}(A)}{\operatorname{argmax}} \sum_{i=1}^{n} \rho(v_i, u). \tag{8.5}$$

Intuitively, $\rho(v, u)$ assigns a score to v based on the similarity between v and u, and f chooses u so as to maximize the total score of the given profile. We say that a mapping $\rho : \mathcal{L}(A) \times \mathcal{L}(A) \to \mathbb{R}$ is *neutral* if $\rho(v', u') = \rho(v, u)$, where rankings v' and u' are obtained by renaming alternatives in v and u according to some permutation $\pi : A \to A$. Conitzer et al. (2009b) show that a simple ranking scoring function f is neutral if and only if there exists a neutral mapping ρ satisfying (8.5).

Example 8.11. Every distance d on $\mathcal{L}(A)$ defines a simple ranking scoring function: we can set $\rho(v, u) = -d(v, u)$. The corresponding social preference function maps a profile $R = (v_1, \ldots, v_n)$ to the set of rankings $\text{argmin}_{u \in \mathcal{L}(A)} \sum_{i=1}^{n} d(v_i, u)$. Observe that this social preference function is closely related to the voting rule that is distance rationalizable via $\hat{d}$ and the strong unanimity consensus $\mathcal{S}$.

Every SRSF corresponds to an infinite family of r-noise models: If f is the SRSF defined by a mapping ρ, then for every $\varphi \in (1, +\infty)$ we can set

$$\mathcal{P}_{\rho, \varphi}(v \mid u) = \frac{1}{\mu_{\rho, \varphi, u}} \varphi^{\rho(v, u)}, \quad \text{where} \quad \mu_{\rho, \varphi, u} = \sum_{v \in \mathcal{L}(A)} \varphi^{\rho(v, u)}; \qquad (8.6)$$

Conitzer et al. (2009b) use $\varphi = 2$ in their paper. By construction, f is the maximum likelihood estimator for $\mathcal{P}_{\rho, \varphi}$ for every $\varphi \in (1, +\infty)$.

Conitzer et al. (2009b) show that for social preference functions that are neutral (i.e., their output does not depend on the names of the candidates) the converse is also true. More precisely, they prove the following characterization result.

Theorem 8.12. *A neutral social preference function is an MLE if and only if it is an SRSF.*

Theorem 8.12 provides a convenient way to show that a given social preference function f is an MLE: it suffices to exhibit a mapping ρ witnessing that f is an SRSF. Conitzer et al. (2009b) apply this method to show that for every score vector $\alpha = (\alpha_1, \ldots, \alpha_m)$ the corresponding social preference function f_α is an MLE. In the rest of this section, we give a sketch of their argument.

Recall that f_α is the social preference function that orders the candidates by their α-scores, where the α-score of a candidate a in a profile $R = (v_1, \ldots, v_n)$ is given by $s_\alpha(R, a) = \sum_{i=1}^{n} \alpha_{\text{pos}(v_i, a)}$; if some candidates have the same score, f_α outputs all rankings that can be obtained by breaking such ties in some way.

To show that f_α is an SRSF, let $\beta_1, \ldots, \beta_m$ be a monotonically decreasing sequence (e.g., we can take $\beta_j = m - j$), and set

$$\rho_\alpha(v, u) = \sum_{a \in A} \beta_{\text{pos}(u, a)} \alpha_{\text{pos}(v, a)}, \qquad (8.7)$$

We claim that f_α is the simple ranking scoring function that corresponds to ρ_α. Indeed, for a given profile $R = (v_1, \ldots, v_n)$ we obtain

$$\sum_{i=1}^{n} \rho_\alpha(v_i, u) = \sum_{a \in A} \beta_{\text{pos}(u, a)} \left(\sum_{i=1}^{n} \alpha_{\text{pos}(v_i, a)} \right) = \sum_{a \in A} \beta_{\text{pos}(u, a)} s_\alpha(R, a).$$

Thus, for u to maximize the expression $\sum_{i=1}^{n} \rho_\alpha(v_i, u)$, we should have $\beta_{\text{pos}(u, a)} > \beta_{\text{pos}(u, b)}$ (and hence $\text{pos}(u, a) < \text{pos}(u, b)$) whenever $s_\alpha(R, a) > s_\alpha(R, b)$, that is, u orders the candidates by their α-score from the highest to the lowest, breaking ties arbitrarily. Theorem 8.12 then implies the following corollary.

Corollary 8.13. *The social preference function f_α is an MLE.*

8.3.4 MLE for Choosing a Winner

In the previous section we described an MLE approach to selecting the best ranking(s). However, typically our goal is to select a single winner (or possibly a set of winners) rather than a ranking of the candidates. To extend the MLE framework to this setting, we can simply output the top candidate(s) in the best ranking(s). Alternatively, we can estimate the likelihood that a given candidate is the best. To this end, for each candidate we determine the total probability mass (with respect to the uniform distribution) of the rankings where she is the top choice, and output the candidate(s) that maximize this quantity; the validity of this method follows from the Bayes rule. We will now discuss these approaches in more detail.

Deducing Winners from Rankings: MLERIV Rules

In Section 8.2.1 we transformed the social preference function associated with the Kemeny rule into a voting rule, by picking the top candidate in each ranking output by this social preference function. By extending this procedure to arbitrary MLE social preference functions, we obtain a class of rules known as MLERIV (Conitzer and Sandholm, 2005a).

Definition 8.10. Let f be a social preference function that is MLE for an r-noise model $\mathcal{P}$. Let $\hat{f}$ be a voting rule defined by $\hat{f}(R) = \{\text{top}(u) \mid u \in f(R)\}$, where $\text{top}(u)$ denotes the top candidate in ranking u. This rule is called the *maximum likelihood estimator for ranking under identically distributed independent votes (MLERIV) for* $\mathcal{P}$.

According to Definition 8.10, the Kemeny rule is MLERIV for the Mallows noise model. Another family of MLERIV rules is provided by Example 8.11: Theorem 8.12 implies that for every neutral distance d over $\mathcal{L}(A)$ the $(\mathcal{S}, \widehat{d})$-rationalizable voting rule is MLERIV. Furthermore, Corollary 8.13 implies that every scoring rule is MLERIV.

Estimating the Winners: Young's Interpretation of Condorcet's Proposal

The MLERIV-based approach provides a simple way to cast many voting rules within the MLE framework. However, it is not appropriate if our goal is to output the candidate that is most likely to be ranked first. Indeed, under an r-noise model the probability that a candidate is ranked first in the true ranking is obtained by adding together the probabilities of all rankings where she appears on top, and it is entirely possible that the top candidate in the most likely ranking is a, but the cumulative probability of rankings that have a on top is lower than the cumulative probability of rankings that have some other candidate b on top.

This was clearly understood by Condorcet himself, who probably did not have the technical skills to pursue this line of reasoning. Young (1988) argues that this approach would lead him to the Borda rule, at least when p is sufficiently close to $1/2$. Young also speculates on reasons why Condorcet might have chosen to abandon this train of thought (see Young, 1988, for an amusing account of the relationship between Condorcet and Borda).

We will now present Young's extension of Condorcet's analysis. While it aims to estimate the most likely winner under the Mallows model, it makes the simplifying assumption that in the prior distribution over the states of the world all pairwise comparisons between the alternatives are independent from each other. For the Mallows model this assumption is not true: if $A = \{a, b, c\}$ and the prior distribution over the states of the world is uniform over $\mathcal{L}(A)$, knowing that in the true state of the world a is ranked above b influences our beliefs about the outcome of the comparison between a and c. Thus, Young's analysis can be seen as a heuristic algorithm for computing the most likely winner; later, we will see that its output may differ from that of the exact algorithm (see also Xia, 2014a).

Given a pair of candidates $a, b \in A$, let n_{ab} denote the number of voters in a given profile $(v_1 \ldots, v_n)$ who prefer a to b. Let S be a fixed set of voters of size n_{ab}, and consider the event that the voters in S prefer a to b, while the remaining voters prefer b to a; denote this event by $\mathcal{E}_S$. If in the true state of the world a is preferred to b, then the probability of $\mathcal{E}_S$ is exactly $p^{n_{ab}}(1 - p)^{n_{ba}}$. Conversely, if in the true state of the world b is preferred to a, then the probability of $\mathcal{E}_S$ is $(1 - p)^{n_{ab}} p^{n_{ba}}$. The prior probability that in the true state of the world a is preferred b is exactly $1/2$. Therefore, the probability of the event $\mathcal{E}_S$ is $\frac{1}{2}(p^{n_{ab}}(1 - p)^{n_{ba}} + (1 - p)^{n_{ab}} p^{n_{ba}})$. Hence, by the Bayes rule, the probability that in the true state of the world a is preferred to b is proportional to

$$\frac{p^{n_{ab}}(1 - p)^{n_{ba}}}{p^{n_{ab}}(1 - p)^{n_{ba}} + (1 - p)^{n_{ab}} p^{n_{ba}}}. \tag{8.8}$$

To compute the probability that in the true state of the world a is preferred to every other candidate, we take the product of probabilities (8.8) over all $b \neq a$; note that this step makes use of the assumption that in the prior distribution over the states of the world all pairwise comparisons are independent. It follows that the probability that a is the true winner given that the observed profile is $(v_1, \ldots, v_n)$ is given by

$$\prod_{b \in A \setminus \{a\}} \frac{p^{n_{ab}}(1 - p)^{n_{ba}}}{p^{n_{ab}}(1 - p)^{n_{ba}} + (1 - p)^{n_{ab}} p^{n_{ba}}} = \prod_{b \in A \setminus \{a\}} \frac{1}{1 + \left(\frac{1-p}{p}\right)^{n_{ab} - n_{ba}}}.$$

Thus, the most likely winners are the candidates that minimize the expression

$$\kappa_a(\varphi) = \prod_{b \in A \setminus \{a\}} \left(1 + \varphi^{n_{ba} - n_{ab}}\right), \quad \text{where} \quad \varphi = \frac{p}{1-p}. \tag{8.9}$$

Now, the behavior of this expression crucially depends on the value of $\varphi = \frac{p}{1-p}$. We will consider two cases: (1) p is very close to 1 and hence $\varphi \to +\infty$ (i.e., a voter is almost always right) and (2) p is very close to $1/2$ and hence $\varphi \to 1$ (a voter has only a slight advantage over a random coin toss). We denote the corresponding voting rules by $\text{MLE}_{\text{intr}}^{\infty}$ and $\text{MLE}_{\text{intr}}^{1}$, respectively (the reasons for this notation are explained in Remark 8.14). The following analysis is based on the work of Elkind and Shah (2014).

$p \to 1, \varphi \to +\infty.$ The rate of growth of $\kappa_a(\varphi)$ as $\varphi \to +\infty$ depends on the degree of its highest-order term, that is, $\sum_{b \in A \setminus \{a\}: n_{ba} > n_{ab}} (n_{ba} - n_{ab})$: slowest-growing functions correspond to the most likely candidates.

Thus, to determine the $\text{MLE}_{\text{intr}}^{\infty}$-winners, we first compute the score of each candidate $a \in A$ as the sum of a's loss margins in all pairwise elections she loses: $s_T(a) = \sum_{b \in A \setminus \{a\}: n_{ba} > n_{ab}} (n_{ba} - n_{ab})$. If there is a unique candidate with the minimum score, this candidate wins. In case of a tie among $a_1, \ldots, a_k$, $\mathrm{MLE}^{\infty}_{\mathrm{intr}}$ takes into account the coefficients of the highest-order terms as well as the lower-order terms of $\kappa_{a_1}(\varphi), \ldots, \kappa_{a_k}(\varphi)$; the resulting tie-breaking procedure is quite complicated (but can be shown to be polynomial-time computable). The voting rule that outputs the set $\arg\min_{a \in A} s_T(a)$ was proposed by Tideman (1987) as an approximation to the Dodgson rule, and is now known as the Tideman rule; thus, our analysis shows that $\mathrm{MLE}^{\infty}_{\mathrm{intr}}$ is a refinement of the Tideman rule. The Tideman rule has been studied by McCabe-Dansted et al. (2008), as well as by Caragiannis et al. (2014b), who refer to it as the simplified Dodgson rule; an overview of their results can be found in Chapter 5.[4]

$p \to 1/2, \varphi \to 1$. In this case, we are interested in the behavior of $\kappa_a(\varphi)$ as $\varphi \to 1$. We have $\kappa_a(1) = 2^{m-1}$ for all $a \in A$. Furthermore, the derivative of $\kappa_a(\varphi)$ at $\varphi = 1$ is $\sum_{c \neq a}(n_{ca} - n_{ac})2^{m-2} = \sum_{c \neq a}(n - 2n_{ac})2^{m-2}$. To minimize this expression, we need to maximize $\sum_{c \neq a} n_{ac}$, which is the Borda score of a. Hence, $\mathrm{MLE}^1_{\mathrm{intr}}$ is a refinement of the Borda rule: it selects the Borda winner when it is unique, and if there are several Borda winners, it breaks ties by taking into account higher-order derivatives of $\kappa_a(\varphi)$ at $\varphi \to 1$.

Remark 8.14. One can think of Young's procedure as estimating the most likely winner under a different noise model, namely, one where the prior distribution assigns equal probability to all tournaments over A, that is, the state of the world is described by the outcomes of $\binom{m}{2}$ comparisons, and all vectors of outcomes are considered to be equally likely. Voters' preferences are tournaments as well; in each vote, the direction of every edge agrees with the ground truth with probability p and disagrees with it with probability $1 - p$, with decisions for different edges made independently from each other. We emphasize that this distribution assigns nonzero probability to "states of the world" that violate transitivity. For this noise model, Young's procedure correctly identifies the candidate with the largest cumulative probability of the states of the world where she wins all her pairwise elections.

It is often claimed that $\mathrm{MLE}^1_{\mathrm{intr}}$ is the Borda rule. We will now show that this claim is inaccurate: while $\mathrm{MLE}^1_{\mathrm{intr}}$ chooses among the Borda winners, it may fail to select some of them.

Example 8.15. Let $A = \{a, b, c, d\}$ and consider a 4-voter profile over A given by $(adcb, bcad, abdc, bcad)$ (where we write $xyzt$ as a shorthand for $x \succ y \succ z \succ t$). The Borda winners in this profile are a and b, and their Borda score is 8. On the other hand, we have $\kappa_a(\varphi) = 4(1 + \varphi^{-4})$, $\kappa_b(\varphi) = 2(1 + \varphi^{-2})^2$. The reader can verify that $\kappa_a(1.2) \approx 5.93$, $\kappa_b(1.2) \approx 5.74$, and

$$\left.\frac{d\kappa_a}{d\varphi}\right|_{\varphi=1} = \left.\frac{d\kappa_b}{d\varphi}\right|_{\varphi=1} = -16, \quad \text{but} \quad \left.\frac{d^2\kappa_a}{(d\varphi)^2}\right|_{\varphi=1} = 48, \quad \left.\frac{d^2\kappa_b}{(d\varphi)^2}\right|_{\varphi=1} = 32,$$

so b emerges as the unique winner under $\mathrm{MLE}^1_{\mathrm{intr}}$.

---

[4] Young (1988) appears to suggest that $\mathrm{MLE}^{\infty}_{\mathrm{intr}}$ is Maximin; our argument shows that this is not the case.

Estimating the Winners under an r-Noise Model

It is natural to ask whether we can estimate the most likely winner under the Mallows model without making the simplifying assumption that in the prior distribution over the states of the world all pairwise comparisons are independent. To the best of our knowledge, Procaccia et al. (2012) were the first to do this for $p \to 1/2$; their argument extends to more general noise models and to settings where the goal is to select a fixed-size subset of candidates. They have also considered the case $p \to 1$ (see also the work of Elkind and Shah, 2014). Just as in Young's analysis, the result turns out to depend on the value of p: when $p \to 1$ (and $\varphi = \frac{p}{1-p} \to +\infty$), we obtain a refinement of the Kemeny rule, and when $p \to 1/2$ (and $\varphi \to 1$), we obtain a refinement of the Borda rule. We will now present the arguments both for $\varphi \to +\infty$ and for $\varphi \to 1$; we refer to the resulting rules as $\mathrm{MLE}_{\mathrm{tr}}^{\infty}$ and $\mathrm{MLE}_{\mathrm{tr}}^{1}$, respectively.

For every candidate $a \in A$ let $\mathcal{L}_a$ denote the set of all rankings in $\mathcal{L}(A)$ where a is ranked first. Recall that under the Mallows noise model the probability of a profile $(v_1, \ldots, v_n)$ given that the true state of the world is described by a ranking u is proportional to $\varphi^{-\sum_{i=1}^{n} d_{\mathrm{swap}}(v_i, u)}$. Thus, to compute the most likely winner, we need to find the candidates that maximize the expression

$$\tau_a(\varphi) = \sum_{u \in \mathcal{L}_a} \varphi^{-\sum_{i=1}^{n} d_{\mathrm{swap}}(v_i, u)}.$$

$p \to 1, \varphi \to +\infty$. The rule $\mathrm{MLE}_{\mathrm{tr}}^{\infty}$ returns a set of candidates S such that for every $a \in S$, $b \in A \setminus S$ we have $\tau_a(\varphi) > \tau_b(\varphi)$ for all sufficiently large values of φ. To see that S is not empty, note that functions $\tau_a(\varphi)$, $a \in A$, are Laurent polynomials (i.e., sums of powers of φ), and therefore any two of these functions either coincide or have finitely many intersection points. Moreover, for each $a \in A$ the most significant summand of $\tau_a(\varphi)$ at $\varphi \to +\infty$ is

$$\varphi^{-\sum_{i=1}^{n} d_{\mathrm{swap}}(v_i, u')}, \quad \text{where} \quad u' \in \operatorname*{argmin}_{u \in \mathcal{L}_a} \sum_{i=1}^{n} d_{\mathrm{swap}}(v_i, u).$$

Hence, $\mathrm{MLE}_{\mathrm{tr}}^{\infty}$ is a refinement of the Kemeny rule.

$p \to 1/2, \varphi \to 1$. We have $\tau_a(1) = (m-1)!$ for all $a \in A$. Furthermore, the derivative of $\tau_a(\varphi)$ at $\varphi = 1$ is given by

$$\left. \frac{d\tau_a}{d\varphi} \right|_{\varphi=1} = -\sum_{u \in \mathcal{L}_a} \sum_{i=1}^{n} d_{\mathrm{swap}}(v_i, u) = -\sum_{i=1}^{n} \sum_{u \in \mathcal{L}_a} d_{\mathrm{swap}}(v_i, u).$$

It is easy to show by induction on j that if $\mathrm{pos}(v_i, a) = j$ then we have $\sum_{u \in \mathcal{L}_a} d_{\mathrm{swap}}(v_i, u) = j(m-1)! + C_m$, where C_m is a function of m (i.e., does not depend on v_i). As $\sum_{i=1}^{n} (m - \mathrm{pos}(v_i, a))$ is exactly the Borda score of a, it follows that $a \in \operatorname{argmin}_{c \in A} \left. \frac{d\tau_c}{d\varphi} \right|_{\varphi=1}$ if and only if a is a Borda winner. Hence, $\mathrm{MLE}_{\mathrm{tr}}^{1}$ is a refinement of the Borda rule. Furthermore, it can be checked that it is distinct from the Borda rule, that is, it may fail to elect some Borda winners; this can happen when $\tau_a(\varphi)$ and $\tau_b(\varphi)$ are different from each other, even though their derivatives at $\varphi = 1$ coincide. Furthermore, it can also be shown that

$\mathrm{MLE}_{\mathrm{tr}}^1 \neq \mathrm{MLE}_{\mathrm{intr}}^1$ (Elkind and Shah, 2014), that is, these two rules are two distinct refinements of the Borda rule.

We can apply a similar procedure to other r-noise models. It turns out that for noise models that are derived from neutral simple ranking scoring functions via Equation 8.6 in the case $\varphi \to 1$ we obtain a voting rule that is a refinement of some scoring rule.

In more detail, consider a neutral SRSF given by a mapping $\rho : \mathcal{L}(A) \times \mathcal{L}(A) \to \mathbb{R}$, a value $\varphi \in (1, +\infty)$, and the corresponding r-noise model $\mathcal{P}_{\rho,\varphi}(v \mid u) = \frac{1}{\mu_{\rho,\phi,u}} \varphi^{\rho(v,u)}$. Because ρ is neutral, $\mu_{\rho,\varphi,u}$ is the same for all $u \in \mathcal{L}(A)$. Assume that each ranking of the alternatives is a priori equally likely. A direct application of the Bayes rule shows that the probability that the true state of the world is a ranking where a is placed first given that the input profile is $(v_1, \ldots, v_n)$ is proportional to

$$\sum_{u \in \mathcal{L}_a} \varphi^{\sum_{i=1}^n \rho(v_i, u)}. \tag{8.10}$$

Let MLE_{ρ}^1 be the voting rule that maps $(v_1, \ldots, v_n)$ to the set of candidates that maximize expression (8.10) for values of φ that are close to 1.

We can view expression (8.10) as a function of φ; its derivative at $\varphi = 1$ equals

$$\sum_{u \in \mathcal{L}_a} \sum_{i=1}^n \rho(v_i, u) = \sum_{i=1}^n \sum_{u \in \mathcal{L}_a} \rho(v_i, u).$$

This means that the set of MLE_{ρ}^1-winners is a (possibly strict) subset of $W = \mathrm{argmax}_{a \in A} \sum_{i=1}^n \sum_{u \in \mathcal{L}_a} \rho(v_i, u)$. Let $\overline{\mathrm{MLE}_{\rho}^1}$ be a coarsening of MLE_{ρ}^1 that, given a profile $(v_1, \ldots, v_n)$, outputs the entire set W. Because ρ is neutral, the value of the expression $\sum_{u \in \mathcal{L}_a} \rho(v_i, u)$ only depends on the position of a in v_i. Thus, $\overline{\mathrm{MLE}_{\rho}^1}$ is a scoring rule. Conversely, every scoring rule can be obtained as $\overline{\mathrm{MLE}_{\rho}^1}$ for a suitable function ρ: for example, for the rule f_α we can use the function ρ_α defined by (8.7).

Noise Models for Winners: MLEVIW Rules

We have seen how to derive a voting rule from an r-noise model by considering the cumulative probability of rankings with a given winner. Conitzer and Sandholm (2005a) put forward a direct MLE-based approach for defining voting rules. It is based on a simplified noise model, where the "state of the world" is simply the identity of the best candidate, and the likelihood of a given vote depends on the position of this candidate in the vote.

Definition 8.11. A *noise model for winners*, or a *w-noise model*, over a candidate set A, $|A| = m$, is a family of probability distributions $\overline{\mathcal{P}}(\cdot \mid a)_{a \in A}$ on $\{1, \ldots, m\}$. For a given $a \in A$, $\overline{\mathcal{P}}(j \mid a)$ is the probability of a vote where a is ranked in position j given that a is the correct winner. We require $\overline{\mathcal{P}}(j \mid a) > 0$ for all $a \in A$, $j = 1, \ldots, m$.

A voting rule f over a candidate set A is a *maximum likelihood estimator for winner under identically distributed independent votes (MLEWIV)* with respect to a w-noise model $\overline{\mathcal{P}}$ over A if for every positive integer n and every preference profile

$R = (v_1, \ldots, v_n) \in \mathcal{L}(A)^n$ it holds that

$$f(R) = \operatorname*{argmax}_{a \in A} \prod_{i=1}^{n} \overline{\mathcal{P}}(\operatorname{pos}(v_i, a) \mid a). \tag{8.11}$$

However, the power of this approach is somewhat limited, at least if we require neutrality: neutral MLEWIV rules are simply scoring rules (Conitzer and Sandholm, 2005a; Elkind et al., 2010b). Note the some form of neutrality is implicit in the definition of a w-noise model: by construction, this model assigns the same probability to any two votes that rank a in the same position, irrespective of how they rank the remaining candidates.

Proposition 8.16. *For every score vector* $\alpha = (\alpha_1, \ldots, \alpha_m)$ *the scoring rule* f_α *is MLEWIV. Conversely, every neutral MLEWIV rule is a scoring rule.*

Proof. Given a score vector $\alpha = (\alpha_1, \ldots, \alpha_m)$, define a w-noise model $\overline{\mathcal{P}}_\alpha$ as $\overline{\mathcal{P}}_\alpha(j \mid a) = \frac{1}{\mu_\alpha} 2^{\alpha_j}$, where $\mu_\alpha = \sum_{j=1}^{m} 2^{\alpha_j}$. Now, consider an arbitrary profile $R = (v_1, \ldots, v_n)$ over A and a candidate $a \in A$. For each $i = 1, \ldots, n$, let $p_i = \operatorname{pos}(v_i, a)$. The α-score of a in R is given by $s_\alpha(R, a) = \sum_{i=1}^{n} \alpha_{p_i}$. On the other hand, we have

$$\prod_{i=1}^{n} \overline{\mathcal{P}}_\alpha(\operatorname{pos}(v_i, a) \mid a) = \frac{1}{\mu_\alpha^n} \prod_{i=1}^{n} 2^{\alpha_{p_i}} = \frac{1}{\mu_\alpha^n} 2^{s_\alpha(a, R)}. \tag{8.12}$$

Hence, the set of most likely candidates under $\overline{\mathcal{P}}_\alpha$ is exactly the set of f_α-winners.

Conversely, let f be a neutral MLEWIV rule for a w-noise model $\overline{\mathcal{P}}$. It is easy to verify that $\overline{\mathcal{P}}$ is neutral, that is, $\overline{\mathcal{P}}(j \mid a) = \overline{\mathcal{P}}(j \mid b)$ for every $j = 1, \ldots, m$ and every $a, b \in A$. Now, fix some $a \in A$ and set $\alpha_j = \log_2 \overline{\mathcal{P}}(j \mid a)$ for all $j = 1, \ldots, m$. Equation (8.12) shows that the scoring rule f_α coincides with f. $\square$

Proposition 8.16 provides an alternative characterization of scoring rules, thus complementing the well-known results of Smith (1973) and Young (1975). Equivalently, one can say that the results of Smith and Young provide a characterization of MLEWIV rules in terms of standard axiomatic properties. A natural open question, which was suggested by Conitzer et al. (2009b), is whether a similar characterization can be obtained for MLERIV rules.

To conclude our discussion of the MLEWIV rules, we note that these rules arise naturally from the ranking-based model considered in the previous section. Indeed, for a neutral function ρ the rule $\overline{\mathrm{MLE}}_\rho^1$ is MLEWIV. To see this, note that given a candidate $a \in A$, we can pick $\varphi \in (1, +\infty)$ and m rankings $v^1, \ldots, v^m$ such that $\operatorname{pos}(v^j, a) = j$ for $j = 1, \ldots, m$, and set

$$\overline{\mathcal{P}}(j \mid a) = \frac{1}{\mu} \varphi^{\sum_{u \in \mathcal{L}_a} \rho(v^j, u)}, \quad \text{where} \quad \mu = \sum_{j=1}^{m} \varphi^{\sum_{u \in \mathcal{L}_a} \rho(v^j, u)}.$$

It is easy to verify that for any choice of $\varphi \in (1, +\infty)$ and $v^1, \ldots, v^m$ the MLEWIV rule that corresponds to this noise model is exactly $\overline{\mathrm{MLE}}_\rho^1$.

Finally, we remark that Ben-Yashar and Paroush (2001) consider another approach to estimating winners under noise: in their model, each voter has to specify one candidate (rather than a ranking of the candidates), and a voter's probability of voting for the true winner depends on the identity of the winner, and may vary from one voter to another. Ben-Yashar and Paroush present an extension of Condorcet's Jury Theorem (see Section 8.3.1) to this setting.

8.4 Conclusions and Further Reading

We have discussed two approaches to rationalizing voting rules: a consensus-based approach that leads to the distance rationalizability framework and a probabilistic approach that leads to the MLE framework. We showed how to rationalize many common voting rules in each of these frameworks. For some rules, such as the Kemeny rule, the rationalizations provided by both frameworks are closely related, while for others (e.g., scoring rules), they seem to be quite different, and thus provide different perspectives on the rule in question.

Due to space constraints, we were not able to overview the entire body of research on these two frameworks; we will now briefly mention some of the relevant papers.

Service and Adams (2012a) consider randomized strategyproof approximations to distance rationalizable voting rules. Boutilier and Procaccia (2012) relate the concept of distance rationalizability to the framework of dynamic social choice (Parkes and Procaccia, 2013). Distance-based approaches have also been considered in the context of judgment aggregation (Lang et al., 2011; Dietrich, 2014), as well as in other areas of social choice (see Eckert and Klamler, 2011, and references therein).

Xia et al. (2010a) apply the MLE framework to voting in multi-issue domains, and Xia and Conitzer (2011b) extend it to partial orders, and a more general notion of "state of the world"; for instance, they consider settings where the goal is to estimate the top k alternatives for $k \geq 1$. The latter problem is explored in more detail by Procaccia et al. (2012).

Caragiannis et al. (2013) investigate a complementary issue: given a noise model and a fixed voting rule, how many samples do we need to generate so that this rule identifies the correct winner? They also consider voting rules that perform well with respect to *families* of noise models; such rules are further explored by Caragiannis et al. (2014a) and Xia (2014b). Drissi-Bakhkhat and Truchon (2004) modify the Mallows model by relaxing the assumption that the probability of correctly ordering two alternatives is the same for all pairs of alternatives. They let this probability increase with the distance between the two alternatives in the true order, to reflect the intuition that a judge or voter is more prone to errors when confronted with two comparable alternatives than when confronted with a good alternative and a bad one. Truchon (2008) shows that when this probability increases exponentially with the distance, the resulting ranking orders the candidates according to their Borda scores. MLE analysis admits a Bayesian interpretation: if we assume the uniform prior over the true states of the world, then an MLE rule outputs the maximum a posteriori estimate. Pivato (2012) considers a more general class of statistical estimators (in particular, settings where the prior distribution over the possible states of the world need not be uniform) and domains other than preference aggregation (including judgment aggregation and committee selection).

Acknowledgments

We would like to thank Shmuel Nitzan, Nisarg Shah, and the editors of this volume for their very useful feedback, which was instrumental in improving this chapter. We are grateful to Piotr Faliszewski for his permission to use material from our joint papers.

CHAPTER 9

Voting in Combinatorial Domains

Jérôme Lang and Lirong Xia

9.1 Motivations and Classes of Problems

This chapter addresses preference aggregation and voting on domains which are the Cartesian product (or sometimes, a subset of the Cartesian product) of finite domain values, each corresponding to an issue, a variable, or an attribute.

As seen in other chapters of this handbook, voting rules map a profile (usually, a collection of rankings, see Chapter 1) to an alternative or a set of alternatives. A key question has to do with the structure of the set of alternatives. Sometimes, this set has a simple structure and a small cardinality (e.g., in a presidential election). But in many contexts, it has a complex combinatorial structure. We give here three typical examples:

- *Multiple referenda.* On the day of 2012 U.S. presidential election, voters in California had to decide whether to adopt each of 11 propositions.[1] Five referenda were categorized as budget/tax issues. Specifically, two of them (Propositions 30 and 38) both aimed to raise taxes for education, with different details on the type and rate of the tax. Similarly, in Florida voters had to vote on 11 propositions, eight of which were categorized as budget/tax issues.
- *Group configuration or group planning.* A set of agents sometimes has to make a common decision about a complex object, such as a common menu (composed for instance of a first course, a main course, a dessert and a wine, with a few possible values for each), or a common plan (for instance, a group of friends have to travel together to a sequence of possible locations, given some constraints on the possible sequences).
- *Committee elections* and more generally *multiwinner elections*. A set of agents has to choose a group of delegates or representatives of some given size, from a larger set of candidates. As another example, a group of friends wants to choose a set of DVDs to purchase collectively, from a larger set, subject to some budget constraints.

---

[1] http://en.wikipedia.org/wiki/California_elections,_November_2012.

In these three examples, the set of alternatives has a combinatorial structure: it is a Cartesian product $A = D_1 \times \ldots \times D_p$, where for each i, D_i is a finite value domain for a variable X_i, or, in the third example, a subset of a Cartesian product (see further). For the menu example, we may have for instance $D_1 = \{soup, salad, quiche\}$, $D_2 = \{beef, salmon, tofu\}$, and so on. For the multiple referenda example, or more generally in the case of *binary* variables (which for the sake of simplicity we assume in most of the chapter), we write $D_i = \{0_i, 1_i\}$ for each i. Also, when all variables are binary, we usually drop indices and parentheses: for instance, $(1_1, 0_2, 1_3)$ is denoted simply by 101.

Each of these examples has specific properties that may call for specific ways of solving them, which we review in this chapter. Still, the major issue for all classes of problems mentioned, is the *trade-off between expressivity and cost*. This is illustrated in the following example for multiple referenda by Lacy and Niou (2000):

Example 9.1. We have three issues, and three voters with the following preferences:

- Voter 1: $110 \succ 101 \succ 011 \succ 001 \succ 100 \succ 010 \succ 000 \succ 111$
- Voter 2: $101 \succ 011 \succ 110 \succ 010 \succ 100 \succ 001 \succ 000 \succ 111$
- Voter 3: $011 \succ 110 \succ 101 \succ 100 \succ 010 \succ 001 \succ 000 \succ 111$

At one extreme, we can allow the voters to be fully expressive: each voter submits a full ranking over all 2^3 alternatives. The number of alternatives grows exponentially in the number of issues, which imposes a high cognitive cost on the voters to construct their rankings as well as a high communication cost to report these rankings to the central authority that has to gather the votes and compute the outcome (cf. Chapter 10).

At the other extreme, we could ask each voter to report only her top-ranked alternative. This approach is almost cost-free, but the lack of expressivity can cause serious problems. Applying plurality voting (see Chapter 1) for winner selection is quite arbitrary, because three alternatives are tied in the first place by receiving a single vote. Applying the majority rule (see Chapter 1) to each issue separately, as commonly done for multiple referenda, leads to an even worse outcome: the winner, 111, is ranked last by *all* voters!

We consider separately the case where the common decision to be taken consists of choosing the members of a committee. Benoît and Kornhauser (1991) consider two classes of committee elections: *designated post committees*, and *at-large committees*. In designated post committees, candidates run for a specific post (and the size of the committee is the number of posts); in at-large committees, they do not run for a specific post, and the size of the committee is specified explicitly. Designated post committee elections are naturally expressed as elections on a combinatorial domain: variables correspond to posts, and the domain of each variable is the set of candidates applying for the post. The case of at-large elections is more subtle. An obvious choice consists in having binary variables corresponding to candidates, but then the cardinality constraint restricts the set of feasible committees: we are here in a case of *constrained voting on a combinatorial domain*, where the set of alternatives is not simply the Cartesian product of the domains but a subset of it. Voting for at-large committees takes this cardinality constraint into account for restricting the set of admissible outputs[2] (and, sometimes, the set of admissible inputs), and gives rise to widely used voting rules for *multiwinner elections* (Brams and Fishburn, 2002).

Consider again Example 9.1. At one extreme, one could view all these domains as ordinary domains, and proceed as usual by eliciting voters' preferences over the set of alternatives A and then applying a given voting rule. Because the number of alternatives grows exponentially with the number of variables, this is unrealistic as soon as one has more than a few variables; we can definitely not expect individuals to spend hours or days expressing rankings explicitly on thousands of alternatives. At the other extreme, one may think of considering each variable or issue separately, and then organizing votes in parallel for each of them. (This is the way it is usually done in multiple referenda, where each voter has to cast a yes/no ballot for each of the variables simultaneously.) This is much less expensive in terms of communication and computation, but amounts to making the very strong assumption that voters have *separable preferences*, that is, voters' preferences for the value of any variable do not depend on the values of other variables. This assumption is patently unrealistic in many contexts. In multiple referenda, it is likely that a voter's preference over some of these referenda depends on the outcomes of the other referenda, especially when budget/tax issues are concerned, because voters typically have some maximal budget or tax amount they are willing to pay. In group configuration, the value taken by a variable (such as the main course) may have a dramatic influence on a voter's preferences on other variables (such as the wine). In a committee election, it is often the case that a voter's preference for having A over B in the committee depends on whether C is also in the committee, because for instance she wants some balance between genders or between members of different communities.

There are several criteria on which we may assess the practical implementability of a method for voting in combinatorial domains. Perhaps the most important one is the *communication cost* necessary to elicit the votes. Because the communication burden is borne by the voters, making sure that it is reasonably low is a crucial requirement. A second criterion is the *computational cost* needed to compute the outcome. A third criterion is the *generality* of the approach, that is, its applicability to a large variety of profiles: some are widely applicable, whereas some rely on strong domain restrictions. Lastly, and crucially, is the *quality of the outcome*: as we shall soon see, some approaches may lead to extremely controversial, sometimes absolutely unacceptable, outcomes, while others may satisfy desirable social choice axiomatic properties such as Pareto Optimality that give a guarantee about the quality of the solution.

Each of the following sections focuses on families of methods for implementing elections on combinatorial domains. Section 9.2 considers simultaneous voting. As we shall see, simultaneous voting may perform extremely poorly when separability does not hold (and may perform poorly—although much less so—even when separability holds); more precisely, we will list a few important criteria for evaluating methods for implementing elections in combinatorial domains, and will show that simultaneous voting performs poorly on all of them except communication and computation

---

[2] Designated post committees also need constraints if some candidates apply for more than one post.

cost. In Section 9.3 we discuss methods that assume that voters' preferences are partially specified and then completed automatically using some *completion principle*. Various completion principles are discussed in subsections: using a distance between alternatives is discussed in Section 9.3.1; using a preference extension from singletons to subsets is discussed in Section 9.3.2; and more generally, using a language for compact preference representation such as CP-nets (Section 9.3.3), lexicographic preferences trees (Section 9.3.4), and languages for cardinal preference representation (Section 9.3.5). In Section 9.4 we present methods based on sequential voting, where variables (or groups of variables) are voted on one after another. Section 9.5 concludes by discussing the respective merits and drawbacks of different classes of methods, and briefly addresses related problems.

9.2 Simultaneous Voting and the Separability Issue

9.2.1 Preliminaries

In this chapter, $\mathcal{X} = \{X_1, \ldots, X_p\}$ is a set of *variables*, or *issues*, where each issue X_i takes a value in a finite *local domain* D_i. The set of alternatives, or the *domain*, is $A = D_1 \times \ldots \times D_p$. For $\vec{x} = (x_1, \ldots, x_p) \in A$, and $I \subseteq \{1, \ldots, p\}$, we denote $\vec{x}_I = (x_i)_{i \in I}$. We also make use of the notational convention $-i = \{1, \ldots, p\} \setminus \{i\}$.

Let $\succ$ be a linear order (a transitive, irreflexive and complete preference relation) on A. We say that $\succ$ is *separable* (Debreu, 1954) if and only if for all $i \leqslant p$, $x_i, y_i \in D_i$ and $(\vec{x}_{-i}, \vec{y}_{-i}) \in D_{-i}$ we have $(x_i, \vec{x}_{-i}) \succ (y_i, \vec{x}_{-i})$ if and only if $(x_i, \vec{y}_{-i}) \succ (y_i, \vec{y}_{-i})$. When $\succ$ is separable, the $\succ^i$ is defined by $x_i \succ^i y_i$ if and only if $(x_i, \vec{x}_{-i}) \succ (y_i, \vec{x}_{-i})$ for an arbitrary $\vec{x}_{-i}$.

Given n voters, a *profile* is a collection $R = \langle \succ_1, \ldots, \succ_n \rangle$ of linear orders on A. A profile R is separable when each of $\succ_i$ is separable. Given a separable profile over a domain composed of binary variables, the *simultaneous*[3] *majority outcome* $m(R)$ is defined by $m(R) = (x_1^*, \ldots, x_p^*)$, where a majority of voters prefer x_i^* to the opposite value $1 - x_i^*$ (for the sake of simplicity we assume an odd number of voters, so that there are no ties and the majority outcome is uniquely defined). When variables are not binary, simultaneous voting uses a specific voting rule for each variable. *In the rest of this section, for the sake of simplicity we focus on binary variables.*

In simultaneous voting, each voter only has to report a ranking over D_i for each i, therefore the communication requirement of simultaneous voting is $O(n \sum_i |D_i| \log |D_i|)$. Because all variables are binary, each voter has only to report a ballot consisting of a (preferred) value for each variable, hence the requirement complexity is $O(np)$. For instance, if a voter prefers 1_1 over 0_1, 0_2 over 1_2 and 1_3 over 0_3, then she reports the ballot 101, which represents $1_1 0_2 1_3$. In this case, separability

---

[3] The terminology "simultaneous voting" is used by Lacy and Niou (2000). It is also called *standard voting* by Brams et al. (1997a), *propositionwise aggregation* by Brams et al. (1998), and *seat-by-seat voting* by Benoît and Kornhauser (2010). We choose the terminology 'simultaneous voting' although it is a little bit ambiguous: it does not only mean that voters vote simultaneously, but also that they vote *simultaneously and separately on all issues*. Approaches reviewed in Section 9.3 do not satisfy that, although, in some sense, they may also be considered as being 'simultaneous' in the sense that all voters vote simultaneously.

implies that this ballot also corresponds to her most preferred alternative: in other words, simultaneous voting is a *tops-only* voting rule.

How good is simultaneous voting? We know already that it has a low communication cost, as well as a very low computation cost when variables are binary (and more generally for most commonly used voting rules, when variables are not binary). Things become much worse when we turn to the *quality* of the outcome. Even though there is no single way of measuring the quality of the outcome, in most cases a popular type of negative results is to show that simultaneous voting is prone to *paradoxes*, called *multiple election paradoxes*, or *paradoxes of multiple referenda* (see next subsection). Positive results, on the other hand, proceed by showing that some desirable axiomatic properties are satisfied.

A key issue in assessing the quality of the outcome is whether we assume voters to have separable preferences or not. We start with the general case.

9.2.2 Simultaneous Voting with Nonseparable Preferences

When preferences are not separable, a first problem that arises is that if a voter's preferred alternative is $\vec{x} = (x_1, \ldots, x_p)$, then there is no guarantee that she will report x_1 as her preferred value for X_1. For example, if her preference relation is $111 \succ 000 \succ 001 \succ 010 \succ 100 \succ 110 \succ 101 \succ 011$, then for three of the four combinations of values of X_2 and X_3, 0_1 is preferred to 1_1, and similarly for X_2 and X_3; therefore, even though the value of X_1 in her preferred alternative is 111, she might well report 0_1 as her preferred value for X_1, as well as 0_2 and 0_3 as her preferred values for X_2 and X_3. A voter whose preferred value for X_i is always the value of X_i in her preferred alternative will be called *optimistic*, because reporting in such a way comes down to assuming that the outcome over all other issues will be the most favorable one. In our example, if the voter is optimistic then she should vote for 1_1, for 1_2 and for 1_3. More generally, choosing a preferred value to report for an issue depends on the voter's beliefs about the outcomes of the other issues, which in turn depends on her beliefs about the other voters' behavior. A game-theoretic analysis of this complex phenomenon is given by Ahn and Oliveros (2012).

The multiple election paradoxes studied by Brams et al. (1998) and Scarsini (1998) occur when the winner of simultaneous voting receives the fewest votes.

Example 9.2 (Brams et al., 1998). There are 3 issues and 3 voters voting respectively for 110, 101 and 011. Simultaneous voting outputs 111, whereas 111 receives support from none of the voters.

An even more striking paradox, again due to Brams et al. (1998), is obtained with 4 issues, with the outcome being 1111 whereas 1111 is the *only* alternative that receives no vote and 0000 is the only alternative that receives the most votes.

Whether these are paradoxical outcomes or not depends on the voters' preferences over the whole domain. The implicit assumption in these examples is that voters have *plurality-based preferences*: each voter i submits her preferred alternative $\vec{x}^i$, prefers $\vec{x}^i$ to all other alternatives, and is indifferent between any two alternatives different from $\vec{x}^i$. Such dichotomous, plurality-based preferences are not separable. Under this assumption, in the three-issue example above, 111 is Pareto-dominated by 110, 101 and 011; in the four-issue example, 1111 is Pareto-dominated by *all other alternatives*, which is clearly a very undesirable outcome.

The assumption that preferences are plurality-based is very demanding and is very often not plausible. A weaker assumption is *top-consistency*: which only states that each voter prefers her reported alternative $\vec{x}^i$ to all other alternatives. If, instead of assuming plurality-based preferences, we only assume top-consistency, the quality of the outcome can be even worse, as it can be seen on the following example.

Example 9.3. We have two issues: building a swimming pool or not (1_S or 0_S), and building a tennis court or not (1_T or 0_T). We have $2k + 1$ voters:

- k voters: $1_S 0_T \succ 0_S 1_T \succ 0_S 0_T \succ 1_S 1_T$
- k voters: $0_S 1_T \succ 1_S 0_T \succ 0_S 0_T \succ 1_S 1_T$
- 1 voter: $1_S 1_T \succ 0_S 1_T \succ 1_S 0_T \succ 0_S 0_T$

It is unclear what the first k voters will report when choosing between 1_S and 0_S. Indeed, their preferences are nonseparable: they prefer the swimming pool to be built if the tennis course is not, and vice versa. Now, if they vote for 1_S, their vote, when it is a decisive, leads to either $1_S 0_T$ or $1_S 1_T$, that is, to the voter's best alternative or to her worst alternative. On the other hand, voting for 0_S, again when it is a decisive vote, leads to either $0_S 0_T$ or $0_S 1_T$, that is, to one of the voter's 'intermediate' alternatives. This shows why the first k voters may be hesitant to vote for 1_S or for 0_S. They may also be hesitant to vote for 1_T or for 0_T, although the situation here is a bit different (a decisive vote for 1_T leads to the second-ranked or to the worst alternative, while a decisive vote for 1_T leads to the best or to the third-ranked alternative). If we assume that these first k voters do not have any knowledge about the others' preferences (or even if they do, but do not use this information for voting strategically), then these voters will feel ill at ease when voting and may experience regret once they know the final outcome (e.g., if they vote for 1_S, wrongly believing that the group will decide not to build the tennis court). The case for the next k voters is symmetric (with the roles of S and T being swapped). Only the last voter, who has separable preferences, has no problem voting for 1_S and for 1_T and does not experience regret after the election. The analysis of the paradox by Lacy and Niou (2000) assumes that voters choose to vote optimistically (thus the first k voters would vote for 1_S)[4]: under this assumption, the simultaneous voting outcome $1_S 1_T$ *is ranked last by all but one voters.*

Take the profile in Example 9.1 as another example. Assuming again that voters vote optimistically, the simultaneous voting outcome (111) is ranked *last* by *all voters*, which is, arguably, a very bad decision.

These paradoxes are partly due to the implicit assumption that voters do not have any knowledge about other votes. However, even if voters' preferences are common knowledge, and voters vote strategically, strong paradoxes can still arise (Lacy and Niou, 2000) (see also Section 9.4.2). As argued by Saari and Sieberg (2001), the source of these paradoxes is the loss of information that occurs when separating the input profile into smaller profiles for single issues.

---

[4] This assumption is often reasonable, even if it has a certain level of arbitrariness.

9.2.3 Simultaneous Voting with Separable Preferences

Assuming separability allows us to avoid some of the paradoxes described above. First, when all voters have separable preferences, they can vote safely for their preferred value, for each one of the issues, and without any risk of experiencing regret (this is called *simple voting* by Benoît and Kornhauser (1991)). Second, under the separability assumption, simultaneously voting enjoys some desirable properties, including the election of a Condorcet winner when there is one (Kadane, 1972).[5]

However, some paradoxes still remain. In particular, the outcome may be Pareto-dominated by another alternative (Özkal-Sanver and Sanver, 2006; Benoît and Kornhauser, 2010), as shown in the following example.

Example 9.4 (Özkal-Sanver and Sanver, 2006). We have three issues, and three voters whose preferences are as follows:

- Voter 1: $111 \succ 011 \succ 101 \succ 001 \succ 110 \succ 010 \succ 100 \succ 000$
- Voter 2: $100 \succ 000 \succ 101 \succ 001 \succ 110 \succ 010 \succ 111 \succ 011$
- Voter 3: $010 \succ 011 \succ 000 \succ 001 \succ 110 \succ 111 \succ 100 \succ 101$

Note that these preferences are separable: voter 1 prefers 1_1 to 0_1, whichever the values of X_2 and X_3 (that is, she prefers 100 to 000, 101 to 001, 110 to 010, and 111 to 011), prefers 1_2 to 0_2, whichever the values of X_1 and X_3, and 1_3 to 0_3, whichever the values of X_1 and X_2. Similar reasoning shows that preferences for voters 2 and 3 are also separable. The outcome of simultaneous voting is 110, which is Pareto-dominated by 001, that is, all three voters prefer 001 to 110.

Benoît and Kornhauser (2010) prove a more general result. One may wonder whether there could be rules other than issue-wise majority that would escape the paradox. Unfortunately this is not the case: as soon as there are at least three issues, or when there are exactly two issues, one of which has at least three possible values, then simultaneous voting is efficient if and only if it is dictatorial. This result was generalized to irresolute voting rules by Xia and Lang (2009).

9.2.4 Discussion

Evaluating simultaneous voting on the criteria evoked in the introduction (Section 9.1), it is now clear that simultaneous voting has a low communication cost, and has also a low computation cost, provided that the "local" rules used to determine the outcome for each variable are easy to compute (which is obviously the case if variables are binary). Then, there are two possibilities: either we are able to assume separability, and in that case the outcome has some quality guarantees (even in this case it remains prone to some paradoxes, see Section 9.2.3); or we do not assume separability, and then the quality of the outcome can be extremely bad. We note that separability is a very strong assumption: the proportion of preferences on a combinatorial domain that are separable is very low (Bradley et al., 2005), and there are many domain-specific

---

[5] This holds both in the assumption that voters vote sincerely and in the assumption that voters' preferences are common knowledge and voters vote strategically.

arguments (such as budget constraints) showing that in many domains, it is almost hopeless to expect that voters' preferences are separable.

9.3 Approaches Based on Completion Principles

One way of escaping the paradoxes of simultaneous voting, discussed in particular by Brams et al. (1997a) and Lacy and Niou (2000), consists in having voters *vote on combinations* (or *bundles*) or values. This section discusses various ways of implementing this. Before addressing several classes of more complex methods, we mention three very simple solutions, which are relevant in some cases.

1. Voters rank all alternatives (i.e., all combinations) and a classical voting rule, such as Borda, is used.
2. Voters give only their top alternatives, and the plurality rule is used.
3. Voters rank a small number of pre-selected alternatives, and use a classical voting rule.

The first way is clearly the best method when the set of alternatives is small (say, up to four or five binary variables). It becomes inapplicable when the number of issues becomes more than a few, since asking voters to rank explicitly more than a few dozens of alternatives is already hopeless. The second way, advocated by Brams et al. (1997a), has the obvious advantage that it is relatively inexpensive both in terms of communication and computation; it is feasible provided that the set of alternatives is small enough with respect to the set of voters; when this is not the case, the plurality votes are likely to be completely dispersed (for instance, with 10 binary variables and 100 voters, the number of alternatives (2^{10}) is ten times larger than the number of voters and it may plausibly happen that each alternative will get no more than one vote), which does not help much making a decision. The third way avoids both problems, but the arbitrariness of the preselection phase can make the whole process very biased, and gives too much power to the authority who determines the preselected alternatives.

Ideally, methods should avoid the arbitrariness of methods 2 and 3 and the communication requirement of method 1. Recall that simultaneous voting has a low elicitation cost, at the price of considering all issues independently. One way of introducing links between issues while keeping the low communication cost of simultaneous voting consists in asking voters to specify a small part of their preference relations and then complete them into full (or, at last, more complete) preference relations using a fixed *completion* (or *extension*) *principle*. After this completion has been performed, we may apply a classical voting rule, or a voting rule specifically designed for this extension principle. We consider several families of completion principles, in increasing order of sophistication.

- *Top-based input*: the voters submit their preferred alternative and the completion principle makes use of a predefined distance over alternatives (typically, the Hamming distance); the completion principle ranks all alternatives according to their proximity to the preferred alternative.

- *Singleton ranking-based input*: this completion principle works only for binary variables; voters specify a ranking over single issues; the completion principle then extends it into a preference relation over all alternatives. This class of methods is often used for the selection of a set of items (typically, a committee).
- *Hypercube-based input*: the input consists of a compact representation of each voter's preference between all pairs of alternatives that are identical on all issues but one (this set of pairs of alternatives is also called the hypercube associated with A).
- *Inputs based on more sophisticated inputs*, such as conditionally lexicographic preference trees, weighted or prioritized logical formulas, generalized additive independence networks, or weighted constraints.

9.3.1 Top-Based Inputs and Distance-Based Completion Principles

One way to express a small part of the agents' preferences and to complete them automatically consists of asking each voter to specify *her top alternative* $\vec{x}^*$, and then applying the following intuitive completion principle: the closer to $\vec{x}^*$ with respect to a predefined distance d between alternatives, the more preferred. Formally: given a voter's top alternative $\vec{x}^*$, $\succ$ is *d-induced* if for all $\vec{y}, \vec{z} \in A$, $\vec{y} \succ \vec{z}$ iff $d(\vec{y}, \vec{x}^*) < d(\vec{z}, \vec{x}^*)$, and $\succ$ is *d-consistent* iff for all $\vec{y}, \vec{z} \in A$, $d(\vec{y}, \vec{x}^*) < d(\vec{z}, \vec{x}^*)$ implies $\vec{y} \succ \vec{z}$.

A trivial choice of a distance is the Dirac (or drastic) distance, defined by $d(\vec{x}, \vec{y}) = 0$ if $\vec{x} = \vec{y}$ and $d(\vec{x}, \vec{y}) = 1$ if $\vec{x} \neq \vec{y}$. We recover here the plurality-based extension principle discussed in Section 9.2.2, which can thus be seen as a distance-based extension.

While many choices of a nontrivial distance can be made, the most obvious one is perhaps the *Hamming distance* d_H: for all $\vec{x}, \vec{y} \in A$, $d_H(\vec{x}, \vec{y})$ is the number of issues on which $\vec{x}$ and $\vec{y}$ disagree. We say that $\succ$ is *Hamming-induced* (resp. *Hamming-consistent*) iff it is d_H-induced (resp. d_H-consistent).

Once such a preference extension principle has been fixed, we can apply a voting rule to select the winner. A prominent example of such a rule is *minimax approval voting*, defined by Brams et al. (2007) in the context of committee elections (although there is no reason not to apply it in more general contexts); for this reason, we describe the rule in a committee election setting, thus, with binary variables (also, it is not entirely trivial to extend minimax approval voting to nonbinary domains). There are n voters, p candidates, $k \leqslant p$ positions to be filled; each voter casts an approval ballot $V_i = (v_i^1, \ldots, v_i^p) \in \{0, 1\}^p$, where $v_i^j = 1$ if voter i approves candidate j. Then for every subset S of k candidates, let $d_H(S, (V_1, \ldots, V_n)) = \max_{i=1,\ldots,n} d_H(S, V_i)$ be the largest Hamming distance between S and a ballot. Minimax approval voting selects a committee S minimizing $d_H(S, (V_1, \ldots, V_n))$. Minimax approval voting makes sense if there are few voters, but much less so in large electorates, because a single voter can have a huge influence, even if everyone else agrees. Note that minimizing the *sum* of Hamming distances would be equivalent to outputting the candidates with the k largest approval scores (see Section 9.3.2).

Example 9.5. Let $n = 4$, $p = 4$, $k = 2$. The ballots are defined as follows, together with the computation of Hamming distance between the votes and any subset S composed of 2 candidates (there are 6 such candidates):

	$V_1 : 1110$	$V_2 : 1101$	$V_3 : 1010$	$V_4 : 1010$	max
1100	1	1	2	2	2
1010	1	3	0	0	3
1001	3	1	3	3	3
0110	1	3	2	2	3
0101	3	1	4	4	4
0011	3	3	2	2	3

The winning committee under minimax approval voting is 1100. Minimizing the *sum* of Hamming distances would lead to selecting 1010.

Because there are $\binom{p}{k}$ possible committees, winner determination for minimax approval voting is computationally intractable: finding a winning committee is NP-hard (Frances and Litman, 1997). LeGrand et al. (2007) give a polynomial-time 3-approximation algorithm; a better approximation (with ratio 2) is given by Caragiannis et al. (2010).

Another line of research that makes use of preference extensions based on the Hamming distance is that of Laffond and Lainé (2009) and Cuhadaroğlu and Lainé (2012). Recall from Section 9.2 that even if voters' preferences are separable, the simultaneous voting outcome can be Pareto-dominated. If furthermore voters' preferences are Hamming-consistent, then two positive results arise: (a) the simultaneous voting outcome cannot be Pareto-dominated, (b) the simultaneous voting outcome is in the top cycle (*a fortiori*, simultaneous voting is Condorcet-consistent). However, weaker negative results remain: not only may the outcome be majority-defeated but it can also fail to be in the uncovered set (Laffond and Lainé, 2009). To which extent are the positive results specific to the Hamming extension principle? An answer is given by Cuhadaroğlu and Lainé (2012), who show that under some mild conditions, the largest set of preferences for which the simultaneous voting outcome is Pareto-efficient is the set of Hamming-consistent preferences.

Distance-based approaches have a lot in common with *belief merging* (see a recent survey by Konieczny and Pino Pérez (2011)), which aggregates several propositional formulas $K_1, \ldots, K_n$ into a collective propositional formula $\Delta(K_1, \ldots, K_n)$. The set of alternatives corresponds to the set of propositional valuations (or interpretations). Perhaps the most well-studied family of belief merging operators is the class of *distance-based* merging operators: there is a predefined, integer-valued, agent-independent distance d over propositional valuations (typically, the Hamming distance), and a symmetric, nondecreasing aggregation function $\star$ over integers, and the output is a formula whose models minimize $\star\{d(., K_i) | i = 1 \ldots n\}$, where $d(\vec{x}, K_i) = \min_{\vec{y} \models K_i} d(\vec{x}, \vec{y})$. The complexity of distance-based belief merging is addressed by Konieczny et al. (2004). Although coming from a different area, distance-based belief merging shares a lot with combinatorial voting with distance-based preference extensions (especially minimax approval voting). Two important differences are that in belief merging: (a) the input may consist of a *set* of equally most preferred alternatives, rather than a single one; and (b) the input is represented compactly by a logical formula.

9.3.2 Input Based on Rankings over Single Variables

In this section we focus specifically on the selection of a *collective set of items* S by a group of agents. The meaning we give here to "items" is extremely general and can cover a variety of situations, with two typical examples being *committee elections*, where the "items" are representatives, and *group recommendations*, where items are objects such as books, movies, and so on.

Formally, this can be cast as a combinatorial domain where the set of binary issues is $\mathcal{X} = \{X_1, \ldots, X_p\}$, with $D_i = \{0_i, 1_i\}$ for each i. These binary issues correspond to a set of items $C = \{c_1, \ldots, c_p\}$, where $X_i = 1_i$ (resp. 0_i) means that item c_i is (resp. is not) in the selection S. Because of the focus on the selection of a subset of items, we change the notational convention by denoting an alternative $\vec{x} \in A = \{0_1, 1_1\} \times \ldots \times \{0_p, 1_p\}$ as a *subset of issues* S composed of items c_is with $X_i = 1_i$. Thus, alternatives are elements of 2^C.

In most cases, the set of feasible subsets is a proper subset of 2^C, defined by a *constraint* Γ restricting the set of feasible or allowed subsets. In committee elections, the most common constraints are *cardinality constraints* that restrict the size of a committee, by specifying an exact size k, or a lower and/or an upper bound. More generally, Lu and Boutilier (2011a) consider budget constraints, defined by a price for each item and a maximum total cost—hence the terminology *budgeted social choice*.

The approaches discussed in this section proceed by first eliciting from each agent some preference information (typically, a ranking) over single *items*, then extending these preferences over single items to preferences over sets of items, and finally selecting a set of items S.

The most obvious way of doing so is *multiwinner approval voting* (which can, to some extent, be seen as the multiwinner version of simultaneous voting): each voter approves as many candidates as she wants, and the winners are the k candidates approved most often. In *single nontransferable vote (SNTV)* and *bloc voting*, there is an additional restriction on the number of candidates approved: 1 in SNTV and k in bloc voting (these rules are thus multiwinner versions of plurality and k-approval, respectively). Finally, in *cumulative voting*, voters distribute a fixed number of points among the candidates, and the winners are the k candidates maximizing the number of points. The common point of all these rules is that voters' preferences are assumed to be separable; reformulated in terms of preference extensions, each input defines a score over single candidates, and the total score of a candidate is the *sum* of the scores it gets from the voters. Computational aspects of strategic behavior (manipulation by a single voter and control by the chair) for these multiwinner voting rules have been studied by Meir et al. (2008).

In the remainder of this section, we focus on classes of methods where the input consists of *rankings* over single items.

In committee elections, where the items are individuals supposed to represent the voters, the rationale for the last step is that a committee election is used to elect an assembly whose members will make decisions on behalf of the society. As argued by Betzler et al. (2013), finding a committee of representatives should satisfy two criteria: *representativity* (the composition of the committee should globally reflect the will of the voters), and *accountability* (each voter should be represented by a given member of the committee). In consensus recommendations, the rationale for the last step is that each user will benefit from the best option according to her own preferences (Lu and Boutilier, 2011a); in this case, the "representative" of a voter is her most preferred item in S.[6,7] The latter interpretation leads to an obvious choice for defining representative items for voters: if the set of items S is chosen, then the representative item of voter i is $c \in S$ if $c \succ_i c'$ for all $c' \in C \setminus \{c\}$. Alternatively, we say that each agent is *represented* by an item in S. In committee elections, this principle is the basis of the *Chamberlin and Courant* multiwinner election scheme (discussed later).

We now describe these multiwinner election schemes (grouped under the terminology "fully proportional representation") more formally. For each voter i and each item c there is a *misrepresentation value* $\mu_{i,c}$, representing the degree to which item c misrepresents voter i. A *positional misrepresentation function* makes use of a scoring vector $\vec{s} = \langle s_1, \ldots, s_p \rangle$ such that $s_1 \leqslant \ldots \leqslant s_p$. In particular, the Borda scoring vector $\vec{s_B}$ is defined by $s_k = k$ for all k. By $pos_i(c)$ we mean the position of item c in i's preference ranking (from 1 for the most preferred item to p for the least preferred one). The misrepresentation function induced by $\vec{s}$ is $\mu_{i,c} = s_{pos_i(c)}$. Intuitively, s_i is the amount of dissatisfaction that a voter derives from being represented by an alternative that she ranks in position i. Another simple way of defining a *misrepresentation based on approval ballots* is: every voter submits a subset of candidates that she approves, and $\mu_{i,c}$ is 0 if i approves c, and 1 otherwise.

An *assignment function* π maps every voter to an item in the selected subset S. The misrepresentation of voter i under π is $\mu_{i,\pi(i)}$. Once individual misrepresentation has been defined, we need to define the *global misrepresentation* of the society when selecting a subset S of items. There are two traditional ways of doing so: *utilitarianism* (global misrepresentation is the sum of all individual misrepresentation) and *egalitarianism* (global misrepresentation is the misrepresentation of the least well-represented agent). Formally, the global misrepresentation of assignment π is defined as:

- (utilitarianism) $\mu_U(\pi) = \sum_{i \leqslant n} \mu_{i,\pi(i)}$.
- (egalitarianism) $\mu_E(\pi) = \max_{i \leqslant n} \mu_{i,\pi(i)}$.

Finally, let $\mathcal{F}$ be the set of feasible subsets of items; typically, if k items are to be elected then $\mathcal{F}$ is the set $\mathcal{S}_k$ of all subsets of C of size k.

The *Chamberlin and Courant* scheme (Chamberlin and Courant, 1983) simply outputs the committee of size k that minimizes μ_U. Because there is no constraint on the assignment function, every voter is assigned to her preferred item in the selected subset S. That is, $\pi(i) = \arg\min_{c \in S} \mu_{i,c}$. Then, her misrepresentation when selecting the feasible subset S is equal to $\mu_{i,S} = \min_{c \in S} \mu_{i,c}$. The best committee is then the feasible subset S minimizing $\mu_U(\pi)$ (under utilitarianism) or S that minimizes $\mu_E(\pi)$ (under egalitarianism). The *Monroe* scheme (Monroe, 1995) additionally requires that

---

[6] As discussed by Lu and Boutilier (2011a), this can also be seen as a segmentation problem (Kleinberg et al., 2004), where one more generally seeks k solutions to some combinatorial optimization problem that will be used by $n \geqslant k$ different users, each with a different objective value on items; optimization requires segmenting users into k groups depending on which of the k items gives them the greatest benefit.

[7] Skowron et al. (2015) generalize this scheme by taking into account more than one item by agent, but still giving more importance to an agent's most preferred item than to her second best preferred item, etc.

the assignment π is balanced: each candidate in S must be assigned to at least $\lfloor n/k \rfloor$ voters.[8] Formally, the Monroe scheme selects the allocation π minimizing $\mu_U(\pi)$ subject to the constraints $|\pi^{-1}(s)| \geqslant \lfloor \frac{n}{k} \rfloor$ for all $s \in Range(\pi)$.

Budgeted social choice (Lu and Boutilier, 2011a) generalizes Chamberlin-Courant by redefining feasibility via a budget constraint: Each item c has a fixed cost (to be counted if x is selected) and a unit cost (to be counted k times if k agents are represented by the item), the maximum budget is K, and $\mathcal{F}$ is the set of all assignments with total cost $\leqslant K$.

The egalitarian version of multiwinner schemes is due to Betzler et al. (2013). Elkind et al. (2014a) discuss some properties of multiwinner voting schemes.

Example 9.6. Let $C = \{c_1, c_1, c_3, c_4\}$, $K = 2$, and the following 4 agents' preferences:

$$\langle\ c_1 \succ c_2 \succ c_3 \succ c_4,$$
$$c_1 \succ c_2 \succ c_3 \succ c_4,$$
$$c_1 \succ c_3 \succ c_2 \succ c_4,$$
$$c_1 \succ c_3 \succ c_2 \succ c_4,$$
$$c_2 \succ c_4 \succ c_3 \succ c_1,$$
$$c_4 \succ c_3 \succ c_2 \succ c_1\ \rangle.$$

For the Borda misrepresentation function, the optimal Chamberlin-Courant committee of 2 items is $\{c_1, c_4\}$, whereas for Monroe it is $\{c_1, c_2\}$. For the egalitarian versions, both $\{c_1, c_4\}$ and $\{c_2, c_3\}$ are optimal for Chamberlin-Courant and $\{c_2, c_3\}$ is optimal for Monroe.

Because the set of feasible subsets is generally exponentially large, finding the optimal subset is highly nontrivial. Brams and Potthoff (1998) were the first to discuss the computation of the Chamberlin-Courant and the Monroe voting schemes, showing that the optimal committee can be determined using integer programming. This provides a method that works in practice when the number of voters and items are small, but may not scale up well. They formulate an improved integer program for settings where the number of agents is large, but this modified integer program is still too large to be solved when the number of items is large.

One cannot really do better in the general case; indeed, we have the following hardness results:

- Winner determination for the Chamberlin-Courant and the Monroe schemes with approval ballots are both NP-complete (Procaccia et al., 2008)
- Winner determination for the Chamberlin-Courant scheme with the Borda misrepresentation function is NP-complete (Lu and Boutilier, 2011a)
- Winner determination for the minimax versions of the Chamberlin-Courant and Monroe schemes is NP-complete (Betzler et al., 2013)

---

[8] In indirect democracy, that is, when the set of representatives has to make a decision on behalf of the society, it may be a good idea to give more power to people who represent more people than to those who represent less people; for instance, Chamberlin and Courant suggested to give to each committee member a weight equal to the number of voters she represents.

Some slightly more positive results are obtained:

- *Parameterized complexity*. Procaccia et al. (2008) show that winner determination for Chamberlin-Courant and Monroe is tractable for small committees: if the size of the subset to be selected is constant, then winner determination is polynomial for both voting schemes. Betzler et al. (2013) investigate further the parameterized complexity of fully proportional representation by establishing a mixture of positive and negative results: they mainly prove fixed-parameter tractability with respect to the number of candidates or the number of voters, but fixed-parameter intractability with respect to the number of winners.
- *Approximation*: Lu and Boutilier (2011a) give a polynomial algorithm with approximation ratio $1 - \frac{1}{e}$ for Chamberlin-Courant with the Borda misrepresentation function. Skowron et al. (2013a,c) give further approximability results.
- *Domain restrictions*: for single-peaked profiles, most multiwinner problems discussed above become polynomial; the only rule that remains NP-hard for single-peaked electorates is the classical Monroe rule (Betzler et al., 2013). These results are extended by Cornaz et al. (2012) to profiles with bounded *single-peaked width*, and by Yu et al. (2013) who consider profiles that are more generally *single-peaked on a tree*. Skowron et al. (2013b) address the case of single-crossing profiles.

Finally, the generalization of full proportional representation schemes to incomplete preferences was considered by Lu and Boutilier (2013) (see also Chapter 10).

The notion of *Condorcet winning set* (Elkind et al., 2015a) also evaluates a subset according to a best item in it. The criteria for selecting a "best" subset does not use a misrepresentation function but is simply based on the Condorcet principle: $S \subseteq C$ is a Condorcet winning set if for every $z \notin S$, a majority of voters prefers *some* $s \in S$ to z. For every m-candidate profile, there is a Condorcet winning set of size at most $\log_2 m + 1$, therefore, finding a Condorcet winning set can be done by enumerating all subsets of candidates of size $\lfloor \log_2 m \rfloor + 1$, i.e., in *quasipolynomial* time. It may actually be even easier: it is an open issue whether for all k there exists a profile for which the smallest Condorcet winning set has size k.

9.3.3 Hypercube-Based Inputs

Specifying top-based inputs (respectively, rankings over variables) needs $O(np)$ (respectively, $O(np \log p)$) space, hence the communication requirement of the two previous subclasses of methods is low: each agent needs only to report $O(np)$ (respectively, $O(np \log p)$) bits to the central authority. On the other hand, their applicability is very weak, because only a tiny fraction of preference relations comply with the required domain restrictions. We now consider more expressive approaches that are based on *compact representations*: the votes, or a significant part of the votes, are not given extensively but are described in some formal language that comes with a function mapping any input of the language to a (partial or complete) vote (Lang, 2004). Formally, a *compact preference representation language* is a pair $L = \langle \Sigma_L, I_L \rangle$ where Σ_L is a formal language, and I_L is a function from Σ_L to the set of preference relations over A. $I_L(\Sigma_L)$ is the set of all preference relations expressible in L. A language L_1 is more expressive than L_2 if $I_{L_1}(\Sigma_{L_1}) \supset I_{L_2}(\Sigma_{L_2})$ and more succinct than L_2 if there is a function $f : \Sigma_{L_2} \to \Sigma_{L_1}$ and a polynomial function pol such that for all $\sigma \in \Sigma_{L_2}$, we have (i) $|f(\sigma)| \leqslant pol(|\sigma|)$ and (ii) $I_{L_1}(f(\sigma)) = I_{L_2}(\sigma)$. Conditions (i) and (ii) together mean that any preference relation expressible in L_2 can also be expressed in L_1 without a superpolynomial increase in the size of expression.

If a language L is totally expressive (i.e., $I_L(\Sigma_L)$ is the set of *all* rankings over D) then the worst-case size necessary for expressing a ranking is exponentially large in the number of variables.[9] Therefore, there is a trade-off to be made between having a fully expressive language which, at least for some preference relations, will not be compact at all, or making a domain restriction that will allow for a compact input in all cases.

Some of the solutions advocated in the previous sections were, to some extent, making use of very rough compact preference representation languages. Expressing only the top alternative, say 111, is a compact representation of the partial preference relation

$$111 \succ A \setminus \{111\}$$

or, in the case of the Hamming distance completion, of the complete preorder

$$111 \succ \begin{matrix} 110 \\ 101 \\ 001 \end{matrix} \succ \begin{matrix} 100 \\ 010 \\ 001 \end{matrix} \succ 000.$$

Expressing a ranking over single items is a compact representation of a partial or complete preorder over committees: for 2-committees and the Chamberlin-Courant scheme, for instance, $1 \succ 2 \succ 3 \succ 4$ is a compact representation of

$$\begin{matrix} \{1,4\} \\ \{1,2\} \\ \{1,3\} \end{matrix} \succ \begin{matrix} \{2,3\} \\ \{2,4\} \end{matrix} \succ \{3,4\}.$$

As already discussed, these first two compact representation languages are admittedly very compact, but also very inexpressive. We now give some examples of more expressive languages.

The first compact representation language we consider is that of *conditional preference networks* (CP-nets). CP-nets (Boutilier et al., 2004) allow for a compact representation of the *preference hypercube* associated with a preference relation over D. Given a preference relation $\succ$ over $D = \prod_{i=1}^{n}\{0_i, 1_i\}$, the preference hypercube $\succ_H$ is the restriction of $\succ$ to the set of pairs of alternatives $\vec{x}, \vec{y}$ differing on only one variable (such as, for instance, 0101 and 0111). CP-nets are based on the notion of *conditional preferential independence* (Keeney and Raiffa, 1976): given a strict preference relation $\succ$, $X_i \in \mathcal{X}, Y \subseteq \mathcal{X} \setminus \{X_i\}$ and $Z = \mathcal{X} \setminus (\{X_i\} \cup Y)$, we say that X_i is preferentially independent of Y given Z with respect to $\succ$ if for any $x_i, x_i' \in D_i, \vec{y}, \vec{y}' \in D_Y$, and $\vec{z} \in D_Z$, we have $(x_i, \vec{y}, \vec{z}) \succ (x_i', \vec{y}, \vec{z})$ if and only if $(x_i, \vec{y}', \vec{z}) \succ (x_i', \vec{y}', \vec{z})$. A CP-net $\mathcal{N}$ over A consists of two components.

---

[9] A simple proof of this fact in the case of binary variables: for p variables there are $(2^p)!$ possible rankings, and the best we can do to express a ranking is to use $\log((2^p)!)$ bits in the worst case; and $\log((2^p)!)$ is exponential in p.

- The first component is a directed graph G expressing preferential independence relations between variables: if $Par_G(X_i)$ denotes the set of the parents of X_i in G, then every variable X_i is preferentially independent of $\mathcal{X} \setminus (Par(X_i) \cup \{X_i\})$ given $Par(X_i)$.
- The second component is, for each variable X_i, a set of linear orders $\succ_{\vec{u}}^i$ over D_i, called conditional preferences, for each $\vec{u} \in D_{Par_G(X_i)}$. These conditional preferences form the *conditional preference table* for issue X_i, denoted by $CPT(X_i)$.

The preference relation $\succ_{\mathcal{N}}$ induced by $\mathcal{N}$ is the transitive closure of

$$\{(a_i, \vec{u}, \vec{z}) \succ (b_i, \vec{u}, \vec{z}) \mid i \leqslant p; \vec{u} \in D_{Par_G(X_i)}; a_i, b_i \in D_i, a_i \succ_{\vec{u}}^i b_i$$
$$\vec{z} \in D_{-(Par_G(X_i) \cup \{X_i\})}\}.$$

When all issues are binary, $\succ_{\mathcal{N}}$ is equivalent to a preference hypercube and $\mathcal{N}$ is a compact representation of this preference hypercube, whose size is the cumulative size of all its conditional preference tables.

Example 9.7. Let $p = 3$. The following represents a CP-net $\mathcal{N}$ together with its induced preference hypercube $\succ_{\mathcal{N}}$. For the sake of simplicity, 000 represents the alternative $0_1 0_2 0_3$, and so on.

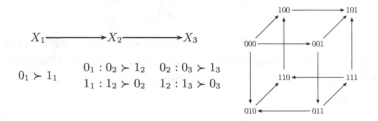

Group decision making in multi-issue domains via CP-net aggregation has been considered in a number of papers, which we briefly review in a nonchronological order. We will discuss in Section 9.4 the role of CP-nets in sequential voting (Lang and Xia, 2009; Airiau et al., 2011): this way of proceeding sequentially leads to interleave elicitation and aggregation, and elicits only a small part of the voters' CP-nets. Another way of proceeding consists in first eliciting the voters' CP-nets entirely, then proceeding to aggregation. Then, two ways are possible.

The first aggregation consists of mapping each of the individual CP-nets to its associated preference relation, and aggregating these into a collective preference relation. This method was initiated by Rossi et al. (2004), who consider several such aggregation functions, and was studied further by Li et al. (2010), who give algorithms for computing Pareto-optimal alternatives with respect to the preference relations induced by the CP-nets, and fair alternatives with respect to a cardinalization of these preference relations.

A second technique, considered by Xia et al. (2008), Li et al. (2011), and Conitzer et al. (2011b), consists of aggregating the individual CP-nets into a collective CP-net, and then outputting the nondominated alternatives of this collective CP-net. No domain restriction is made on the individual CP-nets. For every set of "neighboring" alternatives (differing only in the value of one issue), a local voting rule (typically majority if domains are binary) is used for deciding the common preferences over this set, and finally, optimal outcomes are defined based on the aggregated CP-net.

Example 9.8. We have two issues, X_1 and X_2, and the following three CP-nets.

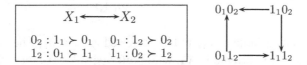

The majority aggregation of $\mathcal{N}_1$, $\mathcal{N}_2$ and $\mathcal{N}_3$ is the following CP-net, depicted with its induced preference relation.

The dependency graph of this collective CP-net contains an edge from X_1 to X_2 (resp., from X_2 to X_1) because the dependency graph of voters 1 (resp., 2) CP-net does. In the preference table for X_1, we have $0_2 : 1_1 \succ 0_1$ because voters 2 and 3 (unlike voter 1) prefer 1_1 to 0_1 when $X_2 = 0_2$.

Once the CP-nets from agents have been aggregated to a common CP-net $\mathcal{N}^*$, the next task consists of finding a set of solutions. Because $\mathcal{N}^*$ only specifies pairwise preferences between neighbor alternatives, usual solution concepts are not directly applicable. In particular, there is generally no way of checking whether a Condorcet winner exists; however, we can check if there are *hypercubewise Condorcet winners* (HCW), that is, alternatives that dominate all of their neighbours in $\mathcal{N}^*$. Unlike Condorcet winners, a profile may possess no HCW, one HCW, or several HCW (in Example 9.8 there are two, namely, $0_1 1_2$ and $1_1 0_2$). The notion of a HCW was first defined by Xia et al. (2008) and studied further by Li et al. (2011), who study some of its properties and propose (and implement) a SAT-based algorithm for computing them, whereas the probability of existence of a HCW is addressed by Conitzer et al. (2011b). More solution concepts (such as the top cycle, Copeland, maximin, or Kemeny) can also be generalized to profiles consisting of preference hypercubes (Xia et al., 2008; Conitzer et al., 2011b), while new solution concepts, based on distances between alternatives in the hypercube, have been proposed by Xia et al. (2010a).

9.3.4 Conditionally Lexicographic Preferences

A *conditionally lexicographic preference* can be represented compactly by a *lexicographic preference tree (LP-tree)* (Booth et al., 2010), consisting of (*i*) a *conditional importance tree*, where each node is labeled by a variable X_i and has either one child, or two children associated with the values 0_i and 1_i taken by X_i; (*ii*) and, for each node v of the tree, labeled by X_i, a *conditional preference table* expressing a preference order on D_i for all possible combination of values of (some of) the ancestor variables that have not yet assigned a value in the branch from the root to v.

Example 9.9. An LP-tree with $p = 3$ is illustrated in the following.

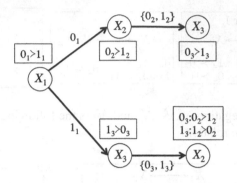

The most important variable is X_1, and its preferred value is 0_1; when $X_1 = 0_1$ then the second most important variable is X_2, with preferred value 0_2, then X_3 with preferred value 0_3; when $X_1 = 1_1$ then the second most important variable is X_3, with preferred value 1_3, then X_2, with preferred value 0_2 if $X_3 = 0_3$ and 1_2 if $X_3 = 1_3$. The preference relation induced by an LP-tree compares two alternatives by looking for the first node (starting from the root) that discriminates them: for instance, for $\vec{x} = 111$ and $\vec{y} = 100$, this is the node labeled by X_3 in the branch associated with $X_1 = 1_1$. Because $1_3 \succ 0_3$ at that node, $\vec{x}$ is preferred to $\vec{y}$. The complete preference relation associated with the preceding LP-tree is $001 \succ 000 \succ 011 \succ 010 \succ 111 \succ 101 \succ 100 \succ 110$.

Assuming preferences are conditionally lexicographic imposes an important domain restriction (as does separability), but for some voting rules, determining the outcome is efficient in communication and computation (Lang et al., 2012a). We give an example with 2^{p-2}-approval. Given an LP-tree T compactly expressing a ranking $\succ_T$, an alternative is one of the 2^{p-2} best alternatives (i.e., in the top quarter) if and only if it gives the preferred value to the most important variable (in the preceding example, $X_1 = 0_1$) and the preferred value to the second most important variable given this value ($X_2 = 0_2$). This gives, for every voter, a conjunction of two literals (here $\neg X_1 \wedge \neg X_2$); the 2^{p-2}-approval winners are exactly those who satisfy a maximal number of such formulas, thus the winner determination problem can be solved using a MAXSAT solver. Note that, although the problem is NP-hard, there are efficient MAXSAT solvers (and a MAXSAT track of the SAT competition). Results about other rules can be found in the work of Lang et al. (2012a).

Example 9.10. Let $n = 3$, $p = 3$, and consider the three LP-trees in Figure 9.1. The first LP-tree is the same as that in Example 9.9, and an alternative is ranked in its top $2^{p-2} = 2$ positions if and only if $\neg X_1 \wedge \neg X_2$ is satisfied. In the second LP-tree, the top 2^{p-2} alternatives can be represented as $\neg X_1 \wedge X_2$. In the third LP-tree, the top 2^{p-2} alternatives can be represented as $X_2 \wedge X_3$. These are the formulas in the MAXSAT instance and the winner for 2-approval is 011.

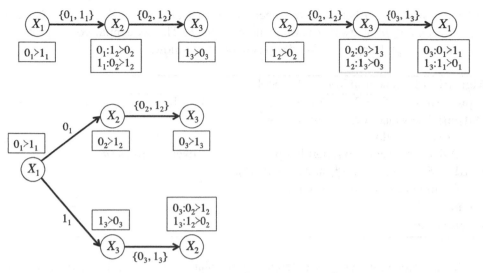

Figure 9.1. Three LP-trees.

9.3.5 Cardinal Preferences

In general, voting rules are using ordinal inputs. Allowing for a numerical representation of preferences (and possibly assuming interpersonal comparison of preference) opens the door to a different class of approaches, based on the maximization of an aggregation function. Many languages for compact preference representation of numerical preferences have been defined and equipped with efficient algorithms, especially valued CSPs (Bistarelli et al., 1999) and GAI-nets (Bacchus and Grove, 1995; Gonzales and Perny, 2004). In both cases, local utility functions are defined over small (and possibly intersecting) subsets of variables $S_1, \ldots, S_q$, and the global utility function is the sum (or more generally the aggregation, for some suitable aggregation function) of the local utilities obtained from the local tables by projecting the alternatives on each of the S_is. Gonzales et al. (2008) use such a representation based on GAI-nets and study algorithms for finding a Pareto-optimal alternative. Lafage and Lang (2000) and Uckelman (2009) assume that individual preferences are compactly represented using weighted propositional formulae, and that a collectively optimal alternative is defined through the maximization of a collective utility function resulting in the aggregation of individual utilities, for some suitable aggregation function (which requires not only that preferences be numerical but also that they be interpersonally comparable). See also the work by Dalla Pozza et al. (2011), discussed in Section 9.4.

9.4 Sequential Voting

The basic principle of sequential voting is that at each step voters' preferences over the values of a single issue are elicited, the decision about this variable is taken using a local voting rule, and the outcome is communicated to the voters before they vote on the next variable. Formally, a sequential voting protocol on A is defined by (1) an order $\mathcal{O}$ over $\mathcal{X}$ – without loss of generality, we let $\mathcal{O} = X_1 \rhd X_2 \rhd \cdots \rhd X_p$; and (2) for each $i \leqslant p$, a resolute voting rule r_i over D_i. The sequential voting protocol $Seq_{\mathcal{O}}(r_1, \ldots, r_p)$ (Lang and Xia, 2009) is defined as follows.

Algorithm 1 Sequential Voting Protocol

Input: An order $\mathcal{O} = X_1 \rhd X_2 \rhd \cdots \rhd X_p$ over $\mathcal{X}$; p local voting rules $r_1, \ldots, r_p$.
Output: The winner $(d_1, \ldots, d_p)$
1 **for** $t = 1$ *to* p **do**
2 | Ask every agent i to report her preferences $\succ_t^i$ over D_t given $(d_1, \ldots, d_{t-1})$.
3 | Let $P_t = \langle \succ_t^1, \ldots, \succ_t^n \rangle$ and $d_t = r_t(P_t)$.
4 | Communicate d_t to the voters.
5 **end**
6 **return** $(d_1, \ldots, d_p)$

This definition can easily be extended to irresolute voting rules. In the remainder of this section, we will use $Seq_{\mathcal{O}}$ as a shorthand notation for $Seq_{\mathcal{O}}(r_1, \ldots, r_p)$.

We have not discussed yet agents' behavior in each step. The main complication is that a preference for one issue may depend on the results for other issues, hence the difficulty for a voter to decide her local preferences to report.

Example 9.11. Let X_1 and X_2 be two binary issues and let P denote the following 3-voter profile:

$$1_1 1_2 \succ 0_1 1_2 \succ 1_1 0_2 \succ 0_1 0_2$$
$$1_1 0_2 \succ 1_1 1_2 \succ 0_1 1_2 \succ 0_1 0_2$$
$$0_1 1_2 \succ 0_1 0_2 \succ 1_1 0_2 \succ 1_1 1_2$$

If the order $\mathcal{O}$ is $X_2 \rhd X_1$, then voters 2 and 3 cannot unambiguously report their preferences over X_2, because they depend on the value of X_1 (for instance, voter 2 prefers 0_2 to 1_2 when $X_1 = 1_1$ and 1_2 to 0_2 when $X_1 = 0_1$), which has not been fixed yet. In other terms, marginal (or local) preference over X_2 does not have a precise meaning here.

9.4.1 Safe Sequential Voting

The condition that ensures that voters can report their preferences unambiguously is $\mathcal{O}$-*legality*: given $\mathcal{O} = X_1 \rhd X_2 \rhd \cdots \rhd X_p$, a preference relation $\succ$ over A is *O-legal* if for every $k \leqslant p$, X_k is preferentially independent of $X_{k+1}, \ldots X_p$ given $X_1, \ldots, X_{k-1}$; or, equivalently, $\succ$ extends the preference relation $\succ_N$ induced by a CP-net whose dependency graph is compatible with $\mathcal{O}$ (i.e., does not contain any edge from X_i to X_j such that $X_j \rhd X_i$). Let $Legal(\mathcal{O})$ denote the set of all $\mathcal{O}$-legal profiles.

Example 9.11, continued. P is not $(X_2 \rhd X_1)$-legal, because voters 2 and 3 have preferences over X_2 that depend on X_1. On the other hand, P is $(X_1 \rhd X_2)$-legal, because all voters have unconditional preferences on X_1: voters 1 and 2 prefer 1_1 to 0_1, and voter 3 prefers 0_1 to 1_1, independently of the value of X_2.

In presence of the O-legality domain restriction, we say that sequential voting is *safe*. In this section we assume $\mathcal{O}$ to be fixed and apply sequential voting to the domain of $\mathcal{O}$-legal profiles only. A crucial property of simultaneous voting under the separability restriction carries over to safe sequential voting: it makes sense for a voter to report her local preferences on the current issue given the value of earlier issues, without having to wonder about the values of issues that have not been decided yet.

When all agents' preferences are $\mathcal{O}$-legal, a sequential voting protocol can also be considered *as a voting rule*, because a voter's preference on the values of X_i given the values of earlier variables is unambiguously defined given her preference relation over A. More precisely, given any $\mathcal{O}$-legal profile P, $Seq_\mathcal{O}(P)$ is defined to be the output of the sequential voting protocol where in step 2, $P_t = \langle \succ_t^1, \ldots, \succ_t^n \rangle$ where $\succ_t^i$ represents local preferences of agent i over D_t given $X_1 = d_1, \ldots, X_{t-1} = d_{t-1}$.

Example 9.12. Suppose there are two binary issues X_1 and X_2. Let P denote the same profile as in Example 9.11. Let $\mathcal{O} = X_1 \rhd X_2$. As we discussed, P is $\mathcal{O}$-legal. To apply $Seq_\mathcal{O}(maj, maj)$, where maj denote the majority rule, in step 1 the voters are asked to report their (unconditional) preferences on X_1, which gives $P_1 = \langle 1_1 \succ 0_1, 1_1 \succ 0_1, 0_1 \succ 1_1 \rangle$. Therefore, $d_1 = maj(P_1) = 1_1$. In step 2, the voters report their preferences over D_2 given $X_1 = 1_1$, which leads to $P_2 = \langle 1_2 \succ 0_2, 0_2 \succ 1_2, 0_2 \succ 1_2 \rangle$, and then $d_2 = maj(P_2) = 0_2$. Therefore, $Seq_\mathcal{O}(maj, maj)(P) = 1_1 0_2$.

Normative Properties

We recall from Chapter 2 that one classical way to assess voting rules is to study whether they satisfy certain normative properties. In this subsection we examine the normative properties of safe sequential voting.

Classical normative properties are defined for voting rules where the input is composed of linear orders over the alternatives. We note that $Seq_\mathcal{O}(P)$ is only defined for $\mathcal{O}$-legal profiles. Some normative properties can be easily extended to $Seq_\mathcal{O}(P)$, for example *anonymity* and *consistency*, while others need to be modified. For example, the classical *neutrality* axiom states that for any profile P and any permutation M of the alternatives, $r(M(P)) = M(r(P))$. However, even if P is $\mathcal{O}$-legal, $M(P)$ might not be $\mathcal{O}$-legal. Therefore, we will focus on a weaker version of neutrality that requires $r(M(P)) = M(r(P))$ for all P and M such that both P and $M(P)$ are $\mathcal{O}$-legal. *Monotonicity* can be modified in a similar way.

Whether $Seq_\mathcal{O}$ satisfies a specific normative property often depends on whether the local voting rules satisfy the same property. Some properties are inherited by sequential compositions from their local rules r_i; for others, satisfaction of the property by the local voting rules is merely a necessary but not sufficient condition.

Theorem 9.13 (Lang and Xia, 2009).

- $Seq_\mathcal{O}(r_1, \ldots, r_p)$ *satisfies* anonymity *(respectively,* consistency*) if and only if* r_i *satisfies* anonymity *(*consistency*) for all* $i = 1, \ldots, p$;

- *if $Seq_{\mathcal{O}}(r_1, \ldots, r_p)$ satisfies* neutrality *(respectively,* Condorcet-consistency, *participation, and* Pareto-efficiency*) then r_i satisfies neutrality (respectively, Condorcet-consistency, participation, and Pareto-efficiency) for all $i = 1, \ldots, p$;*
- *$Seq_{\mathcal{O}}(r_1, \ldots, r_p)$ satisfies* monotonicity *if and only if r_p satisfies monotonicity.*

Proofs for the normative properties mentioned in Theorem 9.13 follow a similar pattern. Take consistency, for example. Recall that a voting rule r satisfies consistency if for all disjoint profiles P_1 and P_2 such that $r(P_1) = r(P_2)$, we have $r(P_1 \cup P_2) = r(P_1)$ (see Chapter 1). We first prove that consistency can be lifted from all local rules to their sequential composition $Seq_{\mathcal{O}}(r_1, \ldots, r_p)$. For any disjoint sets of profiles P_1 and P_2 such that $Seq_{\mathcal{O}}(r_1, \ldots, r_p)(P_1) = Seq_{\mathcal{O}}(r_1, \ldots, r_p)(P_2)$, let $\vec{d}$ denote the outcome. We then prove that $Seq_{\mathcal{O}}(r_1, \ldots, r_p)(P_1 \cup P_2) = \vec{d} = (d_1, \ldots, d_p)$ by induction on the round t of sequential voting. When $t = 1$, let P_1^1 and P_2^1 denote the agents' preferences over X_1, which are well-defined because P_1 and P_2 are $\mathcal{O}$-legal. Due to consistency of r_1, we have $r_1(P_1^1 \cup P_2^1) = d_1$. Suppose the outcome of sequential voting is the same as in $\vec{d}$ up to round $k - 1$. It is not hard to verify that in round k, the winner is d_k by considering agents' preferences over X_t conditioned on previous issues taking $d_1, \ldots, d_{k-1}$. This proves that $Seq_{\mathcal{O}}(r_1, \ldots, r_p)$ satisfies consistency.

Conversely, if $Seq_{\mathcal{O}}(r_1, \ldots, r_p)$ satisfies consistency and for the sake of contradiction suppose that a local rule does not satisfy consistency. Let t denote the smallest number such that r_t is not consistent, and let P_1^t, P_2^t denote the profiles over X_t with $r_t(P_1^t) = r_t(P_2^t) \neq r_t(P_1^t \cup P_2^t)$. Let $r_1, \ldots, r_{t-1}, r_{t+1}, \ldots, r_p$ be rules that always output the same winner regardless of the local profile. We can extend P_1^t and P_2^t to profiles P_1, P_2 over the whole combinatorial domain so that $Seq_{\mathcal{O}}(r_1, \ldots, r_p)(P_1) = Seq_{\mathcal{O}}(r_1, \ldots, r_p)(P_2)$, and agents' local preferences over X_t are P_1^t and P_2^t. It is not hard to verify that $Seq_{\mathcal{O}}(r_1, \ldots, r_p)(P_1) \neq Seq_{\mathcal{O}}(r_1, \ldots, r_p)(P_1 \cup P_2)$, which contradicts the assumption that $Seq_{\mathcal{O}}(r_1, \ldots, r_p)$ satisfies consistency.

In fact, for neutrality and Pareto-efficiency, a stronger result has been proved for *irresolute* sequential voting rules: Xia and Lang (2009) show that except in the case where the domain is composed of two binary issues, the only neutral irresolute sequential voting rules are dictatorships, antidictatorships,[10] and the trivial irresolute rule that always outputs the whole set of alternatives; and the only Pareto-efficient irresolute sequential voting rules are dictatorships and the trivial irresolute rule. When the domain is composed of two binary issues, sequential majority is neutral and Pareto-efficient.

Strategic Behavior

In the previous subsection, when we talked about normative properties, it was implicitly assumed that agents were truthful. However, in practice an agent may misreport her preferences at step 2 of the sequential voting protocol (Algorithm 1). If some variables are nonbinary, then sequential voting will inherit manipulability from the local rules, even if the profile is separable. However, in case all variables are binary, it is not immediately clear if a sequential voting rule defined over $\mathcal{O}$-legal profiles is strategyproof

---

[10] A rule is an antidictatorship if there exists an agent such that the winner is always her least preferred alternative.

(see Chapters 2 and 6), since the Gibbard-Satterthwaite Theorem is not directly applicable. The following example shows that sequential voting is not strategyproof, even when all variables are binary, and the agents' preferences are $\mathcal{O}$-legal for some $\mathcal{O}$.

Example 9.14. Let P be the profile defined in Example 9.11. If agent 1 knows the preferences of agent 2 and agent 3, then she has no incentive to vote truthfully on issue X_1, *even though her preference relation is separable*: if she votes for 1 sincerely, then the outcome is 10. If she votes for 0 instead, then the outcome is 01, which is better to her.

The problem of characterizing strategyproof voting rules in binary multi-issue domains has received some attention. Barberà et al. (1991) characterize strategyproof voting rules when the voters' preferences are separable, and each issue is binary. Ju (2003) characterizes all strategyproof voting rules on binary multi-issue domains (satisfying a mild additional condition) where each issue can take three values: "good," "bad," and "null." Le Breton and Sen (1999) prove that if the voters' preferences are separable, and the restricted preference domain of the voters satisfies a richness condition, then a voting rule is strategyproof if and only if it is a simultaneous voting rule for which each local voting rule is strategyproof over its respective domain.

We may wonder whether this extends to safe sequential voting. However, the following impossibility theorem of Xia and Conitzer (2010a) answers the question negatively: there is no strategyproof sequential voting rule on $Legal(\mathcal{O})^n$ that satisfies nonimposition, except a dictatorship. Xia and Conitzer (2010a) also prove a positive result in the further restricted case of $\mathcal{O}$-legal conditionally lexicographic preferences: essentially, the strategyproof rules on this domain are generalized sequential voting rules, where the choice of the local rule to apply on a given issue may depend on the values taken by more important issues.

9.4.2 Sequential Voting: The General Case

In the absence of $\mathcal{O}$-legality, sequential voting suffers from the same problem as simultaneous voting in the absence of separability: there is no clear way for voters to report their local preferences on the domain of an issue, since it may depend on the value of issues yet to be decided. Moreover, choosing the agenda (the order on which the issues are decided) can be tricky: What is a good agenda? Who chooses it? This problem is raised by Airiau et al. (2011), who suggest designing a voting procedure for choosing the agenda: each voter reports its dependency graph and these graphs are aggregated into an acyclic graph, for instance using a distance-based aggregation function. Another approach to unrestricted sequential voting is described by Dalla Pozza et al. (2011), who assume that at each stage, voters report their local preferences according to the projection of a weighted CSP on the current variable.

Another challenge in the analysis of sequential voting without the $\mathcal{O}$-legality assumption is that the outcome may depend on the order in which the issues are decided. This can give the chair (or whoever chooses the order) an effective way of controlling the election (see Chapter 7). This can be seen in the following example:

Example 9.3, continued. Suppose the voters report their preferences optimistically, which is known to the chair. If S is decided before T, then we get $k + 1$ votes for 1_S, k votes for 0_S, leading to the local outcome 1_S; then, given $S = 1_S$, we have $2k$ votes for 0_T and 1 vote for 1_T, therefore the final outcome is $1_S 0_T$. Symmetrically, if T is decided before S, the final outcome is $0_S 1_T$. Therefore, the chair's strategy can be to choose the order S $\triangleright$ T if she prefers $1_S 0_T$ to $0_S 1_T$, and the order T $\triangleright$ S otherwise. (Note that $1_S 1_T$ and $0_S 0_T$ cannot be obtained).

This shows that the chair can sometimes, and to some extent, control the election by fixing the agenda (see also Chapter 7). This drawback of sequential voting is however tempered by the fact that under some reasonable assumptions about the way the voters's behaviors are represented, in most cases, most of these agenda control problems are NP-hard (Conitzer et al., 2009a).

We mentioned above that in the absence of $\mathcal{O}$-legality, there is no clear way for voters to report their local preferences on the domain of a variable. However, there is a case where voters may in fact be able to determine valid reports of their local preferences. When voters' preferences are assumed to be common knowledge, the sequential voting protocol can be framed as an extensive-form game, called a *strategic sequential voting process*, denoted by $SSV_{\mathcal{O}}$ (Xia et al., 2011a). We assume that all variables are binary. Without loss of generality, let $\mathcal{O} = X_1 \triangleright \cdots \triangleright X_p$. The game is defined as follows:

- The players are the voters; their preferences are linear orders over A; their possible actions at stage $t \leqslant p$ are 0_t and 1_t.
- In each stage t, all voters vote on X_t simultaneously, r_t is used to choose the winning value d_t for X_t, and d_t is reported back to the voters.
- We assume complete information: all voters know the other voters' preferences, the local voting rules $r_1, \ldots, r_p$ and the order $\mathcal{O}$.

When all issues are binary, $SSV_{\mathcal{O}}$ can be solved by backward induction where in each stage all voters move simultaneously and perform a dominant strategy, as illustrated in the following example.

Example 9.15. Let P be the profile defined in Example 9.11. If the outcome of the first stage of sequential voting is 1_1, then in the second stage it is voter 1's dominant strategy to vote for 1_2 because $1_1 1_2 \succ_1 1_2 0_2$ and the majority rule is strategyproof. Similarly, in this case voters 2 and 3 will vote for 0_2. Therefore, by the majority rule, the winner will be $1_1 0_2$. Similarly, if the outcome of the first stage of sequential voting is 0_1, then the votes at the second stage will be unanimously 0_2, and the winner will be $0_1 1_2$. Given this reasoning, in the first stage, each agent is comparing $1_1 0_2$ to $0_1 1_2$, and will vote 1_1 if he prefers $1_1 0_2$ to $0_1 1_2$ and 0_1 if he prefers $0_1 1_2$ to $1_1 0_2$. Again we have two alternatives, and the majority rule is strategyproof. This means that voter 1 will vote for 0_1, voter 2 will vote for 1_1, and voter 3 will vote for 0_1. Hence, the winner for X_1 is 0_1, and the overall winner is $0_1 1_2$. This backward induction process is shown in Figure 9.2.

In Example 9.15, the backward induction winner is unique. This observation can be extended to an arbitrary number of binary issues. Let $SSV_{\mathcal{O}}(P)$ denote the backward

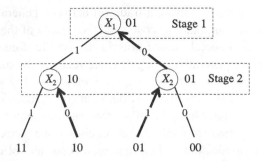

Figure 9.2. Backward induction tree for Example 9.15.

induction winner when the voters' true preferences are P.[11] Despite being unique, this outcome is extremely undesirable in the worst case: Xia et al. (2011a) prove that for any $p \in \mathbb{N}$ and any $n \geqslant 2p^2 + 1$, there exists a profile P such that (1) $SSV_{\mathcal{O}}(P)$ is ranked within the bottom $\lfloor p/2 + 2 \rfloor$ positions in *every* voter's true preferences, and (2) $SSV_{\mathcal{O}}(P)$ is Pareto-dominated by $2^p - (p+1)p/2$ alternatives. We note that when p is not too small, $\lfloor p/2 + 2 \rfloor$ and $(p+1)p/2$ are much smaller than $|A| = 2^p$. Therefore, the SSV winner can indeed be extremely undesirable. A stronger form of the theorem and a similar negative result for $\mathcal{O}$-legal profiles are given by Xia et al. (2011a).

9.4.3 Discussion

The key property of sequential voting is that it interleaves preference elicitation and winner determination, whereas the approaches outlined in Sections 9.2 and 9.3 proceed in a more usual fashion, by eliciting preferences in one round, and determining the winner afterward. As a result, sequential voting can save a lot in communication costs, but is applicable only when it is realistic to elicit preferences step by step. Now, the quality of the outcome obtained by sequential voting primarily depends on whether it is realistic to assume that voters' preferences are $\mathcal{O}$-legal for some common order $\mathcal{O}$: if so, then sequential voting enjoys some good properties; if not, it offers far fewer quality guarantees. Therefore, one criticism of sequential voting is that it still needs a strong domain restriction to work well (Xia et al., 2008); but still, when compared to the separability restriction needed for simultaneous voting, $\mathcal{O}$-legality is much weaker (Lang and Xia, 2009). Conitzer and Xia (2012) evaluate the quality of the outcome of sequential voting w.r.t. a scoring function, which can be seen as numerical versions of multiple election paradoxes.

There could be other ways of interleaving elicitation and winner determination. A completely different way of proceeding was proposed very recently by Bowman et al. (2014), who propose an iterative protocol that allows voters to revise their votes based on the outcomes of previous iterations.

9.5 Concluding Discussion

After reviewing several classes of methods for voting in combinatorial domains, we are left with the (expected) conclusion that none of them is perfect. More precisely, when

---

[11] This should be distinguished from the classical social choice setting, where the input consists of the reported preferences.

choosing a method, we have to make a trade-off between generality, communication (and, to a lesser extent, computation) costs, and the quality of the outcome, evaluated with respect to classical social choice criteria. If specific domain restrictions such as separability or, more generally, $\mathcal{O}$-legality, are realistic for the case at hand, then many of the methods discussed in this chapter work reasonably well. Otherwise, one has to be prepared to make some trade-off between communication requirements and the quality of the outcome. One possibility that has not really been developed yet is to choose some intermediate method that requires some weak domain restriction, some reasonable communication and computation costs, and offers some reasonable guarantees about the quality of the outcome.

Voting in combinatorial domains is related to several other issues studied in this book and elsewhere:

- *Incomplete information and communication* (Chapter 10): as some communication saving can be made by eliciting only a part of the voters' preferences, winner determination in combinatorial domains can benefit from approaches to winner determination from incomplete preferences as well as from the design of communication-efficient voting protocols.
- *Judgment aggregation* (Chapter 17) is also concerned with making common decisions about possibly interrelated issues. There are interesting parallels between judgment aggregation and voting in combinatorial domains. Simultaneous voting corresponds to some extent to proposition-wise voting: while the first works well when preferences are separable, the second outputs a consistent outcome if the agenda enjoys an independence property that resembles separability. Note that in judgment aggregation, difficulties are often caused by the logical relations between the elements of the agenda, while in voting in combinatorial domains, they are mainly due to preferential dependencies. Relating both areas is a promising research direction; see Grandi and Endriss (2011) for some first steps in this direction.
- *Fair division of indivisible items* (Chapter 12) is another field where a common decision has to be made on a combinatorial space of alternatives (the set of all allocations). In the settings we reviewed in this chapter, we assumed that all agents were equally concerned with all issues (which is patently false in fair division, where agents are primarily – sometimes even exclusively – concerned by their share); but in some settings, some issues concern some (subsets of) voters more than others, which will call for introducing fairness criteria into multi-issue voting.

Acknowledgments

We would like to thank Craig Boutilier, Vince Conitzer, Ulle Endriss, and Umberto Grandi for very helpful feedback.

CHAPTER 10

Incomplete Information and Communication in Voting

Craig Boutilier and Jeffrey S. Rosenschein

Many voting schemes (and other social choice mechanisms) make stringent assumptions about the preference information provided by voters, as well as other aspects of the choice situation. Realizing these assumptions in practice often imposes an undesirable and unnecessary burden on both voters and mechanism designers with respect to the provision of such information. This chapter provides an overview of a variety of topics related to the information and communication requirements of voting. One theme underlying much of the work discussed in this chapter is its focus on determining winners or making decisions with incomplete or stochastic information about voter preferences—or in some cases, about the alternatives themselves. This includes work on the computational complexity of determining possible/necessary winners and regret-based winner determination; the query or communication complexity of eliciting preferences; practical schemes for preference elicitation; winner determination under alternative uncertainty; the sample complexity of learning voting rules; and compilation complexity.

10.1 Introduction

Voting methods are extremely attractive as a means for aggregating preferences to implement social choice functions. However, many voting schemes (and other social choice mechanisms) make stringent assumptions about the preferences provided by voters. For instance, it is usually assumed that each voter provides a *complete* preference ranking of all alternatives under consideration. In addition, such schemes are often implemented assuming complete knowledge of the set of alternatives under consideration, and over which voters provide their preferences.

While these modeling requirements are reasonable in many domains—especially high-stakes settings such as political elections—increasingly we see the methods of social choice applied to lower-stakes, higher frequency domains, including web search, product recommendation, market segmentation, meeting scheduling, group travel planning, and many others. For such problems, demanding complete preference information is not viable for several key reasons. First, the number of options from which a winning alternative is to be selected is often extremely large (e.g., the set of possible products under consideration) and may even be combinatorial in nature (e.g., the set of feasible schedules or plans). Second, requiring the complete specification of a preference ordering may impose unwarranted cognitive and communication demands given the stakes involved. It may even be unnecessary in many instances—partial information may be sufficient to reach the correct decision. Third, the frequency of decisions often gives rise to considerable data that allows (statistical) prediction of voter preferences. Finally, the set of alternatives over which decisions are made may be uncertain or change dynamically. This all argues for a deeper analysis of the communication and informational requirements of voting rules, and methods for reducing such requirements, even to the point of "approximating" the ultimate decision. Such methods may allow for the broader practical application of voting methods. Understanding informational requirements is equally important in high-stakes domains, and may provide significant benefits. For instance, reducing cognitive and communication complexity may reduce voting errors (e.g., due to choice confusion), increase voter participation, and decrease the time needed to reach decisions.

In this chapter, we overview a number of models and techniques developed to address such issues, namely, the information and communication requirements of voting. One theme underlying much of the work discussed in this chapter is its focus on determining winners or making decisions with incomplete or stochastic information about voter preferences—or in some cases, about the alternatives themselves. This includes: models for determining winners with partial preference information, including *possible and necessary winners* and *regret-based winner computation*; theoretical analyses of the *communication complexity* of eliciting preferences, as well as practical schemes for eliciting preferences from voters; methods for determining winners when the set of viable alternatives is unknown or uncertain; results on the *compilation complexity* of voting rules, that is, the ability to concisely summarize voter preferences; and techniques for *learning* voting rules, that is, designing voting rules that "perform well" given some model of voter utility.

The remainder of the chapter is organized as follows. We describe basic notation and the models of partial preferences used throughout the chapter in Section 10.2. In Section 10.3 we introduce several key solution concepts for winner determination with partial preferences. In Sections 10.4 and 10.5 we outline key theoretical results on communication and query complexity for vote elicitation and describe recent elicitation techniques and their analysis. We present several models for dealing with uncertainty in the set of alternatives in Section 10.6. Section 10.7 focuses on recent results in compilation complexity, or the summarization of vote profiles. In Section 10.8 we describe models and methods that support the analysis and design of voting rules that are intended to maximize social welfare assuming voters have cardinal utilities over alternatives. We conclude in Section 10.9 with some general observations and a brief discussion of open issues.

10.2 Models of Partial Preferences

While incomplete information for various elements of a voting situation has been mentioned, incomplete information about voter preferences is almost certainly the most fundamental. Furthermore, *communicating voter preferences* to the mechanism represents probably the most critical communication bottleneck in voting. We begin by introducing notation and defining several models of *partial preferences* that will be used throughout this chapter.

10.2.1 Basic Notation and Concepts

We assume a set of *alternatives* $A = \{a_1, \ldots, a_m\}$, representing the space of possible choices, and a set of voters $N = \{1, \ldots, n\}$. Each voter i has a *preference order* $\succ_i$ over A, which is a total order over A, with $a_j \succ_i a_k$ denoting that i prefers a_j to a_k.[1] We sometimes view this ordering as a permutation σ_i of A, in which case: $\sigma_i(j)$ denotes the position of a_j in i's ranking; and $\sigma_i^{-1}(j)$ denotes the alternative ranked in the jth position. Let $\mathcal{R}(A)$ denote the set of all such preference orders over A. A *preference profile* $R = \langle \succ_1, \ldots, \succ_n \rangle$ is a collection of preferences for each voter.

Given a preference profile R, a *social choice function* or *voting rule* f selects a winning alternative $f(R) \in A$ for that profile.[2] We refer to Chapters 2–5 for further discussion of various voting rules and approaches.

Many voting rules are defined by schemes that explicitly *score* each alternative $a \in A$ given a preference profile R, using some "natural" *scoring function* $s(a, R)$ that measures the quality of a given R. The rule selects an alternative $f(R) \in \text{argmax}_{a \in A} s(a, R)$ with maximum score. Usually some method of breaking ties is assumed, but the precise method used has little impact on the discussion in this chapter. In some cases, however, we will use the term *co-winner* to refer to any alternative a with maximum score $s(a, R)$ (independent of tie-breaking), especially in Section 10.3. If one interprets the scoring function s as a measure of social welfare, such voting rules can be viewed as maximizing social welfare. Voting rules based on scoring rules (e.g., plurality, Borda, veto, k-approval), Copeland, Bucklin, maximin, and many others can be defined this way.[3]

10.2.2 Partial Votes and Profiles

One natural way to reduce the communication and informational requirements of voting is to elicit or otherwise obtain *partial information* about voter preferences and attempt to implement a voting rule using only the information at hand.

Abstractly, we let π_i denote the *partial preference* of voter i, and $\Pi = \langle \pi_1, \ldots, \pi_n \rangle$ a *partial profile*. In what follows, we will usually assume that π_i is a *partial order* over A, or equivalently (the transitive closure of) a consistent collection of *pairwise comparisons* of the form $a_j \succ_i a_k$.

---

[1] Allowing indifference between alternatives has little impact on the main concepts that follow, though it does sometimes affect algorithmic details and complexity analysis.

[2] Not all voting rules *require* the specification of the complete rankings (e.g., plurality), and certain rules, such as approval voting or range voting cannot be defined purely as a function of a voter's ranking.

[3] We emphasize that *natural* measures of quality are the norm; trivially, *any* rule can be defined using a scoring function that is a simple indicator function for the winner. We note that while Xia and Conitzer (2008a) propose a class of *generalized* scoring rules, they show that it is not broad enough to encompass all voting rules, not even all anonymous rules; however, this class does seem to capture most "natural" scoring functions.

A partial vote π_i can represent information about voter i's preferences gleaned from a variety of sources: revealed preference data (e.g., based on past choices), collaborative filtering predictions, or responses to queries about her preferences. We note that the responses to most natural preference queries induce constraints on preferences that can be represented as a partial order. These include: arbitrary pairwise comparisons (is a preferred to b?); top-k queries (what are your k most preferred alternatives?), choice queries (which alternative in set S is most preferred?), and others.[4]

Let π_i be the partial ranking of voter i. A *completion* of π_i is any vote $\succ_i$ that extends π_i. Let $C(\pi_i)$ denote the set of *completions* of π_i, that is, the set of all (complete) votes $\succ_i$ that extend π_i. A *partial profile* is a collection of partial votes $\Pi = \langle \pi_1, \ldots, \pi_n \rangle$. Let $C(\Pi) = C(\pi_1) \times \ldots \times C(\pi_n)$ be the set of *completions* of Π. We take the perspective in this chapter that partial votes and profiles reflect the *epistemic* or *information state* of a voting mechanism, agent, decision maker or other party implementing a voting rule or social choice function. We assume that voter i has true preferences corresponding to some completion of π_i. The partial vote *does not* reflect uncertainty, incompleteness or indecision on the part of the voter, merely the mechanism's incomplete information about those preferences.[5]

10.2.3 Probabilistic Preference Models

If one is given partial information about the preferences of voters, but is forced to make a decision (e.g., select the winner of an election), or evaluate the value of eliciting further information, several styles of approach can be used, including worst-case or probabilistic analyses. We consider both in what follows. Probabilistic analysis requires the specification of some prior distribution over voter preferences or preference profiles, so we briefly review several key probabilistic models.

Probabilistic analysis has a rich history in social choice, though until recently it has been used primarily to study the likelihood that various phenomena (e.g., Condorcet cycles, manipulability) occur in randomly drawn voter populations, rather than as a basis for decision making or elicitation with incomplete information. Abstractly, a distribution over $\succ \in \mathcal{R}(A)$ can be viewed as a "culture" indicating the probability that a random voter will hold a particular preference ranking (Garman and Kamien, 1968). By far the most commonly studied distribution is the *impartial culture (IC)*, in which each ranking $\succ \in \mathcal{R}(A)$ is equally likely to be a voter's preference, and all voter preferences are independent (Black, 1958; Gehrlein and Fishburn, 1976; Regenwetter et al., 2006). Related, but taking a slightly different form, is *impartial anonymous culture (IAC)* which provides a uniform distribution over all preference *profiles*. Berg (1985) proposes a general Polyá-Eggenberger *urn* model that encompasses both of these (and has been used, e.g., to study the probability and empirical hardness of manipulation (Walsh, 2009)). See Regenwetter et al. (2006) for a discussion of other cultures studied in social choice.

---

[4] One exception involves constraints that are naturally disjunctive, e.g., a response to the question "What alternative is ranked k^{th}?" cannot generally be mapped to a set of pairwise preferences unless the positions k are queried in ascending or descending order.

[5] For approaches to voting with truly incomplete preferences represented by partial orders, see (Pini et al., 2009; Xia and Conitzer, 2011b), and a discussion of approaches based on maximum likelihood in Chapter 8.

It is widely recognized that impartial cultures do not accurately reflect real-world preferences (Regenwetter et al., 2006). More realistic probabilistic models of preferences, or parameterized families of distributions over rankings, have been proposed in statistics, econometrics and psychometrics. These models typically reflect some process by which people rank, judge or compare alternatives. Many models are unimodal, based on a "reference ranking" from which user rankings are generated as noisy perturbations. A commonly used model, adopted widely in machine learning is the *Mallows ϕ-model* (Mallows, 1957). It is parameterized by a modal or *reference ranking* σ and a *dispersion parameter* $\phi \in (0, 1]$; and for any ranking r we define: $P(r; \sigma, \phi) = \frac{1}{Z}\phi^{d(r,\sigma)}$, where d is the Kendall tau distance and $Z = \sum_{r'} \phi^{d(r',\sigma)} = 1 \cdot (1+\phi) \cdot (1+\phi+\phi^2) \cdots (1+\cdots+\phi^{m-1})$ is a normalization constant.[6] When $\phi = 1$ we obtain the uniform distribution over rankings (i.e., impartial culture), and as $\phi \to 0$ we approach the distribution that concentrates all mass on σ. A variety of other models have been proposed that reflect different interpretations of the ranking process (e.g., Plackett-Luce, Bradley-Terry, Thurstonian) and many of these have found application in computer science, machine learning, and recommender systems; we refer to Marden (1995) for a comprehensive overview of these models. Mixtures of such models, which offer additional modeling flexibility (e.g., by admitting multimodal distributions), are also commonly used (Murphy and Martin, 2003; Meilă and Chen, 2010; Lebanon and Mao, 2008; Lu and Boutilier, 2011b). A variety of statistical techniques have been developed to learn the parameters of such models from (partial, noisy) voting or preference data.

The *riffle independence model* (Huang and Guestrin, 2009), has a somewhat different nature, partitioning A into two sets: a ranking of each set is generated stochastically (and independently); then a stochastic process is used to interleave or "riffle" the two resulting rankings to produce a combined ranking. The model can also be defined hierarchically, with the same process used to generate the subrankings.

10.3 Solution Concepts with Partial Preferences

Two fundamental questions arise in voting situations in which we have access to incomplete preference profiles. First, is the information provided sufficient to determine the winner (or have certain alternatives have been ruled out as possible winners)? Second, if required to choose a winning alternative under such conditions, what are the right criteria for doing so? We discuss both questions in this section.

10.3.1 Possible and Necessary Winners

Suppose we are given a voting rule f but have only a partial profile Π. This partial information may or may not be sufficient to determine the true winner under f. However, if the winner cannot be determined, Π may still contain enough information to rule out certain alternatives as potential winners. Konczak and Lang (2005) introduce the notions of *possible* and *necessary winners* to reflect these possibilities. We say that

---

[6] See Chapters 4 and 8 for a discussion of the Kemeny rule, a voting method based on the same distance function.

a is a *possible winner* under Π iff there is some $R \in C(\Pi)$ such that $f(R) = a$; and a is a *necessary winner* under Π iff $f(R) = a$ for all $R \in C(\Pi)$. The applications of these concepts are many. For instance, if a is a necessary winner under Π, no further elicitation or assessment of voter preferences is needed to make a decision (as we discuss later). Knowing whether a is a possible winner is tightly related to the *coalitional manipulation problem* as well (see Chapter 6). Assume a partial profile Π in which the votes of the nonmanipulators are fully specified, while no information is given for the manipulators: if a is not a possible winner with respect to Π, the manipulating coalition cannot (constructively) manipulate the election to install a; conversely if a is a possible winner, then a is susceptible to (constructive) manipulation;[7] related connections between destructive manipulation and necessary winners also exist. The computation of possible and necessary winners under various voting rules is thus of key importance.

Computationally, the complexity of the possible and necessary winner problems, denoted PW and NW, respectively, varies considerably with the voting rule in question and the setting. We focus our attention here primarily on results that allow for general partial profiles (for results on the special case where some votes are completely known and others are completely unknown, see Chapter 6 on manipulation). First, it is easy to observe that if the number m of alternatives A is bounded—assuming voters are not weighted (we briefly discuss weighted voters in what follows) and the voting rule satisfies anonymity—then both PW and NW are computable in polynomial time if the voting rule supports polynomial winner determination (Conitzer et al., 2007; Walsh, 2007). This is so because there are only a constant number of distinct votes $b = m!$ that may be cast by any voter. By anonymity, the *number* of voters casting each vote is sufficient to determine a winner, and there are at most $(n + 1)^b$ such "count" profiles that need to be enumerated.

However, the complexity as a function of the number of alternatives can vary considerably. The first result along these lines was due to Bartholdi and Orlin (1991), who, in the context of manipulation, show that PW is NP-complete and NW is coNP-complete for STV (even with the restricted partial profiles allowed in manipulation settings). Konczak and Lang (2005) show that PW and NW are polytime solvable for the Condorcet winner problem (i.e., is a necessarily or possibly a Condorcet winner). Xia and Conitzer (2011a) analyze a wide collection of common voting rules. For example, they show that: PW and NW are both polytime solvable for plurality and veto; for maximin and Bucklin, NW is polytime solvable but PW is NP-complete; and for Copeland, ranked pairs, and voting trees (including Cup), NW is coNP-complete and PW is NP-complete. They also analyze a special class of positional scoring rules which include Borda and k-approval as special cases, showing that NW is polytime solvable, while PW is NP-complete. Betzler and Dorn (2010) and Baumeister and Rothe (2010) fully characterize PW for positional scoring rules, showing that it is NP-complete for all such rules apart from plurality and veto.

Many of the hardness results are shown by reduction from problems such as EXACT-3-COVER (Xia and Conitzer, 2011a; Betzler and Dorn, 2010). Easiness of NW is

---

[7] A "hybrid" question when nonmanipulator votes are partial—is a a possible winner given any completion of nonmanipulators' votes—seems to have been unaddressed in the literature.

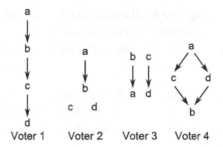

Voter 1   Voter 2   Voter 3   Voter 4

Figure 10.1. A partial profile illustrating necessary winner computation.

generally shown by constructing algorithms that will effectively find a completion of a vote profile that disproves the claim. For instance, suppose we have a rule based on a scoring function $s(a, R)$. To determine if a is a necessary winner, one can attempt to find a completion of partial profile Π that makes some competing alternative w beat a by maximizing the difference between the score of w and the score of a. If such a completion is found that gives w a higher score than a, then a cannot be a necessary winner. If this is tested for all $w \neq a$ without any w "defeating" a, then a is a necessary winner. As long as constructing such a profile for any fixed $w \neq a$ is polytime solvable in the number of alternatives, then NW is also polytime solvable.

Example 10.1. We illustrate the technique developed by Xia and Conitzer (2011a) for determining whether an alternative a is a necessary winner for the Borda scoring rule. Consider the simple partial vote profile in Figure 10.1, over four voters and four alternatives. Notice that this partial profile has 144 possible completions: voter 1 has only 1 completion since it is fully specified; voter 2 has 12 completions; voter 3 has 6 completions; and voter 4 has 2 completions.

To test whether a is a necessary winner, we try to "disprove" this fact by showing that one of b, c or d has a higher Borda score s_B in *some completion* of the profile. We test each of the alternatives $w \in \{b, c, d\}$ in turn, attempting to find a completion of the vote profile that maximizes the score difference $s_B(w) - s_B(a)$. If this difference is positive, then w beats a in some completion, hence a is not a necessary winner or co-winner. If it is negative, w is not a possible winner (since there is no completion in which it even beats a). Finally, if the maximum score difference *for each of the* w is negative, then a is a necessary winner. (If each difference is nonpositive, a is a necessary co-winner.)

It is straightforward to compute the maximum score difference—since the contribution $s_B(w, i)$ of each vote i to alternative w's Borda score is independent, we can complete each voter's partial vote *independently* to maximize this difference. Consider alternative b:

- Since voter 1's vote is complete, the score difference $s_B(b, 1) - s_B(a, 1) = -1$ is fixed.
- Voter 2's vote can be completed in several different ways, but a must be positioned above b, so $s_B(b, 2) - s_B(a, 2) \leqslant -1$ in any completion. To maximize this (negative) difference, any completion that places neither of c or d *between* a and b ensures $s_B(b, 2) - s_B(a, 2) = -1$.

- Voter 3's vote can be completed by placing c and d between b and a, giving completion $b \succ c \succ d \succ a$ and a maximum difference of $s_B(b, 3) - s_B(a, 3) = 3$.
- Voter 4's vote can be completed in two ways, but in each case we have a maximum difference of $s_B(b, 3) - s_B(a, 3) = -3$.

Summing these maximum differences gives a profile that maximizes the score difference $s_B(b) - s_B(a) = -2$. Hence b does beat a in any completion, so cannot be used to refute the fact that a is a necessary co-winner. (This also shows that b is not a possible winner).

We can apply the same reasoning to construct a profile that maximizes $s_B(c) - s_B(a)$. Vote by vote it is not hard to see that the maximum possible difference between c and a is: -2 in vote 1; 2 in vote 2 (using completion $c \succ d \succ a \succ b$); 3 in vote 3 (using completion $c \succ d \succ b \succ a$); and -1 in vote 4 (using completion $a \succ c \succ d \succ b$). In other words, we have a profile where $s_B(c) - s_B(a) = 2$.[8] This means a is not a necessary winner (or co-winner). For completeness, we note that $s_B(d) - s_B(a) = 0$ is the maximum difference for alternative d.

These intuitions can be translated straightforwardly into an $O(nm)$ algorithm for computing completions, hence an $O(nm^2)$ algorithm for testing whether an alternative a is a necessary winner (or co-winner) (Xia and Conitzer, 2011a).

We note that in this partial profile:

- a is a possible winner: the completions $a \succ b \succ c \succ d, b \succ a \succ c \succ d, a \succ d \succ c \succ b$, of votes 2, 3, and 4, respectively, render a the unique Borda winner.
- b is not a possible winner (the detailed reasoning sketched earlier shows that b's maximum score advantage over a is negative, so b cannot beat a in any completion).
- c is a possible winner (using the completion and detailed reasoning sketched previously).
- d is a possible co-winner: the completions $d \succ c \succ a \succ b, c \succ d \succ b \succ a, a \succ d \succ c \succ b$, of votes 2, 3, and 4, respectively, give d a Borda score of 7, that is, equal to that of both a and c and higher than that of b. Note that there is no completion that renders d a unique Borda winner.
- There is no necessary winner, because there are at least two possible winners. □

While computing possible and necessary winners is generally easy with a bounded number of alternatives, this is no longer the case for many rules when voters are weighted. For instance, rules such as Borda, Copeland, maximin, and veto have NP-complete possible winner problems for a bounded number of voters. We do not discuss weighted models in depth, but refer to recent work by Conitzer and Sandholm (2002), Walsh (2007), and Lang et al. (2012b) for a selection of results using this model.

10.3.2 Minimax Regret

While possible and necessary winners are valuable concepts for providing (normative) constraints on the decisions one might make given a partial profile, they do not provide a general means for selecting winners given arbitrary partial profiles. Specifically,

---

[8] It is easy to verify that c also has a higher score than both b and d in this completion—hence c is a possible winner.

necessary winners generally will not exist without a substantial amount of preference information, while possible winners can only be used to narrow the set of alternatives. In circumstances when one is required to make a decision without complete information— or where the cost of obtaining further preferences outweighs the benefit—the following questions remain: which of the possible winners should one select? and is it reasonable to select an alternative that is not a possible winner?

Lu and Boutilier (2011c) propose the use of *minimax regret* to address this problem.[9] Assume a voting rule f defined using some scoring function $s(a, R)$. In this section, we treat this score as a measure of societal "utility" or social welfare. Given a partial profile Π, the quality of a proposed winning alternative a under Π is defined to be the difference between the score of a and the score of the winner (i.e., alternative with the optimal score), in the worst case (i.e., given any completion of Π). The *minimax optimal* alternative is that which is closest to optimal in the worst case. More formally, define:

$$Regret(a, R) = \max_{a' \in A} s(a', R) - s(a, R) \tag{10.1}$$

$$= s(f(R), R) - s(a, R),$$

$$PMR(a, a', \Pi) = \max_{R \in C(\Pi)} s(a', R) - s(a, R), \tag{10.2}$$

$$MR(a, \Pi) = \max_{R \in C(\Pi)} Regret(a, R)$$

$$= \max_{a' \in A} PMR(a, a', \Pi), \tag{10.3}$$

$$MMR(\Pi) = \min_{a \in A} MR(a, \Pi), \tag{10.4}$$

$$a_\Pi^* \in \operatorname*{argmin}_{a \in A} MR(a, \Pi). \tag{10.5}$$

Here $Regret(a, R)$ is the loss (or regret) of selecting a as a winner instead of choosing the true winning alternative under rule f (or scoring function s). $PMR(a, a', \Pi)$ denotes the *pairwise max regret* of a relative to a' given partial profile Π, namely, the worst-case loss—under all possible realizations of the full profile—of selecting a rather than a'. The *maximum regret* $MR(a, \Pi)$ is the worst-case loss associated with a, assuming an adversary selects some completion R of Π to maximize the loss between the selected alternative a and the true winner under R. The goal is thus to find the a with *minimum max (minimax) regret*: here $MMR(\Pi)$ denotes minimax regret under partial profile Π, while a_Π^* denotes the minimax optimal alternative. Note that the minimax winner may not be unique (indeed, given a complete profile R several alternatives may be tied with the best score, requiring some form of tie-breaking).

Measuring the loss of choosing an incorrect alternative using scores in this way is not without controversy, but has been used in other contexts; for example, Smith (2000)

---

[9] Minimax regret was proposed by Savage (1951) as a means for making decisions in the context of *strict* (or nonprobabilistic) uncertainty over world states. It has since been advocated for robust decision making with partial preference or utility functions in both single-agent and multiagent settings; see Boutilier (2013) for an overview.

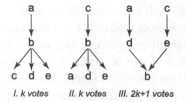

I. k votes   II. k votes   III. 2k+1 votes

Figure 10.2. A partial profile where the minimax-optimal alternative is not a possible winner under 2-approval (Lu and Boutilier, 2011c).

uses score-based (indeed, utility-based) regret to measure the performance of various voting rules, including range voting.

Minimax regret has strong connections to possible and necessary winners. First, notice that if $MR(a, \Pi) = 0$ then a is a necessary (co-)winner w.r.t. Π. This implies that the max-regret decision problem (i.e., determining whether $MR(a, \Pi) \leqslant \varepsilon$) is at least as computationally difficult as the necessary (co-)winners problem for any rule f; thus voting rules such as Copeland and ranked pairs have coNP-hard max-regret decision problems. Interestingly, the alternative a_{Π}^* with minimax regret given Π need *not* be a possible winner w.r.t. Π: Lu and Boutilier (2011c) describe a partial profile under 2-approval where every possible winner has higher max regret than the minimax optimal a_{Π}^*.

Example 10.2. Consider the partial profile Π in Figure 10.2 under 2-approval voting. Notice that b has score $2k$ in each completion. One of a or c must be in the first position of every vote in set III, so either a or c receive at least $k + 1$ approvals from set III. Hence $\max(s(a), s(c)) \geqslant 2k + 1$, and both of a and c are possible winners, while b is not. At the same time, $MR(b, \Pi) = k + 1$—simply consider a completion that places a in position one of all votes in set III. But $MR(a, \Pi) = MR(c, \Pi) = 2k + 1$: if a (resp., c) is chosen as the winner, placement of e and c (resp., d and a) above a (resp., c) in each vote in set III gives $s(a) = k$ and $s(c) = 3k + 1$ (resp., $s(c) = k$ and $s(a) = 3k + 1$). ☐

The connections to possible and necessary winners also extend to algorithms for computing minimax regret. By Equations (10.3) and (10.4) we see that minimax regret can be computed by determining the pairwise max regret $PMR(a, a', \Pi)$ for all pairs (a, a'), maximizing regret for each a, and selecting a_{Π}^* with minimum max regret. Lu and Boutilier (2011c) describe polytime algorithms, based on the same intuitions for forming profile completions used for necessary winner computation (Xia and Conitzer, 2011a), for positional scoring rules, maximin, Bucklin, and "egalitarian" voting.[10]

Example 10.3. Example 10.1, which demonstrates necessary winner computation for alternative a in Borda voting, also illustrates max regret computation for a under Borda scoring. Indeed, the maximum of the three score differences (in this case $s_B(b) -$

---

[10] An "egalitarian" scheme chooses a winner whose lowest rank position taken over all voters (i.e., it maximizes the worst rank of the selected alternative, making the worst-off voter as well off as possible, realizing a Rawlsian form of social welfare maximization). This can be expressed in the distance rationalizability framework discussed in Chapter 8 using the distance metric $\widehat{d}_{swap}^{\infty}$ (i.e., maximum *swap distance*) and the *unanimity* consensus class $\mathcal{U}$.

$s_B(a) = 2$) is precisely the max regret of alternative a under the partial profile in question. Computing max regret for all four alternatives shows that minimax regret can be computed in $O(nm^3)$ time for Borda scoring. In this example, a is the minimax-optimal alternative.   □

10.3.3 Probabilistic Solution Concepts

A different approach to the analysis of winners with partial information uses probabilistic information about voter preferences. Notice that possible and necessary winners are purely epistemic notions that do not prescribe a general method for choosing winners under partial profiles. Minimax regret does provide a general method for selecting winners in such circumstances, but quantifies loss using a worst-case analysis, ignoring the probability of specific completions. By contrast, at least in cases where probabilistic preference models are available, a more refined analysis of the likelihood of various completions can be used to make decisions.

Naturally, probabilistic models have been used extensively in the analysis of voting, but typically they are used to assess the odds of certain phenomena arising in (complete knowledge) voting settings under specific culture or other preference assumptions. For example, theoretical and empirical analysis of the probability of a Condorcet cycle occurring in a vote profile are very common (Gehrlein and Fishburn, 1976; Regenwetter et al., 2006; Mattei, 2011). Probabilistic models are used to study, both theoretically and empirically, the probability that manipulation opportunities can arise in elections as well as to offer average-case analysis of the computational hardness of manipulation (see Chapter 6 or Faliszewski and Procaccia (2010) for an overview). Such models are also required to analyze voting equilibria (i.e., Bayes-Nash equilibria in the incomplete information game played by strategic voters against one another; Majumdar and Sen, 2004; Ángel Ballester and Rey-Biel, 2009), and have been used to analyze the expected loss induced by the use of voting rules under certain social welfare measures (Hillinger, 2005; Smith, 2000) (see connections to our discussion in Section 10.8).

Here we focus on the probabilistic analysis of partial profiles, which can be used to answer several important questions. The probabilistic analog of the possible winner problem is computing the probability $\Pr(win(a)|\Pi)$ that a specific alternative a wins under a voting rule f given partial profile Π. Bachrach et al. (2010b) consider a restricted form of this problem—counting the number of completions in $C(\Pi)$ of partial profile Π for which a is the winner, which they dub #PW. Given that counting the number of linear extensions of a partial order is #P-hard (Brightwell and Winkler, 1991), they show that #PW is also #P-hard for plurality and veto. However, they also provide a polytime (randomized) approximation algorithm for #PW that can be used for any voting rule for which winner determination is polytime solvable. By sampling completions uniformly at random (which can be done in polynomial time), and applying Hoeffding bounds to determine the requisite number of samples, they prove that the fraction of sampled profiles in which a wins is close to the true fraction of such completions with high probability. This work is restricted in that it assumes voter preferences are independent and drawn from a uniform distribution (i.e., impartial culture).

Hazon et al. (2012) consider a model that allows for arbitrary distributions of voter preferences (though they still assume independence of voter preferences) and provide a general dynamic programming algorithm to compute the probability that (any) a wins under a variety of voting rules under fairly general circumstances. For example, given a constant-bounded number of alternatives and weighted votes—where weights are themselves polynomially bounded in n—they show that computing the probability of an alternative winning is polytime solvable for any voting rule with polytime winner determination. The dynamic programming model uses a compact representation of *voting scenarios* tightly tied to work on compilation complexity (see Section 10.7). The approach assumes that each voter i's distribution is given in explicit form; that is, a probability is specified for each possible ranking the voter may hold (e.g., one for each $\succ_i \in C(\pi_i)$). This representation is straightforward when m is small, but becomes problematic for larger m, where prior distributions are usually represented using parametric distributions, and for which conditioning on partial preferences is often intractable (Lu and Boutilier, 2011b). Much like Bachrach et al. (2010b), when the number of alternatives is taken as a parameter, Lu and Boutilier (2011b) show the problem to be #P-hard for k-approval, Borda, Copeland, Bucklin, and plurality. For such larger problems, they propose using a sampling approach to estimate the probability that a specific a wins, treating this as a binomial experiment and providing confidence bounds (in contrast to the Hoeffding approach used by Bachrach et al. (2010b)).

Computing the probability that specific alternatives win, just like computing possible winners, may not be sufficient to support selection of a winner given a partial profile Π. Given a partial profile Π, the probabilistic approach can be combined with the decision-making capabilities of score-based voting or regret-based optimization to make decisions that exploit distributional information. For example, given a partial profile Π, the dynamic programming and sampling algorithms of Hazon et al. (2012) could be adapted, or in some cases used directly, to compute the expected score or expected regret (assuming a score-based voting rule) of each alternative, allowing Bayesian-optimal winners to be chosen given Π. Suitable sample-complexity results would need to be derived to provide confidence in the results. Lu and Boutilier (2011d) take such a decision-making perspective on the use of probabilistic models, but use this to drive a particular elicitation process (see Section 10.5). This probabilistic, decision-making perspective is also adopted in the analysis of manipulation given partial vote profiles offered by Lu et al. (2012). However, in general, truly decision theoretic analysis of voting and preference aggregation mechanisms remains a relatively under-studied topic.

10.4 Communication and Query Complexity

One of the main reasons to implement social choice functions with partial profiles is to minimize the amount of information needed to reach a group decision. While the previous section described several techniques for making decisions given a specific partial profile, in this section and the next we describe techniques for eliciting the "right" (partial) preference information needed to implement a voting rule. In this section we overview formal models of communication and query complexity that quantify the amount of information needed in the worst case to realize specific voting rules. In the next section, we turn our attention to more practical, heuristic elicitation methods that tend to reach correct (or good) decisions with relatively small amounts of preference information.

Formal models of the communication demands of voting rules come in two varieties. One approach uses the tools of *communication complexity* (Yao, 1979; Kushilevitz and Nisan, 1996), measuring the number of bits of information that need to be communicated by voters to the voting mechanism before a winner can be determined using some voting rule. The other approach measures the number of queries that voters need to answer in order to allow the determination of a winner. In this model, results can be very sensitive to the precise form of query used, since certain queries may carry significantly more information than others. Notice, however, that some queries may be more or less natural for voters, and more or less difficult to answer—their *cognitive complexity* may not stand in direct relation to the information they carry (in bits), and may vary from one voter to another.[11] Naturally, bounds on the number of queries needed can be translated directly into upper bounds on communication complexity by simply using the number of bits needed to respond to a query of the type in question.

Before outlining these models, we list several natural forms of queries that can be used to communicate information about voter preferences:

- *Full ranking queries:* a voter i provides her entire ranked list of alternatives $\succ_i$.
- *Set ranking:* voter i is asked to rank all alternatives (w.r.t. each other) in a subset $S \subseteq A$. If $S = A$, this corresponds to a full ranking.
- *Top-k queries:* i provides the top k (ranked) alternatives from $\succ_i$ for some $1 \leqslant k \leqslant m$. Notice that setting $k = 1$ corresponds to plurality, while the use of full ranking queries corresponds to setting $k = m$ (or $k = m - 1$). Bottom k queries can be defined similarly.
- *Next-best-alternative queries:* in sequential elicitation schemes, voter i can be asked to state her "next most preferred alternative;" the kth such query asks for her kth-ranked alternative, assuming that the first $k - 1$ have already been provided (the complete information set corresponds to answering a top-k query).
- *Pairwise comparisons:* voter i is asked to state which of two alternatives, a or a', is preferred to the other.
- *Set choice:* voter i is presented with a subset $S \subseteq A$, and asked which alternative in S is most preferred. If $|S| = k$, the response is equivalent to answering (a specific set of) $k - 1$ pairwise comparisons.[12]
- *Positional:* voter i is asked which alternative is ranked in position t in her ranking $\succ_i$.
- *Approval:* voter i is asked to approve of any number of alternatives, or a fixed number k of alternatives. For fixed k-approval, such queries are similar to top k queries in that the

---

[11] For instance, a pairwise comparison of the form "do you prefer a to a'?" may be more difficult for a voter who is almost indifferent between the two than for a voter who strongly prefers one of the two and strongly dislikes the other. Yet both responses can be communicated to a voting mechanism using one bit. Certain psychometric models of choice (e.g., the Luce-Shepard model (Luce, 1959; Shepard, 1959)) capture choice "errors" that are exponentially less likely the more distinguishable two alternatives are w.r.t. their utility.

[12] Specifically, if $a \in S$ is revealed as most preferred, this response contains the same information as the $k - 1$ comparisons: $a \succ a'$, for all $a' \in S \setminus \{a\}$. Of course, one cannot determine which $k - 1$ pairwise comparisons would "simulate" this set choice *prior* to the received response.

top k alternatives are identified, but differ because these are not ranked relative to one another. Veto is defined analogously and bears the same relation to bottom k queries; and for a fixed k, k-veto is equivalent to $(m - k)$-approval.

- *Split queries:* voter i is asked to partition a subset $S \subseteq A$ into two or more blocks of alternatives, each of some specified size, and an ordering of these blocks, such that each alternative in a higher ranked block is preferred to all alternatives in any lower ranked block. k-approval is a special case where two blocks are used of sizes k and $m - k$.

Conitzer and Sandholm (2005b) study the communication complexity of a variety of common voting rules using the standard model used in the study of distributed algorithms (Yao, 1979; Kushilevitz and Nisan, 1996). A *protocol* that implements a voting rule can be interpreted (somewhat informally) as follows: each voter i has an input $\succ_i$ corresponding to its ordering of alternatives, and the collection of voters wants to compute the function $f(R)$, where R is the profile and f is the voting rule in question. A (deterministic) protocol proceeds in stages: at each stage, one voter i reveals a single bit of information based on her ranking, where the choice of voter and the bit revealed are dependent on all bits revealed at prior stages. The process terminates when the output $f(R)$ of the voting rule can be determined (i.e., the bits revealed are sufficient to determine a necessary winner). The *(deterministic) communication complexity* of a voting rule f is the number of bits required by the best (information minimizing) protocol in the worst case (i.e., given the input profile R that maximizes the number of bits communicated through this protocol). Nondeterministic protocols can be defined similarly.

To determine upper bounds on the communication complexity of a voting rule, Conitzer and Sandholm (2005b) provide deterministic protocols that realize the rule. For example, a universal upper bound of $O(nm \log m)$ bits is easy to see for any rank-based rule: each voter can communicate the rank (one of m positions) of each of m alternatives using $\log m$ bits. An upper bound of $O(n \log m)$ for plurality is easy to see since each voter need only communicate the identity (using $\log m$ bits) of its most preferred alternative. We discuss additional upper bounds later.

Lower bounds are shown for many voting rules using the *fooling set technique*: a fooling set of size k for rule f is any set of k distinct profiles $R^1, \ldots, R^k$—where each $R^j = \langle \succ_1^j, \ldots, \succ_n^j \rangle$—such that for each $i \leqslant k$, $f(R^i) = a$ for some $a \in A$ (i.e., each profile has the same winner); but for any $i, j \leqslant k$ there is some mixture of the two profiles of the form $R^{ij} = \langle \succ_1^x, \ldots, \succ_n^x \rangle$, where $\succ_\ell^x = \succ_\ell^i$ or $\succ_\ell^x = \succ_\ell^j$, such that $f(R^{ij}) \neq a$. If such a fooling set exists, then the communication complexity of f is at least $\log k$. This must be so since any protocol must distinguish each pair of inputs in the fooling set (Kushilevitz and Nisan, 1996): if it failed to distinguish R^i from R^j, it could not tell if the input profile was actually R^{ij} and thus could not in fact implement f. By constructing fooling sets of the appropriate size, lower bounds are provided on a variety of rules.

For many rules, Conitzer and Sandholm (2005b) are able to provide matching lower and upper bounds: for plurality (including with runoff), $O(n \log m)$ and $\Omega(n \log m)$; and for Borda, ranked pairs and Copeland, $\Omega(nm \log m)$, which matches the universal upper bound. Other rules analyzed include maximin, approval, cup, Bucklin and Condorcet, which have upper bounds of $O(nm)$ and lower bounds of $\Omega(nm)$; and STV, which is $O(n(\log m)^2)$ and $\Omega(n \log m)$.[13]

To illustrate, we outline the proof sketch of Conitzer and Sandholm (2005b) demonstrating the $O(mn)$ upper bound for Bucklin (which is tighter than the universal $O(nm \log m)$ upper bound). Recall that the (simplified) Bucklin rule chooses as the winner the alternative a such that a lies within the top l positions of the rankings of at least half of the voters for the minimum value of l for which the property holds (see Chapters 2–4).

Proof sketch. The following protocol for Bucklin essentially performs a binary search for the minimum value $l \leq m$ such that at least half of the voters rank some a within the top l positions, maintaining upper and lower bounds U, L on this position. Given the current upper and lower bounds (initialized at $m, 0$ resp.), we need to test whether $k = \lfloor (U + L)/2 \rfloor > l$ (and update the appropriate bound based on the answer). To do so, we can ask each voter to report, for each alternative a, whether a lies within the top k positions of their ranking. This can be answered with m bits per voter (a yes-no response for each alternative); and since the binary search requires at most $\log m$ iterations, this straightforward approach requires at most $O(nm \log m)$ bits.

However, the number of bits required per voter can be cut in half at each iteration. Simply observe that at any iteration $t + 1$, the past responses of voter i reveal the identities of $\frac{2^t - 1}{2^t} m$ alternatives that lie above or below the queried threshold k at that iteration. For example, the first query asks each voter to indicate which alternatives are in their top $m/2$ positions. Suppose we determine $l \leq m/2$, so that each voter is next asked to reveal which alternatives lie in their top $m/4$ positions: since in response to the prior query, each voter indicated $m/2$ alternatives that lie *outside their top half*, these same $m/2$ alternatives must also lie outside their top quarter. Hence at iteration two, each voter needs to reveal only $m/2$ bits (denoting which alternatives in their top half also lie in their top quarter). Ignoring rounding due to imperfect splitting, we have that each voter reveals $\sum_{t=0}^{\log m} \frac{1}{2^t} m \leq 2m$ bits in total. This proves the upper bound of $O(nm)$ bits. $\square$

The communication complexity of determining approximate winners is also of interest. For instance, for voting rules defined using natural scoring functions, we can use the score difference between alternatives as a measure of approximation as discussed in Section 10.3.2; it may be that the communication complexity of approximate winner determination is less than that of exact winner determination. Service and Adams (2012b) analyze several voting rules in this fashion. Borda voting, for example, can benefit from approximation—the communication complexity of determining a $(1 - \varepsilon)$-approximate winner is $O(\frac{1}{\varepsilon} nm)$, which stands in contrast to the $\Omega(nm \log m)$

---

[13] The cup voting rule is essentially a tournament specified by a balanced binary tree. Each alternative is initially assigned to a single leaf. Each pair of siblings (children of the same parent in the tree) "face off" against each other in a pairwise election, with the winner assigned to the parent. The winner of the tournament is the alternative assigned to the root of the tree.

needed for exact winner determination described earlier.[14] By contrast, they show that approximating Bucklin to degree ρ requires $\Omega(\frac{nm}{\rho^2})$ communication, meaning that any constant factor approximation offers little savings in the worst case relative to exact winner determination (which is $O(nm)$). They also provide an analysis of Copeland and consider several nonconstant approximation bounds.

An example using a slightly different model of query complexity, rather than direct communication complexity, is provided by Procaccia (2008). He analyzes the number of queries needed to determine a Condorcet winner, where each query is allowed to ask about the existence of a directed edge between two alternatives in the tournament graph induced by a profile R. Notice that the answer to such a query does not provide direct information about the preferences of any individual voter—thus, a set of such responses does not correspond to a partial profile under our preceding definition. However, it still constrains possible vote profiles. Procaccia shows that a Condorcet winner can be determined using $2m - \log m - 2$ such edge queries. Since each edge query could be determined by asking each of the n voters to answer a single pairwise comparison query, this provides an upper bound of $O(nm)$ on communication complexity. He also provides a matching lower bound on the number of edge queries (note, however, that this does not provide a lower bound on communication complexity, since the analogous $\Omega(nm)$ bound only applies if one is restricted to edge queries).

A very different axiomatic perspective on the complexity of communication is provided by Sato (2009). He considers the number of distinct messages each voter can send in various (one-shot) protocols associated with specific voting rules and considers the impact of minimizing the number of messages allowed. Define the *informational size* of a voting rule to be the total number of distinct messages (across all voters) that can be sent (e.g., the information size of plurality is nm since each of n voters can send one of m messages). Assume that each voter preference determines a unique message (hence messages partition the space of orderings or preferences $\mathcal{R}(A)$). Sato then characterizes the voting rules that are *informationally minimal*, with respect to their informational size, among all rules satisfying certain combinations of axiomatic properties. As one example, he shows that among (nontrivial) anonymous, neutral and monotonic voting rules, only those (loosely) corresponding to either plurality or veto are informationally minimal. This perspective is somewhat different than that taken above in that (a form of) informational complexity is being suggested as a property by which one might choose to use one voting rule rather than another, in the same spirit as much axiomatic analysis of voting.

When voter preferences have special structure, specific mechanisms can be used to exploit this structure for a variety of purposes. One of the most widely studied such structures is *single-peakedness* (Black, 1948) for which the *median mechanism* and various generalizations are strategyproof, and require that voters simply reveal their most preferred alternative rather than their entire ranking (see Chapters 2 and 6 for further discussion of single-peaked preferences). While single-peaked preferences

---

[14] Service and Adams (2012b) derive multiplicative approximation ratios, rather than the additive error used to define max regret in Section 10.3.2. Hence, a ρ-approximate winner a is one whose (Borda, or other) score ratio w.r.t. the true winner w satisfies $s(a)/s(w) \geqslant \rho$.

and the median mechanism already support making decisions with relatively little information, Conitzer (2009) addresses the communication complexity of additional voting problems when preferences are single-peaked. He considers several different settings, including cases where voter preferences are both ordinal and cardinal (e.g., determined by some distance metric), and the *axis* (i.e., positions of the alternatives) may be known or unknown a priori. Restricting our attention to the case of ordinal preferences with a known axis, he first observes that the median rule can be implemented with $n \log m$ (pairwise comparison) queries using a binary search to determine each voter's most preferred alternative—all that is needed to determine the median—giving an $O(n \log m)$ upper bound on communication complexity. Determining a voter's complete ranking can be accomplished with $O(m)$ queries, with $\log m$ queries needed to determine the peak and $m - 1$ queries needed to "interleave" the induced left and right subrankings. He also addresses the problem of determining the full tournament graph (which, assuming n is odd, is acyclic and can be interpreted as a consensus ranking). He shows that this requires $\Omega(nm)$ queries, and thus essentially requires enough information to construct each voter's ranking.[15]

10.5 Preference Elicitation

In the previous section, we discussed several forms of analysis that provided upper and lower bounds on the number of queries or bits required to determine the outcome of various voting rules. These theoretical analyses show the limits of what is possible; but algorithms that minimize worst-case communication complexity may sometimes elicit more information than necessary in practice. Furthermore, these analyses do not address the informational complexity of determining decisions (or winners) that "approximate" the optimal decision (one exception is the work of Service and Adams (2012b)). In this section, we discuss approaches to preference elicitation that are driven by more practical considerations, although several of the models also offer theoretical analyses of these practical aims (e.g., how much information is needed to determine approximate winners, or true winners with high probability).

10.5.1 Incremental and Partial Preference Elicitation

The abstract goal of any preference elicitation technique is to elicit a partial profile from voters with "just enough" information to determine a winning outcome of "sufficiently high quality." The notion of "just enough" information can be measured formally using the communication or query complexity measures described in the previous section. Many of the methods discussed in this section focus on heuristic minimization of query complexity. More critically, elicitation schemes may use different measures for the *quality of the resulting outcome* selected using the elicited partial profile. Among the elicitation goals considered in this section are the following:

---

[15] Lackner (2014) considers the problem of determining whether a partial profile can be completed in such a way that it is single-peaked, showing that it is computationally difficult in general, but providing polytime methods for specific classes of partial profiles.

- determining the optimal outcome (i.e., a winner or a necessary co-winner) w.r.t. the underlying (complete) vote profile
- determining the optimal outcome (i.e., true winner) with high probability
- determining an outcome that is close to optimal (e.g., has low max regret)
- determining an outcome that is close to optimal with high probability

Each of the models described in what follows assumes one (or more) of these abstract objectives, and uses specific metrics to formalize decision quality and error probability.

10.5.2 The Computational Complexity of Preference Elicitation

One early line of research in vote elicitation deals with the computational complexity of various elicitation questions. Conitzer and Sandholm (2002) consider two classes of elicitation schemes, with a focus on determining the true winner (no approximation, no probabilistic guarantees). *Coarse elicitation* methods are restricted to asking a voter for her entire preference ranking or vote. The aim in coarse elicitation is to minimize the number of voters who provide their votes while still determining the true winner. By contrast, *fine elicitation* schemes can ask more general queries, for example, of the form described in Section 10.4—abstractly, a query corresponds to some partitioning of the space $\mathcal{R}(A)$ of votes, with each response selecting some element of the partition (those votes consistent with the response).

Conitzer and Sandholm analyze two main classes of computational questions. *Elicitation Not Done (END)* asks, given a partial profile consisting of the votes from a subset $S \subseteq N$ of voters and an alternative a, can the remaining votes be cast so that a loses. This question anticipates subsequent developments in the theory of possible and necessary winners: if the answer is no, a must be a necessary co-winner, and in certain circumstances this may be sufficient to terminate the vote elicitation procedure. Indeed, the problem is equivalent to the necessary co-winner problem (given this restricted form of partial profile).[16] They show that END is NP-complete for STV, even when the partial profile consists of all votes but one (exploiting a result of Bartholdi and Orlin (1991), see Section 10.3.1). Since the result is cast in terms of coarse elicitation, it naturally applies to any fine elicitation scheme that can simulate coarse elicitation (as most would). They show, by contrast, that END can be solved in polynomial time for plurality, Borda, Copeland, approval and maximin (for fine or coarse elicitation).

They consider a second problem as well: *Effective Elicitation (EE)* asks whether, given a partial profile of votes from $S \subseteq N$, there is a subset of the remaining voters, of size at most k, whose votes determine the winner. From an elicitation perspective, this question assumes the protocol *knows the responses* it will obtain (or has "perfect suspicions"). While unrealistic, this suggests the computational problem given less that perfect knowledge will be even more difficult. Conitzer and Sandholm (2002) show that EE is NP-complete for several different voting rules, including approval, Borda, Copeland and maximin.

---

[16] Since they cast the problem in terms of coarse elicitation, this is also equivalent to the problem of (coalitional) destructive manipulation; see Chapter 6.

Walsh (2008) continues this line of investigation, analyzing the END problem for a variety of other voting rules and considers weighted voting schemes as well. Of special note, Walsh shows that END is computationally easier using coarse elicitation than fine elicitation for several different (weighted) voting rules under various conditions. For instance, END for the Cup rule is coNP-complete (with four or more alternatives) using fine elicitation, but can be solved in polynomial time if we restrict attention to coarse elicitation.

10.5.3 Incremental Vote Elicitation

We now describe several approaches for the elicitation of voter preferences. In many cases, the methods have been analyzed empirically to assess their effectiveness in practical circumstances. Several are supported by theoretical analyses as well to determine how much information is required to reach "high quality" decisions.

Kalech et al. (2011) were among the first to develop and evaluate significant, practical vote elicitation schemes that allowed the selection of winners using partial profiles. They propose two elicitation schemes designed for use with scoring-based rules (e.g., Borda, range voting), using specific forms of queries and possible and necessary winners as the primary solution concept. Their first technique, dubbed *Iterative Voting*,[17] is used to determine a true winner (no approximation) and proceeds in *rounds*. At each round, each voter is queried for their next best alternative; hence by round t each voter has (incrementally) answered a top-t query. At the end of each round, necessary and possible winner computation on the current partial profile is used to determine termination: if every possible winner is a necessary (co-)winner, the process stops and returns the full set of necessary winners. (The algorithm could also be terminated once *any* necessary winner is found.) Empirical analysis of range voting and Borda voting, using small vote profiles (up to 30 voters and 50 alternatives) generated randomly and from real-world ratings data, shows that this scheme can reduce the number of alternatives the average voter has to rank by 10%–40%, with the larger gains possible when user preferences are more uniform.

Kalech et al.'s second algorithm, *Greedy Voting*, proceeds for a predetermined number of rounds T. Given the current partial profile Π^t at round t, each alternative is evaluated to determine its minimum and maximum possible scores (over all completions R of Π^t) relative to the scoring function $s(a, R)$ for the voting rule in question. Then each voter is asked to rank the set of Q alternatives with the largest minimum scores (maximum scores are used to break ties), for some small Q. Since termination is predetermined after T rounds, necessary winners may not result, so possible winners are returned. One attractive feature of this model is the batching of queries (voters are only queried a fixed, ideally small, number of times, though each query may request more information than in the other schemes discussed later). Such batching can minimize user interruption as well as user *latency* (since voters are required to wait until the responses of other voters are delivered before their next query is received). This scheme provides no guarantee of winner optimality or any bounds on quality, hence Kalech

---

[17] This should not be confused with iterative schemes in which voters change their votes in response to the current vote profile.

et al. (2011) empirically evaluate the (post hoc) quality of the resulting winners relative to the true winners that would have resulted had the full vote profile been available.[18] In small domains, winner quality is shown to be relatively high and naturally improves with the number of rounds permitted.

Lu and Boutilier (2011c) propose an elicitation scheme that exploits minimax regret to determine winners given a partial profile and that uses the solution of the MMR problem to guide the selection of queries. Two different forms of queries are considered: simple pairwise comparisons, and "next best alternative queries." As earlier, the process proceeds in rounds. Let Π^t be the partial profile at round t with minimax regret $MMR(\Pi^t)$ and minimax optimal solution $a^* = a^*_{\Pi^t}$. Let a' be an alternative that maximizes the regret of a^*, that is, an a' that maximizes Equation 10.3. This a' is an "adversarial witness" that has maximum advantage (w.r.t. scoring function s) over a^* in the worst-case.

If $MMR(\Pi^t)$ falls below some threshold τ, elicitation can stop and an approximate winner (with an additive error bound of τ) is returned. Thus the Lu-Boutilier scheme supports approximate winners (note that setting $\tau = 0$ guarantees true winners are returned). If not, a query is selected that will refine the partial profile. They propose a *current solution heuristic* for selecting queries. Specifically, the alternatives a^* and a' are used to identify: (*i*) the voter for whom the worst-case profile completion provides the maximum "controllable" advantage of a' over a^*, where the advantage is controllable if it can be reduced using a different completion; and (*ii*) a pairwise comparison query such that a positive response would provide the greatest reduction in that advantage.[19] They provide techniques for effectively determining these queries for positional scoring rules.

Example 10.4. In Example 10.1 (see discussion in Example 10.3) a's max regret is 2 (it is easy to verify that a is minimax optimal). A query to voter 3 that asks if $a \succ c$, if answered positively, reduces c's advantage over a in vote 3 from 3 to -1, thus reducing $PMR(a, c)$ from 2 to -2 and the max regret of a from 2 to 0, hence proving a is a necessary (co)-winner. □

Lu and Boutilier (2011c) evaluate their method, using Borda voting, on both randomly generated and real-world preference and electoral data sets (with up to 20 items and up to 5000 voters). They show that on the real-world data sets, the current solution scheme can reduce the number of queries needed to find the true winner by 50%–65% relative to the number of (comparable) queries needed to construct the entire profile; and on synthetic Mallows profiles they show that reductions of up to 80% are possible when preferences are very correlated; but even 25% reductions are possible under fully random (impartial culture) preferences. Just as importantly, their scheme has the ability to provide approximate winners with provable quality guarantees. Indeed, approximate winners with low max regret can be found using a small fraction of the queries needed to find the true winner.

---

[18] Note that this is possible only in experimental situations. In any practical deployment, the true profile will be unavailable and no such evaluation is possible.

[19] For next-best-alternative queries, no choice of query needs to be made, only choice of a voter.

Other approaches to incremental vote elicitation exploit the use of probabilistic models of voter preferences (e.g., Goel and Lee, 2012; Dery et al., 2010). We examine two other models that exploit probabilistic models in the next section.

One drawback of the Lu-Boutilier scheme is that it asks one query of a single voter at each round. By contrast, the scheme of Kalech et al. (2011) asks all voters to answer a particular query simultaneously, and (at least in the Greedy Voting scheme) can vary the granularity of that query to effectively reduce the number of rounds. In essence, there are important trade-offs among several key metrics that should addressed when designing practical elicitation schemes:

1. *Winner quality*: approximating the winner usually allows for less preference information, but at the cost of outcome quality.
2. *Amount of information elicited*: higher quality outcomes and fewer rounds of elicitation can usually be achieved at the cost of additional preference information.
3. *Number of rounds of elicitation*: multiple rounds of elicitation can often reduce the amount of information needed to reach a decision of the same quality by conditioning queries on past responses. However, additional rounds of elicitation impose costs in terms of interruption, cognitive/context switching and latency (voters waiting on the responses of other voters).

Lu and Boutilier (2011d) develop a general framework for framing these trade-offs using multiround elicitation protocols. They evaluate this model in the specific context of single-round protocols, as we discuss next.

10.5.4 One-Shot Partial Vote Elicitation

Lu and Boutilier (2011d) address the question of whether high quality winners (as measured using max regret) can be guaranteed using a *single round of elicitation*. In more detail, they ask whether one can determine a value k such that asking a top-k query of every voter allows one to determine an approximate winner with low max regret (assuming a scoring-function based voting rule that admits max regret computation). In general, such guarantees are not possible in the worst-case for most voting rules (see Section 10.4), so they assume that voter preferences (or vote profiles if voter preferences can be correlated) are drawn according to some distribution P. Rather than assuming a specific form of the distribution, they assume only that it can be sampled effectively. They then defined a sampling procedure that determines the minimum value of k such that top-k voting results in a profile with low minimax regret (hence an alternative that is an approximate winner) with high probability. Specifically, given a desired *solution accuracy* $\varepsilon > 0$, *solution confidence* $\delta > 0$, *sampling accuracy* $\xi > 0$, and *sampling confidence* $\eta > 0$, they determine the number of sampled profiles that must be drawn to determine an empirical estimate of k that ensures that if a top-k partial profile $\Pi[k]$ is elicited, then $P[MMR(\Pi[k]) \leqslant \varepsilon] > 1 - \delta - 2\xi$ (where the number of sampled profiles is proportional to $\ln 2m/\eta$ and $1/\xi^2$). Empirically, they show that the sampling approach can be used not only to determine the appropriate value of k for top-k voting, but also to assess the trade-offs between the amount of preference information elicited (value of k) and the distribution over solution quality (resulting MMR).

Oren et al. (2013) also analyze top-k voting, but rather than sampling profiles from an unknown distribution, they assess the values of k needed to ensure the true winner is found with high probability for specific preference distributions. Their focus is on asymptotic analysis, specifically whether top-k voting determines a correct winner with probability approaching 1 as the number of alternatives m (and indirectly, the number of voters n) increases.[20] They show that top-k voting may not offer significant savings for Borda voting under impartial culture—they provide a lower bound of $k = \Omega(m/\log m)$ (for n sufficiently large relative to m). They also consider the extreme case of *zero-elicitation protocols*: assuming voter preferences are drawn from a Mallows model, under what conditions will selecting the alternative at the top of the (modal) reference ranking be the winner with high probability? In other words, can setting $k = 0$ still determine the true winner? They provide a bound on the number of voters required to ensure this holds that depends logarithmically on m and in a complex way on ϕ (the Mallows dispersion parameter). For distributions that are not too uniform (say, $\phi \leqslant 0.75$), relatively few voters are needed to ensure zero elicitation works.

It is also interesting to consider the difficulty of the possible and necessary winner problems for *restricted* classes of partial preferences, such as those of the top-k form. For certain voting rules, these restricted problems may be computationally easier than with unrestricted partial profiles. Baumeister et al. (2012a) explicitly consider *truncated ballots* of the top-k form, the bottom-k form, as well as "doubly truncated" votes (with top and bottom segments provided). They discuss the relationship of the possible winner problem for these forms of truncated ballots to each other and to the unweighted coalitional manipulation problem.[21]

10.6 Voting with an Uncertain Set of Alternatives

We now turn our attention to the incompleteness or uncertainty regarding the set of alternatives A that may be available for selection by our voters N. As we've seen, several key questions regarding incomplete preferences are related to strategic questions of misreporting and manipulation. Similarly, models in which alternatives may or may not materialize are closely related to strategic questions regarding control by adding or deleting alternatives (see Chapter 7) and questions of strategic candidacy (Dutta et al., 2001). We only briefly mention such connections in this section, but refer to Chapter 7 for deeper discussion of such strategic considerations.

In this section, we generally assume that the set of alternatives A is a "potential set," but that some of the alternatives may in fact be unavailable for selection by voters. Voter preferences are defined over the entire potential set A, but the voters are uncertain as to which alternatives are in fact *available* at the time they vote. The question is how voting mechanisms should be modified or analyzed under such conditions.

---

[20] They add the wrinkle of considering determining winners when alternatives may become "unavailable" (as defined in Section 10.6), which means that, even in plurality voting, voters may need to provide more than their top alternative to ensure a feasible winner is found. We ignore this variation here. They also provide several worst-case analyses.

[21] They also describe various other forms of manipulation and campaigning in such cases, but this analysis is less relevant here.

Several motivations can be offered for models of this type. In labor markets, alternatives may declare themselves eligible for multiple positions, but hiring committee decisions may require voting (or aggregating preferences) over interviewed candidates who may ultimately take jobs elsewhere. In some group decision contexts, determining the availability or feasibility of specific alternatives may be quite costly (e.g., calling restaurants to see if reservations are possible; planning a public project or family vacation to determine whether it satisfies feasibility, time and budget constraints). In these cases, it often makes sense to cast votes to determine the most preferred (or reasonable consensus) alternatives *prior* to investing time, effort or money to determine the feasibility of options that may not be selected given voter preferences.

Lu and Boutilier (2010) develop the *unavailable candidate model* to capture such situations. In this model, the set of available alternatives $V \subseteq A$ is unknown at the time votes are cast. Assume a distribution P over 2^A, where $P(V)$ is the probability that V is the true set of available alternatives. Given a vote profile R and voting rule f, the fundamental difficulty is that we may have $f(A) \notin V$, that is, the winner of the full vote may not be available. Of course, one could simply collect preferences and then apply f to the available set V once it is revealed. But in some settings this may not be viable, for example, when the availability of an alternative may only be determined by declaring them the winner (e.g., offering a job to a candidate, or attempting a booking at an exclusive restaurant). Under this assumption, one can aggregate the preferences into a *ranking policy*, an ordering $\succ$ of A such that each alternative will be "offered the win" in turn until an available alternative is discovered. In other words, $\succ$ is effectively a *rationalizable* group choice function.

Since no nondictatorial, unanimity preserving voting rule is robust to the deletion of nonwinning alternatives (Dutta et al., 2001), selecting alternatives in this fashion may produce a winner that is not in fact the true winner relative to the realized set V. This is so not just because of the restrictive nature of the rationalizable policy, but also because the process may never discover the true set V. For this reason, one requires methods for computing the policy that *minimizes the expected disagreement* (difference in winner choice) between the ranking policy and the true voting rule f, where expectation is taken w.r.t. $P(V)$. Lu and Boutilier (2010) show that this problem is NP-hard in certain circumstances. As a result, they offer a polynomial-time approximation scheme (PTAS), as well as a greedy algorithm with a $\frac{1+p^2}{(1-p)^2}$ approximation ratio when all alternatives are (independently) unavailable with probability p. Empirical results show this greedy algorithm to provide excellent results in practice. Other forms of rank aggregation may not provide good ranking policies. For instance, the Kemeny consensus of the profile R need not be a good ranking policy in general; but for large values of p, any Kemeny consensus is close to optimal (in terms of expected disagreement), and at least one Kemeny consensus is in fact optimal (Lu and Boutilier, 2010).

Baldiga and Green (2013) independently developed a model virtually identical to the unavailable candidate model, using rather different motivations, and also draw connections to the Kemeny consensus.

Notice that Lu and Boutilier assume that availability can only be tested by actually selecting a tentative winner—hence they attempt to minimize the odds of selecting an "incorrect" winner. Boutilier et al. (2014) approach the unavailable candidate model from a different perspective: they assume that testing availability is expensive, but can be accomplished without actually selecting a winner. They address the problem of minimizing the number (or cost) of such tests needed to determine the true winner. Specifically, assume some voting rule f, a given vote profile R. Suppose the alternative set A is partitioned into three sets: KA (known available alternatives), KU (known unavailable), and U (unknown availability). The true available set V can be any $KA \subseteq V \subseteq KA \cup U$. They define a *robust winner* to be any a such that $f(R[V]) = a$ for all $V \subseteq KA \cup U$, that is, a is a winner for any realizable available set V (here $R[V]$ is the restriction of profile R to available set V). Of course, determining robust winners is difficult for some voting rules f and easy for others; as the authors point out, this problem has tight connections to the problem of control by candidate addition (see Chapter 7).

If no robust winner exists, then determining the true winner requires testing the availability of certain additional alternatives until we reach a point (state of information about KA and KU) that admits a robust winner. Boutilier et al. (2014) develop a dynamic programming method that will produce the *optimal (minimum cost) availability testing policy*, as well as a myopic search technique based on decision tree induction that heuristically minimizes the cost of the policy. They also provide simple worst-case analysis of the "availability test complexity" of plurality, Borda and Copeland that shows essentially all alternatives must be tested in the worst case. They also describe simple test policies that are optimal for extreme availability probabilities.

Chevaleyre et al. (2012) study a different issue associated with alternative uncertainty, namely, the possible winner problem when votes are provided over some initial set of alternatives A, then a fixed number c of *new alternatives are added to the set*. They study the computational complexity of determining whether an alternative $a \in A$ (i.e., one of the initial alternatives) is a possible winner given the addition of the new alternatives for various voting rules—here uncertainty lies over voter preferences for these new alternatives. Note that this problem (as in possible and necessary winner determination with a known set of alternatives as discussed earlier) bears a tight connection to certain forms of manipulation, specifically, the notions of *cloning* and *control by adding candidates* (see Chapter 7).

Chevaleyre et al. (2012) provide a complete classification of the family of k-approval rules (including plurality). For $k \in \{1, 2\}$ (i.e., plurality and 2-approval), they show that the possible winner problem can be solved in polynomial time for any fixed c (the construction for 2-approval uses a reduction to a max-flow problem). For $k \geqslant 3$ and $c = 2$ they show that the problem can also be solved in polynomial time; but for $k \geqslant 3$ and $c \geqslant 3$, they use a reduction from 3D MATCHING to show that the possible winner problem is NP-complete. They also provide a polytime method for Borda voting (indeed, for a more general class of scoring rules that includes Borda). Xia et al. (2011b) adopt the same model and show that several additional voting rules have NP-complete possible winner problems with new alternatives, namely, Bucklin, Copeland (with pairwise ties in voting giving a score of 0 for both alternatives), maximin and approval.[22]

---

[22] In fact, they consider several different ways in which a voter can extend her approval vote given c new alternatives. In the arguably most natural, the problem is NP-complete, while for the others it is straightforwardly polytime solvable or a trivial problem.

10.7 Compilation Complexity

A subset of voter preferences embodies some inherent partial information regarding the ultimate result of a vote. Such a subset of preferences, or partial profile Π, can of course be held in its raw form, as the original linear orders of the subset of voters. However, several researchers have considered the idea of compressing this information into a smaller number of bits, which still represents the *essence of the partial information* in that it allows one to determine the ultimate winner of an election once the remaining votes are received (Chevaleyre et al., 2009; Xia and Conitzer, 2010b; Chevaleyre et al., 2011). The minimum number of bits required to represent this relevant information, for a given voting rule f, is called the *compilation complexity* of f.

There are several reasons one might want to compile a partial (or complete) vote profile in this way. Compilation may offer privacy benefits by discarding full voter information in favor of statistical or other summaries. It may allow for faster computation of the final result once all votes become available.[23] It may also ease communication complexity when partial vote results from multiple locations need to be aggregated. Finally, if vote profiles need to be stored for future validation or audits, compilation may reduce space requirements. There are also some possible drawbacks of compilation; for example, it may make further elicitation more costly in some circumstances, when a specific voter has to be questioned again.

Research on compilation complexity to date has largely focused on the following questions: the space needed for storing compiled partial voting results when the number of remaining voters is unknown (Chevaleyre et al., 2009); the space needed when that number is known along with the number who have already voted, or one or the other might be unknown (Xia and Conitzer, 2010b); and the relationship between compilation complexity and communication complexity (see Section 10.4) when the set of alternatives is dynamic (Chevaleyre et al., 2011).

To illustrate the main ideas behind compilation complexity, consider the summarization of partial results in plurality voting. Suppose k voters, from an ultimate electorate of size $n > k$, have already expressed their ordered preferences among m alternatives. Since each alternative can be specified using $\lceil \log m \rceil$ bits, this partial vote could be stored in its raw form and used to compute the winner once the remaining votes are received. This very naive storage scheme required $k \lceil \log(m!) \rceil$ bits to store all ballots (namely, specifying for each voter which of $m!$ possible permutations matches their vote). However, the partial input can be represented more concisely, recording only the number of first-place votes received by each of the m alternatives—this uses $m \lceil \log(k + 1) \rceil$ bits. When the remaining $n - k$ votes are submitted, the only data that *matters* from the initial k votes for the purposes of winner computation are alternative first-place vote totals.

Of course, we can do even better. Rather than store all first-place vote totals, we can normalize them by subtracting the score of the lowest-scoring alternative from all alternative scores, hence needing to represent smaller totals (assuming no alternative received zero votes). Moreover, if the difference between the partial votes already

---

[23] Note that when faster computation of the final result is the primary objective, it may sometimes be useful to 'compile' into a structure using more space.

received by the front-runner and those received by the second-place alternative is greater than the number of votes yet to be cast by the remaining $n - k$ voters—assuming this number of votes yet to be cast is known—the ultimate result of the election is already determined, and the only thing that needs to be stored is the identity of the winning alternative.

Based on these intuitions, we can immediately make several simple observations (Chevaleyre et al., 2009). First, the compilation complexity of any voting rule is at most $k\lceil\log(m!)\rceil$ bits—we simply store all voters' votes. For any anonymous voting rule, the compilation complexity will be at most the minimum of $k\lceil\log(m!)\rceil$ and $m!\lceil\log(k + 1)\rceil$, since with an anonymous rule we can store, for each ballot (linear order), the number of voters that chose it, if that requires fewer bits. A dictatorial voting rule has compilation complexity of $\lceil\log m\rceil$—only the choice of the dictator needs to be stored if she is among the original voters (and nothing otherwise).

To formalize the compilation complexity problem, following Xia and Conitzer (2010b), consider a set of voters divided into a subset of k known votes, and a subset of u unknown votes. The k votes, constituting a partial profile Π, are summarized by a string of bits via a *compilation function* c: $c(\Pi) \in \{0, 1\}^*$. For the function to be an effective summary for voting rule f, if we have profiles Π_1 and Π_2, and $c(\Pi_1) = c(\Pi_2)$, then for any profile of the remaining u votes Q it must be the case that $f(\Pi_1 \cup Q) = f(\Pi_2 \cup Q)$. We say that Π_1 and Π_2 are *f-equivalent* in this case.

The minimum number of bits required to summarize a partial profile Π of a subelectorate of size k, for a given voting rule f, u unknown votes, and m alternatives, is called the *compilation complexity* of f, and is denoted by $C_{m,k,u}(f)$. It reflects the most space-effective function c. Chevaleyre et al. (2009) also consider the case where u is unknown. This can be represented using the preceding notation as $C_{m,k,?}(f)$ (the question mark replacing u). This is the minimum number of bits required to summarize the profile of a sub-electorate of size k, for a given voting rule f, when there are m alternatives, and the remaining number of votes u is unknown.

The definition of f-equivalence establishes equivalence classes among profiles and allows one to store a partial profile by storing the index of its equivalence class. If $g(f, k, m)$ denotes the number of equivalence classes for voting rule f, already-voted sub-electorate k, and m alternatives, then the compilation complexity of a voting rule f is precisely $\lceil\log g(f, k, m)\rceil$. To derive the compilation complexity for various voting rules, we can count the relevant equivalence classes for each.

$C_{m,k,?}(f)$ is related to several of the problems described in earlier sections:

1. *The complexity of terminating elicitation (Section 10.5.2)*: is the winner already determined after we have been given a subset of the votes?
2. *The complexity of possible and necessary winner determination (Section 10.3.1)*: if we have a set of incomplete votes (partial orders), is there an extension where a given alternative c is the winner?
3. *Communication complexity of voting rules (Section 10.4)*: what is the smallest number of bits that needs to be communicated among voters and the central authority to compute the winner of an election? Note that compilation complexity can be interpreted as "one-round communication complexity" (the message being sent by the initial voters).

4. Chevaleyre et al. (2011) consider a variant of the communication complexity problem, namely, the relationship of compilation complexity and communication complexity when the set of alternatives is dynamic, that is, new alternatives can be added over time (see Section 10.6).

Results

It is clear that the compilation complexity of plurality is at most $m \lceil \log(k + 1) \rceil$ (storing the score between 0 and k for each alternative). Chevaleyre et al. (2009) show that this can be improved (with an unknown number of additional voters) to

$$\left\lceil \log \binom{m + n - 1}{k} \right\rceil.$$

Exploration of compilation complexity concerns variations on the basic model. As mentioned, Chevaleyre et al. consider $C_{m,k,?}(f)$, where the remaining number of votes u (replaced by a question mark) was the only unknown. Xia and Conitzer (2010b) expand this by considering the relationship among $C_{m,k,?}(f)$, $C_{m,?,u}(f)$ (where the number of already-cast votes is the unknown), and $C_{m,k,u}(f)$ (where the number of already-cast and the number of yet-to-be cast votes are both known). Chevaleyre et al. show that $C_{m,k,?}(f)$ and $C_{m,?,u}(f)$ furnish upper bounds on $C_{m,k,u}(f)$. Xia and Conitzer prove that one can find upper bounds on $C_{m,k,?}(f)$ and $C_{m,?,u}(f)$ from the upper bound of $C_{m,k,u}(f)$, assuming the voting rule f is anonymous and there exists an h-profile Π that always "cancels out"; this simply means that, for some $h \in \mathbb{N}$ there exists an h-profile Π that always "cancels out," that is, $f(\Pi \cup \Pi') = f(\Pi')$ for every profile Π'. Most common voting rules satisfy "h-canceling-out" for some h.

Xia and Conitzer also derive upper and lower bounds on the compilation complexity of many common voting rules, including l-approval, Borda, Bucklin, Copeland, maximin, plurality with runoff, ranked pairs, and voting trees. They derive asymptotically tight bounds on all three types of compilation complexity (i.e., $C_{m,k,?}(f)$, $C_{m,?,u}(f)$, and $C_{m,k,u}(f)$) for some rules. Notably, when k and u are both larger than $m^{1+\epsilon}$ for some $\epsilon > 0$, their bounds are asymptotically tight. Xia and Conitzer's (2010b) results, along with Chevaleyre et al.'s (2009) results, are summarized in Table 10.1 which appears in Xia and Conitzer (2010b). WMG-based rules refer to voting rules that rely on the weighted majority graph to uniquely determine a winner (see Chapter 4); OPE-based rules refer to voting rules where winner determination can be done by comparing the magnitudes of pairwise results; UMG-based rules refer to voting rules in which winner determination is done using the signs (but not magnitudes) of pairwise results (see Chapter 3).

As mentioned above, Chevaleyre et al. (2011) consider the relationship of compilation complexity and communication complexity when the set of alternatives is dynamic. They show that bounds on communication complexity can be derived from the type of storage used to hold partial results; they consider three types of storage, namely, full storage of initial votes of the sub-electorate, null storage where nothing is held, and anonymous storage, where for each possible ranking over initial alternatives, the number of voters who had that preference is stored. They show that certain communication protocols for a given voting rule are asymptotically optimal by deriving their communication complexity for a given type of storage.

10.8 Social Choice from a Utilitarian Perspective

Much of the research in computational social choice takes the classical perspective in which voters are assumed to have ordinal preferences that can be aggregated via social choice functions that satisfy certain normative criteria. There is, however, a different, *utilitarian* approach to the aggregation of group preferences that assumes individuals have *cardinal utility functions* that quantify the desirability of various outcomes. The aggregation of these utility functions typically focuses on choosing an outcome that maximizes the sum of the individual utilities, that is, *social welfare*. Social welfare maximization is a clear criterion by which to evaluate an aggregation scheme (though see later), whereas the choice of normative criteria to use in ordinal voting can be more controversial.

In this section, we consider computational social choice techniques that adopt this utilitarian perspective, that is, that assume voters have cardinal utilities over alternatives. Work is this area can be broadly broken down into two main streams. The first considers the *distortion* of social welfare induced by applying ordinal preference aggregation methods to cardinal preferences, assuming that some mapping is used to transform individual voter utilities into ordinal preferences. The second develops *learning-theoretic* models to compute "sample-optimal" ordinal social choice functions, based on sampled utility profiles from some distribution.

The connections between the use of ordinal and cardinal preferences are subtle. In various settings, one or the other might be the appropriate approach. For example, it is generally assumed that ordinal preferences are easier to extract from voters, who may not be able to compute or articulate their cardinal utilities for outcomes (easily or at all). Even when utility functions can be assumed to (explicitly or implicitly) exist and to be accessible, there exists little basis for valid interpersonal comparisons of those utilities. Some researchers assume that voter utility functions are normalized, which "solves" the problem of the interpersonal comparison; in effect, all voters are assumed to carry equal weight in any utility maximization or voting calculation. It is also not clear that the maximization of the sum of individual utilities ought to be the goal of aggregation—while this criterion is clearly defined, it may not be appropriate in all circumstances.

The most direct aggregation approach to utility maximization, of course, is simply for each individual to provide the center with its utility for each alternative, and have the center choose the outcome that maximizes the sum.[24] The models described in this section assume either that communication bandwidth is limited, and ordinal preferences can be expressed more concisely than utility values for all alternatives, or that it is too difficult or unnatural to extract cardinal preferences from the voters. Hence, a mapping from cardinal utilities to a linear ordering is used to reduce the communication or elicitation burden. This linear ordering is then used by a suitable

---

[24] Ensuring that such reports are truthful of course requires careful *mechanism design*.

preference aggregation or voting rule, and ideally approximates the maximization of social welfare.

The decentralized transformation of utility functions over alternatives to prescriptive votes has the potential to dramatically reduce the communication required to find an alternative that maximizes social welfare. Consider an example due to Caragiannis and Procaccia (2011). Suppose each voter must communicate a utility score, on a scale of 1 to one million, for each of one million alternatives. This requires the transmission of $10^6 \times \log(10^6)$ bits from each voter. If plurality voting is used, an embedding of that utility function into plurality votes requires the transmission of only 20 bits. There are scenarios where power restrictions, communication bandwidth limitations, cognitive costs, or privacy concerns make this kind of reduced communication attractive. The maximization of social welfare is particularly relevant in scenarios where the agents are part of a cooperative multiagent system, for example, where they have been designed to cooperatively carry out some task (such as distributed sensing).

10.8.1 Distortion

In cases where cardinal scores/utilities exist, it is natural to select the alternative that maximizes social welfare as the winner. However, if the cardinal scores are mapped into ordinal rankings for use by a voting rule, the potential for "distortion" of the original cardinal preferences arises. In other words, when a particular voting rule, for example Borda, uses the induced ordinal rankings to choose a winning alternative, the winner may not be the alternative that maximizes social welfare.

Procaccia and Rosenschein (2006) consider several issues relating to this distortion of cardinal scores when mapped into ordinal preferences. They define *distortion of a social choice function* as the *worst-case* ratio of the total utility of the alternative that maximizes social welfare to that of the selected alternative (where the worst-case is with respect to all possible utility profiles, i.e., profiles of utilities that are consistent with the reported rankings).

The formal definition is as follows. Let f be a social choice function, A a set of alternatives, R a preference profile over A, and $\mathrm{sw}(x, R)$ the social welfare of alternative x given profile R. Then the *distortion* dist of social choice function f on a preference profile R is defined as

$$\mathrm{dist}(v, R) = \frac{\max_{y \in A} \mathrm{sw}(y, R)}{\min_{x \in f(R)} \mathrm{sw}(x, R)}.$$

This is the worst-case ratio of the most popular alternative's social welfare, and the least popular winner's social welfare ("least popular winner" handles the case where there are ties, and the worst-case analysis assumes the worst of the tied alternatives is ultimately chosen, as in the preceding definition).

Consider the case where the sum of utilities assigned to the alternatives by each of the voters is identical (i.e., as if each voter has a fixed number of "utility points" to distribute across the alternatives). Every social choice function in this model has distortion greater than 1. In other words, the social-welfare maximizing alternative has greater utility than the selected alternative in the worst case, even when the number of voters and of alternatives are small; several well-known scoring protocols have

Table 10.1. *The misrepresentation of common voting protocols*

Voting Protocol	Misrepresentation
Borda	1
Veto	Unbounded
Plurality	$= m - 1$
Plurality with Runoff	$= m - 1$
Copeland	$\leqslant m - 1$
Bucklin	$\leqslant m$
Maximin	$\leqslant 1.62(m - 1)$
STV	$\leqslant 1.5(m - 1)$

unbounded distortion. With the removal of the assumption that all voters have an equal "sum of utilities," the situation is even worse, as it is not possible to bound the distortion (Procaccia and Rosenschein, 2006).

Now consider an alternative model in which voters may have different sums of utilities to distribute among the alternatives, but winner selection using the mapped ordinal rankings is realized using a weighted election, with each voter's ballot weighted by its utility sum. The reformulated model is, in fact, equivalent to the original unweighted version (Procaccia and Rosenschein (2006) also prove that a particular problem associated with calculating distortion is NP-complete when utilities are unconstrained).

Procaccia and Rosenschein also reformulated the concept of distortion as *misrepresentation*, a concept originally defined by Monroe (1995). The main difference between the two settings is that in misrepresentation the voters' cardinal preferences are defined in a very restricted way. The misrepresentation of voter i for alternative j is the alternative's ordinal position from the top of the ranking minus 1 (e.g., the misrepresentation of the most-preferred alternative is 0), and the overall misrepresentation of an alternative is the sum of its misrepresentations over all voters. Misrepresentation values can be interpreted as very restricted cardinal preferences, where voter i's utility for alternative j is precisely the number of total alternatives m, minus j's misrepresentation, minus 1 (e.g., the utility of the most-preferred alternative is $m - 1$). They establish a necessary and sufficient condition for a social choice function to be optimal with respect to misrepresentation, and also characterize those scoring protocols that have unbounded misrepresentation. Bounds are provided—including several tight bounds—for the misrepresentation of specific voting protocols (summarized in Table 10.1).

Caragiannis and Procaccia (2011) expand the work on distortion. Their basic setting is similar: a group of voters are assumed to have utility functions that assign values to alternatives. These utility functions are then transformed or "reduced" in some fashion, voters transmit the reduced information to the voting protocol, and a winner is chosen. While the original work on distortion proposed such mappings or transformations as a way of descriptively characterizing voting rules—seeing which voting rules cause more or less distortion of the socially optimal result—this later work adopted an algorithmic approach, introducing the notion of *embeddings into voting rules*, mappings from a voter's utility function into a *prescription* of how that voter should vote (given the specific voting rule). This generalizes the straightforward mapping in which the alternative with the kth highest utility is ranked in the kth position; but more fundamentally, it takes a different perspective on distortion. Instead of using the distortion of specific voting rules as a criterion for evaluating and comparing them, Caragiannis and Procaccia attempt to *design* embeddings that minimize distortion.

More specifically, one can generalize the notion of distortion, by defining it for general embeddings. The distortion of a deterministic embedding into a specific voting rule can be defined, as earlier, as the worst-case ratio of the most popular alternative's social welfare, and the least popular winner's social welfare. In the case of randomized embeddings, distortion can be defined using the expected minimum social welfare among the winners, again looking at the worst-case ratio between the most popular alternative's social welfare, and the expected minimum social welfare among the winners.

Consider the distortion of embeddings into the plurality, approval, and veto voting rules. All of these voting rules have low communication overhead: $\log(m)$ bits per voter for plurality and veto, and m bits per voter for approval, where m is the number of alternatives. Any deterministic embedding into the plurality voting rule (when $n \geqslant m$) has distortion $\Omega(m^2)$. A simple randomized embedding into plurality—where the voter selects an alternative with probability proportional to its utility—gives constant distortion when the number of voters n is equal to $\Omega(m \log(m))$, and even for larger values of n has extremely low distortion, specifically, $1 + o(1)$. With approval voting, where $n \geqslant m$, there is a lower bound of $\Omega(m)$ for deterministic embeddings. Here the randomized upper bounds for plurality imply the randomized upper bounds for approval (since an embedding into plurality is also an embedding into approval). Caragiannis and Procaccia (2011) carry out simulations for the case where $n \leqslant m$, with results supporting the conclusion that low distortion can be achieved if n is not too small. They also show that any deterministic embedding into the veto rule has infinite distortion, as is also the case for randomized embeddings if $n < m - 1$. However, when there are many voters, low-distortion embeddings into veto can be achieved.

The work of Boutilier et al. (2012) is strongly related to the distortion analysis described previously. Taking a utilitarian perspective on social choice, two separate distortion models are examined, each with a different assumption about the information that is available, and each with its own optimality criterion. The first model assumes that there is no information about voter utility functions, and considers the *worst-case optimal* social choice function that minimizes distortion on every preference profile; upper and lower bounds are proven on the minimal possible distortion, given randomized social choice functions. There exists a preference profile where every randomized social choice function has distortion at least $\Omega(\sqrt{m})$, where m is the number of alternatives, and there is a randomized social choice function whose distortion on every preference profile is $O(\sqrt{m} \cdot \log^*(m))$. The worst-case optimal social choice function can be computed in polynomial time.

Assume that for each agent i, the sum of the agent's utilities over all alternatives a in A is 1. Let $\mathcal{R}(A)$ be the set of permutations on $[m]$. Formally, we have the following theorem (from Boutilier et al., 2012): Assume that $n \geqslant \sqrt{m}$. Then there exists a preference profile $R \in \mathcal{R}(A)^n$ such that for any randomized social choice function f, $\text{dist}(f, R) = \Omega(\sqrt{m})$.

Proof. For ease of exposition assume that $\sqrt{m}$ divides n. Partition the agents into $\sqrt{m}$ equal subsets $N_1, \ldots, N_{\sqrt{m}}$. Consider the preference profile R where $\sigma_i(a_k) = 1$, for all $i \in N_k$, and the remaining alternatives are ranked arbitrarily.

For any randomized f there must be a $k^* \in \{1, \ldots, \sqrt{m}\}$ such that $\Pr[f(R) = a_{k^*}] \leq \frac{1}{\sqrt{m}}$. Let $\vec{u}$ be a utility profile such that for all $i \in N_{k^*}$, the value of a_{k^*} is 1, and the value of all alternatives other than a_{k^*} is 0. For all $i \notin N_{k^*}$ and alternatives $a \in A$, the value for i of a is $\frac{1}{m}$. It holds that

$$\frac{n}{\sqrt{m}} \leq \mathrm{sw}(a_{k^*}, \vec{u}) \leq \frac{2n}{\sqrt{m}},$$

and for all $a \in A \setminus \{a_{k^*}\}$, $\mathrm{sw}(a, \vec{u}) \leq \frac{n}{m}$. Therefore:

$$\mathrm{dist}(f, R) \geq \frac{\frac{n}{\sqrt{m}}}{\frac{1}{\sqrt{m}} \cdot \frac{2n}{\sqrt{m}} + \frac{\sqrt{m}-1}{\sqrt{m}} \cdot \frac{n}{m}} \geq \frac{\sqrt{m}}{3}.$$

$\square$

In a second, *average-case model*, there is a (known) distribution D over voter utility functions. The *average-case optimal* social choice function is defined as one that chooses an alternative that maximizes expected social welfare, given a profile produced by drawing each voter's utility function independently from D. When D is symmetric with respect to alternatives, this average-case optimal social choice function must be a scoring rule (Boutilier et al., 2012).

The focus of Boutilier et al. (2012) on randomized social choice functions differentiates their work from that of Procaccia and Rosenschein (2006), which deals with deterministic social choice functions. Although Caragiannis and Procaccia (2011) also consider randomized social choice functions, their motivations and hence the models and assumptions are different. Caragiannis and Procaccia cite communication limitations as a primary motivation for voting using rankings (rather than transmitting utility functions). As a consequence, they focus on social choice functions with low communication requirements, with the primary goal being to optimize the embedding of cardinal preferences into ordinal votes. Boutilier et al. (2012) assume that voters translate utility functions into preference orders in the straightforward way (i.e., the alternative with kth-highest utility mapped to the kth position in the vote), and therefore focus on optimization of the social choice function rather than the embedding function.

10.8.2 Learnability

Consider the scenario where there is a *designer* who is able, for each input of voter preferences, to designate a winner. This black box approach assumes that the designer is, perhaps, applying a set of external properties to determine the winner, so that for every vote profile a winner that satisfies those properties can be specified by the designer. It is assumed that the voting rule that (implicitly or explicitly) drives the choice of winners by the designer comes from a family $\mathcal{R}$ of rules. Procaccia et al. (2009) address the problem of finding, via some *probably approximately correct (PAC) learning process*, a voting rule from $\mathcal{R}$ that is as close as possible to the designer's (implicit or explicit) rule. Ideally, the number of sampled profiles given to the designer should be small (perhaps because of the computational or communication costs associated with the process). An algorithm is developed whose input is a collection of "vote profile-winning alternative" pairs drawn according to the fixed distribution D over profiles. The output is a voting rule that maximizes expected agreement (expectation taken w.r.t. D) between the output voting rule and the actual rule from which the samples are derived, in the PAC sense.

One way of conceptualizing this problem is as the "automated design of voting rules"; if there exists a specification of properties that can be used to determine a winner, then the process can find a voting rule that in some sense embodies or operationalizes those properties. The scenario is particularly compelling if there does exist a prior set of criteria for establishing who the winner is, given voter preferences, but no succinct voting rule that is known to capture those criteria.

There are several interesting results in this model (Procaccia et al., 2009). Given a set of examples, it is possible to efficiently compute a scoring rule consistent with the examples (if one exists). That, together with the proven dimensionality of the class of scoring rules (given m alternatives, that dimensionality is bounded by m and $m - 3$), implies that the class of scoring rules with m alternatives and n voters is learnable in polynomial time for all m and n.

The situation when $\mathcal{R}$ is the family of voting trees is somewhat more complicated; the number of different pairwise voting rules that can be represented as voting trees is doubly exponential in the number of alternatives. In general, a large number of examples would need to be provided to allow learning—this is true even in the seemingly simpler case of balanced voting trees, to which arbitrary unbalanced trees can be transformed. In the special case of "small" voting trees (where the number of leaves in the tree is polynomial in the number of alternatives, rather than exponential in the number of alternatives), however, voting trees are efficiently learnable. Extensions to general voting rules can also be considered, but there exist many voting rules that cannot be approximated by scoring rules nor by small voting trees (assuming a uniform distribution over voter profiles). This does not preclude the possibility that there exist important families of general voting rules that can be approximated by scoring rules or small voting trees (Procaccia et al., 2009).

Boutilier et al. (2012) extend the work on learnability further, by considering a learning-theoretic model that is consistent with their overall examination of optimal social choice functions from a utilitarian perspective. They assume one has access only to sampled utility profiles from some unknown distribution D, and wishes to find a *sample-optimal* social choice function, relative to those sampled profiles (in contrast to the worst-case optimal and average-case optimal social choice functions considered earlier). The quality of the sample-optimal social choice function is then assessed relative to the expected social welfare of the (unknown) true optimal social choice function for D. Necessary and sufficient bounds are derived on the number of samples needed to ensure the sample-optimal social choice function has expected social welfare close to that of the optimal function with high probability. These are provided for both k-approval social choice functions, as well as general scoring functions. Finding the sample-optimal scoring function is APX-hard; however, there is a mixed-integer programming formulation that generally enables reasonably effective computation of the sample-optimal function.

10.9 Conclusions and Future Directions

We have seen that a number of interesting and challenging issues arise when we consider the implementation of voting schemes with incomplete information, both conceptually and computationally. At the same time, resolution of these issues allows one to design mechanisms for preference aggregation that have less stringent informational requirements, are more robust with respect to missing information, and minimize the cognitive and communication burden on voters.

We have focused on a few select topics related to voting and partial information. Many interesting avenues are uncovered in this chapter, indeed, several important topics have yet to be addressed in the literature. We list a few here:

- *Manipulation, strategic voting, and equilibrium analysis*: Manipulation and control of elections—and more generally the strategic revelation of preferences—is a topic of great importance (see Chapter 6 and Chapter 7), but much of this work assumes that manipulators have full knowledge of the vote profile. Equilibrium analysis of various voting rules (Majumdar and Sen, 2004; Ángel Ballester and Rey-Biel, 2009) usually assumes (more realistically) that voters have incomplete knowledge in the form of a common prior. Algorithmic and computational study of the complexity and impact of manipulation under more realistic incomplete knowledge assumptions has been sparse, but is clearly of vital importance. See Conitzer et al. (2011a) and Lu et al. (2012) for some steps in this direction. At the same time, many of the models discussed in this chapter—those for vote elicitation, dealing with uncertain alternatives, and learning voting rules in particular—bring with them new opportunities for vote manipulation and control which require novel forms of analysis. Equilibrium analysis for these new models is also required (e.g., see the work of Dutta et al. (2001); Lang et al. (2013), who provide an equilibrium analysis of candidates who choose to enter or abstain from an election).
- *Combinatorial domains*: Effective means for voting in combinatorial domains is clearly vital to the practical deployment of the sophisticated preference aggregation mechanisms (see Chapter 9). We have left unaddressed issues associated with incomplete information in such settings. Incremental vote elicitation schemes for combinatorial domains have been few (though see Chapter 9 for discussion of sequential voting mechanisms using combinatorial representations). Preference elicitation schemes in nonvoting contexts have been developed for multiattribute preference representations such as CP-networks and soft constraint formalisms (Koriche and Zanuttini, 2010; Dimopoulos et al., 2009; Gelain et al., 2010), and these could be adapted to vote elicitation. However, many of the other topics touched on in this chapter have not been addressed in combinatorial settings.
- *Other forms of social choice*: Our focus in this chapter has been on social choice in the "voting" sense. Of course, a variety of other social choice problems are amenable

to the same types of partial information analysis discussed here, including two-sided matching (Chapter 14), coalitional matching and group formation (Chapter 15), assignment problems, multiwinner (or committee) voting problems (Chapter 9), fair division (Chapters 11–13) among others. For example, communication complexity, matching with incomplete information, and incremental preference elicitation have begun to garner attention in the stable matching domain (Chou and Lu, 2010; Pini et al., 2011b; Drummond and Boutilier, 2013; Rastegari et al., 2013; Liu et al., 2012).

PART II
Fair Allocation

CHAPTER 11

Introduction to the Theory of Fair Allocation

William Thomson

11.1 Introduction

The purpose of this chapter is to briefly introduce the theory of fair allocation in the context of concretely specified economic environments. There, requirements of fairness are expressed in terms of resources and opportunities understood in their physical sense. Thus, it contrasts with abstract social choice theory as this expression is commonly understood: in the canonical Arrovian model (Part I), the alternatives available to society are not structured in any particular way, whereas in models of resource allocation, the space of feasible alternatives is equipped with a variety of mathematical structures, topological, vectorial, and order structures. This enrichment has implications on several levels. First, when we specify the model itself, we can include properties of preferences reflecting these structures that would not be meaningful without them. Second, we can formulate properties of allocation rules referring to the structures. Finally, we can define allocation rules that are based on the structures.

Abstract social choice theory and the theory of fair allocation have the same constructive objective, however, namely, to identify the "best" way of reconciling the conflicting interests of the participants. In each case, we can distinguish two branches of the literature. The normative branch focuses on the distribution of welfare throughout the population. It starts with the formulation of criteria of fairness, and it studies their implications. The strategic branch is concerned with the fact that agents have some control over resources, technologies, and the information about the outside world or their own preferences, and that they may try to take advantage of this control. Ideally, the allocation process should be safe from manipulation of resources or technologies, by individual or by groups, and from misrepresentation of their knowledge of the environment or of their preferences. We focus on the normative branch here but there is not a complete conceptual separation between normative and strategic considerations; some properties of rules can be interpreted from either viewpoint; also, from a technical perspective, the two branches are linked in multiple ways.

The primary aim of abstract social choice theory is to define social orderings over the set of alternatives, whereas most of the theory we review here deals with how to choose,

261

for each economy, one (or several) allocation(s) from a set. These allocations can of course be understood as maximizing an implicit social ordering (the two-indifference-class ordering in which the higher indifference class consists of the allocations that are chosen, and the lower one consists of the allocations that are not chosen), but no attempt is made at elucidating these orderings themselves, and in particular, at deriving fine orderings from desirable properties of the process of preference aggregation. For an up-to-date treatment and new perspectives on such derivations, see Fleurbaey and Maniquet (2011).

Given the space constraints we face, we are unable to give extensive references to primary sources and instead, we refer to surveys. They concern either a specific principle or a particular type of allocation problems. General references are Young (1995b), Brams and Taylor (1996), Moulin (1995), Moulin (2004), Barbanel (2005), Thomson (2011), and Thomson (2014d). We focus on the axiomatic approach to fairness. We ignore the experimental literature, how lotteries can be used to achieve fairness in the ex ante sense, and strategic issues. Among the multiple types of allocation problems in which fairness have recently been addressed, we chose some that we felt were representative of the literature as a whole. A large number of papers focus on the interaction of normative and strategic requirements, in particular the incentive that allocation rules provide agents to be truthful about their preferences (Barberà, 2011). We have chosen not to review this literature. Also, several of the chapters in this volume address such issues (Chapters 1, 6, and 14).

Finally, we do not consider computational issues. These are already the central focus of many of the other chapters in this volume. It has been very rewarding to economists who have been involved in the development of the theory of fairness to see the increasing interest that the computer science community has taken in the subject. This interest has been uneven, however. The concept of an envy-free allocation, the classical problem of fair division, the division of a measure space, and various types of allocation problems with discrete structures, such as object allocation or reallocation problems and two-sided matching, have indeed received considerable attention in this community, but there are other facets of the theory, a range of other concepts and other types of allocation problems on which it has not yet brought to bear its own perspectives and techniques, and we hope that this survey will help further cross-fertilization between computer science and economics. Examples are the punctual notions of egalitarian-equivalence and of equal opportunities, and the many relational solidarity requirements that have been critical in axiomatic analysis. As for types of allocation problems that would benefit from being more closely examined from the computational angle, are problems with satiated preferences, claims problems, cost allocation problems (they come in a great variety), and public goods problems. Here is not the place to be formal; these terms are defined in what follows.

We first describe a generic allocation problem, listing its components. We introduce several standard, and some not so standard, classes of allocation problems. Next, we introduce the principles that constitute the conceptual core of the literature under review. We hope to show that in spite of the great diversity in the axioms that have been studied, they can all be seen as expressions of just a few general principles. However, because each class of problems has its own mathematical structure, these principles often have to be adapted. Also, the implications of a particular combination of principles often

differ significantly from one class to the other. It is also the case that for some classes
of problems, additional concepts may be available that are not meaningful in others.

11.2 What Is a Resource Allocation Problem?

We begin with a presentation of the data needed to specify an allocation problem, and
we continue with a sample of problem types. We chose them to illustrate the scope of
the program surveyed here.

11.2.1 The Components of an Allocation Problem

An *economy* has several of the following components:

1. A set of *agents*: this term may refer to individual people, to government agencies, to
   firms, or to other entities, such as "artificial" agents acting on behalf of "real" agents.
2. *Resource data* concerns unproduced endowments of goods that can be either consumed
   as such or, when production opportunities are specified, used as input in the production
   process; in that case, we also specify production sets and we may attach productivity
   parameters to agents or to groups. From all of the data we derive feasible sets or opportunity sets open to agents or to groups. In general equilibrium theory, a production plan
   is a point in commodity space interpreted as a feasible input-output combination. Some
   of the inputs may be labor inputs, and because people may be differently productive,
   productivity parameters may be specified, giving the rate at which each person's labor
   time can be converted into abstract labor.
3. *Ownership data* may concern unproduced resources or production processes. Ownership
   may be *individual*: a particular agent may own a particular resource, his house, his own
   self. It can be *semi-collective*: a particular group of agents may own a particular resource,
   for example a married couple may jointly own the house in which they live. It may be
   collective: the entire agent set may own a particular resource; for example, a nation owns
   its cultural patrimony. It may be *mixed*: some resources may be owned privately; other
   resources may be owned by a group of agents; yet others may be owned by the entire agent
   set; an example here consists of the housing units to which some students are returning
   at the beginning of the academic year and that they have the right to keep—in a sense,
   these resources are owned by these students—and the units that have been vacated by the
   students who graduated and left—these constitute a collective endowment. Ownership
   may be contested, disagreement over it resulting in incompatible *claims*.
4. *Priority data* indicates the precedence to be given to particular agents over others.
   Priority can be *absolute*, as when a linear order is specified on the agent set, no two agents
   being at the same level. Alternatively, it may be *relative*, with nontrivial indifference
   classes. It may be restricted and structured, because of upper bounds on how much
   agents are allowed to get. Then, once the highest-priority agent has been given his
   assignment—here, it is difficult to describe the data without suggesting how they may
   be used—we need to specify who comes next, who comes after this second agent, and
   so on. The structure may take the form of a limit on the scope of priorities, as when
   a priority is attached to only some of the resources, or when different priorities are

attached to different resources. In any of these situations, giving priority to an agent does not mean giving him control over, or access to, every single resource.

5. *Preference data* concerns natural properties that, for each class of problems under investigation, we expect preferences to satisfy; these properties depend in an important way on the mathematical structure of the set of possible consumptions for an agent, that is, on the nature of the resources to be assigned. To illustrate, when goods are infinitely divisible, consumption bundles are vectors in a Euclidean space. This space is equipped with topological, order, and convex structures, and we can require preferences to satisfy continuity, monotonicity, and convexity properties. Using the notation $a \succsim b$ to mean that a is at least as desirable as b, and $a \succ b$ to mean that a is preferred to b, these properties can be written as follows: (i) if $x_i \succ_i y_i$, x_i' is sufficiently close to x_i and y_i' is sufficiently close to y_i, then $x_i' \succ_i y_i'$; (ii) if $y_i \geqslant x_i$, then $y_i \succ_i x_i$, and (iii) given any bundle x_i, $\{y_i \mid y_i \succsim_i x_i\}$ is a convex set.

6. *Bounds* may be imposed on consumptions. They may be lower bounds or upper bounds. We may require a minimal consumption of a particular good (education), or we may require a maximal consumption of a good (only one time slot per person for some activity).

We will not discuss models that include utility information. We will not attempt to measure welfare gains and losses on cardinal scales, let alone compare such quantities across agents. Indeed, an important development of the last decades is that purely ordinal criteria have gained general acceptance. They save us from having to address the delicate conceptual and practical issues raised by the use of utilities. Besides, as we will see, we will have to present a number of negative results and the mild form of our ordinal criteria will make these results all the more striking. When positive results emerge, they are often uniqueness results, and in such cases, even if cardinal information were available, it would have to be ignored. We do not mean to suggest that an ordinal approach is superior to a utility based approach, but it is its ordinal character that makes the recent literature on fairness particularly noteworthy as compared to traditional welfare economics, and it is the literature that we survey.

Once we have specified all of this data, we have a *domain* of economies. Our objective is not just to make a recommendation for the particular allocation problem that we happen to face today, but to make a recommendation for each problem in some domain of interest. This takes us to the concept of a solution or rule (Section 11.3).

11.2.2 A Range of Resource Allocation Problems

Fairness issues have been studied in the context of a great variety of resource allocation problems. We have chosen several of them to illustrate the central concepts.

1. *Classical fair division problems.* A social endowment $\Omega \in \mathbb{R}_+^\ell$ of ℓ infinitely divisible goods has to be distributed among a group N of agents. Each agent $i \in N$ is equipped with a preference relation $\succsim_i$ over ℓ-dimensional commodity space $\mathbb{R}_+^\ell$. These preferences satisfy "classical" assumptions of continuity, monotonicity, and convexity.

2. *Fair division problems with single-peaked preferences* (Sprumont, 1991). A social endowment $\Omega \in \mathbb{R}_+$ of a single commodity has to be *fully* (there is no possibility of disposal) distributed among a group N of agents. Each agent $i \in N$ has preferences

$\succsim_i$ with the following features: up to some critical level, his *peak amount*, denoted $p(\succsim_i)$, an increase in agent i's consumption increases his welfare, but beyond that level, the opposite holds: for each pair x_i, x_i' such that either $x_i' < x_i \leqslant p(\succsim_i)$ or $p(\succsim_i) \leqslant x_i < x_i'$, we have $x_i \succ x_i'$. Such preferences are *single-peaked*. An example is the parceling out among workers of a task that must be completed, when each worker is paid a fixed wage and has convex preferences in leisure-income space. Thus, the model differs from the previous one (essentially) in that there is only one commodity here and the assumption of monotonicity of preferences is dropped; however, the assumption of convexity is retained. Violations of monotonicity raise challenging questions even in the one-commodity case.

3. *Claims problems* (O'Neill, 1982). A social endowment $\Omega \in \mathbb{R}_+$ of a single good has to be distributed among a group N of agents with incompatible *claims* on it. Denoting by $c_i \in \mathbb{R}_+$ the claim of agent $i \in N$, incompatibility means that $\sum c_i > \Omega$. Agents have monotonic preferences. (Thus there is no need to include preferences explicitly in the formal description of a problem: there is only one monotone preference relation defined over the nonnegative reals.) A typical application is to bankruptcy: the liquidation value of a bankrupt firm does not allow to fully satisfy all of its creditors. Mathematically, the problem of raising taxes from the users of a public project as a function of their incomes to cover the cost of the project, or as a function of the benefits they derive from it, is equivalent. Surveys are Thomson (2003) and Thomson (2014a). A related class of problems are surplus-sharing problems. They differ from claims problems in that the endowment exceeds the sum of the claims. It is also meaningful to jointly study both claims and surplus-sharing problems.

4. *Partitioning nonhomogeneous continua.* A social endowment consisting of an infinitely divisible and nonhomogeneous continuum has to be partitioned among a group N of agents. The dividend is a measure space and each agent $i \in N$ has preferences defined over its measurable subsets. In the base model, agent i's preferences $\succ_i$ are monotonic with respect to set inclusion (if $I \supset I'$, then $I \succ_i I'$).

It is also common to take the dividend to be a subset of a finite-dimensional Euclidean space and the one-dimensional case is of special interest. Think of an interval of time $I \subset \mathbb{R}_+$ during which a service is provided, for example, maintenance or repair work on a machine, or instruction on how to use it. The value of the service to an agent depends on how long it lasts and when it is provided, and it varies from agent to agent. In many situations, such as the service example just mentioned, it makes sense to require that each agent be assigned an interval, but not always, as when the issue is to schedule when students in a group will be assigned weekly individual review or practice sessions with tutors. (Chapter 13 discusses algorithmic issues in this context.)

The one-dimensional continuum may be circular. An example here is a market around a lake in a mountain resort that has to be partitioned into intervals to be assigned to ice-cream or souvenir vendors, their potential customers being unevenly distributed around the lake. A cake on which frosting and decorations are distributed unevenly and that has to be partitioned into slices is another example.

The dividend may be undesirable in the sense that of two intervals related by inclusion, the smaller one is preferred to the larger one. Here, and in the context of the tutoring example mentioned previously, think of the teaching assistants who have to staff the office where they will help out students with their homework assignments, and of police patrolling the road around the lake.

As illustrations of the two-dimensional case, consider the problem of partitioning farmland bequeathed by a farmer to his children, or assigning tracts of land to mining companies for gas or oil exploration, or the ocean floor for nations to exploit minerals lying there.

Much of the literature concerns the case of preferences that can be represented by atomless measures. This additivity assumption is restrictive, as it precludes the possibility that a subset be valuable only if some other subset is consumed with it (that is, it rules out complementarities), or conversely that a subset not be valuable because some other subset is already included in someone's assignment (the two subsets are substitutes then). Additional topological and geometric—we could say "geographic" in the case of land—criteria are sometimes meaningful. For instance, it may make sense to require connectedness of each component of the partition, or contiguity of each agent's assignment to some prespecified endowment that is not part of the redistribution.

5. *Object allocation problems.* A social endowment O of indivisible goods, or *objects*, has to be assigned to a group N of agents. Each agent $i \in N$ can consume only one and has preferences $\succ_i$ defined over O. The objects are the only resources. This is the base case of an *object allocation problem*. Think of offices to assign to the members of an academic department moving to a new building, or of tasks to be assigned by a foreman to the workers in his team (see also Chapter 12).

More generally, each agent $i \in N$ may consume several objects and have preferences defined over 2^O. Estate or divorce settlements often involve multiple indivisible items (painting, silverware) and each heir will receive several. Selling these resources and dividing the proceeds among the intended recipients may come to mind as a solution but this may be very imperfect. Indeed, these resources may have value to them that are not recognized on the market (family heirlooms), or legal constraints may prevent appealing to a market altogether (organs).

The simplest case is when the numbers of objects and agents are equal. When there are fewer objects than agents, some agents have to go without one. We allow for this possibility and augment the set of objects by a *null object*; by definition, there are always enough copies of it for each agent to receive one (real or null) object. An object is *desirable* for an agent if he prefers it to the null object, and *undesirable* if the opposite holds. When there are fewer agents than objects, some objects have to be unassigned. In some applications, it is natural to require that the null object not be assigned until all real objects are, even if these objects are undesirable, or undesirable for some agents. An example here is the problem of assigning household tasks to housemates. None of them may enjoy a particular task; yet, the task has to be performed (cleaning, for example); alternatively, some of them may find a particular task desirable and others not (cooking a meal illustrates the possibility).

6. *Objects-and-money allocation problems.* We enrich the previous model by adding a social endowment of one infinitely divisible good that, with some abuse of language, we call "money." Each agent $i \in N$ can consume some amount of money and one object. Consumptions of money may be unrestricted in sign, or they may be required to meet a lower bound (for example zero). Thus, each agent has preferences defined over the cross-product $\mathbb{R} \times O$, perhaps $[a, \infty[\times O$ for some $a \in \mathbb{R}$. They are continuous,

strictly monotonic with respect to money, and such that, starting from any bundle, replacing the object it contains by any other object can always be compensated by an appropriate change in the consumption of money. Here too, the base situation is when the numbers of objects and agents are equal. An example is the problem of assigning students to rooms in the house they are renting together, and specifying for each of them his share of the rent.

As in plain object-allocation problems, when there are fewer objects than agents, some agents have to go without one. As before, we then augment the set of objects by a null object. In the room-assignment–and–rent-division example, the null object can be interpreted as "looking for other accommodation." When the null object is available, we say that a real object is "desirable" for an agent if, given any bundle that includes it (that is, no matter how much of the divisible good is consumed with it), replacing it by the null object leads to a bundle that is at most as desirable. An object is "undesirable" if the opposite always holds.

7. *Priority-augmented object allocation problems* (Balinski and Sönmez, 1999; Abdulkadiroğlu and Sönmez, 2003). Here, we enrich the object allocation problem in a different way, by imagining that each object $a \in O$ is equipped with a *priority order* π_a over its possible recipients. An example is "school choice": the objects are seats in schools; at each school, a priority order over students is given (the order may depend on several factors: whether a student already has a sibling in the school; whether he lives in the "walk-zone" of the school; how long he has been on the waiting list; his academic record; and so on). At each school $a \in O$, a capacity κ_a is specified. In that application, indifference has to be allowed: two seats at a given school have to be considered equivalent by a student, but indifference is very structured in the sense that any two students are indifferent between all the seats at each school. (For a survey, see Abdulkadiroglu (2013).)

8. *Matching agents to each other.* Now, we a priori partition the agent set into two sets. Each agent has preferences over the agents in the component of the partition to which he does not belong. The objective is to make pairs containing one agent from each set. There is a wide variety of matching models, however: (*i*) the option of not being matched may be present or not; (*ii*) in the base model, matching is one-to-one, an example here is when men and women have to be paired for a dance class, or when medical students have to be matched to hospital programs for residency; matching may also be several-to-one, an example being when high-school graduates have to be assigned to colleges; several-to-several matching are possible in some situations, an application here being when a worker can work for several firms and a firm can employ several workers; (*iii*) preferences may be strict or indifference may be allowed; (*iv*) there may also be some amount of an infinitely divisible good, typically money, to distribute, and here, how much of it there is may be derived from the pairs that are formed. There, agents may only care about how much of the divisible resource they are assigned, not about to whom they are paired, or they may care about both. An application here is the assignment of workers to firms, when each pair of a worker and a firm is worth so many dollars (or when each pair consisting of a set of workers and a firm is worth so many dollars), and the amount to divide is the sum of the worths generated by all the pairs that are created. In the simplest case, illustrated by the men-women metaphor, $N = M \cup W$, each $i \in M$ has preferences over W and each $i \in W$

has preferences over M. For the problem of pairing workers and firms, to each pair (w, f) is associated a number $a(w, f)$, and the amount to divide is $\sum a(w, f)$ over all pairs (w, f) that are formed. An introduction to the literature is Roth and Sotomayor (1990) (also see Chapter 14). Related to two-sided pairing problems are *roommate problems*, which are one-to-one pairing problems in which each agent can be matched to any other agent. The theory of coalition formation is a generalization. There, the agent set has to be partitioned into subsets, taking the preferences of each agent over all subsets into account.

Listing the components of an allocation problem in the manner we did earlier raises a number of questions. What does it mean to say that a resource is a "social endowment," that an agent "owns" a resource, that a priority order on the possible recipients is attached to a resource, that a priority order on the possible recipients is attached to each of several resources? What is the operational meaning of these expressions? How should they be reflected in properties of allocation mappings?

11.3 Solutions and Rules

A *solution* associates with each problem in the class under investigation a non-empty subset of its set of feasible allocations. A *rule* is a *single-valued* solution. Thus, a rule provides a complete answer to the question of how to allocate resources in each particular problem in the class under investigation. A solution only achieves a first-round elimination of alternatives, the process through which a final outcome is determined being left unspecified.

We can arrive at solutions and rules in a variety of ways.

(*i*) A solution may formally describe what we observe in actual practice. It is important to understand what is done in the real world, to know the desirable features as well as the undesirable features of common practices. Societies have occasionally hit upon attractive procedures to resolve conflicts over allocation of resources, and we may be able to draw useful lessons from scrutinizing these procedures. Examples are rules based on equality, proportionality, priority, lotteries, and prices. Of course, for this exercise to be meaningful, we have to formulate criteria of desirability. We turn to them next.

(*ii*) The core of the second approach are principles of good behavior of solutions or rules. An "axiom" is the mathematical expression of some intuition we have about how a solution or rule should behave in certain situations. An axiomatic study starts with a list of axioms and its goal is to describe the implications of the axioms when imposed in various combinations. The ultimate goal of the axiomatic program is to trace out the boundary that separates those combinations of axioms that are compatible from those that are not. (Chapter 2 is an example of a chapter that is mainly axiomatic, but axioms are discussed throughout the book.)

The scope of certain principles is very broad, that is, these principles can be meaningfully expressed in almost any model. An example is the economist's central notion of "Pareto-efficiency": an allocation x is *efficient* (for short) for some economy if there is no other allocation x' that all agents find at least as desirable and at least one agent prefers, that is, such that for each $i \in N$, $x'_i \succsim_i x_i$ and for some $j \in N$, $x'_j \succ x_j$. Other principles, although not totally model-free, still have a broad range of applicability. An example is the *no-envy* notion (Foley, 1967),[1] according to which no agent prefers someone else's assignment to his own: there is no pair $i, j \in N$ such that $x_j \succ_i x_i$. The permutations on which it is based presume that all agents' preferences are defined over the same space, and that if agents differ in some relevant dimension other than preferences, some adjustments can be made to place them on the same footing. For instance, when the issue is to reallocate bundles that agents privately own, and calling ω_i and ω_j agent i and j's endowments, we can adapt it by requiring that there is no pair $i, j \in N$ such that $[\omega_i + (x_j - \omega_j)] \succ_i x_i$. This is the notion of *no-envy in trades* (Kolm, 1972; Schmeidler and Vind, 1972). The no-envy notion makes the most sense when applied to the distribution or redistribution of private resources. It is silent in models of "pure" public choice, where by definition, all agents consume the same thing and a compromise has to be found on what that common assignment should be because agents differ in how they value it.

Other principles may be applicable in several contexts but in each particular one, some adaptation is needed, and various expressions of the idea may be meaningful. Monotonicity requirements come to mind here and we will give several examples to illustrate the point.

Some of the principles directly define solutions and rules, and others only place constraints on how the choice of an allocation may vary in response to changes in the data of a problem. For instance, efficient allocations exist almost always. Thus, we can speak of the solution that selects for each economy its set of efficient allocations. By contrast, the self-explanatory requirement of *equal treatment of equals* does not suggest the definition of a solution, because there are many economies in which no two agents have the same characteristics. And even if some agents do have the same characteristics, what should their common consumption be and what are we supposed to assign to the others?

(*iii*) The well-developed theory of cooperative games is also a good source of inspiration for solution concepts and principles. However, the models that are studied in that theory are "abstract" in the sense that only sets of achievable utility vectors are given. The description of the actual physical choices that agents have is typically not included in their specification. By contrast, we are interested here in settling concretely specified resource allocation problems. Part of the conceptual work to undertake when exploiting the theory of cooperative games is to find the most natural expressions in the context of the model under study of the principles that have been important in that theory. Alternatively, we can map the allocation problems under investigation into games and apply solutions introduced in the theory of games to solve these games. A resource allocation problem can often be mapped into a game in more than one way, however (the result may be a bargaining problem, a transferable utility game, or a nontransferable utility game), and proceeding in this way will give us the opportunity to apply different solution concepts of game theory to solve our allocation problem.

(*iv*) Rules that are common in one area may serve as a source of inspiration in defining new rules in other areas. For example, for the standard model of general

---

[1] This notion is also called "envy-freeness."

equilibrium, in which agents may have different endowments, the central rule is the *Walrasian rule*: given some prices p in the simplex of $\mathbb{R}_+^\ell$, we let each agent i maximize his preferences $\succsim_i$ in his budget set (the set of bundles x_i whose value px_i does not exceed the value $p\omega_i$ of his endowment ω_i), and adjust prices so as to obtain equality of demand and supply: $\sum x_i^* = \sum x_i$, where x_i^* designates agent i's maximizing bundle.[2] To solve classical fair division problems, we operate this rule from equal division, that is, we endow each agent with an equal share $\frac{\Omega}{|N|}$ of the social endowment. We thereby obtain the *equal-division Walrasian rule*, the rule that comes to the minds of most economists first. It has the merit of offering to all agents the same opportunities, these opportunities being defined through prices. For single-peaked allocation problems, the *uniform rule U* can also be seen in the light of equal opportunities (Sprumont, 1991). "Budget sets" here are intervals from the origin to some upper bound if the sum of the peak amounts exceeds the social endowment, and from some lower bound to the social endowment otherwise: given $e \equiv (\Omega, \succ) \in \mathcal{E}_{sp}^N$, if $\sum p(\succsim_i) \geqslant \Omega$, then for some $\lambda \in \mathbb{R}_+$ and for each $i \in N$, $U_i(e) = \min\{p(\succ_i), \lambda\}$; if $\sum p(\succsim_i) \leqslant \Omega$, then for some $\lambda \in \mathbb{R}_+$ and for each $i \in N$, $U_i(e) = \max\{p(\succ_i), \lambda\}$;

For priority-augmented object allocation problems, the theory of two-sided matching has been important in defining solutions. Prominent rules are the *immediate acceptance rule*, according to which we identify the various agents' most preferred objects and we assign each object to the agents listing it first, in the order of their priority for that object, until its supply is exhausted; we reject the others; at the next round, each rejected agent "applies" to his second most preferred object. We repeat the operation with them, after adjusting the supplies of the objects down by the number of times it has been assigned at the first round. We proceed until each agent has been assigned an object. For the *tentative acceptance rule*[3] (Chapter 14), at each round we only tentatively assign objects and keep as potential assignees of each object those recipients who have the highest priority among those we kept on as potential assignees at the previous round and the agents who are newly requesting it. As for the immediate acceptance rule, each agent whom we reject at some round applies to his next most preferred object at the next round. The algorithms stop when no one is rejected.

11.3.1 Axioms

Our goal here is not just to try to understand the implications of fairness requirements for allocation rules; we have to define fairness to begin with. Perhaps we should begin by requiring that all agents should be treated equally, that they should be put "on the same level." The objective of treating all "equal" agents "equally" seems rather limited if by "equal" agents we mean agents that nothing distinguishes in their formal descriptions. Indeed, it would not cover many situations. Because in discrete allocation problems, there are finitely many possible preferences, it is applicable to a positive fraction of all preference profiles but otherwise, there may be few agents with the same

---

[2] A pair (p, x) as just described is often called an "equal-income competitive equilibrium," and the allocation x an "equal-income equilibrium allocation." The mapping that associates with each economy its equilibrium allocations is also known as the "equal-income competitive equilibrium correspondence."

[3] Commonly known as the "deferred acceptance rule."

characteristics, or none. Besides, it will not be enough: equal assignments may not be compatible with efficiency. They may not even exist. Again, an example here is, when the resources to allocate present indivisibilities. In an object allocation problem in which all agents have the same preferences, it obviously cannot be met.

The real challenge is to recognize differences between agents when they exist, and to treat these differences appropriately. What should we do when two agents have different preferences? When they have contributed differently to the production of the resources available for distribution, either in labor time, or because they are differently productive, or both? When they differ which respect to claims they have, resources they control, or characteristics that are not related to economic activities, such as record of service or medical condition?

Recognizing departures from fairness, measuring them, assessing their significance, and perhaps redressing them, is also part of the study of fairness. Developing menus of parameterized rules from which the user of the theory can choose so as to best fit his need for a differential treatment of different agents is another objective of the theory of fairness.

11.3.2 Punctual Axioms

We can distinguish between different types of requirements on solutions and rules. We begin with *punctual requirements*, that is, requirements that apply to each economy separately, "point by point." The question to be addressed then concerns the existence, for each economy in the domain under consideration, of allocations satisfying the axiom. When a punctual axiom meaningfully restricts the set of possible allocations of each economy—we could say that it has *full coverage* then—it defines a solution or a rule. Here are the central ideas.[4]

(*i*) *Bounds on physical assignments or on welfares* can be defined agent by agent, in an "intra-personal" way. They are usually *lower bounds*, offering each agent a guarantee that at the allocation chosen by a rule, his welfare will be above a certain level, defined in terms of the social endowment and his preferences. Others are *upper bounds*, specifying for each agent a ceiling on his welfare. Imposing such a ceiling can be seen as another way of preventing the others from being unduly burdened by his presence.

To illustrate, for classical fair division problems, an allocation satisfies *no-domination of, or by, equal division*, if (*i*) no agent is assigned at least as much as an equal share of the social endowment of each good and more than an equal share of the social endowment of at least one good, or (*ii*) at most as much as an equal share of the social endowment of each good and less than an equal share of the social endowment of at least one good, that is, there is no $i \in N$ such that either $x_i \geq \frac{\Omega}{|N|}$ or $x_i \leq \frac{\Omega}{|N|}$.

The notion just defined is preference-free, by contrast with the next ones. An allocation x satisfies the *equal-division lower bound* if each agent finds his assignment at

---

[4] In social choice theory (Part I), the distinction is often made between intra-profile axioms and inter-profile axioms, but we prefer avoiding this language because a relational axiom may have to do with a change in a single parameter, not a change in a profile of parameters.

least as desirable as equal division: for each $i \in N$, $x_i \succsim \frac{\Omega}{|N|}$ (among many others, Kolm, 1972; Pazner, 1977).[5]

Having all agents *share the benefit, or the burden, of their diversity* is another important idea. If one had the choice of joining an economy in which agents have different preferences from one's own or joining one in which they have similar preferences, which decision should one make? Of course, it depends on how the resources would be allocated but in an economy of clones, *efficiency* and the minimal requirement of *equal treatment of equals* together usually determine the allocation. It also depends on the nature of the goods and, when they have to be produced, on the properties of the technologies under which they are produced. Let us answer the question in the context of some of our models.

In a classical fair division problem, diversity is a good thing. When agents have the same convex preferences, equal division is efficient. Introducing diversity allows distributions that all agents prefer to equal division, and ensuring that all agents benefit from their diversity is a meaningful objective. One way to implement it is as follows: for each agent, imagine the hypothetical situation in which everyone else would have his preferences. Then, if preferences are convex, under efficiency and equal treatment of equals, the common welfare of these clones would be what they experience at equal division. Returning to the actual economy, sharing the benefits of diversity would be translated into the requirement that each agent's welfare level at his assignment be at least as high as the common welfare level that he and his clones would experience in this counterfactual economy. This is simply the equal-division lower bound. In other models, the reference to economies of clones has led to new lower bounds, however.

In other situations, diversity is a burden. When it comes to the production of private goods under increasing returns-to-scale, or the production of public goods, similarity of preferences is preferable.

In yet others, diversity may be a good thing or a bad thing depending upon particular features of the economy, and we can refer to economies of clones to define a bound that is a lower bound or an upper bound.

(*ii*) *Requirements based on inter-personal comparisons of assignments, or more generally, "opportunities"* can also be defined. We can base these comparisons on exchanges of these objects, or perhaps on other operations performed on them.

Recall the definition of an envy-free allocation. The no-envy notion can be adapted to assess the relative treatment of groups of agents too: an allocation x is *group envy-free* if given any two groups of the same size, G and G', we cannot redistribute among the members of G what has been assigned in total to the members of G', namely, $\sum_{G'} x_i$, so as to make each member of G at least as well off as he was at x, and at least one of them better off. We can adapt the definition to accommodate groups of different sizes, by performing calculations on a per capita basis, that is, by making available to G the bundle $\frac{|N|}{|N'|} \sum_{G'} x_i$.

The next definition is based on evaluating an allocation by comparison to a counterfactual allocation at which all agents would receive the same bundle: equivalently, the allocation x is *egalitarian-equivalent* if there is a "reference" bundle x_0 that each agent

---

[5] This requirement is usually called "individual rationality from equal division."

finds indifferent to his assignment: for each $i \in N$, $x_i \sim_i x_0$ (Pazner and Schmeidler, 1978). Then, the "obvious" fairness of a hypothetical allocation composed of multiple copies of the same bundle x_0—hypothetical because this list of identical bundles is not usually feasible—is transferred to the allocation x that is being evaluated through Pareto indifference. The definition is not very restrictive; in fact, one can argue that it is too permissive. For instance in the context of classical fair division problems, it is easy to construct examples in which some agent is assigned a share of the resources that is arbitrarily close to one. However, for this model, we can define various selections from this correspondence that have considerable interest. Fix a direction r in commodity space. An allocation x is *r-egalitarian-equivalent* if there is $\lambda \in \mathbb{R}_+$ such that for each $i \in N$, $x_i \sim_i \lambda r$. When $r = \Omega$, the resulting rule is particularly attractive. For example, it also meets the equal-division lower bound.

More generally, we may require the reference bundle to belong to some path G in commodity space that emanates from the origin, is monotone and whose projection on each axis is unbounded. Then, x is *G-egalitarian-equivalent* if there is $x_0 \in G$ such that for each $i \in N$, $x_i \sim_i x_0$. The considerations underlying the no-envy and egalitarian-equivalence criteria (and variants) seem to be far removed from each other but in fact, they can be seen as special cases of a general definition (Thomson, 1994b). We can construct for each agent $i \in N$, a representation of his preferences by "calibrating on G" as follows: to each bundle $x_0 \in \mathbb{R}^\ell_+$, declare the agent's welfare to be equal to the length of the part of G that extends from the origin to the point of G that he finds indifferent to x_0. Then, a G-egalitarian-equivalent allocation can be described as one at which all agents experience the same welfare. Note that the definition is entirely ordinal; it involves no utility considerations.

The success of the no-envy notion comes in part from the fact that it is well-defined in models in which equal division, and comparisons to equal division, are not meaningful or possible: they pertain to object allocation, object-and-money allocation, priority-augmented object-allocation, one-to-one matching, and the partitioning of nonhomogenous continua. The same comment applies to egalitarian-equivalence and some of its variants. Now, to say that a concept is meaningful is not to say that allocations satisfying it necessarily exist. In fact, we will see that discreteness of an allocation space raises serious existence problems.

The requirements discussed so far are most meaningful when ownership of resources is collective, but they can sometimes be adapted so as to take account of private ownership. This is particularly so in the context of classical fair division problems, because one can measure the vectorial difference between an agent's assignment and his endowment, and compare these differences across agents. For instance, the no-envy notion can be applied to trades, as we have seen. For object allocation problems for example, such tests are not meaningful.

11.3.3 Relational Requirements

A relational requirement prescribes how a rule should respond to changes in some parameter(s) of the economy. The most central notion here is that of *solidarity*: if the environment in which a group of agents find themselves changes, and if no one in this group is responsible for the change, that is, if no one deserves any credit or blame for it, the welfare of all of these agents should be affected in the same direction: either they should all be made at least as well off as they were made initially, or they should all be made at most as well off. The terms "credit" and "blame" suggest that the change is good and bad respectively, but in what sense? One possibility is that it causes an expansion of opportunities in the first case and a shrinking of opportunities in the second case. A narrower meaning is when the change is evaluated in relation to the choice made by the rule initially. In the first case, the change is good if a Pareto improvement over that initial choice is possible; in the second case, when it is not, the initially chosen profile of welfares is not feasible anymore.

In applications, the parameter often belongs to a space equipped with an order structure. Then, we can speak of the parameter being given a "greater" or "smaller" value in that order. Then, together with efficiency, and given the assumptions made on preferences, the solidarity requirement often implies a specific direction in which welfares be affected. We require then that when a Pareto improvement is possible, all agents be made at least as well off as they were made initially; otherwise, that they should all be made at most as well off. In such cases, solidarity takes the form of a "monotonicity" requirement.

Note, however, that efficiency considerations come into the picture here. Solidarity in its "pure" form simply says that when a change in the environment of a group of agents occurs for which none of them bears any particular responsibility, the welfares of all of its members should move in the same direction. Making all agents worse off when opportunities expand could only be described as a perverse application of the idea, but it is important to see that insisting on a weak improvement for everyone has to implicate more than solidarity considerations. It does not imply the full force of efficiency because an inefficient choice could of course be followed, after opportunities have expanded, by a Pareto-dominating choice that is also inefficient.

In some models, the general idea may be given several expressions, expressions that are based on the data of the problem. For example, when applied to object-and-money allocation problems, two requirements can be expressed, first a requirement of monotonicity with respect to expansions of the object set and second, a requirement of monotonicity with respect to the amount of money available. In the context of single-peaked allocation problems, the structure of the situation gives us no choice but to consider the general expression of the solidarity idea, not its "efficiency-inclusive" monotonicity expression. It simply says that any change in the endowment should affect the welfares of all agents in the same direction.

The parameter that varies may not belong to a space that is equipped with an order structure. Then, whether a change in its value is beneficial to society or not depends on the other parameters of the problem. The requirement of solidarity retains its general form, namely, that all agents be affected in the same direction, but this direction is not specified.

Finally, even if the parameter that varies belongs to a space that has an order structure, the solidarity requirement can be imposed whether or not the variation can be evaluated in that order.

In a model in which resources are valuable (whether that is the case is not intrinsic to these resources; it is deduced from monotonicity properties that preferences have), *resource monotonicity* says that if the social endowment increases, all agents should end up at least as well off as they were made initially (Roemer, 1986; Chun and Thomson, 1988): if $\Omega' \geqslant \Omega$, then for each $i \in N$, $x'_i \succsim_i x_i$.

Production opportunities may be part of the model and when the technology improves, *technology monotonicity* says that as a result of such an improvement, all agents should be made at least as well off as they were made initially (Roemer, 1986).

When variations in populations are within the scope of the analysis, and resources are valuable, *population monotonicity* says that if population enlarges, all agents initially present should be made at most as well off as they were made initially (Thomson, 1983; Chichilnisky and Thomson, 1987; for a survey, see Thomson, 2014c). For a formal definition, we imagine an infinite set of potential agents, and we call $\mathcal{N}$ the class of finite subsets of this population. Then, we require that for each pair N, $N' \in \mathcal{N}$ with $N \subset N'$, each pair of economies that differ only in their populations, and calling x and x' the choices made when the agent sets are N and N', then for each $i \in N$, $x_i \succsim_i x'_i$.

The order on the Euclidean space to which a social endowment of infinitely divisible resource belongs (the usual vectorial order) is incomplete. Thus, the restriction of the solidarity idea to situations in which two social endowments Ω and Ω' can be compared in these orders, that is when either $\Omega \geq \Omega'$ or the reverse hold suggests that we mostly feel comfortable imposing it in those situations. However, it is meaningful also when social endowments cannot be compared in these orders. For instance, Ω_1 may be greater than Ω'_1 and Ω_2 smaller than Ω'_2. A technology is a subset of commodity space and set inclusion is an incomplete order. Two technologies need not be related by inclusion, even when restricted to the region of the space in which they will have to be operated given input availability. Here too, the solidarity requirement with respect to technologies takes two forms, a weaker one for technologies that are related by inclusion and a stronger one, when they may not be.

Also, the solidarity idea does not only apply to "social," as opposed to "individual," parameters. When a parameter attached to a particular agent changes, it is meaningful to require that all others be affected in the same direction. This is the case for instance, in a classical fair division problem, if some agent's private endowment of a resource increases. That agent, with all of his characteristics, is part of the environment of the others.

Welfare dominance under preference replacement says that if the preferences of some agents change, each of the others should be made at least as well off as he was made initially, or that each of these agents should be made at most as well off (Moulin, 1990; for a survey, see Thomson, 1999). Let $N' \subset N$. Calling x and x' the choices made when the preferences of the group $N \setminus N'$ are given the values $(\succsim_i)_{N \setminus N'}$ and $(\succsim_i)_{N \setminus N'}$, then either for each $i \in N'$, $x_i \succsim_i x'_i$ or for each $i \in N'$, $x'_i \succsim_i x_i$. Indeed, for these agents, the members of $N \setminus N'$, are part of their environment, so once again, if none of the agents in N' has anything to do with the change, why should some be made better off and others worse off?

A problem with insisting on any of these solidarity requirements is that the change in the parameter that is contemplated may have very different impacts on the range of welfare levels attainable by the different agents. Insisting that all should be affected in the same direction may prevent realizing large welfare gains for some agents that would only be at a small cost for the others. Admittedly, the language of this limitation seems to rely on cardinal notions of welfare gains and losses as well as on interpersonal comparisons of these notions, but the idea can be expressed in a purely ordinal way.

Another application of the idea of solidarity in the context of a variable population is to situations in which some agents leave with their assignments, that is, after the solution is applied. Then, both the population of agents and the resources at their disposal vary, but they do not vary independently. The requirement that all remaining agents be affected in the same direction, when imposed together with efficiency, often means that these agents be indifferent between their new assignments and their initial assignments, and even, in some cases, that they be assigned the same bundles as initially. This is essentially what *consistency* expresses more directly, as follows: given an allocation chosen by a solution for some economy, let some agents leave with their assignments. In the resulting "reduced economy," require that the remaining agents be assigned the same bundles as initially. Returning to the variable-population model introduced in connection with population monotonicity, and calling x the choice made for some economy with agent set N, N' a subset of N, and x' the choice made for the economy with agent set N' when the endowment is what remains after the members of $N \setminus N'$ have left with their components of x, then x' should be equal to $x_{N'}$. Other interpretations of the principle are possible and some are discussed later (Thomson, 2012; for a survey, see Thomson, 2014b).

Converse consistency says that the desirability of an allocation for some economy can be deduced from the desirability of all of its restrictions to two agents for the associated reduced economy these agents face. If an allocation x that is feasible for some economy with agent set N is such that for each two-agent subgroup N' of N, its restrictions $x_{N'}$ is the choice made for the problem of dividing $\sum_{N'} x_i$ among them, then x should be chosen for the initial economy. The property does not have a straightforward fairness interpretation but we mention it here, as it is a natural complement to consistency. For some models, the property can also provide the basis for the iterative calculation of the allocations that a solution would select. The *Elevator Lemma* has been an important tool in the literature we review. It says that if a rule is consistent, a second rule is conversely consistent, and they coincide in the two-agent case, then they coincide in general.

Fairness also means that irrelevant considerations should not influence the allocation we choose. In particular, when having to deal with a change in a parameter of a problem, several equally legitimate perspectives may often be taken. Requiring the *robustness* of the choice we make with respect to which perspective is taken is desirable: these different perspectives should not produce welfare redistributions that favor some agents and hurt others. Here is a more concrete description of the idea. Consider some allocation problem and apply the chosen rule to obtain a recommendation for it. Now, suppose that, as we are about to implement this decision, a parameter of the problem takes a new value. One possibility is to ignore the initial situation, declare the initial choice irrelevant, and focus on the new situation. The other consists in taking the initial choice as point of departure and only be concerned about distributing the new opportunities or obligations associated with the change. After all, agents may have made plans on the expectation that a certain allocation will be implemented. Again, and because these two viewpoints appear equally legitimate, it is natural to impose the robustness requirement that all agents be indifferent between the two choices that can be made. Certain *composition* properties that have been formulated and extensively explored in the context of claims problems are applications of the idea, and they are beginning to be studied in other contexts, such as single-peaked allocation problems or object allocation problems.

Composition down is a property of rules to solve claims problems that pertains to the following scenario. After solving some initial problem in which the endowment is Ω, we discover it to be only $\Omega' < \Omega$. Two options present themselves. One is to ignore the initial awards vector we have chosen. The other is to take it as claims vector in dividing Ω'. The requirement is that both ways of proceeding lead to the same outcome.

Consistency itself can be seen from that robustness perspective. When some agents have taken their assignments and left, should we look at the situation anew for the remaining agents, redefine their opportunities and solve the reduced problem they now face, or should we stick with the initial choices we have made for them? Consistency says that it should not matter.

In practice, it is rarely the case that specific protocols are specified to handle changes in our environment. Not all contingencies are covered by the contracts we sign. And even if we think ahead of time about a particular contingency, there may not be a clear way of specifying which is the "right" way of dealing with it. A solution or rule that is robust to choices of perspectives is more likely to elicit a consensus among the agents whose application it would affect.

The comparisons on which all of the requirements just discussed are based can involve actual changes in the parameters of a problem; alternatively, they can be "thought experiments." Relational requirements are not necessarily meant to deal with the possibility that some parameter will change, but thinking about the possibility helps us assess the choice we make in the particular situation we face today, even if we will face no other similar situation.

11.4 A Sample of Results

How demanding is each of the requirements just introduced? What kinds of rules come out of the analysis? Are there some general answers? Given the great variety of the models that we have reviewed, and remember that we chose only a few to illustrate the scope of the axiomatic program, the reader should not expect sweeping statements about the state of the arts. Nevertheless, some useful observations can be made that apply across several domains.

11.4.1 Punctual Requirements

For classical fair division problems, the existence of efficient allocations satisfying the equal-division lower bound is easily established. That of efficient allocations satisfying no-envy holds under any set of assumptions guaranteeing the existence and efficiency of Walrasian allocations, because the Walrasian rule, when operated from equal division, delivers such allocations. In fact, these allocations are group envy-free. If preferences are not convex, efficient and envy-free allocations may not exist. On the other hand, efficient and egalitarian-equivalent allocations exist under very general assumptions. In particular, preferences need not be convex.

For single-peaked allocation problems, the issue of existence of efficient and envy-free allocations is easily settled thanks to the uniform rule. Indeed, recall our definition of the rule as selecting an allocation such that, for some common choice set, each agent maximizes his preferences at his component of the allocation. Because the choice set is the same for all agents, no-envy is automatically satisfied. Because this set is convex, the uniform rule meets the equal-division lower bound as well. However, for this model, egalitarian-equivalence is not a useful notion. Efficient and egalitarian-equivalent allocations almost never exist.

For object-and-money allocation problems, if consumptions of money are unrestricted in sign, general existence results for envy-free allocations are available (Alkan et al., 1991). The main assumption is that no object be infinitely more valuable than any other; this means that, given any bundle and any object not contained in that bundle, some change in the consumption of money should be possible to exactly compensate for the switch to that object. If consumptions of money are required to be nonnegative, or are bounded below, it is equally clear that efficient and envy-free allocations may not exist. Suppose for instance that, in the nonnegative case, the amount of money available is in fact equal to zero. Then, the situation reduces to that described in a forthcoming paragraph concerned with plain object allocation problems. If people have the same preferences over the objects in a set, envy is unavoidable. Keeping everything else fixed, as the amount of money increases from 0, the possibility of compensation progressively increases and an amount is eventually reached beyond which existence is guaranteed (Maskin, 1987). This critical amount obviously depends on preferences.

The specification of a priority-augmented object allocation problem includes reasons not to place agents on the same footing, namely, the priorities over agents attached to objects. It identifies circumstances under which envy is justified: an agent may prefer someone else's assignment to his own but his envy should be ignored if the priority attached to that second agent's assignment places him, the first agent, on a lower level. The existence of allocations at which there is no justified envy can be proved by applying the tentative acceptance rule developed in the theory of two-sided matching. Unfortunately, and unless the profile of priorities satisfies a strong correlation property, it may be that none of the allocations at which there is no justified envy is efficient.

For claims problems, there is no reason to require no-envy between two agents whose claims differ: the agent whose claim is higher should be allowed to receive more. If imposed on two agents with equal claims, no-envy simply means that they should be awarded equal amounts, the requirement of equal treatment of equals, a very weak requirement. We can go further, however: a natural strengthening is *order preservation in awards*, which says that awards should be ordered as claims are. We could be concerned about the losses that agents occur and add to order preservation that losses should be ordered as claims are (Aumann and Maschler, 1985). These ideas can be applied to groups of agents. Given two groups, aggregate awards should be ordered as aggregate claims, and so should aggregate losses. Allocations satisfying these stronger requirements always exist (Chambers and Thomson, 2002).

As mentioned earlier, for object allocation problems, it is obvious that no-envy cannot be guaranteed. Consider two objects and two agents, when both agents prefer the same object. Envy is unavoidable then. Criteria based on differences between the relative ranks in each agent's preferences of his assignment and the assignment of each other agent can be formulated, however.

For one-to-one matching problems, the scope of the envy relation should of course be restricted to agents of the same type, say between men, or between women, but again, because of the discrete nature of the resources to be allocated, envy-free matches will rarely exist. What about an equal treatment of the two groups, men and women? Discreteness gets in the way as well, but some things can be done. Say that a match is *stable* if there is no pair of a man and a woman who prefers each other to their assigned mates. It turns out that the set of stable matches has a lattice structure, one stable match being uniformly preferred by all the men to all other stable matches and another stable match being uniformly preferred by all the women to all other stable matches. Also, there is sort of middle to that lattice, a set of matches at which men and women, as groups, are treated "similarly" (Klaus and Klijn, 2006).

11.4.2 Relational Requirements

Turning now to relational requirements, the situation largely depends on the complementary punctual fairness requirements that are imposed. Indeed, the central notion of solidarity is often incompatible with no-envy, but broadly compatible with egalitarian-equivalence.

Resource monotonicity. For classical fair division problems, no selection from the efficiency–and–no-envy correspondence is resource monotonic (Moulin and Thomson, 1988). However, fix a monotone and unbounded path in commodity space emanating from the origin. Consider the selections from the egalitarian-equivalence correspondence defined by requiring the reference bundle to belong to this path: given $(\Omega, \succ)$, select the efficient allocation x such that for some x_0 on the path, and for each $i \in N$, $x_i \sim_i x_0$. Any rule defined in this way is efficient, egalitarian-equivalent, and resource monotonic.

For single-peaked allocation problems, and because preferences are not monotonic, it would of course make no sense to impose the same requirement (that if the social endowment increases, all agents end up at least as well off as they were made initially). However, remembering the central idea of solidarity that underlies our monotonicity properties, we could instead require that an increase in the social endowment—in fact, any change in it—be accompanied by a uniform, in direction, change in the welfares of all agents. Unfortunately, no selection from the no-envy correspondence, nor from the equal-division lower bound correspondence, is resource monotonic in this sense (note that these negative results do not implicate efficiency). However, if the proviso is added that the change should not cause the direction of the inequality between the social endowment and the sum of the peak amounts to reverse direction—let us add the prefix *one-sided* to resource monotonicity to designate this weaker version—it is met by many rules. A characterization of the uniform rule can be obtained on a large subdomain of our primary domain if one-sided resource monotonicity is imposed in conjunction with efficiency and no-envy.

On the other hand, for claims problems, the requirement that, as the endowment increases, all claimants end up with at least as much as they were assigned initially, is met by virtually all of the rules that have been encountered in the literature.

For all models with a discrete structure, the property is quite demanding.

Population monotonicity. As for population monotonicity, the same patterns of positive and negative results have been established for the various models under discussion. For classical fair division problems, no selection from the efficiency–and–no-envy correspondence is population monotonic (Kim, 2004). However, the selections from the efficiency–and–egalitarian-equivalence correspondence that we identified as resource monotonic are also population monotonic. If the reference bundle is required to be proportional to the social endowment, we gain the equal-division lower bound (but lose resource monotonicity).

For single-peaked allocation problems and again because preferences are not monotonic, it would also not be appropriate to require that if the population increases, all agents initially present be made at most as well off as they were made initially. If there is too much of the commodity, having more people around to consume it may be a good thing for the agents who are initially present. Solidarity in response to population changes takes the form that an increase in population—in fact, any change in population—should be accompanied by a uniform, in direction, change in the welfares of all agents who are present before and after. It turns out that no selection from the no-envy correspondence, or from the equal-division lower bound correspondence, is population monotonic in this sense. However, if the proviso is added that the change should not cause the direction of the inequality between the endowment and the sum of the peak amounts to reverse direction, it is met by many rules, in particular by the uniform rule. Yet, on a large subdomain of our primary domain, the uniform rule is the only rule to satisfy efficiency, no-envy, replication invariance (which says that, given an economy and an allocation chosen for it, then for each $k \in \mathbb{N}$, the k-replica of the allocation should be chosen for the k-replica of the economy), and this one-sided version of population monotonicity.

For claims problems, the property is easily met. All of the rules that have been discussed in the literature satisfy it.

For object-and-money allocation problems, population monotonicity can be met only in some limited way by selections from the efficiency–and–no-envy correspondence.

For discrete models, it is very demanding. For object allocation problems, certain sequential priority rules do satisfy it but obviously, the priority orders used for the various populations should be related. If two agents belong to two different groups related by inclusion, their order should be the same in both. This is achieved by inducing them from a single reference priority order on the entire set of potential agents. The rules obtained in this way are certainly not very satisfactory from the viewpoint of punctual fairness.

Welfare-dominance under preference replacement. Welfare-dominance under preference replacement has not been studied as thoroughly as the various properties just discussed, but for several models, a number of negative results have been established for selections from the no-envy solution.

In particular, for classical fair division problems, no selection from the efficiency–and–no-envy solution satisfies the property in general. However, here too, selections from the efficiency–and–egalitarian-equivalence solution can easily be defined that do satisfy it. The equal-division lower bound can also be met.

For single-peaked allocation problems, the property is also incompatible with efficiency and no-envy, but a one-sided version of it, defined as the one-sided versions of resource monotonicity and population monotonicity, is satisfied by many rules. When imposed in conjunction with these two properties and replication invariance, however, only the uniform rule qualifies.

For object-and-money allocation problems, the property is in general incompatible with no-envy (in this context, no-envy implies efficiency), even if preferences are quasi-linear. In the one-object case—say when a single agent has to be given access to the object—it can be met, but in a unique way. In that case, there is (essentially) a unique envy-free allocation that is least favorable to the recipient of the object (obtained when he is indifferent between his assignment and the common assignment of the other agents), and the rule that selects that allocation is the only selection from the no-envy solution to satisfy welfare-dominance under preference replacement.

Consistency. Consistency has been the central axiom in a large number of characterizations in virtually all of the classes of problems that we have discussed: For classical fair division problems, the equal-division Walrasian rule is *consistent* and on the domain of economies with smooth preferences, if a subsolution of the efficiency–and–equal-division-lower-bound correspondence is consistent and *replication invariant*, it is in fact a subsolution of the equal-division Walrasian correspondence.

For single-peaked allocation problems, the uniform rule is the smallest subsolution of the efficiency–and–no-envy solution to be consistent and to satisfy a mild continuity requirement (Thomson, 1994a; Dagan, 1996).

For claims problems, several characterizations of important rules have been obtained in which consistency plays a central role. They are the proportional rule, the constrained equal awards rule (which makes awards as equal as possible subject to no one receiving more than his claim), the constrained equal losses rule (which makes awards so that all claimants experience losses that are as equal as possible subject to no award being negative), and the Talmud rule (which is a hybrid of these last two). It is the central axiom in the characterization of an important family of "parametric rules," the other two being the mild requirements of continuity and equal treatment of equals (Young, 1987). Together with composition properties, it has also led to a family of rules that can be seen as hybrids of the proportional rules, weighted generalizations of the constrained equal awards and constrained equal losses rules, these components being applied after partitioning of the claimant set into priority classes (Moulin, 2000).

For general object-and-money allocation problems, no proper subsolution of the no-envy solution is consistent. In the one-object case, the solution that selects the envy-free allocation(s) at which the agent who is assigned the object is indifferent between his assignment and the common assignment of the other agents (these agents only receive money so by no-envy between them, they have to receive the same amount of that good) is the smallest subsolution of the no-envy solution to be consistent and closed under Pareto-indifferent reassignments.

For priority-augmented object allocation problems, the stable correspondence is consistent, but for the tentative acceptance rule to be consistent, the priorities attached to the various objects have to satisfy a restrictive correlation condition. Then, the rule is quite close to being a sequential priority rule.

For one-to-one matching problems, the stable solution as a whole has emerged from considerations of consistency. It is the only correspondence to be anonymous, consistent, and conversely consistent (Sasaki and Toda, 1992).

For object allocation problems, the sequential priority rules are consistent provided the various orders applied in the various populations are "consistent."

Consistency is preserved under arbitrary intersections and unions. Because the feasibility correspondence is consistent, and given any solution, there is a smallest consistent correspondence that contains it, its *minimal consistent enlargement.*

Model-specific requirements. Turning to model-specific requirements, it is for claims problems that the greatest number of ideas have been formulated and explored. The central notion here is that of *duality* (Aumann and Maschler, 1985) . It too is an expression of a robustness principle. First, say that two problems are dual if their claims vectors are equal and their endowments average to the half-sum of the claims. Two rules are dual if for each claims vector, one divides each endowment in the same way as the other divides what is missing for the dual endowment. Two properties are dual if whenever a rule satisfies one of them, the dual rule satisfies the other. Two theorems are dual if one is obtained from the other by replacing each rule by its dual and each property by its dual. Composition properties have also been examined in this context. In spite of the large inventory of rules that have been defined for claims problems, it is mainly the proportional, constrained equal awards, constrained equal losses, and Talmud rules, as well as various extensions and generalizations, that have come out of axiomatic work.

What about proofs? Because most of the punctual fairness notions that we have discussed are not local, proof techniques that are common in standard economic analysis, being based on tools of differential calculus, are not available, and for many of the proofs for models in which consumption spaces are Euclidean spaces, geometric techniques have had to be developed. The various discrete models that we have discussed have required tools of discrete mathematics, and algorithmic definitions have been critical. The set of allocations satisfying punctual notions such as no-envy or stability have been important in the study of money-and-object allocation problems or two-sided matchings problems for example.

11.5 Conclusion

Summarizing this short survey, we see that punctual concepts can be grouped in several main categories; various types of lower and upper bounds on physical assignments and on welfare, requirements based on inter-personal comparisons of assignments or opportunities, no-envy, egalitarian-equivalence and related concepts, being central concepts. As for relational concepts, and in spite of the great diversity in the axioms that have been studied in various branches of the literature on fair allocation, two central themes have emerged. One is solidarity. The other is robustness under choice of perspective when handling a change in the situation; fairness in part means not letting irrelevant or unimportant issues matter in the decision we make.

We have seen that for each type of allocation problems, something interesting can almost always be said about fairness. The appeal of several well-known rules has been strengthened by axiomatic analysis involving considerations of both punctual and relational fairness, and new rules have also been identified. The conceptual apparatus that we have presented is ripe for other applications. We should all look forward to being better able to formally address questions about distributional issues in other contexts.

Acknowledgments

I thank Jérôme Lang, John Weymark, and especially Sylvain Bouveret and Ulle Endriss for their comments.

CHAPTER 12

Fair Allocation of Indivisible Goods

Sylvain Bouveret, Yann Chevaleyre, and Nicolas Maudet

As introduced in Chapter 11, *fair allocation* (or *fair division*) refers to the general problem of fairly dividing a common resource among agents having different—and sometimes antagonistic—interests in the resource. But under this general term one can actually gather a cluster of very different problems, all calling for different solution concepts: after all, one can easily figure out that we cannot allocate a set of objects like a bicycle, a car or a house like we allocate pieces of land.

In this chapter, we will focus on fair division of *indivisible goods*. In other words, the resource is here a set $\mathcal{O} = \{o_1, \ldots, o_p\}$ of *objects* (that may also be called *goods* or *items*). Every object must be allocated *as is*, that is, an object loses its value if it is broken or divided into pieces to be allocated to several individuals. This assumption makes sense in a lot of real-world situations, where indivisible goods can be for example physical objects such as houses or cars in divorce settlements, or "virtual" objects like courses to allocate to students (Othman et al., 2010) or Earth observation images (Lemaître et al., 1999). Moreover, we assume in this chapter that the objects are *nonshareable*, which means that the same item cannot be allocated to more than one agent. This assumption seems to be questionable when the objects at stake are rather nonrival, that is, when the consumption of one unit by an agent will not prevent another one from having another unit (what we referred to as "virtual" objects). In most applications, such nonrival objects are available in limited quantity though (e.g., number of attendants in a course). This kind of problems can always be modeled with nonshareable goods by introducing several units of the same good.

What mainly makes fair division of indivisible goods specific, if not more difficult, is that classical fairness concepts like envy-freeness or proportionality are sometimes unreachable, unlike in the divisible (aka cake-cutting) case. As an illustration of this difference, consider a (infinitely divisible) piece of land which has to be split among two individuals, Alice and Bob. One classical way to proceed (see Chapter 13) is to let Alice propose a cut, and then let Bob take the share he prefers. If Alice acts rationally, she will cut the land into two pieces of the same value to her (if she acts differently she may end up with a worse piece), and hence will not envy Bob's piece. Such an *envy-free* allocation is always reachable with a divisible resource, but computing this allocation may require an unbounded number of cuts, as we will see in Chapter 13, Section 13.4. Even in the presence of indivisible items, the use of a special divisible resource (money) allows to "transfer utility" and suffices to guarantee this existence (Beviá, 1998). This is not the case when only indivisible goods are available: if, in the extreme case, there is a single good and two agents, one of the two will obviously be despoiled. Worse, in the general case, figuring out for a given instance whether such a fair solution even exists can be very complex (see Section 12.3).

To circumvent this issue, some authors reintroduce some divisibility in the process, either by relaxing the integrity of some goods and allocating *fractions* of these goods, as in the Adjusted Winner procedure proposed by Brams and Taylor (2000) and explained in Section 12.4, or by using *money* as an *ex-post* compensation for despoiled agents. When these kinds of solutions are not available, some authors (among which Brams et al., 2014) propose to relax the assumption that all the objects should be allocated. Another option is to relax our fairness requirement and focus on weaker solution concepts. These two last options correspond to the two possible solutions to the classical fairness versus efficiency trade-off (Section 12.2).

We cannot conclude this overview of distinctive features of indivisible goods without mentioning *preferences*. Preferences are at the heart of fair division, because fairness is often related to what the agents prefer to get from the allocation, may it be what they need, or what they just would like to have. To be able to compare two different allocations, we should first be able to figure out how the agents at stake evaluate their shares. This may come down to answering questions like: "does Alice prefer the bike and the boat together or the car alone?" While the number of shares to compare is finite, this number is huge, and makes the explicit representation of agents' preferences unrealistic. Concise preference representation is yet not out of reach, and can be achieved at the price of restricting assumptions—like additivity—or increased complexity (see Section 12.1). However, as can be seen in Chapter 13, such preference representation languages do not really transpose to the divisible case, which makes the design of *centralized* one-shot procedures less relevant to this case. This may explain why many works in fair division of indivisible goods focus on complexity and algorithmic issues of centralized allocation procedures (see Section 12.3), while the literature in cake-cutting is more concerned with the design of interactive protocols for fair division. There are nevertheless prominent protocols for the allocation of indivisible items, we review some of them in Section 12.4.

Preliminary Definitions

We will now introduce a few formal definitions which will be used all along the chapter. In this chapter, $N = \{1, \ldots, n\}$ will be a set of n *agents*, and $\mathcal{O} = \{o_1, \ldots, o_p\}$ a set of p (indivisible, nonshareable) *objects*. Each subset S of $\mathcal{O}$ is called a *bundle*. In the following, we will sometimes write $o_1o_2o_3$ as a shortcut for bundle $\{o_1, o_2, o_3\}$. An *allocation* is a function $\pi : N \to 2^{\mathcal{O}}$ mapping each agent to the bundle she receives, such that $\pi(i) \cap \pi(j) = \emptyset$ when $i \neq j$ because the items cannot be shared. The subset of objects $\pi(i)$ will be called agent i's *bundle* (or *share*). When $\bigcup_{i \in N} \pi(i) = \mathcal{O}$, the allocation is said to be *complete*. Otherwise, it is *partial*. The set of all allocations is denoted Π.

Following Chevaleyre et al. (2006), a *MultiAgent Resource Allocation setting* (MARA setting for short) denotes a triple $(N, \mathcal{O}, R)$, where N is a finite set of agents, $\mathcal{O}$ is a finite set of indivisible and nonshareable objects, and R is a sequence of n *preference relations* on the bundles of $\mathcal{O}$. The notion of "preference relation" has to be properly defined, which is not straightforward, and is the topic of the entire next section.

12.1 Preferences for Resource Allocation Problems

In order to allocate the indivisible goods properly to the agents, the community (or the benevolent arbitrator acting on behalf of it) needs to take into account the agents' wishes about the goods they want to receive. In other words, one has to be able to compare the different allocations based on the preferences the agents have on what they receive.[1] As we have seen in the introduction, the particular structure of the set of allocations is the main distinctive feature of resource allocation of indivisible goods, that makes the expression of preferences and the resolution of this kind of problems particularly difficult from a computational point of view.

12.1.1 Individual Preferences: From Objects to Bundles

The minimal and most natural assumption we can reasonably make on the agents is that they are at least able to compare each pair of individual items, just like voters are able to compare each pair of candidates in an election setting (see Chapter 2). In other words, we can minimally assume that each agent i is equipped with a preorder $\trianglerighteq_i$ on $\mathcal{O}$. Two further assumptions that are commonly made are that this relation is:

- either a *linear order* $\triangleright_i$, which basically means that each agent is able to rank each item from the best to the worst, with no ties allowed (this is the classical preference model in voting theory)
- or represented by a *utility function* $w_i : \mathcal{O} \to \mathbb{F}$, mapping each object to a score taken from a numerical set (that we will assume to be $\mathbb{N}$, $\mathbb{Q}$ or $\mathbb{R}$ for the sake of simplicity)

Unlike in voting theory, ranking items is generally not enough to provide valuable information about the agents' preferences concerning different allocations. Consider for example a setting where four objects $\{o_1, o_2, o_3, o_4\}$ have to be allocated to two different agents. Suppose that agent 1 ranks the objects as follows: $o_1 \triangleright o_2 \triangleright o_3 \triangleright o_4$. Does it mean that she would prefer an allocation that would give her o_1 and o_4 to an allocation that would give her o_2 and o_3? Or an allocation that would give her o_1 to an allocation that would give her o_2 and o_4?

The technical problem that lies behind this kind of questions is the problem of *lifting* the preference relation $\trianglerighteq$ (or the utility function w) on individual objects to a

---

[1] We assume that the agents only care about what they receive, and not what the others receive. This assumption of *nonexogenous preferences* is commonly made in the context of fair division.

preference relation $\succsim$ (or a utility function u) on *bundles* of objects.[2] There are two possible ways of doing it:

1. either by automatically lifting preferences to bundles of objects using some natural assumptions
2. or by asking the agents to rank not only the individual objects but also the bundles of objects

12.1.2 Additive Preferences

The first approach has been considered by several authors, either in economics (Brams and King, 2005; Herreiner and Puppe, 2009) or in computer science (Lipton et al., 2004; Bansal and Sviridenko, 2006; Bouveret et al., 2010). These works are usually based on a cardinal property and its ordinal counterpart, which can be reasonably assumed in many resource allocation contexts:

Definition 12.1 (Modularity). A utility function $u : 2^{\mathcal{O}} \to \mathbb{F}$ is *modular* if and only if for each pair of bundles $(\mathcal{S}, \mathcal{S}')$, we have $u(\mathcal{S} \cup \mathcal{S}') = u(\mathcal{S}) + u(\mathcal{S}') - u(\mathcal{S} \cap \mathcal{S}')$.

An equivalent definition is that for each bundle $\mathcal{S}$, $u(\mathcal{S}) = u(\emptyset) + \sum_{o \in \mathcal{S}} u(\{o\})$.

If we further assume that the utility of an agent for the empty set $(u(\emptyset))$ is 0, then we can compute the utility of an agent for each bundle of objects $\mathcal{S}$ by just summing the scores given by this agent to each individual object in $\mathcal{S}$. In this case, the utility function is said to be *additive*. This is one of the most classical settings in fair division of indivisible goods.

Additivity is a very strong property that forbids any kind of synergy between objects. Going back to our previous example with four objects, additivity implies that because agent 1 prefers o_1 to o_2, she will also prefer $\{o_1, o_3\}$ to $\{o_2, o_3\}$. This makes sense if o_3 is rather uncorrelated to o_1 and o_2: for example, if o_1 is a voucher for a train ticket in France, o_2 is a voucher for a night in Paris, and o_3 is a camera, it seems reasonable to assume that my preference on taking the train rather than spending a night in Paris will hold, no matter whether a camera is delivered with the voucher or not. Another way to state it is to say that if in bundle $\{o_2, o_3\}$ o_2 is replaced by a better object (e.g., o_1), then it makes a better bundle. This feature corresponds to a notion called pairwise-dominance, or *responsiveness* (Barberà et al., 2004), which can be stated formally in a purely ordinal context: $\forall \mathcal{S} \subset \mathcal{O}$ and all $o \in \mathcal{S}$ and $o' \in \mathcal{O} \setminus \mathcal{S}$, $(\mathcal{S} \succ \mathcal{S} \setminus \{o\} \cup \{o'\} \Leftrightarrow \{o\} \succ \{o'\})$ and $(\mathcal{S} \setminus \{o\} \cup \{o'\} \succ \mathcal{S} \Leftrightarrow \{o'\} \succ \{o\})$.[3]

Responsiveness is used among others by Brams et al. (2004); Brams and King (2005) to lift preferences defined as a linear order $\rhd$ over single objects to a preference relation over bundles of objects of the same cardinality.[4] To be able to compare bundles of different cardinalities, some authors (Bouveret et al., 2010; Brams et al., 2012b)

---

[2] The problem of lifting preferences over items to preferences over bundles has actually been studied in depth in social choice theory (Barberà et al., 2004).

[3] To be precise, in the original definition by Barberà et al. (2004) the comparisons are not strict, but some authors, for example, Brams et al. (2012b) use this strict version of responsiveness.

[4] Such a lifting is called the *responsive set extension*.

add a monotonicity assumption stating that if $S \supset S'$, $S \succ S'$.[5] Responsiveness (in its strict form, or with possible indifferences) plays an important role in fair division under ordinal preferences, because it has an interesting implication. An agent with responsive preferences will always be able to pick unambiguously the object that she prefers among a set, this choice being independent from what she has already received, and what she will receive later on. This property guarantees that some protocols for fair division such as the undercut procedure (see Section 12.4.1) or picking sequences (see Section 12.4.2) work properly. As mentioned earlier, this property, in its strict form, is also at the basis of a few works (Brams et al., 2004; Brams and King, 2005; Bouveret et al., 2010), the latter having been extended by Aziz et al. (2014d) to deal with (responsive) preferences with indifferences.

Note that, interestingly, it can be easily shown that any preference relation $\succ$ obtained by lifting a linear order $\rhd$ over single objects using pairwise dominance and monotonicity can be represented by any additive utility function u (i.e., $u(S) > u(S') \Leftrightarrow S \succ S'$), as soon as u is compatible with the linear order (i.e., $u(o) > u(o') \Leftrightarrow S \rhd S'$). However, things are not so simple as soon as indifferences between bundles are allowed: as mentioned by Barberà et al. (2004), additive representability only entails *responsiveness*, but is not equivalent.[6]

12.1.3 Beyond Additivity

Going back to the previous example, additivity makes sense when the objects at stake are rather unconnected (a train ticket and a camera in the example). However, things are different if the objects are of similar nature or are closely coupled. For example, if o_3 is now a plane ticket for the same day as the train ticket, we can reasonably assume that my preferences will be reversed, because now only the night in Paris is compatible with the plane ticket (so by getting the night and the plane ticket I can enjoy both, whereas by getting the train and plane tickets I will have to drop one of the two). This is a case where additive preferences fail to represent what the agents really have in mind, because there are some *dependencies* between objects. These dependencies (or synergies) can be of two kinds: *complementarity* or *substitutability*. Complementarity occurs when having a group of objects is worth more than the "sum" of their individual values: the agent benefits from using them jointly. Going back to our previous example, the plane ticket and the night in Paris can be considered as complementary (if I am not living in Paris): I can use the plane ticket to fly to Paris, and then spend the night there. Substitutability occurs when objects are of very similar nature and when their use is mutually exclusive. In our example, the plane and the train tickets are exclusive, and thus their joint value is not more than the value of one of the two.

A way to circumvent this problem is to allocate the items by pre-made bundles instead of proposing them individually (just like most shoe retailers sell shoes by pairs, not individually). However, in most cases the preferential dependencies are of subjective nature, and complementary and substitutable items are simply not the same

---

[5] Monotonicity will be formally introduced in Definition 12.9.
[6] Another important property is *extended independence*, which states that for every pair of bundles (S, S'), and every bundle S'' such that $(S \cup S') \cap S'' = \emptyset$, we have: $S \succ S' \Rightarrow S \cup S'' \succsim S' \cup S''$. Additive representability entails extended independence which in turn entails responsiveness.

for everyone.[7] In that case, we just cannot do anything else than asking the agents to rank all the possible bundles of objects. As the reader might guess, however, the number of possible bundles obviously grows exponentially with the number of objects, which renders the explicit ranking of all bundles simply impossible as soon as the number of objects exceeds 4 or 5. To illustrate this combinatorial blow-up, consider a resource allocation problem with just 16 objects, which seems to be a setting of very reasonable (if not small) size. In such a problem, each agent will have to compare $2^{16} = 65536$ bundles, which comes down to a tremendous (and unrealistic) amount of work for the agents.

As we can see, the community of agents or the benevolent arbitrator acting on behalf of it faces a dilemma: either restricting the set of expressible preferences to additive ones and hence ruling out the expression any kind of preferential dependencies, or letting the agents compare all pairs of possible bundles and falling in the combinatorial blow-up trap.

12.1.4 Compact Preference Representation

Compact preference representation languages can be seen as a compromise, often made at the price of increased computational complexity. The idea here is to use an intermediate language which can represent the agents' preferences as closely as possible, while formulas in that language remain as compact as possible. One formula in this language simply represents one preference relation on the bundles of objects. More formally:

Definition 12.2 (Preference representation language). An ordinal (resp. a cardinal) preference representation language is a pair $\langle L, I(L) \rangle$ that associates to each set of objects:[8]

- a language $L(\mathcal{O})$ (i.e., a vocabulary and a set of well-formed formulas)—the syntactical part of the language;
- an interpretation $I(L)(\mathcal{O})$ that maps any well-formed formula φ of $L(\mathcal{O})$ to a preorder $\succsim_\varphi$ of $2^{\mathcal{O}}$ (resp. a utility function $u_\varphi : 2^{\mathcal{O}} \to \mathbb{F}$)—the semantical part of the language.

A trivial example of preference representation language is the *bundle form*, which can be seen as a form of explicit representation. A formula in this language is just made of a set of pairs $\langle S, u_S \rangle$, where S is a bundle of objects, and u is a nonzero numerical weight. The utility of a given bundle S is just u_S if $\langle S, u_S \rangle$ belongs to the set, and 0 otherwise.

One might wonder what in the use of an intermediate language for representing ordinal or numerical preferences makes the representation "compact." Actually, reconciling (full) expressivity and succinctness is an unsolvable equation for the following reason. If for the sake of example we consider numerical preferences, the number

---

[7] For example, a laptop computer and a tablet-PC might be complementary for individuals doing a lot of writing at home (they would need a good keyboard) and a lot of reading while traveling (they would require a lightweight device). For others, these devices might be substitutable.

[8] Preference representation languages can be used more generally to represent a preference relation on any combinatorial set of alternatives. For the sake of simplicity, we choose to restrict the definition here to sets of objects.

of utility functions from $2^{\mathcal{O}} \to \{0, \dots, K-1\}$ is K^{2^p} (with $p = |\mathcal{O}|$). Following an information-theoretic argument recalled by Cramton et al. (2006), it means that if our language is fully expressive, some utility functions will need at least $2^p \frac{\ln K}{\ln 2}$ bits to be encoded as a formula, because no encoding of t bits is able to discriminate more than 2^t words. Hence, compact preference representation is not a matter of representing all preference relations in reasonable (polynomial) size, but just the *interesting* ones, that is the ones that are more likely to correspond to what the agents will naturally express. For example, the bundle form language described earlier can be considered compact only if it is reasonable to assume that the agents will value positively only a small number of bundles.

Additivity Generalized

Let us take another example of what we mean by "interesting preference relations." Consider additive utility functions introduced earlier. Their main advantages are their conciseness (each agent just needs to provide one weight for each object) and their simplicity. However, their annoying drawback is that they are unable to encode even the slightest complementarity or substitutability between objects. On the other hand, allowing any kind of synergy exposes us to the computational blow-up, whereas it is very likely that an agent would be willing to express only synergies concerning a limited number of objects (do we really need to give the agents the opportunity of expressing the added value of owning a bundle of 42 objects compared to the values of its proper subsets?). This is the idea behind k-additive numerical preferences:

Definition 12.3 (k-additive preference representation language). A formula in the k-additive representation language is a set $\mathcal{B}$ of pairs $\langle \mathcal{S}, w_{\mathcal{S}} \rangle$, where $\mathcal{S} \subseteq \mathcal{O}$ is a bundle of size at most k, and $w_{\mathcal{S}}$ is a nonzero numerical weight. Given a formula $\mathcal{B}$ in this language, the utility of each bundle $\mathcal{S}$ is defined as:

$$u(\mathcal{S}) = \sum_{\substack{\langle S', w_{S'} \rangle \in \mathcal{B} \\ S' \subseteq S, |S'| \leq k}} w_{S'} \qquad (12.1)$$

The weight $w_{\mathcal{S}}$ represents the added value of $\mathcal{S}$, beyond the value of its proper subsets, or in other words, the synergistic potential of $\mathcal{S}$.[9] If this number is positive, it means that the objects in $\mathcal{S}$ work in complementarity, if it is negative, these objects are probably substitutable. A utility function u whose weights of size 2 or more are positive (resp. negative) has the *supermodularity* (resp. *submodularity*) property. In other words, it holds that $u(\mathcal{S} \cup \mathcal{S}') \geq u(\mathcal{S}) + u(\mathcal{S}') - u(\mathcal{S} \cap \mathcal{S}')$ (resp. $u(\mathcal{S} \cup \mathcal{S}') \leq u(\mathcal{S}) + u(\mathcal{S}') - u(\mathcal{S} \cap \mathcal{S}')$).

Example 12.1. Let $\mathcal{O} = \{o_1, o_2, o_3, o_4\}$ be a set of objects, and let u be the k-additive utility function defined from the following set of weights: $\langle o_1, 2 \rangle$, $\langle o_2, 2 \rangle$, $\langle o_1 o_2, -2 \rangle$, $\langle o_3 o_4, 10 \rangle$. All other bundles have weight zero. We have for example $u(o_1) = u(o_2) = 2$,

---

[9] These weights are also called *Möbius masses* in the context of fuzzy measures, where this kind of representation is extensively used (see e.g., Grabisch, 1997).

and $u(o_1o_2) = 2 + 2 - 2$, which is 2 as well. This probably means that objects o_1 and o_2 are *substitutes* (having both does not give more utility than having just one). On the contrary, o_3 and o_4 alone are useless ($u(o_4) = u(o_3) = 0$), but having them together is interesting ($u(o_3o_4) = 10$), which means that they act as *complementary objects*. We can also notice that u is neither modular, nor sub- or supermodular.

The succinctness of the language is ensured by the parameter k, that bounds the size of formulas representing our utility functions to $\sum_{i=0}^{k} \binom{p}{i} = O(p^k)$ This parameter k can be seen as a value that represents the trade-off between full expressivity (and formulas of potentially exponential size) if $k = p$ and limited expressivity (and formulas of linear size), that is, additive functions, if $k = 1$.

Graphical Models

Interestingly, the k-additive preference representation coincides, for the special case of bundle combinatorial spaces we have to deal with in resource allocation problems, with a more general preference representation language: *GAI-nets* (Bacchus and Grove, 1995; Gonzales and Perny, 2004). The language of GAI-nets is a *graphical model* for preference representation. Graphical models are a family of knowledge representation languages, which have been introduced decades ago in the context of uncertainty (e.g., influence diagrams, see Howard and Matheson, 1984) probabilistic modeling (e.g., Bayesian networks, see Pearl, 1988), constraint satisfaction (Montanari, 1974) or valued constraint optimization (Schiex et al., 1995). In all these contexts, graphical models are based upon the same components: (*i*) a graphical component describing directed or undirected dependencies between variables; (*ii*) a collection of local statements on single variables or small subsets of variables, compatible with the dependence structure. In the particular case of GAI-nets, the preferential (in)dependence notion upon which this language is built is *generalized additive independence* (GAI), introduced by Fishburn (1970), further developed by Keeney and Raiffa (1976) in the context of multiattribute decision making. The k-additive representation introduced earlier can be seen as a GAI representation on a bundle space, where the size of the local relations (synergies) is explicitly bounded by k, and with no associated graphical representation.

GAI-nets are not the only graphical model for compact preference representation. Boutilier et al. (1999, 2004) have developed a very powerful and popular preference representation language: CP-nets. Unlike GAI-nets, CP-nets are dedicated to the representation of *ordinal preferences*. Here, the graphical structure describes the (directed) preferential dependencies between variables. The local statements, for each variable, describe the agents' ordinal preferences on the values of the variable's domain, given all the possible combinations of values of its parents (hence "CP" standing for "Conditional Preferences"), and all other things being equal (*ceteris paribus*).

CP-nets have been extended to a family of preference representation languages with different features (see e.g., Brafman et al., 2006, for TCP-nets, Boutilier et al., 2001, for UCP-nets and Wilson, 2004, for CP-theories). One of these languages, CI-nets (Bouveret et al., 2009) is especially dedicated to the representation of ordinal preferences on sets of objects, hence well-suited to fair division problems. Formally, a CI-net $\mathcal{N}$ is a set of CI statements (where CI stands for Conditional Importance) of the form $\mathcal{S}^+, \mathcal{S}^- : \mathcal{S}_1 \rhd \mathcal{S}_2$ (where $\mathcal{S}^+, \mathcal{S}^-, \mathcal{S}_1$ and $\mathcal{S}_2$ are pairwise-disjoint subsets of $\mathcal{O}$). The informal reading of such a statement is: "if I have all the items in $\mathcal{S}^+$ and none of those in $\mathcal{S}^-$, I prefer obtaining all items in $\mathcal{S}_1$ to obtaining all those in $\mathcal{S}_2$, all other things being equal (ceteris paribus)." Formally, the interpretation of a CI-net $\mathcal{N}$ is the smallest monotonic strict partial order $\succ$ that satisfies each CI-statement in $\mathcal{N}$, that is, for each CI-statement $\mathcal{S}^+, \mathcal{S}^- : \mathcal{S}_1 \rhd \mathcal{S}_2$, we have $\mathcal{S}' \cup \mathcal{S}^+ \cup \mathcal{S}_1 \succ \mathcal{S}' \cup \mathcal{S}^+ \cup \mathcal{S}_2$ as soon as $\mathcal{S}' \subseteq \mathcal{O} \setminus (\mathcal{S}^+ \cup \mathcal{S}^- \cup \mathcal{S}_1 \cup \mathcal{S}_2)$.

Example 12.2. Let $\mathcal{O} = \{o_1, o_2, o_3, o_4\}$ be a set of objects, and let $\mathcal{N}$ be the CI-net defined by the two following CI-statements: $S1 = (o_1, \emptyset : o_4 \rhd o_2 o_3)$; $S2 = (\emptyset, o_1, : o_2 o_3 \rhd o_4)$.

From $\mathcal{N}$, we can deduce for example that $o_1 o_4 \succ o_1 o_2 o_3$ ($S1$) and $o_2 o_3 \succ o_4$ ($S2$). We can notice that obviously $\succ$ is not responsive, as having o_1 or not in the bundle reverses the preference between $o_2 o_3$ and o_4.

CI-nets are a quite natural way of expressing preferences on subsets of objects. However, as we shall see later on, computational complexity is the price to pay for this cognitive relevance. A strict subset of this language, SCI-nets, that coincides with responsive monotonic preferences, have been further investigated from the point of view of fair resource allocation (Bouveret et al., 2010).

Logic-Based Languages

Another family of compact representation languages, which, unlike k-additive representation or graphical models, is not based on limited synergies, is the family *logical languages*. As we will see, propositional logic is well-suited to represent preferences on subsets of objects, because any set of subsets of objects can be represented (often compactly) by a propositional formula.

In the following, given a set of objects $\mathcal{O}$, we will denote by $\mathcal{L}_\mathcal{O}$ the propositional language built upon the usual propositional operators $\wedge$, $\vee$ and $\neg$, and one propositional variable for each object in $\mathcal{O}$ (for the sake of simplicity we use the same symbol for denoting the object and its associated propositional variable). Each formula φ of $\mathcal{L}_\mathcal{O}$ represents a *goal* that an agent is willing to achieve. From any bundle $\mathcal{S}$ we can build a logical interpretation $\mathcal{I}(\mathcal{S})$ by setting all the propositional variables corresponding to an object in $\mathcal{S}$ to $\top$ and the other to $\bot$. A bundle $\mathcal{S}$ *satisfies* a goal φ (written $\mathcal{S} \vDash \varphi$) if and only if $\mathcal{I}(\mathcal{S}) \vDash \varphi$. A goal φ thus stands for a compact representation of the set of all bundles that satisfy φ.

Example 12.3. Let $\mathcal{O} = \{o_1, o_2, o_3\}$ be a set of objects. The goal $\varphi = o_1 \vee (o_2 \wedge o_3)$ is a compact representation of the set of bundles $\{o_1, o_1 o_2, o_1 o_3, o_2 o_3, o_1 o_2 o_3\}$.

The most obvious way of interpreting a goal as a preference relation is to consider that the agent is only happy if the goal is satisfied, and unhappy otherwise. This leads to a dichotomous preference relation $\succsim^\varphi$ that is defined as follows: for each pair of bundles $\langle \mathcal{S}, \mathcal{S}' \rangle$, we have $\mathcal{S} \succ^\varphi \mathcal{S}'$ if and only if $\mathcal{S} \vDash \varphi$ or $\mathcal{S}' \nvDash \varphi$.

This approach is not very subtle: the agent is not even able to express the tiniest preference between two different objects she both desires. We can do better:

- The first idea is to allow an agent to express several goals (a *goal base*) at the same time. Counting the number of goals satisfied by a given bundle for example gives a good idea of how interesting the bundle is for an agent.
- The second idea is to further allow an agent to *prioritize* the goals of her goal base (bundles are then evaluated in terms of the higher priority goal they satisfy).
- A third idea is that, beyond prioritizing her goal, an agent gives a weight (or a score) to each of them. This idea leads to the weighted logic-based preference representation language that is described in what follows.

Definition 12.4 (Weighted logic-based preference representation language). A formula in the weighted logic-based representation language is a set Δ of pairs $\langle \varphi, w_\varphi \rangle$, where φ is a well-formed formula of the propositional language $\mathcal{L}_\mathcal{O}$, and w_φ is a nonzero numerical weight.

Given a formula Δ in this language, the utility of each bundle $\mathcal{S}$ is defined as

$$u(\mathcal{S}) = \sum_{(\varphi, w_\varphi) \in \Delta \ | \ \mathcal{S} \vDash \varphi} w_\varphi. \tag{12.2}$$

Note that in Equation 12.2 any other aggregation operator can be used, such as for example the maximum that selects only the highest weight among the satisfied goals (Bouveret et al., 2005).

Example 12.4. Let $\mathcal{O} = \{o_1, o_2, o_3\}$ be a set of objects. The goal $\Delta = \{\langle o_1 \vee o_2, 1 \rangle, \langle o_2 \wedge o_3, 2 \rangle\}$ is a compact representation of the utility function:

$\mathcal{S}$	$\emptyset$	o_1	o_2	o_3	$o_1 o_2$	$o_1 o_3$	$o_2 o_3$	$o_1 o_2 o_3$
$u(\mathcal{S})$	0	1	1	0	1	1	3	3

The interested reader can refer to Lang (2004) for an extensive survey on logic-based preference representation languages. Coste-Marquis et al. (2004) and Uckelman (2009) provide some detailed results about the expressivity, succinctness, and computational complexity of these languages.

Bidding Languages

We conclude this introduction about compact preference representation for resource allocation by discussing a domain closely related to ours: *auctions*. Auctions are only distinguished from a general resource allocation problem with indivisible goods by the fact that money is at the heart of the evaluation scale (utility here actually represents the amount an agent is ready to pay to obtain some object), and that auctioneers do not care about end-state fairness issues in general. Beyond these "ethical" differences, nothing formally distinguishes an auction setting from a general resource allocation problem.

In the classical auction setting, buyers (or sellers if we deal with reverse auctions) can only bid on individual objects. As a result, the same expressivity problem as the one aforementioned for additive preferences occurs: a bidder is simply unable to express her preference in a proper way if she has preferential dependencies between the objects to be sold. This issue has led Rassenti et al. (1982) to define a new auction setting, where bidders can actually bid on *bundles* of items, instead of just individual items: *combinatorial auctions* (Cramton et al., 2006). To overcome the combinatorial blow-up caused by the explicit representation of set functions, this community has developed its own stream of compact preference representation languages: *bidding languages*. We will not describe these languages here, but the interested reader can refer to the book by Cramton et al. (2006) and especially its chapter about bidding languages (Nisan, 2006) for more information.

About Monotonicity

Beyond all these preference representation approaches, a property that is often taken for granted in most fair division contexts is monotonicity:

Definition 12.5 (Monotonicity). A preference relation $\succsim$ on $2^{\mathcal{O}}$ is *monotonic* (resp. *strictly monotonic*) if and only if $\mathcal{S} \subsetneq \mathcal{S}' \Rightarrow \mathcal{S} \precsim \mathcal{S}'$ (resp. $\mathcal{S} \prec \mathcal{S}'$).

Monotonicity formalizes the fact that all the objects have a positive value for each agent, and that the "more" objects an agent receives, the "happier" she will be. Going back to our previous example with four objects, monotonicity implies here that our agent prefers for example o_1 and o_2 together to o_1 alone. This assumption is very natural as long as we are dealing with "positive" objects or "negative" ones, such as tasks or chores (reversing the inequality in this case), but not mixing the two. For most typical compact preference representation languages, the monotonicity assumption has a very natural translation into a simple property on the formulas. For example, for numerical modular preferences, monotonicity is equivalent to the positivity of $w(o_i)$ for every object o_i. For weighted logic-based formulas, a sufficient condition for monotonicity is to require that the weight of every formula is positive, together with forbidding the negation symbol $\neg$.

Unless explicitly stated, we will consider in this chapter that all the preference relations we are dealing with are monotonic.

12.1.5 Multiagent Resource Allocation Settings

After this discussion about preferences, we can update the definition of MARA setting proposed at the end of the introduction and make it more precise. In the following, an *ordinal MultiAgent Resource Allocation setting* (ordinal-MARA setting for short) will be defined as a triple $\langle N, \mathcal{O}, R \rangle$, where N is a finite set of agents, $\mathcal{O}$ is a finite set of indivisible and nonshareable objects, and R is a set $\{\succsim_1, \ldots, \succsim_n\}$ of preorders on $2^{\mathcal{O}}$, defined as well-formed formulas in a (compact) ordinal representation language.

A *cardinal-MARA setting* will be defined accordingly by replacing the set R of preorders by a set $U = \{u_1, \ldots, u_n\}$ of utility functions on $2^{\mathcal{O}}$, defined as well-formed formulas in a (compact) numerical representation language.

12.2 The Fairness versus Efficiency Trade-Off

Now that the setting is properly defined, we will deal with the definition of *fair* allocations. In what follows we will mainly focus on two notions of fairness (see

Chapter 11): *maxmin* allocations and *envy-free* allocations. Note that the former is only defined in the cardinal-MARA setting, because it requires the ability to compare the well-being of different agents, whereas the latter is well defined in both MARA settings.

In cardinal-MARA settings, maxmin allocations optimize the so-called *egalitarian social welfare*:

Definition 12.6 (Maxmin). An allocation is maxmin when the utility of the poorest agent is as high as possible, that is,

$$\max_{\pi \in \Pi} \left\{ \min_{i \in N} u_i(\pi(i)) \right\}.$$

Note that it is still possible to conceive ordinal versions of this notion: for instance we may wish to maximize the worst "rank" of a bundle in the preference orderings of agents (*rank-maxmin*).

Envy-freeness only requires an ordinal-MARA setting to operate:

Definition 12.7 (Envy-freeness). An allocation is envy-free when $\pi(i) \succsim_i \pi(j)$ for all agents $i, j \in N$.

Unfortunately, these fairness objectives may not be compatible with the objective of *efficiency*. Informally, efficiency can be seen as the fact that resources shall not be "under-exploited." At the weakest sense, it means that we should only consider *complete* allocations (objects should not be thrown away). However, usually, efficiency corresponds to the stronger notion of *Pareto-efficiency* or to the even stronger notion of *utilitarian optimality* (for cardinal-MARA settings). This latter notion of efficiency provides a convenient way to quantify the loss of efficiency due to the requirement to meet a fairness criterion: this is the idea of the *price of fairness*, which will also be discussed in Chapter 13 in the context of divisible goods.

12.2.1 Maxmin Allocations

As a warm-up, let us start with maxmin allocations and Pareto-efficiency. Observe that a maxmin allocation is not necessarily Pareto-optimal. This is so because this notion only focuses on the well-being of the agent who is worst-off, and overlooks the rest of the society. But it may well be the case that for the same utility enjoyed by the "poorest" agent, a better allocation of resources exists for the rest.[10] On the other hand, among the set of maxmin optimal allocations, one can easily see that at least one of them must be Pareto-optimal (many of them can be). Assume for contradiction that it is not the case. Then for each maxmin allocation π there is another allocation π' Pareto-dominating π and not in the set of maxmin allocations. Because π' Pareto-dominates π we have $u_i(\pi'(i)) \geqslant u_i(\pi(i)) \geqslant \min_{k \in N}(\pi(k))$ for all $i \in N$. Hence either $\min_{k \in N}(\pi'(k)) = \min_{k \in N}(\pi(k))$, in which case π' is maxmin optimal, or

---

[10] A way to overcome this problem and reconcile maxmin allocations with Pareto-optimality is to use the leximin preorder (Sen, 1970) which can be seen as a refinement of the maxmin fairness criterion: if two allocations yield the same maxmin value, then the leximin criterion will discriminate them based on the second poorest agent if possible, otherwise on the third poorest, and so on.

$\min_{k \in N}(\pi'(k)) > \min_{k \in N}(\pi(k))$, in which case π is not maxmin optimal. In both case, this is a contradiction.

If we now consider the utilitarian notion of efficiency, then no guarantee can be given on the loss of efficiency induced by the requirement to have a maxmin allocation. Let us make this statement more formal using the notion of *price of fairness*. The price of fairness is usually defined as the ratio between the total utility of the optimal utilitarian allocation over the total utility of the best maxmin optimal allocation. The following holds:

Theorem 12.5 (Caragiannis et al., 2012a). *The price of fairness for maxmin allocations is unbounded.*

Proof. Suppose the preferences of n agents regarding n objects are normalized so that they sum up to 1, and are set as follows: each agent i (from 1 to $n-1$) has utility ε for object o_i, $1 - \varepsilon$ for object o_{i+1}, and 0 for the other objects, while agent n has only utility 1 for object o_n. The maxmin allocation assigns object o_i to each agent i, and thus yields $1 + (n-1) \cdot \varepsilon$ overall when we sum utilities. But giving to each agent $i \in 1, \ldots, n-1$ object o_{i+1} (and object 1 to anyone) yields an overall $(n-1) \cdot (1-\varepsilon)$. Hence, the ratio is unbounded as n grows. $\qquad\square$

12.2.2 Envy-Freeness

As an obvious first remark, note that a partial allocation where each good is thrown away is obviously envy-free: all agents own the same empty bundle, so they cannot envy each other. Thus, in this section we will focus on the nontrivial case of complete allocations.

First, as with the maxmin criterion, an envy-free allocation is not necessarily Pareto-efficient, as shown in the following example:

Example 12.6. Let $\mathcal{O} = \{o_1, o_2, o_3, o_4\}$ be a set of objects shared by two agents. Assume $u_1(\mathcal{S}) = \mathbf{1}_{\{\{o_1, o_2\}\}}(\mathcal{S})$ and $u_2(\mathcal{S}) = \mathbf{1}_{\{\{o_3, o_4\}\}}(\mathcal{S})$, where $\mathbf{1}$ is the indicator function. Then, the allocation where agent 1 owns $\{o_1, o_3\}$ and agent 2 owns $\{o_2, o_4\}$ is complete and envy-free, but not Pareto efficient: giving $\{o_1, o_2\}$ and $\{o_3, o_4\}$ respectively to agents 1 and 2 will strictly increase their utility function.

Next, it is easy to show that there does not always exist an envy-free complete allocation. Consider the case where two agents share a single good, and suppose this good is preferred by both agents to the empty bundle. Then, the agent owning the good will be envied by the other agent. More generally, the probability of existence of complete and envy-free allocation has actually been further investigated in a recent work by Dickerson et al. (2014). In particular, this work shows analytically that under several assumptions on the probability distribution of the agents' (additive) preferences, an envy-free allocation is unlikely to exist up to a given threshold on the ratio between the number of goods and the number of agents, and very likely to exist beyond. Experimental results show an interesting phenomenon of phase-transition.

Finally, consider the utilitarian notion of efficiency. Similarly to the price of fairness, the price of envy-freeness has been defined by Caragiannis et al. (2012a) as the ratio between the total utility of the optimal utilitarian allocation over the total utility of the best envy-free allocation. Caragiannis et al. (2012a) show that the price of envy-freeness is $\Theta(n)$. So as more and more agents appear in the system, the gap between envy-free allocations and optimal allocations will grow at a linear rate.

12.2.3 Other Fairness Criteria

Beyond maxmin fairness and envy-freeness, *proportionality* is another prominent fairness criterion. This property, coined by Steinhaus (1948) in the context of continuous fair division (cake-cutting) problems, states that each agent should get from the allocation at least one n^{th} of the total utility she would have received if she were alone. Obviously, this criterion is related to maxmin fairness when utility are normalized (each agent gives the same value to the entire set of objects): if there exists an allocation that satisfies proportionality, then any maxmin-optimal allocation satisfies it. As we will see in Chapter 13, it is always possible to find an allocation that satisfies proportionality. In the case of two agents, the example procedure given in the introduction of the chapter (Alice cuts, Bob chooses) obviously guarantees a proportional share to both agents. Once again, things turn bad when we switch to indivisible objects (just consider again one object and two agents, no allocation can give her fair share to each agent).

Even if it is not possible to guarantee one n^{th} of the resource to each agent, Demko and Hill (1988) have shown that under additive numerical preferences it is always possible to find an allocation guaranteeing a given amount of utility (only depending on the maximum weight α given by the agents to the objects) to each agent. Markakis and Psomas (2011) have significantly extended this result, first by showing that it is actually possible to guarantee that the minimal amount of utility received by each agent i depends on the maximum weight α_i given by this agent to the objects, and secondly by exhibiting a deterministic polynomial-time algorithm to compute it. The same idea has been used by Gourvès et al. (2013), who further refine these results by constructively exhibiting a stronger lower bound, that also works for fair division problems with a particular kind of admissibility constraints represented as a matroid.

Another approach has been proposed by Budish (2011). Instead on focusing on the maximal fraction of absolute utility it is possible to guarantee to each agent, Budish (2011) proposes to start from the "I cut you choose" protocol described earlier in the divisible case, and to adapt it to the indivisible case. According to this definition of fairness, every agent i should receive from the allocation at least what she would receive in the worst case if she had to partition the objects into n bundles and let the other $n - 1$ agents choose first. In other words, each agent should receive at least the best (max), among all possible allocations (cuts), of the worst (min) share of this allocation: Budish (2011) calls it the *maximin share*. Obviously, in the cake-cutting case, this notion coincides with proportionality.

Example 12.7. Consider a MARA setting involving two agents with additive preferences, and four objects $\{o_1, o_2, o_3, o_4\}$. Let agent 1's preferences be defined as follows:

$u_1(o_1) = 7$, $u_1(o_2) = 2$, $u_1(o_3) = 6$ and $u_1(o_4) = 10$. Then agent 1's maximin share is 12, associated to partition $\{o_1 o_3, o_2 o_4\}$.

Contrary to proportionality, in the case of additive preferences, maximin share guarantee is *almost* always possible to satisfy (Bouveret and Lemaître, 2014). Actually, Procaccia and Wang (2014) have exhibited some MARA-settings where no allocation guaranteeing maximin shares to everyone can be found, but these instances are rather rare.[11] Moreover, Bouveret and Lemaître (2014) notice that in the special case of additive preferences, not only envy-freeness implies proportionality, but also proportionality implies maximin share guarantee. It means that these properties form a scale of fairness criteria, from the strongest to the weakest.[12] This suggests another solution to the fairness versus efficiency trade-off: try to satisfy envy-freeness if possible; if not, try to satisfy proportionality if you can; and finally, as a fallback fairness criterion, maximin share guarantee is almost always possible to satisfy.

12.3 Computing Fair Allocations

We will now see how challenging computing optimal fair allocations is. To achieve this, we will among other things study the computational complexity of decision problems associated with the computation of fair allocations. The input of these decision problems will include the preference profiles encoded in a given representation language. Note that if a preference profile is represented with a formula whose size is superpolynomial in p and n, then even if the decision problem is computationally easy, finding a fair allocation may remain prohibitive in practice—hence the relevance of compact representation languages discussed in the previous section.

12.3.1 Maxmin Allocations

We start with a bad news: if we make no assumption on the preferences of agents (beyond monotonicity), then not only is computing an optimal maxmin allocation computationally hard, but even computing an approximation is (Golovin, 2005). The argument is simple, and based as usual on a problem known to be hard. In the PARTITION problem, we are given a collection of (positive) integers $C = \langle c_1, \ldots, c_q \rangle$ such that $\sum_{i=1}^{q} c_i = 2k$, and we are asked whether there exists $I \subseteq \{1, \ldots, n\}$ with $\sum_{i \in I} c_i = k$. But now take $\mathcal{O} = C$ and set the utility functions of two agents as follows:

$$u(\mathcal{S}) = \begin{cases} 1 & \text{if } \sum_{x \in \mathcal{S}} x \geqslant k \\ 0 & \text{otherwise .} \end{cases}$$

The only situation where an allocation with social welfare 1 can be obtained is when agents receive a bundle such that $\sum_{x \in \mathcal{S}} x = k$, otherwise any allocation yields utility 0 (because at least one agent enjoys utility 0). But then any approximation would have to distinguish between these cases, which requires to solve PARTITION. The careful

---

[11] They also show that it is always possible to guarantee at least 2/3 of the maximin share to everyone.
[12] Actually there are two additional criteria in the scale, which we do not discuss here for the sake of clarity and conciseness.

reader should be skeptical at this point: shouldn't the complexity precisely depend on the size of the representation of u? In fact, Golovin (2005) circumvents this problem of compact representation by assuming a "value query model" where an oracle can provide values of bundles of items in unit computation time. But even using the naive bundle form language, similar conclusions can be obtained, as long as allocations are required to be complete (Nguyen et al., 2013).

Getting more positive results requires further restrictions on the preferences of agents. However, even quite severe restrictions turn out to be insufficient. For instance, the problem remains inapproximable as soon as $k \geqslant 3$-additive functions are considered (Nguyen et al., 2013, 2014). Note that, as Nguyen et al. (2014) show, inapproximability results also hold for other "fair" collective utility functions, such as the Nash product for example.[13]

In fact, as we shall see now, even the most basic setting remains very challenging.

The Santa Claus Problem

Take a cardinal-MARA setting, where utility functions are modular. This setting has been popularized as the *Santa Claus problem* (Bansal and Sviridenko, 2006): Santa Claus has p gifts to allocate to n children having modular preferences; Santa Claus allocates the gifts so as to maximize the utility of the unhappiest child (which is exactly the maxmin allocation). First, note that the problem remains NP-hard even in this restrictive setting (Bezáková and Dani, 2005; Bouveret et al., 2005). Furthermore, the problem cannot be approximated within a factor $> 1/2$ (Bezáková and Dani, 2005).

There is a natural integer linear program (ILP) formulation for this problem, usually called the "assignment LP." By taking $x_{i,j}$ to be the binary variable taking value 1 when agent i receives object o_j, and 0 otherwise, we set the objective function to be the maximization of the right-hand side of Inequality 12.6:

$$\text{maximize } y, \tag{12.3}$$

$$\forall i \in N, \forall j \in \mathcal{O}: \quad x_{i,j} \in \{0, 1\}, \tag{12.4}$$

$$\forall j \in \mathcal{O}: \quad \sum_{i \in N} x_{i,j} = 1, \tag{12.5}$$

$$\forall i \in N: \sum_{o_j \in \mathcal{O}} w_i(o_j) \cdot x_{i,j} \geqslant y. \tag{12.6}$$

The bad news is that just solving the relaxation of this ILP (that is, solving the problem by assuming that goods are divisible) is not a good approach since the *integrality gap* (the ratio between the fractional and the integral optimum) can be infinite. Indeed suppose there is a single object to allocate, for which every agent has the same utility, say x. Then the fractional solution would be x/n, while the ILP would yield 0 (Bezáková and Dani, 2005).

The similarity of the problem with scheduling problems is important to emphasize (take agents as being the machines, and objects as being the jobs). In particular the minimum makespan problem, which seeks to minimize the maximal load for an agent, is well studied. While the objective is opposite, this proved to be a fruitful connection,

---

[13] The Nash product is defined as the product of all utilities.

and motivated the use of (adapted) sophisticated rounding techniques (Lenstra et al.,
1990). Bezáková and Dani (2005) were among the first to exploit this connection. They
used job truncations techniques to propose an $O(n)$ approximation, later improved to
$O(\frac{1}{\sqrt{n}\log^3 n})$ by Asadpour and Saberi (2010).

Linear programming is not the only possible approach to this problem: *branch and
bound* techniques have also been investigated (Dall'Aglio and Mosca, 2007). For this
type of algorithms, the quality of the bound is a crucial component. Dall'Aglio and
Mosca (2007) use the "adjusted winner" procedure (that we discuss later on in this
chapter) to compute this bound.

12.3.2 Computing Envy-Free or Low-Envy Allocations

There is a simple algorithm which always returns an envy-free allocation: throw all
the objects away! However, as discussed already, as soon as a very minimal efficiency
requirement of *completeness* is introduced, an envy-free allocation may not exist. In
fact, it is computationally hard to decide whether such an allocation exists (Lipton
et al., 2004). If we now ask for an allocation which meets both envy-freeness and
Pareto-optimality, then for most compact representation languages the problem lies
above NP (Bouveret and Lang, 2008). More precisely, this problem is Σ_2^P-complete
for most logic-based languages introduced in Section 12.1, including the very simple
language leading to dichotomous preferences. It also turns out that the combinatorial
nature of the domain plays little role here: even in additive domains, deciding whether
there exists an efficient and envy-free allocation is Σ_2^P-complete (de Keijzer et al.,
2009).

Given this, a perhaps more realistic objective is to seek to minimize the "degree
of envy" of the society. There are several ways to define such a metric. For example,
Cavallo (2012) defines the *rate of envy* as the average envy of all agents. Here we
follow Lipton et al. (2004) in their definitions:

$$e_{ij}(\pi) = \max\{0, u_i(\pi(j)) - u_i(\pi(i))\}.$$

Now the envy of the allocation is taken to be the maximal envy among any pair of
agents, that is,

$$e(\pi) = \max\{e_{ij}(\pi) \mid i, j \in N\}. \tag{12.7}$$

Allocations with Bounded Maximal Envy

One may ask whether allocations with bounded maximal envy can be found. The
question is raised by Dall'Aglio and Hill (2003) and later addressed by Lipton et al.
(2004). We will see that such bounds can be obtained, by taking as a parameter the
maximal marginal utility of a problem, noted α. The marginal utility of a good o_j, given
an agent i and a bundle $\mathcal{S}$, is the amount of additional utility that this object yields
when taken together with the bundle. Then the maximal marginal utility is simply the
maximal value among all agents, bundles, and objects. In an additive setting, this is
thus simply the highest utility that an agent assigns to a good.

The result by Lipton et al. (2004)—which improves upon a first bound of $O(\alpha n^{3/2})$ given by Dall'Aglio and Hill (2003)—is then simply stated:

Theorem 12.8 (Lipton et al., 2004). *It is always possible to find an allocation whose envy is bounded by α, the maximal marginal utility of the problem.*

Proof sketch. First, we introduce the notion of the envy graph associated with an allocation π, where nodes are agents and there is an edge from i to j when i envies j. Now take a cycle in this envy graph: a key observation is that by rotating the bundles held by agents in the direction opposite to that of the cycle (so that each agent gets the bundle of the agent he envies), we necessarily "break the envy cycle" at some point. This is so because the utility of each agent in this cycle is increased at each step of this rotation. Furthermore, agents outside the cycle are unaffected by this reallocation. Now consider the following procedure. Goods are allocated one by one. First allocate one good arbitrarily. Now consider the end of round k, and suppose $\{o_1, \ldots, o_k\}$ have been allocated, and that envy is bounded by α. At round $k + 1$ we build the envy graph. Next we rotate the bundles as previously described. As already observed, at some point there must be an agent i that no one envies. We then allocate object o_{k+1} to this agent i. Envy is thus at most α. $\square$

Example 12.9. Let $\mathcal{O} = \{o_1, o_2, o_3, o_4, o_5\}$ be a set of objects, and let $\{1, 2, 3\}$ be three agents whose additive preferences are defined as follows:

$\mathcal{S}$	o_1	o_2	o_3	o_4	o_5
$u_1(\mathcal{S})$	1	2	5	3	7
$u_2(\mathcal{S})$	2	6	8	1	5
$u_3(\mathcal{S})$	5	4	4	3	1

The maximal marginal utility is 8. We know that by applying the procedure we are guaranteed to obtain an allocation with a degree of envy at most 8. Suppose we allocate the first three items o_i to agent i, we thus get $\pi(1) = \{o_1\}, \pi(2) = \{o_2\}$, and $\pi(3) = \{o_3\}$. At this step of the procedure, the envy graph is depicted in (*i*). For convenience we indicate the degree of envy on each arrow. There are two cycles. Let us consider for instance the cycle (1,3), and rotate (this corresponds to simply swapping the resources of agents 1 and 3 here). It happens to be sufficient to remove the cycle: we obtain the new envy graph (*ii*). Now we wish to allocate o_4. No one envies 2 nor 3, so we can for instance allocate o_4 to 2, resulting in (*iii*). The graph is without cycle. We can now give o_5 to agent 3, thus obtaining (iv), with a degree of envy of 3.

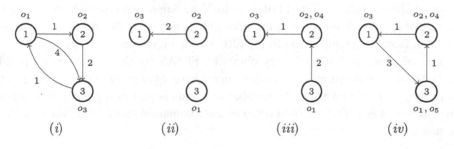

$\qquad(i)\qquad\qquad\qquad(ii)\qquad\qquad\qquad(iii)\qquad\qquad\qquad(iv)$

Note that in that case, by performing a final rotation, we could obtain en envy-free allocation.

Observe that the procedure makes no assumption on the preferences of agents. The result thus shows that it is always possible to have an allocation bounded by the highest marginal value. Of course, such a bound is tight, as is easily observed by a scenario involving a single good and two agents with the same utility for it. In general, however, for a given instance, allocations with a much lower envy than this bound will exist.

Low-Envy Allocations

Is it possible to design algorithms returning an allocation with minimal envy, or at least an approximation of it? A critical problem is that in the case of general preferences, the amount of information that needs to be transmitted to the algorithm is prohibitive (see Section 12.4). It is thus natural to consider the same question in restricting the domain considered.

Another technical issue occurs: the minimum degree of envy as defined by Equation (12.7) is 0 when the allocation is envy-free. While this an intuitive requirement, it has an undesirable consequence: any finite approximation would have to be able to distinguish an envy-free allocation. Unfortunately, as we have seen, this problem is hard, even in the case of modular preferences. Thus, unless P = NP, there is no hope for approximation here (remember the same line of argumentation was used to show inapproximability for maxmin allocations).

To circumvent this, a different measure of envy is considered. The *minimum envy-ratio* is defined as

$$ \max \left\{ 1, \frac{u_i(\pi_j)}{u_i(\pi_i)} \right\}. $$

When the objective function is to minimize this measure, positive results can be obtained. Lipton et al. (2004) were the first to address this version of the problem. They made the additional assumption that agents have the same preferences. In this context, the greedy procedure proposed by Graham (1969) in the context of scheduling yields a 1.4-approximation. The procedure is fairly simple: rank the goods in decreasing order, then allocate them one by one, to the agent whose current bundle has least value. But Lipton et al. (2004) went further: they showed that it is possible to achieve an approximation arbitrarily close to 1 with an algorithm running in polynomial time in the input size (in other words, a Polynomial-Time Approximation Scheme). When the number of agents is bounded, it is even possible to get an FPTAS for this minimization problem. Recently, Nguyen and Rothe (2015) took up this research agenda. When the number of agents is bounded, they obtain an FPTAS for this minimization problem (and other degree measures), *even when agents have different preferences*. On the other hand, they showed that when the number of agents is part of the input, it will not be possible to obtain (in polynomial time) an approximation factor better than 3/2, under the usual P ≠ NP assumption.

Envy-Freeness and Ordinal Preferences

Let us conclude this overview of computational aspects of envy-freeness with a quick look at ordinal preferences. An interesting feature of envy-freeness is that this notion does not require any interpersonal comparison of preferences. As a result, envy-freeness is a *purely ordinal* notion: this fairness criterion is properly defined as soon as the agents are able to compare pairs of bundles (which is not the case for maxmin fairness, requiring cardinal preferences). The ordinal analogous of the problem studied by Lipton et al. (2004) for numerical preferences, namely, the problem of finding an efficient and envy-free allocation with ordinal preferences (using pairwise dominance for lifting preferences from objects to bundles) has been studied by Brams et al. (2004) and Brams and King (2005) and later by Bouveret et al. (2010) and Aziz et al. (2014d).

The main difficulty here is that, unlike additivity for numerical preferences, only requiring responsiveness (and monotonicity, for the two latter references) leaves many pairs of bundles incomparable. For example, if we have $o_1 \rhd o_2 \rhd o_3 \rhd o_4$, responsiveness implies that $o_1 o_2 \succ o_3 o_4$, but leaves $o_1 o_4$ and $o_2 o_3$ incomparable. This calls for an extended version of envy-freeness that takes into account incomparabilities. Brams et al. (2004); Bouveret et al. (2010) propose the two notions of *possible* and *necessary* envy:[14] basically, agent i possibly (resp. necessarily) envies agent j if $\pi(i) \not\succ_i \pi(j)$ (resp. $\pi(j) \succ_i \pi(i)$). The recent work of Aziz et al. (2014d) further extends and refines these notions by introducing a new definition of ordinal dominance based on stochastic dominance.

On the positive side, it turns out that the problem of determining whether a possible envy-free efficient allocation exists is in P (Bouveret et al., 2010) for strict preferences, for different notions of efficiency (completeness, possible and necessary Pareto-efficiency). On the negative side, things seem to be harder (NP-complete) for necessary envy-freeness, and as soon as ties are allowed (Aziz et al., 2014d). Note also that in the case of ordinal preferences, defining measures of envy makes less sense than for numerical preferences. That means that it seems difficult to use approximation to circumvent the computational complexity of the problem.

12.3.3 Other Fairness Measures

In this section we have looked in details at the computation of maxmin or low-envy allocations. Of course, there are many other criteria of fairness of interest. In particular, it is natural to not only focus on the worst-off agent, but to define a more general measure of the inequality of the society and to rely on a *generalized Gini social-evaluation function*. This class of functions is also known as *ordered weighted averages* (Yager, 1988). The computation of these functions has been studied by Lesca and Perny (2010). They investigate in particular how techniques of linear programming (such as the one mentioned in Section 12.3.1) can be adapted so to handle these problems. Recently, the problem of computing inequality indices in combinatorial domains has been considered by Endriss (2013). Also, Vetschera (2010) came up with an approach

---

[14] Actually Brams et al. (2004) use a different terminology, but the idea is the same.

generalizing the branch and bound approach of Dall'Aglio and Mosca (2007) to a wider class of objective functions: more precisely, for any setting involving the division of indivisible goods between *two* agents, and for which the objective function is maximum when the utilities of both players are equal (in the hypothetical continuous case). In that case, the bound based on the "adjusted winner" split, which will be presented in Section 12.4.1, is not valid any longer.

12.4 Protocols for Fair Allocation

The *centralized* "one-shot" approaches to fair resource allocation we have considered so far work in two steps: first the agents fully reveal their preferences (may them be ordinal or numerical) to the benevolent arbitrator, then this arbitrator computes a satisfactory allocation (thanks to an algorithm) and gives the objects to the agents. This approach has two main drawbacks: (*i*) the elicitation process can be very expensive or agents may not be willing to fully reveal their preferences; and (*ii*) agents may be reluctant to accept a solution computed as a black-box.

Regarding (*i*), there is not much we can do in the worst case : when preferences are not modular, the communication load that is required to compute optimal (or indeed approximated) fair solutions becomes a fundamental barrier. This can be stated more formally:

Theorem 12.10 (Lipton et al., 2004; Golovin, 2005). *Any deterministic algorithm would require an exponential number of queries to compute any finite approximation for the minimal envy allocation (Lipton et al., 2004) or the maxmin allocation (Golovin, 2005).*

Such lower bounds can be obtained by borrowing techniques from the communication complexity literature (see also Chapter 10).

The incremental protocols we discuss in this section take a different approach: they prescribe "simple" actions to be taken by the agents at different stages of the process (comparing two bundles, choosing an item, etc.), and they (typically) do not require heavy computation from the central authority. They sometimes do not involve any central computation at all (beyond verification of the legality of agents' actions) nor preference elicitation, and may even work in the absence of a central authority in some cases, as we shall see.

Before we go on and present original protocols, note that some of the algorithms presented earlier in this chapter can be readily interpreted as protocols. This is true in particular of the procedure of Lipton et al. (2004): allocate items sequentially, and each time a new item is assigned, ask agents to point to agents they envy (note that this does not require to elicit preferences). When a cycle occurs, rotate the bundles as indicated in the procedure, and ask again agents who they envy, and so on. Of course, as we have already seen, the guarantees of such a protocol are not so good. We will see that better guarantees can be given, at the price of restrictions on the number of agents, or on the type of preferences.

12.4.1 Protocols for Two Agents

The Adjusted Winner Procedure

This procedure has been used in various contexts (Brams and Taylor, 2000). It works for two agents, with additive utility functions. At the end of the procedure, one item may need to get split, but as we do not know beforehand which one, it has to assume that all items are divisible. The technique is nevertheless inspiring, and can be used to compute a bound in the indivisible case (Dall'Aglio and Mosca, 2007), as already mentioned.

In the first phase of the algorithm (the "winning phase"), goods are allocated efficiently, that is, each good is assigned to the agent who values it the most. At the end of this stage, either $u_1 = u_2$ and we are done, or some agent (say r, the richest) has a higher utility than the other (say p, the poorest) and the "adjusting phase" can begin. During this phase, goods are transferred from the richest to the poorest, in increasing order of the ratio $\frac{u_r(o)}{u_p(o)}$ (note that the ratio is necessarily $\geqslant 1$). The algorithm stops when either both agents enjoy the same utility, or the richest becomes the poorest. Suppose this happens under the transfer of good g: then g is split so as to attain *equitability*, that is, the utility of both agents is equal. To get this equitable outcome, the richest gets a fraction of g computed as follows:

$$\frac{u_p(g) + u_p(\pi(p) \setminus \{g\}) - u_r(\pi(r) \setminus \{g\})}{u_r(g) + u_p(g)}$$

The allocation is thus also a maxmin allocation. In fact, it has several desirable properties:

Theorem 12.11 (Brams and Taylor, 2000). *The adjusted winner procedure returns an equitable, envy-free, and Pareto-optimal allocation.*

Recall that here "equitable" means that the two agents enjoy the same utility at the end of the protocol.

Example 12.12. Let $\mathcal{O} = \{o_1, o_2, o_3, o_4, o_5\}$ be a set of objects.

$\mathcal{S}$	o_1	o_2	o_3	o_4	o_5
$u_1(\mathcal{S})$	1	2	5	3	7
$u_2(\mathcal{S})$	2	6	8	1	5

After the winning phase, agent 2 gets $\{o_1, o_2, o_3\}$ and agent 1 gets $\{o_4, o_5\}$. The utility of agent 2 is $2 + 6 + 8 = 16$ while the utility of agent 1 is 10. Agent 2 will transfer goods to agent 1, starting with o_3 (with ratio $\frac{8}{5}$, while o_1 has $\frac{2}{1}$, and o_2 has $\frac{6}{2}$). But once we do that agent 1 becomes the richest: the good o_3 has to be split, with agent 2 obtaining $(5 + 10 - 8)/13 = 7/13$ of the good g (and the rest for agent 1). This provides each agent a utility $\simeq 12.3$.

The Undercut Procedure

Unlike the adjusted winner, this protocol takes as input ordinal information (a ranking of the items), and assumes that preferences are responsive (in fact, Aziz, 2014 has recently introduced a modified version of the procedure which works for the more general class of *separable* preferences).

As discussed in Section 12.1, the assumption of responsiveness allows to rank some of the bundles only: for instance if $o_1 \rhd o_2 \rhd o_3$, we know among others that $o_1 o_2 \succ o_1 o_3 \succ o_1$. The undercut procedures guarantees to find an envy-free allocation among two agents, whenever one exists. The procedure runs in two phases: in the *generation phase*, agents name their preferred item. If the items are different, they are allocated to agents asking them, otherwise they are placed in the *contested pile*. This is iterated until all the items are either allocated or placed in the pile. Observe that at the end of the generation phase, each agent holds a bundle that she values more than the bundle held by the other agent. The main role of the protocol is then to implement a split of the "contested" items that will lead to an envy-free allocation. The key step is to let agents reveal what is called their *minimal bundles* (they may have several of them): a minimal bundle for agent x is a set of items that is worth at least 50% of the value of the full set of items for x—we say that such a bundle is envy-free (EF) to agent x—and such that it is not possible to find another bundle ordinally less preferred to it, which would also be EF to x. So for instance, with $o_1 \rhd o_2 \rhd o_3$, if $o_1 o_3$ is EF to agent 1, then $o_1 o_2$ cannot be a minimal bundle. Once minimal bundles have been named, the protocol chooses randomly one of them as a proposal (say S_1, that of agent 1). Next agent 2 has the opportunity to either accept the complement of the proposal, or to undercut the proposal, by modifying the proposed split and take for herself a bundle strictly less preferred than S_1.

Theorem 12.13 (Brams et al., 2012b). *If agents differ on at least one minimal bundle, then an envy-free allocation exists and the undercut protocol returns it.*

Example 12.14. We borrow an example from Brams et al. (2012b), where both agents declare the same ranking of five items $o_1 \rhd o_2 \rhd o_3 \rhd o_4 \rhd o_5$. In that case an envy-free split looks unlikely because agents have exactly the same preference: thus, after the generation phase, *all* items go to the contested pile. Now assume agent 1 announces $o_1 o_2$ as her only minimal bundle, while agent 2 announces $o_2 o_3 o_4 o_5$. The minimal bundles differ: there must be an envy-free allocation. Let us see why. Suppose $o_1 o_2$, the minimal bundle of agent 1, is chosen for proposal. Then agent 2 will reject this proposal because $o_3 o_4 o_5$ is not EF to her (as she declared $o_2 o_3 o_4 o_5$ as minimal). It means that $o_1 o_2$ must be EF to agent 2. But as $o_1 o_2$ is not minimal to her, she may propose to take $o_1 o_3$ which is the next ordinally less preferred bundle, and so must still be EF to her. So agent 2 may propose this split, letting agent 1 with $o_2 o_4 o_5$. As on the other hand, $o_1 o_2$ was minimal to agent 1, it must be that $o_1 o_3$ is worth less than 50%, and so $o_2 o_4 o_5$ is EF to agent 1. This allocation is envy-free.

Compared to the adjusted winner, this protocol has the advantage to only require ordinal preferential information. But note that it may not be able to produce a complete envy-free allocation (at least in a deterministic way). Suppose we run the protocol on Example 12.12. Agent 1 reports $o_5 \rhd o_3 \rhd o_4 \rhd o_2 \rhd o_1$, while agent 2 reports

$o_3 \triangleright o_2 \triangleright o_5 \triangleright o_1 \triangleright o_4$. Thus, after the generation phase, agent 1 gets $o_5 o_4$ and agent 2 gets $o_3 o_2$: item 1 is the only contested item and thus no complete envy-free allocation of the pile can be proposed (but assigning this last item randomly may still yield an envy-free allocation).

12.4.2 Protocols for More Than Two Agents

Picking Sequences

Can we take inspiration from the generation phase of the undercut procedure and allocate goods incrementally? This is soon going to be unpractical as the number of agents grows, because all goods will be likely to be contested. But an alternative solution is to fix beforehand a sequence among agents. This is viable even for a large number of agents, and only requires a *partial* elicitation of the agents' preferences (or, at the extreme, no elicitation at all). From the point of view of agents, the assumption of responsiveness of preferences suffices to decide simply which item to pick.

More precisely, the benevolent arbitrator defines a sequence of p agents. Every time an agent is designated, she picks one object out of those that remain. For instance, if $n = 3$ and $p = 5$, the sequence 12332 means that agent 1 picks an object first; then 2 picks an object; then 3 picks two objects; and 2 takes the last object. Such a protocol has very appealing properties: first, it is very simple to implement and to explain[15] and secondly, it frees the central authority from the burden of eliciting the agents' preferences. Seen from the point of view of communication complexity, implementing such a protocol just requires the exchange of $O(m \log(m))$ bits of information (at each of the m steps of the protocol, the chosen agent just needs to send the identifier of the object she wants to pick, which requires $O(\log(m))$ bits). A classical centralized protocol as the ones we discussed earlier would require $\Theta(nm \log(m))$ bits of information to send the agents' preferences to the arbitrator (if they only provide an ordinal information), and $\Theta(m \log(n))$ additional bits for the arbitrator to send the result to the agents.

This protocol has been discussed to some extent by Brams and Taylor (2000), who focus on two particular sequences, namely, *strict alternation*, where two agents pick objects in alternation, and *balanced alternation* (for two agents) consisting of sequences of the form 1221, 12212112, and so on. One can feel intuitively that these kinds of sequences are quite fair, in the sense that alternating the agents in the sequence increases the probability of obtaining a fair allocation in the end (for example, the sequence 1221 is more likely to make both agents happy than 1122, where agent 2 is very likely to be disappointed). The problem of finding the best (fairest) sequence has been investigated by Bouveret and Lang (2011), who proposed a formalization of this problem based on the following hypotheses: (*i*) the agents have additive utilities; (*ii*) a scoring function maps the rank of an object in a preference relation to its utility value—the agents may have different rankings, but this scoring function is the same for all agents; (*iii*) the arbitrator does not know the agents' preferences but only has a probability distribution on the possible profiles. In this framework, the best sequence is just one that maximizes the expected (utilitarian or egalitarian) collective utility.

---

[15] The less understandable an allocation protocol is, the less likely it will accepted by the agents.

Even if the precise complexity of the problem of finding the optimal sequence is still unknown, Kalinowski et al. (2013) have shown, among other things, that the strict alternation policy is optimal with respect to the utilitarian social welfare, if we consider two agents that can have any preference profile with equal probability, and a Borda scoring function. This formally proves the intuitive idea that under mild assumptions, a sequence like 12121212... maximizes the overall utility of the society.

The Descending Demand Procedure

In this protocol proposed by Herreiner and Puppe (2002), agents are assumed to have a linear ordering over all subsets of resources (satisfying monotonicity). An ordering of the agents is fixed beforehand: one by one, they name their preferred bundle, then their next preferred bundle, and so on. The procedure stops as soon as a feasible complete allocation can be obtained, by combining only bundles mentioned so far in the procedure. There may be several such allocations, in which case the Pareto-optimal ones are selected. It does not offer any guarantee of envy-freeness, but produces "balanced" allocations, that is, allocations which maximize the rank in the preference ordering[16] of the bundle obtained by the worst-off agent. As mentioned already, this notion is the natural counterpart of the egalitarian social welfare in this specific case where linear orders are available.

Theorem 12.15 (Herreiner and Puppe, 2002). *The descending demand procedure returns a Pareto-efficient and rank-maxmin-optimal allocation.*

This protocol is simple and can be used by more than two agents, for a moderate number of goods though (since otherwise the requirement to rank all subsets becomes unrealistic).

Distributed Fair Division

When many agents are involved in an allocation, fully distributed approaches can be well adapted. The main idea is that agents will start from an initial allocation, and myopically contract local exchanges (or deals) independently from the rest of the society.[17] In particular, this means that agents can rely on a *local rationality criteria* which tells them whether to accept or not a deal. A rationality criteria is *local* when it can be checked by inspecting only those agents who modified their bundle during the deal. Ideally, such deals should be "simple" (for instance, involving only two agents). For instance, based on the *Pigou-Dalton principle* (Moulin, 1988a), we may conceive a system where only bilateral deals which diminish the inequality among agents involved are allowed.

The question is whether this type of incremental deal-based protocol has any chance in the end to converge to an optimal (fair) solution. As discussed by Endriss et al. (2006), the question is related to the *separability* (Moulin, 1988a, p. 43) of the social welfare ordering considered (not to be confused with the separability of individual

---

[16] Assuming lower ranks correspond to less preferred bundles.
[17] This is similar to the case of housing markets vs. house allocation problems (see Chapter 14).

preferences). The idea behind separability is the following: suppose that only a subset of agents are involved in a deal δ. Then, the change in social welfare caused by δ will always be the same, irrespective of the level of utility of the agents not concerned by the deal. To grasp the intuition, compare the utilitarian social welfare (separable), with maxmin (only separable in the weak sense) and the notion of envy (not separable). Suppose some agents implement a deal (while the rest of the agents do not), and that you can observe its outcome. If the sum of utility among those agents involved in the deal has increased, you know that the overall sum of utility must have increased as well. But you can never be sure that the min utility of the society has increased, even though you observe that the min utility among the agents involved has (because the agent who is currently the worst-off may not be involved in the deal). Still, the allocation cannot become worse (hence separability in the weak sense). This is not even the case with envy: the implementation of a local deal can have negative consequences, since by modifying agents' bundle the envy of agents outside the deal (but observing it) can certainly increase. In a series of papers by Sandholm (1998), Endriss et al. (2006), and Chevaleyre et al. (2010), convergence results are proven for different social welfare measures, domain restrictions, and deal types. These results typically show convergence of *any* sequence of deals to some allocation where no further deal is possible, with guarantees on the quality of such a final allocation.

For instance, convergence to maxmin allocations by means of locally egalitarian deals (that is, deals where the situation of the worst-off agent involved has improved) can still be guaranteed by exploiting the separability of the (stronger) leximin social welfare. Of course the complexity of the problem has not magically disappeared. This is witnessed by two types of "negative" results, affecting the complexity of a single step (i.e., a deal), and the complexity of the sequence of deals as a whole:

- *Any* kind of restriction on deal types ruins the guarantee of convergence in the general domain (Endriss et al., 2006). This is problematic because, as mentioned, deals are likely to be simple in practice (for instance, swapping two resources).
- The upper bound on the length of the sequence of deals can be exponential in the worst case (Sandholm, 1998; Endriss and Maudet, 2005), even when considering only the simplest type of deals, consisting of moving a single resource from one agent to another agent (Dunne, 2005).

On the positive side, these approaches can be deployed in the absence of a central authority, and they enjoy a nice anytime behavior: they return a solution even if stopped before convergence, and the quality of the obtained allocation usually improves as long as the agents can perform deals (though this may not be theoretically guaranteed for all social welfare measures, as briefly discussed earlier).

12.5 Conclusion

In this chapter we have discussed fair division problems involving indivisible items. We have seen that this setting poses several challenges, starting from the mere representation of agents' preferences, to the computation of optimal fair allocations (with maxmin and envy as main illustrations). These difficulties are not necessarily intertwined: we have seen for instance that even with additive preferences, the algorithmic challenge may remain surprisingly high. Of course the usual warning is flashing here: these are typically worst-case results, and recent work suggests that under specific assumptions about the domain considered, it may be possible to obtain satisfying allocations with high probability (and even compute them rather easily). For the design of practical interactive protocols, the preference representation and communication bottleneck seems more stringent, and indeed most efforts have concentrated so far on the setting of two agents equipped with additive, or at least responsive preferences. It is striking though, that very few works have addressed natural preference restrictions beyond such domains. An important question is how such protocols and algorithms will be adopted in practice, for instance whether agents may manipulate, and whether suggested solutions can be easily understood and accepted. While the allocation settings discussed here remain as general as possible, specific features may require dedicated approaches. For instance, agents may have different priority, they may enter the system sequentially, and so on. These aspects (among many others of course) have been investigated in the matching community, and this leads us to strongly encourage the reader interested in fair division to jump to Chapter 14. Indeed, in particular when one resource exactly has to be allocated to each agent, allocation problems can be readily captured in a matching setting (where stability is the primary focus of interest). But if agents have priority when selecting their resource, the notion of envy may only be *justified* when an agent has higher priority over the agent he envies. Interestingly, this corresponds to the notion of stability. This illustrates how the concepts discussed in both chapters can be connected.

Acknowledgments

We would like to thank our editors (in particular Ulle Endriss, Jérôme Lang, and Ariel Procaccia) and our reviewers, Stéphane Airiau and Haris Aziz, for their support, corrections, and very constructive comments.

CHAPTER 13

Cake Cutting Algorithms

Ariel D. Procaccia

13.1 Introduction

Imagine a cake that must be divided between a group of gluttonous children. To complicate matters, the cake is *heterogeneous*: two pieces of cake may differ in terms of their toppings, so the children have different preferences over the pieces (one may prefer a larger proportion of chocolate curls, while another may single-mindedly desire the piece with the cherry). In this chapter we discuss the surprisingly intricate problem of *fairly* dividing the cake—which serves as a metaphor for heterogeneous divisible resources such as land or time.

The cake cutting problem has a long and storied history described, for example, in the books by Brams and Taylor (1996) and Robertson and Webb (1998). The early research on the problem has two main themes: existence results showing that certain fairness guarantees *can* be achieved; and algorithmic results showing *how* such guarantees can be achieved. The focus of this chapter is on the latter theme, which has a more computational flavor.

From a computer scientist's point of view, the cake cutting problem provides a sandbox in which we can explore the role of computational thinking in the allocation of divisible goods. Indeed, the elegant cake cutting model (Section 13.2) distills many of the issues we care about when studying divisible goods more broadly; for example, how to reason about computational complexity in the face of continuous inputs, and how to quantify the trade-offs between individual fairness and global welfare.

13.2 The Model

Our setting includes a set of *agents* denoted $N = \{1, \ldots, n\}$, and a heterogeneous divisible good—the *cake*—represented by the interval $[0, 1]$. We assume that each agent $i \in N$ is endowed with a *valuation function* V_i, which maps a given subinterval $I \subseteq [0, 1]$ to the value assigned to it by agent i, $V_i(I)$. We also write $V_i(x, y)$ as a shorthand for $V_i([x, y])$. These valuation functions are assumed to satisfy several conditions, for every $i \in N$:

- *Normalization:* $V_i(0, 1) = 1$.
- *Divisibility:* For every subinterval $[x, y]$ and $0 \leqslant \lambda \leqslant 1$ there exists a point $z \in [x, y]$ such that $V_i(x, z) = \lambda V_i(x, y)$.
- *Nonnegativity:* For every subinterval I, $V_i(I) \geqslant 0$.

The divisibility property implies that the valuation functions are nonatomic, that is, $V_i(x, x) = 0$ for every $x \in [0, 1]$. This property allows us to ignore the boundaries of intervals, and in particular we can treat two intervals as disjoint if their intersection is a singleton. We denote the length of an interval I by $\ell(I)$, that is, $\ell([x, y]) = y - x$.

A *piece of cake* is a finite union of disjoint intervals. We can alternatively view a piece of cake X as a set of intervals, which allows us to write $I \in X$. To extend the valuation functions to pieces of cake, we also assume:

- *Additivity:* For two disjoint subintervals I, I', $V_i(I) + V_i(I') = V_i(I \cup I')$.

The value of $i \in N$ for a piece X is then simply $V_i(X) = \sum_{I \in X} V_i(I)$, and its length is $\ell(X) = \sum_{I \in X} \ell(I)$.

A slightly more specific model for valuation functions assumes that each agent $i \in N$ has a nonnegative integrable *value density function* v_i. Given a piece of cake X, we let $V_i(X) = \int_{x \in X} v_i(x) dx$. As before we can assume that $\int_{x=0}^{1} v_i(x) dx = V_i(0, 1) = 1$. Importantly, divisibility and additivity follow directly from the basic properties of integration.

In some cases it will prove useful to restrict the agents' valuation functions via the structure of the associated density functions. We say that a valuation function is *piecewise constant* if its associated value density function has this property (see Figure 13.1a). An agent with a piecewise constant valuation function desires a collection of intervals, and each interval is valued uniformly. In other words, crumbs of equal size from the same interval are valued equally, but crumbs from different intervals may have different values. For example, think of the cake as television advertising time; a toy company would be interested in commercial breaks that are associated with children's programs, and its value for a slot would increase with the program's popularity (i.e., the density of different intervals can be different). However, the company may be indifferent between slots within the same commercial break.

Piecewise uniform valuations are a special case of piecewise constant valuations, where the density is either a fixed constant $c > 0$ or 0 (see Figure 13.1b). An agent with a piecewise uniform valuation function has a desired piece of cake that it values uniformly. Such valuations can arise, for instance, if one thinks of cake as access time to a shared backup server. Users are interested in time slots in which their machines are idle, but would be indifferent between two idle time slots of equal length.

We are interested in allocations $\mathbf{A} = (A_1, \ldots, A_n)$, where each A_i is the piece of cake allocated to agent i. These pieces are assumed to form a partition of the cake: They are disjoint and their union is the entire cake. In general each A_i can consist of multiple disjoint intervals, but we are sometimes interested in *contiguous* allocations where each A_i is a single interval. We consider the following fairness properties:

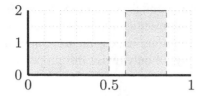

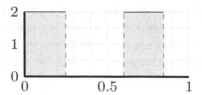

(a) Value density function for a piecewise constant valuation that is not piecewise uniform.

(b) Value density function for a piecewise uniform valuation.

Figure 13.1. An illustration of special value density functions.

- *Proportionality:* for all $i \in N$, $V_i(A_i) \geqslant 1/n$
- *Envy-freeness:* For all $i, j \in N$, $V_i(A_i) \geqslant V_i(A_j)$
- *Equitability:* For all $i, j \in N$, $V_i(A_i) = V_j(A_j)$

Informally, proportionality means that every agent has value at least $1/n$ for its piece of cake; envy-freeness implies that each agent weakly prefers his own piece to any other piece; and equitability means that every two agents assign the exact same value to their own pieces.

It is easy to see that envy-freeness implies proportionality. Indeed, by additivity $\sum_{j \in N} V_i(A_j) = 1$, so there must exist $j \in N$ such that $V_i(A_j) \geqslant 1/n$. Using envy-freeness we have that $V_i(A_i) \geqslant V_i(A_j)$, and therefore $V_i(A_i) \geqslant 1/n$. The converse is true for the case of two agents, because $V_i(A_i) \geqslant 1/2$ and $V_i(A_i) + V_i(A_{3-i}) = 1$ together imply that $V_i(A_i) \geqslant V_i(A_{3-i})$. However, for three agents there are allocations that are proportional but not envy-free: An agent can have value $1/3$ for its own piece, satisfying proportionality, but a value of $1/2$ for another piece, violating envy-freeness. It is also worth mentioning that equitability is incomparable to the other two properties: An allocation where each agent assigns value 0 to its own piece and value 1 to another piece is equitable but not proportional (and hence not envy-free), while most envy-free (and hence proportional) allocations would not satisfy the stringent equality constraint that equitability requires.

13.3 Classic Cake Cutting Algorithms

Although we promised to focus on constructive cake cutting results, we start our formal discussion of cake cutting algorithms with one nonconstructive existence result that tells us what we can expect.

Theorem 13.1 (Alon, 1987). *Let $V_1, \ldots, V_n$ be valuation functions induced by continuous value density functions. Then it is possible to cut the cake in $n^2 - n$ places and partition the $n^2 - n + 1$ intervals into n pieces $A_1, \ldots, A_n$ such that for all $i, j \in N$, $V_i(A_j) = 1/n$.*

So, under a mild assumption (continuity of the value density functions), there are allocations that are equitable (each agent has value exactly $1/n$ for its piece) and envy-free (each agent also has value exactly $1/n$ for any other piece). Moreover, such allocations only require a number of cuts that is polynomial in n, regardless of the valuation functions. Unfortunately, as we shall see constructing allocations satisfying these properties is difficult. In fact, equitable allocations are impossible to achieve in the computational model that we adopt,[1] which is why we only revisit this property in Section 13.5.

13.3.1 Proportionality for $n = 2$: Cut and Choose

When there are two agents, the intuitive *cut and choose* algorithm computes a proportional (and hence also envy-free) allocation. Agent 1 cuts the cake into two equally valued pieces, that is, two pieces X_1 and X_2 such that $V_1(X_1) = V_1(X_2) = 1/2$. Agent 2 then chooses its preferred piece, and agent 1 receives the remaining piece. Formally, if $V_2(X_1) \geqslant V_2(X_2)$ then set $A_2 = X_1$, $A_1 = X_2$; otherwise set $A_1 = X_1$, $A_2 = X_2$. This allocation is clearly proportional.

An important property of the cut and choose algorithm—which is shared by other classic algorithms, described later—is that an agent can obtain its fair share by following the algorithm, regardless of whether others also follow the algorithm. Indeed, agent 1 would receive a piece worth exactly $1/2$ by cutting the cake into two equal pieces, even if agent 2 deviated from the algorithm by choosing its less preferred piece. Similarly, agent 2 would receive a piece worth at least $1/2$, even if agent 1 cut the cake into two uneven pieces. Making a distinction between the prescribed algorithm and the agents' strategies gives rise to intriguing game-theoretic questions, which we do not discuss here; some relevant references can be found in Section 13.6.

13.3.2 Proportionality for Any n: Dubins-Spanier and Even-Paz

An algorithm devised by Dubins and Spanier (1961) guarantees a proportional allocation for any number of agents. The algorithm was originally specified using a continuously moving knife, but we describe its discrete version (and slightly modify it for ease of exposition). In the first round each agent $i \in N$ makes a mark at the point x_i such that $V_i(0, x_i) = 1/n$. The agent i^* that made the leftmost mark—formally an agent in $i^* \in \operatorname{argmin}_{i \in N} x_i$—exits with the piece $A_{i^*} = [0, x_{i^*}]$. The process is repeated with the remaining agents and remaining cake. When there is only one agent left, it receives the unclaimed piece of cake.

Each agent $i \in N$ that exits during the execution of the algorithm receives a piece A_i such that $V_i(A_i) = 1/n$. The proportionality guarantee is also satisfied with respect to the last agent j, because $V_j(A_i) \leqslant 1/n$ for all $i \in N \setminus \{j\}$, and hence $V_j(A_j) \geqslant 1 - (n - 1)/n = 1/n$.

A similar algorithm, proposed more than two decades later by Even and Paz (1984), achieves the same proportionality guarantee but in a more computationally efficient way. Presently we describe the algorithm and establish proportionality; we provide a complexity analysis in Section 13.4. Assume purely for ease of exposition that n is a power of 2. When the algorithm is given a subset of agents $1, \ldots, k$ and a piece $[y, z]$, it asks each agent i to mark the point x_i such that $V_i(y, x_i) = V_i(y, z)/2$. Let $x_{i_1}, \ldots, x_{i_k}$

---

[1] Methods that achieve equitable allocations, like the one by Brams et al. (2006), require "continuous" operations.

be the marks sorted from left to right; that is, $x_{i_j} \leqslant x_{i_{j+1}}$ for $j = 1, \ldots, k - 1$. The algorithm is recursively called with agents $i_1, \ldots, i_{k/2}$ and the piece $[y, x_{i_{k/2}}]$, and agents $i_{k/2+1}, \ldots, i_k$ and the piece $[x_{i_{k/2+1}}, z]$. When the algorithm is called with a singleton set of agents $\{i\}$ and an interval I it assigns $A_i = I$. Initially the algorithm is called with all agents and the entire cake.

At depth k in the recursion tree, $n/2^k$ agents share a piece of cake that each values at least at $1/2^k$. In particular, at depth $\lg n$ the algorithm is called with one agent and a piece of cake it values at least at $1/2^{\lg n} = 1/n$. We conclude that the Even-Paz algorithm is proportional.

However, it is easy to see that the Dubins-Spanier and Even-Paz algorithms are not envy free. For example, in Dubins-Spanier an agent would never envy agents that exited earlier, but may certainly envy agents that exited later.

13.3.3 Envy-Freeness for $n = 3$: Selfridge-Conway

In around 1960, Selfridge and Conway (independently) constructed the following envy-free algorithm for the case of three agents (see, e.g., Brams and Taylor, 1995):

Initialization:

1. Agent 1 divides the cake into three equally valued pieces X_1, X_2, X_3: $V_1(X_1) = V_1(X_2) = V_1(X_3) = 1/3$.
2. Agent 2 trims the most valuable piece according to V_2 to create a tie for most valuable. For example, if $V_2(X_1) > V_2(X_2) \geqslant V_2(X_3)$, agent 2 removes $X' \subseteq X_1$ such that $V_2(X_1 \setminus X') = V_2(X_2)$. We call the three pieces—one of which is trimmed—*cake 1* ($X_1 \setminus X', X_2, X_3$ in the example), and we call the trimmings *cake 2* (X' in the example).

Division of cake 1:

3. Agent 3 chooses one of the three pieces of cake 1.
4. If agent 3 chose the trimmed piece ($X_1 \setminus X'$ in the example), agent 2 chooses between the two other pieces of cake 1. Otherwise, agent 2 receives the trimmed piece. We denote the agent $i \in \{2, 3\}$ that received the trimmed piece by T, and the other agent by $\overline{T}$.
5. Agent 1 receives the remaining piece of cake 1.

Division of cake 2:

6. Agent $\overline{T}$ divides cake 2 into three equally valued pieces.
7. Agents $T, 1, \overline{T}$ select a piece of cake 2 each, in that order.

To establish the envy-freeness of the Selfridge-Conway algorithm, first note that the division of cake 1 is clearly envy free: Agent 3 chooses first; agent 2 receives one of the two pieces that it views as tied for largest; and agent 1 definitely receives an untrimmed piece, which it also views as tied for largest. Now consider the division of cake 2. Agent T chooses first, and agent $\overline{T}$ is indifferent between the three pieces, so these agents do not envy another agent's piece of cake 2. Combining envy-free divisions of two disjoint pieces of cake yields an envy-free division of the combined cake, hence agents T and $\overline{T}$ are not envious overall. At first glance one may worry that agent 1 prefers T's piece of cake 2 to its own. Observe, however, that agent 1 would not envy agent T, even if T received all of cake 2; because then T would merely construct one of the original pieces (X_1 in the example), which agent 1 values at $1/3$—only as much as its own untrimmed piece of cake 1!

13.4 Complexity of Cake Cutting

Some of the previous chapters of this book analyzed the computational complexity of problems in terms of complexity classes such as P and NP. Understanding the complexity of cake cutting calls for a different approach, though, because in general there may not be a finite discrete representation of a problem instance. We must therefore adopt a *concrete complexity* model that specifies which operations a cake cutting algorithm is allowed to use; we will measure complexity via bounds on the number of allowed operations.

The standard concrete complexity model for cake cutting is the *Robertson-Webb* model (Robertson and Webb, 1998), which supports two types of queries:

- $\text{eval}_i(x, y)$: Asks agent i to evaluate the interval $[x, y]$. Formally, $\text{eval}_i(x, y) = V_i(x, y)$.
- $\text{cut}_i(x, \alpha)$: Asks agent i to cut a piece of cake worth a given value α, starting at a given point x. Formally, $\text{cut}_i(x, \alpha) = y$ where y is the leftmost point such that $V_i(x, y) = \alpha$.

The Robertson-Webb model is deceptively simple, but in fact it is powerful enough to capture the cake cutting algorithms described in Section 13.3. For example, to simulate cut and choose the algorithm sends a $\text{cut}_1(0, 1/2)$ query to agent 1. Agent 1 answers with a point y; note that $V_1(0, y) = V_1(y, 1) = 1/2$. It is now sufficient to ask agent 2 an $\text{eval}_2(0, y)$ query. If the answer is at least $1/2$, we know that $A_1 = [y, 1]$, $A_2 = [0, y]$ is a proportional allocation; otherwise we can obtain a proportional allocation by switching the two pieces.

Let us also verify that we can simulate the initialization stage of the Selfridge-Conway algorithm (simulating the other stages is even easier). The algorithm starts with a $\text{cut}_1(0, 1/3) = y$ query, followed by a $\text{cut}_1(y, 1/3) = z$ query. The intervals $[0, y]$, $[y, z]$, $[z, 1]$ are now known to be worth $1/3$ each to agent 1. We next ask agent 2 to evaluate the three intervals (strictly speaking, evaluating two is sufficient). Say that $V_2(0, y) > V_2(y, z) \geqslant V_2(z, 1)$; to trim the largest piece, the algorithm asks a $\text{cut}_2(0, V_2(0, y) - V_2(y, z)) = w$ query. Cake 2 is the interval $[0, w]$.

Earlier we claimed that the Even-Paz algorithm is more computationally efficient than the Dubins-Spanier algorithm. We are now in a position to make this statement formal. The Dubins-Spanier algorithm can be simulated by asking each remaining agent a $\text{cut}_i(x, 1/n)$ query, where x is the left boundary of the remaining cake. The overall number of queries is $\sum_{k=0}^{n-2}(n - k) = \Theta(n^2)$.

The Even-Paz algorithm requires a $\text{cut}_i(y, V_i(y, z)/2)$ query to each agent in each recursive call, where $[y, z]$ is the current piece. If we again assume for ease of exposition that n is a power of 2, there is one recursive call with n agents, two with $n/2$ agents, and in general 2^k recursive calls with $n/2^k$ agents. The overall number of queries is therefore exactly $n \lg n$. When n is not a power of 2, the algorithm and its analysis can be slightly adjusted to yield a bound of $\Theta(n \lg n)$.

13.4.1 A Lower Bound for Proportional Cake Cutting

In light of the significant improvement the Even-Paz algorithm achieves over Dubins-Spanier, one may ask whether it is possible to do even better. The next theorem says that the answer is no: The Even-Paz algorithm is provably the most computationally efficient (in the asymptotic sense) proportional cake-cutting algorithm.

Theorem 13.2 (Edmonds and Pruhs, 2006b). *Any proportional cake-cutting algorithm requires* $\Omega(n \lg n)$ *queries in the Robertson-Webb model.*

To prove the theorem we separate the problem of finding a proportional allocation into problems that must be solved for each agent individually. To this end, we fix an agent $i \in N$, and say that a piece X is *thin* if $\ell(X) \leqslant 2/n$, and *rich* if $V_i(X) \geqslant 1/n$. A piece is *thin-rich* if it satisfies both properties (this terminology is inspired by a quote from Wallis Simpson, the Duchess of Windsor, "A woman can't be too rich or too thin"). The *thin-rich problem* is that of finding a thin-rich piece of cake.

Lemma 13.3. *If the complexity (in the Robertson-Webb model) of the thin-rich problem is $T(n)$, then the complexity of proportional cake cutting (in the Robertson-Webb model) is $\Omega(nT(n))$.*

Proof. First note that in the Robertson-Webb model each query only acquires information about the valuation function of a single agent, hence the interaction with one agent cannot help us find a thin-rich piece with respect to another agent.

Next, note that in any proportional allocation all the pieces must be rich. Moreover, a feasible allocation cannot include more than $n/2$ pieces that are *not* thin, otherwise we would have that $\sum_{i \in N} \ell(A_i) > (n/2)(2/n) = 1$, which is impossible because the length of the entire cake is 1 and the pieces are disjoint. It follows that the computation of a proportional allocation requires finding at least $n/2$ thin-rich pieces, that is, solving the thin-rich problem with respect to at least $n/2$ agents. We conclude that the complexity of proportional cake-cutting is at least $(n/2)T(n) = \Omega(nT(n))$. $\square$

By Lemma 13.3, to prove Theorem 13.2 it is sufficient to establish that the complexity of the thin-rich problem is $\Omega(\lg n)$. In the following, we fix an agent i and hence we can drop the i subscript (i.e., we use V instead of V_i, cut instead of cut_i, and so on).

We represent the valuation function of the fixed agent via a *value tree*. Assume without loss of generality that $n/2$ is a power of 3, and divide the cake into $n/2$ disjoint intervals of length $2/n$ each. The value tree is a rooted complete ternary tree—each internal node has exactly three children—where the leaves are the disjoint intervals. Furthermore, for each internal node u, two of the edges to its children are labeled by $1/4$ (*light* edges), and the third is labeled by $1/2$ (*heavy* edge). We think of an internal node as the union of the intervals at the leaves of the subtree rooted at that node, and the edge labels tell us how the value of a node is split between its children. In particular, the value of the interval that corresponds to a node is the product of the weights on the path from the root to the node. We assume that the value is uniformly distributed on each interval corresponding to a leaf (i.e., V is piecewise constant). See Figure 13.2 for an illustration.

In general an algorithm can return a piece of cake that does not correspond to a leaf of the value tree, or even a union of such leaves. However, the next lemma implies that

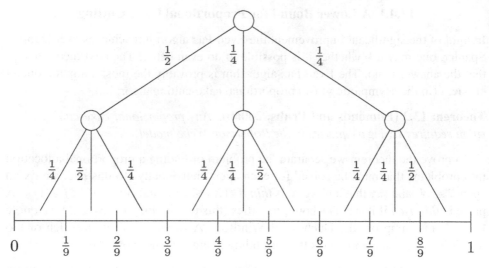

Figure 13.2. An example of a value tree for $n/2 = 9$. In this example, $V(2/9, 3/9) = 1/8$ and $V(3/9, 4/9) = 1/16$.

for the purposes of the proof of Theorem 13.2 we can focus on algorithms that return a single leaf of the value tree.

Lemma 13.4. *When the valuation function is derived from a value tree, if there exists a $T(n)$-complexity algorithm for the thin-rich problem in the Robertson-Webb model, then there exists an $O(T(n))$-complexity algorithm that returns a thin-rich leaf of the value tree.*

Proof. Suppose that after $T(n)$ queries we were able to find a thin-rich piece of cake X. There exists an interval $I^* \in X$ such that $V(I^*) \geqslant \ell(I^*)/2$, otherwise

$$V(X) = \sum_{I \in X} V(I) < \sum_{I \in X} \frac{\ell(I)}{2} = \frac{\ell(X)}{2} \leqslant \frac{1}{n},$$

contradicting the assumption that X is rich. It follows that the average value density on I^* is at least $1/2$. Note that I^* intersects at most two leaves of the value tree because $\ell(I^*) \leqslant \ell(X) \leqslant 2/n$, and the value density function is constant on each of these two leaves. Therefore, one of these two leaves—call it u—has density at least $1/2$, so $V(u) \geqslant \ell(u)/2 = 1/n$.

To pinpoint u using queries in the Robertson-Webb model, note that after $T(n)$ queries the algorithm knows the values of at most $O(T(n))$ intervals; we can therefore assume without loss of generality that $|X| = O(T(n))$.[2] We conclude that using $O(T(n))$ additional eval queries the algorithm can learn the value of each leaf that intersects an interval $I \in X$.   □

Lemma 13.4 tells us that it is sufficient to show that any algorithm for the thin-rich problem that is constrained to return a (rich) leaf of the value tree requires $\Omega(\lg n)$

---

[2] This argument is intuitive and sufficiently formal for the purposes of this chapter, but making it completely formal requires some more work.

queries. Intuitively, the path from the root to a rich leaf must have "many" heavy edges. To find out exactly how many, note that the height of the tree is $H = \log_3(n/2) = \theta(\lg(n))$. Denoting the number of heavy edges on the path from the root to a leaf u by $q(u)$, we have

$$\frac{1}{n} \leqslant V(u) = \left(\frac{1}{2}\right)^{q(u)} \left(\frac{1}{4}\right)^{H-q(u)} = \left(\frac{1}{4}\right)^{H-\frac{q(u)}{2}}.$$

It follows that $4^{H-q(u)/2} \leqslant n$, and hence $2(H - q(u)/2) \leqslant \lg n$. Using the fact that $2H - \lg n = \Omega(\lg n)$ we conclude that $q(u) = \Omega(\lg n)$. In other words, a constant fraction of the edges on the path to u must be heavy.

If the algorithm were only allowed to directly query the edges of the value tree, a lower bound of $\Omega(\lg n)$ would follow almost immediately from the preceding argument. Indeed, unqueried edges could be light, so the algorithm must query a constant fraction of the edges on the path from the root to a leaf in order to find a constant fraction of heavy edges. However, we are interested in algorithms that operate in the Robertson-Webb model, so we must explain how to simulate cut and eval queries by revealing edges of the value tree.

We say that a node u is *revealed* if the weights of *all* edges of *every* node on the path from the root to u are known to the algorithm. Intuitively the approach is to generously answer the algorithm's queries by revealing nodes in a way that provides at least as much information as requested. We note the following facts:

- If u is revealed, its value (formally, the value of the interval associated with the node) $V(u)$ is known to the algorithm.
- If $u = [x, y]$ is revealed then $V(0, x)$ is known to the algorithm: Let $u_0, \ldots, u_k = u$ be the path from the root to u, then $V(0, x)$ is the sum of the values of the nodes to the left of each u_i, all of which are also revealed. Moreover, $V(y, 1) = 1 - V(0, x) - V(x, y)$ is also known.
- If $z \in [x, y]$ where $[x, y]$ is a revealed leaf then $V(0, z)$ can be computed, using the preceding observation and the fact that $V(x, z) = V(x, y) \cdot \frac{\ell([x,z])}{2/n}$.
- If $w \in u$, u is a revealed leaf, and α is a given cake value, then it is possible to compute the least common ancestor of u and the leaf that contains the point z such that $V(w, z) = \alpha$. Indeed, let $u_0, \ldots, u_H = u$ be the path from the root to the leaf u, and let y_i be the rightmost point of u_i. We start from $i = H$ and working our way upward iteratively compute $V(w, y_i)$, where $V(w, y_H) = \frac{\ell([w,y_H])}{2/n}$ and $V(w, y_i)$ is the sum of $V(w, y_{i+1})$ and the values of the children of u_i to the right of u_{i+1}. We return the first u_i (i.e., the one with the largest index) such that $V(w, y_i) \geqslant \alpha$.

Proof of Theorem 13.2. It is sufficient to prove that any algorithm for the thin-rich problem that returns a leaf of the value tree requires $\Omega(\lg n)$ queries. We will answer the algorithm's eval and cut queries by revealing nodes of the value tree in a way that maintains the following invariant: After k queries, there are at most $2k$ edges that are known to be heavy on any path from the root to a leaf. Because we have shown that $\Omega(\lg n)$ edges on the path must be known to be heavy, the theorem will directly follow. Initially the invariant trivially holds.

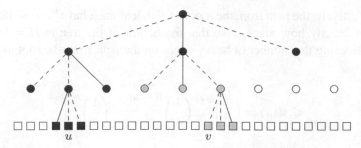

Figure 13.3. Illustration of the proof of Theorem 13.2, with $n/2 = 27$. In this example the first query is an eval(x, y) query, $x \in u$, $y \in v$. Solid edges are revealed to be heavy, dashed edges are revealed to be light. In the process of revealing u, the black nodes are also revealed; note that all the edges from the root to u are light. Next, in the process of revealing v, the gray nodes are revealed. Some paths are revealed to contain two heavy edges, but no path contains more.

Say that the algorithm has already asked k queries, and any root-to-leaf path has at most $2k$ edges that were revealed to be heavy. Assume first that query $k + 1$ is an eval(x, y) query. Let u be the leaf that contains x, and let $u_0, \ldots, u_H = u$ be the path from the root to u; u_t is the lowest revealed node on this path. The weights of the edges on the path $u_t, \ldots, u_H$ are revealed to be light. Moreover, each u_i on this path has two additional edges to its children; one is revealed to be light, and the other heavy. We repeat the same process for y; see Figure 13.3 for an illustration. Since the leaves containing x and y are revealed, the algorithm has enough information to determine $V(x, y)$ and therefore to answer the eval query.

Let us verify that the invariant has been maintained. Revealing the nodes on the path to x adds at most one additional heavy edge on the path to a leaf, because the edges that are revealed to be heavy do not lie on the same path. The same observation holds for y, but it may be the case that each of the two procedures contributed a heavy edge on the path to a leaf. Overall the number of heavy edges on the path to a leaf increased by at most two, and is now at most $2k + 2 = 2(k + 1)$.

Dealing with a cut(w, α) query is slightly trickier. First, the leaf that contains w is revealed as before. Second, we find the least common ancestor u of the leaf that contains w and the leaf that contains the point z such that $V(w, z) = \alpha$. Our goal is to reveal the leaf that contains z in a way that all the currently unrevealed edges between u and the leaf are light. Starting from the first unrevealed node in this path, we set the values so that the path always follows a light edge. Specifically, at node u', let β be the additional value that is required from u'. If $\beta / V(u') > 1/2$ we set the edge from v to its left child to be heavy; the path will then follow the middle or right edge, both of which are light. Otherwise—$\beta / V(u') \leqslant 1/2$—we set the right edge to be heavy, again making the path follow one of the light edges. It can be seen that the invariant is maintained via the same argument given for the case of an eval query.   □

It is worth pointing out that Edmonds and Pruhs (2006b) actually prove a more general lower bound that captures approximate proportionality requirements and approximate queries, and holds even for randomized algorithms.

13.4.2 The Complexity of Envy-Free Cake Cutting

While the complexity of proportional cake cutting is well understood, envy-freeness is a completely different matter. The classic Selfridge-Conway algorithm provides an envy-free solution for the case of three agents, but it took another three decades until their algorithm was extended to any number of agents. The celebrated algorithm of Brams and Taylor (1995) is a discrete envy-free cake cutting algorithm. When viewed through the Robertson-Webb lens, the algorithm can be simulated via eval and cut queries, and is guaranteed to terminate—it is *finite*. But it does have a serious flaw: Its running time is *unbounded*. Specifically, the analysis of the Dubins-Spanier and Even-Paz algorithms bounded the required number of queries as a function of the number of agents: $O(n^2)$ and $O(n \lg n)$, respectively. In contrast, for any $n \geqslant 4$ and any $k \in \mathbb{N}$ there are valuation functions $V_1, \ldots, V_n$ such that the Brams-Taylor algorithm requires at least k queries to terminate.[3]

It is natural to ask whether the envy-free cake cutting problem is inherently difficult: Is it provably impossible to design a bounded envy-free cake cutting algorithm? Currently there are two partial answers to this question. The first result restricts the allocations to be contiguous.

Theorem 13.5 (Stromquist, 2008). *For any $n \geqslant 3$, there is no finite envy-free cake-cutting algorithm that outputs contiguous allocations.*[4]

However, from a technical point of view the restriction to contiguous pieces is severe. Indeed, the Brams-Taylor algorithm is finite and guarantees an envy-free allocation for any number of agents. Moreover, for the case of $n = 3$ (which is captured by Theorem 13.5), the Selfridge-Conway algorithm is actually a *bounded* envy-free algorithm! Interestingly, the latter algorithm even allocates "almost contiguous" pieces, in that the piece of each agent is the union of at most two intervals.

The second result does not make any assumptions, but achieves a relatively weak lower bound.

Theorem 13.6 (Procaccia, 2009). *Any envy-free cake-cutting algorithm requires $\Omega(n^2)$ queries in the Robertson-Webb model.*

This theorem is somewhat unsatisfying, because the gap between $\Omega(n^2)$ and "unbounded" is still, well, unbounded. Nevertheless, it does establish a separation between the $O(n \lg n)$ complexity of proportional cake cutting and the $\Omega(n^2)$ complexity of envy-free cake cutting. In other words, the theorem implies that envy-freeness is provably harder than proportionality, and provides a partial explanation for why envy-freeness has been so elusive.

The running time of the Brams-Taylor algorithm depends on the valuation functions; this fact seems to suggest that the hardness of envy-free cake cutting draws on the possible richness of the valuation functions. This turns out not to be the case: In the Robertson-Webb model, envy-free cake cutting is equally hard when the valuation functions are piecewise uniform.

---

[3] Even when moving knives are allowed, there are no known bounded solutions beyond the case of $n = 5$ (Brams et al., 1997b; Saberi and Wang, 2009).

[4] This theorem was extended by Deng et al. (2012).

Theorem 13.7 (Kurokawa et al., 2013). *Suppose there is an algorithm that computes an envy-free allocation for n agents with piecewise uniform valuations using at most $f(n)$ queries in the Robertson-Webb model. Then the algorithm can compute an envy-free allocation for n agents with general valuation functions using at most $f(n)$ queries.*

Proof. Let $V_1, \ldots, V_n$ be general valuation functions. We let the algorithm interact with these functions via cut and eval queries. Suppose first that the algorithm outputs an allocation **A** using at most $f(n)$ queries. Our goal is to construct piecewise uniform valuation functions $U_1, \ldots, U_n$ that lead to an identical interaction with the algorithm, and identical values for the allocated pieces (i.e., $V_i(A_i) = U_i(A_i)$ for all $i \in N$). Since the algorithm is guaranteed to output an envy-free allocation with respect to $U_1, \ldots, U_n$, these properties would imply that **A** is envy-free with respect to the general valuation functions $V_1, \ldots, V_n$.

To construct the valuation functions $U_1, \ldots, U_n$, we define sets of points M_i as follows. First, M_i contains all "marks" made during the algorithm's interaction with agent i; an $eval_i(x, y)$ query marks the points x and y, and a $cut_i(x, \alpha)$ query marks the point x and the point y that is returned. Second, for each $j \in N$ and each interval $[x, y] \in A_j$, M_i contains x and y; in other words, the allocation **A** induces a partition of $[0, 1]$ into subintervals, and M_i contains the boundaries of these intervals. Third, M_i contains the boundaries of the cake, 0 and 1.

Let $M_i = \{0 = x_{i1}, x_{i2}, \ldots, x_{ik_i} = 1\}$, where $x_{it} < x_{i,t+1}$ for all $t = 1, \ldots, k_i - 1$. Let $\mu_i = \max_t \frac{V_i(x_{it}, x_{i,t+1})}{x_{i,t+1} - x_{it}}$ be the maximum average density on any interval defined by the points in M_i. The valuation function U_i is induced by a piecewise uniform value density function u_i, defined as follows:

$$u_i(x) = \begin{cases} \mu_i & \exists t \text{ s.t. } x \in \left[x_{i,t+1} - \frac{V_i(x_{it}, x_{i,t+1})}{\mu_i}, x_{i,t+1} \right] \\ 0 & \text{otherwise.} \end{cases}$$

For all $i \in N$ and $t = 1, \ldots, k_i - 1$ it holds that

$$U_i(x_{it}, x_{i,t+1}) = \frac{V_i(x_{it}, x_{i,t+1})}{\mu_i} \cdot \mu_i = V_i(x_{it}, x_{i,t+1}).$$

Since the boundaries of intervals in each A_j are contained in M_i (i.e., they are among the points x_{it}), it follows that for every $i, j \in N$, $U_i(A_j) = V_i(A_j)$. We also claim that the algorithm's interaction with $U_1, \ldots, U_n$ is identical to its interaction with $V_1, \ldots, V_n$. Indeed, the answers to $eval_i$ queries are identical because the marks made by the query are contained in the set M_i. To see that the answers to cut_i queries are also identical, consider a $cut_i(x, \alpha) = y$ query. Note that $U_i(x, y) = V_i(x, y) = \alpha$ because $x, y \in M_i$, and crucially for any $\epsilon > 0$, $U_i(x, y - \epsilon) < \alpha$ because u_i is strictly positive in the left neighborhood of y. This concludes the proof under the assumption that the algorithm terminates after at most $f(n)$ queries.

If the algorithm does not terminate after $f(n)$ queries, consider the first $f(n)$ queries, and repeat the process of constructing $U_1, \ldots, U_n$ without including the boundaries of allocated intervals in $M_1, \ldots, M_n$. As before, the algorithm's interaction with $U_1, \ldots, U_n$ is identical to its interaction with $V_1, \ldots, V_n$, and thus the assumption that the algorithm proceeds to query $f(n) + 1$ contradicts the assumption that the number of queries is bounded by $f(n)$ given piecewise uniform valuations. $\square$

Theorem 13.7 has two complementary interpretations. On one hand, the theorem tells us that to design an envy-free algorithm we can focus on handling the seemingly simple case of piecewise uniform valuations. On the other hand, if one seeks to prove a lower bound for envy-free cake cutting, the theorem implies that constructing elaborate valuation functions would not be a fruitful approach.

In order to conclude this section on a positive note, we next relax the envy-freeness requirement, instead asking for ϵ-envy-freeness: $V_i(A_i) \geqslant V_i(A_j) - \epsilon$ for all $i, j \in N$. Despite the difficulties we have discussed, it turns out that this natural relaxation can be solved by a very simple, computationally efficient algorithm. First, the algorithm asks each agent $i \in N$ to cut the cake into $\lceil 1/\epsilon \rceil$ disjoint intervals worth ϵ each (except for maybe the rightmost interval, which is worth at most ϵ); this step requires roughly n/ϵ cut queries. Next the algorithm sorts the cut points made by all the agents, and asks each agent to evaluate each interval between two adjacent cut points; this step requires roughly n^2/ϵ eval queries.

We claim that at this point the algorithm has sufficient information to compute an ϵ-envy-free allocation. Indeed, we can treat the intervals between adjacent cut points as indivisible goods where, crucially, each good is worth at most ϵ to *any* agent. The goods are allocated in a round-robin fashion: each of the agents $1, 2, \ldots, n$ selects its most preferred good in that order, and we repeat this process until all the goods have been selected. To see why this allocation is ϵ-envy-free consider an agent $i \in N$, and consider the sequence of choices starting from the first time i selected a good: $i, i + 1, \ldots, n, 1, \ldots, i - 1, i, \ldots, i - 1, \ldots$. In each subsequence $i, \ldots, i - 1$, i prefers its own good to the goods selected by other agents. The only potential source of envy is the selections made by agents $1, \ldots, i - 1$ before i first selected a good, but these agents received one good each in this phase, and $V_i(g) \leqslant \epsilon$ for each good g.

13.5 Optimal Cake Cutting

So far we were interested in algorithms that achieve fairness guarantees. But if we are also interested in economic efficiency, better allocations may be achieved at the expense of depriving some agents of their fair share.

To quantify the efficiency of an allocation $\mathbf{A}$ we employ the notion of *social welfare*. While this notion has several interpretations, the computer science literature typically adopts the *utilitarian* interpretation, as do we: The social welfare of $\mathbf{A}$ is $\mathrm{sw}(\mathbf{A}) = \sum_{i \in N} V_i(A_i)$. It is important to note that this notion assumes the agents have *comparable* valuation functions. Although earlier we have assumed that $V_i(0, 1) = 1$, the assumption was made for ease of exposition; proportionality and envy-freeness involve inequalities that only constrain the valuation function of a single agent; that is, two valuation functions never appear in the same inequality. In contrast, when discussing social welfare our objective is the sum of all valuation functions, so our assumption that $V_i(0, 1) = 1$ for all $i \in N$ takes a more literal interpretation.

13.5.1 Computation of Optimal Fair Allocations

Our next task is the computation of *optimal* fair allocations; that is, we wish to maximize social welfare under fairness constraints. To circumvent the computational issues

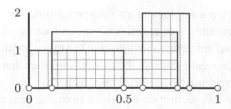

Figure 13.4. An illustration of piecewise constant value density functions, where $n = 2$ and the area under the density function of agent 1 (resp., agent 2) is filled with horizontal (resp., vertical) lines. The boundaries of the segments reported by the agents are marked by white circles. Note that both value density functions are constant between every pair of consecutive marks.

discussed in Section 13.4, the algorithmic results assume that agents' valuation functions are restricted. For ease of exposition we formulate and prove the results for piecewise constant valuations, even though some of them also hold under less restrictive assumptions.

Crucially, we also assume that these valuations are *fully known* to the algorithm. In other words, the algorithm's task is not to elicit information via the kind of interaction with the agents captured by the Robertson-Webb model; rather, the algorithm's goal is to compute an allocation, given an explicit representation of the valuation functions. Such an explicit representation is possible because piecewise constant valuations are concisely representable: For each segment on which the density function is constant, the representation includes the boundaries of the segment and the density.[5]

For the sake of intuition, let us first see why computing allocations that are both envy-free and equitable (but not necessarily optimal) is easy given the full representation of the agents' piecewise constant valuation functions. Mark the boundaries of the agents' reported segments, as well as 0 and 1. Let $\mathcal{J}$ denote the set of intervals that lie between consecutive marks. The crucial observation is that for all $i \in N$ and all $I \in \mathcal{J}$, v_i is constant on I, as can be seen in Figure 13.4. It follows that if $I' \subseteq I$ is such that $\ell(I') = \ell(I)/n$ then $V_i(I') = V_i(I)/n$. To construct the allocation $A_1, \ldots, A_n$, simply partition each $I \in \mathcal{J}$ into n pieces of equal length, and give each piece to a different agent. It holds that for all $i, j \in N$, $V_i(A_j) = 1/n$; that is, each agent values each piece at exactly $1/n$, and in particular the allocation is envy-free and equitable. In other words, under piecewise constant valuation functions we can *compute* the kind of allocations whose *existence* Theorem 13.1 guarantees.

More generally, suppose that the piece A_j allocated to j consists of a fraction f_{jI} interval I, for every $I \in \mathcal{J}$; then for every $i \in N$, $V_i(A_j) = \sum_{I \in \mathcal{J}} f_{jI} V_i(I)$. Because envy-freeness, proportionality, and equitability are linear constraints on the values of allocated pieces, this observation directly allows us to compute optimal allocations among the allocations satisfying any of these fairness properties, or even pairs of properties.[6] For example, to compute optimal proportional allocations we can solve

---

[5] We assume that these parameters are represented as k-bit rationals, that is, numbers of the form a/b where a and b are k-bit integers.

[6] It is pointless to talk about satisfying all three properties together because envy-freeness implies proportionality.

the following linear program (Cohler et al., 2011):

$$\max \sum_{i=1}^{n} \sum_{I \in \mathcal{J}} f_{iI} V_i(I), \tag{13.1}$$

$$\text{s.t.} \sum_{i=1}^{n} f_{iI} \leqslant 1 \; \forall I \in \mathcal{J}, \tag{13.2}$$

$$\sum_{I \in \mathcal{J}} f_{iI} V_i(I) \geqslant \frac{1}{n} \; \forall i \in N, \tag{13.3}$$

$$f_{iI} \geqslant 0 \; \forall i \in N, I \in \mathcal{J}. \tag{13.4}$$

The social welfare objective is formulated as Equation 13.1. Equation 13.2 ensures that the fractions of interval I that are allocated sum up to at most 1, and Equation 13.4 guarantees that these fractions are nonnegative. The proportionality constraint is formulated as Equation (13.3).

In contrast, as in Section 13.4 (cf. Theorem 13.5), when contiguous allocations are required the problem becomes much harder.

Theorem 13.8 (Bei et al., 2012). *Given explicit piecewise constant valuation functions and assuming that the allocation must be proportional and contiguous, the optimal social welfare is NP-hard to approximate to a factor of $\Omega(\sqrt{n})$.*

13.5.2 The Price of Fairness

The results of Section 13.5.1 enable the computation of optimal fair allocations; but how good are these allocations? The fairness constraints cause a degradation in social welfare, which can be measured using the *price of fairness*. The price of proportionality (resp., envy-freeness, equitability) is the worst-case (over agents' valuation functions) ratio between the social welfare of the optimal allocation, and the social welfare of the optimal proportional (resp., envy-free, equitable) allocation.

Theorem 13.9 (Caragiannis et al., 2009). *The price of proportionality is $\Theta(\sqrt{n})$.*

To establish the upper bound, we must show that for any collection of valuation functions, the ratio between the social welfare of the optimal allocation and the optimal proportional allocation is $O(\sqrt{n})$. The lower bound only requires producing one example of valuation functions such that this ratio is $\Omega(\sqrt{n})$.

Proof of Theorem 13.9. To prove the upper bound, let $V_1, \dots, V_n$ be the agents' valuation functions, and let $\mathbf{A}^*$ be the optimal allocation. Let $L = \{i \in N : V_i(A_i^*) \geqslant 1/\sqrt{n}\}$ be the set of "large" agents, and $S = N \setminus L$ be the set of "small" agents. We consider two cases.

Case 1: $|L| \geqslant \sqrt{n}$. It follows from the assumption that $|S| \leqslant n - \sqrt{n}$. Define an allocation $\mathbf{A}$ as follows. For each $i \in S$, reallocate A_i^* among the agents in S so that for each $j \in S$, $V_j(A_j \cap A_i^*) \geqslant V_j(A_i^*)/|S|$; this can even be done algorithmically (although only existence is required), for example, using (a slight variation of) the

Even-Paz protocol. For each $i \in L$, we reallocate A_i^* among the agents in $\{i\} \cup S$ so that

$$V_i(A_i \cap A_i^*) \geqslant \sqrt{n} \cdot \frac{V_i(A_i^*)}{\sqrt{n} + |S|},$$

and for all $j \in S$,

$$V_j(A_j \cap A_i^*) \geqslant \frac{V_j(A_i^*)}{\sqrt{n} + |S|}.$$

This can be done, for example, by creating $\sqrt{n} - 1$ copies of agent i with identical valuations and running the Even-Paz algorithm with the $\sqrt{n}$ identical agents and the agents in S.

Note that the allocation $A_1, \ldots, A_n$ is proportional, because for all $i \in L$,

$$V_i(A_i) \geqslant \sqrt{n} \cdot \frac{V_i(A_i^*)}{\sqrt{n} + |S|} \geqslant \frac{1}{\sqrt{n} + |S|} \geqslant \frac{1}{n},$$

and for all $i \in S$,

$$V_i(A_i) \geqslant \sum_{j \in L} \frac{V_i(A_j^*)}{\sqrt{n} + |S|} + \sum_{j \in S} \frac{V_i(A_j^*)}{|S|} \geqslant \frac{\sum_{j \in N} V_i(A_j^*)}{n} = \frac{1}{n}.$$

Moreover, for each $i \in N$, $V_i(A_i) \geqslant V_i(A_i^*)/\sqrt{n}$, hence it holds that $\mathrm{sw}(\mathbf{A}) \geqslant \mathrm{sw}(\mathbf{A}^*)/\sqrt{n}$; the ratio is at most $\sqrt{n}$.

Case 2: $|L| < \sqrt{n}$. Observe that $\mathrm{sw}(\mathbf{A}^*) \leqslant |L| + |S|/\sqrt{n} < 2\sqrt{n}$, while for any proportional allocation $\mathbf{A}$, $\mathrm{sw}(\mathbf{A}) \geqslant \sum_{i \in N} 1/n = 1$; the ratio is $O(\sqrt{n})$.

To establish the lower bound, consider the following valuation functions. The set of agents $L \subseteq N$ now contains exactly $\sqrt{n}$ agents, each uniformly interested only in a single interval of length $1/\sqrt{n}$, such that for $i, j \in L$ the two desired intervals are disjoint. The set of agents $S = N \setminus L$ contains $n - \sqrt{n}$ agents that desire the entire cake uniformly.

The optimal allocation $\mathbf{A}^*$ gives each agent in L its desired interval, hence $\mathrm{sw}(\mathbf{A}^*) = \sqrt{n}$. In contrast, any proportional allocation $\mathbf{A}$ would have to give an interval of length $1/n$ to each agent in S, leaving only $1/\sqrt{n}$ by length to the agents in L. With their density of $\sqrt{n}$, it must hold that $\sum_{i \in L} V_i(A_i) \leqslant \sqrt{n}/\sqrt{n} = 1$, while $\sum_{i \in S} V_i(A_i) \leqslant 1$. Thus, $\mathrm{sw}(\mathbf{A}) \leqslant 2$; the ratio is $\Omega(\sqrt{n})$.   □

Two comments on the theorem and its proof are in order. First, the lower bound of $\Omega(\sqrt{n})$ also applies to the price of envy-freeness, because every envy-free allocation is proportional. However, no nontrivial $o(n)$ upper bound on the price of envy-freeness is known. Second, the valuation functions used in the lower bound construction are piecewise uniform, so one cannot hope to circumvent this negative result by restricting the valuation functions. It is not hard to see that a similar construction only admits severely suboptimal equitable allocations, and indeed the price of equitability is steep.

Theorem 13.10 (Caragiannis et al., 2009). *The price of equitability is $\Theta(n)$.*

While the price of equitability is significantly higher than the price of proportionality, the comparison relies on a worst-case notion, and it could be the case that there are instances where the optimal equitable allocation is superior to the optimal proportional allocation in terms of social welfare. The last technical result for this chapter rules out this situation, even if we replace proportionality by the stronger envy-freeness requirement; for ease of exposition we formulate and prove the theorem for piecewise constant valuations.

Theorem 13.11 (Brams et al., 2012a). *Given piecewise constant valuation functions* $V_1, \ldots, V_n$, *let* A^* *be the optimal equitable allocation and let* A^{**} *be the optimal envy-free allocation. Then* $sw(A^*) \leqslant sw(A^{**})$.

The theorem's proof draws on a connection between cake cutting and *linear Fisher markets*. Instead of a single heterogeneous divisible good, the market includes a set $G = \{1, \ldots, m\}$ of homogeneous divisible goods. The utility of good j for agent i is denoted by u_{ij}. An allocation gives each agent $i \in N$ a fraction f_{ij} of good j such that for all $j \in G$, $\sum_{i \in N} f_{ij} \leqslant 1$. The utility of agent i for an allocation is $\sum_{j \in G} f_{ij} u_{ij}$.

Consider a cake allocation $\mathbf{A}$, and let the set of goods be the pieces in $\mathbf{A}$, that is, good j corresponds to the piece A_j, and $u_{ij} = V_i(A_j)$. We claim that given an allocation $\mathbf{f} = (f_{ij})_{i \in N, j \in G}$ in the Fisher market, there is an allocation $\mathbf{A}'$ in the corresponding cake cutting setting such that $V_i(A'_j) = \sum_{k \in G} f_{jk} u_{ik}$ for all $i, j \in N$; that is, agents' utilities in the Fisher market can be replicated in the cake cutting setting. This claim can be established via similar arguments to the ones we have seen in Section 13.5.1: Each piece A_j is divides into intervals such that each interval is valued uniformly by all agents, and then an f_{ij}-fraction (by length) of each of these intervals is added to the piece A'_i.

Lemma 13.12 (see, e.g., Vazirani, 2007). *Consider a linear Fisher market where agent* $i \in N$ *has budget* e_i, $\sum_{i \in N} e_i = 1$, *and for every* $j \in G$ *there is* $i \in N$ *such that* $u_{ij} > 0$. *Then there exists a price vector* $\mathbf{p} = (p_1, \ldots, p_m)$ *such that* $p_j > 0$ *for all* $j \in G$ *and* $\sum_{j \in G} p_j = 1$, *and an allocation* $\mathbf{f}$ *such that:*

1. *Goods are fully allocated: For all* $j \in G$, $\sum_{i \in N} f_{ij} = 1$.
2. *Agents only get their most profitable goods under the price vector* $\mathbf{p}$: *For all* $i \in N, j \in G$, *if* $f_{ij} > 0$ *then* $j \in \text{argmax}_{k \in G} u_{ik}/p_k$.
3. *Agents spend their entire budgets: For all* $i \in N$, $\sum_{j \in G} f_{ij} p_j = e_i$.

Proof of Theorem 13.11. Consider the optimal equitable allocation $\mathbf{A}^*$. We construct a linear Fisher market where good j corresponds to A_j^*, and $u_{ij} = V_i(A_j^*)$. We also set the agents' budgets to be identical: $e_i = 1/n$ for all $i \in N$. Using Lemma 13.12 we obtain an allocation $\mathbf{f}$ in the Fisher market satisfying properties 1–3. Construct an allocation $\mathbf{A}$ that corresponds to the Fisher market allocation, as explained earlier. We claim that $\mathbf{A}$ is an envy-free allocation and $sw(\mathbf{A}) \geqslant sw(\mathbf{A}^*)$.

The envy-freeness of $\mathbf{A}$ follows directly from the assumptions that the price of each agent's bundle is exactly $1/n$ and each agent receives only items that maximize the ratio of utility to price. Formally, for an agent $i \in N$ let $r_i^* = \max_{j \in G} u_{ij}/p_j$; then

$$V_i(A_i) = \sum_{j \in G} f_{ij} u_{ij} = \sum_{j \in G} f_{ij} \frac{u_{ij}}{p_j} p_j = \sum_{j \in G} f_{ij} r_i^* p_j = \frac{r_i^*}{n}, \tag{13.5}$$

where the third transition follows from the second property in Lemma 13.12, and the fourth transition follows from the third property and $e_i = 1/n$. Likewise,

$$V_i(A_k) = \sum_{j \in G} f_{kj} u_{ij} = \sum_{j \in G} f_{kj} \frac{u_{ij}}{p_j} p_j \leqslant \sum_{j \in G} f_{kj} r_i^* p_j = \frac{r_i^*}{n}.$$

Next we prove that $\mathrm{sw}(\mathbf{A}) \geqslant \mathrm{sw}(\mathbf{A}^*)$. Because $\mathbf{A}^*$ is equitable there exists $\alpha > 0$ such that $V_i(A_i^*) = \alpha$ for all $i \in N$; hence $\mathrm{sw}(\mathbf{A}^*) = n\alpha$. We also know from Equation (13.5) that $\mathrm{sw}(\mathbf{A}) = \frac{1}{n} \sum_{i \in N} r_i^*$. By definition, $r_i^* \geqslant u_{ii}/p_i$; recall that $u_{ii} = V_i(A_i^*) = \alpha$. We conclude that

$$\mathrm{sw}(\mathbf{A}) = \frac{1}{n} \sum_{i \in N} r_i^* \geqslant \frac{1}{n} \sum_{i \in N} \frac{u_{ii}}{p_i} = \frac{\alpha}{n} \sum_{i \in N} \frac{1}{p_i} \geqslant \frac{\alpha}{n} n^2 = n\alpha = \mathrm{sw}(\mathbf{A}^*),$$

where the fourth transition holds because $\sum_{i \in N} p_i = 1$, and therefore the sum $\sum_{i \in N} (1/p_i)$ is minimized when $p_i = 1/n$ for all $i \in N$. □

13.6 Bibliography and Further Reading

Section 13.4 covers complexity results due to Edmonds and Pruhs (2006b), Stromquist (2008), Procaccia (2009), and Kurokawa et al. (2013). The result of Stromquist (2008) was generalized by Deng et al. (2012). Other papers on the complexity of cake cutting include the ones by Woeginger and Sgall (2007), Magdon-Ismail et al. (2003), and Balkanski et al. (2014). A beautiful paper by Edmonds and Pruhs (2006a) circumvents Theorem 13.2 by designing a *randomized*, approximately proportional algorithm that requires only $O(n)$ queries in the Robertson-Webb model.

Section 13.5 includes results by Caragiannis et al. (2009), Cohler et al. (2011), Brams et al. (2012a), and Bei et al. (2012); all of these papers contain numerous results that are not covered here. The complexity of cake cutting with contiguous pieces but without fairness constraints is explored by Aumann et al. (2013). The price of fairness was independently proposed by Caragiannis et al. (2009) and Bertsimas et al. (2011); the concept is inspired by the *price of stability* (Anshelevich et al., 2004). Aumann and Dombb (2010) study the price of fairness under the restriction that allocations are contiguous. Arzi et al. (2011) show that (when pieces are contiguous) the optimal fair allocation can actually be better if a piece of cake is discarded, and quantify the potential benefit. It is also worth mentioning that the problem of interpersonal comparison of utility has been extensively debated by philosophers and economists; for more information see the survey by Hammond (1991).

This chapter does not attempt to cover game-theoretic issues in cake cutting. A simple randomized strategyproof, envy-free algorithm was independently discovered by Chen et al. (2013) and Mossel and Tamuz (2010). Chen et al. (2013) also design a more intricate deterministic strategyproof envy-free algorithm for piecewise uniform valuation functions, which is generalized by Aziz and Ye (2014); under the same assumption, Maya and Nisan (2012) give a characterization of strategyproof, Pareto-efficient cake cutting algorithms. Nash equilibria of cake cutting algorithms are studied by Nicolò and Yu (2008) and Brânzei and Miltersen (2013).

This chapter also avoids nonconstructive existence results, focusing on algorithmic results instead. The book by Barbanel (2005) is a good source of information about existence results in fair division.

Additional cake cutting research has recently explored a variety of questions. For example, Brams et al. (2013) show that Pareto-efficient, envy-free, and equitable allocations may not exist when $n \geqslant 3$; Lindner and Rothe (2009) aim to design algorithms that provide guarantees with respect to the number of envy relations between pairs of agents; Zivan (2011) establishes a trade-off between the strength of proportionality guarantees (which he interprets as the level of trust between agents) and social welfare; Caragiannis et al. (2011) investigate the approximate fairness guarantees that can be achieved when agents' valuation functions are nonadditive; and Brânzei et al. (2013a) study externalities in cake cutting.

In a recent paper, Ghodsi et al. (2011) suggested that fair division theory can be applied to the problem of allocating computational resources (e.g., CPU, RAM) in cluster computing environments. Users are modeled as having Leontief preferences, meaning that they demand the resources in fixed proportions. While the model is somewhat different, it has much in common with the cake cutting model. Other papers that study this research direction include papers by Dolev et al. (2012), Gutman and Nisan (2012), Parkes et al. (2014), and Kash et al. (2014).

Acknowledgments

The author thanks Yair Dombb and Eric Pacuit for their very helpful reviews of this chapter. The author is partially supported by the National Science Foundation under grants CCF-1215883 and IIS-1350598.

PART III
Coalition Formation

CHAPTER 14

Matching under Preferences

Bettina Klaus, David F. Manlove, and Francesca Rossi

14.1 Introduction and Discussion of Applications

Matching theory studies how agents and/or objects from different sets can be matched with each other while taking agents' preferences into account. The theory originated in 1962 with a celebrated paper by David Gale and Lloyd Shapley (1962), in which they proposed the Stable Marriage Algorithm as a solution to the problem of two-sided matching. Since then, this theory has been successfully applied to many real-world problems such as matching students to universities, doctors to hospitals, kidney transplant patients to donors, and tenants to houses. This chapter will focus on algorithmic as well as strategic issues of matching theory.

Many large-scale centralized allocation processes can be modelled by matching problems where agents have preferences over one another. For example, in China, over 10 million students apply for admission to higher education annually through a centralized process. The inputs to the matching scheme include the students' preferences over universities, and vice versa, and the capacities of each university.[1] The task is to construct a matching that is in some sense optimal with respect to these inputs.

Economists have long understood the problems with decentralized matching markets, which can suffer from such undesirable properties as *unravelling*, *congestion* and *exploding offers* (see Roth and Xing, 1994, for details). For centralized markets, constructing allocations by hand for large problem instances is clearly infeasible. Thus centralized mechanisms are required for automating the allocation process.

Given the large number of agents typically involved, the *computational efficiency* of a mechanism's underlying algorithm is of paramount importance. Thus we seek polynomial-time algorithms for the underlying matching problems. Equally important are considerations of strategy: an agent (or a coalition of agents) may manipulate their input to the matching scheme (e.g., by misrepresenting their true preferences or underreporting their capacity) in order to try to improve their outcome. A desirable

---

[1] In fact, students are first assigned to universities and then to their programme of study within the university (see, e.g., Zhu, 2014).

property of a mechanism is *strategyproofness*, which ensures that it is in the best interests of an agent to behave truthfully.

The study of matching problems involving preferences was begun in 1962 with the seminal paper of Gale and Shapley (1962) who gave an efficient algorithm for the so-called *Stable Marriage problem* (which involves matching men to women based on each person having preferences over members of the opposite sex) and showed how to extend it to the *College Admissions problem*, a many-to-one extension of the Stable Marriage problem which involves allocating students to colleges based on college capacities, as well as on students' preferences over colleges, and vice versa. Their algorithm has come to be known as the *Gale–Shapley algorithm.*

Since 1962, the study of matching problems involving preferences has grown into a large and active research area, and numerous contributions have been made by computer scientists, economists, and mathematicians, among others. Several monographs exclusively dealing with this class of problems have been published (Knuth, 1976; Gusfield and Irving, 1989; Roth and Sotomayor, 1990; Manlove, 2013).

A particularly appealing aspect of this research area is the range of practical applications of matching problems, leading to real-life scenarios where efficient algorithms can be deployed and issues of strategy can be overcome. One of the best-known examples is the National Resident Matching Program (NRMP) in the United States, which handles the annual allocation of intending junior doctors (or *residents*) to hospital posts. In 2014, 40,394 aspiring junior doctors applied via the NRMP for 29,671 available residency positions (NRMP, 2014). The problem model is very similar to Gale and Shapley's College Admissions problem, and indeed an extension of the Gale–Shapley algorithm is used to construct the allocation each year (Roth, 1984a; Roth and Peranson, 1997). Similar medical matching schemes exist in Canada, Japan, and the United Kingdom. As Roth argued, the key property for a matching to satisfy in this context is *stability*, which ensures that a resident and hospital do not have the incentive to deviate from their allocation and become matched to one another.

Similar applications arise in the context of School Choice (Abdulkadiroğlu and Sönmez, 2003). For example in Boston and New York, centralized matching schemes are employed to assign pupils to schools on the basis of the preferences of pupils (or more realistically their parents) over schools, and pupils' *priorities* for assignment to a given school (Abdulkadiroğlu et al., 2005a, 2005b). A school's priority for a pupil might include issues such as geographical proximity and whether the pupil has a sibling at the school already, among others.

Kidney exchange (Roth et al., 2004, 2005) is another application of matching that has grown in importance in recent years. Sometimes, a kidney patient with a willing but incompatible donor can swap their donor with that of another patient in a similar position. Efficient algorithms are required to organize kidney "swaps" on the basis of information about donor and patient compatibilities. Such swaps can involve two or more patient–donor pairs, but usually the maximum number of pairs involved is three. Also altruistic donors can trigger "chains" involving swaps between patient–donor pairs. These allow for a larger number of kidney transplants (compared to those one could perform based on deceased donors only) and thus more lives saved. Centralized clearinghouses for kidney exchange are in operation on a nationwide scale in a number of countries including the United States (Roth et al., 2004, 2005; Ashlagi and Roth, 2012), the Netherlands (Keizer et al., 2005), and the United Kingdom (Johnson et al., 2008). The problem of maximizing the number of kidney transplants performed through cycles and chains is NP-hard (Abraham et al., 2007a), though algorithms based on Mixed Integer Programming have been developed and are used to solve this problem at scale in the countries mentioned (Abraham et al., 2007a; Dickerson et al., 2013; Manlove and O'Malley, 2012; Glorie et al., 2014).

The importance of the research area in both theoretical and practical senses was underlined in 2012 by the award of the Sveriges Riksbank Prize in Economic Sciences in Memory of Alfred Nobel (commonly known as the Nobel Prize in Economic Sciences) to Alvin Roth and Lloyd Shapley for their work in "the theory of stable allocations and the practice of market design." This reflects both Shapley's contribution to the Stable Marriage algorithm among other theoretical advances, and Roth's application of these results to matching markets involving the assignment of junior doctors to hospitals, pupils to schools, and kidney patients to donors. The Nobel prize rules state that the prize cannot be awarded posthumously and hence David Gale (1921–2008) could not be honoured for his important contributions.

Matching problems involving preferences can be classified as being either *bipartite* or *nonbipartite*. In the former case, the agents are partitioned into two disjoint sets A and B, and the members of A have preferences over only the members of B (and possibly vice versa). In the latter case we have one single set of agents, each of whom ranks some or all of the others in order of preference. For space reasons we will consider only bipartite matching problems involving preferences in this chapter.

Bipartite problems can be further categorized according to whether the preferences are *two-sided* or *one-sided*. In the former case, members of both of the sets A and B have preferences over one another, whereas in the latter case only the members of A have preferences (over the members of B). Bipartite matching problems with two-sided preferences arise in the context of assigning junior doctors to hospitals, for example, while one-sided preferences arise in applications including the assignment of students to campus housing and reviewers to conference papers.

Our treatment covers *ordinal preferences* (where preferences are expressed in terms of first choice, second choice, etc.) rather than *cardinal utilities* (where preferences are expressed in terms of real-numbered valuations). In their simplest form, models of kidney exchange problems can involve *dichotomous preferences* (a special case of ordinal preferences, where an agent either finds another agent acceptable or not, and is indifferent among those it does find acceptable), on the basis of whether a patient is compatible with a potential donor. However, in practice, models of kidney exchange are more complex, typically involving cardinal utilities rather than ordinal preferences, and therefore the matching problems defined in this chapter do not encompass theoretical models of kidney exchange.

The problems considered in this chapter sit strongly within the field of computational social choice. This field lies at the interface of economics and computer science, and our approach will involve interleaving key aspects that have hitherto been considered by the two communities in bodies of literature that have largely pertained to the two disciplines separately. Such key considerations involve the existence of structural results and efficient algorithms, and the derivation of strategyproof mechanisms. These topics will be reviewed in each of the cases of bipartite matching problems with two-sided and one-sided preferences. Although space restrictions have necessarily limited our coverage, we have tried to include the results that we feel will be of most importance to the readership of this handbook.

The structure of this chapter is as follows. In Section 14.2, we focus on bipartite matching problems where both sides have preferences. Here the most important property for a matching to satisfy is *stability*. In Section 14.2.1 we define the key matching problems in this class, most notably the *Hospitals / Residents problem*, and we also define stability in this context. We then state fundamental structural and algorithmic results concerning the existence, computation, and structural properties of stable matchings, in Section 14.2.2. Issues of strategy, and in particular the existence (or otherwise) of strategyproof mechanisms, are dealt with in Section 14.2.3. Next, in Section 14.2.4, we outline some further algorithmic results, including decentralized algorithms for computing stable matchings, variants of the Hospitals/Residents problem involving ties and couples, and many-to-many extensions.

Bipartite matching problems where only one side of the market has preferences are considered in Section 14.3. The fundamental problems in this class are the *House Allocation problem* and its extension to *Housing Markets*. We define these problems together with key properties of matchings, including *Pareto optimality* and membership of the *core*, in Section 14.3.1. Section 14.3.2 describes some important mechanisms that can be used to produce Pareto optimal matchings and matchings in the core. Strategyproofness is considered in Section 14.3.3, and then further algorithmic results are described in Section 14.3.4, including the computation of *maximum Pareto optimal*, *popular*, and *profile-based optimal matchings*.

Finally, in Section 14.4 we give some concluding remarks and list some further sources of reading.

14.2 Two-Sided Preferences

14.2.1 Introduction and Preliminary Definitions

The *Hospitals/Residents problem*[2] (HR) (Gale and Shapley, 1962; Gusfield and Irving, 1989; Roth and Sotomayor, 1990; Manlove, 2008) was first defined by Gale and Shapley in their seminal paper "College Admissions and the Stability of Marriage" (Gale and Shapley, 1962).

An instance I of HR involves a set $R = \{r_1, \ldots, r_{n_1}\}$ of *residents* and a set $H = \{h_1, \ldots, h_{n_2}\}$ of *hospitals*. Each hospital $h_j \in H$ has a positive integer *capacity*, denoted by c_j, indicating the number of *posts* that h_j has. Also there is a set $E \subseteq R \times H$ of *acceptable* resident–hospital pairs. Let $m = |E|$. Each resident $r_i \in R$ has an *acceptable* set of hospitals $A(r_i)$, where $A(r_i) = \{h_j \in H : (r_i, h_j) \in E\}$. Similarly each hospital $h_j \in H$ has an acceptable set of residents $A(h_j)$, where $A(h_j) = \{r_i \in R : (r_i, h_j) \in E\}$.

---

[2] The Hospitals/Residents problem is sometimes referred to as the College (or University or Stable) Admissions problem, or the Stable Assignment problem.

The *agents* in I are the residents and hospitals in $R \cup H$. Each agent $a_k \in R \cup H$ has a *preference list* in which she/it ranks $A(a_k)$ in strict order. Given any resident $r_i \in R$, and given any hospitals $h_j, h_k \in H$, r_i is said to *prefer* h_j to h_k if $\{h_j, h_k\} \subseteq A(r_i)$ and h_j precedes h_k on r_i's preference list; the *prefers* relation is defined similarly for a hospital.

An *assignment* M in I is a subset of E. If $(r_i, h_j) \in M$, r_i is said to be *assigned* to h_j, and h_j is *assigned* r_i. For each $a_k \in R \cup H$, the set of assignees of a_k in M is denoted by $M(a_k)$. If $r_i \in R$ and $M(r_i) = \emptyset$, r_i is said to be *unassigned*, otherwise r_i is *assigned*. Similarly, a hospital $h_j \in H$ is *undersubscribed* or *full* according as $|M(h_j)|$ is less than or equal to c_j, respectively. A *matching* M in I is an assignment such that $|M(r_i)| \leqslant 1$ for each $r_i \in R$ and $|M(h_j)| \leqslant c_j$ for each $h_j \in H$. For notational convenience, given a matching M and a resident $r_i \in R$ such that $M(r_i) \neq \emptyset$, where there is no ambiguity the notation $M(r_i)$ is also used to refer to the single member of the set $M(r_i)$.

Given an instance I of HR and a matching M, a pair $(r_i, h_j) \in E \backslash M$ *blocks* M (or is a *blocking pair* for M) if (i) r_i is unassigned or prefers h_j to $M(r_i)$ and (ii) h_j is undersubscribed or prefers r_i to at least one member of $M(h_j)$. M is said to be *stable* if it admits no blocking pair. If a resident–hospital pair (r_i, h_j) belongs to some stable matching in I, r_i is called a *stable partner* of h_j, and vice versa.

Example 14.1 (HR **instance**). Consider the following HR instance:

$$
\begin{array}{ll}
r_1 : h_1 \ h_2 & h_1 : 1 : r_3 \ r_2 \ r_1 \ r_4 \\
r_2 : h_1 \ h_2 \ h_3 & h_2 : 2 : r_2 \ r_3 \ r_1 \ r_4 \\
r_3 : h_2 \ h_1 \ h_3 & h_3 : 1 : r_2 \ r_3 \\
r_4 : h_2 \ h_1 &
\end{array}
$$

Here, r_1 prefers h_1 to h_2 and does not find h_3 acceptable. Also, h_1 has capacity 1 and prefers r_3 to r_2, and so on. $M = \{(r_2, h_1), (r_3, h_2), (r_4, h_2)\}$ is a matching in which each resident is assigned except for r_1, and both h_1 and h_2 are full while h_3 is undersubscribed. M is not stable because (r_1, h_2) is a blocking pair.

The *Stable Marriage problem with Incomplete lists* (SMI) (Gale and Shapley, 1962; Knuth, 1976; Gusfield and Irving, 1989; Roth and Sotomayor, 1990; Irving, 2008) is an important special case of HR in which $c_j = 1$ for all $h_j \in H$, and residents and hospitals are more commonly referred to as *men* and *women* respectively. The classical *Stable Marriage problem* (SM) is the restriction of SMI in which $n_1 = n_2$ and $E = R \times H$.

Finally, the *School Choice problem* (SC) (Balinski and Sönmez, 1999; Abdulkadiroğlu and Sönmez, 2003) is a one-sided preference version of HR where students and schools replace residents and hospitals respectively, and schools are endowed with *priorities* over students instead of preferences. A school's priority ranking over students may reflect a school district's policy choice (e.g., by giving students who are within walking distance or have a sibling in the same school a higher priority) or they may be based on other factors (e.g., grades in an entrance exam, time spent on a waiting list). For SC, schools are not considered to be economic agents: they neither strategize nor is their welfare measured and taken into account. Many results can easily be translated from HR to SC, but often the interpretation changes. For instance, the notion of stability can be interpreted as the elimination of *justified envy* (Balinski and Sönmez, 1999): a student can justifiably envy the assignment of another student to a school if he likes that school better than his own assignment and he has a higher priority (with a lower priority, envy might be present as well but is not justifiable). Two recent and exhaustive surveys on school choice have been written by Abdulkadiroglu (2013) and Pathak (2011).

14.2.2 Classical Results: Stability and Gale-Shapley Algorithms

Gale and Shapley (1962) showed that every instance I of HR admits at least one stable matching. Their proof of this result was constructive, that is, they described a linear-time algorithm for finding a stable matching in I. Their algorithm is known as the *resident-oriented Gale-Shapley algorithm* (or RGS algorithm for short), because it involves residents applying to hospitals. Given an instance of HR,

(1) at the first step of the RGS algorithm, every resident applies to her favourite acceptable hospital. For each hospital h_j, the c_j acceptable applicants who have the highest ranks according to h_j's preference list (or all acceptable applicants if there are fewer than c_j) are placed on the waiting list of h_j, and all others are rejected;

(*l*) at the *l*th step of the RGS algorithm, those applicants who were rejected at step $l - 1$ apply to their next best acceptable hospital. For each hospital h_j, the c_j acceptable applicants among the new applicants and those on the waiting list who have the highest ranks according to h_j's preference list (or all acceptable applicants if there are fewer than c_j) are placed on the waiting list of h_j, and all others are rejected.

Example 14.2 (RGS algorithm). We now illustrate an execution of the RGS algorithm for the HR instance shown in Example 14.1. In the first step, each of r_1 and r_2 applies to h_1, and each of r_3 and r_4 applies to h_2. Whilst h_2 accepts each of r_3 and r_4, h_1 can only accept r_2 (from among r_1 and r_2). Thus r_1 is rejected by h_1 and applies to the next hospital in his preference list, namely, h_2, at the second step. At this point, h_2 accepts r_1, keeps r_3, and rejects r_4. In the third step, r_4 applies to h_1 and is rejected again. Now the algorithm terminates because each resident is either assigned to a hospital or has applied to every hospital on his preference list. The resulting matching is thus $M' = \{(r_1, h_2), (r_2, h_1), (r_3, h_2)\}$, and the reader may verify that M' is stable.

The RGS algorithm is well-defined and terminates with the unique *resident-optimal* stable matching M_a that assigns to each resident the best hospital that she could achieve in any stable matching, while each unassigned resident is unassigned in every stable matching (Gale and Shapley, 1962; Gusfield and Irving, 1989, Section 1.6.3).

It is instructive to give a short sketch of the proof illustrating why M_a is stable. For, consider any resident r_i and suppose that h_j is any hospital that r_i prefers to $M_a(r_i)$ (if r_i is assigned in M_a) or h_j is any hospital that r_i finds acceptable (if r_i is unassigned in M_a). Then r_i applied to h_j during the execution of the RGS algorithm, and was rejected by h_j. This could only happen if h_j was full and preferred its worst assignee to h_j at that point. But h_j cannot subsequently lose any residents and indeed can only potentially gain better assignees. Hence in M_a, h_j is full and prefers its worst assigned resident to r_i. Thus (r_i, h_j) cannot block M_a, and because r_i and h_j were arbitrary, M_a is stable.

Furthermore, M_a is worst-possible for the hospitals in a precise sense: if M is any other stable matching then every hospital $h_j \in H$ prefers each resident in $M(h_j)$ to each resident in $M_a(h_j) \backslash M(h_j)$ (Gusfield and Irving, 1989, Section 1.6.5).

Theorem 14.3 (Gale and Shapley, 1962; Gusfield and Irving, 1989). *Given an* HR *instance, the RGS algorithm constructs, in $O(m)$ time, the unique resident-optimal stable matching, where m is the number of acceptable resident–hospital pairs.*

A counterpart of the RGS algorithm, known as the *hospital-oriented Gale–Shapley algorithm*, or HGS algorithm for short, involves hospitals offering posts to residents. The HGS algorithm terminates with the unique *hospital-optimal* stable matching M_z. In this matching, every full hospital $h_j \in H$ is assigned its c_j best stable partners, while every undersubscribed hospital is assigned the same set of residents in every stable matching (Gusfield and Irving, 1989, Section 1.6.2). Furthermore, M_z assigns to each resident the worst hospital that she could achieve in any stable matching, while each unassigned resident is unassigned in every stable matching (Gusfield and Irving, 1989, Theorem 1.6.1).

Theorem 14.4 (Gusfield and Irving, 1989). *Given an instance of* HR, *the HGS algorithm constructs, in $O(m)$ time, the unique hospital-optimal stable matching, where m is the number of acceptable resident–hospital pairs.*

Note that the RGS / HGS algorithms are often referred to as *deferred acceptance algorithms* by economists (Roth, 2008).

It is easy to check that for Example 14.2, $M_a = M' = M_z$. In general there may be other stable matchings—possibly exponentially many (Irving and Leather, 1986)—between the two extremes given by M_a and M_z. However some key structural properties hold regarding unassigned residents and undersubscribed hospitals with respect to all stable matchings in I, as follows.

Theorem 14.5 (Rural Hospitals Theorem: Roth, 1984a; Gale and Sotomayor, 1985; Roth, 1986). *For a given instance of* HR, *the following properties hold:*

1. *the same residents are assigned in all stable matchings;*
2. *each hospital is assigned the same number of residents in all stable matchings;*
3. *any hospital that is undersubscribed in one stable matching is assigned exactly the same set of residents in all stable matchings.*

The term "Rural Hospitals Theorem" stems from the tendency of rural hospitals to have problems in recruiting residents to fill all available slots. The theorem's name then indicates the importance of the result to the rural hospitals' recruitment problem: under stability one can never choose matchings to help undersubscribed rural hospitals to recruit more or better residents. Additional background to the Rural Hospitals Theorem for HR is given by Gusfield and Irving (1989, Section 1.6.4).

A classical result in stable matching theory states that, for a given instance of SM, the set of stable matchings forms a distributive lattice; Knuth (1976) attributed this result to John Conway (see also Gusfield and Irving, 1989, Section 1.3.1). In fact such a structure is also present for the set of stable matchings in a given instance I of HR

(Gusfield and Irving, 1989, Section 1.6.5). To describe this structure, we will define some preliminary notation and terminology.

Let S denote the set of stable matchings in I and let $M, M' \in S$. We say that $r_i \in R$ *prefers* M to M' if r_i is assigned in both M and M', and r_i prefers $M(r_i)$ to $M'(r_i)$. Also, we say that r_i *is indifferent between* M and M' if either (*i*) r_i is unassigned in both M and M', or (*ii*) r_i is assigned in both M and M', and $M(r_i) = M'(r_i)$. Then, M *dominates* M', denoted $M \succeq M'$, if each resident either prefers M to M', or is indifferent between them.

For $M, M' \in S$ we denote by $M \wedge M'$ (respectively $M \vee M'$) the set of resident-hospital pairs in which either (*i*) r_i is unassigned if she is unassigned in both M and M', or (*ii*) r_i is given the better (respectively poorer) of her partners in M and M' if she is assigned in both stable matchings. It turns out that each of $M \wedge M'$ and $M \vee M'$ is a stable matching in I, representing the *join* and the *meet* of M and M' respectively (Gusfield and Irving, 1989, Section 1.6.5). These operations give rise to a lattice structure for S, as the following result indicates.

Theorem 14.6 (Gusfield and Irving, 1989). *Let I be an instance of* HR, *and let S be the set of stable matchings in I. Then $(S, \succeq)$ forms a distributive lattice, with $M \wedge M'$ representing the meet, and $M \vee M'$ the join, for two stable matchings $M, M' \in S$, where $\succeq$ is the dominance partial order on S.*

14.2.3 Strategic Results: Strategyproofness

Note that both the RGS and HGS algorithms are described in terms of agents taking actions based on their preference lists (one side proposes and the other side tentatively accepts or rejects these proposals). However, unless agents have an incentive to truthfully report their preferences, any preference-based requirement (such as stability) might lose some of its meaning. The following theorem demonstrates that in general, stability is not compatible with the requirement that for all agents truth telling is a weakly dominant strategy (strategyproofness).

To be more precise, we call a function that assigns a matching to each instance of HR (or SMI/SM) a *mechanism*. A mechanism that assigns only stable matchings is called *stable*. The mechanism that always assigns the resident-optimal (hospital-optimal) stable matching is called the *RGS (HGS) mechanism*.

A mechanism for which no single agent can ever benefit from misrepresenting her/its preferences is called *strategyproof*, that is, in game-theoretic terms, it is a weakly dominant strategy for each agent to report her/its true preference list. If we restrict preference misrepresentations to one type of agents only, we obtain the one-sided versions of strategyproofness: a mechanism for which no single resident can ever benefit from misrepresenting her preferences is called strategyproof for residents. Strategyproofness for hospitals is similarly defined.

Theorem 14.7 (Impossibility Theorem: Roth, 1982b). *There exists no mechanism for* SMI *that is stable and strategyproof.*

As SMI is a special case of HR, Theorem 14.7 clearly extends to the HR case. The proof of Theorem 14.7 can be shown with the following example.

Example 14.8 (Impossibility). Consider the following instance:

$$r_1 : h_1 \ h_2 \qquad h_1 : r_2 \ r_1$$
$$r_2 : h_2 \ h_1 \qquad h_2 : r_1 \ r_2$$

The two stable matchings for this instance are $M_a = \{(r_1, h_1), (r_2, h_2)\}$ and $M_z = \{(r_1, h_2), (r_2, h_1)\}$. Assume that the mechanism picks stable matching M_a. Then, if h_1 pretended that only r_2 is acceptable, M_a is not stable anymore and the stable mechanism would have to pick the only remaining stable matching M_z, which h_1 would prefer; a contradiction to strategyproofness. Similarly, if the mechanism picks stable matching M_z, r_1 could manipulate by declaring h_1 uniquely acceptable.

The intuition behind this impossibility result is that an agent who is assigned to a stable partner that is not her/its best stable partner can improve her/its outcome by truncating the preference list just below the best stable partner: this unilateral manipulation will result in the assignment of the best stable partner to the agent who misrepresented her/its preference list. Alcalde and Barberà (1994) and Takagi and Serizawa (2010) further strengthened the impossibility result by considerably weakening the stability requirement.

On the positive side, stable mechanisms that respect strategyproofness for all residents exist.

Theorem 14.9 (Roth, 1985). *The RGS mechanism for* HR *is strategyproof for residents.*

As HR is a generalization of each of SM and SMI, clearly Theorem 14.9 also holds in these latter contexts. This theorem for HR is an extension of an earlier corresponding theorem for SM (Dubins and Freedman, 1981; Roth, 1982a). Strategyproofness for all residents also turns out to be a key property in characterizing the RGS mechanism (Ehlers and Klaus, 2014): almost all real-life mechanisms used in variants of HR (including SC)—including the large classes of priority mechanisms and linear programming mechanisms—satisfy a set of simple and intuitive properties, but once strategyproofness is added to these properties, the RGS mechanism is the only one surviving (and characterized by the respective properties including strategyproofness). For SC, since residents (aka students) are the only economic agents, Theorem 14.9 in fact establishes a possibility result. For HR, the negative result of Theorem 14.7 persists even if restricting attention only to hospitals.

Theorem 14.10 (Roth, 1986). *There exists no mechanism for* HR *that is stable and strategyproof for hospitals.*

This result implies that even when the HGS mechanism is used, hospitals might have an incentive to misrepresent their preferences.

Once the incompatibility of stability and strategyproofness is established (Theorems 14.7 and 14.10), the question arises as to whether we can at least find stable mechanisms that are *resistant* to strategic behavior, meaning that it is computationally difficult (i.e., NP-hard) for agents to behave strategically. This approach is typical in voting theory, which is the subject of Chapter 6 on barriers to manipulation, because no voting rule is strategyproof (Arrow et al., 2002; Bartholdi et al., 1989a). It is possible to exploit such results to define stable mechanisms that are resistant to strategic behaviour. Pini et al. (2011a) showed how to take voting rules that are resistant to strategic behaviour and use them to define stable mechanisms with the same property.

Besides worst-case analysis, we may also consider the occurrence and impact of strategic behavior when stable matching mechanisms are used in real-world instances of HR. Roth and Peranson (1999) showed that, for data from the NRMP, only a few participants could improve their outcomes by changing their preference list. They also showed via simulations that the opportunities for manipulation diminish when the instances of HR grow larger in population. Since then, various articles have provided theoretical explanations for this phenomenon for large population instances of SMI or HR (Immorlica and Mahdian, 2005; Kojima and Pathak, 2009; Lee, 2014).

14.2.4 Further Algorithmic Results

Decentralized Algorithms for SMI

In Section 14.2.2 we described the Gale-Shapley algorithm, which can be regarded as a centralized algorithm for HR. There has also been much interest in the study of decentralized algorithms for finding stable matchings. In particular, Roth and Vande Vate (1990) studied a mechanism for SMI that involves starting from some initial matching M_0 (which need not be stable) and constructing a random sequence of matchings $M_0, M_1, M_2 \ldots$, where for each $i \geqslant 1$, M_i is obtained from M_{i-1} by satisfying a blocking pair (m, w) of M_{i-1} (that is, the partners of m and w in M_{i-1}, if they exist, are both single in M_i, and (m, w) is added to M_i). The blocking pair that is satisfied at each step is chosen at random, subject to the constraint that there is a positive probability that any particular blocking pair (from among those that exist at a given step) is chosen. Roth and Vande Vate (1990) showed that this random sequence converges to a stable matching with probability 1. The algorithm underlying their result became known as the *Roth-Vande Vate Mechanism*. The special case of this mechanism in which $M_0 = \emptyset$ (and some other subtle modifications are made) has been referred to as the *Random Order Mechanism* (Ma, 1996).

When satisfying a blocking pair (m, w), if the "divorcees" ($M(w)$ and $M(m)$) are required to marry one another then the situation is very different. In this case there are SM instances and initial matchings M_0 such that it is not possible to transform M_0 to a stable matching by satisfying a sequence of blocking pairs (Tamura, 1993; Tan and Su, 1995).

Ackermann et al. (2011) categorized decentralized algorithms for SMI into *better response dynamics* and *best response dynamics*. The former description applies to mechanisms that are based on satisfying blocking pairs, while the latter refers to a more specific mechanism where, should a blocking pair be satisfied, it is the best blocking pair for the *active* agent (i.e., the agent who makes the proposal). The authors also considered *random better response dynamics* and *random best response dynamics*. In the former case, a blocking pair is chosen uniformly at random, while in the latter case, a blocking pair that corresponds to the best blocking pair for a given proposer is selected uniformly at random. The authors gave exponential lower bounds for the convergence time of both approaches in uncoordinated markets.

Both sequential and parallel local search algorithms, based on the approach of Roth and Vande Vate (1990), have been implemented and tested on large SMI problem instances, showing a very efficient behavior (Gelain et al., 2013; Munera et al., 2015).

Hospitals/Residents Problem with Ties

In the context of centralised clearinghouses for junior doctor allocation, often large hospitals have many applicants and may find it difficult to produce a strict ranking over all these residents. In practice a hospital may be indifferent between batches of residents, represented by *ties* in its preference list. This naturally leads to the *Hospitals/Residents problem with Ties* (HRT), the generalization of HR in which the preference lists of both residents and hospitals can contain ties.

In the HRT context, several stability definitions have been formulated in the literature, with varying degrees of strength. A matching M is *weakly stable* if there is no resident–hospital pair (r, h), such that by coming together, each would be strictly better off than their current situation in M. In the case of *strong stability*, in a blocking pair (r, h) it is enough for one of (r, h) to be strictly better off, while the other must be no worse off, by forming a partnership. Finally, in the case of *super-stability*, all we require is that each of (r, h) must be no worse off.

Example 14.11 (HRT **instance**). To illustrate these stability concepts, we insert some ties into the preference lists in the HR instance shown in Example 14.1. The resulting instance of HRT is

$$r_1 : h_1 \ h_2 \qquad\qquad h_1 : 1 : r_3 \ (r_2 \ r_1) \ r_4$$
$$r_2 : h_1 \ h_2 \ h_3 \qquad\quad h_2 : 2 : r_2 \ (r_3 \ r_1 \ r_4)$$
$$r_3 : h_2 \ (h_1 \ h_3) \qquad h_3 : 1 : r_2 \ r_3$$
$$r_4 : h_2 \ h_1$$

Here, parentheses indicate ties in the preference lists, so for example, r_3 prefers h_2 to each of h_1 and h_3, and is indifferent between the latter two hospitals. The matchings $\{(r_1, h_2), (r_2, h_1), (r_3, h_2)\}$ and $\{(r_1, h_1), (r_2, h_2), (r_3, h_3), (r_4, h_2)\}$ are both weakly stable, but the instance admits no strongly stable matching, and hence no super-stable matching either.

We continue by considering algorithmic results for HRT under weak stability. Firstly, an HRT instance is bound to admit a weakly stable matching, and such a matching can be found in linear time (Irving et al., 2000). Recall from Theorem 14.5 that all stable matchings in an HR instance have the same size. However in the case of HRT, weakly stable matchings may have different sizes, as illustrated by Example 14.11. Often in the case of centralized clearinghouses, an important consideration is to match as many participants as possible. This motivates MAX HRT, the problem of finding a maximum weakly stable matching, given an HRT instance. This problem is NP-hard (Iwama et al., 1999; Manlove et al., 2002) even if each hospital has capacity 1, and also even under severe restrictions on the number, length and positions of the ties (Manlove et al., 2002). A succession of approximation algorithms has been proposed in the literature for various restrictions of MAX HRT, culminating in the best current bound of $3/2$ for the general problem (McDermid, 2009; Király, 2013; Paluch, 2014).

Although an HRT instance I is bound to admit a weakly stable matching as mentioned above, by contrast a strongly stable matching or a super-stable matching in I may not exist (Irving et al., 2000, 2003). However there is an efficient algorithm to find a strongly stable matching or report that none exists (Kavitha et al., 2007). A faster and simpler algorithm exists in the case of super-stability (Irving et al., 2000). Moreover an analogue of Theorem 14.5 holds in HRT under each of the strong stability and super-stability criteria (Scott, 2005; Irving et al., 2000).

Hospitals/Residents Problem with Couples

Another variant of HR that is motivated by practical applications arises in the presence of *couples*. These are pairs of residents who wish to be jointly assigned to hospitals via a common preferences list over pairs of hospitals, typically in order to be geographically close to one another. Each couple (r_i, r_j) has a preference list over a subset of $H \times H$, where each pair (h_p, h_q) on this list represents the joint assignment of r_i to h_p and r_j to h_q. (There may be single residents in addition, as before.) We thus obtain the *Hospitals/Residents problem with Couples* (HRC).

Relative to a suitable stability definition, Roth (1984a) showed that an HRC instance need not admit a stable matching. Ng and Hirschberg (1988) and Ronn (1990) independently showed that the problem of deciding whether an HRC instance admits a stable matching is NP-complete, even if each hospital has capacity 1 and there are no single residents.

McDermid and Manlove (2010) considered a variant of HRC in which each resident (whether single or in a couple) has a preference list over individual hospitals, and the joint preference list of each couple (r_i, r_j) is *consistent* with the individual lists of r_i and r_j in a precise sense. Relative to Roth's stability definition (Roth, 1984a), they showed that the problem of deciding whether a stable matching exists is NP-complete. However if instead we enforce classical (Gale–Shapley) stability on a given matching relative to the individual lists of residents, then the problem of finding a stable matching or reporting that none exists is solvable in polynomial time (McDermid and Manlove, 2010).

Biró et al. (2011) developed a range of heuristics for the problem of finding a stable matching or reporting that none exists in a given HRC instance, and subjected them to a detailed empirical evaluation based on randomly generated data. They found that a stable matching is very likely to exist for instances where the ratio of couples to single residents is small and of the magnitude typically found in practical applications.

Ashlagi et al. (2014) studied large random matching markets with couples. They introduced a new matching algorithm and showed that if the number of couples grows slower than the size of the market, a stable matching will be found with high probability. If, however, the number of couples grows at a linear rate, with constant probability (not depending on the market size), no stable matching exists.

Further results for HRC are described in the survey paper of Biró and Klijn (2013).

Many-to-Many Stable Matching

Many-to-many extensions of SM (and by implication HR) have been considered in the literature (Roth, 1984b; Roth and Sotomayor, 1990; Sotomayor, 1999; Baïou and

Balinski, 2000; Fleiner, 2003; Martínez et al., 2004; Echenique and Oviedo, 2006; Bansal et al., 2007; Kojima and Ünver, 2008; Eirinakis et al., 2012, 2013; Klijn and Yazıcı, 2014). These matching problems tend to be described in the context of assigning *workers* to *firms*, where each agent can be multiply assigned (up to a given capacity). We will discuss the two main models of many-to-many matching in the literature.

The first version we consider, which we refer to as the *Workers/Firms problem, Version 1*, denoted by WF-1, involves each worker ranking in strict order of preference a set of individual acceptable firms, and vice versa for each firm. Baïou and Balinski (2000) generalized the stability definition for SM to the WF-1 case. They showed that every instance I of WF-1 has a stable matching and such a matching can be found in $O(n^2)$ time, where $n = \max\{n_1, n_2\}$, n_1 is the number of workers and n_2 is the number of firms in I. They also generalized Theorems 14.5 and 14.6 to the WF-1 context. Additional algorithms have been given for computing stable matchings with various optimality properties in WF-1 (Bansal et al., 2007; Eirinakis et al., 2012, 2013).

In the second version, which we refer to as the *Workers/Firms problem, Version 2*, denoted by WF-2, each worker ranks in strict order of preference acceptable subsets of firms, and vice versa for each firm. Two main forms of stability have been studied in the context of WF-2, namely, *pairwise stability* and *setwise stability*.

A matching M in a WF-2 instance is *pairwise stable* (Roth, 1984b) if it cannot be undermined by a single worker–firm pair acting together. A WF-2 instance need not admit a pairwise stable matching (Roth and Sotomayor, 1990, Example 2.7). However Roth (1984b) proved that, given an instance of WF-2 where every agent's preference list satisfies so-called *substitutability* (Kelso and Crawford, 1982), a pairwise stable matching always exists, and he gave an algorithm for finding one. Martínez et al. (2004) gave an algorithm for finding all pairwise stable matchings.

A more powerful definition of stability is *setwise stability*. Informally, a matching M is *setwise stable* (Sotomayor, 1999) if it cannot be undermined by a coalition of workers and firms acting together. More precisely, several definitions of setwise stability have been given in the literature (Sotomayor, 1999; Echenique and Oviedo, 2006; Konishi and Ünver, 2006); the various alternatives were formally defined and analyzed by Klaus and Walzl (2009).

Bansal et al. (2007) noted that, generally speaking, WF-1 has been studied mainly by the computer science community, while the economics community has mainly focused on WF-2. One reason for this is that WF-2 suffers from the drawback that the length of an agent's preference list is in the worst case exponential in the number of agents. A consequence of this is that the practical applicability of any algorithm for WF-2 would be severely limited in general, however, this problem does not arise with WF-1.

14.3 One-Sided Preferences

14.3.1 Introduction and Preliminary Definitions

Many economists and game theorists, and increasingly computer scientists in recent years, have studied the problem of allocating a set H of indivisible goods among a set A of applicants (Shapley and Scarf, 1974; Hylland and Zeckhauser, 1979; Deng et al., 2003; Fekete et al., 2003). Each applicant a_i may have ordinal preferences over a subset of H (the *acceptable* goods for a_i). Many models have considered the case where there is no monetary transfer. In the literature the situation in which each applicant initially owns one good is known as a *Housing Market* (HM)[3] (Shapley and Scarf, 1974; Roth and Postlewaite, 1977; Roth, 1982b). When there are no initial property rights, we obtain the *House Allocation problem* (HA) (Hylland and Zeckhauser, 1979; Zhou, 1990; Abdulkadiroğlu and Sönmez, 1998). A mixed model, in which a subset of applicants initially owns a good has also been studied (Abdulkadiroğlu and Sönmez, 1999).

House Allocation Problems

Formally, an instance I of the *House Allocation problem* (HA) comprises a set $A = \{a_1, a_2, \ldots, a_{n_1}\}$ of *applicants* and a set $H = \{h_1, h_2, \ldots, h_{n_2}\}$ of *houses*. The *agents* in I are the applicants and houses in $A \cup H$. There is a set $E \subseteq A \times H$ of *acceptable* applicant–house pairs. Let $m = |E|$. Each applicant $a_i \in A$ has an *acceptable* set of houses $A(a_i)$, where $A(a_i) = \{h_j \in H : (a_i, h_j) \in E\}$. Similarly each house $h_j \in H$ has an acceptable set of applicants $A(h_j)$, where $A(h_j) = \{a_i \in A : (a_i, h_j) \in E\}$.

Each applicant $a_i \in A$ has a *preference list* in which she ranks $A(a_i)$ in strict order. Given any applicant $a_i \in A$, and given any houses $h_j, h_k \in H$, a_i is said to *prefer* h_j to h_k if $\{h_j, h_k\} \subseteq A(a_i)$, and h_j precedes h_k on a_i's preference list. Houses do not have preference lists over applicants, and it is essentially this feature that distinguishes HA from SMI.

HA is a very general problem model and any application domain having an underlying matching problem that is bipartite, where agents in only one of the sets have preferences over the other, can be viewed as an instance of HA. These include the problems of allocating graduates to trainee positions, students to projects, professors to offices, clients to servers, and so on. The literature concerning HA has largely described this problem model in terms of assigning applicants to houses, so for consistency we also adopt this terminology.

An *assignment* M in I is a subset of E. The definitions of the terms *assigned to*, *assigned*, *unassigned* and *assignees* relative to M are analogous to the same definitions in the HR case (see Section 14.2.1). A *matching* M in I is an assignment such that, for each $p_k \in A \cup H$, the set of assignees of p_k in M, denoted by $M(p_k)$, satisfies $|M(p_k)| \leqslant 1$. For notational convenience, as in the HR case, if p_k is assigned in M then where there is no ambiguity the notation $M(p_k)$ is also used to refer to the single member of the set $M(p_k)$. Let $\mathcal{M}$ denote the set of matchings in I.

Given two matchings M and M' in $\mathcal{M}$, we say that an applicant $a_i \in A$ *prefers* M' to M if either (i) a_i is assigned in M' and unassigned in M, or (ii) a_i is assigned in both M and M', and a_i prefers $M'(a_i)$ to $M(a_i)$. We say that M' *Pareto dominates* M if (i) some applicant prefers M' to M and (ii) no applicant prefers M to M'. A matching $M \in \mathcal{M}$ is *Pareto optimal* if there is no matching $M' \in \mathcal{M}$ that Pareto dominates M. Intuitively M is Pareto optimal if no applicant a_i can be better off without requiring

---

[3] This problem is also referred to as the *House-swapping Game* in the literature.

another applicant a_j to be worse off. For example, M is not Pareto optimal if two applicants could improve by swapping the houses that they are assigned to in M.

Housing Markets

An instance I of a *Housing Market* (HM) comprises an HA instance I where $n_1 = n_2$, together with a matching M_0 in I (the *initial endowment*) such that $|M_0| = n_1$. A matching M in I is *individually rational* if, for each applicant $a_i \in A$, either a_i prefers $M(a_i)$ to $M_0(a_i)$, or $M(a_i) = M_0(a_i)$. Since we are only interested in individually rational matchings, we assume that $M_0(a_i)$ is the last house on a_i's preference list, for each $a_i \in A$. Clearly then, any individually rational matching M in I satisfies $|M| = n_1$.

The notion of Pareto optimality in HA is closely related to the concept of *core* matchings in the HM context (Roth and Postlewaite, 1977): let I be an instance of HM where M_0 is the initial endowment, and let M be an individually rational matching in I. Let M' be a matching in I, and let S be the set of applicants who are assigned in M'. Then M' *weakly blocks* M with respect to the *coalition* S if:

(*i*) the members of the coalition are only allowed to improve by exchanging their own resources (via their initial endowment M_0): $\{M'(a_i) : a_i \in S\} = \{M_0(a_i) : a_i \in S\}$;

(*ii*) some member of the coalition $a_i \in S$ is better off in M': some $a_i \in S$ prefers $M'(a_i)$ to $M(a_i)$;

(*iii*) no member of the coalition $a_i \in S$ is worse off in M' than in M: no $a_i \in S$ prefers $M(a_i)$ to $M'(a_i)$.

M is a *strict core matching*, or M is *in the strict core*, if there is no other matching in I that weakly blocks M. Also M' *strongly blocks* M with respect to S if Condition (*i*) is satisfied, and in addition, every $a_i \in S$ prefers $M'(a_i)$ to $M(a_i)$. M is a *weak core matching*, or M is *in the weak core*, if there is no other matching in I that strongly blocks M.

Note that M is Pareto optimal if and only if M is not weakly blocked by any matching M' such that $|M'| = n_1$ (here the coalition comprises all applicants and is referred to as the *grand coalition*). Hence a strict core matching is Pareto optimal.

Example 14.12 (HM **instance**). Consider the following HM instance in which the initial endowment is $M_0 = \{(a_1, h_4), (a_2, h_3), (a_3, h_2), (a_4, h_1)\}$.

$$a_1 : h_1 \ h_2 \ h_3 \ h_4$$
$$a_2 : h_1 \ h_2 \ h_4 \ h_3$$
$$a_3 : h_4 \ h_1 \ h_3 \ h_2$$
$$a_4 : h_4 \ h_3 \ h_2 \ h_1$$

Now define the matchings $M = \{(a_1, h_4), (a_2, h_3), (a_3, h_1), (a_4, h_2)\}$, $M' = \{(a_1, h_3), (a_2, h_2), (a_3, h_4), (a_4, h_1)\}$ and $M'' = \{(a_1, h_1), (a_2, h_2), (a_3, h_3), (a_4, h_4)\}$. Then M' strongly blocks M with respect to the coalition $S = \{a_1, a_2, a_3\}$, while M'' is a strict core matching and hence Pareto optimal.

We call a function that assigns a matching to each instance of HA (or HM) a *mechanism*. A mechanism that assigns only Pareto optimal matchings is called *Pareto optimal*.

14.3.2 Classical Structural and Algorithmic Results

House Allocation Problems

All Pareto optimal matchings can be constructed using a classical algorithm called the *Serial (SD) Dictatorship Algorithm* (see Theorem 14.14). For any fixed order of applicants $f = (i_1, i_2, \ldots, i_{n_1})$, the SD algorithm is a straightforward greedy algorithm that takes each applicant in turn and assigns her to the most-preferred available house on her preference list. The associated mechanism is called the *Serial Dictatorship (SD) mechanism*. The order in which the applicants are processed will, in general, affect the outcome. If a uniform lottery is used in order to determine the applicant ordering, then we obtain a random mechanism called the *Random Serial Dictatorship Mechanism* or *RSD mechanism* (Abdulkadiroğlu and Sönmez, 1998).

Often, the fixed order of applicants used for the SD mechanism is determined in some objective way. Roth and Sotomayor (1990, Example 4.3) remark that when the U.S. Naval Academy matches graduating students to their first posts as naval officers using an approach based on the SD algorithm, students are considered in nondecreasing order of graduation results. Clearly the SD algorithm may be implemented to execute in $O(m)$ time (m being the number of acceptable applicant–house pairs).

Strictly speaking RSD produces a probability distribution over matchings, and its output can be regarded as a bi-stochastic $n_1 \times n_2$ matrix M in which entry (i, j) gives the probability of applicant a_i receiving house h_j. Independently, Aziz et al. (2013a) and Saban and Sethuraman (2013) proved that computing M is #P-complete. Saban and Sethuraman (2013) also proved the surprising result that determining whether a given entry (i, j) in M has positive probability is NP-complete. This implies NP-completeness for the problem of determining whether, given an applicant a_i and house h_j, there exists a Pareto optimal matching containing (a_i, h_j).

Krysta et al. (2014) gave an $O(n_1^2 \gamma)$ strategyproof adaptation of RSD to the more general extension of HA in which preference lists may include ties, where γ is the maximum length of a tie in any applicant's preference list.

Housing Markets

For a somewhat more general housing market model that allows for indifferences in preference lists, Shapley and Scarf (1974) showed that the weak core is always nonempty by constructing a weak core matching using Gale's *Top Trading Cycles* or *TTC algorithm* (the authors attributed the now famous TTC algorithm to David Gale). They also showed that the weak core matching constructed is a competitive allocation,[4] the strict core may be empty and the nonempty weak core may exceed the (not necessarily singleton) set of competitive allocations. Note that for our housing market model with strict preferences, the weak and the strict core coincide. Given an instance of HM with initial endowment M_0,

---

[4] While housing markets are modelled as pure exchange economies, a competitive allocation of a housing market can be defined using fiat money. Then, an allocation is competitive if there exists a price for each house such that, by selling his house at the given price, each agent can afford to buy his most-preferred house (i.e., market clearance ensues).

(1) at the first step of the TTC algorithm, every applicant points to the owner of her favourite house (possibly to herself). Because there are finitely many applicants, there is at least one cycle (where a cycle is an ordered list $(i_1, i_2, \ldots, i_k)$, $1 \leqslant k \leqslant n_1$, of applicants with each applicant pointing to the next applicant in the list and applicant a_{i_k} pointing to applicant a_{i_1}; $k = 1$ is the special case of a self-loop where an applicant points to herself). In each cycle the implied cyclical exchange of houses is implemented and the algorithm continues with the remaining applicants and houses;

(l) at the lth step of the TTC algorithm, every remaining applicant points to the owner of her favourite remaining house (possibly to herself). Again, there is at least one cycle and in each cycle the implied cyclical exchange of houses is implemented and the algorithm continues with the remaining applicants and houses, and terminates when no applicants remain.

Note that there is an equivalent two-sided formulation of the TTC algorithm in which agents point to houses, as specified previously, and houses will always point to their owners. The TTC algorithm can be implemented to run in $O(m)$ time (m being the number of acceptable applicant–house pairs) (Abraham et al., 2004). Roth and Postlewaite (1977) demonstrated that the matching found by the TTC algorithm is the unique strict core allocation as well as the unique competitive allocation. The mechanism that assigns to each instance of HM the strict core matching obtained by the TTC algorithm is called the *Core Mechanism* or sometimes simply the *Core*.

Example 14.13. We apply the TTC algorithm to the HM instance shown in Example 14.12. The initial directed graph has four nodes (representing all applicants) where each applicants points to the owner (in M_0) of its most preferred house. Hence there is a directed arc from a_1 to a_4, from a_2 to a_4, from a_3 to a_1, and from a_4 to a_1. Because there is a cycle involving a_1 and a_4, we swap their houses, and thus a_1 receives h_1 and a_4 receives h_4. Now we delete a_1 and a_4 from the graph, as well as their houses from the HM instance. We are thus left with a_2 and a_3, with an arc from a_2 to a_3 (because after having deleted h_1, the most preferred house of a_2 is h_2, owned by a_3) and similarly an arc from a_3 to a_2. Thus we swap their houses and the algorithm stops, returning the matching $M'' = \{(a_1, h_1), (a_2, h_2), (a_3, h_3), (a_4, h_4)\}$ as in Example 14.12.

Recall that the only difference between an instance of HA and an instance of HM is that in the latter case an initial endowment matching M_0 is given as well. Hence, we could define a mechanism for HA that fixes an initial endowment matching M_f and then uses the Core mechanism for the obtained instance of HM. We call such a mechanism a *Core from Fixed Endowments* or *CFE mechanism*. If now a uniform lottery is used in order to determine the initial endowment matching, then we obtain a random mechanism called the *Core from Random Endowments* or *CRE mechanism* (Abdulkadiroğlu and Sönmez, 1998). Abdulkadiroğlu and Sönmez (1998) proved that the two random mechanisms we have introduced are equivalent.

Theorem 14.14 (Abdulkadiroğlu and Sönmez, 1998).

1. All SD mechanisms for HA are Pareto optimal. For each Pareto optimal matching M of an instance of HA, there exists an order of applicants such that the corresponding SD mechanism assigns M.

2. *All Core mechanisms for* HM *are Pareto optimal. For each Pareto optimal matching M of an instance of* HA, *there exists an initial endowment matching* M_f *such that the CFE mechanism assigns M.*
3. *The CRE and the RSD mechanisms for* HA *are equivalent.*

Hylland and Zeckhauser (1979) had already shown that the RSD mechanism is ex-post Pareto optimal, that is, the final matching that is chosen by the RSD lottery is Pareto optimal. Bogomolnaia and Moulin (2001) showed that the RSD mechanism, however, is not ex ante or ordinally efficient (Pareto optimal), that is, for some lotteries chosen by the RSD mechanism there exist Pareto dominating lotteries (with stochastic dominance being used to formulate the dominance relation). They also suggested a new random mechanism, the *Probabilistic Serial mechanism*, that satisfies ex ante efficiency.

14.3.3 Strategic Results: Strategyproofness

As in Section 14.2.1, a mechanism for which no single applicant can ever benefit from misrepresenting her preferences is called *strategyproof* (i.e., in game-theoretic terms, it is a weakly dominant strategy for each applicant to report her true preference list). All mechanisms introduced so far in this section are strategyproof, as the following results indicate.

Theorem 14.15 (Hylland and Zeckhauser, 1979). *The SD mechanisms for* HA *are strategyproof.*

Theorem 14.16 (Roth, 1982b). *The Core mechanism for* HM *is strategyproof. Hence, all CFE mechanisms for* HA *are strategyproof.*

In addition, the Core and CFE mechanisms are *group strategyproof* (i.e., no coalition of applicants can jointly misrepresent their true preferences in order for at least one member of the coalition to improve, while no other coalition member is worse off; see, e.g., Svensson, 1999). Strategyproofness is also one of the properties that characterize the Core mechanism.

Theorem 14.17 (Ma, 1994). *The Core mechanism for* HM *is the only mechanism that is Pareto optimal, individually rational, and strategyproof.*

Abdulkadiroğlu and Sönmez (1999) extended Ma's characterization result to a mixed model that combines HA and HM: in the House Allocation problem with Existing Tenants, a subset of applicants initially owns a house. They defined mechanisms that combine elements of SD as well as Core mechanisms based on the so-called YRMH-IGYT (You Request My House—I Get Your Turn) algorithm. All YRMH-IGYT mechanisms are strategyproof, Pareto optimal, and individually rational (in the sense that no existing tenant receives a house inferior to his own).

In Section 14.2.1 we introduced SC as a one-sided preference variant of HR, but we could also introduce this class of problems as a variant of HA with the additional properties that objects (i.e., houses/schools) have priorities over students, and objects can be multiply assigned up to some capacity. Either way, the RGS mechanism can be used to find a matching for each instance of SC. This mechanism is then strategyproof

$$\begin{array}{lll} a_1 : h_1 \ h_2 & a_1 : h_1 \ h_2 \ h_3 & a_1 : h_1 \ h_3 \\ a_2 : h_1 & a_2 : h_1 \ h_2 \ h_3 & a_2 : h_2 \ h_1 \\ & a_3 : h_1 \ h_2 \ h_3 & a_3 : h_2 \\ (a) & (b) & (c) \end{array}$$

Figure 14.1. (a) HA instance I_1; (b) HA instance I_2; (c) HA instance I_3.

(by Theorem 14.9) and stable (Gale and Shapley, 1962), but it is not Pareto optimal. In fact, no mechanism is both stable and Pareto optimal (Balinski and Sönmez, 1999). However it turns out that no other stable mechanism would do better in the following sense.

Theorem 14.18 (Balinski and Sönmez, 1999). *The RGS mechanism for* SC *Pareto dominates any other stable mechanism.*

Finally, when focusing on strategyproofness and Pareto optimality only, no better mechanism than the RGS mechanism emerges.

Theorem 14.19 (Kesten, 2010). *The RGS mechanism for* SC *is not Pareto-dominated by any other Pareto optimal mechanism that is strategyproof.*

14.3.4 Further Algorithmic Results

Pareto Optimal Matchings

For a given instance of HA, Pareto optimal matchings may have different sizes, as illustrated by Figure 14.1a: for the instance I_1 shown, matchings $M_1 = \{(a_1, h_1)\}$ and $M_2 = \{(a_1, h_2), (a_2, h_1)\}$ are both Pareto optimal. In many applications we seek to match as many applicants as possible. This motivates the problem of finding a Pareto optimal matching of maximum size, which we refer to as a *maximum Pareto optimal matching*.

Toward an algorithm for this problem, Abraham et al. (2004) gave a characterization of Pareto optimal matchings in a given HA instance I. A matching M in I is *maximal* if there is no pair $(a_i, h_j) \in E$, both of which are unassigned in M. Also M is *trade-in-free* if there is no pair $(a_i, h_j) \in E$ such that h_j is unassigned in M, and a_i is assigned in M and prefers h_j to $M(a_i)$. Finally M is *cyclic coalition-free* if M admits no cyclic coalition, which is a sequence of applicants $C = \langle a_{i_0}, a_{i_1}, \dots, a_{i_{r-1}} \rangle$, for some $r \geqslant 2$, all assigned in M, such that a_{i_j} prefers $M(a_{i_{j+1}})$ to $M(a_{i_j})$ $(0 \leqslant j \leqslant r - 1)$ (with subscripts taken modulo r). Abraham et al. gave the following necessary and sufficient conditions for a matching to be Pareto optimal in terms of these concepts:

Proposition 14.20 (Abraham et al., 2004). *Let I be an instance of HA and let M be a matching in I. Then M is Pareto optimal if and only if M is maximal, trade-in-free and coalition-free. Moreover there is an $O(m)$ algorithm for testing M for Pareto optimality, where m is the number of acceptable applicant–house pairs in I.*

Abraham et al. also gave a three-phase algorithm for finding a maximum Pareto optimal matching in I, with each phase enforcing one of the conditions for Pareto optimality given in Proposition 14.20. In Phase 1 they construct a maximum matching

M in the *underlying graph* of I, which is the bipartite graph with vertex set $A \cup H$ and edge set E. This step can be accomplished in $O(\sqrt{n_1}m)$ time and ensures that M is maximal. Phase 2 is based on an $O(m)$ algorithm in which assigned applicants repeatedly trade in their own house in M for any preferred vacant house. Once this step terminates, M is trade-in-free. Finally, cyclic coalitions are eliminated during Phase 3, which is based on an $O(m)$ implementation of the TTC algorithm. Putting these three phases together, they obtained the following result.

Theorem 14.21 (Abraham et al., 2004). *Let I be an instance of* HA. *A maximum Pareto optimal matching in I can be found in $O(\sqrt{n_1}m)$ time, where n_1 is the number of applicants and m is the number of acceptable applicant–house pairs in I.*

Popular Matchings

Pareto optimality is a fundamental solution concept, but on its own it is a relatively weak property. A stronger notion is that of a *popular matching*. Intuitively a matching M in an HA instance I is *popular* if there is no other matching that is preferred to M by a majority of the applicants who are not indifferent between the two matchings. This concept was first defined by Gärdenfors (1975) (using the term *majority assignment*) in the context of SMI.

To define the popular matching concept more formally, let $M, M' \in \mathcal{M}$, and let $P(M, M')$ denote the set of applicants who prefer M to M'. We say that M' is *more popular than M*, denoted $M' \succ M$, if $|P(M', M)| > |P(M, M')|$. Define a matching $M \in \mathcal{M}$ to be *popular* (Abraham et al., 2007b) if M is $\succ$-maximal (i.e., there is no other matching $M' \in \mathcal{M}$ such that $M' \succ M$).

Clearly a matching M is Pareto optimal if there is no other matching M' such that $|P(M, M')| = 0$ and $|P(M', M)| \geq 1$. Hence a popular matching is Pareto optimal. However in contrast to the case for Pareto optimal matchings, an HA instance need not admit a popular matching. To see this, consider the HA instance I_2 shown in Figure 14.1b. It is clear that a matching in I_2 cannot be popular unless all applicants are assigned. The unique matching up to symmetry in which all applicants are assigned is $M = \{(a_i, h_i) : 1 \leq i \leq 3\}$, however, $M' = \{(a_2, h_1), (a_3, h_2)\}$ is preferred by two applicants, which is a majority. The relation $\succ$ in this case cycles, hence the absence of a $\succ$-maximal solution (therefore, in general, $\succ$ is not a partial order on $\mathcal{M}$).

The potential absence of a popular matching in a given HA instance can be related all the way back to the observation of Condorcet (1785) that, given k voters who each rank n candidates in strict order of preference, there may not exist a "winner," namely, a candidate who beats all others in a pairwise majority vote. See also Chapter 2.

Abraham et al. (2007b) derived a neat characterization of popular matchings, leading to an $O(m)$ algorithm to check whether a given matching M in I is popular. The same characterization also led naturally to an $O(n + m)$ algorithm for finding a popular matching or reporting that none exists, where $n = n_1 + n_2$. We remark that popular matchings in I can have different sizes, and the authors showed how to extend their algorithm in order to find a maximum popular matching without altering the time complexity. This discussion can be summarized as follows.

Theorem 14.22 (Abraham et al., 2007b). *Let I be an instance of* HA. *There is an* $O(n + m)$ *algorithm to find a maximum popular matching in I or report that no popular matching exists, where n is the number of applicants and houses, and m is the number of acceptable applicant–house pairs.*

A more complex algorithm, with $O(\sqrt{n}m)$ complexity, can be used to find a maximum popular matching in I or report that no popular matching exists, in the case that preference lists include ties (Abraham et al., 2007b).

McDermid and Irving (2011) showed that the set of popular matchings in an HA instance can be characterized succinctly via a structure known as the *switching graph*. Using this representation they showed that a number of problems can be solved efficiently, including counting popular matchings, sampling a popular matching uniformly at random, listing all popular matchings and finding various types of "optimal" popular matchings.

As a given HA instance need not admit a popular matching, it is natural to weaken the notion of popularity, and seek matchings that are "as popular as possible" in cases where a popular matching does not exist. To this end, McCutchen (2008) defined two versions of "near-popular" matchings, namely, a *least unpopularity factor matching* and a *least unpopularity margin matching*. Also Kavitha et al. (2011) studied the concept of a *popular mixed matching*, which is a probability distribution over matchings that is popular in a precise sense.

Profile-Based Optimal Matchings

Further notions of optimality are based on the *profile* $p(M)$ of a matching M in an HA instance I. Informally, $p(M)$ is an r-tuple whose ith component is the number of applicants who have their ith-choice house, where r is the maximum length of an applicant's preference list.

A matching M is *rank-maximal* (Irving et al., 2006) if $p(M)$ is lexicographically maximum, taken over all matchings in $\mathcal{M}$. Intuitively, in such a matching, the maximum number of applicants are assigned to their first-choice house, and subject to this condition, the maximum number of applicants are assigned to their second-choice house, and so on. A rank-maximal matching need not be of maximum cardinality. To see this, consider the HA instance I_3 in Figure 14.1c and the following matchings in I_3: $M_1 = \{(a_1, h_1), (a_2, h_2)\}$ and $M_2 = \{(a_1, h_3), (a_2, h_1), (a_3, h_2)\}$. Clearly M_1 is rank-maximal and $|M_1| = 2$, whereas $|M_2| = 3$.

In many applications we seek to assign as many applicants as possible. With this in mind, consider $\mathcal{M}^+$, the set of maximum matchings in a given HA instance I. A *greedy maximum matching* is a matching $M \in \mathcal{M}^+$ such that $p(M)$ is lexicographically maximum, taken over all matchings in $\mathcal{M}^+$. Both rank-maximal and greedy maximum matchings maximize the number of applicants with their sth-choice house as a higher priority than maximizing the number of those with their tth-choice house, for any $1 \leqslant s < t \leqslant r$. As a consequence, both of these types of matchings could end up assigning applicants to houses relatively low down on their preference lists.

Consequently, define a *generous maximum matching* to be a matching $M \in \mathcal{M}^+$ such that $p^R(M)$ is lexicographically minimum, taken over all matchings in $\mathcal{M}^+$, where $p^R(M)$ is the reverse of $p(M)$. That is, M is a maximum cardinality matching that assigns the minimum number of applicants to their rth-choice house, and subject to this, the minimum number to their $(r-1)$th-choice house, and so on.

We collectively refer to rank-maximal, greedy maximum and generous maximum matchings as *profile-based optimal matchings*. Returning to instance I_3 shown in Figure 14.1c, the matching M_2 defined previously is the unique maximum matching and is therefore both a greedy maximum matching and a generous maximum matching.

The following results indicate the complexity of the fastest current algorithms for constructing rank-maximal, greedy maximum and generous maximum matchings in a given HA instance.

Theorem 14.23 (Irving et al., 2006). *Let I be an instance of* HA. *A rank-maximal matching M in I can be constructed in* $O(\min(n_1 + r^*, r^*\sqrt{n_1})m)$ *time, where n_1 is the number of applicants, m is the number of acceptable applicant–house pairs, and r^* is the maximum rank of an applicant's house in M.*

Theorem 14.24 (Huang and Kavitha, 2012). *Let I be an instance of* HA. *A greedy maximum matching M in I can be constructed in* $O(r^*\sqrt{n}m \log n)$ *time, where n is the number of applicants and houses, m is the number of acceptable applicant–house pairs, and r^* is the maximum rank of an applicant's house in M. The same time complexity holds for computing a generous maximum matching.*

The algorithms referred to in Theorems 14.23 and 14.24 are also applicable in the more general case that preference list contain ties.

14.4 Concluding Remarks and Further Reading

In this chapter we have tried to cover some of the most important results on matching problems with preferences. However the literature in this area is vast, and due to space limitations, we could only cover a subset of the main results in a single survey chapter. Chapter 11 introduces some of our matching problems within the context of fair resource allocation, namely, *object allocation problems* (HA), *priority-augmented object allocation problems* (SC), and *matching agents to each other* (SMI and HR). The following nonexhaustive list of articles contains normative results for these problems and basic axioms of fair allocation as introduced in Chapter 11 (e.g., resource-monotonicity, population-monotonicity, consistency, converse consistency): Ehlers and Klaus (2004, 2007, 2011), Ehlers et al. (2002), Ergin (2000), Kesten (2009), Sasaki and Toda (1992), and Toda (2006).

One obvious omission has been the Stable Roommates problem (SR), a non-bipartite generalization of SM. However a wider class of matching problems, known as *hedonic games*, which include SR as a special case, are explored in Chapter 15.

Looking ahead, it seems likely that the level of interest in matching under preferences will show no sign of diminishing, and if anything we predict that this field will continue to grow. This is due in no small part to the exposure that the research area has had on a global stage following the award of the Nobel Prize in Economic Sciences to Alvin Roth and Lloyd Shapley in 2012. Another contributing factor is the increasing engagement by more and more elements of society in forms of electronic communication, thereby easing preference elicitation and centralization of allocation processes.

To conclude, we give some sources for further reading. For more details on structural and algorithmic aspects of SM, HR and SR, we recommend Gusfield and Irving (1989). The second author's monograph (Manlove, 2013) provides an update to Gusfield and Irving (1989) and also expands the coverage to include HA. It expands on the algorithmic results presented in this chapter in particular. For more depth from an economic and game-theoretic viewpoint, the reader is referred to Roth and Sotomayor (1990), which considers issues of strategy in SM and HR in much more detail, and also covers monetary transfer and the Assignment Game. Finally, more recent results that also include economic applications (e.g., school choice and kidney exchange) are reviewed by Sönmez and Ünver (2011) and Vulkan et al. (2013).

Acknowledgments

Bettina Klaus acknowledges financial support from the Swiss National Science Foundation (SNFS). David Manlove is supported by grant EP/K010042/1 from the Engineering and Physical Sciences Research Council. Francesca Rossi is partially supported by the project "KIDNEY—Incorporating patients' preferences in kidney transplant decision protocols," funded by the University of Padova. The authors would like to thank Peter Biró, Felix Brandt, Vincent Conitzer, and Ulle Endriss for detailed comments, which have helped us to improve the presentation of this chapter.

CHAPTER 15

Hedonic Games

Haris Aziz and Rahul Savani

15.1 Introduction

Coalitions are a central part of economic, political, and social life, and coalition formation has been studied extensively within the mathematical social sciences. Agents (be they humans, robots, or software agents) have preferences over coalitions and, based on these preferences, it is natural to ask which coalitions are expected to form, and which coalition structures are better social outcomes. In this chapter, we consider coalition formation games with hedonic preferences, or simply hedonic games. The outcome of a coalition formation game is a partitioning of the agents into disjoint coalitions, which we will refer to synonymously as a partition or coalition structure.

The defining feature of *hedonic preferences* is that every agent only cares about which agents are in its coalition, but does not care how agents in other coalitions are grouped together (Drèze and Greenberg, 1980). Thus, hedonic preferences completely ignore inter-coalitional dependencies. Despite their relative simplicity, hedonic games have been used to model many interesting settings, such as research team formation (Alcalde and Revilla, 2004), scheduling group activities (Darmann et al., 2012), formation of coalition governments (Le Breton et al., 2008), clusterings in social networks (see, e.g., Aziz et al., 2014b; McSweeney et al., 2014; Olsen, 2009), and distributed task allocation for wireless agents (Saad et al., 2011).

Before we give a formal definition of a hedonic game, we give a standard hedonic game from the literature that we will use as a running example (see, e.g., Banerjee et al., 2001).

Example 15.1. The hedonic game has three agents, 1, 2, and 3, and their preferences over coalitions are as follows.

- All agents prefer coalitions of size two to coalitions of size one or three.
- All agents prefer coalitions of size one to coalitions of size three.
- Agent 1 prefers to be with agent 2 than to be with agent 3.
- Agent 2 prefers to be with agent 3 than to be with agent 1.
- Agent 3 prefers to be with agent 1 than to be with agent 2.

A coalition is as nonempty subset of $\{1, 2, 3\}$. The outcomes of the game are the partitions of the set of all agents into coalitions: $\{\{1, 2, 3\}\}$, $\{\{1, 2\}, \{3\}\}$, $\{\{1, 3\}, \{2\}\}$, $\{\{2, 3\}, \{1\}\}$ and $\{\{1\}, \{2\}, \{3\}\}$. Agent 1 is indifferent between the last two outcomes, because its own coalition is the same in both.

We now formally define a hedonic game. The description of a hedonic game can be exponentially large in the number of agents, because for every agent it must describe the preferences of this agent over all possible coalitions to which the agent may belong.

Definition 15.1. Let N be a finite set of agents. A *coalition* is a nonempty subset of N. Let $\mathcal{N}_i = \{S \subseteq N : i \in S\}$ be the set of all coalitions (subsets of N) that include agent $i \in N$. A *coalition structure* is a partition π of agents N into disjoint coalitions. A *hedonic coalition formation game* is a pair $(N, \succsim)$, where $\succsim$ is a *preference profile* that specifies for every agent $i \in N$ a reflexive, complete, and transitive binary relation $\succsim_i$ on $\mathcal{N}_i$. We call $\succsim_i$ a *preference relation*.

Given a coalition structure, a deviation by a single agent is a move by this agent to leave its current coalition and join a different (possibly empty) coalition. If this different coalition is empty, by deviating, the agent has broken away from a non-singleton coalition to go alone. We say that an agent has an *incentive to deviate* if there exists a deviation of this agent to a new coalition that it prefers to its old coalition; we call such a deviation a *profitable deviation*. Sometimes, we restrict which deviations are allowed, for example, based on what effect the deviation has on coalitions that lose members via the deviation.

A coalition structure is *stable* with respect to a class of allowable single-agent deviations if no agent has a profitable allowable deviation (Bogomolnaia and Jackson, 2002). Stability is the main criterion that has been used to analyze which coalition structures will form. Later in this chapter, in addition to single-agent deviations, we will also consider deviations by groups of agents.

Before we formally define notions of stability in Section 15.2, we discuss stability under deviations by single agents in the context of Example 15.1. In this example, no coalition structure is stable under single-agent deviations, abbreviated in the subsequent argument to simply "not stable." Suppose that all three agents are together in a single coalition. All three agents have an incentive to deviate and "go alone," so this coalition structure is not stable. Now consider the coalition structure $\{\{1, 2\}, \{3\}\}$. This coalition structure is not stable, because agent 2 would prefer to deviate and join agent 3. Likewise, the other two coalition structures that consist of one coalition of size two and one coalition of size one, are also not stable, because exactly one of the players in the coalition of size two wants to join the agent in the singleton coalition. Finally, the coalition structure where all three agents are alone is not stable, because all three agents prefer being with another agent than to being alone. Technically, this shows that the example does not admit a *Nash stable* partition, which is a solution concept that we will define formally in Section 15.2.

In order to achieve some weaker notion of stability, one can consider situations where the types of allowable deviations are more restricted. For example, for every coalition S in a coalition structure, we give every member of S the power to veto the deviation of a member of S who would like to leave S, and to veto a deviation by an agent from another coalition that would like to join S. In our example, every partition of the three agents into two nonempty coalitions is stable under the allowed deviations. For example, the partition $\{\{1\}, \{2, 3\}\}$ is stable because the only agent that has an incentive to deviate is agent 3, and although agent 1 would be happy for agent 3 to join it, agent 2 would not want 3 to leave and would veto this move. Technically, we have shown that the example admits a *contractually individually stable* partition, which is another solution concept that we will define formally in Section 15.2.

A significant amount of research has been undertaken to understand what stability requirements and what restrictions on preferences guarantee that stable partition exists (see, e.g., Alcalde and Revilla, 2004; Aziz and Brandl, 2012; Banerjee et al., 2001; Bogomolnaia and Jackson, 2002; Dimitrov et al., 2006; Dimitrov and Sung, 2007; Karakaya, 2011). In this chapter we consider a number of standard stability requirements and restrictions on preferences from a computational viewpoint. We consider questions such as the following ones. What is the most expressive or compact way to represent hedonic games? What is the computational complexity of deciding if a stable partition exists, or finding a stable partition if one is known to exist? Two other surveys on the computational aspects of hedonic games are presented by Hajduková (2006) and Cechlárová (2008).

15.1.1 Relationship with Cooperative Game Theory

Coalitions have always played a central role in *cooperative game theory*. Initially, coalition formation was understood in the context of *transferable utility cooperative games*, which are defined by a valuation function that assigns a value to every coalition, and it is assumed that the value of a coalition can be split between its members in every possible way. A common assumption in transferable utility cooperative games is that the valuation function is super-additive, which means that the union of two disjoint coalitions has a value greater than or equal to sum of the values of the separate coalitions. Under this assumption, the formation of the coalition structure consisting of the grand coalition with all agents together maximizes the total value achieved. In these settings, the question of which coalition structures form is not relevant, and the focus has been on the question of how the values of smaller coalitions should determine the division of the value of the grand coalition among its members (Curiel, 1997; Chalkiadakis et al., 2011; Deng and Fang, 2008; Elkind et al., 2013; Peleg and Sudhölter, 2007). In case a transferable utility cooperative game is *not* super-additive, then a natural approach that has been considered in the literature is to first compute a coalition structure that maximizes social welfare, that is, the sum of values of coalitions (Aziz and de Keijzer, 2011; Michalak et al., 2010; Rahwan et al., 2009a, 2009b; Sandholm et al., 1999).

Hedonic games are a sub-class of *nontransferable utility cooperative games*. A nontransferable utility game describes the possibilities open to a coalition as a set of outcomes, where each outcome specified the payoff to each agent in the coalition. These possible outcomes can be thought of as different ways for the coalition to organize itself, which in turn can result in different utilities for the members of the coalition. An outcome is represented as a payoff vector that assigns a payoff to every member of the coalition. In a hedonic game, *the set of payoff vectors for every possible coalition that may form can be viewed as being a singleton*. For more details on cooperative games and in particular nontransferable utility cooperative games and the eventual formalization of hedonic games, we refer to the introductory section of the survey of Hajduková (2006).

Hedonic games are a strict generalization of various well-studied matching models such as the marriage market (Gale and Shapley, 1962), roommate market, and many-to-one market (see, e.g., Roth and Sotomayor, 1990). These are all models with hedonic preferences but where not all partitions are permitted. We refer the reader to Chapter 14, which is on Matching under Preferences.

15.1.2 Roadmap

The rest of the chapter is organized as follows. In Section 15.2, we present the standard solution concepts used for hedonic games. In Section 15.3, we consider the most common representations of hedonic games as well as standard restrictions on preferences. In Section 15.4, we give an overview of computational aspects of hedonic games. Finally, we conclude the chapter with suggestions for further reading in Section 15.5.

15.2 Solution Concepts

In this section, we describe the most prominent solution concepts for hedonic games. We use the following notation throughout the chapter. For two coalitions $S, T \in \mathcal{N}_i$ that contain agent i, we use $S \succ_i T$ to denote that i strictly prefers S over T, $S \sim_i T$ to denote that i is indifferent between S and T, and $S \succsim_i T$ to denote that either $S \succ_i T$ or $S \sim_i T$ holds. Given a coalition structure π we use $\pi(i)$ to denote the (unique) coalition of π that includes agent i.

The first solution concept that we consider is *individual rationality*. A partition π is *individually rational (IR)* if every agent is at least as happy in its coalition $\pi(i)$ as it would be alone, that is, for all $i \in N$, $\pi(i) \succsim_i \{i\}$. This is really a minimal requirement for a solution to be considered stable, and many solution concepts that we consider will satisfy individual rationality.

Next, we introduce the concept of a *perfect partition*. This solution concept is stronger than *all* other solution concepts that we will consider in this chapter. A partition is *perfect* if each agent belongs to one of its most preferred coalitions (Aziz et al., 2013e). Thus, no matter what deviations we allow, a perfect partition is always stable. However, in general a perfect partition does not exist. In our running example (Example 15.1, each agent has a unique most preferred coalition ({1,2}, {2,3}, and {3,1} for agents 1, 2, and 3, respectively), but these are not consistent with any partition, and so there is no perfect partition.

We next discuss *Pareto optimality*, which is a concept that has been used throughout the economics literature. A partition π is *Pareto optimal (PO)* if there is no partition π' with $\pi'(j) \succsim_j \pi(j)$ for all agents j and $\pi'(i) \succ_i \pi(i)$ for at least one agent i. Pareto optimality can also be considered a group-based stability concept in the sense that if a partition is not Pareto optimal, then there exists another partition that each agent weakly prefers and at least one agent strictly prefers.

The remaining solution concepts that we consider are all based on stability with respect to deviations by agents or groups of agents, which we deal with separately.

15.2.1 Solution Concepts Based on Group Deviations

The core is one of the most fundamental solution concepts in cooperative game theory. In the context of coalition formation games, we say that a coalition $S \subseteq N$ *strongly blocks* a partition π, if every agent $i \in S$ strictly prefers S to its current coalition $\pi(i)$ in the partition π. A partition which admits no strongly blocking coalition is said to be in the *core (C)*, or *core stable*.

Returning to Example 15.1, it is easy to check that no core stable partition exists. If all agents are together in a single coalition, then every coalition of size two is a strongly blocking coalition. If all agents are alone, then again every coalition of size two is a strongly blocking coalition. Thus, if there is a core stable partition, exactly one agent is alone. Suppose agent 1 is alone. Then agent 1 and agent 3 together form a strongly blocking coalition. Due to the cyclic nature of the preference of agents over coalitions of size two, we can similarly rule out a core stable partition in which either agent 2 or 3 is alone.

A weaker definition of blocking (that gives rise to a more stringent solution concept) has also been considered. We say that a coalition $S \subseteq N$ *weakly blocks* a partition π, if each agent $i \in S$ weakly prefers S to $\pi(i)$ and there exists at least one agent $j \in S$ who strictly prefers S to its current coalition $\pi(j)$. A partition which admits no weakly blocking coalition is said to be in the *strict core (SC)*, which is sometimes referred to as the strong core (Bogomolnaia and Jackson, 2002).

One can also define other stability concepts based on more complex deviations by coalitions of agents. For partition π, $\pi' \neq \pi$ is called *reachable* from π by movements of players $S \subseteq N$, denoted by $\pi \xrightarrow{S} \pi'$, if $\forall i, j \in N \setminus S, i \neq j : \pi(i) = \pi(j) \Leftrightarrow \pi'(i) = \pi'(j)$. A subset of players $S \subseteq N$, $S \neq \emptyset$ *strong Nash blocks* π if a partition $\pi' \neq \pi$ exists with $\pi \xrightarrow{S} \pi'$ and $\forall i \in S : \pi'(i) \succ_i \pi(i)$. If a partition π is not strong Nash blocked by any set $S \subseteq N$, π is called *strong Nash stable (SNS)* (Karakaya, 2011). The stability concept strong Nash stability can be suitably weakened or strengthened to obtain other stability concepts such as *strict strong Nash stability (SSNS)* and *strong individual stability (SIS)*. We refer to Aziz and Brandl (2012) for the definitions.

15.2.2 Solution Concepts Based on Single-Agent Deviations

In this subsection, we define a number of solution concepts based on single-agent deviations. The most basic is *Nash stability* which is named after Nash equilibrium. A partition is Nash stable if no agent would gain by unilaterally moving to a different (possibly empty) coalition. The other solution concepts restrict which deviations are allowed based on the preferences of other agents in the coalitions that may lose or gain an agent through the deviation. We say that a partition π is:

- *Nash stable (NS)* if no agent can benefit by moving from its coalition to another (possibly empty) coalition, that is, for all $i \in N$, $\pi(i) \succsim_i S \cup \{i\}$ for all $S \in \pi \cup \{\emptyset\}$.
- *Individually stable (IS)* if no agent can benefit by moving from its coalition to another (possibly empty) coalition while not making the members of that coalition worse off, that is, for all $i \in N$, if there exists a coalition $S \in \pi \cup \{\emptyset\}$ with $S \neq \pi(i)$ s.t. $S \cup \{i\} \succ_i \pi(i)$ then there exists a $j \in S$ with $S \succ_j S \cup \{i\}$.

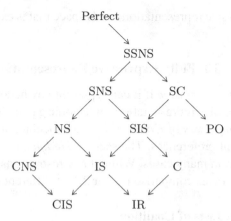

Figure 15.1. Logical relationships between stability concepts for hedonic games. For example, every NS partition is also IS. NS, SC, PO, C, and IR are classic stability concepts. IS was formulated by Bogomolnaia and Jackson (2002); CNS by Sung and Dimitrov (2007b); SNS (strong Nash stability) by Karakaya (2011); and perfect partitions by Aziz et al. (2013e). SSNS (strict strong Nash stability) and SIS (strong individual stability) were introduced by Aziz and Brandl (2012). Partitions satisfying CIS, PO, and IR, respectively, are guaranteed to exist for all hedonic games.

- *Contractual Nash stable (CNS)* if no agent i can benefit by moving from its coalition $\pi(i)$ to another (possibly empty) coalition $S \in \pi \cup \{\emptyset\}$ with $S \neq \pi(i)$ while not making the members of $\pi(i)$ worse off (Sung and Dimitrov, 2007b). Formally, for all $i \in N$, if there exists a coalition $S \in \pi \cup \{\emptyset\}$ with $S \neq \pi(i)$ s.t. $S \cup \{i\} \succ_i \pi(i)$ then there exists a $j' \in \pi(i)$ with $\pi(i) \succ_{j'} \pi(i) \setminus \{i\}$.
- *Contractually individually stable (CIS)* if no agent can benefit by moving from its coalition to another existing (possibly empty) coalition while making no member of either coalition worse off. Formally, for all $i \in N$, if there exists a coalition $S \in \pi \cup \{\emptyset\}$ with $S \neq \pi(i)$ s.t. $S \cup \{i\} \succ_i \pi(i)$ then there exists a $j \in S$ with $S \succ_j S \cup \{i\}$ or there exists a $j' \in \pi(i)$ with $\pi(i) \succ_{j'} \pi(i) \setminus \{i\}$.

All of the preceding concepts (except contractual Nash stability) have been defined by Bogomolnaia and Jackson (2002). In Figure 15.1, we show relationships between these and other solution concepts. For example, the figure shows that if a partition is perfect, then it satisfies all the stability concepts defined earlier. The hedonic game in Example 15.1 admits no IS partition (and therefore no NS) but has multiple CIS partitions. For example, the partition $\{\{1\}, \{2, 3\}\}$ is CIS, but not IS, because agent 3 has incentive to deviate to agent 1 and form coalition $\{1, 2\}$.

15.3 Preference Restrictions and Game Representations

When hedonic games are represented, we would ideally prefer a representation that not only allows agents to be as flexible as possible in describing their preferences but which also requires less space to succinctly store the preferences of the agents. In this section, we discuss different representations of hedonic games and, in particular the trade-off that occurs between the expressiveness of a representation and its size;

typically a fully expressive representation needs space that is exponentially large in the number of agents.

15.3.1 Fully Expressive Representations

A representation is *fully expressive* if it can represent any hedonic game. We describe two types of fully expressive representations of hedonic games. The first, representation by *Individually Rational Lists of Coalitions*, is nonsuccinct and involves a complete enumeration of relevant preferences. The second, *Hedonic Coalition Nets*, allows for succinct representation in many cases. Without any restrictions, a representation of an agent's preferences involves comparisons over $2^{|N|-1}$ different coalitions.

Individually Rational Lists of Coalitions

Most reasonable solution concepts require that an agent will be in a coalition that is *individually rational* (*IR*), that is, the agent prefers to be in that coalition over being alone. Therefore, instead of expressing preferences over all coalitions that include an agent, the agent may express preferences only over individually rational coalitions. Such a representation is called an *Individually Rational Lists of Coalitions* (*IRLC*) (Ballester, 2004). Of course such representations are essentially still complete enumerations and can be exponentially large in the number of agents.

Example 15.2 (An example of an IRLC). Let us examine a preference relation of agent 1 in the hedonic game defined in Example 15.1. Agent 1's preference list contains all coalitions that are at least as preferred as the singleton coalition:

$$\succsim_1: \quad \{1, 2\} \succ_1 \{1, 3\} \sim_1 \{1\}.$$

Hedonic Coalition Nets

Hedonic coalition nets are a representation of hedonic games that are both *expressive*, that is, able to capture potentially nonsuccinct IRLC, and also capable of allowing compact representations of games that have structured preferences. They were introduced by Elkind and Wooldridge (2009). In such a representation, each agent's preference relation is represented by a collection of rules of the form $\phi \mapsto_i b$ where ϕ is a predicate over coalitions and b is a real number. The value of an agent for a coalition is obtained by adding the values on the right hand side of those rules that are satisfied by the coalition. Hedonic coalition nets are inspired by *marginal contribution nets*, which were introduced in the context of transferable utility cooperative games by Ieong and Shoham (2005).

Hedonic coalition nets use the framework of propositional logic. Let Φ be a vocabulary of Boolean variables, and let $\mathcal{L}_\Phi$ be the set of propositional logic formulae over Φ. Given a truth assignment to the variables $\varphi \subseteq \Phi$, a *valuation* ξ is the subset of the variables such that we have $x \in \xi$ iff x is true. Given a valuation ξ and a formula $\phi \in \mathcal{L}_\varphi$, we say that $\xi \models \phi$ if and only if ϕ is true under valuation ξ.

In a hedonic coalition net, $\Phi = N$, each agent corresponds to a propositional variable and every coalition S defines a valuation over $\mathcal{L}_N$ where the variable $i \in N$ is set to true if $i \in S$ and set to false if $i \notin S$. A *rule* for agent $i \in N$ is $\phi \mapsto_i \beta$ where $\phi \in \mathcal{L}_N$ is a formula and $\beta \in \mathbb{R}$ is the *value* associated with the rule. A hedonic coalition net is a structure $(N, R_1, \ldots, R_n)$ where R_i specifies a set of rules for each $i \in N$. It specifies the utility of a coalition $S \in \mathcal{N}_i$ for an agent i in the following way:

$$u_i(S) = \sum_{\substack{\phi \mapsto_i \beta \in R_i \\ S \models \phi}} \beta.$$

In other words, for every coalition $S \in \mathcal{N}_i$, the utility of agent i for being in S is the sum of the values corresponding to those rules ϕ in R_i that the coalition S satisfies. Given a hedonic coalition net, the corresponding hedonic game is $(N, \succsim)$ such that for all $i \in N$ and for all $S, S' \in \mathcal{N}_i$, we have that $S \succsim_i S'$ if and only if $u_i(S) \geqslant u_i(S')$.

Hedonic coalition nets are fully expressive because they can represent an IRLC. In an IRLC with n agents, the preference list of agent i is represented as

$$S_1 *^1 S_2 *^2 \cdots *^{r-1} S_r$$

where $r \leq 2^{n-1}$, $*^j \in \{\succ_j, \sim_j\}$, $S_j \in \mathcal{N}_i$, and $S_r = \{i\}$. Based on an IRLC, we can construct a hedonic coalition net where there are r rules and the value of the r'th rule is $x_r = 0$, and for $j = r - 1, \ldots, 1$, we set $x_j = x_{j+1}$ if $S_j \sim_i S_{j+1}$ and $x_j = x_{j+1} + 1$ if $S_j \succ_i S_{j+1}$. Now, for $j \in \{1, \ldots, r\}$, the j'th rule in R_i is

$$\left(\bigwedge_{k \in S_j} k \right) \wedge \left(\bigwedge_{l \in N \setminus S_j} \neg l \right) \mapsto_i x_j.$$

In other words, if agents in S_j are in the coalition and agents not in S_j are not in the coalition, then agent i gets utility x_j (exactly one rule is satisfied by a given coalition).

Example 15.3 (An example of hedonic coalition nets). Let us consider how a hedonic coalition net can represent the preferences of agent 1 in Example 15.2.

$\neg i_1 \mapsto -\infty$	$i_2 \mapsto 3$
$i_2 \mapsto -\epsilon$	$i_3 \wedge \neg i_2 \mapsto 2$
$i_3 \mapsto -\epsilon$	$i_4 \wedge \neg i_3 \wedge \neg i_2 \mapsto 1$
$i_4 \mapsto -\epsilon$	

The symbol ϵ represents an arbitrarily small positive real number. The symbol ∞ represents a sufficiently large number. Let us see how agent 1 compares coalition $\{1, 2\}$ with $\{1, 3, 4\}$. For coalition $\{1, 2\}$, the rules $i_2 \mapsto -\epsilon$ and $i_2 \mapsto 3$ are satisfied and the total utility of agent 1 for coalition $\{1, 2\}$ is $3 - \epsilon$. In fact, the rules $i_2 \mapsto -\epsilon$ and $i_2 \mapsto 3$ can simply be combined into a single rule $i_2 \mapsto 3 - \epsilon$. For coalition $\{1, 3, 4\}$, the rules $i_3 \wedge \neg i_2 \mapsto 2, i_3 \mapsto -\epsilon$ and $i_4 \mapsto -\epsilon$ are satisfied, so the total utility of agent 1 for coalition $\{1, 3, 4\}$ is $2 - 2\epsilon$.

In contrast to IRLC, hedonic coalition nets can be used to succinctly represent various classes of hedonic games such as additively separable hedonic games and games with $\mathcal{B}$-preferences, which we will introduce in Section 15.3.4.

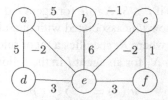

Figure 15.2. Example of an additively separable symmetric hedonic game.

The use of weighted logics for succinct representations is prevalent in computational social choice (see Chapter 12). More generally, succinct representations are discussed in several chapters (e.g., Chapters 9, 12, and 14).

15.3.2 Additively Separable Hedonic Games

Separability of preferences is a property of certain preferences that allows for a succinct representations. The main idea of separability is that adding a liked (unliked) agent to a coalition makes the coalition more (less) preferred.

Definition 15.2 (Separability). A game $(N, \succsim)$ is called *separable* if for every agent $i \in N$, coalition $S \in \mathcal{N}_i$, and agent j not in S, we have the following:

- $S \cup \{j\} \succ_i S$ if and only if $\{i, j\} \succ_i \{i\}$
- $S \cup \{j\} \prec_i S$ if and only if $\{i, j\} \prec_i \{i\}$
- $S \cup \{j\} \sim_i S$ if and only if $\{i, j\} \sim_i \{i\}$

Additive separable preferences are a particularly appealing (strict) subclass of separable preferences. In an *additively separable hedonic game (ASHG)* $(N, \succsim)$, each agent $i \in N$ has value $v_i(j)$ for agent j being in the same coalition as i and for any coalition $S \in \mathcal{N}_i$, i gets utility $\sum_{j \in S \setminus \{i\}} v_i(j)$ for being in S. The utility that an agent gets for being alone in a singleton coalition is assumed to be 0. For coalitions $S, T \in \mathcal{N}_i$, we have $S \succsim_i T$ if and only if $\sum_{j \in S \setminus \{i\}} v_i(j) \geq \sum_{j \in T \setminus \{i\}} v_i(j)$. Therefore an ASHG can be represented by a weighted directed graph in which every vertex corresponds to an agent and weight of an arc (i, j) represents $v_i(j)$. Additively separable preferences are *symmetric* if $v_i(j) = v_j(i)$ for every two agents $i, j \in N$.

A *nonsymmetric* ASHG need not have a Nash stable partition (Bogomolnaia and Jackson, 2002), and deciding whether there is one is NP-complete (Sung and Dimitrov, 2010). A symmetric ASHG is represented by an *undirected* weighted graph, and always has a Nash stable partition as we will explain after an example.

Example 15.4. Figure 15.2 gives an example of a symmetric additively separable hedonic game. Consider the partition $\{\{a, b, d\}, \{c, e, f\}\}$. The utilities of the agents a, b, c, d, e, f are $10, 5, -1, 5, 1, 4$, respectively. Agents a, b, d, f have no profitable single-agent deviations, c has a profitable deviation to go alone and start a singleton coalition, and e has a profitable deviation to join the other coalition. This is a contractually individually stable partition. The partition $\{\{a, b, d\}, \{c\}, \{e, f\}\}$ is an individual stable partition, and $\{\{a, b, d, e, f\}, \{c\}\}$ is Nash stable.

For an additively separable *symmetric* hedonic game, the existence of a Nash stable (NS) partition (and therefore also a CNS, CIS, and IS partition) is guaranteed by an argument based on a "potential function," which was noted by Bogomolnaia and Jackson (2002). We will construct an *exact potential function*. For every partition the exact potential function assigns a potential value equal to half the sum of agents' utilities under this partition. A deviation by a single agent from its coalition to another will change the value of this potential function by exactly the change in the utility of this deviating agent (every edge gained or lost in the sum of agents' utilities counts twice). Because the potential function is bounded, and there are finitely many partitions, and every profitable deviation by a single agent improves the value of the potential function, we have the following: starting from any partition, every maximally long sequence of profitable deviations by agents terminates with a Nash stable partition. Note that symmetry is key for this potential function argument to work.

15.3.3 Games Based on the Best or Worst Agents

We now describe classes of hedonic games in which the agents' preferences over coalitions are induced by their *ordinal* preferences over the other individual agents via *set extensions* (Hajduková, 2006; Barberà et al., 2004). Two of the most natural ways to extend preferences is based on the most preferred or least preferred agent in the coalition. For a subset J of agents, we denote by $\max_{\succsim_i}(J)$ and $\min_{\succsim_i}(J)$ the sets of the most and least preferred agents in J by i, respectively. In $\mathcal{B}$ (where $\mathcal{B}$ stands for best) and $\mathcal{W}$ (where $\mathcal{W}$ stands for worst) games each agent's appreciation of a coalition depends on the most preferred (best) or least preferred (worst) agent in the coalition. Note that roommate markets can also be considered in the framework with the additional constraint that coalitions of size three or more are not feasible.

In *hedonic games with $\mathcal{B}$-preferences* (which we will refer to as $\mathcal{B}$-hedonic games), $S \succ_i T$ if and only if, we have either:

(i) for each $s \in \max_{\succsim_i}(S \setminus \{i\})$ and $t \in \max_{\succsim_i}(T \setminus \{i\})$, $s \succ_i t$, or
(ii) for each $s \in \max_{\succsim_i}(S \setminus \{i\})$ and $t \in \max_{\succsim_i}(T \setminus \{i\})$, $s \sim_i t$ and $|S| < |T|$.

So an agent's appreciation of a coalition depends on its most favoured agents in the coalition. If two coalitions have equally preferred agents, then a smaller coalition is strictly preferred (Cechlárová and Hajduková, 2002; Cechlárová and Romero-Medina, 2001).

Example 15.5 (A $\mathcal{B}$-hedonic game). Let $(N, \succsim)$ be a game with $N = \{1, 2, 3, 4\}$ and let the agents have preferences over other agents as follows:

$$2 \succ_1 3 \succ_1 4 \succ_1 1,$$

$$3 \succ_2 4 \succ_2 1 \succ_2 2,$$

$$1 \succ_3 2 \succ_3 4 \succ_3 3,$$

$$3 \succ_4 2 \succ_4 1 \succ_4 4.$$

For the $\mathcal{B}$-hedonic game, the preferences of each agent over other agents are extended over the preferences over sets of agents. The preferences of the agents are as follows (the preference of agent 1 is the same as in Example 15.2). For brevity, we omit the commas separating agents in each coalition.

$$\{12\} \succ_1 \{123\} \sim_1 \{124\} \succ_1 \{1234\} \succ_1 \{13\} \succ_1 \{134\} \succ_1 \{14\} \succ_1 \{1\},$$

$$\{23\} \succ_2 \{234\} \sim_2 \{123\} \succ_2 \{1234\} \succ_2 \{24\} \succ_2 \{124\} \succ_2 \{12\} \succ_2 \{2\},$$

$$\{13\} \succ_3 \{123\} \sim_3 \{134\} \succ_3 \{1234\} \succ_3 \{23\} \succ_3 \{234\} \succ_3 \{34\} \succ_3 \{3\},$$

$$\{34\} \succ_4 \{134\} \sim_4 \{234\} \succ_4 \{1234\} \succ_4 \{24\} \succ_4 \{124\} \succ_4 \{14\} \succ_4 \{4\}.$$

In *hedonic games with W-preferences* (which we will refer to as W-hedonic games), $S \succsim_i T$ if and only if for each $s \in \min_{\succsim_i}(S \setminus \{i\})$ and $t \in \min_{\succsim_i}(T \setminus \{i\})$, we have $s \succsim_i t$. So an agent's appreciation of a coalition depends on its least preferred favoured agents in the coalition (Cechlárová and Hajduková, 2004b; Cechlárová and Romero-Medina, 2001).

Other games can be defined based on preferences that depend on both the best and worst agents in the coalition (Hajduková, 2006) or in which the presence of an unacceptable agent in the coalition makes the coalition unacceptable (Aziz et al., 2012a, 2013e). B-hedonic games, in which agents express strict preferences over other agents, are known to admit a core stable partition (Cechlárová and Romero-Medina, 2001). For further details on games based on the best or worst agents, we refer the reader to Aziz et al. (2012a, 2013e); Cechlárová and Romero-Medina (2001); Cechlárová and Hajduková (2004b); Hajduková (2006). B-hedonic games with strict preferences form a subclass of a larger class of hedonic games that satisfy *top responsiveness*.

15.3.4 Top Responsiveness

Identifying sufficient and necessary conditions for the existence of stability in coalition formation has been a very active area of research. Perhaps the most celebrated result in this field is the existence of a (core) stable matching for the stable marriage problem, which is shown constructively via the *deferred-acceptance* algorithm (Gale and Shapley, 1962). For hedonic games, more generally, a number of preference restrictions have been identified for which a stable partition is guaranteed to exist for some notion of stability (see, e.g., Alcalde and Revilla, 2004; Aziz and Brandl, 2012; Banerjee et al., 2001; Bogomolnaia and Jackson, 2002; Dimitrov et al., 2006; Dimitrov and Sung, 2007; Karakaya, 2011). In this subsection, we present an example of hedonic games that satisfy *top responsiveness* (Alcalde and Revilla, 2004) that always admit a core stable partition.

Every coalition contains subset subcoalitions over which the agents also have preferences. Top responsiveness captures the situation in which each agent's appreciation of a coalition depends on the most preferred subset within the coalition. If two coalitions have the same most preferred subcoalition, then the coalition with the smaller size is preferred. Top responsiveness is based on *choice sets*, which are sets of agents that an agent wants to be with. We use $Ch(i, S)$ to denote the *choice sets* of agent i in coalition S. It is formally defined as follows:

$$Ch(i, S) := \{S' \subseteq S : (i \in S') \wedge (S' \succsim_i S'' \ \forall S'' \subseteq S)\}.$$

If $|Ch(i, S)| = 1$, we denote by $ch(i, S)$ the unique subset of S that is maximally preferred by agent i on under $\succsim_i$: A game satisfies *top responsiveness* if $|Ch(i, S)| = 1$ for each $i \in N$ and $S \in \mathcal{N}_i$ and the following conditions hold for each $i \in N$ and all $S, T \in \mathcal{N}_i$,

(i) $S \succ_i T$ if $ch(i, S) \succ_i ch(i, T)$;
(ii) $S \succ_i T$ if $ch(i, S) = ch(i, T)$ and $S \subset T$.

Example 15.6 (An example of top responsive preferences). The hedonic game specified in Example 15.5 satisfies top responsiveness. For example, for agent 1, its choice set of the grand coalition is $\{1, 2\}$. It likes each coalition that is a superset of $\{1, 2\}$ more than any coalition that is not a superset of $\{1, 2\}$. Moreover, it prefers a smaller coalition that is a superset of $\{1, 2\}$ more than a bigger coalition.

In Section 15.4.3, we show how to exploit the top responsiveness property algorithmically.

15.4 Algorithms and Computational Complexity

In this section we give an overview of computational results concerning hedonic games. For a given solution concept α, such as core stability, we consider the following natural computational problems:

VERIFICATION: Given $(N, \succsim)$ and a partition π of N, does π satisfy α?
EXISTENCE: Given $(N, \succsim)$, does there exist a partition satisfying α?
CONSTRUCTION: Given $(N, \succsim)$, if a partition satisfying α exists, find one.

15.4.1 Hardness to Check Non-emptiness of Core

We next consider the problem EXISTENCE for core stability for a hedonic game given as an IRLC, which was shown by Ballester (2004) to be NP-complete.

Theorem 15.7 (Ballester, 2004). *For hedonic games in IRLC, the problem of checking whether there exists a core stable partition is NP-complete.*

Proof. Given an IRLC, VERIFICATION for core stability can be solved in polynomial time because each agent explicitly lists all the individually rational coalitions, and these are also all the potentially blocking coalitions. Thus the problem of deciding whether a core stable partition exists is in NP.

We now show that it is NP-hard and thus NP-complete, via a reduction from EXACTCOVERBY3SETS.

EXACTCOVERBY3SETS (X3C).
Instance: Set X and set T that consists of 3-element subsets of X.
Question: Does there exist a subset of T that partitions X?

We construct a hedonic game where $N = \{x, x', x'' : x \in X\}$ and $\succsim$ is defined as follows. For each $i \in \{x, x', x''\}$, let $X_1^i, \ldots, X_m^i$ be the elements in T such that they include i.

- For each x, $X_1^x \sim_x \cdots \sim_x X_m^x \succ_x \{x, x''\} \succ_x \{x, x'\} \succ_x \{x\}$
- For each x', $\{x, x'\} \succ_{x'} \{x', x''\} \succ_{x'} \{x'\}$
- For each x'', $\{x', x''\} \succ_{x''} \{x, x''\} \succ_{x''} \{x''\}$

It can be shown that $(N, \succsim)$ admits a core stable partition if and only if the X3C instance is a yes instance. If the X3C instance is a yes instance, then there exists a partition π of N that puts each $x \in X$ in one of its most preferred coalitions. As for each x' and x'', they can be paired up in a coalition so that x'' is in its most preferred coalition, and x' is in its second most preferred coalition. Hence the partition is core stable.

If X3C is a no instance, then there exists no partition in which each x gets a most preferred coalition. Hence, in each partition, at least one $x \in X$ is in one of the following coalitions: $\{x, x''\}, \{x, x'\}, \{x\}$. For any partition containing coalition $\{x, x''\}$, the coalition $\{x', x''\}$ is blocking. For any partition containing coalition $\{x, x'\}$, the coalition $\{x, x''\}$ is blocking. For any partition containing coalition $\{x\}$, the coalition $\{x, x'\}$ is blocking. Hence each partition admits a blocking coalition and is not core stable. $\quad\square$

NP-hardness of checking existence of core is not restricted to IRLC but also holds for various other representations and classes of games. For a survey on this topic, see Woeginger (2013).

15.4.2 Symmetric Additively Separable Hedonic Games

In this section, we focus on the class of symmetric additively separable games. As described in Section 15.3.2, an argument that uses a potential function shows that every instance from this class possesses a Nash stable outcome. This places the computational problem of finding a Nash stable outcome for a game of this type, as well as the problem of finding any stable outcome based on more restrictive (polynomial-time checkable) notions of deviation, in the complexity class PLS, which stands for polynomial local search. In this section, we first give a brief overview of the complexity class PLS and PLS-reductions (Johnson et al., 1988). Then, we give an overview of some negative results (PLS-completeness) and positive results (polynomial-time algorithms) for the problem of finding stable outcomes for hedonic games in this class.

A problem in PLS comprises a finite set of candidate solutions. Every candidate solution has an associated nonnegative integer cost, and a neighbourhood of candidate solutions. In addition, a PLS problem is specified by the following three polynomial-time algorithms that

(i) construct an initial candidate solution
(ii) compute the cost of any candidate solution in polynomial time
(iii) given a candidate solution, provide a neighbouring solution with lower cost if one exists

The goal in a PLS problem is to find a local optimum, that is, a candidate solution whose cost is smaller than all of its neighbors.

Suppose A and B are problems in PLS. Then A is PLS-reducible to B if there exist polynomial-time computable functions f and g such that f maps instances I of A

to instances $f(I)$ of B, and g maps the local optima of instances $f(I)$ of B to local optima of instance I. A problem in PLS is PLS-complete if all problems in PLS are PLS-reducible to it. PLS captures the problem of finding pure Nash equilibria for many classes of games where pure equilibria are guaranteed to exist, such as congestion games Fabrikant et al. (2004).

On one hand, it is very unlikely that a PLS problem is NP-hard because this would imply NP = coNP (Johnson et al., 1988). On the other hand, a polynomial-time algorithm for a PLS-complete problem would resolve a number of long open problems, for example, because it would show that *simple stochastic games* can be solved in polynomial time (Yannakakis, 2008). Thus, PLS-complete problems are believed not to admit polynomial-time algorithms.

Observation 15.8 (Gairing and Savani, 2010). *For symmetric additively separable hedonic games,* CONSTRUCTION *for Nash Stability is PLS-complete.*

Proof. We reduce from the PLS-complete problem PARTYAFFILIATION, which is to compute an equilibrium of a party affiliation game. The input of PARTYAFFILIATION is an undirected edge-weighted graph. A solution is a partition of the nodes into two parties such that for every node v the sum of edge weights of edges from v to other nodes in v's part is greater that the sum of edge weights to nodes in the other party. A party affiliation game is essentially a symmetric additively separable hedonic game where at most two coalitions are permitted.

Consider an instance $G = (V, E, w)$ of PARTYAFFILIATION. We augment G by introducing two new agents, called *super nodes*. Every agent $i \in V$ has an edge, of weight $W > \sum_{e \in E} |w_e|$, to each of the super nodes. The two super nodes are connected by an edge of weight $-M$, where $M > |V| \cdot W$. Use the resulting graph to define a corresponding hedonic additively separable game and consider Nash stable outcomes. By the choice of M the two super nodes will be in different coalitions in any Nash stable outcome of the resulting hedonic game. Moreover, by the choice of W, each agent will be in a coalition with one of the super nodes. So, in each Nash stable outcome we have exactly two coalitions. The fact that edges to super nodes have all the same weight directly implies a one-to-one correspondence between the Nash stable outcomes in the hedonic game and in the party affiliation game. $\qquad\square$

Every Nash stable outcome is also an individually stable outcome and thus CONSTRUCTION is no harder for individual stability than for Nash stability. It turns out that CONSTRUCTION for individual stability is still PLS-hard, though the simplest reduction we know that shows this result is much more involved than the proof of Observation 15.8 for Nash stability (Gairing and Savani, 2010, 2011). When deviations of players are restricted even further, and we move from individual stability to contractual individual stability, the problem CONSTRUCTION becomes efficiently solvable:

Observation 15.9 (Gairing and Savani, 2010). *For symmetric additively separable hedonic games,* CONSTRUCTION *for CIS can be solved in* $\mathcal{O}(|E|)$ *time. Moreover, local improvements converge in at most* $2|V|$ *steps.*

Proof. Consider the following algorithm to solve the game $G = (V, E, w)$:

Delete all negative edges from G and put every connected component in a separate coalition.

Consider any coalition formed by this algorithm. If the coalition consists of only one agent, then this agent has no positive edges to any agent and staying alone is a (weakly) dominant strategy. Agents in larger coalitions are connected by a positive edge to some agent within the same coalition. Therefore, they are not allowed to leave the coalition. Thus, we have computed a CIS stable state. Finding the connected components of an undirected graph can be done by depth-first search in $\mathcal{O}(|E|)$ time.

Now consider local improvements. Observe that whenever an agent joins a non-empty coalition then this agent (and all agents to which it is connected by a positive edge in the coalition) will never move again. Moreover, an agent can only start a new coalition once. It follows that each agent can make at most two strategy changes. In total we have at most $2|V|$ local improvements. $\square$

For further results on additively separable hedonic games, we refer the reader to Aziz et al. (2013b), Sung and Dimitrov (2010), Olsen (2009), and Sung and Dimitrov (2007a).

15.4.3 Top Covering Algorithm

In Section 15.3.4, we discussed games that satisfy top responsiveness that are guaranteed to admit a core stable partition. Next, we define the *Top Covering Algorithm* to compute a core stable partition for hedonic games satisfying top responsiveness (Alcalde and Revilla, 2004; Dimitrov and Sung, 2006). For this we need the following definitions. For each $X \subseteq N$, we denote by $\smallfrown_X$ the relation on $X \times X$ where $i \smallfrown_X j$ if and only if $j \in ch(i, X)$. In this case j is called a *neighbour* of i in X. The connected component $CC(i, X)$ of i with respect to X is defined as follows:

$$CC(i, X) = \{k \in X : \exists j_1, \ldots, j_l \in X : i = j_1 \smallfrown_X \cdots \smallfrown_X j_l = k\}.$$

Based on the concept of connected components, we can specify the Top Covering Algorithm. The algorithm is formally specified as Algorithm 1 and is based on similar ideas as that of the *Top Trading Cycle Algorithm* for exchange of indivisible objects (Shapley and Scarf, 1974). We maintain a partition π and a set R^k as the set of remaining agents in round k. In each round, an agent i is selected from R^k for which the size of the connected component of i with respect to R^k is at most the size of the connected component of some other agent $j \in R^k$ with respect to R^k. Such a connected component is a new coalition in partition π. The process is iterated until no more agents remain. For hedonic games that satisfy top responsiveness, the Top Covering Algorithm returns a core stable partition. Alcalde and Revilla (2004) also proved that, for top responsive preferences, the Top Covering Algorithm is strategyproof. If the preference profile satisfies some natural constraints in addition to top responsiveness, the Top Covering Algorithm returns a partition which satisfies even stronger notions of stability than core stability (Aziz and Brandl, 2012).

Example 15.10 (An example illustrating the Top Covering Algorithm). We run the Top Covering Algorithm on the hedonic game specified in Example 15.5. Example 15.6 pointed out that the hedonic game satisfies top responsiveness. First, we examine the connected components. Initially, $R^1 = \{1, 2, 3, 4\}$, $CC(1, \{1, 2, 3, 4\}) =$

Algorithm 1 Top Covering Algorithm

Input: A hedonic game $(N, \succsim)$ satisfying top responsiveness.
Output: A core stable partition π.

1: $R^1 \leftarrow N; \pi \leftarrow \emptyset$.
2: **for** $k = 1$ to $|N|$ **do**
3:     Select $i \in R^k$ such that $|CC(i, R^k)| \leqslant |CC(j, R^k)|$ for each $j \in R^k$.
4:     $S^k \leftarrow CC(i, R^k)$
5:     $\pi \leftarrow \pi \cup \{S^k\}$
6:     $R^{k+1} \leftarrow R^k \setminus S^k$
7:     **if** $R^{k+1} = \emptyset$ **then**
8:         **return** π
9:     **end if**
10: **end for**
11: **return** π

$CC(2, \{1, 2, 3, 4\}) = CC(3, \{1, 2, 3, 4\}) = \{1, 2, 3\}$ and $CC(4, \{1, 2, 3, 4\}) = \{1, 2, 3, 4\}$.

Because $|CC(1, \{1, 2, 3, 4\})| < |CC(4, \{1, 2, 3, 4\})|$, hence $S^1 = \{1, 2, 3\}$ and $R^2 = \{1, 2, 3, 4\} \setminus \{1, 2, 3\} = \{4\}$. Thus the coalition $S^1 = \{1, 2, 3\}$ is fixed and the next fixed coalition is $S^2 = \{4\}$. Hence the final partition $\pi = \{\{1, 2, 3\}, \{4\}\}$.

Recall from Section 15.3.4 that $\mathcal{B}$-hedonic games are one well-studied class of games that satisfy top responsiveness. For more details on computational aspects of games based on the best or worst agents, we refer the reader to Aziz et al. (2012a); Cechlárová and Romero-Medina (2001); Cechlárová and Hajduková (2004b); Hajduková (2006).

15.4.4 Preference Refinement Algorithm

We outline the Preference Refinement Algorithm (PRA) to compute individually rational and Pareto optimal partitions (Aziz et al., 2013e). The idea of PRA is to relate the problem of computing a Pareto optimal partition to PerfectPartition — the problem of checking whether a perfect partition exists. First note that if there exists a polynomial-time algorithm to compute a Pareto optimal partition, then it returns a perfect partition if a perfect partition exists. For the opposite direction, we show that an oracle to solve PerfectPartition can be used by PRA to compute a Pareto optimal partition.

In PRA, the bottom preference $\succsim_i^{\perp}$ of each agent i is initially completely 'coarsened' so that each agent is indifferent among all acceptable coalitions. The top preference $\succsim_i^{\top}$ of each agent is set to $\succsim_i$. The preference profiles $\succsim^{\perp}$ and $\succsim^{\top}$ are updated during the running of PRA while ensuring that a perfect partition exists for $\succsim^{\perp}$. Because the partition of singletons is a perfect partition for the coarsest profile $(\succsim_1^{\perp}, \ldots, \succsim_n^{\perp})$, we know that a perfect partition exists. Before we formally specify PRA, we must define *coarsening*, *refinement*, and *cover* in preference relations.

Let $\succsim = (\succsim_1, \ldots, \succsim_n)$ and $\succsim' = (\succsim_1', \ldots, \succsim_n')$. We say that $\succsim_i'$ refines $\succsim_i$ if $\succsim_i$ is exactly like $\succsim_i'$, except that in $\succsim_i'$ agent i may have strict preferences among some of his most preferred coalitions according to $\succsim_i$. Equivalently $\succsim_i$ is *coarser* than $\succsim_i'$. We

---

Algorithm 2 Preference Refinement Algorithm (PRA).

Input: Hedonic game $(N, \succsim)$

Output: Pareto optimal and individually rational partition

1 $\succsim_i^\top \leftarrow \succsim_i$, for each $i \in N$
2 $\succsim_i^\perp \leftarrow \succsim_i \cup \{(X, Y) : X \succsim_i \{i\} \text{ and } Y \succsim_i \{i\}\}$, for each $i \in N$
3 **while** $\succsim_i^\perp \neq \succsim_i^\top$ for some $i \in N$ **do**
4     $i \leftarrow \text{Choose}(\{j \in N : \succsim_j^\perp \neq \succsim_j^\top\})$
    $\{\text{Choose specifies some way to choose an agent from a set of agents.}\}$
5     $\succsim_i' \leftarrow \text{Refine}(\succsim_i^\perp, \succsim_i^\top)$
6   **if** $\text{PerfectPartition}(N, (\succsim_1^\perp, \ldots, \succsim_{i-1}^\perp, \succsim_i', \succsim_{i+1}^\perp, \ldots, \succsim_n^\perp)) = \emptyset$ **then**
7       $\succsim_i^\top \leftarrow \succsim_i''$ where $\succsim_i'$ covers $\succsim_i''$
8   **else**
9       $\succsim_i^\perp \leftarrow \succsim_i'$
10   **end if**
11 **end while**
12 **return** $\text{PerfectPartition}(N, \succsim^\perp)$

---

say that $\succsim_i'$ is *strictly refines* $\succsim_i$ if $\succsim_i'$ refines $\succsim_i$ but $\succsim_i$ does not refine $\succsim_i$. If a partition is perfect for some preference profile $\succsim$, then it is also perfect for any profile in which the preferences are coarsened. The same holds for Pareto optimal partitions. We say that $\succsim_i$ *covers* $\succsim_i'$ if $\succsim_i$ is a minimal refinement of $\succsim_i'$ with $\succsim_i' \neq \succsim_i$, that is, if $\succsim_i$ strictly refines $\succsim_i'$ and there is no $\succsim_i''$ such that $\succsim_i$ strictly refined $\succsim_i''$ and $\succsim_i''$ strictly refined $\succsim_i'$.

PRA can be viewed as gradually improving the minimum guaranteed welfare of agents while using binary search. When an agent i is chosen for whom $\succsim_i^\perp$ and $\succsim_i^\top$ do not coincide, $\succsim_i^\perp$ is temporarily set to some preference relation $\succsim_i'$ which is finer than $\succsim_i^\perp$ but coarser than $\succsim_i^\top$. If a perfect partition still exists for the given preference preference profile, then $\succsim_i^\perp$ is set to the updated preference. If no perfect partition exists, then we can restrict our attention to preferences of agent i that are not as fine as $\succsim_i'$. The main idea is that if no refinement of some preference profile with perfect partition π allow for a perfect partition, then π is Pareto optimal. PRA is specified more formally as Algorithm 2 where $\text{Choose}(\{j \in N : \succsim_j^\perp \neq \succsim_j^\top\})$ returns a player in the set $\{j \in N : \succsim_j^\perp \neq \succsim_j^\top\}$ and $\text{Refine}(\succsim_i^\perp, \succsim_i^\top)$ returns a preference $\succsim_i'$ that strictly refines $\succsim_i^\perp$ and is a coarsening of $\succsim_i^\top$.

Example 15.11 (An example illustrating PRA). We run PRA on the hedonic game specified in Example 15.6. In the beginning, $\succsim_i^\top = \succsim_i$ and $\succsim_i^\perp$ specifies indifference between all coalitions.

Let us say that agent 4 is chosen in Step 4 of the algorithm and we consider its preferences $\succsim_4'$.

$$\{34\} \succ_4' \{134\} \sim_4' \{234\} \succ_4' \{1234\} \succ_4' \{24\} \succ_4' \{124\} \succ_4' \{34\} \succ_4' \{4\}$$

We check whether a perfect partition still exists or not for $(\succsim_1^\perp, \succsim_2^\perp, \succsim_3^\perp, \succsim_4')$. A perfect partition indeed exists: $\{\{3, 4\}, \{1\}, \{2\}\}$. Thus $\succsim_4^\perp$ is set to $\succsim_4'$. Let us now take agent 2 and consider its preference $\succsim_2'$.

$$\{23\} \sim_2' \{234\} \sim_2' \{213\} \sim_2' \{1234\} \sim_2' \{24\} \sim_2' \{214\} \succ_2' \{12\} \succ_2' \{2\}$$

However, no perfect partition exists for $(\succsim_1^\perp, \succsim_2', \succsim_3^\perp, \succsim_4^\perp)$. Hence $\succsim_2^\top$ is changed as follows:

$$\{23\} \sim_2^\top \{234\} \sim_2^\top \{213\} \sim_2^\top \{1234\} \sim_2^\top \{24\} \sim_2^\top \{214\} \sim_2^\top \{12\} \succ_2^\top \{2\}$$

The process goes on until top and bottom preferences of the agents are as follows in the end:

$$\{12\} \succ_1^\perp \{123\} \sim_1^\perp \{124\} \succ_1^\perp \{1234\} \succ_1^\perp \{13\} \succ_1^\perp \{134\} \succ_1^\perp \{14\} \succ_1^\perp \{1\},$$

$$\{23\} \sim_2^\perp \{234\} \sim_2^\perp \{213\} \sim_2^\perp \{1234\} \sim_2^\perp \{24\} \sim_2^\perp \{214\} \sim_2^\perp \{12\},$$

$$\{13\} \sim_3^\perp \{123\} \sim_3^\perp \{134\} \sim_3^\perp \{1234\} \sim_3^\perp \{23\} \sim_3^\perp \{234\} \sim_3^\perp \{34\} \succ_3^\perp \{3\},$$

$$\{34\} \succ_4^\perp \{134\} \sim_4^\perp \{234\} \succ_4^\perp \{1234\} \succ_4^\perp \{24\} \succ_4^\perp \{124\} \succ_4^\perp \{14\} \succ_4^\perp \{4\}.$$

The perfect partition for $(\succsim_1^\perp, \succsim_2^\perp, \succsim_3^\perp, \succsim_4^\perp) = (\succsim_1^\top, \succsim_2^\top, \succsim_3^\top, \succsim_4^\top)$ is $\{\{3, 4\}, \{1, 2\}\}$. which is Pareto optimal for $\succsim$.

Any Pareto optimal and individually rational partition can be returned by PRA depending on how the refinements of preferences are carried out. The behaviour of PRA may depend on the specific settings of Choose and Refine. In particular the following are two interesting versions of PRA. In PRA_{SD}, Choose selects players according to a fixed order of the players and Refine returns a player's finest preference relation, that is, generally $\text{Refine}(\succsim_i^\perp, \succsim_i^\top) = \succsim_i^\top$. In PRA_{Egal}, Choose selects a player that has been selected the fewest number of times during the execution of PRA. Refine is defined such that $\text{Refine}(\succsim_i^\perp, \succsim_i^\top) = \text{Cover}(Q_i^\perp)$. Both versions have their merits. If all coalitions are acceptable then PRA_{SD} is strategyproof. On the other hand, PRA_{Egal} satisfies the following property: for any $k \in \mathbb{N}$ for which there exists a Pareto optimal partition in which none of the players get one of their kth lowest-ranked or worse coalitions, PRA_{Egal} will return such a partition.

PRA can be adapted for various specific classes of hedonic games by formulating specific algorithms to solve PerfectPartition for those classes. For example, applying this idea yields a polynomial-time algorithm to compute a Pareto optimal partition for $\mathcal{W}$-hedonic games (Aziz et al., 2013e).

15.5 Further Reading

There are a number of topics that we have not touched on in this chapter. We have not discussed strategic issues in detail (see, e.g., Demange, 2009). One reason is that impossibility results hold even for restricted classes of hedonic games (Barberà and Gerber, 2007; Rodríguez-Álvarez, 2009).

Various classes of hedonic games can be represented by graphs. Some of them are special subclasses of additively separable hedonic games, which we have discussed. An additively separable hedonic game (N, v) is an *appreciation of friends* game if for all $i, j \in N$ such that $i \neq j$, $v_i(j) \in \{-1, +n\}$. It is an *aversion to enemies* game if for all $i, j \in N$ such that $i \neq j$, $v_i(j) \in \{-n, +1\}$. These games were introduced in Dimitrov et al. (2006).

There are other interesting graph based hedonic games that we did not discuss. *Social distance games* were introduced by Branzei and Larson (2011). Each social distance game is represented by an unweighted undirected graph. Agent i in coalition $C \subseteq N$ has utility for this coalition equal to $v_i(C) = \frac{1}{|C|} \sum_{j \in N \setminus \{i\}} \frac{1}{d_C(i,j)}$ where $d_C(i, j)$ is the shortest path distance between i and j in the subgraph induced by coalition C on the graph G. If i and j are disconnected in C, then $d_C(i, j) = \infty$. Another class of graph based game that has been recently proposed is that of *fractional hedonic games* (Aziz et al., 2014b). As in additively separable hedonic games, each agent i has a value function $v_i: N \to \mathbb{R}$, assigning a value to each agent $i \in N$ with $v_i(i) = 0$. A value function v_i can be extended to a value function over coalitions $S \subseteq N$ in such a way so that $v_i(S) = \frac{\sum_{j \in S} v_i(j)}{|S|}$. A hedonic game $(N, \succsim)$ is said to be a *fractional hedonic game* if for each agent i in N there is a value function v_i such that for all coalitions $S, T \subseteq N$, $S \succsim_i T$ if and only if $v_i(S) \geq v_i(T)$. Unlike additively separable hedonic games, even if the weights are all positive, the grand coalition need not be core stable for fractional hedonic games.

The class of *roommate games*, which are well-known from the literature on matching theory, can be defined as those hedonic games in which only coalitions of size one or two are feasible (see, e.g., Aziz, 2013). A *marriage game* is a roommate game in which the set N of agents can be partitioned into two sets *male* and *female* and an agent finds a member of the same sex unacceptable. For further reading on computational aspects of marriage, roommate and related games, we refer the reader to Ronn (1990); Irving (1985); Scott (2005); Irving (1994); Manlove (1999); Aziz (2013); Deineko and Woeginger (2013). Cechlárová and Hajduková (2004a) examined more complex preferences in which agents' appreciation of coalition depends on both the worst and best agents in the coalition.

There are also various classes of hedonic games in which agent's appreciation of a coalition depends on the size of the coalition. *Anonymous games* are a subclass of hedonic games in which an agent's preferences over coalitions *only* depends on the coalition sizes (see, e.g., Ballester, 2004). Anonymous games are closely related to congestion games (see, e.g., Milchtaich, 1996) in noncooperative game theory. A setting that is related to anonymous games is that of *group activity selection game* in which each agent has preference over pairs of activity and number of agents participating in the activity. A number of variants of the games are defined by Darmann et al. (2012). Another class of hedonic games that is based on the number of agents is *Gamson's hedonic game*. This class of hedonic games is of considerable importance in modeling coalition formation in the parliament in which each political party wants to be in a majority coalition in which it has a maximum proportion of seats. Each agent $i \in N$ representing a party has weight $w(i)$. For each coalition $S \subset N$ such that $i \in S$, $v_i(S) = \frac{w(i)}{\sum_{j \in S} w(j)}$ if $\sum_{j \in S} w(j) > \sum_{j \in N} w(j)/2$ and zero otherwise (Le Breton et al., 2008; Deineko and Woeginger, 2014; Gamson, 1961).

Research issues and future directions

An important area of future research is to model and capture realistic scenarios via hedonic games. There is a need to bring together the work on behavioral game theory and mathematical game theory. This may help identify other interesting classes of hedonic games and preference restrictions. Identifying other natural set extensions for compact representations of hedonic games will be fruitful.

Another issue is that in many realistic scenarios, most agents are part of overlapping coalitions. Although there is interesting work on overlapping coalitions in transferable utility cooperative game theory (see, e.g., Chalkiadakis et al., 2010), there is scope for more work on overlapping coalitions in hedonic games. We have focussed on outcomes in which each agent is in one of the coalitions of the partition. The setting can be generalized to allow agents to be partial members of various coalitions. This could, for example, represent the proportion of time different coalitions are formed. Formally, a *fractional hypergraph matching* is a function w assigning nonnegative weights to coalitions such that $\sum_{S \in \mathcal{N}_i} w(S) \leqslant 1$ for all $i \in N$. A fractional hypergraph matching is *stable* if for every $S \in 2^N$, there exists an $i \in S$ such that $\sum_{\substack{i \in T \in \mathcal{N}_i \\ T \succsim_i S}} w(T) = 1$.

Aharoni and Fleiner (2003) used a connection with Scarf's Lemma to show that a stable fractional hypergraph matching is guaranteed to exist. In general, the complexity of computing a fractional stable matching is PPAD-complete (Kintali et al., 2009). There are other ways to define stability for fractional hypergraph matchings (Manjunath, 2013) and each of the concepts leads to corresponding computational problems.

Although hedonic games have been examined computationally, their algorithmic treatment has been somewhat piecemeal. The hope is to come up with general algorithms that are not tailor-made for a specific representation of hedonic games and can compute solutions of different classes of games. A plethora of intractability results indicates that a fixed parameter tractability approach (Niedermeier, 2006) may also be fruitful. Finding faster exact exponential algorithms is also a natural avenue (Fomin and Kratsch, 2010). Another research direction is to have logical representations of hedonic games and propose logical characterizations of solution concepts which would enable SAT solvers to compute stable partitions (see, e.g., Aziz et al., 2014a). Finally, given that it is computationally hard to find many types of (exactly) stable outcomes, it is natural to study the computational complexity of finding approximately stable partitions. A first step in this direction for cut and party affiliation games, which are closely related to additively separable hedonic games, was taken by Bhalgat et al. (2010).

Characterizing conditions under which stable partitions are guaranteed to exist is one of the main research questions concerning hedonic games. Although various sufficient conditions have been identified in the literature, there is scope for a better understanding of sufficient and necessary conditions. Another interesting question is studying the conditions under which a game has a *unique* stable partition. Pápai (2004) characterized conditions under which a hedonic game has a unique core stable partition. There are various interesting questions regarding the complexity of checking whether the game has a unique core stable partition. It is not clear whether this question is easier or harder than checking the existence of a core stable partition.

Deviation dynamics in uncoordinated matching markets have been examined within computer science (see, e.g., Ackermann et al., 2011). The rich landscape of hedonic games provides fertile ground for interesting research on dynamics of deviations.

Finally, the solutions of hedonic games based on graphs can be used as desirable ways to perform network clustering and community detection (Aziz et al., 2014b; Olsen, 2013). Aziz et al. (2014b) suggested core stable and welfare-maximizing partitions of the fractional hedonic game corresponding to the graph as an interesting way of clustering the vertices of the network. Further work (see, e.g., Bilò et al., 2014) in this area may be of interest to other communities working in network analysis (McSweeney et al., 2014).

Acknowledgments

The authors acknowledge Martin Aleksandrov, Sajid Aziz, Felix Brandt, Vince Conitzer, Paul Harrenstein, Jérôme Lang, Dominik Peters, and Gerhard Woeginger for their helpful and constructive comments. The authors acknowledge numerous useful discussions with Florian Brandl, Felix Brandt, Martin Gairing, Paul Harrenstein, and Hans Georg Seedig and thank them for their permission to adapt material from joint papers for this chapter. NICTA is funded by the Australian government through the Department of Communications and the Australian Research Council through the ICT Centre of Excellence Program. Rahul Savani would like to acknowledge support from the EPSRC under grant EP/L011018/1.

CHAPTER 16

Weighted Voting Games

Georgios Chalkiadakis and Michael Wooldridge

16.1 Introduction

In this chapter, we consider *weighted voting games*: a form of social choice system that seems much simpler than most schemes considered in this handbook, but which is, nevertheless, widely used for many important real-world social choice problems. There are at least two very good reasons for studying weighted voting systems: first, as we have already mentioned, they are widely used in practice; and second, for all their apparent simplicity, they possess interesting mathematical and computational properties, making them interesting objects from the point of view of scientific study.

Weighted voting games originated in the domain of *cooperative game theory* (Chalkiadakis et al., 2011). They model decision-making situations in which a set of voters must make a binary (yes/no) decision on some particular issue; each voter is allocated a numeric *weight*, and the decision is carried if the sum of weights of voters in favour of it meets or exceeds some specific given threshold, called the *quota*. Weighted voting games have many applications beyond social choice theory. For example, they can be used to model settings where each player has a certain amount of a given resource (say, time, money, or manpower), and there is a goal that can be reached by any coalition that possesses a sufficient amount of this resource.

The remainder of this chapter is structured as follows.

- In Section 16.2, we present the basic models and solution concepts that will be used throughout the remainder of the chapter. We start by defining cooperative games in characteristic function form, and then introduce weighted voting games. We go on to describe some key solution concepts for cooperative games: the core, the Shapley value, and the Banzhaf index.
- In Section 16.3, we consider computational properties of weighted voting games: in particular, the complexity of computing the core, the Shapley value, and the Banzhaf index.
- In Section 16.4, we consider the (sometimes unintuitive) relationship between the weight that a voter is assigned in a weighted voting game and the power that this voter then wields.

- In Section 16.5, we consider the extent to which weighted voting games can be considered as a representation scheme for yes/no voting systems (i.e., simple cooperative games). We give a condition on yes/no voting systems that is both necessary and sufficient for such a system to be representable as a weighted voting game.

Throughout the chapter, we assume familiarity with the basic notation and terminology of computational complexity theory (big-O notation, the classes P, NP, coNP, and #P) (Garey and Johnson, 1979; Papadimitriou, 1994).

16.2 Basic Definitions

Weighted voting games are a special case of a class of cooperative games, and the solution concepts that we consider for weighted voting games are in fact those developed within cooperative game theory. In this section, we begin by presenting the key game model from cooperative game theory, and then introduce weighted voting games as a special case of such game. We then define the key solution concepts for such games.

16.2.1 Cooperative Games

We start by defining the game model that underpins weighted voting games: formally, these are *cooperative games with transferable utility in characteristic function form*, but we will refer to them as *cooperative games*.

Definition 16.1. A *cooperative game*, G, is given by a pair $G = (N, v)$, where $N = \{1, \ldots, n\}$ is the set of *players* of the game, and $v : 2^N \to \mathbb{R}$ is the *characteristic function* of the game. Unless otherwise stated, we assume that $v(\emptyset) = 0$, and moreover that $v(\{i\}) = 0$ for all $i \in N$. We will say a cooperative game $G = (N, v)$ is *simple* if $v(C) \in \{0, 1\}$ for all $C \subseteq N$, in which case we say $C \subseteq N$ are *winning* if $v(C) = 1$, and *losing* otherwise. A simple game is *nontrivial* if $v(N) = 1$. We will usually assume games are nontrivial.

The basic idea behind this model is that any subset $C \subseteq N$ of the players can cooperate with each other, and, by joining forces, they can obtain the value $v(C)$. The model does not specify *how* the players cooperate; it only specifies *what value* they could obtain through cooperation. It is conventional to refer to (sub)sets of players $C \subseteq N$ as *coalitions*: in everyday use the term "coalition" implies a collection of people with some common cause or commitment to joint action, but we will mean it simply in the sense of a set of players, who may or may not choose to cooperate. We will refer to the set of all players N as the *grand coalition*.

16.2.2 Weighted Voting Games

We are now ready to define weighted voting games. A weighted voting game is a simple cooperative game (i.e., a game in which every coalition has a value of either 0 or 1), which is defined by each player in the game having a *weight*, and where a coalition obtains the value 1 if the sum of their values meets or exceeds a given *quota*. Formally:

Definition 16.2. A *weighted voting game* G with a set of players $N = \{1, \ldots, n\}$ is given by a list of *weights* $\mathbf{w} = (w_1, \ldots, w_n) \in \mathbb{R}^n$ and a *quota* $q \in \mathbb{R}$; we will write $G = [N; \mathbf{w}; q]$. The characteristic function $v : 2^N \to \{0, 1\}$ of the game is defined as follows:

$$
v(C) = \begin{cases} 1 & \text{if } \sum_{i \in C} w_i \geqslant q \\ 0 & \text{otherwise.} \end{cases}
$$

We write $w(C)$ to denote the total weight of a coalition C, that is, we set $w(C) = \sum_{i \in C} w_i$. It is usually assumed that all weights and the quota are nonnegative; in what follows, we will make this assumption as well. Under this assumption, weighted voting games are *monotone*: if a coalition wins, then adding players to the coalition cannot turn it into a losing coalition. It is common to assume that $0 < q \leq w(N)$; this condition ensures that the empty coalition is losing and the grand coalition is winning (and hence the game is nontrivial).

Our definition of weighted voting games allows for arbitrary real number weights. However, it is not clear how to efficiently store and manipulate such weights, which presents a difficulty from the algorithmic point of view. Fortunately, it turns out that *any weighted voting game is equivalent to a game with fairly small integer weights*. More precisely, we have the following theorem, which follows from results on linear threshold functions (Muroga, 1971).

Theorem 16.1. *Let us say two weighted voting games* $G = [N; \mathbf{w}; q]$ *and* $G' = [N; \mathbf{w}'; q']$ *are equivalent iff for all coalitions* $C \subseteq N$ *we have* $w(C) \geqslant q$ *iff* $w'(C) \geqslant q'$. *Then, for any weighted voting game* $G = [N; \mathbf{w}; q]$ *with* $|N| = n$, *there exists an equivalent weighted voting game* $G' = [N; \mathbf{w}'; q']$ *with* $\mathbf{w}' = (w_1', \ldots, w_n')$ *such that all* w_i', $i = 1, \ldots, n$, *and* q' *are nonnegative integers, and* $w_i' = O(2^{n \log n})$ *for all* $i = 1, \ldots, n$.

We can therefore assume without loss of generality that *all weights and the quota are integers given in binary*. We remark that, even though the entries of the weight vector $\mathbf{w}'$ are exponential in n, they can be represented using $O(n \log n)$ bits—that is, a weighted voting game with n players can be described using poly(n) bits. Thus, *any weighted voting game has an equivalent "compact" representation*: this fact is useful when considering questions relating to computational complexity.

Before proceeding, let us say a few words about the applications of weighted voting games. These games can be used to describe many real-world situations. In particular, they are very well suited to model coalition formation in *legislative bodies*. In more detail, each party in a parliament can be associated with a player in a weighted voting game; the weight of the player is given by the total number of the representatives of this party. The quota corresponds to the number of votes needed to pass a bill; while in most cases a simple majority $q = \lfloor w(N)/2 \rfloor + 1$ suffices, in some circumstances a bill can only be passed if it is supported by two thirds of the legislators (i.e., $q = 2w(N)/3$), or even the entire legislative body ($q = w(N)$). Another example of a weighted voting game is *shareholder voting*: the weight of each voter is proportional to the number of shares she holds. A weighted voting game also arises in a setting where there is a task that requires q hours of work, and there is a group of agents $N = \{1, \ldots, n\}$ such that each agent i can dedicate w_i of his time to this task.

16.2.3 Solution Concepts

The basic assumption in cooperative game theory is that players will make strategic decisions about who they will cooperate with. The best-known solution concept in cooperative game theory, the core, formalizes an answer to the question of which players will cooperate. The idea of the core is that a *stability* is a necessary condition for coalition formation: a coalition will not form if some sub-coalition can do better by defecting and working together as a team. To formulate the core, we need some further definitions.

Definition 16.3. An *imputation* for a cooperative game $G = (N, v)$ is a tuple of real numbers $\mathbf{x} = (x_1, \ldots, x_n) \in \mathbb{R}^n$ satisfying the following conditions:

- $\sum_{i=1}^n x_i = v(N)$
- $x_i \geqslant v(\{i\})$ for all $i \in N$

Where $\mathbf{x} = (x_1, \ldots, x_n)$ is an imputation and $C \subseteq N$ is a set of players, we denote by $x(C)$ the value $\sum_{i \in C} x_i$.

We think of an imputation as an indication of how the value of the grand coalition should be divided among players in the game. The first requirement relates to *efficiency*: it simply says that the total value available should be distributed. The second requirement relates to *individual rationality*: it says that no player should receive a payoff that is lower than it could obtain alone.

The core then attempts to characterize a set of "acceptable" imputations: imputations to which no coalition could realistically object. We will see the formal definition first, and then discuss it.

Definition 16.4. The *core*, $\mathcal{C}(G)$, of a cooperative game $G = (N, v)$ is the set:

$$\mathcal{C}(G) = \{\mathbf{x} \mid \forall C \subseteq N : x(C) \geqslant v(C)\}.$$

Thus, if an imputation $\mathbf{x}$ is *not* in the core, then there exists some coalition $C \subseteq N$ such that $v(C) > x(C)$. Such a coalition would *object* to the imputation $\mathbf{x}$, because they could do better by working together as a team: the value they would obtain in this way could be distributed among the members of C in such a way that all the players in C receive a higher payoff than they do under the imputation $\mathbf{x}$. Note that *the core of a game may be empty*, as the following example illustrates.

Example 16.2. Consider a game G with $N = \{1, 2, 3\}$ and the characteristic function v defined as follows:

$$v(C) = \begin{cases} 1 & \text{if } |C| \geqslant 2 \\ 0 & \text{otherwise.} \end{cases}$$

Thus, a coalition obtains a value of 1 *iff* the coalition contains at least 2 members. Now consider any imputation for the game. The imputation $(1/3, 1/3, 1/3)$ is not in the core, because any pair of agents could defect, obtaining the value 1 which can be shared among themselves. No other imputation $\mathbf{x} = (x_1, x_2, x_3)$ can be in the core because two players will always be able to defect and share the value assigned to the third player among themselves. For example, if $\mathbf{x} = (0, 0.5, 0.5)$ then players 1 and 2 could benefit by defecting.

The core formalizes the idea of the grand coalition being *stable*, in the sense that no coalition can profitably defect from it. However, it is easy to construct examples where the core contains imputations that seem unreasonable:

Example 16.3. Suppose $G = (\{1, 2\}, v)$ is such that:

$$v(\{1\}) = v(\{2\}) = 5$$
$$v(\{1, 2\}) = 20.$$

The reader may easily verify that the imputation $(5, 15)$ *is* in the core, but from the point of view of player 1, this seems unreasonable: it gives all the surplus obtained by cooperation to player 2, while there seems to be nothing in the game to distinguish the contribution that player 1 makes from the contribution that player 2 makes.

Thus, the core is not appropriate as a framework for deciding how to divide coalitional value. The *Shapley value* is the best known solution concept for this purpose. Formulated by Nobel Laureate Lloyd Shapley in the early 1950s (Shapley, 1953), the Shapley value is defined in terms of the *marginal contribution* that players make in games. Formally, where $C \subseteq N \setminus \{i\}$, the marginal contribution that player i makes to C is denoted by $\delta_i(C)$, and is simply the value that i would add to the coalition C by joining it:

$$\delta_i(C) = v(C \cup \{i\}) - v(C).$$

We will say a player is a *dummy* if $\delta_i(C) = 0$ for all $C \subseteq N \setminus \{i\}$. Thus, a dummy player is a player that *never adds any value to a coalition*. We will say players $i \neq j \in N$ are *symmetric* if $\delta_i(C) = \delta_j(C)$ for all $C \subseteq N \setminus \{i, j\}$. Thus, symmetric players are players who always make *identical* contributions to coalitions. We let Π denote all possible orderings of the players N, and denote members of Π by $\pi, \pi', \ldots$ and so on. Where $\pi \in \Pi$ and $i \in N$, we denote by π_i the set of players that precede i in the ordering π. Then:

Definition 16.5. The Shapley value for a game G is the imputation $\varphi(G) = (\varphi_1(G), \ldots, \varphi_n(G))$ defined as follows:

$$\varphi_i(G) = \frac{1}{n!} \sum_{\pi \in \Pi} \delta_i(\pi_i). \tag{16.1}$$

Thus, player i's Shapley value is *the average marginal contribution that player i makes, over all possible orderings of the players, to the set of players preceding i in the ordering*.[1] Before proceeding, we note that the Shapley value can be presented in several different ways; one important equivalent formulation is as follows:

$$\varphi_i(G) = \sum_{S \subseteq N \setminus \{i\}} \frac{(n - |S| - 1)! |S|!}{n!} \delta_i(S). \tag{16.2}$$

---

[1] Put otherwise, pick a value $k = 0 \ldots n - 1$ uniformly at random, and then select a set S of size k uniformly at random from the possible subsets of $N \setminus i$. The expected marginal contribution of i to S is the Shapley value.

This latter formulation is less common than the former, but we will make use of it in one of our proofs.

Now, much of the interest in the Shapley value derives from the fact that it can be shown to be the *unique* solution to a set of axioms characterizing *fair* imputations—that is, fair ways to divide the value $v(N)$ among the players N. To define these axioms, we need a little more notation. Where $G = (N, v)$ and $G' = (N, v')$ are games with the same set of players, the game $G + G'$ is the game with the same player set, and characteristic function $v'' : 2^N \to \mathbb{R}$ defined by $v''(C) = v(C) + v'(C)$. We can now state Shapley's characterization of the value.

Theorem 16.4 (Shapley). *For all games G, the $\varphi(G)$ payoff division scheme satisfies the following properties:*

- Efficiency: $\sum_{i=1}^{n} \varphi_i(G) = v(N)$
- Dummy Player: *If i is a dummy player in G then $\varphi_i(G) = 0$*
- Symmetry: *If i and j are symmetric in G then $\varphi_i(G) = \varphi_j(G)$*
- Additivity: *The value is additive over games: For all games $G = (N, v)$ and $G' = (N, v')$, and for all players $i \in N$, we have $\varphi_i(G + G') = \varphi_i(G) + \varphi_i(G')$*

Moreover, $\varphi(G)$ is the only *payoff division scheme that simultaneously satisfies all these properties.*

In weighted voting game settings, the Shapley value has an important interpretation: it essentially measures the probability that a player will be able to turn a losing coalition into a winning one—that is, the probability that a player is *pivotal* for a coalition. As such, the Shapley value can be interpreted as a measure of the *power* wielded by a voter: the greater the Shapley value of a player, the more power that player wields. When used to analyze the power of voters in social choice settings, the Shapley value is called the *Shapley-Shubik voting index*.

A closely related, but simpler measure of voting power is the *Banzhaf index* (Banzhaf, 1965; Dubey and Shapley, 1979). The Banzhaf index for a player i in game G is denoted $\beta_i(G)$, and is defined as follows:

$$\beta_i(G) = \frac{1}{2^{n-1}} \sum_{C \subseteq N \setminus \{i\}} \delta_i(C).$$

Thus, $\beta_i(G)$ measures the probability that i will be able to turn a losing coalition into a winning one, assuming that all members of that coalition have already assembled (the more "refined" Shapley value considers all possible ways that the coalition could form). The Banzhaf index has properties similar to the Shapley value, but does not satisfy efficiency (Chalkiadakis et al., 2011, p. 22). Two axiomatisations for this index are provided in Dubey and Shapley (1979) and in Lehrer (1988).

We end this section by noting that the Shapley value and the Banzhaf index are not the only measures of power used in (weighted) voting games. Examples of other *power indices* include the *Deegan-Packel* index (Deegan and Packel, 1978), which attempts to measure a player's expected gain from participating in minimal-sized winning coalitions; the *Public Good index* (Holler, 1982), which measures a player's power as the number of all minimal winning coalitions in which the player participates, divided by the sum of all such numbers over all players; and the *Coleman initiative and preventive power indices* (Coleman, 1971), which, respectively, correspond to the fraction of losing coalitions that a given player can turn into winning, and vice versa.

16.3 Basic Computational Properties

In this section, we consider computational questions associated with weighted voting games. The main questions relate to the solution concepts for cooperative games—the core and the Shapley value—that we discussed earlier. However, we will start by considering some simpler properties. First, consider the following definition:

Definition 16.6. Let $G = (N, v)$ be a cooperative game, and let i be a player in G. Then i is said to be a *veto player* in G if $v(C) = 0$ for all $C \subseteq N \setminus \{i\}$.

Thus, a veto player is one whose presence is necessary for a coalition to be winning. The obvious decision problem associated with veto players is as follows:

Name: VETO PLAYER.
Instance: Weighted voting game $G = [N; \mathbf{w}; q]$, player $i \in N$.
Question: Is i a veto player in G?

We start our survey of computational problems with some good news:

Lemma 16.5. *The* VETO PLAYER *problem is polynomial time solvable for weighted voting games.*

Proof. Given a player i, it suffices check whether the coalition $N \setminus \{i\}$ is losing, which is simple arithmetic. □

The significance of this result is made apparent by the following:

Theorem 16.6. *A simple cooperative game $G = (N, v)$ has a nonempty core iff it has a veto player. It follows that it is possible to check in polynomial time whether a weighted voting game has a nonempty core.*

Proof. For the left-to-right implication of the first statement, suppose for sake of contradiction that G has a nonempty core but no veto player. Take an imputation $\mathbf{x}$ in the core. Because $x(N) = 1$, we have $x_i > 0$ for some $i \in N$, and hence $x(N \setminus \{i\}) = 1 - x_i < 1$. However, because i is not a veto player then $v(N \setminus \{i\}) = 1 > x(N \setminus \{i\})$; contradiction. Now for the right-to-left implication. Suppose i is a veto player, and consider the imputation in which $x_j = 0$ for all $j \neq i$. This imputation is in the core: because i is a veto player, any deviating coalition would have value 0, and so no such coalition could profitably deviate. The second statement then follows from Lemma 16.5. □

Now consider the following problem.

Name: DUMMY PLAYER.
Instance: Weighted voting game $G = [N; \mathbf{w}; q]$, player $i \in N$.
Question: Is i a dummy player in G?

In contrast to checking for veto players, identifying dummy players is computationally hard. To show this, we provide a reduction from the classic PARTITION problem (Garey and Johnson, 1979, p. 223).

Theorem 16.7. DUMMY PLAYER *is* coNP-*complete*.

Proof. If a player i is not a dummy player, this can be proved by exhibiting a coalition C such that $w(C) < q$, $w(C \cup \{i\}) \geq q$. Thus, DUMMY PLAYER is in coNP. To show coNP-hardness, we will transform an instance $I = (a_1, \ldots, a_k, K)$ of PARTITION into a weighted voting game $G = [N; \mathbf{w}; q]$, which is constructed as follows. We set $N = \{1, \ldots, k, k + 1\}$, $w_i = 2a_i$ for $i = 1, \ldots, k$, $w_{k+1} = 1$, and $q = 2K + 1$. It is easy to see that I is a "yes"-instance of PARTITION if and only if player $k + 1$ is not a dummy in G. Indeed, suppose that there is a subset of indices J such that $\sum_{i \in J} a_i = K$. Then we have $w(J) = 2K$, $w(J \cup \{k + 1\}) = 2K + 1 = q$, that is, $k + 1$ is pivotal for $J \cup \{k + 1\}$. Conversely, suppose that $k + 1$ is pivotal for some coalition C. Then we have $w(C \setminus \{k + 1\}) < q$, $w(C) \geq q$. Because $w_{k+1} = 1$ and all weights are integer, this means that $w(C \setminus \{k + 1\}) = 2K$, that is, $\sum_{i \in C \setminus \{k+1\}} a_i = K$. We conclude that I is a "yes"-instance of PARTITION if and only if (G, k) is a "no"-instance of DUMMY PLAYER; and thus, DUMMY PLAYER is coNP-hard. $\qquad \square$

Another important observation is that in our hardness reduction, the weights are derived from the numbers in the instance of PARTITION. Thus, our hardness result is relevant only if the weights are fairly large. Put differently, we have shown that DUMMY PLAYER is unlikely to admit an algorithm that runs in time polynomial in the input size, that is, $\text{poly}(n, \log w_{\max})$. Now, in some applications of weighted voting games, such as shareholder voting, the weights (i.e., numbers of shares held by individual shareholders) can be huge. However, in parliamentary voting the weight of each party is usually fairly small: for instance, at the time of writing the U.K. House of Commons has 650 seats, and the Hellenic Parliament has 300 seats. In such settings, we might be satisfied with a *pseudopolynomial* algorithm, that is, an algorithm that runs in time $\text{poly}(n, w_{\max})$, or, equivalently, runs in polynomial time if all numbers in the input are given in unary. It turns out that DUMMY PLAYER admits such an algorithm. This will follow from Theorem 16.9, which shows that each player's Shapley value in a weighted voting game can be computed in pseudopolynomial time. Indeed, because weighted voting games are monotone, a player is a dummy in a weighted voting game if and only if her Shapley value is 0. Therefore, an algorithm for computing players' Shapley values can be used to identify dummies.

In order to use the Shapley value and the Banzhaf index to measure the agents' power in weighted voting games, we would like to have an efficient algorithm for computing these indices. However, such an algorithm is unlikely to exist: Theorem 16.7, combined with the dummy player axiom and the fact that weighted voting games are monotone, directly implies that checking whether an agent's Shapley value is 0 is coNP-hard. In fact, computing the Shapley value and the Banzhaf index in weighted voting games is computationally hard, and we will now investigate the complexity of this problem in more detail (see also Deng and Papadimitriou, 1994; Faliszewski and Hemaspaandra, 2009; Matsui and Matsui, 2001; Prasad and Kelly, 1990).

To understand just how hard the problem is, we need to recall some concepts from computational complexity that are not quite as well known as notions such as NP-hardness. We want to know how hard it is to compute the Shapley value in a weighted voting game. Such a problem is not a *decision* problem like DUMMY PLAYER, because the output of the problem is not "yes" or "no": we want a numeric answer. In fact, it is a *counting problem*. To understand what we mean by a counting problem, consider the following problem: We are given a propositional logic formula ψ, and we are asked *how many satisfying assignments the formula has*. This problem is known as #SAT. Notice that the output of #SAT is not "yes" or "no": it is a natural number. Also notice that #SAT can be seen to trivially subsume the canonical NP-complete problem SAT, because if we can count the number of satisfying assignments a formula has, we can certainly tell whether it has at least one (which is what the SAT problem asks). The relevant complexity class through which to understand the complexity of problems like #SAT is called #P (Papadimitriou, 1994, p. 442). A problem is in #P if there is a nondeterministic polynomial time Turing machine T such that the number of accepting computations of T on a given input x gives the answer to the problem. For the case of #SAT, for example, such a Turing machine simply guesses a valuation for the problem instance ψ, accepts if that valuation satisfies ψ, and rejects otherwise; clearly, the number of accepting runs is exactly the number of satisfying assignments. Hardness can be shown in the usual way for computational complexity classes, for example by showing how we can reduce #SAT. We will now show that computing the Shapley value in weighted voting games is #P-complete.

Theorem 16.8 (Deng and Papadimitriou, 1994). *The problem of computing the Shapley value of a player i in a given weighted voting game G is #P-complete.*

Proof. For membership, consider a Turing machine such that the computations of the machine each correspond to an ordering π of the players; a computation accepts if $\delta_i(\pi_i) = 1$. Clearly, the number of accepting computations is $n!\varphi_i(G)$.

For hardness, we reduce the counting version of the well-known KNAPSACK problem. In this problem, we are given positive integers $a_1, \ldots, a_m$ and a further positive integer K, and we are asked to compute the number of subsets S of $\{1, \ldots, m\}$ such that $\sum_{i \in S} a_i = K$. Computing the number of such sets is known to be #P-hard. In fact, we work with a simplified version of this problem, which is also known to be #P-hard (Papadimitriou, 1994). In this version it is first assumed that $K = \frac{M}{2}$, where $M = \sum_{i=1}^{m} a_i$, and further, that all solutions have equal cardinality.

We create a weighted voting game with $n = m + 1$ players, as follows. For players $1 \leqslant i \leqslant m$ we set $w_i = a_i$, and we set $w_n = 1$. The quota is set to be $q = \frac{\sum_{i \in N} w_i}{2}$.

Now, it is easy to see that for all $S \subseteq N$, we have $v(S) - v(S \setminus \{n\}) = 1$ *iff* the following conditions hold:

1. $n \in S$
2. $\sum_{j \in S} w_j > (M + 1)/2$
3. $\sum_{j \in S \setminus \{n\}} w_j < (M + 1)/2$

But, because $w_n = 1$, this is the same as saying that

$$\sum_{j \in S \setminus \{n\}} w_j = \frac{M}{2} = K.$$

But in this case, $S \setminus \{n\}$ is clearly a solution to the original instance of KNAPSACK. It follows from the alternate form of the Shapley value—recall Equation 16.2—that $\varphi_i(G)$ is exactly

$$\frac{(n-k)!(k-1)!}{n!}$$

times the number of solutions to the instance of knapsack (recall that k is the common size of any solution instance).   □

However, just as in the case of DUMMY PLAYER, these hardness results are only relevant when the weights can be assumed to be large. For small weights both the Shapley value and the Banzhaf index can be computed by a pseudopolynomial algorithm, as shown by Matsui and Matsui (Matsui and Matsui, 2000).

Theorem 16.9. *Given an n-player weighted voting game* $G = [N; \mathbf{w}; q]$ *and a player* $i \in N$, *we can compute* $\beta_i(G)$ *and* $\varphi_i(G)$ *in time* $O(n^2 w_{\max})$ *and* $O(n^3 w_{\max})$, *respectively.*

Proof. We will first describe the algorithm for the Shapley value; later, we will explain how to simplify it for the Banzhaf index.

By renumbering the players if necessary, we can assume that $i = n$, that is, our goal is to compute the Shapley value of the last player. We can assume without loss of generality that $w_n > 0$, because otherwise we clearly have $\varphi_n(G) = \beta_n(G) = 0$. Observe first that it suffices to determine, for each $s = 0, \ldots, n-1$, the number N_s of s-element subsets of $N \setminus \{n\}$ that have weight $W \in \{q - w_n, \ldots, q - 1\}$. Indeed, whenever i is pivotal for a coalition C, $|C| = s + 1$, it is pivotal for all permutations in which the agents in $C \setminus \{i\}$ appear in the first s positions, followed by i; there are exactly $s!(n - s - 1)!$ such permutations (where we use the convention that $0! = 1$). Therefore, the formula for the Shapley value can be rewritten as

$$\varphi_i(G) = \frac{1}{n!} \sum_{s=0}^{n-1} s!(n-s-1)!N_s. \tag{16.3}$$

To compute N_s, we use dynamic programming. Specifically, we define $X[j, W, s]$ to be the number of s-element subsets of $\{1, \ldots, j\}$ that have weight W; here, j ranges from 1 to $n-1$, s ranges from 0 to $n-1$, and W ranges from 0 to $w(N)$. For $s = 0$, $j = 1, \ldots, n-1$, we have

$$X[j, W, 0] = \begin{cases} 1 & \text{if } W = 0 \\ 0 & \text{otherwise.} \end{cases}$$

Furthermore, for $j = 1$, $s = 1, \ldots, n-1$ we have

$$X[1, W, s] = \begin{cases} 1 & \text{if } W = w_1 \text{ and } s = 1 \\ 0 & \text{otherwise.} \end{cases}$$

Now, having computed the values $X[j', W', s']$ for all $j' < j$, all $W' = 0, \ldots, w(N)$, and all $s' = 0, \ldots, n - 1$, we can compute $X[j, W, s]$ for $W = 0 \ldots, w(N)$ and $s = 1, \ldots, n - 1$ as follows:

$$X[j, W, s] = X[j - 1, W, s] + X[j - 1, W - w_j, s - 1].$$

In the preceding equation, the first term counts the number of subsets that have weight W and size s and do not contain j, whereas the second term counts the number of subsets of this weight and size that do contain j.

Thus, we can inductively compute $X[n - 1, W, s]$ for all $W = 0, \ldots, w(N)$ and all $s = 0, \ldots, n - 1$. Now, $N_s, s = 0, \ldots, n - 1$, can be computed as

$$N_s = X[n - 1, q - w_n, s] + \cdots + X[n - 1, q - 1, s].$$

By substituting this expression into Equation 16.3, we can compute the Shapley value of player n.

The running time of this algorithm is dominated by the time needed to fill out the table $X[j, W, s]$. The size of this table can be bounded by $n \times n w_{\max} \times n$, and each of its entries can be computed in $O(1)$ steps, which proves our bound on the running time.

For the Banzhaf index, the dynamic program can be simplified by omitting the third index, s: indeed, to compute the Banzhaf index, we simply need to know how many subsets of $N \setminus \{n\}$ have weight that is at least $q - w_n$ and at most $q - 1$. This allows us to reduce the running time from $O(n^3 w_{\max})$ to $O(n^2 w_{\max})$. $\square$

When the weights are large, Theorem 16.9 is not very useful, and we may want to resort to heuristics and/or *approximation algorithms* for computing the power indices. Now, Theorem 16.7 implies that, unless P= NP, no efficient algorithm can approximate the Shapley value within a constant factor on all instances. However, it does not rule out the existence of *randomized algorithms* that are *probably approximately correct* (*PAC*), that is, produce a good solution with high probability. In fact, the good news is that such algorithms do actually exist.

Take the recent algorithm by Bachrach et al. (2010a), for instance. The main idea of this algorithm, dating back to Mann and Shapley (1960), is to randomly sample a coalition and check whether the given player is pivotal for it. It is not hard to see that the fraction of coalitions for which i is pivotal provides an unbiased estimator of i's Banzhaf index. Bachrach et al. show that, by averaging over $\text{poly}(n, \ln 1/\delta, 1/\epsilon)$ samples, we can obtain an estimate that is within a distance ϵ from i's true Banzhaf index with probability at least $1 - \delta$; this approach can be generalized to the Shapley value. The accuracy and confidence achieved by use of the randomized algorithm are typically very high, and can be achieved with only a fraction of the sample size that is theoretically required by the approach—as verified by empirical results (Bachrach et al., 2010a).

Many other papers consider the problem of computing power indices, either approximately or exactly; an (incomplete) list includes Alonso-Meijide et al. (2012), Fatima et al. (2008), Leech (2003), Mann and Shapley (1962), Merrill (1982), and Owen (1975). Moreover, there are several recent attempts to efficiently compute power indices in *restricted* settings, taking advantage of specific domain characteristics (see, e.g., Durán et al., 2003; Bachrach and Shah, 2013; See et al., 2014).

16.4 Voter Weight versus Voter Power

In weighted voting games, one might expect that there is a close correlation between the weight w_i that a player i is assigned, and the power that player i wields. After all, a player's ability to turn a losing coalition into a winning coalition derives from their weight. This intuition is not entirely incorrect: it is not hard to show that power is monotone in weight—that is, for any weighted voting game $G = [N; \mathbf{w}; q]$ and any two players $i, j \in N$ we have $\varphi_i(G) \leq \varphi_j(G)$ if and only if $w_i \leq w_j$. However, the power of an agent cannot be simply represented by its weight, in general: in that sense, "weighted voting doesn't work" (Banzhaf, 1965). Indeed, two agents may have identical voting power even if their weights differ dramatically.

Example 16.10. After the May 2010 elections in the United Kingdom, the Conservative Party had 307 seats, the Labour Party had 258 seats, the Liberal Democrats (LibDems) had 57 seats, and all other parties shared the remaining 28 seats (with the most powerful of them getting 8 seats). The U.K. Parliament is a simple majority system, so the quota is 326. To keep things simple in this analysis, we will treat the "other" parties as a single block (the other parties would be unlikely to act as a block in practice).

Now, it is easy to see that in this weighted voting game there are two two-party coalitions (Conservatives+Labour and Conservatives+LibDems) that can get a majority of seats. Moreover, if Labour or LibDems want to form a coalition that does not include Conservatives, they need each other and the others. Thus, Labour and LibDems have the same Shapley value, despite being vastly different in size. In more detail, the Shapley values are as follows:

i	φ_i
Conservative	1/2
Labour	1/6
LibDem	1/6
Other	1/6

The phenomenon illustrated in Example 16.10 has been observed in many decision-making bodies. It explains why major parties often end up making concessions to smaller parties in order to form a winning coalition: the small parties may wield substantial voting power. Example 16.10 also indicates that to determine an agent's power, we have to take into account the distribution of the other players' weights as well as the quota. In particular, if we keep the weights fixed, but alter the quota, an agent's power can change considerably.

Example 16.11. Consider a weighted voting game with two players of weight 4 and two players of weight 1. If the quota is set to 10, the only winning coalition is the grand coalition, so each player's Shapley value is 1/4. If the quota is set to 8, the smaller players are dummies, so their Shapley value is 0. Finally, if the quota is set to 5, a player of weight 1 is pivotal only if it appears in the second position, and a player of weight 4 appears in the first position. There are four permutations that satisfy this condition, so for $q = 5$ the Shapley value of each of the smaller players is $1/6$.

The role of the quota in determining the agents' power in weighted voting games was studied in detail by Zuckerman et al. (2008), and then by Zick et al. (2011). Zuckerman et al. considered how a central authority might manipulate the quota of a game from a worst-case point of view, and also from an algorithmic points of view. They demonstrated that given a collection of voter weights and a specific undesirable voter, it was possible to compute in polynomial time the quota that would minimize the Banzhaf index of that voter. They also showed that checking whether a player was more powerful with one quota than another, with respect to both the Shapley value and Banzhaf index, is complete with respect to probabilistic polynomial time (i.e., PP-complete (Papadimitriou, 1994, p. 256)).

16.4.1 Paradoxes of Power

An agent's Shapley value and his Banzhaf index may behave in an unexpected way if we modify the game. For example, we might naively expect that adding players to a game would reduce the power of players already present in the game, but this is not necessarily the case: when a new player joins the game, the power of some existing players may in fact increase! Consider the following example.

Example 16.12. Consider a weighted voting game $G = [\{1, 2, 3\}; (2, 2, 1); 4]$. Clearly, player 3 is a dummy in this game, so $\varphi_3(G) = 0$. Now, suppose that a new player with weight 1 joins this game. In the resulting game G', player 3 is pivotal for the coalition consisting of himself, the new player and one of the other two players, so $\varphi_3(G') > 0$.

Another interesting observation is that, when a player i in a game G splits into two different players—that is, distributes his weight between two identities i' and i''—the sum of the new identities' Shapley values in the resulting game can be considerably different from i's Shapley value in the original game.

Example 16.13. Consider an n-player weighted voting game $G = [N; \mathbf{w}; q]$ with $\mathbf{w} = (2, 1, \ldots, 1)$ and $q = n + 1$. In this game the only winning coalition is the grand coalition, so $\varphi_i(G) = \frac{1}{n}$ for all $i = 1, \ldots, n$. Now, suppose that player 1 decides to split into two unit-weight players $1'$ and $1''$. In the resulting game $G' = [N \setminus \{1\} \cup \{1', 1''\}; (1, \ldots, 1); n + 1]$ all players are symmetric, and therefore have equal Shapley value, namely, $\frac{1}{n+1}$. Thus, the joint power of the two new identities of player 1 is $\frac{2}{n+1}$, that is, almost twice his original power!

However, weight-splitting may also lead to a reduction in power. To see this, consider an n-player weighted voting game $G = [N; \mathbf{w}; q]$ with $\mathbf{w} = (2, 2, \ldots, 2)$ and $q = 2n - 1$. By symmetry, we have $\varphi_i(G) = \frac{1}{n}$ for all $i = 1, \ldots, n$. However, it can be shown that if player 1 splits into two unit-weight players $1'$ and $1''$, the sum of their Shapley values in the new game $G' = [N \setminus \{1\} \cup \{1', 1''\}; (1, 1, 2, \ldots, 2); 2n - 1]$ is only $\frac{2}{n(n+1)}$; the proof of this fact is left as an exercise for the reader. Thus, weight-splitting lowers the agent's power by a factor of $(n + 1)/2$.

The phenomena illustrated in Examples 16.12 and 16.13 are known as *the paradox of new members* and *the paradox of size*, respectively. There are several other forms of counterintuitive behavior exhibited by the power indices; jointly, they are referred to as *the paradoxes of power*. These paradoxes are discussed by Felsenthal and Machover (1998) and subsequently by Laruelle and Valenciano (2005) (see also the references therein). The paradox of size is studied in detail by Aziz et al. (2011), who show that the games described in Example 16.13 exhibit the strongest form of this paradox possible: in an n-player weighted voting game, splitting into two identities can increase (respectively, decrease) an agent's Shapley value by at most a factor of $2n/(n + 1)$ (respectively, $(n + 1)/2$). Aziz et al. (2011) also show that deciding whether a given player can split so as to increase his power is NP-hard. Rey and Rothe (2014) show similar hardness results for coalitional splitting, merging and annexation in weighted voting games.

16.5 Simple Games and Yes/No Voting Systems

At this point, let us step back from considering weighted voting games specifically, and consider the wider class of social choice systems of which weighted voting games are an instance. *Yes/No voting systems* are voting systems in which a proposal (e.g., a new law, or a change to tax regulations) is pitted against the status quo (Taylor and Zwicker, 1999). Decision making in many political bodies can be understood as a yes/no voting system (e.g., in the United Kingdom, the voting system of the House of Commons; in the European Union, the voting system in the enlarged EU; in the United States, the U.S. federal system; in the United Nations, the voting system of the Security Council (Taylor, 1995)). Formally, yes/no voting systems have a very simple structure:

Definition 16.7. A *yes/no voting system* is a pair $Y = (N, W)$, where $N = \{1, \dots, n\}$ is the set of voters, and $W \subseteq 2^N$ is the set of *winning coalitions*, with the intended interpretation that, if $C \in W$, then C would be able to determine the outcome (either "yes" or "no") to the question at hand, should they collectively choose to.

Notice that yes/no voting systems can alternatively be understood as *simple cooperative games*. Formally, we can understand a simple game $G = (N, v : 2^N \to \{0, 1\})$ as defining a yes/no voting system $Y_G = (N, W_G)$ in which

$$W_G = \{C \subseteq N \mid v(C) = 1\}.$$

Results relating to simple games can thus be applied directly to yes/no voting systems, and we can therefore choose to work with whichever model we find most convenient.

Several possible conditions on yes/no voting games suggest themselves as being appropriate for some (though of course not all) scenarios:

- *Nontriviality*: There are some winning coalitions, but not all coalitions are winning—formally, $\emptyset \subset W \subset 2^N$.

- *Monotonicity*: If C wins, then every superset of C also wins—formally, if $C_1 \subseteq C_2$ and $C_1 \in W$ then $C_2 \in W$.
- *Zero-sum*: If a coalition C wins, then the agents outside C do not win—formally, if $C \in W$ then $N \setminus C \notin W$.
- *Empty coalition loses*: $\emptyset \notin W$.
- *Grand coalition wins*: $N \in W$.

Of course, these conditions are not independent: the final two conditions imply the first, for example.

Now, we can think of weighted voting games as being a *compact representation* for yes/no voting systems; the set W is simply

$$W = \{C \subseteq N \mid w(C) \geqslant q\}.$$

The representation is compact because we do not need to explicitly list all winning coalitions; we simply specify the weights and quota. This suggests an interesting question: Are weighted voting games a *complete* representation for yes/no voting systems? Is it the case that, for every yes/no voting system $Y = (N, W)$ we can find a weighted voting game G with player set N such that W is exactly the set of winning coalitions in G? The answer is no:

Theorem 16.14. *There are yes/no voting systems for which there exist no weighted voting game with the same set of winning coalitions.*

Proof. Consider a yes/no voting system $Y = (N, W)$ such that $C \in W$ *iff* C contains an odd number of players. Take an odd number k and consider the coalition $C = \{1, \dots, k\}$. By definition we have

1. $C \in W$
2. $C \cup \{k + 1\} \notin W$
3. $C \cup \{k + 2\} \notin W$
4. $C \cup \{k + 1, k + 2\} \in W$

But now consider the weight w_{k+2}: the first and third conditions imply $w_{k+2} < 0$, while the second and fourth imply $w_{k+2} > 0$. There can thus be no weighted voting game representing the yes/no voting system in which the winning coalitions are those containing an odd number of players. $\square$

This raises a further interesting question: Can we identify a condition on yes/no voting systems that is necessary and sufficient to ensure that they *can* be represented by a weighted voting game? The answer is yes. The property of *trade robustness* was identified by Taylor and Zwicker as a necessary and sufficient condition for a yes/no voting system to be representable as a weighted voting game (Taylor and Zwicker, 1999). "Trade robustness" is easily explained. Suppose we have some collection of disjoint coalitions $C_1, \dots, C_k$ with members drawn from the set of voters N. Now discard the losing coalitions from this list—that is, the coalitions C_i such that $C_i \notin W$—leaving us with winning coalitions only. Let us then say a *trade* is an exchange of players between two of the winning coalitions. For example, it may be that coalition C_1 gives players $\{3, 4\}$ to coalition C_2, and in return coalition C_2 gives player 7 to C_1. Of course, for such a trade to be "legal," we would have to have $\{3, 4\} \subseteq C_1$ and $7 \in C_2$. (We will permit the possibility of empty sets of players being transferred in a trade.) Then we have:

Definition 16.8. A yes/no voting game is said to be *trade robust* if, after an any legal sequence of trades starting with a set of winning coalitions, at least one of the resulting coalitions is still winning.

We have:

Theorem 16.15 (Taylor and Zwicker, 1999). *For every yes/no voting system $Y = (N, W)$, there exists a weighted voting game that is equivalent to Y iff Y is trade robust.*

To further illustrate trade robustness, let us consider a richer example.

Example 16.16. Consider a game $G = (N, v)$ with $N = \{1, 2, 3, 4\}$ given by

$$v(C) = 0, \qquad \text{if } |C| \leq 1$$

$$v(C) = 1, \qquad \text{if } |C| \geq 3$$

$$v(\{1, 2\}) = v(\{3, 4\}) = v(\{1, 4\}) = v(\{2, 3\}) = 1,$$

$$v(\{1, 3\}) = v(\{2, 4\}) = 0.$$

This game is not trade robust, because when two winning coalitions $C_1 = \{1, 2\}$ and $C_2 = \{3, 4\}$ trade members (2 moves from C_1 to C_2 and 3 moves from C_2 to C_1), both of the resulting coalitions are losing.

Notice, however, G can be represented as an *intersection* of two weighted voting games, in the following sense. Let $\mathbf{w}^1 = (1, 0, 1, 0)$, $\mathbf{w}^2 = (0, 1, 0, 1)$, $q^1 = q^2 = 1$, and set $G^1 = [N; \mathbf{w}^1; q^1]$, $G^2 = [N; \mathbf{w}^2; q^2]$. Observe that a coalition C is winning in both G^1 and G^2 if and only if it contains both an even-numbered player and an odd-numbered player—that is, if and only if $v(C) = 1$.

The construction presented in Example 16.16 can be used to describe other simple games in the language of weighted voting games. That is, we can take $k \geq 1$ weighted voting games $G^1, \ldots, G^k$ over the same set of players N, and define a new simple game $G = (N, v)$ by setting $v(C) = 1$ if and only if C is a winning coalition in each of the underlying games $G^1, \ldots, G^k$. It turns out that any yes/no game can be obtained in this manner.

Theorem 16.17. *For any simple game $G = (N, v)$, there exists a list of weighted voting games $G^1, \ldots, G^k$, where $G^j = [N; \mathbf{w}^j; q^j]$ for $j = 1, \ldots, k$ such that for any coalition $C \subseteq N$ it holds that $v(C) = 1$ if and only if $w^j(C) \geq q^j$ for each $j = 1, \ldots, k$.*

Proof. Let $C^1, \ldots, C^k$ be the list of losing coalitions in G. We define the jth weighted voting game G^j by setting $w_i^j = 0$ if $i \in C^j$ and $w_i^j = 1$ if $i \notin C^j$ (here w_i^j denotes the weight of the ith player in G^j) and $q^j = 1$. That is, a coalition C is winning in G^j if and only if it contains an agent $i \notin C^j$, or, equivalently, if and only if it is not a subset of C^j.

Consider a coalition C with $v(C) = 1$. By monotonicity, C is not a subset of any losing coalition, so we have $w^j(C) \geq q^j$ for any $j = 1, \ldots, k$. On the other hand, if

$v(C) = 0$, then $C = C^j$ for some $j = 1, \ldots, k$, so $w^j(C) = 0 < q^j$. Thus, the theorem is proved.   □

Games that are represented as intersections of k weighted voting games are known as *k-weighted voting games* or *vector weighted voting games*. More formally, a *k-weighted voting game* is given by a set of players N, $|N| = n$, for each player $i \in N$, a k-dimensional weight vector $\mathbf{w}_i = (w_i^1, \ldots, w_i^k)$ whose entries are nonnegative integers, and k nonnegative integer quotas $q^1, \ldots, q^k$; we write $G = [N; \mathbf{w}_1, \ldots, \mathbf{w}_n; q^1, \ldots, q^k]$. A coalition $C \subseteq N$ is deemed to be winning in G if and only if $\sum_{i \in C} w_i^j \geq q^j$ for all $j = 1, \ldots, k$.

Observe that G can be associated with k weighted voting games $G^1, \ldots, G^k$, where $G^j = [N; (w_1^j, \ldots, w_n^j); q^j]$; these games are called the *component games* of G, and the weight vector of the jth game is denoted by $\mathbf{w}^j$. Clearly, any vector voting game is a simple game, and Theorem 16.17 shows that the converse is also true.

It is important to note that vector weighted voting games are not theoretical constructs: they feature quite prominently in our lives. For example, the following political systems can be understood as vector weighted voting games (Bilbao et al., 2002; Taylor, 1995; Taylor and Zwicker, 1999):

- The U.S. federal system is a 2-weighted voting game, in which the components correspond to the two chambers (the House of Representatives and the Senate). The players are the president, vice president, senators, and representatives. In the game corresponding to the House of Representatives, senators have zero weight, while in the game corresponding to the Senate, representatives have zero weight. The president is the only player to have nonzero weight in *both* games.
- The voting system of the European Union is a 3-weighted voting game (Bilbao et al., 2002). Specifically, in the Council of the European Union, a law requires the support of 50% of the countries, 62% of the population of the European Union, and 74% of the "commissioners" of the EU. Each member state is a player, so (as of 2011) the players are as follows:

  > Germany, United Kingdom, France, Italy, Spain, Poland, Romania, The Netherlands, Greece, Czech Republic, Belgium, Hungary, Portugal, Sweden, Bulgaria, Austria, Slovak Republic, Denmark, Finland, Ireland, Lithuania, Latvia, Slovenia, Estonia, Cyprus, Luxembourg, Malta.

The three component games in the EU voting system are shown in Figure 16.1 (we omit the player set $N = \{1, \ldots, 27\}$, as well as all brackets and parentheses, from the notation). Weights in the first game are assigned according to the number of commissioners the respective member state has. The second game is a simple majority game: every member state gets one vote, and a law must have the support of at least 14 member states. In the third game, weights are assigned in proportion to the population of the respective member state.

Theorem 16.17 allows us to represent any simple game G as a vector weighted voting game; however, the number k of the component games can be quite large (and, in particular, exponential in the number of players n). The number of the component

G^1 : 29 29 29 29 27 27 14 13 12 12 12 12 12 10 10 10   7   7   7 7 7 4 4 4 4 4 3   255
G^2 :   1   1   1   1 1 1 1   1 1 1   1   1 1 1 1 1   1   1   1 1 1 1 1 1 1 1 1   14
G^3 :170 123 122 120 82 80 47 33 22 21 21 21 21 18 17 17 11 11 11 8 8 5 4 3 2 1 1   620

Figure 16.1. Voting in the Council of the European Union is a 3-weighted voting game.

games in a minimal such representation can be interpreted as the inherent complexity of the game. Therefore, given a simple game G, we may be interested in finding the smallest value of k such that G can be represented as a k-weighted voting game. This value of k is called the *dimension* of G; we write $\dim(G) = k$. We emphasize that even if we are given a representation of G as a k-weighted voting game, this does not mean that $\dim(G) = k$: indeed, there may exist a $k' < k$ such that G can be represented as a k'-weighted voting game, so the only conclusion that we can derive is that $\dim(G) \leq k$.

It turns out that there exist simple games of exponentially large dimension. More precisely, for any odd value of n there exists an n-player simple game G such that $\dim(G) \geq 2^{n/2-1}$ (see Taylor and Zwicker (1999) for a proof).

Vector weighted voting games can be interpreted as *conjunctions* of weighted voting games. One can also combine weighted voting games according to more complex Boolean formulas: for instance, to win in the game $(G^1 \vee G^2) \wedge G^3$, a coalition must win in one of the games G^1 and G^2 as well as in G^3. This representation for simple games is studied in detail by Faliszewski et al. (2009a); in particular, Faliszewski et al. show that it can be considerably more compact than the representation via vector weighted voting games.

16.6 Conclusions

Despite their simple mathematical structure, weighted voting games are surprisingly rich with respect to their computational and mathematical properties. In this chapter, we have presented a survey of the key weighted voting games properties, with particular emphasis on computing solution concepts.

16.7 Further Reading

For an outstanding introduction to cooperative game theory set in the wider context of game theory, see Maschler et al. (2013). There seem to be relatively few texts that focus specifically on cooperative games; some examples are Brânzei et al. (2005), Curiel (1997), and Driessen (1988). A good introduction to the mathematics of cooperative games is Peleg and Sudhölter (2007). Simple games in general are discussed in detail in Taylor and Zwicker (1999). For an introduction to the computational aspects of cooperative game theory, see Chalkiadakis et al. (2011). For a detailed survey of the computational complexity of solution concepts for weighted voting games, see Elkind et al. (2009b).

Acknowledgments

We would like to thank Edith Elkind for her permission to adapt co-authored material for this chapter, and in particular, material from our book (Chalkiadakis et al., 2011). We would also like to thank our editors (in particular Jérôme Lang and Ariel Proccacia) and our reviewers, Yair Zick and Yoram Bachrach, for their invaluable corrections and comments. Wooldridge was supported by the European Research Council under grant 291528 ("RACE").

PART IV
Additional Topics

CHAPTER 17

Judgment Aggregation

Ulle Endriss

17.1 Introduction

Social choice theory deals with the aggregation of information supplied by several individuals into a collective decision that appropriately reflects the views of the group as a whole. The most widely considered type of information is preference information. For example, in an election each voter supplies information regarding her preferences over the set of candidates and the voting rule in operation aggregates this information into the collective decision of which candidate wins the election. But the methodology of social choice theory may just as well be applied to other types of information, such as beliefs about whether certain statements are true or false. *Judgment aggregation* (JA from here on), the topic of this chapter, is an elegant formal framework for modeling this form of aggregation.

Let us begin with a famous example from the work of legal scholars Lewis A. Kornhauser and Lawrence G. Sager (Kornhauser and Sager, 1993). Suppose three judges together have to decide on a case regarding an alleged breach of contract. They will try to establish whether (a) the document in question really is a binding contract and whether (b) the promise given in that document really has been breached. Legal doctrine stipulates that the defendant is liable if and only if there have been both a contract and a breach. The three judges differ in their assessment regarding the two premises (and thus also regarding the conclusion):

	Contract?	Breach?	Liable?
Judge Joe:	Yes	Yes	Yes
Judge Judy:	Yes	No	No
Judge Jules:	No	Yes	No

What should be their collective decision regarding the defendant's liability? If they implement a majority vote on the conclusion (the rightmost column), then they will find the defendant *not liable* (by a 2:1 majority). If instead they vote on the premises, they will have to accept that the contract was binding (by a 2:1 majority) and that it has been breached (again, by a 2:1 majority). In the latter case, legal doctrine requires them to find the defendant *liable*. Thus, in the presence of this doctrine, two seemingly reasonable procedures lead to contradictory outcomes. This is known as the *doctrinal paradox*.

Now consider a more abstract rendering of the problem. Three judges have to assess the truth of three formulas of propositional logic: p ("contract"), q ("breach"), and their conjunction $p \wedge q$ (which we said was equivalent to "liable"). This time we also include the result of applying majority voting to each formula:

	p	q	$p \wedge q$
Judge 1:	Yes	Yes	Yes
Judge 2:	Yes	No	No
Judge 3:	No	Yes	No
Majority:	Yes	Yes	No

Thus, we again obtain an unexpected, that is, paradoxical, outcome: despite the fact that each individual judge provides a logically consistent set of judgments, the majority rule results in a judgment set that is inconsistent (there exists no assignment of truth values to propositional variables that would make p true, q true, and $p \wedge q$ false). So, our example demonstrates not merely a dilemma between premise-driven and conclusion-driven approaches to collective decision making, but rather a dilemma between a certain *responsiveness* to the views of decision makers (by respecting their majority decisions) and the *consistency* of collective decisions. This point was first made by the political philosopher Philip Pettit, who noted that this dilemma is not only relevant to analytical jurisprudence, but may strike whenever a group of people engage in a democratic decision making process involving several mutually dependent propositions (Pettit, 2001). Pettit introduced the term *discursive dilemma* for this problem, both to stress its relevance to the political discourse in general and to reflect the fact that we do not actually require the external legal doctrine from the original example to exhibit the problem.

Is there a way around this dilemma? Maybe the majority rule is the root of the problem and there are other methods of aggregation that can ensure a consistent outcome? In a seminal paper that introduced a formal framework for JA that permits us to ask and answer such questions, Christian List and Philip Pettit showed that this is not the case (List and Pettit, 2002): it is *impossible* to devise an aggregation rule that avoids the discursive dilemma—at least if we wish to maintain some of the most basic properties of the majority rule that, arguably, are fundamental features of any reasonable form of aggregation. These properties are *anonymity* ("treat all judges symmetrically"), *neutrality* ("treat all propositions symmetrically"), and *independence* ("base the collective decision regarding a given proposition only on the individual judgments regarding that same proposition"). We formally state and prove this surprising result in Section 17.2.4.

The work of List and Pettit employs the *axiomatic method* commonly used in economic theory, and specifically in social choice theory, for example, to establish impossibility results in preference aggregation. This—together with the fact that JA is a natural framework in which to embed other frameworks of aggregation, specifically preference aggregation (see Section 17.2.2)—has triggered a sustained interest in JA among economic theorists. Their work has led to a deeper understanding of the circumstances under which it is either possible or impossible to perform consistent aggregation. In particular, these results clarify the role of the *agenda*, the set of propositions to be judged. For instance, it is easy to see that when the agenda consists solely of literals (i.e., propositional variables and their negations), then the majority rule will never produce an inconsistent outcome. We review some representative examples of such results later on in Section 17.4.

Besides analytical jurisprudence, political philosophy, and economic theory, JA is also relevant to computer science, particularly to artificial intelligence (AI). For instance, JA suggests itself as a framework in which to study collective decision making in systems of autonomous software agents, given that logic is the preferred language in which to model the beliefs of a single such agent (we will discuss this and other applications of JA in computer science in Section 17.6). In fact, there are close connections between some of the work on *belief merging* in AI and the model of JA under consideration here (we briefly comment on some of these connections in Section 17.5.1). Once computer scientists got interested in JA, this naturally led to a view of aggregation procedures as *algorithms* and, more generally, of reasoning about questions in JA as *computational problems*. We will adopt this perspective also in parts of this chapter and report, for instance, on the computational difficulty of recognizing whether an agenda is sufficiently simple to avoid all occurrences of the discursive dilemma for a given aggregation procedure.

The remainder of this chapter is organized as follows. Section 17.2 defines the *formal framework* of JA and, to exemplify the expressive power of the framework, shows how *preference aggregation* can be embedded into JA. The same section also introduces the most commonly used *axioms* in JA and then proves the basic *impossibility theorem* of List and Pettit mentioned earlier. Section 17.3 reviews three specific types of aggregators in some detail: *quota rules*, *distance-based aggregators*, and the *premise-based rule*. In the context of quota rules, we also discuss examples of the *axiomatic characterization* of aggregators; we use distance-based aggregation to exemplify the analysis of the complexity of *winner determination* in JA; and we review questions of *strategic manipulation* in the section dedicated to premise-based aggregation. Section 17.4 is devoted to *agenda characterization* results that clarify the extent to which instances of the discursive dilemma depend on the structural complexity of the agenda on which judges are asked to vote. Section 17.5 discusses related frameworks for collective decision making and Section 17.6 sketches possible applications in computer science. To improve readability, bibliographic references are kept to a minimum in the body of the chapter; such details are instead supplied in Section 17.7, which also provides pointers to further reading.

Throughout this chapter we shall assume familiarity with the very basics of propositional logic (see, e.g., van Dalen, 2013), particularly the notion of logical consistency. In a few selected places we furthermore assume familiarity with basic concepts from the theory of computational complexity (see, e.g., Arora and Barak, 2009, or the introductory chapter of this volume).

17.2 Basics

In this section we define the formal framework of JA, which originally was laid down by List and Pettit (2002) and since then has been further refined by several authors, notably Dietrich (2007).[1] We also sketch how to embed preference aggregation problems into JA, review the most important axioms encoding desirable properties of aggregators proposed in the literature, and discuss a basic impossibility theorem.

17.2.1 Formal Framework

Let $\mathcal{L}$ be a set of propositional formulas built from a finite set of propositional variables using the usual connectives $\neg$, $\wedge$, $\vee$, $\rightarrow$, $\leftrightarrow$, and the constants $\top$ ("true") and $\bot$ ("false"). For every formula φ, define $\sim\varphi$ to be the *complement* of φ, that is, $\sim\varphi = \neg\varphi$ if φ is not negated, and $\sim\varphi = \psi$ if $\varphi = \neg\psi$ for some formula ψ. We write $\Delta \models \varphi$ in case formula φ is true whenever all formulas in the set Δ are true.

An *agenda* is a finite nonempty subset $\Phi \subseteq \mathcal{L}$ that does not contain any doubly-negated formulas and that is closed under complementation (i.e., if $\varphi \in \Phi$ then $\sim\varphi \in \Phi$).[2] For ease of exposition, we shall assume that Φ is *nontrivial* in the sense of including (at least) two logically independent formulas α and β (i.e., all of $\{\alpha, \beta\}$, $\{\alpha, \sim\beta\}$, $\{\sim\alpha, \beta\}$, and $\{\sim\alpha, \sim\beta\}$ are consistent).[3] Some authors exclude the possibility of Φ including a tautology or a contradiction, but we do not make this assumption here. A *judgment set* J for Φ is a subset $J \subseteq \Phi$. For example, the discursive dilemma sketched in the introduction involved the agenda $\Phi = \{p, \neg p, q, \neg q, p \wedge q, \neg(p \wedge q)\}$. The judgment set of judge 3 was $J_3 = \{\neg p, q, \neg(p \wedge q)\}$, that is, rather than labeling formulas φ with "yes" and "no," as we did earlier, we now either include φ or $\sim\varphi$ in the relevant judgment set.

We call a judgment set J *complete* if $\varphi \in J$ or $\sim\varphi \in J$ for all $\varphi \in \Phi$; we call it *complement-free* if for no $\varphi \in \Phi$ we have both $\varphi \in J$ and $\sim\varphi \in J$; and we call it *consistent* if there exists an assignment of truth values (*true* or *false*) to propositional variables under which all formulas in J are true. Note that every consistent set is complement-free, but the converse is not true. For instance, the majority judgment set from our introductory example, $\{p, q, \neg(p \wedge q)\}$, is clearly complete and complement-free, but it is not consistent: if we set both p and q to be true, then the third formula $\neg(p \wedge q)$ necessarily comes out as false. Let $\mathcal{J}(\Phi)$ denote the set of all complete and consistent subsets of Φ.

Let $N = \{1, \ldots, n\}$ be a set of $n > 1$ *judges* (or *individuals*, or *agents*). For ease of exposition, we shall assume that n is odd. We often refer to subsets $C \subseteq N$ as *coalitions* and we write $\overline{C} := N \setminus C$ for the complement of C. A *profile* is a vector of judgment sets $\boldsymbol{J} = (J_1, \ldots, J_n) \in \mathcal{J}(\Phi)^n$, one for each judge. We write $N_\varphi^{\boldsymbol{J}} := \{i \in N \mid \varphi \in J_i\}$ for the set of judges accepting the formula φ in profile $\boldsymbol{J}$.

---

[1] The particular mode of exposition chosen here is closely based on the author's joint work with Umberto Grandi and Daniele Porello (Endriss et al., 2012).

[2] The reason for introducing the notion of complement is that it often simplifies presentation. For example, if $\varphi \in \Phi$, then the "*negation of φ*" will only be in Φ if φ is not a negated formula, while we can speak of the "*complement of φ*" without having to take any such precautions.

[3] For example, this nontriviality condition is satisfied if α and β are propositional variables.

A (resolute) *judgment aggregation rule* (or *aggregator* for short) for agenda Φ and judges $N = \{1, \ldots, n\}$ is a function $f : \mathcal{J}(\Phi)^n \to 2^\Phi$ mapping every profile into a single (collective) judgment set (2^Φ denotes the powerset of Φ).[4] Note that the resulting judgment set need not be complete and consistent, but the individual sets in the profile are always assumed to have these properties. An example of an aggregator is the (strict) *majority rule* $f_{\text{maj}} : \boldsymbol{J} \mapsto \{\varphi \in \Phi \mid |N_\varphi^J| > \frac{n}{2}\}$, which accepts a formula φ if more than half of the individual judges do.

We conclude this review of the formal framework with two technical definitions. First, we occasionally require a means of measuring how dissimilar two judgment sets are. The *Hamming distance* $H(J, J')$ of two complete and complement-free judgment sets J and J' is the number of nonnegated agenda formulas on which they differ. That is, $H(J, J') := |J \setminus J'| = |J' \setminus J|$. Second, to better understand the sources of inconsistency in aggregation we require a means of abstracting away from formulas that do not contribute to an observed inconsistency. We call an inconsistent set X *minimally inconsistent* if every proper subset of X is consistent.

17.2.2 An Example: Simulating the Condorcet Paradox

To demonstrate the versatility of JA, let us briefly sketch how we can use it to simulate the standard framework of preference aggregation. Suppose three *voters* each express a strict preference order (i.e., a complete, antisymmetric, and transitive binary relation) over a set of *alternatives* $A = \{a, b, c\}$:

Ann:	$a \succ b \succ c$
Bob:	$c \succ a \succ b$
Chloé:	$b \succ c \succ a$

If we try to aggregate these individual preferences using the majority rule (now in the sense of accepting $x \succ y$ if at least two of the three individuals do), then we obtain a cycle: $a \succ b \succ c \succ a$ (two out of three voters prefer a over b, and so forth). This is the classical *Condorcet paradox* (McLean and Urken, 1995).

Now construct a JA scenario as follows. Let $\mathcal{L}$ be the propositional language built from the propositional variables $\{p_{a \succ b}, p_{a \succ c}, p_{b \succ a}, p_{b \succ c}, p_{c \succ a}, p_{c \succ b}\}$. Let Φ consist of all literals in $\mathcal{L}$ as well as these formulas (and their complements):

- $p_{a \succ b} \leftrightarrow \neg p_{b \succ a}, \quad p_{a \succ c} \leftrightarrow \neg p_{c \succ a}, \quad p_{b \succ c} \leftrightarrow \neg p_{c \succ b}$
- $p_{a \succ b} \wedge p_{b \succ c} \to p_{a \succ c}$, and similarly for all other permutations of a, b, c

Observe how, when we interpret $p_{a \succ b}$ as "*I consider a being preferable over b*" and so forth, we get the first group of formulas to encode the fact that our preference order should be complete and antisymmetric, while the second group expresses that it should be transitive. Let us call Φ the *preference agenda* (for three alternatives). Now consider a consistent and complete profile for judges Ann, Bob, and Chloé, in which all three

---

[4] *Irresolute* aggregators, which allow for ties between several collective judgment sets in the outcome, while also of some interest, are studied less frequently (but see, e.g., Lang and Slavkovik, 2013).

of them accept the positive formulas listed. Such a profile is fully determined once we fix each judge's stance on $p_{a \succ b}$, $p_{b \succ c}$, and $p_{a \succ c}$:

	$p_{a \succ b}$	$p_{b \succ c}$	$p_{a \succ c}$
Ann:	Yes	Yes	Yes
Bob:	Yes	No	No
Chloé:	No	Yes	No
Majority:	Yes	Yes	No

This corresponds directly to the Condorcet paradox. If we translate back to preference aggregation, then $\{p_{a \succ b}, p_{b \succ c}, \neg p_{a \succ c}, \ldots\}$, which is part of the judgment set returned by the majority rule, corresponds to the cycle $a \succ b \succ c \succ a$. If we stay in JA, then that same set becomes inconsistent once we add $p_{a \succ b} \wedge p_{b \succ c} \rightarrow p_{a \succ c}$ (which must also be part of the majority outcome, as it is accepted by all judges).

17.2.3 Axioms: Desirable Properties of Aggregation Rules

We have seen that using the majority rule can lead to problems. It does not meet all of our requirements. But what are those requirements? Following is a list of properties of aggregators that are intuitively appealing. In the jargon of social choice theory, such desirable properties are called *axioms*.

- An aggregator f is (proposition-wise) *unanimous* if $\varphi \in J_i$ for all $i \in N$ entails $\varphi \in f(J)$, for all $\varphi \in \Phi$ and all $J \in \mathcal{J}(\Phi)^n$. That is, if every individual judge accepts φ, then so should the collective represented by f.[5]
- An aggregator f is *anonymous* if $f(J) = f(J_{\pi(1)}, \ldots, J_{\pi(n)})$, for all $J \in \mathcal{J}(\Phi)^n$ and all permutations $\pi : N \rightarrow N$. That is, f should treat all judges the same.
- An aggregator f is *neutral* if $\varphi \in J_i \Leftrightarrow \psi \in J_i$ for all $i \in N$ entails $\varphi \in f(J) \Leftrightarrow \psi \in f(J)$, for all $\varphi, \psi \in \Phi$ and all $J \in \mathcal{J}(\Phi)^n$. That is, f should treat all formulas the same (if φ and ψ are accepted by the same judges, then the collective must accept either both or neither of them).[6]
- An aggregator f is *independent* if $\varphi \in J_i \Leftrightarrow \varphi \in J_i'$ for all $i \in N$ entails $\varphi \in f(J) \Leftrightarrow \varphi \in f(J')$, for all $\varphi \in \Phi$ and all $J, J' \in \mathcal{J}(\Phi)^n$. That is, whether we accept φ should only depend on the pattern of individual acceptances of φ.
- An aggregator f is *monotonic* if $\varphi \in J_i' \setminus J_i$ entails $\varphi \in f(J) \Rightarrow \varphi \in f(J_{-i}, J_i')$, for all $i \in N$, all $\varphi \in \Phi$, all $J \in \mathcal{J}(\Phi)^n$, and all $J_i' \in \mathcal{J}(\Phi)$.[7] That is, if a collectively accepted formula φ is accepted by an additional judge i (switching her judgment set from J_i to J_i'), then φ should still get accepted.

---

[5] Another common formulation of unanimity requires only $f(J, \ldots, J) = J$ for all $J \in \mathcal{J}(\Phi)$.

[6] For some very simple agendas, such as $\Phi = \{p, \neg p\}$, all aggregators are vacuously neutral (because $p \in J_i \Leftrightarrow \neg p \in J_i$ is never true), even though, intuitively, they do not all treat all formulas the same. To exclude such pathological cases, we have made the assumption that the agenda is nontrivial.

[7] Here (J_{-i}, J_i') denotes the profile we obtain when we replace J_i in J by J_i'.

Neutrality and independence together are also known as *systematicity*.[8] Note that we do not claim, or even wish, that every aggregator satisfies *all* of these axioms. They merely are strong candidates to consider when drawing up a list of requirements. The majority rule, however, clearly satisfies all of them.

Our remaining axioms express that we would like to see properties such as consistency be *lifted* from the individual to the collective level:

- An aggregator f is *complete* if $f(\boldsymbol{J})$ is complete for all $\boldsymbol{J} \in \mathcal{J}(\Phi)^n$.
- An aggregator f is *complement-free* if $f(\boldsymbol{J})$ is complement-free for all $\boldsymbol{J} \in \mathcal{J}(\Phi)^n$.
- An aggregator f is *consistent* if $f(\boldsymbol{J})$ is consistent for all $\boldsymbol{J} \in \mathcal{J}(\Phi)^n$.

Consistency and completeness together are often referred to as *collective rationality*. Observe that the majority rule is both complete and complement-free (at least in case n is odd), but that we have seen that it is *not* consistent.

It is useful to reformulate the independence axiom as follows: f is independent if (and only if) for every $\varphi \in \Phi$ there exists a family of sets of judges $\mathcal{W}_\varphi \subseteq 2^N$ such that for all $\boldsymbol{J} \in \mathcal{J}(\Phi)^n$ it is the case that $\varphi \in f(\boldsymbol{J})$ if and only if $N_\varphi^{\boldsymbol{J}} \in \mathcal{W}_\varphi$. We call $\mathcal{W}_\varphi$ the set of *winning coalitions* for φ. That is, under an independent aggregator we only need to look at the coalition of judges accepting φ to be able to decide whether φ should be collectively accepted (and those coalitions with the power of getting φ accepted are what we call its winning coalitions). Understanding the structure of the space of winning coalitions provides a crucial key to understanding the dynamics of JA. For now, we pin down some basic facts about it:

Lemma 17.1 (Winning Coalitions). *Let f be an independent aggregator and, for every formula $\varphi \in \Phi$, let $\mathcal{W}_\varphi \subseteq 2^N$ be the corresponding family of winning coalitions, that is, $\varphi \in f(\boldsymbol{J}) \Leftrightarrow N_\varphi^{\boldsymbol{J}} \in \mathcal{W}_\varphi$ for all $\boldsymbol{J} \in \mathcal{J}(\Phi)^n$. Then the following are all true:*

(i) *f is unanimous if and only if $N \in \mathcal{W}_\varphi$ for all $\varphi \in \Phi$.*

(ii) *f is anonymous if and only if $\mathcal{W}_\varphi$ is closed under equinumerosity, that is, if and only if $C \in \mathcal{W}_\varphi$ and $|C| = |C'|$ entail $C' \in \mathcal{W}_\varphi$ for all $C, C' \subseteq N$ and all $\varphi \in \Phi$.*

(iii) *f is neutral if and only if $\mathcal{W}_\varphi = \mathcal{W}_\psi$ for all $\varphi, \psi \in \Phi$.*

(iv) *f is monotonic if and only if $\mathcal{W}_\varphi$ is upward closed, that is, if and only if $C \in \mathcal{W}_\varphi$ and $C \subseteq C'$ entail $C' \in \mathcal{W}_\varphi$ for all $C, C' \subseteq N$ and all $\varphi \in \Phi$.*

(v) *f is complement-free if and only if $\mathcal{W}_\varphi$ does not contain complementary coalitions, that is, if and only if $C \notin \mathcal{W}_\varphi$ or $\overline{C} \notin \mathcal{W}_\varphi$ for all $C \subseteq N$ and all $\varphi \in \Phi$.*

(vi) *f is complete if and only if $\mathcal{W}_\varphi$ is maximal, that is, if and only if $C \in \mathcal{W}_\varphi$ or $\overline{C} \in \mathcal{W}_\varphi$ for all $C \subseteq N$ and all $\varphi \in \Phi$.*

Proof. These claims follow immediately from the relevant definitions. Only the case of neutrality requires closer inspection. Clearly, $\mathcal{W}_\varphi = \mathcal{W}_\psi$ for all $\varphi, \psi \in \Phi$ implies the symmetric treatment of all formulas and thus neutrality in the technical sense. For the converse, we make use of our assumption that Φ contains two formulas α and β

---

[8] To be precise, any statement regarding the equivalence of axioms must be made w.r.t. a specific class of agendas. The equivalence mentioned here holds for nontrivial agendas.

such that all of $\{\alpha, \beta\}$, $\{\alpha, \sim\beta\}$, $\{\sim\alpha, \beta\}$, and $\{\sim\alpha, \sim\beta\}$ are consistent. So let f be an aggregator that is independent and neutral.

First, consider two formulas φ and ψ for which both $\{\varphi, \psi\}$ and $\{\sim\varphi, \sim\psi\}$ are consistent and take any coalition $C \in \mathcal{W}_\varphi$. We can construct a profile J with $N_\varphi^J = N_\psi^J = C$. From C being winning for φ, we get $\varphi \in f(J)$. From neutrality we then get $\psi \in f(J)$, and from independence $C \in \mathcal{W}_\psi$. Thus, from $\{\varphi, \psi\}$ and $\{\sim\varphi, \sim\psi\}$ being consistent we get $\mathcal{W}_\varphi = \mathcal{W}_\psi$, so in particular $\mathcal{W}_\alpha = \mathcal{W}_{\sim\alpha} = \mathcal{W}_\beta = \mathcal{W}_{\sim\beta}$.

Note that α is contingent (i.e., it is neither a tautology nor a contradiction). Consider any other formula φ that is also contingent. If both $\{\varphi, \alpha\}$ and $\{\sim\varphi, \sim\alpha\}$ are consistent, then $\mathcal{W}_\varphi = \mathcal{W}_\alpha$ and we are done. So suppose it is not the case that both $\{\varphi, \alpha\}$ and $\{\sim\varphi, \sim\alpha\}$ are consistent. Observe that when we negate one of the formulas in an inconsistent set of two contingent formulas, we obtain a consistent set. Thus, if $\{\varphi, \alpha\}$ is inconsistent, then both $\{\sim\varphi, \alpha\}$ and $\{\varphi, \sim\alpha\}$ are consistent. And also in case $\{\sim\varphi, \sim\alpha\}$ is inconsistent, both $\{\sim\varphi, \alpha\}$ and $\{\varphi, \sim\alpha\}$ are consistent. Thus, in either case we get $\mathcal{W}_\varphi = \mathcal{W}_{\sim\alpha}$. To summarize, so far we have shown that $\mathcal{W}_\varphi = \mathcal{W}_\psi$ for any two contingent formulas φ and ψ in the agenda.

If φ is a tautology, then there exists a profile $J \in \mathcal{J}(\Phi)^n$ with $N = N_\varphi^J = N_\alpha^J$. Thus, by neutrality and independence, $N \in \mathcal{W}_\varphi \Leftrightarrow N \in \mathcal{W}_\alpha$. As no coalition other than the grand coalition N can ever accept φ, it does not matter which other coalitions belong to $\mathcal{W}_\varphi$ and we may simply assume that $\mathcal{W}_\varphi = \mathcal{W}_\alpha$. The proof for contradictions φ (using $\emptyset$ in place of N) is analogous. $\qquad\square$

As a first simple example of the power of Lemma 17.1, let us see how we can use it to prove that every aggregator f that is neutral, independent, monotonic, and complete is also unanimous: From neutrality and independence we get that f is fully defined by a single family $\mathcal{W}$ of winning coalitions. By completeness, either $N \in \mathcal{W}$ (in which case we are done) or $\overline{N} = \emptyset \in \mathcal{W}$. But also in this latter case, by monotonicity and due to $\emptyset \subseteq N$, we get $N \in \mathcal{W}$, that is, f is unanimous.

17.2.4 A Simple Impossibility Theorem

We conclude our run through the basic theory of JA with a simple impossibility theorem. It shows that it is not just the majority rule that fails to reliably produce consistent outcomes, but that we cannot get consistency for any aggregator that satisfies what would appear to be rather innocent axiomatic requirements. This is the original impossibility theorem of JA, due to List and Pettit, which we had already mentioned in the introduction.

Theorem 17.2 (List and Pettit, 2002). *No aggregator for an agenda of the form $\Phi \supseteq \{p, q, p \wedge q\}$ can be anonymous, neutral, independent, complete, and consistent.*

Proof. Let f be an aggregator for an agenda Φ with $\{p, q, p \wedge q\} \subseteq \Phi$. For the sake of contradiction, assume f is anonymous, neutral, independent, complete, and consistent. By Lemma 17.1 and the first three properties, if two formulas φ and ψ are accepted by the same number of judges, then f must accept either both or neither of them. Now consider a profile J in which $\frac{n-1}{2}$ judges accept both p and q; one judge accepts p but not q; one judge accepts q but not p; and the remaining $\frac{n-3}{2}$ judges accept neither

p nor q.[9] Observe that for this profile we get $|N_p^J| = |N_q^J| = |N_{\neg(p \wedge q)}^J| = \frac{n+1}{2}$. So we must accept either all of p, q, and $\neg(p \wedge q)$, or none of them. The former immediately clashes with consistency. If we take the latter route, completeness forces us to accept all of $\neg p$, $\neg q$, and $p \wedge q$, which again leads to a clash with consistency. $\quad\square$

Theorem 17.2 is a negative result. Still, it can help us to pinpoint how we need to relax our requirements to make consistent aggregation possible after all.

One approach is to weaken the axioms. For instance, it is easy to define certain (trivial) aggregators that meet all but one of our requirements: the *dictatorship* that always returns a copy of the judgment set of the first judge only violates anonymity, while a *constant* aggregator that always returns some fixed judgment set in $\mathcal{J}(\Phi)$ only violates neutrality. Of course, such aggregators are of little practical interest. In Section 17.3 we discuss some more practically useful aggregation rules, which account for the impossibility by violating independence or completeness.

A second approach is to restrict the range of agendas on which we require our aggregator to perform satisfactorily. Section 17.4 will be devoted to results that identify, for a given (class of) aggregator(s), the precise class of agendas for which consistent aggregation is possible. This also takes care of a somewhat unsatisfactory feature of Theorem 17.2, namely, its restriction to an overly specific class of agendas (those including p, q, and $p \wedge q$).

A third approach, finally, is to not restrict the agenda, but to instead assume that not every possible profile will be encountered in practice. We shall not discuss such *domain restrictions* in any detail here. They are similar to domain restrictions studied in voting theory, but arguably lack the intuitive appeal of, say, Black's *single-peakedness*, a domain restriction for preference profiles avoiding paradoxical election outcomes (Black, 1948). The most powerful result along these lines in JA is due to Dietrich and List (2010). They showed that, if a profile is *value-restricted* in the sense that for every minimally inconsistent (nonsingleton) subset X of the agenda Φ there exist two formulas $\varphi_X, \psi_X \in X$ such that no individual accepts both φ_X and ψ_X, then the outcome of the majority rule will be consistent. The proof is immediate: For the sake of contradiction, assume the majority outcome is inconsistent. Then it must include some minimally inconsistent set X with associated formulas φ_X and ψ_X, each of which must have been accepted by a (strict) majority. But then, by the pigeonhole principle, at least one judge must have accepted both of them, which contradicts the assumption of value restriction.

17.3 Aggregation Rules

The majority rule is but one method of aggregation. In this section we introduce three families of aggregators (quota rules, distance-based rules, and premise-based rules), and for each of them discuss to what extent they allow us to address the deficit of the

---

[9] Note how we make use of our general assumption that n is odd. If n is even, we obtain a much more fundamental impossibility: there can be no anonymous, neutral, complete and *complement-free* aggregator even for simple agendas such as $\Phi = \{p, \neg p, q, \neg q\}$. To see this, consider what to do in case the number of judges accepting p equals that accepting $\neg p$.

majority rule highlighted by the discursive dilemma. For each family, we then exemplify a specific research direction in JA: the axiomatic characterization of aggregators, the complexity of winner determination, and strategic manipulation.

17.3.1 Quota-Based Aggregation/Axiomatic Characterizations

Under a *quota rule* we accept a given formula φ if the number of individual judges accepting φ reaches a certain threshold. Formally, a quota rule f_q is induced by a function $q : \Phi \to \{0, 1, \ldots, n+1\}$, mapping formulas to thresholds:

$$f_q(\boldsymbol{J}) = \{\varphi \in \Phi \mid |N_\varphi^{\boldsymbol{J}}| \geqslant q(\varphi)\}$$

Note that if the quota of a given formula is 0, then this means that that formula will always get accepted, while quota $n+1$ means that the formula in question will never get accepted. The rule f_q is called a *uniform* quota rule if q maps all formulas to the same number λ (in such a case, we simply write f_λ). For example, the (strict) majority rule is the uniform quota rule $f_{\lceil \frac{n+1}{2} \rceil}$, while f_n is the *intersection rule*, mapping any given profile $\boldsymbol{J}$ to the judgment set $J_1 \cap \cdots \cap J_n$.

It is intuitively clear that, if we increase the quota, then it should be less likely that we obtain a collective judgment set that is inconsistent. For example, take once more the agenda $\Phi = \{p, \neg p, q, \neg q, p \wedge q, \neg(p \wedge q)\}$. Then, provided we impose a uniform quota strictly greater than $\frac{2}{3}n$, the collective judgment set will be consistent for every possible profile.[10] This is a consequence of the following result:

Proposition 17.3 (Dietrich and List, 2007a). *Let k be the size of the largest minimally inconsistent subset of the agenda* Φ*. Then every uniform quota rule* f_λ *with a quota of* $\lambda > \frac{k-1}{k} \cdot n$ *is consistent.*

Proof. For the sake of contradiction, suppose there exists a profile $\boldsymbol{J} \in \mathcal{J}(\Phi)^n$ for which $f_\lambda(\boldsymbol{J})$ is inconsistent. Take an arbitrary minimally inconsistent subset $X \subseteq f_\lambda(\boldsymbol{J})$. By assumption, we have $|X| \leqslant k$. For each formula $\varphi \in X$, there must have been at least λ judges accepting it. Hence, summing over all the formulas in X, there must have been at least $|X| \cdot \lambda$ occasions of a formula in X being accepted by some judge. By the pigeon hole principle, at least one of the n judges must have accepted at least $\frac{|X| \cdot \lambda}{n}$ of these formulas. But due to $\lambda > \frac{k-1}{k} \cdot n$, we get $\frac{|X| \cdot \lambda}{n} > |X| - \frac{|X|}{k}$, that is, (as $\frac{|X|}{k} \leqslant 1$) that judge must have accepted *all* of the formulas in X, contradicting our assumption of individual consistency. $\qquad\qquad\square$

Thus, if we are willing to give up completeness (which is violated by quota rules with high quotas), then we can circumvent the impossibility of Theorem 17.2.

Proposition 17.3 can be strengthened to say that for any quota *not* satisfying the constraint $\lambda > \frac{k-1}{k} \cdot n$ the corresponding rule is *not* consistent. In our earlier example, $\{p, q, \neg(p \wedge q)\}$ with size 3 is the largest minimally inconsistent subset of the agenda $\Phi = \{p, \neg p, q, \neg q, p \wedge q, \neg(p \wedge q)\}$. So if, for example, $n = 30$, then any quota of 21 or higher will guarantee consistency, while quota 20 does not.

---

[10] On the downside, the collective judgment set may not always be complete (namely, when both φ and $\sim\varphi$ are accepted by fewer than two thirds of the judges).

An important question in social choice theory is whether a given set of axiomatic requirements fully characterizes a particular aggregator (or family of aggregators). If this is the case and if we have strong normative support for the axioms in question, then this forces us to adopt the corresponding aggregator. Let us briefly review a number of such characterization results for quota rules.

Proposition 17.4 (Dietrich and List, 2007a). *An aggregator is anonymous, independent, and monotonic if and only if it is a quota rule.*

Proof. For the right-to-left direction, observe that every quota rule clearly has those three properties. For the left-to-right direction, the claim follows from Lemma 17.1: By independence, we can decide formula by formula. By monotonicity, the set of winning coalitions is upward closed. By anonymity, only the size of coalitions matters. Taken together, this means that for every formula φ there exists a number λ_φ such that φ is collectively accepted if and only if at least λ_φ judges accept φ. In other words, λ_φ is the quota associated with φ, that is, $q(\varphi) = \lambda_\varphi$. $\qquad\square$

A quota rule is neutral if and only if it is a uniform quota rule.[11] Thus, as an immediate consequence of Proposition 17.4, we obtain the following characterization:

Corollary 17.5. *An aggregator is anonymous, neutral, independent, and monotonic if and only if it is a uniform quota rule.*

We now want to add completeness and complement-freeness to our requirements (but not consistency, which we already know to be impossible from Theorem 17.2). Intuitively speaking, low quotas should favor completeness (as generally more formulas will get accepted), while high quotas should favor complement-freeness (as generally fewer formulas will get accepted). Let λ be the uniformly imposed quota. If k individuals accept φ, then $n-k$ individuals accept $\sim\varphi$. Thus, to guarantee completeness, we require $\max\{k, n-k\} \geqslant \lambda$ for all $k \leqslant n$, as that way at least one of φ and $\sim\varphi$ will get accepted under all circumstances. Similarly, to guarantee complement-freeness, we require $\lambda > \min\{k, n-k\}$ for all $k \leqslant n$. The closer k is to $\frac{n}{2}$, the harder it gets to satisfy *both* of these constraints. Recall that we assume n to be odd. For $k = \frac{n+1}{2}$, there is only a single value for λ that will satisfy both constraints, namely, $\lambda = \frac{n+1}{2}$. That is, only the majority rule satisfies all of our requirements and we obtain the following corollary to Corollary 17.5:

Corollary 17.6. *An aggregator is anonymous, neutral, independent, monotonic, complete, and complement-free if and only if it is the (strict) majority rule.*

We stress that Corollary 17.6 is true only when the number n of individual judges is odd. As pointed out in Footnote 9 already, when n is even, there exists no aggregator that satisfies all of these requirements. For the special case of an agenda with just a single pair of complementary formulas, Corollary 17.6 reduces to May's Theorem on the characterization of the majority rule in voting theory (May, 1952).[12]

---

[11] This characterization holds, provided the agenda is nontrivial. See also Footnote 6.

[12] May allows for ties and uses a more sophisticated monotonicity axiom, known as *positive responsiveness*, so as to be able to also cover the case of an even number of individuals. Refer to Chapter 2 for full details.

17.3.2 Distance-based Aggregation/Winner Determination

Another approach to aggregation is to select as outcome a judgment set that, in some sense, minimizes the distance to the profile. If we measure distances between judgment sets using the *Hamming distance* and if we interpret the distance from an outcome to a profile as the *sum* of the distances between that outcome and each of the individual judgment sets, then we obtain the following aggregator:

$$f_{\text{kem}}(\boldsymbol{J}) = \operatorname*{argmin}_{J \in \mathcal{J}(\Phi)} \sum_{i \in N} H(J, J_i).$$

That is, we go through all complete and consistent judgment sets J and return the one that minimizes the sum of the Hamming distances to the individual judgment sets. This rule, discussed under a variety of different names in the literature, is the most widely used distance-based aggregator in JA. If we apply it to the preference agenda (see Section 17.2.2), then we obtain the *Kemeny rule* familiar from preference aggregation (Kemeny, 1959) and discussed in depth in Chapter 4 this is why we shall refer to it as the *generalized Kemeny rule*. To be precise, f_{kem} is an *irresolute* aggregator, as it may return a *set* of several judgment sets (that are all equally close to the profile). To obtain a resolute rule fitting our definition of Section 17.2.1, we have to combine f_{kem} with a *tie-breaking* rule.

The generalized Kemeny rule is clearly consistent: only consistent judgment sets are considered as possible outcomes during the optimization process. It achieves consistency by sacrificing independence.

A fundamental question in computational social choice concerns the computational complexity of the *winner determination* problem of a given method of aggregation. For a resolute aggregator f this can be cast as a decision problem by asking, for a given profile $\boldsymbol{J}$ and a given formula $\varphi \in \Phi$, whether it is the case that $\varphi \in f(\boldsymbol{J})$. By answering this question for every formula φ in the agenda, we can compute the outcome, the "winning" judgment set. Thus, the complexity of our decision problem is directly relevant to the algorithmic feasibility of the pragmatic problem of applying rule f. For irresolute aggregators, such as the generalized Kemeny rule, an appropriate formulation of the question is whether, for a given profile $\boldsymbol{J}$ and a given set $L \subseteq \Phi$, there exists a winning set $J^\star \in f(\boldsymbol{J})$ such that $L \subseteq J^\star$. For the generalized Kemeny rule, winner determination is highly intractable:

Theorem 17.7 (Endriss et al., 2012). *The winner determination problem of the generalized Kemeny rule is Θ_2^P-complete.*

The complexity class Θ_2^P is the class of problems that can be solved, in polynomial time, by a (hypothetical) machine that has access to an oracle capable of deciding NP-complete problems in an instant, with the restriction that the number of queries to the oracle must be at most logarithmic in the size of the problem. Equivalently, we may ask a polynomial number of oracle queries, provided we ask them all in parallel. That is, the generalized Kemeny rule is *complete for parallel access to NP*. The proof of Theorem 17.7 is beyond the scope of this chapter. It is based on a reduction from the KEMENY WINNER problem in voting theory, for which Θ_2^P-completeness was established by Hemaspaandra et al. (2005). For a discussion of that problem we refer to Chapter 4. For comparison, it is easy to see that for any quota rule the winner determination problem is polynomial.

The generalized Kemeny rule is not the only distance-based aggregator in JA. We may use other distance metrics than the Hamming distance and we may vary the way we define the distance to a profile in terms of that basic metric. Here we only give one further example of a generalization of a rule familiar from preference aggregation: Under the *Slater rule* we first compute the *majority graph* and then return the preference order that minimizes the number of edges in the majority graph we have to invert before we obtain a transitive order (Slater, 1961).[13] This idea is easily transposed to JA to obtain a *generalized Slater rule:*

$$f_{\text{sla}}(J) = \operatorname*{argmin}_{J \in \mathcal{J}(\Phi)} H(J, f_{\text{maj}}(J)).$$

That is, we first compute the majority outcome $f_{\text{maj}}(J)$ and then find the complete and consistent judgment set closest to it (again, more than one judgment set may be closest and we may have to break ties if we need a unique winner).

The following example, with φ_1 and φ_2 representing two syntactically distinct formulas that are both semantically equivalent to $p \vee (q_1 \wedge q_2) \vee (r_1 \wedge r_2 \wedge r_3)$, demonstrates that the Kemeny rule and the Slater rule do not always coincide:

	p	q_1	q_2	r_1	r_2	r_3	φ_1	φ_2
1 judge:	Yes	No	No	No	No	No	Yes	Yes
10 judges:	No	Yes	Yes	No	No	No	Yes	Yes
10 judges:	No	No	No	Yes	Yes	Yes	Yes	Yes
Kemeny:	No	Yes	Yes	No	No	No	Yes	Yes
Slater:	Yes	No	No	No	No	No	Yes	Yes

Consult Section 17.7 for references to other distance-based aggregators.

17.3.3 Premise-based Aggregation/Strategic Manipulation

For some application scenarios it will be natural to think of certain formulas in the agenda as *premises* and the others as *conclusions*. Suppose we can partition the agenda Φ into a set Φ^p of premises and a set Φ^c of conclusions such that each of them is closed under complementation, $\Phi = \Phi^p \cup \Phi^c$, and $\Phi^p \cap \Phi^c = \emptyset$.

The *premise-based rule* f_{pre} works by first applying the majority rule to the premises and then accepting those conclusions that logically follow from the collectively accepted premises:

$$f_{\text{pre}}(J) = \Delta \cup \{\varphi \in \Phi^c \mid \Delta \models \varphi\}, \text{ where } \Delta = \left\{\varphi \in \Phi^p \,\middle|\, |N_\varphi^J| > \frac{n}{2}\right\}$$

Clearly, in the general case f_{pre} inherits all the problems of the majority rule and cannot guarantee consistency (e.g., when *every* formula is declared a premise). In addition, f_{pre} may fail to be complete. For example, when $p \wedge q$ and $\neg(p \wedge q)$ are

---

[13] For an in-depth discussion of the Slater rule we refer to Chapter 3.

conclusions and no premise has either p or q as a subformula, then neither $p \wedge q$ nor $\neg(p \wedge q)$ will be logically entailed by whatever (consistent) set of premises we end up accepting. However, if we impose suitable constraints on the definition of premises and conclusions, we can obtain a well-behaved aggregator. The most common set of assumptions, which we shall also adopt here, is the following:

(i) The set of premises is the set of literals in the agenda.
(ii) The agenda is closed under propositional variables, that is, if φ is a formula in the agenda, then so is every propositional variable occurring within φ.

Assumption (i) guarantees consistency; a set of collectively accepted premises now directly corresponds to an assignment of truth values to propositional variables. Assumption (ii) then guarantees completeness, because, for every conclusion φ, either φ or $\sim\varphi$ will be satisfied by that truth assignment. That is, we obtain the following result (given our assumption of n being odd):

Fact 17.8. *For any agenda that is closed under propositional variables, the premise-based rule, with the premises being the literals, is complete and consistent.*

Thus, by sacrificing both neutrality and independence, the premise-based rule allows us to circumvent the impossibility of Theorem 17.2.

We have seen that distance-based aggregators achieve consistency at the price of high computational complexity. This is not the case for f_{pre}:

Fact 17.9. *The winner determination problem of the premise-based rule, with the premises being the literals, is polynomial.*

Indeed, applying the majority rule to the premises is certainly polynomial. Deciding whether a given conclusion should be accepted then amounts to a model checking problem for propositional logic, which can also be done in polynomial time.

One of the central phenomena studied in social choice theory is strategic behavior. Under what circumstances do individuals have an incentive to truthfully report their private information to the aggregation mechanism? This is a very natural question in the context of voting or resource allocation, where this private information concerns the individuals' preferences and where we can use these very same preferences to define what it means for an individual to have an incentive to perform a given action. In JA, on the other hand, individuals do not have preferences, so it is not obvious what it may mean for an individual to have an incentive one way or the other. To be able to analyze strategic behavior in JA, we need to endow our judges with preferences. For the purposes of this brief exposition, let us assume that every judge's preferences are induced by her true judgment set and the Hamming distance: judge i with true judgment set J_i prefers J to J', denoted as $J \succ_i J'$, if and only if $H(J_i, J) < H(J_i, J')$. We say that she has *Hamming preferences*.[14] Now suppose three judges truthfully report their judgment sets:

---

[14] Preferences induced by the Hamming distance are also discussed in Chapter 9 on voting in combinatorial domains.

	p	q	r	$p \vee q$	$p \vee r$
Judge 1:	No	No	No	No	No
Judge 2:	Yes	No	No	Yes	Yes
Judge 3:	No	Yes	Yes	Yes	Yes

Under the premise-based rule, all three premises will get rejected, which means that also the two conclusions get rejected. For judge 3 the Hamming distance from this outcome to her own judgment set is 4. But if she lies and answers "yes" for p, then p will get accepted and thus also the two conclusions. Her distance to this new outcome is only 3, that is, she has an incentive to *manipulate* in this manner. We say that an aggregator f is *immune to manipulation* for a given method of deriving preferences from judgment sets, if every judge i (at least weakly) prefers the sincere outcome $f(\boldsymbol{J})$ to the manipulated outcome $f(\boldsymbol{J}_{-i}, J_i')$ for any profile $\boldsymbol{J} \in \mathcal{J}(\Phi)^n$ and any alternative insincere judgment set $J_i' \in \mathcal{J}(\Phi)$ for judge i.

Proposition 17.10 (Dietrich and List, 2007c). *Any independent and monotonic aggregator is immune to manipulation by judges with Hamming preferences.*

Proof. Independence means that the would-be manipulator can consider one formula at a time. Monotonicity then means that it is always in her best interest to drive up the support for formulas in her judgment set and to reduce the support for those not in her judgment set, that is, it is in her best interest to report truthfully. □

As discussed in depth in Chapter 6 for aggregators that are not immune to manipulation a relevant question is whether it may be the case that manipulation is a computationally intractable problem, as this may provide at least some level of protection against unwanted strategic behavior. The *manipulation problem* for a given aggregator f and a given method of deriving preferences from judgment sets is the problem of deciding whether a judge may obtain a preferred outcome by misreporting her judgment set. While we have seen that the premise-based rule can be manipulated, doing so is hard, at least in the worst case and for agendas involving large formulas:[15]

Proposition 17.11 (Endriss et al., 2012). *The manipulation problem for the premise-based rule and judges with Hamming preferences is NP-complete.*

The proof is not difficult, but beyond the scope of this chapter. It involves a reduction from the NP-hard *satisfiability problem* for propositional logic to our manipulation problem. Given a formula φ, the core idea is to build a profile where one judge has an incentive to misreport her judgment set if and only if φ is satisfiable.

It is important to stress that the particular manipulation problem of Proposition 17.11 is just one of several natural definitions for which complexity results are known (Baumeister et al., 2013a). For instance, we may vary the way in which preferences are induced from judgment sets or we may assume that the manipulator is only interested in some of the formulas in the agenda.

---

[15] Given that for distance-based aggregators the winner determination problem is already intractable, questions regarding the complexity of manipulation are considerably less interesting here.

17.4 Agenda Characterization Results

Suppose we are given an agenda Φ and an aggregator f. Then we may want to ask: can we be certain that the outcome $f(J)$ will be consistent for every possible consistent profile $J \in \mathcal{J}(\Phi)^n$ over this agenda?

We want to answer such questions not only for one specific agenda Φ, but would like to be able to offer a full *characterization* of *all* agendas for which the answer is positive. In this section, we provide such characterizations in terms of *agenda properties* that tally the structural richness of an agenda. Going beyond individual aggregators f, we also prove agenda characterization results for *families of aggregators* $\mathcal{F}$, defined in terms of the axioms they satisfy. Such results come in two forms: *existential results* talk about conditions under which at least *some* aggregator in $\mathcal{F}$ is consistent, while *universal results* establish conditions under which *all* aggregators in $\mathcal{F}$ are. For the latter, in particular, a relevant question is how difficult it is to verify whether a given agenda satisfies certain agenda properties. Therefore, we briefly discuss the computational complexity of this problem.

17.4.1 Consistent Aggregation under the Majority Rule

In the introduction we have seen that for one specific aggregator and one specific agenda, namely, the majority rule and the agenda $\{p, \neg p, q, \neg q, p \wedge q, \neg(p \wedge q)\}$, we may encounter a discursive dilemma. That is, for this agenda it is possible to construct a consistent profile such that the majority rule will return a judgment set that is inconsistent. In Section 17.2.4 we have seen a generalization of this insight: the problem persists for any aggregator belonging to an entire *class of aggregators* (cf. Theorem 17.2). We now want to discuss a different generalization and ask: what is the *class of agendas* for which the majority rule has this deficiency?

Intuitively speaking, the discursive dilemma comes about when there is an inconsistent subset $X \subseteq \Phi$, such that each judge accepts *sufficiently few* of the formulas in X to be individually consistent, but at the same time *sufficiently many* to ensure that every formula in X gathers a majority. That is, the *size* of inconsistent sets, or more precisely *minimally inconsistent sets*, that we can build from the formulas in the agenda seems to matter. We say that an agenda Φ satisfies the *median property* if every inconsistent subset of Φ does itself have an inconsistent subset of size at most 2.[16] For example, the agenda $\{p, \neg p, q, \neg q, p \wedge q, \neg(p \wedge q)\}$ does not have the median property, because one of its minimally inconsistent subsets, namely, $\{p, q, \neg(p \wedge q)\}$, has three elements. This agenda property allows us to give a full characterization of the agendas on which the majority rule is consistent:

Lemma 17.12 (Nehring and Puppe, 2007). *The majority rule is consistent for a given agenda Φ if and only if Φ has the median property.*

Proof. The right-to-left direction is an instance of Proposition 17.3 for $k = 2$, because Φ having the median property means that the largest minimally inconsistent subset of

---

[16] The term *median property* is due to Nehring and Puppe (2007), who coined this term in the context of work on social choice theory over a class of vector spaces known as median spaces. Agendas that satisfy the median property are sometimes also called *simple* agendas.

Φ has at most size 2. For the other direction, let Φ be an agenda that violates the median property, that is, there exists a minimally inconsistent set $X = \{\varphi_1, \ldots, \varphi_k\} \subseteq \Phi$ with $k \geqslant 3$. Now consider the profile J, in which judge i accepts all formulas in X except for $\varphi_{1+(i \bmod 3)}$. Note that J is consistent. But the majority rule will accept all formulas in X, that is, $f_{\text{maj}}(J)$ is inconsistent. $\square$

Deciding whether a given agenda has the median property is Π_2^P-complete (Endriss et al., 2012). Π_2^P, a complexity class located at the second level of the polynomial hierarchy, is the class of decision problems for which a certificate for a negative answer can be verified in polynomial time by a machine that has access to an oracle for answering NP-complete problems in an instant. Deciding whether a quantified Boolean formula of the form $\forall x_1 \cdots \forall x_n \exists y_1 \cdots \exists y_m \varphi$ is true is the canonical example of a problem that is complete for this class. Π_2^P includes the other complexity classes featuring in this chapter, particularly NP and Θ_2^P (and this inclusion is believed, but not known, to be proper).

Thus, we have a doubly negative result: not only do we have to restrict ourselves to highly simplistic agendas if we want to be certain to avoid instances of the discursive dilemma (this is the import of Lemma 17.12), but on top of this determining whether a given agenda is sufficiently simplistic is very difficult.

17.4.2 Existential Agenda Characterization

Next we want to go beyond specific aggregators (such as the majority rule), and instead prove agenda characterization results for *classes* of aggregators, defined in terms of certain axioms. For the first such result we take the axioms defining the majority rule (cf. Corollary 17.6), except that we substantially weaken anonymity and instead only require that our aggregator is not a dictatorship. Formally, an aggregator f is a *dictatorship* if there exists an individual $i^\star \in N$ (the dictator) such that $f(J) = J_{i^\star}$ for every profile J; otherwise f is *nondictatorial*.[17] Lemma 17.12 shows that only agendas with the median property guarantee consistent outcomes under the majority rule. We will now see that, even if we allow ourselves to pick freely from the much larger class of aggregators we obtain when we replace anonymity by nondictatoriality, we cannot do better than that.

Before we state this result formally, let us say something about the technique we are going to use to prove it. Recall that any independent and neutral aggregator is defined by a family $\mathcal{W} \subseteq 2^N$ of winning coalitions (cf. Lemma 17.1). In mathematics, a set $\mathcal{W}$ of subsets of a set N is called an *ultrafilter* if it satisfies the following three conditions (see, e.g., Davey and Priestley, 2002):[18]

(*i*) $\mathcal{W}$ does not include the empty set: $\emptyset \notin \mathcal{W}$.
(*ii*) $\mathcal{W}$ is closed under taking intersections: $C \in \mathcal{W}$ and $C' \in \mathcal{W}$ entail $C \cap C' \in \mathcal{W}$ for all $C, C' \subseteq N$.
(*iii*) $\mathcal{W}$ is maximal: $C \in \mathcal{W}$ or $\overline{C} \in \mathcal{W}$ for all $C \subseteq N$.

---

[17] To appreciate that anonymity really is much stronger than nondictatoriality, observe that the former rules out all weighted majority rules, while the latter does not.

[18] Sometimes being upward closed is stated as a fourth defining condition of an ultrafilter. But note that we do not need to do so, as this already follows from the other three conditions.

An ultrafilter is called *principal* if it is of the form $\mathcal{W} = \{C \subseteq N \mid i^\star \in C\}$ for some $i^\star \in N$. By a well-known fact, every ultrafilter $\mathcal{W}$ on a *finite* set N is principal (Davey and Priestley, 2002).[19] Translating back into the world of winning coalitions, this means that if we can show that the set $\mathcal{W}$ of winning coalitions corresponding to a given (independent and neutral) aggregator f meets the three preceding conditions, then, given that the set N of judges is finite, f must be dictatorial (with the principal element $i^\star$ of the ultrafilter being the dictator).

We are now ready to prove a first important existential agenda characterization theorem, for a class of aggregators defined by a natural combination of axioms:

Theorem 17.13 (Nehring and Puppe, 2007). *There exists a neutral, independent, monotonic, and nondictatorial aggregator that is complete and consistent for a given agenda Φ if and only if Φ has the median property.*

Proof. The right-to-left direction follows from Lemma 17.12: if Φ has the median property, then the majority rule is consistent (and the majority rule is also neutral, independent, monotonic, nondictatorial, and complete).

The left-to-right direction in effect establishes an impossibility result. It is equivalent to the following claim: if a given neutral, independent, and monotonic aggregator f is complete and consistent (and thus also complement-free) for a given agenda Φ that violates the median property, then f must be a dictatorship. By Lemma 17.1, neutrality and independence mean that f is determined by a single family $\mathcal{W}$ of winning coalitions. Let us show that $\mathcal{W}$ must be an ultrafilter on N:

(i) $\emptyset \notin \mathcal{W}$: If we had $\emptyset \in \mathcal{W}$, then $N \in \mathcal{W}$ by monotonicity (because $\emptyset \subseteq N$), which is in direct conflict with the requirement of being complement-free (as $\overline{\emptyset} = N$).

(ii) $\mathcal{W}$ is closed under taking intersections: This will be the (only) part in the proof where we make use of the assumption that Φ violates the median property. The median property being violated means that there exists a minimally inconsistent subset $X = \{\varphi_1, \ldots, \varphi_k\} \subseteq \Phi$ with $k \geqslant 3$. Take any two winning coalitions $C, C' \in \mathcal{W}$. (We need to show that $C \cap C' \in \mathcal{W}$.) Observe that it is possible to construct a complete and consistent profile $\boldsymbol{J}$ with the following properties:

- $N^{\boldsymbol{J}}_{\varphi_1} = C$
- $N^{\boldsymbol{J}}_{\varphi_2} = C' \cup (N \setminus C)$
- $N^{\boldsymbol{J}}_{\varphi_3} = N \setminus (C \cap C')$
- $N^{\boldsymbol{J}}_{\varphi_\ell} = N$ for all ℓ with $4 \leqslant \ell \leqslant k$

That is, each judge accepts exactly $k-1$ of the formulas in X (which means that every judge is consistent). Note that $N^{\boldsymbol{J}}_{\sim\varphi_3} = C \cap C'$. Now, C being winning implies $\varphi_1 \in f(\boldsymbol{J})$. By monotonicity, any superset of C' is winning, including $C' \cup (N \setminus C)$. The latter implies $\varphi_2 \in f(\boldsymbol{J})$. Finally, from $\emptyset \notin \mathcal{W}$ we get $N \in \mathcal{W}$ (i.e., f is unanimous) and therefore all judges accepting all of $X \setminus \{\varphi_1, \varphi_2, \varphi_3\}$ entails $X \setminus \{\varphi_1, \varphi_2, \varphi_3\} \subseteq$

---

[19] The proof is immediate: Let $C^\star := \bigcap_{C \in \mathcal{W}} C$. As N is finite, we can apply (ii) inductively and obtain $C^\star \in \mathcal{W}$. By construction, $C^\star$ must be the smallest element of $\mathcal{W}$. If we can show that $C^\star$ is a singleton, then we are done. First, by (i), $C^\star \neq \emptyset$. Second, for the sake of contradiction, suppose $|C^\star| \geqslant 2$. Take any nonempty proper subset C of $C^\star$. By (iii), either $C \in \mathcal{W}$ or $\overline{C} \in \mathcal{W}$. If it is the latter, then from (ii) and $C^\star \in \mathcal{W}$ we get $C^\star \cap \overline{C} = C^\star \setminus C \in \mathcal{W}$. Hence, in either case a proper subset of $C^\star$ must be an element of $\mathcal{W}$. This is the required contradiction and concludes the proof.

$f(\boldsymbol{J})$. Taken together, this means $X \setminus \{\varphi_3\} \subseteq f(\boldsymbol{J})$. Thus, to ensure consistency of the outcome, we must have $\varphi_3 \notin f(\boldsymbol{J})$. But then, to ensure completeness, we are forced to accept $\sim\varphi_3 \in f(\boldsymbol{J})$. That is, we are forced to accept a formula that was accepted by precisely the judges in the intersection $C \cap C'$. In other words, $C \cap C'$ is winning, that is, $C \cap C' \in \mathcal{W}$.

(*iii*) $\mathcal{W}$ is maximal: This follows immediately from completeness (cf. Lemma 17.1).

As N is finite, $\mathcal{W}$ must in fact be a principal ultrafilter. But we have already seen that this is equivalent to f being dictatorial, so we are done. $\qquad\square$

The ultrafilter method is very powerful. We will see one more example of its use. Our next theorem concerns independent and unanimous aggregators. The most important difference is that this time we do not want to assume neutrality, that is, we cannot work with a single family $\mathcal{W}$ of winning coalitions from the outset. To still make the ultrafilter method applicable, we have to *derive* neutrality. As we shall see, this is possible for agendas that are sufficiently rich. Merely violating the median property is not sufficient: for example, if the positive formulas in the agenda are $\{p, q, p \wedge q, r\}$, then the aggregator under which judge 1 dictates the outcome for $\{p, q, p \wedge q\}$ and r is decided upon by majority is nondictatorial, independent, and unanimous. That is, we require an agenda with sufficiently strong connections between its formulas to rule out such "localized" aggregators.

Write $\varphi \overset{\Phi}{\to} \psi$ in case there exists a minimally inconsistent set $X \subseteq \Phi$ with $\varphi, \sim\psi \in X$. This notation indicates that, in the context of the remaining formulas in X, accepting φ forces us to also accept ψ. Let $\overset{\Phi}{\Rightarrow}$ be the transitive closure of $\overset{\Phi}{\to}$. An agenda Φ is called *totally blocked* if $\varphi \overset{\Phi}{\Rightarrow} \psi$ for every two formulas $\varphi, \psi \in \Phi$.

Lemma 17.14 (Neutrality). *Every unanimous and independent aggregator f that is complete and consistent for a totally blocked agenda Φ is neutral.*

Proof. Let Φ be a totally blocked agenda and let f be a unanimous and independent aggregator that is complete and consistent for Φ. By independence, for each $\varphi \in \Phi$ there exists a $\mathcal{W}_\varphi \subseteq N$ such that $\varphi \in f(\boldsymbol{J}) \Leftrightarrow N_\varphi^{\boldsymbol{J}} \in \mathcal{W}_\varphi$ for all profiles $\boldsymbol{J}$.

Consider two formulas $\varphi, \psi \in \Phi$ such that $\varphi \overset{\Phi}{\to} \psi$. We show that this implies $\mathcal{W}_\varphi \subseteq \mathcal{W}_\psi$: Let X be the minimally inconsistent set establishing $\varphi \overset{\Phi}{\to} \psi$. Take any winning coalition $C \in \mathcal{W}_\varphi$. Construct a complete and consistent profile $\boldsymbol{J}$ in which all judges accept all of $X \setminus \{\varphi, \sim\psi\}$, those in C also accept φ and ψ, and the rest also accept $\sim\varphi$ and $\sim\psi$. By unanimity, $X \setminus \{\varphi, \sim\psi\} \subseteq f(\boldsymbol{J})$. Due to $C \in \mathcal{W}_\varphi$, furthermore $\varphi \in f(\boldsymbol{J})$. Hence, consistency forces $\sim\psi \notin f(\boldsymbol{J})$ and thus completeness forces $\psi \in f(\boldsymbol{J})$. As it was exactly the judges in C who accepted ψ, this means that C is also a winning coalition for ψ, that is, $C \in \mathcal{W}_\psi$.

Now, by induction, not only $\varphi \overset{\Phi}{\to} \psi$ implies $\mathcal{W}_\varphi \subseteq \mathcal{W}_\psi$, but also $\varphi \overset{\Phi}{\Rightarrow} \psi$ implies $\mathcal{W}_\varphi \subseteq \mathcal{W}_\psi$. Total blockedness means that $\varphi \overset{\Phi}{\Rightarrow} \psi$ for all $\varphi, \psi \in \Phi$. Hence, $\mathcal{W}_\varphi = \mathcal{W}_\psi$ for all $\varphi, \psi \in \Phi$, that is, by Lemma 17.1, f is indeed neutral. $\qquad\square$

We require one further agenda property: Φ is *even-number-negatable* if it has a minimally inconsistent subset X for which $(X \setminus Y) \cup \{\sim\varphi \mid \varphi \in Y\}$ is consistent for some set $Y \subset X$ of even cardinality. Any minimally inconsistent set X can be made consistent by flipping exactly one of its elements; even-number-negatability requires that for at least one X we can also get consistency by flipping an even number of formulas in X. The agenda property used in the following theorem is intuitively weaker than the median property used in Theorem 17.13. This is exactly what we would expect, as the axioms we impose are also weaker.

Theorem 17.15 (Dokow and Holzman, 2010). *There exists a unanimous, independent, and nondictatorial aggregator that is complete and consistent for a given agenda Φ if and only if Φ is not both totally blocked and even-number-negatable.*

Proof. For the right-to-left direction, for any agenda Φ that is either not totally blocked or not even-number-negatable, we show how to construct an aggregator that meets our requirements.

First, suppose Φ is *not totally blocked*. Then we can partition Φ into two disjoint sets Φ_1 and Φ_2 (i.e., $\Phi_1 \cup \Phi_2 = \Phi$ and $\Phi_1 \cap \Phi_2 = \emptyset$) such that there exist no $\varphi_1 \in \Phi_1$ and $\varphi_2 \in \Phi_2$ with $\varphi_1 \overset{\Phi}{\Rightarrow} \varphi_2$. We use this partition to define an aggregator f: judge 1 dictates acceptance for formulas φ with $\{\varphi, \sim\varphi\} \subseteq \Phi_1$; judge 2 dictates acceptance for formulas φ with $\{\varphi, \sim\varphi\} \subseteq \Phi_2$; and for formulas φ with $\varphi \in \Phi_1$ and $\sim\varphi \in \Phi_2$ we accept φ unless there is unanimous support for $\sim\varphi$. This rule is easily seen to be unanimous, independent, nondictatorial, and complete. It also is consistent: For if not, there would be a profile for which f accepts some minimally inconsistent set X. But X cannot be fully included in Φ_1, as then judge 1 would be inconsistent. It cannot be fully included in Φ_2 either, as then judge 2 would be inconsistent. Finally, X cannot be split across Φ_1 and Φ_2: if $\sim\varphi_2 \in \Phi_1$ for all $\varphi_2 \in X \cap \Phi_2$, then all of $X \cap \Phi_2$ would have had to be accepted unanimously, meaning that judge 1 would have had to accept all of X (contradicting consistency of judge 1); and if $\sim\varphi_2 \in \Phi_2$ for some $\varphi_2 \in X \cap \Phi_2$, then $\varphi_1 \overset{\Phi}{\to} \sim\varphi_2$ for all $\varphi_1 \in X \cap \Phi_1$ (in contradiction to how the partition into Φ_1 and Φ_2 has been defined).

Second, suppose Φ is *not even-number-negatable*. Consider the *parity rule* f_{par} that accepts a formula if and only if an odd number of the judges does.[20] This rule clearly is unanimous, independent, nondictatorial, and complete. To show that it is also consistent we will make use of the fact that Φ is not even-number-negatable. Assume, for the sake of contradiction, that there exists a profile $\boldsymbol{J} \in \mathcal{J}(\Phi)$ for which $f_{\mathrm{par}}(\boldsymbol{J})$ is inconsistent. Let X be a minimally inconsistent subset of $f_{\mathrm{par}}(\boldsymbol{J})$. Suppose $|X|$ is odd (the case where $|X|$ is even works analogously). As Φ is not even-number-negatable, every set of the form $(X \setminus Y) \cup \{\sim\varphi \mid \varphi \in Y\}$ with $Y \subset X$ and $|Y|$ even must be inconsistent. Hence, every judge must accept a subset of X of even cardinality. So, if we sum over all judges, we obtain an *even* number of instances of an acceptance of an X-formula by a judge. On the other hand, by definition of f_{par}, each of the odd number of formulas in X must have been accepted by an odd number of judges, which implies that the overall number of acceptances of X-formulas must be *odd*. Thus, we obtain the desired contradiction.

---

[20] Here we will make use of our assumption that n, the total number of judges, is odd.

For the left-to-right direction, we have to prove that for any agenda Φ that is totally blocked and even-number-negatable, any aggregator f that is unanimous, independent, complete, and consistent must be dictatorial. As Φ is totally blocked we can apply Lemma 17.14 and infer that f must be neutral. As Φ is even-number-negatable, it is also *pair-negatable* in the sense that there must exist a minimally inconsistent set X such that $(X \setminus Y) \cup \{\sim\varphi \mid \varphi \in Y\}$ is consistent for some $Y \subset X$ of cardinality 2.[21] In other words, Φ has a minimally inconsistent subset X including at least three formulas $\varphi_1, \varphi_2, \varphi_3$ such that all of $(X \setminus \{\varphi_1\}) \cup \{\sim\varphi_1\}$, $(X \setminus \{\varphi_2\}) \cup \{\sim\varphi_2\}$, and $(X \setminus \{\varphi_1, \varphi_2\}) \cup \{\sim\varphi_1, \sim\varphi_2\}$ are consistent. In summary, we now have all the conditions of the left-to-right direction of Theorem 17.13 in place, except for monotonicity; and in addition we can make use of slightly stronger assumptions on Φ. Recall that the only points in the proof of Theorem 17.13 where we required monotonicity were the derivations of the first two ultrafilter conditions. The first of them, $\emptyset \notin \mathcal{W}$, can instead be inferred from maximality, the third ultrafilter condition, together with $N \in \mathcal{W}$ (which follows from unanimity). We are left with establishing the second ultrafilter condition, closure under taking intersections. Take any two winning coalitions $C, C' \in \mathcal{W}$. We can construct a complete and consistent profile J with $N_{\varphi_1}^J = C$, $N_{\varphi_2}^J = C'$, $N_{\varphi_3}^J = N \setminus (C \cap C')$, and $N_{\varphi}^J = N$ for all $\varphi \in X \setminus \{\varphi_1, \varphi_2, \varphi_3\}$. Observe that this slightly simplified construction was not available to us in the proof of Theorem 17.13, because in the absence of pair-negatability we would have had no guarantee that the judgment set of judges in $N \setminus (C \cap C')$, missing two of the formulas in X, is consistent. Now φ_1 gets accepted by virtue of C being winning, φ_2 gets accepted by virtue of C' being winning, and all of $X \setminus \{\varphi_1, \varphi_2, \varphi_3\}$ get accepted by virtue of unanimity. So we must reject φ_3 and thus accept $\sim\varphi_3$. But it is exactly the judges in $C \cap C'$ who support $\sim\varphi_3$, so $C \cap C'$ must be winning. $\square$

Interestingly, independence and unanimity are also the core axioms in *Arrow's Theorem* in preference aggregation (Arrow, 1963). Indeed, using the embedding of preference aggregation into JA sketched in Section 17.2.2, we can obtain a proof of Arrow's Theorem in the same way as we have shown the left-to-right direction of Theorem 17.15 (this involves showing that the preference agenda is both totally blocked and even-number-negatable). To be precise, the JA encoding given here allows individuals to, for instance, not accept the formulas for transitivity, while Arrow's Theorem applies even under the assumption that they always do. This can be accounted for by altering the underlying logic and adding the formulas expressing properties of preference orders as logical axioms on top of those of the propositional calculus, rather than including them in the agenda (Dietrich and List, 2007b).

17.4.3 Universal Agenda Characterization

Let us call an agenda Φ *safe* for a given aggregator f if $f(J)$ is consistent for every admissible profile $J \in \mathcal{J}(\Phi)^n$. That is, Theorems 17.13 and 17.15 talk about properties

---

[21] This may be proved as follows: Suppose Φ is even-number-negatable by virtue of X and Y, with $|Y| = k > 2$. If Φ is not also pair-negatable by virtue of X and some Y' with $|Y'| = 2$, then $(X \setminus \{\varphi_1, \varphi_2\}) \cup \{\sim\varphi_1, \sim\varphi_2\}$ for some $\varphi_1, \varphi_2 \in Y$ is also minimally inconsistent, and we get even-number-negatability by virtue of that set together with $Y \setminus \{\varphi_1, \varphi_2\}$ of cardinality $k - 2$. The claim then follows by induction on $|Y|$.

of agendas that guarantee safety for at least one aggregator from a given class. Now we want to establish conditions under which *every* aggregator of a given class guarantees safety. We will see one example of such a universal agenda characterization theorem. As is to be expected, the conditions we have to impose on our agendas will be more restrictive than for existential agenda characterization theorems. We shall work with a restriction of the median property: agenda Φ is said to satisfy the *simplified median property* if every nonsingleton minimally inconsistent subset of Φ consists of two formulas that are logical complements, that is, every such set is of the form $\{\varphi, \psi\}$ with $\models \varphi \leftrightarrow \neg\psi$.[22]

Theorem 17.16 (Endriss et al., 2012). *An agenda Φ is safe for all unanimous, anonymous, neutral, independent, complete and complement-free aggregators if and only if Φ has the simplified median property.*

Proof. First, suppose Φ has the simplified median property. Take any aggregator f that is unanimous, neutral, and complement-free (we will not need the other axioms) and for the sake of contradiction assume there exists a profile $J \in \mathcal{J}(\Phi)^n$ such that $f(J)$ is inconsistent. By unanimity and complement-freeness, this inconsistency cannot be due to a single inconsistent formula (as no judge would accept that formula), so we must have $\{\varphi, \psi\} \subseteq f(J)$ with $\models \varphi \leftrightarrow \neg\psi$ for some $\varphi, \psi \in \Phi$. By completeness and consistency of the profile, φ and $\sim\psi$ must be accepted by the same coalition. Thus, by neutrality, $\varphi \in f(J)$ implies $\sim\psi \in f(J)$, that is, $\{\psi, \sim\psi\} \subseteq f(J)$. But this contradicts complement-freeness of f. Hence, $f(J)$ cannot be inconsistent.

For the opposite direction, suppose Φ violates the simplified median property. If Φ also violates the (normal) median property, then we are done, as we already know that the majority rule is inconsistent (cf. Lemma 17.12) and satisfies all the required axioms (cf. Corollary 17.6). So, w.l.o.g., suppose Φ has a minimally inconsistent subset consisting of two formulas that are not logical complements, that is, there exist $\varphi, \psi \in \Phi$ with $\varphi \models \neg\psi$ but $\neg\psi \not\models \varphi$. But now consider the parity rule f_{par}, accepting all those formulas that are accepted by an odd number of judges. It is easy to see that f_{par} is unanimous (as n is odd), anonymous, neutral, independent, complete and complement-free. However, f_{par} is not safe: If one judge accepts (the consistent set) $\{\varphi, \sim\psi\}$, one judge accepts (the consistent set) $\{\sim\varphi, \psi\}$, and all other judges (an odd number) accept (the consistent set) $\{\sim\varphi, \sim\psi\}$, then f will accept the inconsistent set $\{\varphi, \psi\}$. This concludes the proof. $\square$

Let us consider two examples. First, an agenda that consists solely of literals satisfies the simplified median property. Thus, any such agenda will be safe, not only for the majority rule, but for every aggregator that meets the axioms of Theorem 17.16. Second, consider the agenda $\{p, \neg p, p \wedge q, \neg(p \wedge q), r, \neg r\}$, which violates the simplified median property, and the following profile:

---

[22] An example of a set that satisfies the median property but not the simplified median property is $\{\neg p, p \wedge q\}$: the two formulas together are inconsistent, but they are not logical complements.

	p	$p \wedge q$	r
Judge 1:	Yes	Yes	Yes
Judge 2:	No	No	Yes
Judge 3:	Yes	No	Yes

All three judgment sets are consistent. Yet, if we aggregate using the parity rule f_{par}, we have to reject p but accept $p \wedge q$, which corresponds to an inconsistent judgement set. Thus, as predicted by Theorem 17.16, our agenda is not safe for f_{par}.

Suppose we have some limited information on the method of aggregation a group of agents is going to use (e.g., we might know that they will respect certain axioms). Results such as Theorem 17.16 allow us to give consistency guarantees in such situations. Unfortunately, however, respecting the simplified median property severely limits the expressive power of the JA framework, and verifying whether a given agenda satisfies the simplified median property is computationally intractable; more specifically, this problem is Π_2^p-complete (Endriss et al., 2012).

To conclude our discussion of agenda characterization results, let us briefly compare existential and universal theorems. For a given class $\mathcal{F}$ of aggregators, the former speak about agenda properties ensuring *some* aggregators in $\mathcal{F}$ are consistent, while the latter speak about agenda properties ensuring that *all* of them are.[23] The former is a natural question from the perspective of economics. For instance, a mechanism designer who is working in a specific application domain (determining the agenda properties) and who wants to respect certain axioms (determining $\mathcal{F}$), must ask this question to find out whether her desiderata are feasible. The latter problem is more likely to surface in computer science. For instance, a system designer may only have partial knowledge of the decision making methods employed by the users of a platform she is providing (say, enough to determine $\mathcal{F}$, but not enough to single out a specific aggregator), but still wants to be able to issue guarantees against inconsistencies in the agreements forged over this platform.

17.5 Related Frameworks

In this section, we briefly review three approaches to collective decision making that are closely related to JA, namely, belief merging, binary aggregation, and voting in combinatorial domains.

17.5.1 Belief Merging

In computer science, specifically in artificial intelligence and database theory, the problem of *belief merging* had been investigated already some time before the emergence of the modern literature on JA in philosophy and economics (see, e.g., Baral et al., 1992; Liberatore and Schaerf, 1998; Konieczny and Pino Pérez, 2002). Suppose we are given

---

[23] If $\mathcal{F}$ is a singleton, then the two notions coincide, as for Lemma 17.12.

several knowledge bases encoding knowledge provided by experts in a logical language and we want to integrate these individual bases to obtain a large overall knowledge base. The naïve approach of simply taking the union of all individual bases will, in most cases, lead to an inconsistent knowledge base. One possible refinement is to choose a maximally consistent subset of the union (Baral et al., 1992), but this and similar approaches do not track which individual provided which formulas in the knowledge base, that is, it is not possible to give equal weight to different individuals. The latter is possible using distance-based procedures (Konieczny and Pino Pérez, 2002), which are also briefly discussed in Chapter 9.

There are important differences between JA and typical work in belief merging. In JA we have an *agenda* and we usually assume that every individual expresses a judgment regarding every formula in the agenda, while in belief merging the knowledge/belief bases coming from distinct individuals need not concern the same set of formulas. Furthermore, in JA we (implicitly) impose the same constraints on different individuals and the collective, while in belief merging we typically impose an *integrity constraint* to be satisfied by the merged base that need not be satisfied by every individual base. Like in JA, work in belief merging often evokes the notion of "*axiom*" to define what makes a good procedure for merging, but most of the axioms used in the literature are inspired by work in *belief revision* (and typically are "outcome-oriented," talking about consistency requirements) rather than social choice theory (where axioms tend to have more of an "agent-oriented" flavor).

17.5.2 Binary Aggregation

Binary aggregation (see, e.g., Dokow and Holzman, 2010; Grandi and Endriss, 2013) has its origins in the work of Wilson (1975) and Rubinstein and Fishburn (1986) on abstract (algebraic) aggregation. In binary aggregation, each individual is asked to supply a vector of 0's and 1's of some fixed length, and we then have to aggregate this information into a single such vector. The application domain under consideration determines which vectors are *feasible*. This is very closely related to the formula-based framework of JA we have discussed in this chapter. For example, if the set of feasible vectors is $\{000, 010, 100, 111\}$, then this induces the same domain of aggregation as the agenda formulas p, q, and $p \wedge q$. In fact, in the literature the term "judgment aggregation" is sometimes taken to encompass both JA in the narrow sense (i.e., formula-based JA) and binary aggregation.

In the economics literature the set of feasible vectors is usually assumed to be specified explicitly (Dokow and Holzman, 2010), while in the computer science literature the set of feasible vectors is usually defined implicitly by means of an *integrity constraint* expressed in the language of propositional logic (Grandi and Endriss, 2013). For example, the integrity constraint $x_1 \wedge x_2 \wedge x_3 \leftrightarrow x_4$ defines the domain $\{0000, 0010, 0100, 0110, 1000, 1010, 1100, 1111\}$. The advantage of using integrity constraints is that they provide a *compact representation* of the domain of aggregation, which is important when we are interested in algorithmic aspects of aggregation. Integrity constraints also allow for alternative characterizations of aggregators. For instance, an aggregator is unanimous if and only if it maps feasible profiles to feasible outcomes for every integrity constraint expressible as a conjunction of literals; and the only aggregators that "lifts" *all* possible integrity constraints in this sense are the *generalized dictatorships*, that is, those aggregators that amount to first selecting one of the individuals and then copying that individual's input vector to produce the output (Grandi and Endriss, 2013).

17.5.3 Voting in Combinatorial Domains

When voting on complex matters, such as the composition of a committee or the outcome of a referendum involving a set of proposals, each of which has to be either accepted or rejected, we face problems not dissimilar to those faced in JA. In such a *multiattribute election* we have a number of variables, each ranging over a finite domain, and we ask each voter for her preferences regarding the assignment of values to these variables. For instance, in the committee example the variables are the seats on the committee and the values are the candidates. When each variable is binary (as is the case for referenda), we obtain a similar problem as in binary aggregation. However, a crucial difference is that in binary aggregation we assume that each individual can only communicate one vector (i.e., one set of variable assignments), while in general we may ask each individual to report a complex preference structure over the set of all possible outcomes. This raises interesting questions, not only regarding the aggregation of such information, but also regarding the compact representation of the preferences themselves.

Such questions are studied in the field of *voting in combinatorial domains*. Chapter 9 is devoted to this important topic.

17.6　Applications in Computer Science

In the introduction we have already alluded to the fact that JA has important applications in analytical jurisprudence and political philosophy. We want to conclude this chapter with a few words about possible *applications in computer science*. Maybe the most important of these, and certainly the one most often quoted as an example, is collective decision making in systems of autonomous software agents. In such a *multiagent system* we have several agents, which may have been designed and programmed by different developers and which may act on behalf of different users, and these agents need to interact, both cooperating and competing with each other. Social choice theory is part of the basic repertoire available for modeling the fundamental features of multiagent systems (Wooldridge, 2009; Shoham and Leyton-Brown, 2009). Given that important aspects of the agents themselves, such as their beliefs or goals, are often represented using logic, JA is a useful formalism for modeling agreements made by those agents.

Another important formal tool for modeling the dynamics of multiagent systems is the theory of *abstract argumentation*, widely studied in artificial intelligence, which is concerned with high-level representations of the relationships that hold between arguments for and against a given position. Given a network of arguments together with information on which argument attacks which other argument, different agents may hold competing views on which arguments to accept. JA then is a useful framework for modeling the process of finding a common view in such situations (see, e.g., Caminada and Pigozzi, 2011).

Besides multiagent systems, another potential application for JA is *information merging*, for example, the merging of knowledge bases provided by different experts briefly discussed in Section 17.5.1. This includes the merging of *ontologies*, which play a central role in the development of the Semantic Web (Porello and Endriss, 2011).

JA and particularly the closely related binary aggregation are also relevant to *crowdsourcing*. Several areas in or related to computer science, such as, computer vision or computational linguistics, rely on the availability of annotated data, such as images labeled with object names or text corpora annotated with semantic information. Crowdsourcing platforms provide fast and cheap means for labeling large amounts of data using nonexpert annotators. The annotations provided by different workers then need to be aggregated to obtain a collective annotation, a task that shares many similarities with JA (Endriss and Fernández, 2013).

It is important to stress that, at the time of writing, none of the applications of JA sketched here has been developed in depth. Still, JA certainly holds great potential for these, as well as other, areas of computer science.

17.7 Bibliographic Notes and Further Reading

In this section we supply additional bibliographic references and explanations regarding some of the material covered in this chapter. We also provide pointers to further reading on specific topics. Let us begin by pointing out that, while research on JA *proper* started with the work of List and Pettit (2002), the work of Guilbaud (1952) on what he called "the logical problem of aggregation" may be considered an early precursor of JA (Eckert and Monjardet, 2010).

Following the publication of the original impossibility theorem of List and Pettit (our Theorem 17.2), several other authors derived technically stronger results of a similar nature, replacing in particular anonymity by absence of dictatorships (see, e.g., Pauly and van Hees, 2006; Dietrich, 2007). Gärdenfors (2006) showed that giving up the requirement of completeness amounts to moving from dictatorships to oligarchic aggregators, that is, aggregators where the outcome is the set of those propositions a fixed set of individuals completely agrees on (dictatorships and the intersection rule are extreme cases of such oligarchic rules). We refer to List (2012) for a systematic discussion on how to cope with impossibility results by relaxing certain desiderata, and to Grossi and Pigozzi (2014) for an in-depth discussion of proofs of impossibility results using the ultrafilter method.

In work integrating the classical axiomatic method with ideas from computer science, Nehama (2013) showed that relaxing the cornerstones of most impossibility theorems, consistency and independence, to *approximate* variants of these desiderata does not allow us to significantly improve on known negative results.

The simulation of preference aggregation in JA sketched in Section 17.2.2 follows Dietrich and List (2007b), who for notational convenience use predicate rather than just propositional logic (which, as we have seen, is not technically required). Also the idea of deriving Arrow's Theorem from results in JA, as briefly mentioned at the end of the Section 17.4.2, is due to Dietrich and List (2007b).

While initial work in JA had focused on impossibility results and the axiomatic method, work on the design of concrete practically useful methods of aggregation only started several years later. Distance-based methods originally entered JA via the field of belief merging (Revesz, 1997; Konieczny and Pino Pérez, 2002; Pigozzi, 2006). We have only discussed two such methods here; several others are analyzed in the work of Miller and Osherson (2009), Lang et al. (2011), and Lang and Slavkovik (2013). The premise-based rule has been part of the JA literature from the very beginning, due to its importance in the context of legal decision making in practice (Kornhauser and Sager, 1993). Other approaches for designed JA rules not discussed here include *support-based methods* (Lang et al., 2011; Porello and Endriss, 2011; Everaere et al., 2014), where aggregation is guided by the numbers of judges accepting a given formula, methods inspired by *scoring rules* in voting theory (Dietrich, 2014), and methods that copy the choice of the judge that, in some sense, is the "*most representative*" in the group (Endriss and Grandi, 2014).

The analysis of strategic behavior is a major topic in social choice theory. As we have discussed in Section 17.3.3, how to best model an individual's preferences, and thus her incentives, is debatable in JA. Our definition of strategic manipulation in terms of preferences induced by the Hamming distance is but one possibility (Dietrich and List, 2007c; Baumeister et al., 2013b). Manipulation is not the only type of strategic behavior of interest in JA. Baumeister et al. (2011) have initiated a study of the computational complexity of related problems in JA, namely, bribery and control problem. For the former, we ask whether a given budget suffices to bribe sufficiently many judges to obtain a particular outcome. An example for a control problem is the question of whether we can obtain a given outcome by removing at most k judges. Alon et al. (2013) have focussed on a specific control problem, where we ask whether a desired outcome can be enforced by conducting separate elections for certain subsets of the agenda.

In Section 17.4, we have seen that the normal and the simplified median property are both Π_2^p-complete (Endriss et al., 2012). For most other commonly used agenda properties, at the time of writing, no complexity results are known.

The agenda characterization results in Section 17.4.2 have been adapted to our framework of formula-based JA from original results in binary aggregation (Dokow and Holzman, 2010) and the "property space" formulation of abstract aggregation (Nehring and Puppe, 2007). For a comprehensive review of existential agenda characterization results we refer to List and Puppe (2009). The ultrafilter method we employed in Section 17.4.2 is useful also in other areas of social choice theory, where it was pioneered by Kirman and Sondermann (1972).

Finally, JA uses logic to define the structure of the domain of aggregation. A broader review of uses of logic in computational social choice, for example, to describe properties of aggregators in a logical language or to use techniques from automated reasoning to support the verification or discovery of results in social choice theory, is available elsewhere (Endriss, 2011).

Acknowledgments

I would like to thank Dorothea Baumeister, Franz Dietrich, Roosmarijn Goldbach, Umberto Grandi, Davide Grossi, Jérôme Lang, and Daniele Porello for their helpful feedback on earlier versions of this chapter.

CHAPTER 18

The Axiomatic Approach and the Internet

Moshe Tennenholtz and Aviv Zohar

18.1 Introduction

The Internet reinforces types of multiagent systems which can effectively utilize this new media. Reputation systems, ranking systems, trust systems, recommendation systems, affiliate marketing in social networks, and more, are flowering in its midst. This recent wave of online social systems is typically associated with a large amount of data that is collected online, which leads to the "big data" approach to the utilization of such information. Quite surprisingly, however, the abundance of available data does not help system designers to come up with the right design for online systems in the first place. Indeed, available data is typically generated by the use of a particular system, and mining the data generated by users while interacting with one system does not provide a tool for exploring the overwhelmingly large design space. Interestingly, the main practical approach to software and hardware design, the formal specification of clear system requirements and the implementation of a system satisfying these exact requirements, has not been used often. This classical approach, when adapted to the context of multiagent systems, coincides with extensions of a standard tool of social choice theory and cooperative game theory, namely, *the axiomatic approach*.

The use of axioms can be either in a descriptive or in a normative context. In both cases basic properties of a system are phrased as axioms. In the descriptive approach a basic set of properties of a known system is sought out, with the aim of finding one that characterizes the system uniquely, hence teaching us much about its essence. The normative approach, on the other hand, starts from a specification of a basic set of requirements which is followed by an attempt to construct a system that satisfies them. Our goal in this chapter is to demonstrate both approaches in the context of the Internet.

Perhaps the best known axiomatic theory in the social sciences is the theory of social choice. In the classical social choice setting we have a set of voters and a set of alternatives, where each voter has a ranking over the set of alternatives, and our aim is to find a good aggregation of the individual rankings into a global (or social) ranking. Various properties of such aggregation functions have been considered and have led to different characterizations of particular systems as well as impossibility results showing no system can satisfy certain sets of properties all at once. In the Internet setting, the study of ranking and reputation systems, such as page-ranking systems, defines a natural extension of classical social choice to the case where the set of voters and the set of alternatives coincide. For example, in graph ranking systems, one wishes to obtain a ranking of the nodes based on the structure of the graph. In this case, the nodes in the graph serve the dual role of both the voters and of the objects being ranked, with their outgoing edges determining their votes. In a particular application, the nodes can represent Internet pages and the search for an aggregated ordering of the pages is in fact the page ranking problem. The edges which are formed from the links between the pages represent votes in support of the page being linked to. In such a setting the classical axioms of social choice become less relevant, and are replaced with new axioms which lead to a completely new theory. Indeed, we will use the axiomatic approach in the context of graph ranking systems, applicable to page ranking algorithms, as our first illustrative study. In particular, we will present an axiomatic treatment of the classical PageRank algorithm.

Further removed from direct extensions of social choice, one can find systems originating from personalized versions of ranking and reputation systems. Here we no longer consider the aggregation of preferences into a global or social ranking, but instead seek to provide personalized rankings or recommendations to each agent. Such recommendations are still aggregate measures, based on trust between agents and their own local rankings. Examples of these extensions include trust systems in which we aim to derive an agent's trust toward other agents he does not directly know based on the aggregate of localized trust-relationships between agents in the system. The designer is then faced with questions like the following that define the way trust should be used in the system: Who should an agent trust more, a participant which is unknown to others and whom the agent alone trusts directly, or an agent who is trusted only indirectly but by many trustworthy sources? Perhaps even more interestingly, what is the best way to aggregate both measures of trust and of preference? Based on trust-relationships among the agents, and their expressed opinions about a service or a product, we may be interested in *trust-based recommendation systems*, in which a recommendation about a service or a product is provided to agents who did not evaluate it personally. The puzzling challenge of generating useful trust-based recommendation systems is amenable to an axiomatic treatment, beginning with an attempt to characterize the systems satisfying different sets of desired properties. We will use trust-based recommendation systems as our second illustrative study as they show how the spirit of axiomatic social choice can be brought into personalized systems and not only to global preference aggregation.

In addition to the two application areas mentioned earlier, other domains for which axiomatic approaches have been suggested can be viewed as extensions of topics typically covered in cooperative game theory. Cooperative game theory typically deals with issues such as the distribution of monetary gains or the attribution of credit to participating agents. Traditional solution concepts used in cooperative games such as the Shapley value, which originate from a purely axiomatic treatment, aim to tackle such issues. These, however, do not immediately extend to the design of practical incentive and credit distribution systems that are found in some of the emerging settings on the Internet. An illuminating study in this context is the axiomatic approach to multilevel marketing (also known as affiliate marketing). In this form of marketing, which is facilitated by social networks, products may be sold through referrals generated by previous customers. Affiliate marketing systems offer credit in exchange for such referrals (especially for successful ones). We will use the axiomatic approach to multilevel marketing as our third illustrative study.

In this chapter we have selected to focus on the preceding illustrative studies, showing technical details of the related axiomatic approaches, but omitting most of the proofs. We add some informal discussion of complementary treatments such as the normative approach to ranking systems and axiomatic treatments of personalized trust systems at the end of the chapter.

We believe the axiomatic approach is one of the fundamental messages theory brings to the flowering industry designing Internet mechanisms in the multiagent context. While the recent trend in the research and design of social systems is to employ data mining heavily because "data is everywhere," this approach alone is not informative enough to design new systems from scratch, but rather leads to ad-hoc design that is only incrementally improved by mining data and revising the system. The axiomatic approach is a solid complementary alternative, and the illustration of its power in the preceding settings, augmented with its conceptual depth, provides clear evidence for that.

18.2 An Axiomatic Characterization of PageRank

The ranking of agents based on other agents' input is fundamental to Internet-based systems (see, e.g., Resnick et al., 2000), and has become a central ingredient of a variety of sites, where perhaps the most famous examples are Google's PageRank algorithm (Page et al., 1998) which ranks web pages, and eBay's reputation system (Resnick and Zeckhauser, 2001) in which both buyers and sellers are ranked based on trustworthiness.

In the classical theory of social choice, as manifested by Arrow (1950), a set of voters is called upon to rank a set of alternatives. Given the agents' input, that is, the agents' individual rankings, a social ranking of the alternatives is generated. The theory studies desired properties of the aggregation of agents' rankings into a social ranking.

The setting of ranking systems introduces a new social choice model. The novel feature of this setting is that the set of agents and the set of alternatives *coincide*. Therefore, in such a setting one may need to consider the transitive effects of voting. For example, if agent a reports on the importance of (i.e., votes for) agent b then this may influence the credibility of a report by b on the importance of agent c; these indirect effects should be considered when we wish to aggregate the information provided by the agents into a social ranking.

A natural interpretation of this setting is the ranking of Internet pages. In this case, the set of agents represents the set of Internet pages, and the links from a page p to a set of pages Q can be viewed as a two-level ranking where agents in Q are preferred by p over pages which are not in Q. The problem of finding an appropriate social ranking in this case is in fact the problem of (global) page ranking. Particular approaches for obtaining a useful page ranking and to quantify the so called importance of web pages using the link structure have been implemented by search engines (Page et al., 1998).

Due to Arrow-like impossibility results and inspiration from the page ranking setting, we limit the discussion to ranking systems in which agents have dichotomous preferences (see Bogomolnaia et al., 2005, for a discussion in the social choice setting). In these settings agents have only two levels of preferences: either they vote for some agent, or they do not.

18.2.1 Ranking Systems

We begin by formally defining the term "ranking system" in the context of graphs and linear orderings:

Definition 18.1. Let A be some set. A relation $R \subseteq A \times A$ is called a *linear ordering* on A if it is reflexive, transitive, antisymmetric, and complete. Let $\mathcal{L}(A)$ denote the set of all linear orderings on A.

Notation 18.1. Let $\preceq$ be a linear ordering, then $\sim$ is the equality predicate of $\preceq$, and $\prec$ is the strict order induced by $\preceq$. Formally, $a \sim b$ if and only if $a \preceq b$ and $b \preceq a$; and $a \prec b$ if and only if $a \preceq b$ but not $b \preceq a$.

Given the preceding, we can define a ranking system f, which for each graph G generates a ranking of its vertices.

Definition 18.2. Let $\mathbb{G}_V$ be the set of all directed graphs $G = (V, E)$ with no parallel edges, but possibly with self-loops. A *ranking system* f is a functional that for every finite vertex set V maps graphs $G \in \mathbb{G}_V$ to corresponding orderings $\preceq_G^f \in \mathcal{L}(V)$.

18.2.2 PageRank

In this section we present the PageRank algorithm, which among its many other uses forms the basis for Google's search technology[1] (Brin and Page, 1998).

The current practice of the ranking of Internet pages is based on the idea of computing the limit stationary probability distribution of a random walk on the Internet graph, where the nodes are pages, and the edges are links among the pages. Roughly speaking, page p_1 will be ranked higher than page p_2 if the probability of reaching p_1 is greater than the probability of reaching p_2.

The version of PageRank we present is slightly idealized form of the original algorithm. In its original form, small adaptations were included to deal with vertices without outgoing edges (sinks, and dangling vertices as they were called). In particular, in order for the result of that process to be well defined, we restrict our attention to strongly connected aperiodic graphs in which such corrections are not necessary.[2]

---

[1] Its use can indeed be found in other contexts. See Pinski and Narin (1976) for the use of PageRank-like procedure in the comparison of journals' impact, or Newman (2008) for its use as a measure of centrality in social network analysis studies.

[2] A graph is aperiodic if the greatest common divisor of its circles' lengths is 1. This is a common restriction which guarantees, along with strong connectivity, a unique limiting distribution for the Markov chain defined by the random walk process on a finite graph.

Definition 18.3. A directed graph $G = (V, E)$ is called *strongly connected* if for all vertices $v_1, v_2 \in V$ there exists a path from v_1 to v_2 in E.

In order to define the PageRank ranking system, we first recall the following standard definitions:

Definition 18.4. Let $G = (V, E)$ be a directed graph, and let $v \in V$ be a vertex in G. Then: The *successor set* of v is $S_G(v) = \{u | (v, u) \in E\}$, and the *predecessor set* of v is $P_G(v) = \{u | (u, v) \in E\}$.

We now define the PageRank matrix which is the matrix which captures the random walk created by the PageRank procedure. Namely, in this process we start in a random page, and iteratively move to one of the pages that are linked to by the current page, assigning equal probabilities to each such page.

Definition 18.5. Let $G = (V, E)$ be a directed graph, and assume $V = \{v_1, v_2, \ldots, v_n\}$. the *PageRank Matrix* A_G (of dimension $n \times n$) is defined as:

$$[A_G]_{i,j} = \begin{cases} 1/|S_G(v_j)| & (v_j, v_i) \in E \\ 0 & \text{Otherwise.} \end{cases}$$

The PageRank procedure will rank pages according to the stationary probability distribution obtained in the limit of the preceding random walk; this is formally defined as follows:

Definition 18.6. Let $G = (V, E)$ be some strongly connected graph, and assume $V = \{v_1, v_2, \ldots, v_n\}$. Let $\mathbf{r}$ be the unique solution of the system $A_G \cdot \mathbf{r} = \mathbf{r}$ where $r_1 = 1$.[3] The *PageRank* $PR_G(v_i)$ of a vertex $v_i \in V$ is defined as $PR_G(v_i) = r_i$. The *PageRank ranking system* is a ranking system that for the vertex set V maps G to $\preceq_G^{PR}$, where $\preceq_G^{PR}$ is defined as: for all $v_i, v_j \in V$: $v_i \preceq_G^{PR} v_j$ if and only if $PR_G(v_i) \leqslant PR_G(v_j)$.

The preceding defines a powerful heuristic for the ranking of Internet pages, as adopted by search engines (Page et al., 1998). This is, however, a particular numeric procedure, and another may have been chosen in its stead. We therefore treat the general question from an axiomatic social choice perspective, providing a graph-theoretic, ordinal representation theorem for PageRank.

18.2.3 The PageRank Axioms

From the perspective of the theory of social choice, each page in the Internet graph is viewed as an agent, where this agent prefers the pages (i.e., agents) it links to over pages it does not link to. The problem of finding a social aggregation rule will therefore become the problem of page ranking. The idea is to search for simple axioms, that is, requirements we wish the page ranking system to satisfy. Most of these requirements will have the following structure: page a is preferable to page b when the graph is G if and only if a is preferable to b when the graph is G'. Our aim is to exhibit a small

---

[3] The solution is unique up to a scaling factor that can be applied to both sides of the equation. This is guaranteed for finite, strongly connected aperiodic graphs.

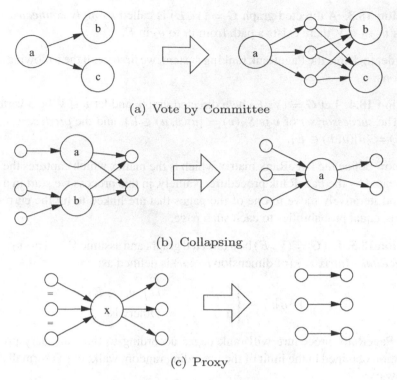

(a) Vote by Committee

(b) Collapsing

(c) Proxy

Figure 18.1. Sketch of several axioms.

set of axioms that can be shown to be satisfied by PageRank. The axioms will thus be simple graph-theoretic, ordinal properties.

In explaining some of the axioms we will refer to Figure 18.1. For simplicity, while the axioms are stated as "if and only if" statements, we will sometimes emphasize in the intuitive explanation of an axiom only one of the directions (in all cases similar intuitions hold for the other direction).

The first axiom is straightforward:

Axiom 18.2 (Isomorphism). A ranking system f satisfies *Isomorphism* if for every isomorphism function $\varphi : V_1 \mapsto V_2$, and two isomorphic graphs $G \in \mathbb{G}_{V_1}$, $\varphi(G) \in \mathbb{G}_{V_2}$: $\preceq^f_{\varphi(G)} = \varphi(\preceq^f_G)$.

The isomorphism axiom tells us that the ranking procedure should be independent of the names we choose for the vertices. It resembles the anonymity and neutrality properties often discussed in social choice.

The second axiom is also quite intuitive. It tells us that if a is ranked at least as high as b in the graph G, where in G vertex a does not link to itself, then a should be ranked higher than b if all that we add to G is a link from a to itself. Moreover, the relative ranking of other vertices in the new graph should remain as before. Formally, we have the following notation and axiom:[4]

---

[4] One may claim that this axiom makes no sense if self loops are not allowed. This is, however, only a simple technical issue. If we disallow self loops, the axiom should be replaced by a new one, where the addition of

Notation 18.3. Let $G = (V, E) \in \mathbb{G}_V$ be a graph and a let $v \in V$ s.t. $(v, v) \notin E$. Let $G' = (V, E \cup \{(v, v)\})$. Let us denote $\textbf{SelfEdge}(G, v) = G'$ and $\textbf{SelfEdge}^{-1}(G', v) = G$.

Axiom 18.4 (Self Edge). A ranking system f satisfies the *Self Edge* axiom if for every vertex set V and for every vertex $v \in V$ and for every graph $G = (V, E) \in \mathbb{G}_V$ s.t. $(v, v) \notin E$, and for every $v_1, v_2 \in V \setminus \{v\}$: Let $G' = \textbf{SelfEdge}G, v$. If $v_1 \preceq_G^f v$ then $v \npreceq_{G'}^f v_1$; and $v_1 \preceq_G^f v_2$ iff $v_1 \preceq_{G'}^f v_2$.

The third axiom (titled *Vote by Committee*) captures the following idea, which is illustrated in Figure 18.1a. If, for example, page a's successors are b and c, then the relative ranking of all pages should be the same as in the case where the direct links from a to b and c are replaced by links from a to a new set of pages, which link (only) to b and c. The idea here is that the amount of importance a provides to b and c by linking to them, should not change due to the fact that a assigns its power through a committee of (new) representatives, all of which behave as a. More generally, and more formally, we have the following:

Axiom 18.5 (Vote by Committee). A ranking system f satisfies *Vote by Committee* if for every vertex set V, for every vertex $v \in V$, for every graph $G = (V, E) \in \mathbb{G}_V$, for every $v_1, v_2 \in V$, and for every $m \in \mathbb{N}$: Let $G' = (V \cup \{u_1, u_2, \ldots, u_m\}, E \setminus \{(v, x) | x \in S_G(v)\} \cup \{(v, u_i) | i = 1, \ldots, m\} \cup \{(u_i, x) | x \in S_G(v), i = 1, \ldots, m\})$, where $\{u_1, u_2, \ldots, u_m\} \cap V = \emptyset$. Then, $v_1 \preceq_G^f v_2$ iff $v_1 \preceq_{G'}^f v_2$.

The 4th axiom, termed *Collapsing* is illustrated in Figure 18.1b. The idea of this axiom is that if there is a pair of pages, with no link between them, say a and b, where both a and b link to the same set of pages, but the sets of pages that link to a and b are disjoint, then if we collapse a and b into a singleton, say a, where all links to b become now links to a, then the relative ranking of all pages (excluding a and b) should remain as before. The intuition here is that if there are two voters (i.e., pages), a and b, who vote similarly (i.e., have the same outgoing links), and the power of each of them stems from the fact a set of (other) voters who have voted for him, where the sets of voters for a and for b are disjoint, then if all voters for a and b would vote only for a (dropping b) then a should provide the same importance to other agents as a and b did together. This of course relies on having a and b voting for the same individuals. As a result, the following axiom is quite intuitive:

Axiom 18.6 (Collapsing). A ranking system f satisfies *Collapsing* if for every vertex set V, for every $v, v' \in V$, for every $v_1, v_2 \in V \setminus \{v, v'\}$, and for every graph $G = (V, E) \in \mathbb{G}_V$ for which $S_G(v) = S_G(v')$, $P_G(v) \cap P_G(v') = \emptyset$, and $[P_G(v) \cup P_G(v')] \cap \{v, v'\} = \emptyset$: Let $G' = (V \setminus \{v'\}, E \setminus \{(v', x) | x \in S_G(v')\} \setminus \{(x, v') | x \in P_G(v')\} \cup \{(x, v) | x \in P_G(v')\})$. Then, $v_1 \preceq_G^f v_2$ iff $v_1 \preceq_{G'}^f v_2$.

The last axiom we introduce, termed the *Proxy* axiom, is illustrated in Figure 18.1c. Roughly speaking, this axiom tells us that if there is a set of k pages, all having the same importance, which link to a, where a itself links to k pages, then if we drop a and

---

self-loop to a is replaced by the addition of a new page, a', where a links to a' and where a' links only to a. All results remain similar.

connect directly, and in a 1-1 fashion, the pages which linked to a to the pages that a linked to, then the relative ranking of all pages (excluding a) should remain the same. This axiom captures equal distribution of importance. The importance of a is received from k pages, all with the same power, and is split among k pages; alternatively, the pages that link to a could pass directly the importance to pages that a link to, without using a as a proxy for distribution. More formally, and more generally, we have the following:

Axiom 18.7 (Proxy). A ranking system f satisfies *Proxy* if for every vertex set V, for every vertex $v \in V$, for every $v_1, v_2 \in V \setminus \{v\}$, and for every graph $G = (V, E) \in \mathbb{G}_V$ for which $|P_G(v)| = |S_G(v)|$, for all $p \in P_G(v)$: $S_G(p) = \{v\}$, and for all $p, p' \in P_G(v)$: $p \sim_G^f p'$: Assume $P_G(v) = \{p_1, p_2, \ldots, p_m\}$ and $S_G(v) = \{s_1, s_2, \ldots, s_m\}$. Let $G' = (V \setminus \{v\}, E \setminus \{(x, v), (v, x) | x \in V\} \cup \{(p_i, s_i) | i \in \{1, \ldots, m\}\})$. Then, $v_1 \preceq_G^f v_2$ iff $v_1 \preceq_{G'}^f v_2$.

18.2.4 A Representation Theorem for PageRank

Although we have provided some intuitive explanation for the axioms, one may argue that particular axiom(s) are not that reasonable. As it turns out, however, all the preceding axioms are satisfied by the PageRank procedure:

Proposition 18.8 (Altman and Tennenholtz, 2005). *The PageRank ranking system satisfies isomorphism, self edge, vote by committee, collapsing, and proxy.*

This proposition assures us of the soundness of the axioms. Moreover, it can be shown that the preceding axioms are not only satisfied by PageRank, but also completely and uniquely characterize the PageRank procedure:

Theorem 18.9 (Altman and Tennenholtz, 2005). *A ranking system f satisfies isomorphism, self edge, vote by committee, collapsing, and proxy if and only if f is the PageRank ranking system.*

The way this is shown, given Proposition 18.8, is by proving the uniqueness of the system satisfying the preceding axioms. Namely:

Proposition 18.10. *Let f_1 and f_2 be ranking systems that satisfy isomorphism, self edge, vote by committee, collapsing, and proxy. Then, f_1 and f_2 are the same ranking system (notation: $f_1 \equiv f_2$).*

The proof in can therefore be viewed as "inefficient" procedure for computing PageRank. It starts from a graph which it slowly changes by application of the axioms. The sequence of graphs that are created maintain the ordering of a given pair of nodes, but get progressively "simpler." In the end, the graph shrinks to only this single pair of nodes, where the ordering of PageRank is determined by the number of their self loops. Technically, the axioms are not used directly to derive all of the graphs in the sequence. Instead, the transitions between graphs are based on higher level properties derived from the axioms (the complete definition of these properties and their use is quite lengthy).

An interesting open problem is whether the preceding axioms are independent. The current conjecture, offered by Altman and Tennenholtz (2005), is that they are.

18.3 Trust-Based Recommendations

Reputation, recommendation, and trust systems have become fundamental and essential ingredients of multiagent systems, especially in e-commerce applications (e.g., Kleinberg, 1999; Resnick et al., 2000; Bakos and Dellarocas, 2003; Tennenholtz, 2004; Dash et al., 2004). All of these systems aggregate agents' reviews of one another, as well as about external events, into valuable information. Notable commercial examples include Amazon and E-Bay's recommendation and reputation systems (Resnick and Zeckhauser, 2001), and the Epinions web of trust/reputation system (Massa and Avesani, 2005). *Personalized* recommendations add value to an agent's experience and may also be naturally paired with personalized advertising.

In a typical application, there is an item of interest (e.g., a product, service, candidate, restaurant). A subset of the agents have prior opinions about this item. Any of the remaining agents might want to estimate whether they would like the item or not, based on the opinions of others. In the real world, a person might first consult friends for their recommendations. In turn, the friends (who do not have opinions of their own) may consult their friends, and so on. Based on the cumulative feedback that is received, an agent might form its own subjective opinion. An automated trust-based recommendation system aims to simulate such a process to provide high-quality *personalized* recommendations to agents.

The model we present here (which was originally presented by Andersen et al., 2008) represents the social connections using a directed graph, partially labeled with $\pm$ votes. A node in the graph represents an agent, an edge from a to b represents the fact that agent a trusts agent b, and a subset of the nodes are labeled by $+$ or $-$, indicating prior opinions. Based on this input, the recommendation system must output a recommendation for each unlabeled node. We call such an abstraction a *voting network* because it models a variety of two-candidate voting systems, where the candidates are $+$ and $-$.

We first show that a number of elementary axioms lead to an impossibility theorem. This set is minimal in the sense that any proper subset of the axioms is satisfied by some recommendation system. We then explore relaxations that lead to a unique system that is most easily described in terms of random walks. Then we show a second axiomatization that leads to a unique "min-cut" system on graphs. For simplicity, the focus is placed on the case of unweighted graphs and binary votes.

18.3.1 Notation and Definitions

We now formally define the basic setting of a *trust-based recommendation system*.

Definition 18.7. A *voting network* is a directed annotated multigraph $G = (N, V_+, V_-, E)$ where N is a set of nodes, $V_+, V_- \subseteq N$ are disjoint subsets of positive and negative voters, and $E \subseteq N^2$ is a multiset of edges with parallel edges allowed but no self loops.

Edges in the voting network imply trust relations between participants, and multiple parallel edges, signify a stronger degree of trust. When V_+ and V_- are clear from context, we denote the set of *voters* by $V = V_+ \cup V_-$ and the set of *nonvoters* by $\overline{V} = N \setminus V$.

Definition 18.8. A *recommendation system* R takes as input a voting network G and source $s \in \overline{V}$ and outputs *recommendation* $R(G, s) \in \{-, 0, +\}$. We denote $R(G) = \langle R_+(G), R_-(G), R_0(G) \rangle$ where $R_+(G) = \{s \in \overline{V} \mid R(G, s) = +\}$ and similarly for $R_-(G), R_0(G)$.

We denote by $sgn : \mathbb{R} \to \{-, 0, +\}$ the function that computes the sign of its input. We denote by $\text{Pred}_E(v)$ and $\text{Succ}_E(v)$ the multisets of nodes that point to v and that v points to, respectively.

Given a multiset of recommendations, $S \subseteq \{-, 0, +\}$, we define the *majority* $\text{MAJ}(S)$ to be $+$ if a strict majority of S is $+$, $-$ if a strict majority of S is $-$, and 0 otherwise (a strict majority simply means more than half).

18.3.2 Five Appealing Properties and an Impossibility

We now consider various properties of recommendation systems as candidate axioms. The first property, *Symmetry*, is purely structural. Symmetry implies that the names of the agents do not matter for the source node; all that matters is the structure of the trust graph and the votes provided. In addition we treat the values +/- as arbitrary, and require that they be treated symmetrically.

Axiom 18.11 (Symmetry). A recommendation system R satisfies *Anonymity* if for every voting network $G = (N, V_+, V_-, E)$: For any permutation $\pi : N \to N$, let G', be the isomorphic voting network under π. Then $R_+(G') = \pi(R_+(G))$ and $R_-(G') = \pi(R_-(G))$.

A recommendation system R satisfies *Neutrality* if for every voting network $G = (N, V_+, V_-, E)$: Let $G'' = (N, V_-, V_+, E)$. Then $R_+(G) = R_-(G'')$ and $R_-(G) = R_+(G'')$.

A recommendation system R satisfies *Symmetry* if it satisfies both Anonymity and Neutrality.

The next axiom states that if a node s has recommendation 0 (or $+$) and a brand new $+$-voter is added to the network along with an edge from s to the new node, then s's new recommendation should be $+$. It reflects a razor's-edge view of a 0 recommendation. The axiom "pushes" the systems toward strict recommendations. (Without such an axiom, systems may almost always recommend 0.)

Axiom 18.12 (Positive Response). A recommendation system R satisfies *Positive Response* if for every voting network $G = (N, V_+, V_-, E)$: for every $w \notin N$, $s \in \overline{V}$, and $G' = (N \cup \{w\}, V_+ \cup \{w\}, V_-, E \uplus \{(s, w)\})$; If $s \notin R_-(G)$ then $s \in R_+(G')$.

Note that this axiom is presented asymmetrically in terms of $\pm$ votes and recommendations. In combination with the Symmetry axiom, the corresponding version with $-$ votes and recommendations follows directly. We use an asymmetric presentation for readability in several of the axioms.

The next axiom, *Independence of Irrelevant Stuff (IIS)*, captures the fact that voters have already made up their minds. This means that when considering the recommendation for a particular source node in a particular trust graph, where part of the agents vote (perhaps based on first-hand experience), feedback from these agents is independent of who they trust (i.e., they trust themselves infinitely more than others) and the recommendation system should consider only reachable nodes and should ignore links out of voters. While one may consider other types of semantics, this one is (approximately) quite typical for actual systems.

Axiom 18.13 (IIS). A recommendation system R satisfies *Independence of Irrelevant Stuff (IIS)* if for every voting network $G = (N, V_+, V_-, E)$: for any edge $e \in V \times N$ leaving a voter, and the subgraph $G' = (N, V_+, V_-, E \setminus \{e\})$ in which e has been removed, $R(G) = R(G')$. In addition, for every $s \in \overline{V}$ and $v \in N$ not reachable from s, for the subgraph G'' in which node v (and its associated edges) have been removed, we have $R(G, s) = R(G'', s)$.

When we write $R(G) = R(G')$, as earlier, the recommendations in the two voting networks are identical.

Notice that IIS captures two aspects of relevant information. First, when one experiences a service, trust relations are irrelevant, as his opinion is completely framed by his direct experience; second, the opinion of a person unreachable in the trust network is irrelevant.

The following requirement deals with some minimal rationality we wish to attribute to the agents; as in the classical theory of choice we are willing to assume something about the vote of an agent who has no a priori opinion only in extreme cases. The Neighborhood Consensus axiom does just that: if all the outgoing neighbors of (i.e., agents trusted by) a node v in a trust network vote $+$, and no other nodes point to v's neighbors, then v might be considered to vote $+$ as well. Formally, we have:

Axiom 18.14 (Neighborhood Consensus). A recommendation system R satisfies *Neighborhood Consensus* if for every voting network $G = (N, V_+, V_-, E)$, and for every distinct nonvoters $s, u \in \overline{V}$, where u has at least one outgoing edge and each outgoing edge $(u, v) \in E$ points to v such that $v \in V_+$ and v has no (incoming or outgoing) neighbors other than u: Let $G' = (N, V_+ \cup \{u\}, V_-, E)$, then $R(G, s) = R(G', s)$.

Transitivity is a central concept in the axiomatization of voting, and in our intuition regarding trust relations. In this context, we consider the case when the underlying trust graph is fixed, while the system needs to deal with more than one item, where different subsets of nodes vote on different items. The idea is that if a source node is recommended, say, $+$, then it means that the system assigns higher trust to the agents who report $+$ than to the agents who report $-$.

Definition 18.9. Let $G = (N, V_+, V_-, E)$ be a voting network, $s \in \overline{V}$, and R a recommendation system. If $s \in R_+(G)$, then we say that s *trusts V_+ more than V_-* relative to multigraph (N, E) under the recommendation system R.

In this case, a partial ordering among sets of nodes is generated, and we wish this relation to be transitive. This axiom is not only natural, but also builds a strong tie between trust systems and recommendation systems.

Axiom 18.15 (Transitivity). A recommendation system R satisfies *Transitivity* if for all multigraphs (N, E), and mutually disjoint $A, B, C \subseteq N$, and $s \notin A \cup B \cup C$: if s trusts A more than B and s trusts B more than C, then s trusts A more than C.

Unfortunately, the following result, says that the five axioms cannot be obtained simultaneously by any system.

Theorem 18.16 (Andersen et al., 2008). *The axioms Symmetry, Positive Response, Independence of Irrelevant Stuff (IIS), Neighborhood Consensus, and Transitivity are inconsistent. Any proper subset of these axioms is satisfied by some reputation system.*

18.3.3 Alternatives to Transitivity and the Random Walk System

In this section, we consider propagation of *trust*. Intuitively, if u trusts v and v trusts w, then u trusts w as well. Much has been written about trust propagation within social networks (see, e.g., Guha et al., 2004) and the following axiom is a conservative interpretation that agrees with much of the literature.

One would like to say that if u trusts nonvoter v, and v trusts w, then we can simply add an edge from u to w without changing anything. However, the system is supposed to reflect degrees of trust, and this would falsely inflate such trust. Instead, edges are counted as follows. Suppose there are k edges leaving v (that do not point to u). Suppose that there happen to be k edges from u to v. Then we can remove k edges from u to v and replace them by k new edges from u to the k nodes that v trusts (besides u), and no recommendations should change.

Axiom 18.17 (Trust Propagation). A recommendation system R satisfies *Trust Propagation* if for every voting network $G = (N, V_+, V_-, E)$: for every distinct $u, v \in \overline{V}$, suppose that the edges leaving v (besides those to u) are $(v, w_1), \ldots, (v, w_k)$, $(w_i \neq u)$ for some integer k, and that E contains exactly k copies of (u, v). Then, for $E' = \left(E \uplus \{(u, w_1), \ldots, (u, w_k)\}\right) \setminus \{(u, v) * k\}$ and $G' = (N, V_+, V_-, E')$, we have that $R(G) = R(G')$.

Another natural axiom is *Scale Invariance*. Loosely speaking, this means that the amount of trust placed in a node is relative.

Axiom 18.18 (Scale Invariance). A recommendation system R satisfies *Scale Invariance* if for every voting network $G = (N, V_+, V_-, E)$: for every $u \in \overline{V}$, and $k \geq 1$, let $G' = (N, V_+, V_-, E \uplus E')$, where E' is the multiset containing k copies of each of the edges leaving u, then $R(G) = R(G')$.

It states that we can duplicate all edges leaving a node an arbitrary number of times without changing recommendations.

Theorem 18.19. *Axioms Symmetry, Positive Response, Independence of Irrelevant Stuff (IIS), Neighborhood Consensus, Trust Propagation and Scale Invariance are satisfied uniquely by the Random Walk System (see later).*

Input: $G = (N, V_+, V_-, E), s \in \overline{V}$.
Output: recommendation $\in \{-, 0, +\}$.

1. Let $S \subseteq \overline{V}$ be the set of nonvoters that cannot reach any voter.
2. For each $v \in N$, create a variable $r_v \in \mathbb{R}$. Solve the following from r_v:

$$
r_v = \begin{cases}
0, & \text{if } v \in S \\
1, & \text{if } v \in V_+ \\
-1, & \text{if } v \in V_- \\
\frac{\sum_{w \in \text{Succ}_E(v)} r_w}{|\text{Succ}_E(v)|}, & \text{otherwise}
\end{cases}
$$

3. Output $\text{sgn}(r_s)$.

Figure 18.2. The random walk algorithm. (Recall that $V = V_+ \cup V_-$ is the set of voters and $\overline{V} = N \setminus V$ is the set of nonvoters.)

The Random Walk System

We first give a recommendation system for the case of directed graphs. Undirected graphs will be considered later. The recommendation of the system for $G = (N, V_+, V_-, E)$ to source $s \in \overline{V}$ is most easily described in terms of the following random walk. It originates at node s and, at each step, chooses a random outgoing edge and follows it to the destination node. This terminates when a node with a +/- vote is reached, or when a node with no outgoing edges is reached. Let p_s be the probability that the random walk terminates at a node with positive vote and q_s be the probability that the random walk terminates at node with negative vote. Let $r_s = p_s - q_s$. (Note that $p_s + q_s \leqslant 1$ and it is possible that this random walk never terminates.) The *random walk recommendation system* recommends $\text{sgn}(r_s)$ to s.

The algorithm in Figure 18.2 correctly computes the recommendations defined by this system.

18.3.4 The Groupthink Axiom and the Min-Cut Mechanism

Groupthink refers to a social phenomenon in which an entire group of people arrive at a ridiculous conclusion, simply by unfounded group interactions. The No Groupthink axiom rules this out and imposes a strong semantics on the system. There are two parts to this axiom. First, we consider the case that an entire group of nonvoters are all recommended +. This strong position should be based on something external, because no member voted. The requirement is that, among the edges leaving the group, a majority must point to nodes with + votes or recommendations. Conversely, if a majority of the edges leaving the group point to nodes with + votes or recommendations, then the group must contain at least one node with + recommendation.

For example, the reader may consider the following situation. There are three undecided people, each connected to the two others. In addition each of the three individuals has a friend of his own who expresses a negative opinion about a product. A "wrong" recommendation system may provide positive recommendations to each of the undecided persons, saying that now each one of them is consistent with the majority of his friends. This is a typical example of group thinking that we wish to avoid.

Formally, we say that a recommendation system R *avoids Groupthink for* $G = (N, V_+, V_-, E)$ if the following holds.

Axiom 18.20 (No Groupthink). A recommendation system R satisfies *No Groupthink* if for every voting network $G = (N, V_+, V_-, E)$, and $S \subseteq \overline{V}$, a nonempty set of nonvoters: Let E' be the multiset of edges in E from S to $N \setminus S$. (a) If $S \subseteq R_+(G)$ (resp. $R_-(G)$), then a strict majority of the edges in E' must point to nodes in $R_+(G) \cup V_+$ (resp. $R_-(G) \cup V_-$). (b) Conversely, if a strict majority of the edges in E' point to nodes in $R_+(G) \cup V_+$ (resp. $R_-(G) \cup V_-$), then $S \cap R_+(G) \neq \emptyset$ (resp. $S \cap R_-(G) \neq \emptyset$).

As it turns out, the No Groupthink axiom can not be satisfied in general directed graphs. We define it here for specific graphs, namely, undirected graphs, as the ones employed, for example, by Facebook. An undirected graph is a (directed) graph where node v links to node u iff node u links to node v.

Theorem 18.21. *Axiom No Groupthink on an undirected graph implies the min-cut recommendation system (see later).*

The Min-Cut System

Let $G = (N, V_+, V_-, E)$ be a voting network. Let $E' \subseteq E$ be the set of edges in E that originate at nonvoters, that is, eliminate edges out of voters. We say that cut $C \subseteq E'$ is a V_+-V_- cut of G if there is no path from V_+ to V_- using edges in $E' \setminus C$. We say that C is a min cut of G if its *size* $|C|$ is minimal among all such cuts.

More intuitively, a cut in a voting network is a set of the edges, originating from nonvoters, such that any path from a $+$ voter to a $-$ voter must pass through at least one of them. A min-cut is such a cut of minimal size.

The *min-cut system* can be defined as follows. The recommendation of a source s is $+$ (resp. $-$) if and only if in *all* min-cuts there is a path from s to V_+ (resp. V_-) among edges in $E' \setminus C$. If neither is the case, then the recommendation is 0.

This is easily computed as follows. Compute a min-cut C. Then, consider the graph when adding an edge from source s to a $+$ (resp. $-$) voter and compute C_+ (resp. C_-). If $|C| < |C_-|$ then the recommendation is $+$. If $|C| < |C_+|$ then the recommendation is $-$. Otherwise, the recommendation is 0. The computation can be done efficiently because min s-t cut can be found in polynomial time. To see that this procedure matches the preceding definition, note that if s is connected to V_+ in all min-cuts then adding an edge from s to a $-$ voter will create a path from V_- to V_+ in any min-cut and necessarily increase the min-cut cost by 1. Similarly if s is connected to V_- in all min-cuts. In the remaining case, the sizes of all three min-cuts will be the same because there are some min-cuts in which s is not connected to V_- and some in which s is not connected to V_+.

18.4 Mechanisms for Multilevel Marketing

Social networks have existed long before the Internet, but their recent web-based form, as exhibited by companies like Facebook, Twitter, or LinkedIn, made them more tangible. In this new manifestation, social networks have become an attractive playground for viral marketing: the dream of any marketer is to successfully market products via "word of mouth" thus utilizing social networks. In order to make that dream a reality, various forms of marketing have been advocated. The so-called affiliate marketing, direct marketing, and multilevel marketing all refer to (overlapping) approaches that facilitate viral marketing.

The fundamental idea behind multilevel marketing is that one customer, who already purchased the product, is rewarded for *referrals*, that is, for purchases made by another as a result of his promotion. The *reward mechanism* associated with multi-level marketing may take various forms. In particular, agents may be rewarded for both purchases made by direct referrals and for indirect ones in a recursive manner.

The potential to accumulate small rewards from each person to a sizable sum, a feature which is now manageable thanks to the Internet and information technology, is important as it allows advertisers to attract early adopters and trendsetters that are of great value to them. (On the downside, the possibility of gathering a large sum has also inspired more illicit versions of multilevel marketing, which are not really intended to promote a product, namely, *pyramid schemes*.) Needless to say that selecting an appropriate reward mechanism is inherent to the design of a successful multilevel marketing scheme.

The design of mechanisms for social settings is widely relevant. Kleinberg and Raghavan (2005) consider a setting that is perhaps the most similar in spirit to the one presented here, in which they elicit effort from agents that forward queries in a social network. In their setting, the final rewards are only allocated along the path to the agent that gave the answer, and not to all those who forwarded the question. Similar reward mechanisms were used by the team from MIT that won the DARPA network challenge (Pickard et al., 2011), in the context of incremental deployment on the Internet (Douceur and Moscibroda, 2007), and in the context of message passing within the Bitcoin protocol (Babaioff et al., 2012).

18.4.1 The Referral Tree Model

There are many possible ways to take the social network that forms the basis of the referral process into account. In principle, one may wish to consider the times at which promoting messages were sent from one user to another, to consider referrals that were not followed up by a purchase of the product being promoted, or even to consider the social links along which a referral was *not* made. However, this information may not be all available to the original seller.[5] We therefore take the straightforward

---

[5] In some social networks such as Facebook there is often more explicit knowledge of social connections, but general referral systems do not necessarily have all the information about the underlying social structure and may not be able to track messages in the network.

approach of looking only at the structure of successful referrals. For each buyer, we mark only a single referrer for introducing the product to her (in reality, this would typically be specified at the time of purchase). The induced structure of referrals forms a collection of directed trees, each rooted at a node that corresponds to some buyer that has purchased the product directly from the seller.

To better illustrate why trees (and more generally forests) are considered, picture the following tracking procedure for Internet affiliate marketing: Upon purchasing a product the buyer gets a code; this code can be now shared by him/her in any way (SMS, email, Facebook page, etc.); when another user makes a purchase and provides that code, this fact is recorded. The original owner of the code may then get some reward for a successful referral. The new buyer then gets another code, which may be used further. Notice that a code is delivered only upon purchase, and a buyer shows a particular code (associated with another buyer) upon purchase following a referral. This creates a well-define forest structure which will be used to allocate the rewards.

We shall refer to this tree collection as the *referrals forest*, denoted $\mathcal{T}$, and to the rooted trees in $\mathcal{T}$ as the *referrals trees*. We find the assumption that $\mathcal{T}$ can be maintained by the seller sufficiently weak.

It should be clarified that the referrals forest corresponds to a single multilevel marketing campaign (typically associated with a single product). Moreover, social network users that did not purchase the product are not represented in $\mathcal{T}$ even if some of their friends have sent them referrals. For ease of presentation, we assume that $\mathcal{T}$ is fully known when the rewards are to be distributed, although all the mechanisms explored in this section are also suited for incremental payments performed online. It will also be convenient to identify the buyers with their corresponding nodes in $\mathcal{T}$, denoting the reward of (the buyer corresponding to) node u under the referrals forest $\mathcal{T}$ by $R_\mathcal{T}(u)$.

18.4.2 Properties of Reward Mechanisms

The reward mechanism is essentially a function that maps the referrals forest $\mathcal{T}$ to the nonnegative real rewards of its nodes. However, not every such function should be considered; specifically, we impose three constraints on the reward mechanisms. Through the remainder of the chapter, these axioms will not be questioned, but will rather be considered a part of every reward mechanism. The first one is the *Subtree* constraint:

Axiom 18.22 (SubTree (ST)). A reward mechanism R satisfies the *Subtree* axiom if: $R_\mathcal{T}(u)$ is uniquely determined by $\mathcal{T}_u$, namely, by the subtree of $\mathcal{T}$ rooted at u.

This is sensible, as each user u can really be credited only for bringing in users she promoted the product to, either directly (the children of u in $\mathcal{T}$) or indirectly (lower level descendants of u). Moreover, a dependence of $R_\mathcal{T}(u)$ on the position of u within $\mathcal{T}$ (rather than on $\mathcal{T}_u$ only) may result in an undesirable behavior on behalf of u: in some cases u is better off delaying the purchase of the product after receiving a referral in hope for a "better" offer, that is, for a referral that would place u in a better position within $\mathcal{T}$.

One of the consequences of the subtree constraint is that there is no point in dealing with the referrals forest $\mathcal{T}$ in full, but rather focus on trees which are rooted at the nodes whose reward we are trying to calculate. In other words, the reward mechanism is completely specified by the function $\mathrm{R}(T)$ that maps the rooted tree T to the nonnegative real reward of its root (which may be an internal node within the whole referrals forest).

The second constraint that we impose on the reward mechanism is the *Budget* constraint: the seller is willing to spend at most a certain fraction $\phi \leqslant 1$ of her total income on rewarding her buyers for referrals. Given that the price of the product is π, this means that the total sum of rewards given to all nodes is at most $\phi \cdot \pi |\mathcal{T}|$. We assume without loss of generality that π and ϕ are scaled so that $\phi \cdot \pi = 1$. Thus,

Axiom 18.23 (Budget Constraint (BC)). A reward mechanism R satisfies the *Budget Constraint* if:

$$\sum_{u \in \mathcal{T}} \mathrm{R}(T_u) \leqslant |\mathcal{T}| .$$

The third requirement is the *Unbounded Reward* constraint: there is no limit to the rewards one can potentially receive even under the assumption that each user has a limited circle of friends in the underlying social network (imposing a limited number of direct referrals). This requirement is a way to capture the high motivation that is given in affiliate marketing schemes even to those with a bounded number of friends. Formally,

Axiom 18.24 (Unbounded Reward (UR)). A reward mechanism R satisfies *Unbounded Reward* if: there exists some positive integer d (a property of the reward mechanism) such that for every real R_θ, there exists some tree T of maximum degree d (i.e., every node has at most d children) such that $\mathrm{R}(T) \geqslant R_\theta$.

In particular, this constraint implies that the reward mechanisms we consider must take indirect referrals into account. From this point on, we restrict discussion only to mechanisms for which the three preceding axioms (ST, BC, UR) hold. We term these *proper* reward mechanisms.

18.4.3 Geometric Mechanisms

We now focus on characterizing the following well-known family of reward mechanisms, referred to as *geometric mechanisms*. Given two constants $0 < a < 1$ and $b > 0$ such that $b + 1 \leqslant 1/a$, the reward from a referral tree T under the (a, b)-*geometric mechanism* is defined to be

$$\mathrm{R}(T) = \sum_{u \in T} a^{\mathrm{dep}(u)} \cdot b .$$

Where $\mathrm{dep}(u)$ is the depth of node u in the referral tree. The constraints on a and b ensure that the amount contributed by each node to the reward of its ancestors will not exceed 1.

Let us begin by defining and discussing three additional properties (that will prove useful in the context of geometric mechanisms). We define the operation $\cup$ on trees such that if T_1, T_2 are trees, then $T_1 \cup T_2$ is the tree formed by contracting (or merging) the roots of T_1 and T_2. This allows us to define the Additivity axiom as follows:

Axiom 18.25 (Additivity (ADD)). A reward mechanism R satisfies *Additivity* if: for any two disjoint trees T, T'

$$R(T) + R(T') = R(T \cup T').$$

This property suggests that if two disjoint trees are merged at the root, then the reward of the root is exactly the sum of the rewards of the two original trees. Generally speaking this property implies that the reward to each node can be independently attributed to the subtrees rooted at its children.

The next axiom, Child Dependence, determines the reward of the root uniquely from the rewards of its children. This property ensures that the actual computation of the rewards can be performed locally. In fact, we shall consider a weaker condition for this property:

Axiom 18.26 (Child Dependence (CD)). A reward mechanism R satisfies *Child Dependence* if: given that the root of T has a single child u, then $R(T)$ is uniquely determined by $R(T_u)$.

This is captured by a function $\chi : \mathbb{R}_{\geq 0} \to \mathbb{R}_{\geq 0}$ (a property of the mechanism) so that $R(T) = \chi(R(T_u))$.

The next axiom states that the reward $R(T)$ is uniquely determined by the number of nodes on each depth level in T. We denote by d_k the number of nodes of T at depth level $k > 0$, and the infinite vector containing these numbers for all depth levels by $d = (d_1, \ldots, d_h, 0, 0, \ldots)$, where h is the height of the tree. Let $\mathcal{D}$ be the set of all such vectors, that is, the set of all infinite vectors over $\mathbb{Z}_{\geq 0}$ with a strictly positive prefix followed by a countably infinite suffix of zeros.

Axiom 18.27 (Depth Level Dependence (DLD)). A reward mechanism R satisfies *Depth Level Dependence* if: There exists some function $f : \mathcal{D} \to \mathbb{R}_{\geq 0}$ (a property of the mechanism) such that $R(T) = f(d)$.

This property essentially means that the credit for a referral depends solely on how direct (or better said, indirect) this referral is.

The preceding axioms characterize the family of geometric mechanisms:

Theorem 18.28 (Emek et al., 2011). *A proper reward mechanism satisfies DLD, ADD, and CD if and only if it is a geometric mechanism.*

An appealing property of geometric mechanisms is that the contribution of descendants to their ancestor decreases with distance. This reflects the fact that the ancestor gets less credit for more distant indirect referrals.

It is important to point out that each of the three properties we used to characterize the family of geometric mechanisms is needed, that is, if we remove one of the three properties then there exists another proper mechanism (outside the geometric family) for which the remaining two hold.

To prove the theorem, we will need the definition of the following additional property:

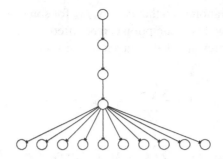

Figure 18.3. $T(n, m)$ for $n = 4$ and $m = 10$.

Definition 18.10. We say that a proper reward scheme satisfies the *Summing Contributions (SC)* property if and only if there exists a sequence $\{c_k\}_{k \geqslant 1}$ of non-negative reals such that

$$\mathrm{R}(T) = \sum_{u \in T} c_{\mathrm{dep}(u)} = \sum_{k=1}^{\infty} \#\text{nodes at depth level } k \cdot c_k \, .$$

That is, SC implies that each node in the tree T contributes some independent amount to the root, and that amount depends only on its depth. The following lemma reveals the connection between this property and the ones we have already defined.

Lemma 18.29 (Emek et al., 2011). *A proper reward mechanism satisfies SC if and only if it satisfies DLD and ADD.*

Theorem 18.28 is established by showing that the contribution values c_k form a geometric progression.

Lemma 18.30 (Emek et al., 2011). *A proper reward mechanism satisfies SC and CD if and only if it is a geometric mechanism.*

Proof. It is trivial to show that a geometric mechanism satisfies both properties, so we focus on the converse direction. Let us restrict our attention to a specific class of trees: For $n > 1$ and $m > 0$, we denote by $T(n, m)$ the tree consisting of $n + m$ nodes organized as a path of length $n - 1$ emerging from the root with the last node in this path having m children, all of which are leaves. Refer to Figure 18.3 for illustration.

We first argue that c_ks implied by SC must be strictly positive for every $k \geqslant 1$. To that end, suppose that $c_{k^*} = 0$ for some $k^* \geqslant 1$ and consider the trees $T(k^*, m)$ and $T(k^*, m')$ for some $m, m' > 0$, $m \neq m'$. SC implies that $\mathrm{R}(T(k^*, m)) = \mathrm{R}(T(k^*, m'))$ because $c_{k^*} = 0$. By CD, we conclude that the same holds for $T(k^* + 1, m)$ and $T(k^* + 1, m')$, namely, $\mathrm{R}(T(k^* + 1, m)) = \mathrm{R}(T(k^* + 1, m'))$, because both the root of $T(k^* + 1, m)$ and that of $T(k^* + 1, m')$ have a single child whose reward is $\mathrm{R}(T(k^*, m)) = \mathrm{R}(T(k^*, m'))$. This implies that c_{k^*+1} must also be 0 and by induction, that $c_k = 0$ for every $k \geqslant k^*$. But this contradicts the unbounded reward constraint: if $c_k = 0$ for every $k \geqslant k^*$, then no tree T of maximum degree d can provide a reward greater than $2 \cdot d^{k^*}$.

So, assume hereafter that $c_k > 0$ for every $k \geqslant 1$. In attempt to simplify the analysis, we shall impose another assumption on the contribution values c_k. Specifically, we assume that each c_k is rational, so that $c_k = x_k/y_k$ for some positive integers x_k and y_k. We later on outline how this assumption can be lifted.

Let us compare the reward that is given to the root node in two specific $T(n, m)$ trees:

$$R(T(k - 1, x_k \cdot y_{k-1} + 1)) = \sum_{i=1}^{k-2} c_i + (x_k \cdot y_{k-1} + 1) \cdot c_{k-1}$$

$$= \sum_{i=1}^{k-1} c_i + x_{k-1} \cdot x_k = \sum_{i=1}^{k-1} c_i + x_{k-1} \cdot y_k \cdot c_k = R(T(k, x_{k-1} \cdot y_k)). \qquad (18.1)$$

Now, observe that CD implies that if $R(T(n, m)) = R(T(n', m'))$, then $R(T(n + 1, m)) = R(T(n' + 1, m'))$. By applying this observation to Equation 18.1, we conclude that

$$R(T(k, x_k \cdot y_{k-1} + 1)) = R(T(k + 1, x_{k-1} \cdot y_k)).$$

SC then implies that

$$\sum_{i=1}^{k-1} c_i + (x_k \cdot y_{k-1} + 1) \cdot c_k = \sum_{i=1}^{k} c_i + (x_{k-1} \cdot y_k) \cdot c_{k+1},$$

hence $x_k \cdot y_{k-1} \cdot c_k = (x_{k-1} \cdot y_k) \cdot c_{k+1}$. It follows that

$$(c_k)^2 = c_{k-1} \cdot c_{k+1}, \qquad (18.2)$$

which implies a geometric progression (c_k is the geometric mean of c_{k-1} and c_{k+1}).

Recall that our proof thus far only works if all c_ks are rational numbers. We can extend the proof to irrational numbers if we add a requirement on the continuity of the function that determines the rewards of a parent from the reward of its children. If the c_ks are not rational, it is possible to approximate them as closely as one wishes with rational numbers x_k/y_k and with the extra assumption, the preceding derivation results in an equation similar to Equation 18.2 which is modified with terms that represent the error in the approximation of c_k. As this error can be made arbitrarily small, Equation 18.2 holds even for irrational values.   □

18.4.4 Sybil Attacks

The goal of this section is to exhibit proper reward mechanisms that are not vulnerable to forging identities on behalf of the users (something which is very easily done in most online scenarios). Fake identities may allow users to create fictitious referrals, and perhaps to collect a greater reward.

We model such fake identities (Sybils) in this context using the notion of a *split*. Consider some tree T and some node $v \in T$ and let $u_1, \ldots, u_k$ be the children of v in T. Intuitively speaking, a split of v refers to a scenario in which v presents itself as *several* nodes—aka *replicas*—thus modifying the (sub)tree T_v that determines its reward (possibly turning it into several trees), while keeping its subtrees $T_{u_1}, \ldots, T_{u_k}$ intact. The subtrees are kept intact in order to model the fact that while v may create several false identities, it does not gain additional new social connections through them,

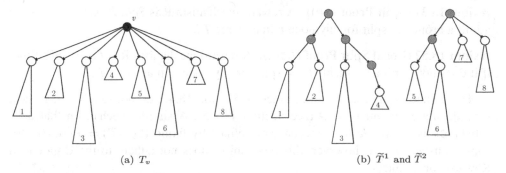

(a) T_v (b) $\widetilde{T}^1$ and $\widetilde{T}^2$

Figure 18.4. The tree collection $\{\widetilde{T}^1, \widetilde{T}^2\}$ can be obtained from T_v by a split of v. The white circles depict the (a) children of v in T and (b) their positions in $\widetilde{T}^1$ and $\widetilde{T}^2$ after the split. The gray circles in 18.4b depict the replicas of v under that split.

and the referrals directly and indirectly attributed to him remain the same. In the same manner, the initial referral to node v is through the same original ancestor, and v cannot "implant" its newly created identities elsewhere in the tree.

A *local split* refers to the special case of a split in which $u_1, \ldots, u_k$ are forced to share the same parent in the resulting tree. In this way, we model cases where nodes do not readily accept referrals from fake identities (that they do not know), and will only accept referrals from the agent's true identity.

Formally, we say that the tree collection $\{\widetilde{T}^1, \ldots, \widetilde{T}^m\}$ can be obtained from T_v by a *split* of v if

(1) for every $1 \leqslant i \leqslant k$, there exists a single $1 \leqslant j(i) \leqslant m$ such that $u_i \in \widetilde{T}^{j(i)}$; and

(2) $\widetilde{T}_{u_i}^{j(i)} = T_{u_i}$ for every $1 \leqslant i \leqslant k$.

The nodes in

$$\left(\widetilde{T}^1 \cup \cdots \cup \widetilde{T}^m\right) - \left(\widetilde{T}_{u_1}^{j(1)} \cup \cdots \cup \widetilde{T}_{u_k}^{j(k)}\right)$$

are referred to as the *replicas* of v under that split. By definition, u_i must be a (direct) child of some replica of v for every $1 \leqslant i \leqslant k$ as otherwise, at least one of the subtrees rooted at $u_1, \ldots, u_k$ must have been changed, thus violating condition (2). Refer to Figure 18.4 for an illustration of a split. The split is called *local* if $u_1, \ldots, u_k$ are all children of the same replica of v.

When does a node v gain from a split? Clearly, v has to invest $\pi \times$ #replicas in introducing the new replicas (purchasing new copies of the product). However, she now collects the rewards from all her replicas, which sums up to

$$\sum_{i=1}^{m} \sum_{\text{replica } u \text{ of } v \text{ in } \widetilde{T}^i} R(\widetilde{T}_u^i) .$$

Thus, the profit of v changes from $R(T_v) - \pi$ to

$$\sum_{i=1}^{m} \sum_{\text{replica } u \text{ of } v \text{ in } \widetilde{T}^i} R(\widetilde{T}_u^i) - \pi \times \text{\#replicas} ;$$

the split is called *profitable* for v if this change is positive. This leads to the definition of the following two properties of reward mechanisms:

Axiom 18.31 (Split Proof (SP)). A reward mechanism R is *Split Proof* if it does not admit a profitable split for any node v in any tree T.

Axiom 18.32 (Local Split Proof (LSP)). A reward mechanism R is *Local Split Proof* if it does not admit a profitable *local* split for any node v in any tree T.

The geometric mechanisms presented in Section 18.4.3 do not satisfy SP. In fact, they do not even satisfy LSP (see Section 18.4.5). A simple mechanism that does satisfy SP is the *single level* mechanism defined by fixing $R_{\mathcal{M}_{sl}}(T) = \alpha \cdot \deg(r)$ for some constant $\alpha \leqslant 1$, however, this mechanism does not adhere to the Unbounded Reward constraint.

18.4.5 Negative Results

Let us now exhibit two negative results regarding the design of split-proof mechanisms. The first result shows that the reward guaranteed to a node in a split-proof mechanism cannot be a constant fraction of even its least influential child.

Lemma 18.33 (Emek et al., 2011). *A proper reward mechanism that satisfies LSP cannot guarantee a node some fraction $0 < \alpha \leqslant 1$ of the reward of its least rewarded child.*

Next, we see that even a family of reward mechanisms much wider than geometric mechanisms is still not split-proof. This requires the introduction of another axiom which is clearly satisfied by every geometric mechanism (thus, it is not independent), yet, cannot replace any of the characterizing properties listed in Theorem 18.28.

Axiom 18.34 (Monotonicity (MONO)). A reward mechanism R satisfies *Monotonicity* if: for every pair of trees T, T' such that the tree T can be obtained from the tree T' by removing some leaf, then $R(T) < R(T')$.

Lemma 18.35 (Emek et al., 2011). *A proper reward mechanism that satisfies MONO and ADD cannot satisfy SP.*

18.4.6 A Split-Proof Mechanism

In this section we present a split-proof reward mechanism, denoted $\mathcal{M}_{split}$. Informally, the mechanism $\mathcal{M}_{split}$ is defined in two stages: in the first stage, we define a simple *base* mechanism, denoted $\mathcal{M}_{base}$; $\mathcal{M}_{split}$ is then defined with respect to the maximum profit a node can make under $\mathcal{M}_{base}$ from splits.

Mechanism $\mathcal{M}_{base}$

The base mechanism $\mathcal{M}_{base}$ is defined by setting $R_{\mathcal{M}_{base}}(T)$ to be the maximum $h \in \mathbb{Z}_{\geqslant 0}$ such that T exhibits as a subtree, a perfect binary tree[6] B rooted at r whose height is h. In that case we say that B *realizes* $R_{\mathcal{M}_{base}}(T)$ (see Figure 18.5). If there are several

---

[6] A perfect binary tree is a rooted tree in which all leaves are at the same distance from the root and all nonleaves have exactly two children.

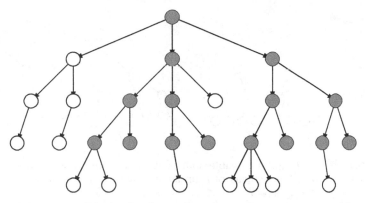

Figure 18.5. The tree T and the perfect binary tree that realizes $R_{\mathcal{M}_{base}}(T)$ (nodes depicted by gray circles).

perfect binary trees that can realize $R_{\mathcal{M}_{base}}(T)$, then it will be convenient to take the first one in a lexicographic order based on a breadth-first-search traversal and consider it as *the* perfect binary tree that realizes $R_{\mathcal{M}_{base}}(T)$.

A node $u \in T$ is said to be *visible* in T if it belongs to the perfect binary tree that realizes $R_{\mathcal{M}_{base}}(T)$; otherwise, u is said to be *invisible* in T. This definition is extended as follows: given some ancestor v of u in T, u is said to be *visible* to v if u is visible in T_v, and *invisible* otherwise. The parent of a (nonroot) node u in T is denoted $p_T(u)$. Note that if u is invisible to v, then it is also invisible to $p_T(v)$ (assuming of course that $v \neq r$). The contrary is not necessarily true: u may be visible to v but invisible to $p_T(v)$. By definition, for every node $u \in T$ and for every $j \in \mathbb{Z}_{\geqslant 1}$, it holds that u admits either 2^j or 0 visible depth-j descendants.

We denote the *distance* from u to v by $\delta_T(u, v)$, that is, the number of edges along the unique path in T leading from u to v. The mechanism $\mathcal{M}_{base}$ can now be redefined by setting

$$R_{\mathcal{M}_{base}}(T) = \sum_{\text{visible } u \in T} 2^{-\delta_T(u,r)} .$$

This alternative view of mechanism $\mathcal{M}_{base}$ calls for the definition of *contributions*: a node $u \in T$ *contributes* 2^{-k} to the reward of its kth ancestor v, $k \geqslant 1$, if u is visible to v; otherwise, u does not contribute anything to the reward of v. Let $C_{\mathcal{M}_{base}}(u, v)$ denote the contribution of u to the reward of v under $\mathcal{M}_{base}$. The reward of a node can now be calculated by summing the contributions that its descendants make to it. This implies that $\mathcal{M}_{base}$ satisfies the budget constraint: the total contribution made by a node $u \in T$ to all its ancestors is bounded from above by the geometric sum $\sum_{j=1}^{\delta(u,r)} 2^{-j} < 1$, hence, by changing the summation, we conclude that $\sum_{v \in T} R_{\mathcal{M}_{base}}(T_v) < |T|$.

Mechanism $\mathcal{M}_{split}$

The mechanism $\mathcal{M}_{split}$ is defined by setting $R_{\mathcal{M}_{split}}(T)$ so that it reflects the maximum profit that r can get under $\mathcal{M}_{base}$ from splits. More formally, let S be the collection of all tree collections that can be obtained from T by a split of r. Then $\mathcal{M}_{split}$ is defined

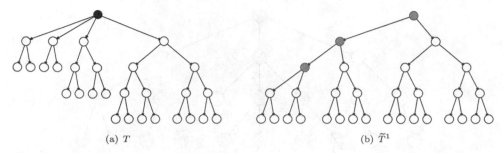

(a) T (b) $\widetilde{T}^1$

Figure 18.6. The tree T and a possible split of its root r (into a single tree $\widetilde{T}^1$). The gray circles in 18.6b depict the replicas of r under that split. If $\pi = 1$, then this split realizes $R_{\mathcal{M}_{\text{split}}}(T) = 2 + 3 + 4 - 2 \cdot \pi = 7$.

by setting

$$R_{\mathcal{M}_{\text{split}}}(T) = \sup_{\widetilde{\mathcal{T}} = \{\widetilde{T}^1 \ldots, \widetilde{T}^m\} \in \mathcal{S}} \left\{ \left(\sum_{i=1}^{m} \sum_{\text{repl. } v \text{ of } r \text{ in } \widetilde{T}^i} R_{\mathcal{M}_{\text{base}}}(\widetilde{T}_v^i) \right) \right.$$

$$\left. - \pi \cdot \left(\left| \widetilde{T}^1 \cup \cdots \cup \widetilde{T}^m \right| - |T| \right) \right\} .$$

To avoid cumbersome notation, we shall denote

$$\rho(\widetilde{\mathcal{T}}) \equiv \sum_{i=1}^{m} \sum_{\text{replica } v \text{ of } r \text{ in } \widetilde{T}^i} R_{\mathcal{M}_{\text{base}}}(\widetilde{T}_v^i)$$

and $\bigcup \widetilde{\mathcal{T}} \equiv \widetilde{T}^1 \cup \cdots \cup \widetilde{T}^m$ so that $R_{\mathcal{M}_{\text{split}}}(T) = \sup_{\widetilde{\mathcal{T}} \in \mathcal{S}} \{ \rho(\widetilde{\mathcal{T}}) - \pi \cdot (|\bigcup \widetilde{\mathcal{T}}| - |T|) \}$. Refer to Figure 18.6 for illustration.

It is easy to see that $\mathcal{M}_{\text{split}}$ satisfies the SubTree constraint and the Unbounded Reward constraint ($\mathcal{M}_{\text{base}}$ already satisfies the Unbounded Reward constraint and the rewards under $\mathcal{M}_{\text{split}}$ dominates those of $\mathcal{M}_{\text{base}}$). Moreover, by definition, $\mathcal{M}_{\text{split}}$ satisfies SP, that is, a node cannot increase its profit by splitting (recall that the mechanism takes every possible split into account). The difficult part is to show that $\mathcal{M}_{\text{split}}$ satisfies the budget constraint, that is, $\sum_{v \in T} R_{\mathcal{M}_{\text{split}}}(T_v) \leqslant |T|$. This is indeed the case:

Theorem 18.36 (Emek et al., 2011). *Mechanism $\mathcal{M}_{split}$ satisfies the budget constraint and is therefore a proper referral reward mechanism with the SP property.*

Additional work on mechanisms for this setting appears in the work by Drucker and Fleischer (2012).

18.5 Discussion: Additional Applications

Earlier we surveyed three major applications of the axiomatic approach to Internet settings. In this section we briefly mention and discuss additional applications with complementary views.

18.5.1 Normative Approach to Ranking Systems

Reasoning about agent preferences on a set of alternatives, and the aggregation of such preferences into some social ranking is a fundamental issue in reasoning about multiagent systems. When the set of agents and the set of alternatives coincide, we get the ranking systems setting for which we have explored the descriptive approach via PageRank. Altman and Tennenholtz (2008) present an extensive axiomatic study of the normative approach to such systems. In particular, two fundamental axioms are considered: Transitivity and Consistency. Surprisingly, it is shown that there is no general social ranking rule that satisfies both requirements. Furthermore, it is shown that this impossibility result holds under various restrictions on the class of ranking problems considered. However, when transitivity is weakened, an interesting positive result is obtained.

Incentive Compatibility

Altman and Tennenholtz (2007) introduce a study of incentives in ranking systems, where agents act in order to maximize their position in the ranking. Several basic properties of ranking systems are considered, and fully characterize the conditions under which incentive compatible ranking systems exist, demonstrating that, in general, no system satisfies all the properties together.

Altman and Tennenholtz (2006) consider three measures for quantifying the incentive compatibility of ranking systems. These measures are applied to several known ranking systems, yielding tight bounds on their level of incentive compatibility. The paper also introduce two novel nonimposing ranking systems (i.e., in which each agents' ranking can be materialized), in which the measure of manipulation is such that manipulation is not severely harmful.

18.5.2 Selection Systems

In the selection system setting, agents elect representatives from within their groups. Voting profiles are represented by directed graphs over the set of agents, where an edge (i, j) is taken to mean that agent i trusts or supports agent j. Given such a graph, the goal is to select a subset of agents of fixed size that maximizes the sum of indegrees, that is, a subset of most popular or most trusted agents. On the other hand, each agent is only interested in being selected, and may misreport its outgoing edges to this end. This problem formulation captures realistic scenarios where agents choose among themselves, in the context of, for example, social networks such as Twitter, reputation systems such as Epinions, and Internet search (Alon et al., 2011; Fischer and Klimm, 2014) consider the design of mechanisms that satisfy two constraints: strategyproofness, that is, agents cannot benefit from misreporting their outgoing edges; and approximation, that is, the mechanism must always select a subset of agents that is close to optimal in terms of the sum of indegrees. The paper shows a surprising impossibility: no deterministic strategyproof mechanism can yield a finite approximation ratio for any $k \in \{1, 2, \ldots, n - 1\}$, where k is the size of the selected subset and n is the number of agents. However, the paper also shows that a randomized strategyproof mechanism yields an approximation ratio of four for any value of k, and provides a ratio that approaches one as k grows.

18.5.3 Link Prediction

The link prediction problem is central to the field of complex network analysis. Link prediction functions essentially map a graph to a ranking over pairs of vertices it. Highly ranked pairs constitute links that are likely to form, or may exist in the social network (such as Facebook friends the users have not yet reported about). Cohen and Zohar (2015) discuss the axiomatic approach to link prediction, and characterize several well known link prediction functions.

18.5.4 Trust Systems

Trust systems are in fact personalized ranking systems in which trust relations between many agents are aggregated to produce a personalized trust rating of the agents. Altman and Tennenholtz (2010) present an extensive axiomatic study of this setting, and explores a wide array of well-known and new trust / personalized ranking systems. Several axioms are adapted from the literature on (global) ranking systems to the context of trust systems / personalized ranking systems, and fully classify the set of systems that satisfy all of these axioms. It is also shown that all these axioms are necessary for this result.

18.5.5 Axioms for Collaborative Filtering

Pennock et al. (2000a) present several requirements from collaborative filtering methods, and show that they fit the classical setting of social choice. This allows the authors to deduce that the set of systems satisfying the related requirements is extremely narrow. While this treatment is still in the setting of Arrow's Theorem (applied before to other CS settings, see, e.g., Kfir-Dahav and Tennenholtz, 1996) it also illustrates the power of axiomatization in Internet settings.

CHAPTER 19

Knockout Tournaments

Virginia Vassilevska Williams

19.1 Introduction

The theory of social choice has developed an immense variety of voting rules, ranging from simple rules such as plurality to more complicated rules such as the tournament equilibrium set studied in Chapter 3. Even though the variety may seem vast, most voting rules can be grouped into a small number of types. The main two types are *scoring* rules and *Condorcet-consistent* rules (also called Condorcet extensions). The former contain rules such as Borda and approval voting. A large portion of the latter type of rules consists of *majority* rules that determine the winner by using pairwise comparisons between candidates using the majority rule. Examples of such rules include the binary cup and the *tournament solutions* such as the Slater, Banks and uncovered sets (see Chapter 3).

Majority voting rules can be viewed as tournaments:[1] competitions between the candidates that determine the winner using some rule based solely on the results of matches, that is pairwise comparisons.

Besides as voting rules, tournaments are prevalent in many social settings, most commonly in sports competitions, but also in patent races (Lita, 2008; Durant, 2010), hiring employees (Ryvkin, 2010), and even drug trials (these are commonly referred to as "head-to-head" drug trials).

Tournaments have a wide variety of formats; their common feature is that they proceed in stages. In each stage several pairwise comparisons called *matches* take place. As mentioned earlier, in social choice, a match is typically implemented by a simple majority rule. The outcome of the matches in a stage influences (using some rule) which matches take place in the next stage. In the final stage a winner is determined. Different types of tournaments differ in how matches in different stages are selected and how the final winner is determined.

---

[1] Unlike in Chapter 3, in this chapter, a tournament refers to a competition, and not to the majority graph which we call the tournament graph in this chapter.

A very common type of tournament is the so-called *knockout* or *single-elimination* tournament. In a knockout tournament, no ties are allowed, so that every match produces a match winner. The important property of a knockout tournament is that once a player loses a match, he is eliminated, that is, "knocked-out," from the tournament. Thus the winner of a knockout tournament has won all of her matches. Knockout tournaments are typically represented by a binary tree the leaves of which are labeled by players and each internal node is labeled by the winner between the two children. In social choice such a tree is called a *voting tree* or an *agenda*. (We give a formal definition of a knockout tournament later.)

In this chapter we will focus on knockout tournaments and issues related to manipulating the winner that they pick by changing something about their structure. The latter is perhaps the most central topic in the study of knockout tournaments within computational social choice. Other topics around knockout tournaments are mentioned in Section 1.5.

19.2 Formal Definition and Some Properties

We begin by formally defining a knockout tournament.

Definition 19.1. Given a set C of m players, a *knockout tournament* (T, S) is defined by a binary tree T with m leaves $L(T)$ and a bijective function $S : C \to L(T)$ called the *seeding*, mapping the m players to the m leaves. Suppose that in addition to C, for each two $u, v \in C$ one and exactly one of u and v is picked to be the winner of the *match* between u and v. Then the *winner* of a knockout tournament (T, S) is determined recursively: the winner at a leaf l is the player j with $l = S(j)$, and the winner of the subtree rooted at a node v is the winner of the match between the winners of the two subtournaments rooted at the children of v.

In sports tournaments such as the tennis tournament Wimbledon or the basketball tournament March Madness, the tree T is often referred to as the *bracket*. There T is typically a complete balanced binary tree, and the seeding depends on the prior match history of the players. In the *sequential majority comparisons* voting rule, T is a path on n nodes with an extra edge attached to each node except the last, that is, in each stage, a new candidate is compared to the current winner and if the current winner loses, the new candidate replaces him.

Properties

As mentioned in the introduction, all natural majority voting rules are Condorcet extensions (see Chapter 2), that is, if there is a Condorcet winner, it is elected. This is easy to see for knockout tournaments—regardless of the tree structure and the seeding, if a candidate is preferred over any other candidate by a majority of the voters, then that candidate will win all matches and will be the winner.

Knockout tournaments satisfy an even stronger property—they are *Smith-consistent*: if the set A of candidates is split into A_1 and $A_2 = A \setminus A_1$ so that every candidate in A_1 is preferred (by a majority) over every candidate in A_2, then regardless of the

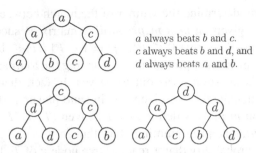

a always beats b and c.
c always beats b and d, and
d always beats a and b.

Figure 19.1. Here, for each of the three players that can beat at least two others, there is a seeding that guarantees that they can win. For seeding a, b, c, d, player a wins. For seeding a, d, c, b, player c wins, and for seeding a, c, b, d, player d wins.

seeding of the candidates at the leaves, a knockout tournament using pairwise majority comparisons always elects a candidate in A_1. (The smallest nonempty set satisfying the requirement for A_1 is called the *Smith set* or the *top cycle*; see Chapter 3.)

Knockout tournaments suffer from all the drawbacks of all resolute Condorcet-consistent voting rules—they do not satisfy the *reinforcement* and *participation* criteria (see Chapter 2 and Moulin, 1988a, pp. 237 and 239). Participation states that no voter has an incentive to not vote. Reinforcement[2] states that if the voter set N is split into two sets N_1 and N_2 that both elect a candidate a, then N should also elect a.

In addition, knockout tournaments have other drawbacks. For instance, as Figure 19.1 demonstrates, the seeding easily affects the winner, and because the seeding depends on the names of the candidates, knockout tournaments do not satisfy *neutrality*—renaming candidates can change the elected winner. They also do not satisfy *Pareto-optimality* when the number of candidates is at least 5, regardless of T and S (see Moulin, 1988a, p. 245, for a proof). That is, for any (T, S) on more than 5 candidates, there is a voter profile so that there is some other candidate that is unanimously preferred to the elected winner.

Regardless of all these problems, knockout tournaments are extremely popular, largely because of their simplicity. They are popular in sports also because of their efficiency—the number of matches they require is no more than the number of players. They also have the advantage that no player has an incentive to intentionally lose a match because a single loss causes elimination. (Other tournament formats such as double-elimination no longer have this property.) This also makes knockout sports tournaments exciting to watch as in most cases players try to play their best.

Computing the Probability of Winning

The definition of the winner of a knockout tournament is constructive and provides a linear time algorithm to find the winner for a given seeding, provided for any pair

---

[2] Knockout tournaments not satisfying reinforcement means the following: there exists a set of candidates C, a set of voters N with preferences over C, a splitting of N into N_1 and $N_2 = N \setminus N_1$ and a knockout tournament (T, S), such that if one uses either the preferences solely of N_1 or solely of N_2 to compute the winner of (T, S), then that winner is some candidate a, whereas if one uses the preferences of all of N, then the winner is a different candidate b.

of players a, b we can determine the winner of the match between a and b. Suppose, however, that we are given an $m \times m$ *probability* matrix P such that $P[i, j]$ is the probability that i beats j, so that $0 \leqslant P[i, j] = 1 - P[j, i] \leqslant 1$. Can we determine which player has the maximum probability of winning the tournament?

The answer to this question turns out to be yes. In fact, there is an $O(m^2)$ time algorithm that can calculate for any given seeding and player j, the probability that j wins a tournament on m players defined by P. Given (T, S), P and a player j, one runs the following dynamic programming algorithm.

Let $q(j, v)$ be the probability that j reaches tree node v of T. For all players j, we have that $q(j, S(j)) = 1$. If v is a node with children r and l, such that j is seeded at a descendent of r, then $q(j, v) = q(j, r) \cdot \sum_i q(i, l) \cdot P[j, i]$. The runtime is $O(m^2)$ because i and j are only matched at the least common ancestor of their leaves.

Notice that the preceding algorithm does not depend on the structure of T, just on the fact that T is binary. The structure of the tree T does play a role in some settings. For instance, if T is a balanced binary tree on $\leqslant 4$ candidates, then one can show that it selects a Pareto-optimal candidate. In the next section we will show that if one can manipulate the shape of T, then one can almost arbitrarily pick the winner of the tournament.

19.3 Agenda Control for General Knockout Tournaments

We mentioned earlier that no single player has an incentive to lose on purpose in a knockout tournament. However, one can imagine many other different types of manipulation of the tournament outcome. One type of manipulation defined by Bartholdi et al. (1989a, 1992) is called *agenda control*. Here, one considers how much power an election chairman has in affecting the outcome of the election by changing something in the protocol itself.[3] For the special case of knockout tournaments, the chairman (or the tournament organizer) has the freedom to pick two things, the tree T and the seeding S. If the chairman can change T, then we can assume that the seeding is fixed by fixing an ordering of the leaves of T. Hence we will consider only two types of agenda control—when the chairman can change T, and when T is fixed but the chairman can change S.

In order for the chairman to be able to control the agenda, we need to consider what type of information he has about the pairwise comparisons.

In the *deterministic* setting most commonly used in social choice, we may assume that the chairman has access to a *tournament graph*: a directed graph such that for any two vertices[4] i and j exactly one of (i, j) and (j, i) is an edge. The vertices of the tournament graph correspond to the players/candidates in the knockout tournament, and the tournament graph gives the match outcome for any pair of players. In the social choice setting, the tournament graph obtained by adding a directed edge from i to j if and only if i is preferred to j by a majority of voters, is called the *majority graph*.

---

[3] Agenda control should not be confused with the implementation by agenda problem discussed in Chapter 3.
[4] In this chapter we refer to vertices and nodes interchangeably.

In a more general *probabilistic* setting, one is given a probability matrix P with rows and columns indexed by the candidates, so that $P[i, j]$ is the probability that i is preferred to j. Here $P[i, j] \geqslant 0$ and $P[i, j] + P[j, i] = 1$ for all i, j.

Now, the general agenda control problem is as follows:

Definition 19.2 (General Agenda Control for Knockout Tournaments). Let the following be given: a candidate i, a threshold $p \in (0, 1]$, and voter profile information. The voter profile information can be a probability matrix P on the candidates, in which case we say it is probabilistic, or it can be a tournament graph G, in which case we say it is deterministic and we can assume that $p = 1$. The *general agenda control problem* for knockout tournaments asks to determine whether there is a knockout tournament (T, S) so that i wins (T, S) with probability at least p.

We refer to the problem as

- *agenda control* if the chairman can only modify S (T is fixed) and his input is deterministic
- *P-agenda control* if the chairman can only modify S (T is fixed) and his input is probabilistic
- *full agenda control* if the chairman can modify T and his input is deterministic
- *full P-agenda control* if the chairman can modify T and his input is probabilistic

Each of these problems is in NP: when m is the number of candidates, it can be solved by guessing the tree T on m leaves and the seeding S of T, and then computing the probability that the given candidate i wins for the given T and S. In the remainder of the chapter we will discuss the time complexity of the problems, that is, we will try to address the question:

Is there an efficient algorithm that decides each of the preceding four variants of the agenda control problem?

Full Agenda Control

In this deterministic setting, there is a simple algorithm for full agenda control running in time linear in the size of the tournament graph G. The algorithm does depth-first-search in G starting from the input candidate i and returns "yes" if and only if all nodes in G are reachable from i.

To see why this algorithm works, we will prove two claims. Claim 19.1 shows that any winner of a knockout tournament is in the *top cycle* of the tournament graph. Claim 19.2 shows that any candidate in the top cycle is a winner of some knockout tournament. Claim 19.1 is proven for instance by Moulin (1988a), and Claim 19.2 appears in Lang et al. (2007).

Claim 19.1. *Suppose that (T, S) is a knockout tournament that i wins. Then in the tournament graph G, every node j is reachable from i.*

Proof. We prove this by induction on the number of leaves of the tree. Base case: if the tree has a single leaf node, the candidate seeded at that leaf is the single node in the tournament graph so the claim is trivially true.

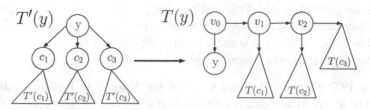

Figure 19.2. The construction of $T(y)$ from $T'(y)$ in Claim 19.2.

Now suppose that for all trees T' on at most $n - 1$ leaves if a candidate c is a winner of the knockout tournament at T' then all nodes in G that are seeded at the leaves of T' are reachable from c. Consider a candidate i that wins the knockout tournament at T. Let r be the root node of T and let T_1 and T_2 be the subtrees rooted at the children of r. Without loss of generality assume that i is seeded at a leaf of T_1. Let j be the winner of T_2. By the induction hypothesis, all candidates seeded at the leaves of T_2 are reachable from j in G and all candidates seeded at the leaves of T_1 are reachable from i in G. Because i beats j in the final match, the candidates seeded at the leaves of T_2 must also be reachable from i by taking the edge (i, j) in G and then the paths from j to them.   □

Claim 19.2. *Suppose that all nodes in G are reachable from i, then there is a tree T (and thus a seeding S) such that i wins (T, S).*

Proof. Let T' be a depth-first-search tree in G rooted at i. Because all nodes of G are reachable from i, T' contains all candidates. We will recursively build T.

For a subtree $T'(y)$ of T' rooted at y, we define a binary tree $T(y)$ with leaves labeled with the nodes of $T'(y)$, such that y wins the knockout tournament defined by $T(y)$. If $T'(y)$ is just the node y, then let $T(y)$ also be a single node labeled y.

Otherwise, let $c_1, \ldots, c_d$ be the children of y in $T'(y)$. Build $T(y)$ from the trees $T(c_1), \ldots, T(c_d)$ as follows; see Figure 19.2. Let $v_0, v_1, \ldots, v_d$ be a path on $d + 1$ nodes, that is, (v_i, v_{i+1}) is an edge. Set v_d to be the root of $T(c_d)$; all other v_j are new nodes. Add an edge from v_j to the root of $T(c_j)$, for each $j \in \{1, \ldots, d - 1\}$. Add an edge (v_0, y). Root the tree at v_0. This completes the description of $T(y)$.

Notice that $T(y)$ is a binary tree and the leaves of $T(y)$ are labeled with distinct candidates because the trees $T(c_j)$ are disjoint. Furthermore, by induction, because c_j is the winner of $T(c_j)$ for every j, y must be the winner of $T(y)$. Because T' contains all candidates, $T(i)$ is a binary tree with all candidates mapped to a unique leaf, and moreover i is the winner of $T(i)$.   □

Full P-Agenda Control

Vu et al. (2009a) consider the full P-agenda control problem and show by induction that for all input matrices P, the best knockout tournament for a candidate i is unbalanced with i only playing in the last round. This restricts the shape of T somewhat. However, no polynomial time algorithm for finding the best tree structure for a given P and i is known.

Open Problem 19.3. *Is the full P-agenda control problem in polynomial time?*

P-Agenda Control

The P-agenda control has been extensively studied, especially for the case of *balanced binary trees*. The complete balanced binary tree is the most widely used tournament tree in practice. It is defined when the number of candidates/players is a power of 2, but the concept can also be extended to arbitrary numbers $2^i - k$ of players by allowing k players a *bye*, that is, these players play their first match in the second round of the tournament.

There are several reasons for why most knockout tournaments in sports are balanced. First, they are considered more fair, because in order to win the tournament, any player must win exactly the same number of matches. In fact, Lang et al. (2007) call the winners of balanced knockout tournaments "fair possible winners." Another reason is that balanced tournaments offer the maximum possible parallelism, so that the tournament can be scheduled to last the shortest possible time.

The history of the P-agenda control problem for *balanced binary trees* is as follows. First, several papers proved that the P-agenda control problem is NP-complete (Lang et al., 2007; Hazon et al., 2008) for arbitrary P. Vu et al. (2009a) then showed that the P-agenda control problem is NP-complete even when the probabilities in P are in $\{0, 1, 1/2\}$. Finally, in a breakthrough result, Aziz et al. (2014e) showed that even the agenda control problem for balanced binary trees (i.e., when P is just over $\{0, 1\}$) is NP-complete.

Besides putting a restriction on the values in P, one can also restrict P in a different way. Suppose that we have some order of the players, so that we think of player i as stronger than any player $j > i$, then a natural way to capture this is to enforce a *monotonicity* property on the probability matrix P. Intuitively, if i is at least as strong as $j > i$, then we would like that i beats j with probability at least $1/2$. Moreover, for any other player k, we would expect that k has a harder time beating i than beating j, that is, $P[k, i] \leqslant P[k, j]$. This motivates the following definition.

Definition 19.3. A probability matrix P is *monotonic* if

- $P[i, j] \geqslant 1/2$ for $i < j$
- $P[i, j] \leqslant P[i, k]$ for every i and $j < k$

A matrix is monotonic exactly when it is sorted in each row and column and has entries $\geqslant 1/2$ above the diagonal. A natural question is whether the P-agenda control problem is still NP-complete when we restrict ourselves to monotonic matrices P, as we would expect probability matrices arising from practical applications to be roughly monotonic. It turns out, however, that the complexity of this version of the problem is still unknown.

Open Problem 19.4. *Is the P-agenda control polynomial time solvable when P is monotonic?*

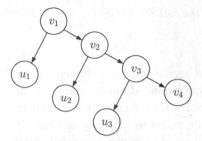

Figure 19.3. An example of an SMC-tree with seven vertices.

Consider relaxing the monotonicity property by allowing for the rows and columns to be "roughly" sorted up to some noise. (From a practical perspective, this makes sense as in the real world there is always noise.) One way to define such a relaxation is that if $j < k$ then for all i, $P[i, j]$ is at most $P[i, k]$, plus some slack ε.

Definition 19.4. A probability matrix P is *ε-monotonic* if

- $P[i, j] \geqslant 1/2$ for $i \leqslant j$
- $P[i, j] \leqslant P[i, k] + \varepsilon$ for every i and all $j < k$

As ε goes closer to 0, such a matrix P becomes closer and closer to monotonic. Interestingly, Vu et al. (2009a) showed that P-agenda control for ε-monotonic P for any $\varepsilon > 0$ is NP-complete, thus almost settling Open Problem 19.4.

Even though the P-agenda control problem is NP-complete even for very structured matrices, it is still interesting to consider how fast it can be solved. Even if $P \neq NP$, it could be that there is a *subexponential*, that is, $O(2^{\varepsilon m})$ time algorithm for all $\varepsilon > 0$, which although not polynomial, is still extremely fast.

Open Problem 19.5. *Is the P-agenda control problem in subexponential time?*

Agenda Control

In the previous paragraph we noted that the agenda control for balanced binary trees is NP-hard (Aziz et al., 2014e). In the following, we show that there exist natural trees T for which the agenda control problem is efficiently solvable. Thus, the complexity of the agenda control problem *crucially* depends on the tree.

Recall the sequential majority comparisons rule from the previous section. The binary tree associated with its tournament is a directed path $v_1 \ldots, v_m$ on m nodes with an extra edge (v_i, u_i) attached to each v_i for $i < m$. We will call this tree an SMC-tree. See Figure 19.3 for an example. The following claim shows that the chairman can always efficiently manipulate the outcome of a sequential majority election.

Claim 19.6. *If T is an SMC-tree, then the agenda control problem for any tournament graph G and candidate i can be solved in polynomial time.*

Proof. Given $G = (V, E)$ on m nodes, let us first compute the strongly connected components of G. This can be done in $O(m^2)$ time as G has $O(m^2)$ edges. The strongly connected components form a directed acyclic graph, the SCC-DAG. The nodes of the SCC-DAG are the strongly connected components, and there is a directed edge from

C to C' if and only if there is some $u \in C$, $v \in C'$ with $(u, v) \in E$. We will show that i is a winner of a knockout tournament if and only if i is in the unique source node of the SCC-DAG of G.

As we proved in Claim 19.1, if i is a winner of a knockout tournament, regardless of the structure of T, i must have a path in G to all other nodes. Thus i is in a source node of the SCC-DAG, and because G is a tournament graph this source node is unique.

On the other hand, suppose that i is in the unique source node of the SCC-DAG. We will show that one can construct (in polynomial time) a Hamiltonian path in G starting from i. (This also proves that tournament graphs always contain a Hamiltonian path and one can be found in polynomial time.) After this, from the Hamiltonian path starting from i we will construct a seeding of an SMC-tree on m leaves so that i wins, as follows. If there is a Hamiltonian path in G starting from i, let this path be $i = x_1 \to x_2 \to \ldots \to x_m$. For each $j < m$, seed x_j at leaf u_j of the SMC-tree, and seed x_m at v_m. It is easy to see by induction that x_j wins the tournament rooted at the parent of its leaf node, and hence i wins the knockout tournament defined by the seeded SMC-tree.

Now, let us show that if i is in the source node of the SCC-DAG, then one can find a Hamiltonian path in G starting with i. Consider $G' = G \setminus \{i\}$. G' is still a tournament graph. By induction, assume that for any vertex j in the source node C of the SCC-DAG of G' we can construct a Hamiltonian path of G' starting from j. This is true for the base case when G' has only one vertex. Now, because i can reach all nodes in G, and all edges incident to C in G' go out of C, i must have an out-neighbor $j \in C$. Build the Hamiltonian path P in G' starting from j. Then i, followed by the edge (i, j) followed by P is a Hamiltonian path of G. □

Although some variants of the agenda control problem are NP-hard, NP-hardness only implies that (unless P $=$ NP) there is no polynomial time algorithm for the problem. How fast can one solve the problem in general? Is exponential time necessary for some T? It is not hard to devise a dynamic programming algorithm that solves the agenda control problem for arbitrary T in $O(3^m \text{poly}(m))$ time. We describe this in what follows.

Theorem 19.7. *Given any tree T, the agenda control problem for T can be solved in $O(3^m \text{poly}(m))$ time.*

Proof. One computes a table entry $\sigma(u, U, j)$ for every node u of T, subset U of the players and every $j \in U$. $\sigma(u, U, j)$ represents a seeding of the leaves of the subtournament T_u of T rooted at u with the players of U for which j wins the tournament T_u. Here we can assume that $|U|$ is exactly the number of leaves $|L(T_u)|$ of T_u, and $\sigma(u, U, j) = \emptyset$ if j cannot win T_u.

If $|T_u| = 1$, then set $\sigma(u, \{j\}, j) = \{j\}$ for all j. Otherwise, suppose that for some integer $s \geqslant 1$ we have computed $\sigma(v, S', i)$ for all $v \in T$, $S' \subseteq V$ and $i \in S'$ such that $|S'| = |L(T_v)| < s$. We show how to compute $\sigma(u, S, j)$ for any particular $u \in T$, $S \subseteq V$ and $j \in S$ with $|S| = |L(T_u)| = s$.

Let v and w be the children of u and let $s' = |L(T_v)|$, so that $|L(T_w)| = s - s'$. Consider all subsets $U \subseteq S$ such that $|U| = s'$. Because $s', s - s' < s$, we have already computed $\sigma(v, U, i)$ for all $i \in U$ and $\sigma(w, S \setminus U, k)$ for all $k \in S \setminus U$.

Now, for each choice of U with $|U| = s'$, $j \in U$ such that $\sigma = \sigma(v, U, j) \neq \emptyset$, we go through all $i \in S \setminus U$ such that j beats i. If $\sigma(w, S \setminus U, i) \neq \emptyset$, then set $\sigma(u, S, j) = \sigma \odot \sigma(w, S \setminus U, i)$. That is, if there is a seeding for U such that j wins T_v and a seeding of $S \setminus U$ such that i wins T_w and j beats i, then the concatenation of those seedings is a seeding for which j wins T_u.

If no choice of U with $j \in U$ works, do the same for choices for U with $|U| = s'$, $j \notin U$, reversing the roles of v and w. Finally, if no partitioning of S gives a good seeding for j, then j cannot win the tournament on S with tree T_u, so set $\sigma(u, S, j) = \emptyset$.

Let us analyze the running time. For each node u of T, we consider all subsets S of size $t = |L(T_u)|$ and to compute $\sigma(u, S, j)$ for some $j \in S$ in the worst case we consider all possible 2^t subsets of S. (For some special cases of T we may consider fewer subsets.) The runtime per subset U of S is $O(t)$. Thus the final runtime over all choices of u, t, S of size t and $j \in S$ is asymptotically

$$m \sum_{t \leq m} t \binom{m}{t} 2^t \cdot t \leq m^3 \sum_{t \leq m} \binom{m}{t} 2^t 1^{m-t} \leq m^3 3^m.$$

□

The fastest known algorithm for the agenda control problem for complete balanced trees is by Vassilevska Williams (2009) and runs in $O(2^m \text{poly}(m))$ time and uses sophisticated machinery such as fast subset convolution (Björklund et al., 2007). However, the algorithm of Vassilevska Williams (2009) uses $\Theta(2^m \text{poly}(m))$ space. Aziz et al. (2014e) present a family of algorithms for the agenda control problem for complete balanced trees with a sophisticated time/space trade-off. The fastest of their algorithms runs in $O(2.8285^m)$ time and uses $O(1.7548^m)$ space.

The algorithm in Theorem 19.7 and the algorithms of Vassilevska Williams (2009) and Aziz et al. (2014e) can be made to *count* the number of seedings for which the given player wins. This counting version of the agenda control problem is called #Agenda Control.

Definition 19.5. The #*Agenda Control problem* is as follows: given a tournament graph G, a tree T and a node $v \in G$, count the number of seedings of T for which v wins the tournament defined by T, using the match outcomes given by G.

The number of winning seedings for a player is an extremely interesting measure. For instance, it immediately gives the probability that the player will win a randomly seeded tournament given by T. Being able to compute the count efficiently would give an interesting new way of ranking players. Unfortunately, even when we restrict ourselves to complete balanced trees, computing the count exactly is NP-hard by the result of Aziz et al. (2014e) mentioned earlier. What about approximations? Unfortunately again, Aziz et al. (2014e) also show that, unless RP = NP, there is not even a fully polynomial randomized *approximation* scheme (FPRAS) for the problem, that is, an algorithm that for all $\varepsilon > 0$, returns in $\text{poly}(m, 1/\varepsilon)$ time a value that is between $c/(1 + \varepsilon)$ and $(1 + \varepsilon)c$ where c is the true answer. Thus #Agenda Control is a truly hard problem.

In the rest of the chapter we will focus on the natural special case of the agenda control problem for complete balanced trees and will present two cases for which the

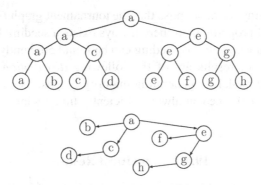

Figure 19.4. A seeded balanced knockout tournament and its outcome, and its corresponding binomial tree.

problem is actually efficiently solvable, thus circumventing the NP-hardness result of Aziz et al. (2014e).

Balanced Tournament Agenda Control as a Graph Problem

Recall that a player v can win the tournament under some seeding if and only if there is a partition of the players V into S and $V \setminus S$ with $v \in S$ and $|S| = m/2$ such that

- v can win a balanced knockout tournament on S under some seeding
- there is a player $u \in V \setminus S$ that v beats and u can win a balanced knockout tournament on $V \setminus S$ under some seeding

Consider the tournament graph G of match outcomes. Because v beating u is the same as the existence of the directed edge (v, u) in G, the preceding conditions are equivalent to the existence of a tree of a particular shape, rooted at v, with edges directed away from v spanning the entire graph. This tree is a *binomial* spanning arborescence of G rooted at v.

A binomial arborescence is the directed version of binomial trees as in Knuth (1973). A binomial arborescence on m nodes rooted at a node v is recursively built by taking two disjoint binomial arborescences on $m/2$ nodes, one rooted at v, and one rooted at a node u, and then adding the directed edge (v, u). The smaller binomial arborescences represent the two subtournaments that u and v win, and the edge (v, u) represents the final match between them. See Figure 19.4 for an illustration.

Thus the balanced tournament agenda control problem is equivalent to the following.

Definition 19.6 (Tournament Fixing Problem (TFP)). Given a tournament graph G and a node v, is there a binomial arborescence rooted at v, spanning G?

19.4 Agenda Control for Balanced Trees Is Easy
for Special Instances

This section provides some proofs that in some cases agenda control for balanced trees is easy. We will consider two different types of results. The first type are *structural* results of the following form: suppose that the tournament graph G or the given player i have some special property, then there always exists a seeding for which i can win the balanced tournament, and this seeding can be found efficiently.

The second type of results are of the following *distributional* form: consider a special probabilistic model for generating majority graphs, then for almost all graphs generated by the model, one can always efficiently find a winning seeding for all (or most) players.

19.4.1 Structural Results

Our goal in this section is to consider various notions of *strength* that a candidate has so that regardless of the individual match outcomes, there is always an efficiently computable winning balanced knockout tournament seeding for any candidate that fulfills the strength criterion.

A requirement for any winner w of a balanced knockout tournament is that in the tournament graph there is a path of length at most $\log m$ between w and all other candidate/player nodes. A natural notion of strength that we can glean from this is that a node is strong if there are short paths between it and all other nodes. The strictest such strength notion is that the player should be a Condorcet winner—in this case the node has distance 1 to all other nodes. The next strictest such strength notion is that the player should be a *king*.

Definition 19.7. A *king* is a node that has a path of length at most two to any other node.

Every tournament graph contains a king as any node that beats the maximum number of other nodes (i.e., every Copeland winner) is a king. To see this, let $\mathcal{K}$ be a Copeland winner and let b be any node that beats $\mathcal{K}$. Then b cannot beat every node that $\mathcal{K}$ beats, as otherwise it would have outdegree that is at least 1 larger than that of $\mathcal{K}$, contradicting the fact that $\mathcal{K}$ is a node of maximum outdegree.

In fact, if there is no node that beats all other nodes, that is, if there is no Condorcet winner, there are at least three kings in any tournament graph. The set of kings is also called the *uncovered* set (see Chapter 3).

Although in general the tournament fixing problem is NP-hard, in the NP-hardness proof of Aziz et al. (2014e) the desired winner of the tournament has long shortest paths to some nodes in the tournament graph instance, so that it is far from being a king. Nevertheless, we can show that the tournament fixing problem is also NP-hard when the favorite player is a king. The proof of the theorem is due to Kim (2014).

Theorem 19.8. *The agenda control problem for balanced binary trees is NP-hard even when the given player is a king in the tournament graph.*

Proof. We will reduce from the agenda control problem where the desired winner is not necessarily a king. Let G be the given tournament graph on m nodes, and let v be the desired winner. Let H be a transitive tournament on m new nodes and let u be the unique node of outdegree $m-1$ in H. Add a directed edge from v to u, and for every $x \in H$ and $y \in G$ add a directed edge (x, y) (except for (u, v) which we already fixed in the opposite direction). Let this new tournament graph be G'. First note that

v is now a king in G', as it beats u and u beats everyone but v. Second, if there is a seeding of G for which v is a winner of a balanced single-elimination tournament over G, then this seeding can be completed to a winning seeding for v over G' by arbitrarily seeding the players of H in the second half of the bracket. Then v wins the first half of the tournament, u wins the second and then v beats u in the final.

Suppose on the other hand that there is a seeding for which v can win a balanced tournament over G'. Then in this seeding, every player of H must be in the same half of the bracket, and the players of G must be in the other half. To see this, suppose that without loss of generality u is in the left half of the seeding, and some nodes of H are in the right half of the seeding. Then, because every node of $H \setminus \{u\}$ beats every node of G, the winner of the right half of the tournament bracket is some node $h \in H \setminus \{u\}$. However, this is already a contradiction, because this means that h will play in the final, and even if v is in the final, it would lose to h. Thus, one half of the seeding is a seeding solely of G which v must win, thus v can win G' if and only if v can win G. $\square$

In this section we consider some further restrictions on the king node that make the player strong enough to *always* be a winner of a balanced knockout tournament.

In the following, we assume that the number m of vertices of G is a power of 2. We also let the input player to the agenda control problem be a king $\mathcal{K}$, and introduce the notation $A = N^{out}(\mathcal{K})$ and $B = N^{in}(\mathcal{K})$ for the out- and in-neighborhood of $\mathcal{K}$.

In all of the results in this section we use the following representation of a seeding of a knockout tournament. When one has deterministic match outcome information, the seeding permutation is equivalent to specifying which matches occur in each of the $\log m$ rounds of the tournament. The matches in round i are $m/2^i$ disjoint edges in the match outcome tournament graph, that is, a *matching* of size $m/2^i$. Because each matching consists of directed edges, we let for each matching M, $sources(M)$ denote $\{u \mid \exists v \text{ with } (u, v) \in M\}$. If M is the set of matches played in round r, then the players surviving till round $r + 1$ is exactly $sources(M)$. Let $V(M)$ denote the vertices that have incident edges in M. We thus use the following representation of a seeding.

Definition 19.8 (Matching Representation of a Seeding). A seeding in a balanced knockout tournament on m players with match outcomes from a tournament graph T is represented by a set of tuples $S = \{(M_1, 1), \ldots, (M_{\log m}, \log m)\}$ where

- for each r, M_r is a matching of size $m/2^r$ in T
- $V(M_{i+1}) = sources(M_i)$

Here if $(M, r) \in S$, then M are the set of matches to be played in round r. Adding the round number is redundant—we could have just had S be an ordered set of matchings. We add the round so that the algorithms would be easier to read.

In the following, we sometimes abuse notation and use M to denote $V(M)$ when it is clear from the context that we are talking about vertices.

For a node v and subset S of the vertex set, we denote by $N_S^{in}(v)$ the set of in-neighbors of v that are in S. Similarly, $N_S^{out}(v)$ denotes the set of out-neighbors of v that are in S. We denote $|N_S^{in}(v)|$ by $indeg_S(v)$ and $|N_S^{out}(v)|$ by $outdeg_S(v)$.

Algorithm SuperSeed$(G, \mathcal{K})$:

1. **If** $E(G) = \{(\mathcal{K}, a)\}$ for some a, **then**
   return $(\{(\mathcal{K}, a)\}, \log m)$.
2. $A' = N_G^{out}(\mathcal{K})$
3. $B' = N_G^{in}(\mathcal{K})$
4. Pick some $a \in A'$, and set $M = \{(\mathcal{K}, a)\}$.
5. $M' = $ maximal matching from $A' \setminus \{a\}$ to B'
6. $M_A = $ maximal matching within $A' \setminus \{a\} \setminus M'$
7. $M_B = $ maximal matching within $B' \setminus M'$
8. $M = M \cup M' \cup M_A \cup M_B$
9. **If** $|B' \setminus M'|$ is odd, **then** let $x \in B' \setminus M$,
   $y \in A' \setminus M$ and set $M = M \cup \{(x, y)\}$.
10. **Return** $\{(M, \log m - \log|G| + 1)\} \cup$
    SuperSeed$(G[sources(M)], \mathcal{K})$.

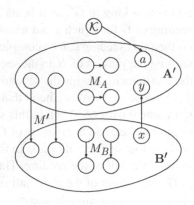

Figure 19.5. Algorithm SuperSeed picks a winning seeding for any given superking $\mathcal{K}$ in G.

Superkings

The notion of a king $\mathcal{K}$ required that each node has at least one path of length at most 2 from $\mathcal{K}$. Here we define a stronger notion that requires that all nodes that are not out-neighbors of $\mathcal{K}$ have at least $\log m$ paths of length 2 from $\mathcal{K}$.

Definition 19.9. A node $\mathcal{K}$ in an m-node directed graph is a *superking* if for every $b \notin N^{out}(\mathcal{K})$, there are at least $\log m$ nodes $c \in N^{out}(\mathcal{K})$ such that (c, b) is an edge.

Superkings do not necessarily exist in tournament graphs. However, if a node is a superking, then finding a winning seeding for it is relatively simple. We give the algorithm for constructing a winning seeding in Figure 19.5, and it serves as a warm-up for the later more complicated construction.

Let m and $\mathcal{K}$ be global variables denoting the number of players in the original tournament and $\mathcal{K}$ is the given superking player. The algorithm is as follows.

Theorem 19.9 (Vassilevska Williams, 2010). *Algorithm SuperSeed computes in polynomial time a winning knockout tournament seeding for any superking $\mathcal{K}$.*

Proof. The runtime is polynomial because in each recursive call the size of the graph reduces in half, and because each individual step takes polynomial (in fact linear) time. It remains to show that the computed seeding makes the superking $\mathcal{K}$ the winner. We prove this by induction. The base case is when G is a single edge. Then the only seeding is to match the two players against each other, as step 1 does.

Suppose now that for all tournament graphs on k vertices the algorithm produces a winning seeding for a superking. Then, we will show that given a graph on $2k$ vertices, SuperSeed picks a perfect directed matching M containing $\mathcal{K}$ as a source and $\mathcal{K}$ is still a superking in the graph induced by the sources of M. Because the latter graph has k vertices, it follows that SuperSeed returns a winning seeding for $\mathcal{K}$ in it, and combined with M this gives a winning seeding for $\mathcal{K}$ in the entire graph.

First, we show that the matching M produced by SuperSeed is a perfect matching. All we need to do is to show that step 9 completes M to a perfect matching. If $|B' \setminus M'|$

is odd, because M has an even number of vertices and because G has an even number of vertices, $|A' \setminus M|$ must also be odd. After step 8, however, all but at most one node of B' and at most one node of A' are matched. Hence $|A' \setminus M| = |B' \setminus M| = 1$, and step 9 just maps the two vertices from these two sets. The direction of the edge (x, y) is also correct because M' was a maximal matching.

Now we show that if $\mathcal{K}$ is a superking in G, then it is also one in $G[sources(M)]$. Consider any $b \in B'$. As $\mathcal{K}$ is a superking, $A' \setminus \{a\}$ must contain at least $\log |G| - 1$ in-neighbors of b. If $b \in sources(M)$, then b was not matched by M', and because M' is a maximal matching, all of the in-neighbors of b that are in $A' \setminus \{a\}$ are also in $sources(M)$. Thus b has at least $\log |G| - 1 = \log(|G|/2)$ in-neighbors in $A' \cap sources(M)$. As $|sources(M)| = |G|/2$ because M is a perfect matching, this makes $\mathcal{K}$ a superking in $G[sources(M)]$. $\qquad\square$

As we will see later on, even though superkings may seem like a restrictive notion, most nodes are superkings in almost all tournament graphs generated by a natural random graph model.

Kings of Highish Outdegree

Here we give a second clean condition under which a king player can be made a winner. Let $\mathcal{H}^{in}(a)$ be the set of in-neighbors of a that have higher outdegree than a. We show that if $\mathcal{K}$ is a node in a tournament graph such that $outdeg(\mathcal{K}) \geqslant |\mathcal{H}^{in}(\mathcal{K})| + 1$, then there is an efficiently constructible seeding for which $\mathcal{K}$ can win a balanced knockout tournament. We present a simplified version of the original proof of Stanton and Vassilevska Williams (2011).

Theorem 19.10 (Kings of Highish Outdegree). *Let G be a tournament graph and $\mathcal{K}$ be a king. If $outdeg(\mathcal{K}) \geqslant |\mathcal{H}^{in}(\mathcal{K})| + 1$, then one can efficiently compute a winning knockout tournament seeding for $\mathcal{K}$.*

This result is *tight* in the sense that there are tournament graphs and kings $\mathcal{K}$ with $outdeg(\mathcal{K}) = |\mathcal{H}^{in}(\mathcal{K})|$ such that $\mathcal{K}$ loses the tournament regardless of the seeding. An example of this is Figure 19.6. In this figure, $\mathcal{K}$ beats exactly $m/2 - 1$ nodes and loses to $m/2$. There is a player a that $\mathcal{K}$ beats that beats all players in $N_{in}(\mathcal{K})$, and all players in $N_{out}(\mathcal{K}) \setminus \{a\}$ lose to everyone in $N_{in}(\mathcal{K})$. Each player in $N_{in}(\mathcal{K})$ beats at least one other player in $N_{in}(\mathcal{K})$, so that the outdegree of each player in $N_{in}(\mathcal{K})$ is at least $m/2$. Thus, $\mathcal{H}^{in}(\mathcal{K}) = N_{in}(\mathcal{K})$ and $outdeg(\mathcal{K}) = |\mathcal{H}^{in}(\mathcal{K})|$. If $\mathcal{K}$ is to be the winner, every player in $N_{in}(\mathcal{K})$ must be eliminated either by a player in $N_{in}(\mathcal{K})$ or by a. However, this means that a must survive at least $\log(|N_{in}(\mathcal{K})| + 1) > (\log m) - 1$ rounds, and hence will be the winner of the tournament because the tournament has exactly $\log m$ rounds. Thus $\mathcal{K}$ cannot win, regardless of the seeding.

An interesting special case of Theorem 19.10 is when $\mathcal{K}$ is a king that beats at least half the graph, that is, $m/2$ players. Figure 19.6 also shows that there are graphs in which even if a king beats $m/2 - 1$ other players, he cannot win regardless of the seeding, so in that special case the result is tight as well.

We give a new algorithm, Algorithm Seed (Figure 19.7) and the algorithm of Theorem 19.10 just runs Seed on input $(G, \mathcal{H}^{in}(\mathcal{K}), \mathcal{K})$.

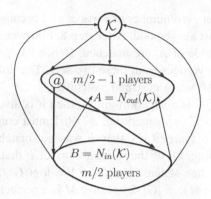

Figure 19.6. An example of an m-node tournament graph and a king $\mathcal{K}$ of outdegree $m/2 - 1$ so that $\mathcal{K}$ cannot win a balanced knockout tournament, regardless of the seeding. Here the set of nodes B does not contain a sink vertex. The outdegree of each node of B is thus at least $m/2$, and so $B = \mathcal{H}^{in}(\mathcal{K})$ and $outdeg(\mathcal{K}) = |\mathcal{H}^{in}(\mathcal{K})|$.

Algorithm Seed$(G, H, \mathcal{K})$:
1. **If** $E(G) = \{(\mathcal{K}, a)\}$ for some a, **then**
    return $(\{(\mathcal{K}, a)\}, \log m)$.
2. $A = N_G^{out}(\mathcal{K})$.
3. $B = N_G^{in}(\mathcal{K})$.
4. M = maximal matching from A to H.
5. M' = maximal matching from $A \setminus M$ to $B \setminus H$.
6. **If** $A \setminus (M' \cup M) \neq \emptyset$, **then** pick $a' \in A \setminus (M' \cup M)$,
    and set $\mathcal{M} = M \cup M' \cup \{(\mathcal{K}, a')\}$.
7. **Else**, pick any $(a', q) \in M'$, and set
    $M' = M' \setminus \{(a', q)\}$, $\mathcal{M} = M \cup M' \cup \{(\mathcal{K}, a')\}$.
8. M_A = maximal matching within $\bar{A} = A \setminus \mathcal{M}$
9. M_B = maximal matching within $\bar{B} = B \setminus H \setminus M'$
10. M_H = maximal matching within $\bar{H} = H \setminus \mathcal{M}$.
11. $\mathcal{M} = \mathcal{M} \cup M_A \cup M_B \cup M_H$.
12. **If** $|\bar{A} \setminus M_A| > 0$ or $|\bar{B} \setminus M_B| > 0$ or
    $|H \setminus \mathcal{M} \setminus M_H| > 0$, **then** pick distinct
    $x, y \in (\bar{A} \setminus M_A) \cup (\bar{B} \setminus M_B) \cup (\bar{H} \setminus M_H)$ and
    set $\mathcal{M} = \mathcal{M} \cup \{(x, y)\}$.
13. **Return** $\{(\mathcal{M}, \log m - \log |G| + 1)\} \cup$
$\mathbf{Seed}(G[sources(\mathcal{M})], H \cap sources(\mathcal{M}), \mathcal{K})$.

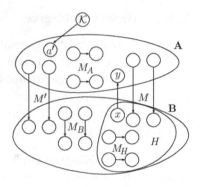

Figure 19.7. Algorithm Seed picks a winning seeding for any highish outdegree king $\mathcal{K}$.

We will first show that the algorithm always returns a valid seeding. To do this, we need to show that steps 7 and 12 make sense.

Claim 19.11. *If $|A| \geqslant |H| + 1$, in step 7, M' is nonempty, so that a' can be picked. In step 12, x and y exist and $\mathcal{M}$ is a perfect matching in G.*

Proof. Because $|A| \geqslant |H| + 1$, $|M| < |A|$ and either step 6 succeeds and step 7 is not run, or $|M'| \geqslant 1$.

For step 12, consider the parity of $|\bar{A}| + |\bar{B}| + |\bar{H}|$. Here m is even, and $m =$

$$|A| + 1 + |B| = (|A \setminus M \setminus M' \setminus \{a'\}| + |M| + |M'| + 1) + 1$$
$$+ (|B \setminus H \setminus M'| + |M'| + |H \setminus M| + |M|)$$
$$= |\bar{A}| + |\bar{B}| + |\bar{H}| + 2(|M| + |M'| + 1),$$

and hence $|\bar{A}| + |\bar{B}| + |\bar{H}|$ must be even.

Thus either 0 or 2 of $|\bar{A}|, |\bar{B}|, |\bar{H}|$ are odd. Hence in step 12, if $|\bar{A} \setminus M_A| > 0$ (i.e., $|\bar{A}|$ is odd) or $|\bar{B} \setminus M_B| > 0$ (i.e., $|\bar{B}|$ is odd) or $|H \setminus M \setminus M_H| > 0$ (i.e., $|\bar{H}|$ is odd), then exactly two of these are the case. Thus in step 12, x and y exist and moreover $(\bar{A} \setminus M_A) \cup (\bar{B} \setminus M_B) \cup (H \setminus M \setminus M_H) = \{x, y\}$, and adding (x, y) to $\mathcal{M}$ makes $\mathcal{M}$ a perfect matching. □

This claim implies that the algorithm gives a valid seeding. To show that the seeding is in fact a winning seeding for $\mathcal{K}$, we will show that an invariant is preserved by the algorithm.

Lemma 19.12. *Algorithm Seed preserves the following invariant:*

$|A| \geqslant |H| + 1$, $\mathcal{K}$ **is a king and the subset of nodes from** $N_G^{in}(\mathcal{K})$ **that have larger outdegree than** $\mathcal{K}$ **is contained in** H.

If the invariant is maintained, $\mathcal{K}$ remains in G after each iteration, so that when $|G| = 1$, G contains only $\mathcal{K}$, and the algorithm computes a winning seeding.

Before we begin the proof of Lemma 19.12, let us assert the following fact.

Claim 19.13. *For any $b \in B$,*

$$outdeg(b) \leqslant outdeg(\mathcal{K}) \iff outdeg_B(b) < indeg_A(b).$$

The proof of the claim is simple: $outdeg(b) = 1 + outdeg_A(b) + outdeg_B(b) = 1 + outdeg(\mathcal{K}) - indeg_A(b) + outdeg_B(b)$.

Proof of Lemma 19.12. Let us assume that in some iteration of the algorithm we have that $|A| \geqslant |H| + 1$, $\mathcal{K}$ is a king and the subset of nodes from $N_G^{in}(\mathcal{K})$ that have larger outdegree than $\mathcal{K}$ is contained in H.

We will first show that $|A \cap sources(\mathcal{M})| > |H \cap sources(\mathcal{M})|$ which of course implies $|A \cap sources(\mathcal{M})| \geqslant |H \cap sources(\mathcal{M})| + 1$.

$$|A \cap sources(\mathcal{M})| \geqslant \lfloor (|A| + |M| + |M'| - 1)/2 \rfloor \geqslant (|A| + |M| + |M'| - 2)/2$$

because all of $A \cap (M \cup M')$ survive and the $\lfloor (|A| - 1 - |M| - |M'|)/2 \rfloor$ sources of M_A survive. On the other hand,

$$|H \cap sources(\mathcal{M})| \leqslant \lceil (|H| - |M|)/2 \rceil \leqslant (|H| - |M| + 1)/2$$

because the only nodes of H that survive are the sources of M_H and potentially a single extra node if $|H| - |M|$ is odd.

If $|A| \geqslant |H| + 2$, then because $|M| \geqslant 1$, $(|A| + |M| + |M'| - 2)/2 \geqslant (|H| + |M|)/2 = (|H| - |M| + 2|M|)/2 > (|H| - |M| + 1)/2$, so that $|A \cap sources(\mathcal{M})| > |H \cap sources(\mathcal{M})|$.

Otherwise, assume that $|A| = |H| + 1$. Then, if $|M| + |M'| \geqslant 2$,

$$|A \cap sources(\mathcal{M})| \geqslant |A|/2 = (|H| + 1)/2 > (|H| - |M| + 1)/2$$

$$\geqslant |H \cap sources(\mathcal{M})|.$$

The final case is that $|A| = |H| + 1$, $|M| = 1$ and $|M'| = 0$. In this case, $|A \cap sources(\mathcal{M})| \geqslant \lfloor(|H| + 1)/2\rfloor$ and $|H \cap sources(\mathcal{M})| \leqslant \lceil(|H| - 1)/2\rceil \leqslant |H|/2$. Because $|A|$ and $|B|$ have different parities, there are only two cases: either $B = H$, or there are at least two nodes b and b' in $B \setminus H$.

Suppose that $B = H$. Then, $|B| < |G|/2$ and $|H \cap sources(\mathcal{M})| \leqslant |H|/2 = |B|/2 < |G|/4$, so that $|A \cap sources(\mathcal{M})| \geqslant |G|/2 - 1 - |H \cap sources(\mathcal{M})| \geqslant |G|/4 > |H \cap sources(\mathcal{M})|$.

Suppose now that there are two nodes b and b' in $B \setminus H$. Without loss of generality, assume that b beats b'. Thus $outdeg_B(b) \geqslant 1$. But then by Claim 19.13, we must have that b has at least two in-neighbors from A, so that if $|H| > 1$, then there is a node to match $\mathcal{K}$ to, while matching b to an in-neighbor from A, and $|M'| \geqslant 1$ but we assumed that $|M'| = 0$. Thus we must have that $|H| = 1$. But then, consider $B \setminus H$. Because the number of nodes in G is a power of 2, we must have that $|B \setminus H| = |G| - 4 \geqslant 4$. However, then there is a node $b \in B \setminus H$ with $outdeg_B(b) \geqslant 2$. By Claim 19.13 this would imply that $indeg_A(b) \geqslant 3 > |A|$, a contradiction. Thus this case never occurs.

We have shown that the algorithm maintains that $|A| \geqslant |H| + 1$. Now let's consider some node $b \in N_G^{in}(\mathcal{K})$ that survives the iteration, in the sense that is among the sources of the matching $\mathcal{M}$. We need to show that b must have at least one in-neighbor in $A \cap sources(\mathcal{M})$, and that if $b \notin H$, then its outdegree in the remaining graph is at most that of $\mathcal{K}$.

Consider the outdegree of b at the beginning of the iteration. Because b was not included in $M \cup M'$, all but possibly one of its in-neighbors (a') are in $sources(\mathcal{M})$. Thus, if b survived by beating another node of B, then its indegree from A must have been at least 2 by Claim 19.13 and thus b must have an in-neighbor in $A \cap sources(\mathcal{M})$. If on the other hand b survived by beating a node in A, then step 7 did not happen and no node a' is removed from M'. Thus all of the in-neighbors of b from A are in $sources(\mathcal{M})$. This proves that $\mathcal{K}$ is still a king after the iteration.

Now consider a node $b \in B \setminus H$ that survives the iteration and is in $sources(\mathcal{M})$. Because $outdeg(b) \leqslant outdeg(\mathcal{K})$, by Claim 19.13, $outdeg_B(b) < indeg_A(b)$. We will show that after the iteration $outdeg_{B \cap sources(\mathcal{M})}(b) < indeg_{A \cap sources(\mathcal{M})}(b)$, completing the proof via Claim 19.13.

If all in-neighbors of b from A also survive the iteration, then

$$outdeg_{B \cap sources(\mathcal{M})}(b) \leqslant outdeg_B(b) < indeg_A(b) = indeg_{A \cap sources(\mathcal{M})}(b).$$

We can therefore assume that Step 7 of the algorithm occurs and that a' was an in-neighbor of b that did not survive. Because all other in-neighbors of b survive, we have that $indeg_{A \cap sources(\mathcal{M})}(b) = indeg_A(b) - 1$. However, because Step 7 happened and b still survived, it must have done so by beating an out-neighbor in B. Thus $outdeg_{B \cap sources(\mathcal{M})}(b) \leqslant outdeg_B(b) - 1 < indeg_A(b) - 1 = indeg_{A \cap sources(\mathcal{M})}(b)$. This completes the proof. $\square$

19.4.2 Distributional Results

So far we have only considered worst case inputs to the agenda control problem. It is natural to ask how the complexity of the problem changes if instead the input is taken from a probability distribution.

For tournament problems, an extremely natural probabilistic generative model was proposed by Condorcet as follows. The players are totally ordered from 1 to m. Let p be a value less than $1/2$. Then, a tournament graph T is sampled as follows. For each i, j with $i < j$, a directed edge (i, j) is added to T with probability $1 - p$ and otherwise, with probability p, edge (j, i) is added.

This model attempts to capture real-world scenarios, where there is a hidden total order of the players but we observe a noisy sample of it, so that with some small probability p, a weaker player actually beats a stronger one, but otherwise, stronger players beat weaker players.

Consider the agenda control problem for balanced knockout tournaments restricted to inputs generated in this way. For any player w and any seeding, apriori the probability that w wins the tournament is at most $(1 - p)^{\log m} \leqslant 1/m^\gamma$ for some γ (depending on p) even for the strongest player. Hence no fixed seeding can give a good probability of winning for w for all tournaments generated by the Condorcet model. The situation changes, however, if we are allowed to see the tournament graph T generated by the model. Then one can show that with high probability, T has some structure so that even for very small p, one can find a winning seeding for *every* player!

Theorem 19.14 (Every Node Is a Winner). *Let $p = C\sqrt{\log m/(m-1)}$ for $C \geqslant 8$. Then for almost all tournament graphs T generated by the Condorcet model, for every player w in T, there is an efficiently computable seeding for which w wins the balanced knockout tournament with outcomes given by T.*

The proof of the preceding theorem appears in Vassilevska Williams (2010). It is based on showing, using standard Chernoff bounds, that in a tournament graph generated with $p = C\sqrt{\log m/(m-1)}$ with $C > 8$, with high probability, every vertex is a superking.

The theorem requires that $p \geqslant \Omega(\sqrt{\log m/m})$. Can anything be said for smaller values of p? In order for the weakest player v_m to be able to win, it needs to be able to win at least $\log m$ matches. In order for this to happen with good probability, p must be $\Omega(\log m/m)$. Such low probability is not sufficient to make every player a possible winner. However, Stanton and Vassilevska Williams (2011) show that if $p \geqslant \Omega(2^i \log m/m)$ for some positive integer i, then any one of the top $1 + m(1 - 1/2^i)$ players have a winning seeding.

19.5 Extensions and Further Reading

There has been a lot of experimental work on tournament seeding. Russell (2010), for instance, extends the distributional results presented in the previous section. He generates tournament graphs from real data and shows experimentally that the agenda control problem for the generated tournaments is typically easily solved, even when one places restrictions on the tournament organizer. The restrictions can be of many different types: some players may be required to play each other before facing anyone else; there may be strict rules on positioning the teams, for instance that geographically close-by teams should play each other, and so on. Russell's results indicate that the agenda control problem may be easy in real life, even if the tournament organizer's hands may seem tied. One catch here is, of course, just as with the distributional results from the previous section, that the tournament organizer needs to be able to see the actual outcomes. Nevertheless, it could be that the probabilistic setting, that is, P-agenda control, is also easy for real-world instances. Indeed, Vu et al. (2009b) investigate how different natural heuristics perform in solving the P-agenda control problem for both balanced and caterpillar voting trees. Their experiments use both randomly generated and real data. Interestingly, the heuristics perform extremely well for real-world tennis data, but poorly for real-world basketball data.

Many sports tournaments such as most major tennis tournaments use a so-called standard seeding that aims to benefit each player according to the player's perceived strength. This seeding matches up the top player with bottom player, the second player with the second-to last (and so on in a specified way) and makes sure that the first and second players are in opposite sides of the bracket. Marchand (2002) compares the standard seeding of a balanced elimination tournament to a random seeding, considering how the seeding affects the probability that a given player wins. Marchand analyzes this change for the strongest player in some interesting special cases and proves that the standard seeding does not increase the probability of winning by much. Marchand conjectures that this is true in general. Under some assumptions on the probability matrix, Marchand shows that for some players, even if they are relatively strong (such as the third out of 16), a random seeding actually increases their probability of winning over the standard seeding. This suggests that the standard seeding only really benefits the very top players.

There have been several studies on what is the optimal seeding of a knockout tournament. For instance, Horen and Riezman (1985) study the following scenario: suppose that one is to seed a balanced knockout tournament on m players, given a monotonic probability matrix P, what is the seeding that maximizes the probability that the best player wins, or that maximizes the expected quality of the winner? Horen and Riezman (1985) give definitive answers to these questions for $m = 4$. However, they show that for $m = 8$, monotonic probability matrices can have a rich structure and depending on the matrix, different seedings may be best, even for just maximizing the probability that the top player wins. Vu and Shoham (2010a) and Vu and Shoham (2010b) continue this study for $m \geqslant 8$. They show that for $m = 8$, the probabilities that the best player wins under the optimal seeding and under the worst seeding differ at most by $1/8$. They also give heuristics with which they can estimate a variety of seeding properties such as the probability that the top player wins for any given seeding. They use these heuristics to experimentally evaluate the standard seeding and some others for values of m up to 128. Groh et al. (2012) use game theoretic techniques to analyze similar measures for four players, obtaining optimal seedings in some settings, and comparing their results to real data from basketball tournaments.

Kräkel (2014) also considers a game theoretic scenario for four players. Here players exert effort and in a match, the winner is the player who exerted substantially more effort than the other player. There are two types of players: strong and weak, and there are two of each. The organizer's goal is either to maximize the total expected effort, or two maximize the probability that a strong player wins. Kräkel (2014) concludes that often the best strategy for the organizer is, in the first stage of the knockout tournament, to match the two strong players against each other and the two weak players against each other, rather than matching players of different types. Kräkel's framework is partially based on work by Lazear and Rosen (1981) and Rosen (1986) that analyzed what the prizes for different finishes in a balanced knockout tournament should look like to maximize the players' effort.

Ryvkin (2010) and Ryvkin and Ortmann (2008) also analyze the expected quality of the winner, the probability that the strongest player becomes the winner and related measures for SMC-trees, balanced knockout tournaments (of arbitrary size) and round-robin tournaments. These works consider a probabistic model of player abilities, where the winner of each match is determined via a comparison of randomly perturbed values of these abilities.

Other research investigates other types of manipulation of the outcome of knockout tournaments. Russell and Walsh (2009) consider manipulations by coalitions of players, where each coalition can decide which players in it are to lose their matches on purpose. They analyze the complexity of both constructive (making a favorite player win) and destructive (preventing a player from winning) manipulations in knockout and round-robin tournaments, showing for instance that one can compute in polynomial time whether a coalition can make a player win a knockout tournament. The results of Russell and Walsh (2009) are based partially on results by Conitzer et al. (2007) that concern whether a coalition of *voters* can manipulate the outcome of a cup election by changing their votes. Altman et al. (2009) further investigate the manipulability of different tournament choice rules such as voting trees or Copeland when players can drop matches or coalitions of players can change the outcome of any matches between them.

A different type of manipulation is *bribery*. Here, an external agent can pay some number of players to intentionally lose matches. Bribery in elections was studied by Faliszewski et al. (2009b). Mattei et al. (2012b) consider bribery questions for seeded SMC-trees, balanced trees and round-robin tournaments. In this work, there are probabilities for match outcomes and costs associated with bribing each particular player. The manipulator wants to raise her favorite player's probability of winning by using a minimal amount of bribe cash. One result is that in polynomial time, one can determine whether the manipulator can raise the probability of their favorite player winning above 0, given a fixed budget of bribery money.

A natural extension of knockout tournaments are tournaments with multiple elimination rounds. In such tournaments, there is a tournament/voting tree for each elimination round. The losers in the ith round are seeded (according to some rule) in the tree for the $(i + 1)$st round. The winner is determined from matches between the winners of all elimination rounds. In a k-elimination tournament, a player is eliminated only when they lose k matches. In double-elimination tournaments, for instance, there are two brackets. The losers of the winner bracket are seeded in the loser bracket. Losers in the loser bracket are eliminated, and the winner of the tournament is the winner of the match between the winners of the loser and the winner bracket.

There are very few papers on the complexity of any type of manipulation for multiple elimination tournaments. Russell and Walsh (2009) consider manipulation of the outcome of a double-elimination tournament by coalitions of players showing that for small enough coalitions the problem is efficiently solvable. Stanton and Vassilevska Williams (2013) extend the results of Russell and Walsh (2009). They also focus on formalizing the definition of a double-elimination tournament. Prior work defined double-elimination only as two tournament trees, where the losers of the first get seeded in the second. However, neither the structure of the trees, nor the seeding of the losers has been formalized before. The definitions in Stanton and Vassilevska Williams (2013) capture the format of most real-world double-elimination tournaments. They also allow for new proofs on the complexity of double-elimination tournament manipulation.

There is some literature analyzing more complex competition formats. Connolly and Rendleman (2011) use Monte Carlo simulations and statistical modeling to analyze the seeding and selection efficiency of the PGA TOUR's FedExCup, a very complex multistage golf competition. Pauly (2014) studies certain complex competition formats used in the soccer world cup and the Olympics. In these formats, there is a round-robin stage followed by a knockout stage. In the round-robin stage, the teams/players are partitioned into groups, each group plays a round-robin tournament and typically the top two players from each group advance and are seeded into a balanced knockout tournament. In such tournaments it is often advantageous for a team to lose intentionally in order to be second in their group, as this may sometimes benefit their seeding into the knockout tournament. This happens in real life, as evidenced by a scandal at the 2012 Olympics in which eight badminton players were disqualified for intentionally losing matches (CNN, 2012). Pauly (2014) investigates whether one can obtain a round-robin-based knockout tournament format resistant to manipulation. He proves an impossibility theorem: any such tournament format satisfying several natural conditions is vulnerable to manipulation by the players.

Acknowledgments

The author is indebted to the diligent reviewers and editors who have helped shape this chapter: Serge Gaspers, Haris Aziz, Marc Pauly, Ariel Procaccia, Felix Brandt, Vincent Conitzer, Ulle Endriss, and Jérôme Lang.

References

Abdulkadiroğlu, A. 2013. School Choice. In *Oxford Handbook of Market Design*, 138–169. New York: Oxford University Press.

Abdulkadiroğlu, A. and Sönmez, T. 1998. Random Serial Dictatorship and the Core from Random Endowments in House Allocation Problems. *Econometrica*, **66**(3), 689–701.

Abdulkadiroğlu, A. and Sönmez, T. 1999. House Allocation with Existing Tenants. *Journal of Economic Theory*, **88**, 233–260.

Abdulkadiroğlu, A. and Sönmez, T. 2003. School Choice: A Mechanism Design Approach. *American Economic Review*, **93**(3), 729–747.

Abdulkadiroğlu, A. Pathak, P. A., Roth, A. E., and Sönmez, T. 2005a. The Boston Public School Match. *American Economic Review*, **95**(2), 368–371.

Abdulkadiroğlu, A., Pathak, P. A., and Roth, A. E. 2005b. The New York City High School Match. *American Economic Review*, **95**(2), 364–367.

Abraham, D. J., Cechlárová, K., Manlove, D. F., and Mehlhorn, K. 2004. Pareto Optimality in House Allocation Problems. In *Proceedings of the 15th Annual International Symposium on Algorithms and Computation* (ISAAC), 3–15. New York: Springer.

Abraham, D. J., Blum, A., and Sandholm, T. 2007a. Clearing Algorithms for Barter Exchange Markets: Enabling Nationwide Kidney Exchanges. In *Proceedings of the 8th ACM Conference on Electronic Commerce* (EC), 295–304. New York: ACM.

Abraham, D. J., Irving, R. W., Kavitha, T., and Mehlhorn, K. 2007b. Popular Matchings. *SIAM Journal on Computing*, **37**, 1030–1045.

Ackermann, H., Goldberg, P. W., Mirrokni, V. S., Röglin, H., and Vöcking, B. 2011. Uncoordinated Two-Sided Matching Markets. *SIAM Journal on Computing*, **40**(1), 92–106.

Aharoni, R. and Fleiner, T. 2003. On a Lemma of Scarf. *Journal of Combinatorial Theory, Series B*, **87**, 72–80.

Ahn, D. S. and Oliveros, S. 2012. Combinatorial Voting. *Econometrica*, **80**(1), 89–141.

Ailon, N., Charikar, M., and Newman, A. 2005. Aggregating Inconsistent Information: Ranking and Clustering. In *Proceedings of the 37th ACM Symposium on Theory of Computing* (STOC), 684–693. New York: ACM.

Ailon, N., Charikar, M., and Newman, A. 2008. Aggregating Inconsistent Information: Ranking and Clustering. *Journal of the ACM*, **55**(5), 1–27.

Airiau, S. and Endriss, U. 2009. Iterated Majority Voting. In *Proceedings of the 1st International Conference on Algorithmic Decision Theory (ADT)*, 38–49. New York: Springer.

Airiau, S., Endriss, U., Grandi, U., Porello, D., and Uckelman, J. 2011. Aggregating Dependency Graphs into Voting Agendas in Multi-issue Elections. In *Proceedings of the 22nd International Joint Conference on Artificial Intelligence (IJCAI)*, 18–23. Palo Alto, CA: AAAI.

Aizerman, M. and Aleskerov, F. 1995. *Theory of Choice*. Amsterdam: North-Holland.

Alcalde, J. and Barberà, S. 1994. Top Dominance and the Possibility of Strategy-Proof Stable Solutions to Matching Problems. *Economic Theory*, **4**(3), 417–435.

Alcalde, J. and Revilla, P. 2004. Researching with Whom? Stability and Manipulation. *Journal of Mathematical Economics*, **40**(8), 869–887.

Aleskerov, F. and Kurbanov, E. 1999. Degree of Manipulability of Social Choice Procedures. In *Current Trends in Economics: Studies in Economic Theory Volume 8*, 13–27. New York: Springer.

Ali, A. and Meilă, M. 2012. Experiments with Kemeny Ranking: What Works When? *Mathematical Social Sciences*, **64**(1), 28–40.

Alkan, A., Demange, G., and Gale, D. 1991. Fair Allocation of Indivisible Goods and Criteria of Justice. *Econometrica*, **59**(4), 1023–1039.

Alon, N. 1987. Splitting Necklaces. *Advances in Mathematics*, **63**, 241–253.

Alon, N. 2006. Ranking Tournaments. *SIAM Journal on Discrete Mathematics*, **20**(1), 137–142.

Alon, N. and Spencer, J. 2008. *The Probabilistic Method*. 3rd ed. New York: John Wiley.

Alon, N., Fischer, F. A., Procaccia, A. D., and Tennenholtz, M. 2011. Sum of Us: Strategyproof Selection from the Selectors. In *Proceedings of the Conference on Theoretical Aspects of Rationality and Knowledge* (TARK), 101–110. New York: ACM.

Alon, N., Falik, D., Meir, R., and Tennenholtz, M. 2013. Bundling Attacks in Judgment Aggregation. In *Proceedings of the 27th AAAI Conference on Artificial Intelligence*, 39–45. Palo Alto, CA: AAAI.

Alonso-Meijide, J. M., Freixas, J., and Molinero, X. 2012. Computation of Several Power Indices by Generating Functions. *Applied Mathematics and Computation*, **219**(8), 3395–3402.

Altman, A. and Tennenholtz, M. 2005. Ranking Systems: The Pagerank Axioms. In *Proceedings of the 6th ACM Conference on Electronic Commerce* (EC), 1–8. New York: ACM.

Altman, A. and Tennenholtz, M. 2006. Quantifying Incentive Compatibility of Ranking Systems. In *Proceedings of the 21st National Conference on Artificial Intelligence* (AAAI), 586–591. Palo Alto, CA: AAAI.

Altman, A. and Tennenholtz, M. 2007. Incentive Compatible Ranking Systems. In *Proceedings of the 6th International Conference on Autonomous Agents and Multiagent Systems* (AAMAS), 546–553. IFAAMAS.

Altman, A. and Tennenholtz, M. 2008. Axiomatic Foundations for Ranking Systems. *Journal of Artificial Intelligence Research (JAIR)*, **31**, 473–495.

Altman, A. and Tennenholtz, M. 2010. An Axiomatic Approach to Personalized Ranking Systems. *Journal of the ACM*, **57**(4), 1–35.

Altman, A., Procaccia, A. D., and Tennenholtz, M. 2009. Nonmanipulable Selections from a Tournament. In *Proceedings of the International Joint Conference on Artificial Intelligence* (IJCAI), 27–32. Palo Alto: AAAI.

Ambos-Spies, K. 1986. Randomness, Relativization, and Polynomial Reducibilities. *Proceedings of the 1st Structure in Complexity Theory Conference*, 23–34. New York: Springer.

Amer-Yahia, S., Roy, S. B., Chawlat, A., Das, G., and Yu, C. 2009. Group Recommendation: Semantics and Efficiency. *Proceedings of the VLDB Endowment*, **2**(1), 754–765.

Andersen, R., Borgs, C., Chayes, J., Feige, U., Flaxman, A., Kalai, A., Mirrokni, V., and Tennenholtz, M. 2008. Trust-Based Recommendation Systems: An Axiomatic Approach. In *Proceedings of the 17th International Conference on the World Wide Web*, 199–208. New York: ACM.

Ángel Ballester, M. and Rey-Biel, P. 2009. Does Uncertainty Lead to Sincerity? Simple and Complex Voting Mechanisms. *Social Choice and Welfare*, **33**(3), 477–494.

Anshelevich, E., Dasgupta, A., Kleinberg, J. M., Tardos, É., Wexler, T., and Roughgarden, T. 2004. The Price of Stability for Network Design with Fair Cost Allocation. In *Proceedings of the 45th Annual Symposium on Foundations of Computer Science* (FOCS), 295–304. New York: IEEE.

Apesteguia, J., Ballester, M. A., and Masatlioglu, Y. 2014. A Foundation for Strategic Agenda Voting. *Games and Economic Behavior*, **87**, 91–99.

Arora, S. and Barak, B. 2009. *Computational Complexity: A Modern Approach*. Cambridge: Cambridge University Press.

Arrow, K. J. 1950. A Difficulty in the Concept of Social Welfare. *Journal of Political Economy*, **58**, 328–346.

Arrow, K. J. 1951. *Social Choice and Individual Values*. 1st ed. New Haven, CT: Cowles Foundation.

Arrow, K. J. 1963. *Social Choice and Individual Values*. 2nd ed. New York: John Wiley.

Arrow, K. J. and Raynaud, H. 1986. *Social Choice and Multicriterion Decision-Making*. Cambridge, MA: MIT Press.

Arrow, K. J., Sen, A. K., and Suzumura, K., eds. 2002. *Handbook of Social Choice and Welfare*. Vol. 1. Amsterdam: North-Holland.

Arrow, K. J., Sen, A. K., and Suzumura, K., eds. 2010. *Handbook of Social Choice and Welfare*. Vol. 2. Amsterdam: North-Holland.

Arzi, O., Aumann, Y., and Dombb, Y. 2011. Throw One's Cake—and Eat It Too. In *Proceedings of the 4th International Symposium on Algorithmic Game Theory* (SAGT), 69–80. New York: Springer.

Asadpour, A. and Saberi, A. 2010. An Approximation Algorithm for Max-min Fair Allocation of Indivisible Goods. *SIAM Journal on Computing*, **39**(7), 2970–2989.

Ashlagi, I. and Roth, A. E. 2012. New Challenges in Multihospital Kidney Exchange. *American Economic Review*, **102**(3), 354–359.

Ashlagi, I., Braverman, M., and Hassidim, A. 2014. Stability in Large Matching Markets with Complementarities. *Operations Research*, **62**(4), 713–732.

Aumann, Y. and Dombb, Y. 2010. The Efficiency of Fair Division with Connected Pieces. In *Proceedings of the 6th International Conference on Web and Internet Economics* (WINE), 26–37. New York: Springer.

Aumann, R. J. and Maschler, M. 1985. Game Theoretic Analysis of a Bankruptcy Problem from the Talmud. *Journal of Economic Theory*, **36**(2), 195–213.

Aumann, Y., Dombb, Y., and Hassidim, A. 2013. Computing Socially-Efficient Cake Divisions. In *Proceedings of the 12th International Conference on Autonomous Agents and Multiagent Systems* (AAMAS), 343–350. Richland, SC: IFAAMAS.

Ausiello, G., Crescenzi, P., Gambosi, G., Kann, V., Marchetti-Spaccamela, A., and Protasi, M. 1999. *Complexity and Approximation: Combinatorial Optimization Problems and their Approximability Properties*. New York: Springer.

Austen-Banks, D. and Smith, J. S. 1994. Information Aggregation, Rationality, and the Condorcet Jury Theorem. *American Political Science Review*, **90**(1), 34–45.

Austen-Smith, D. and Banks, J. S. 2000. *Positive Political Theory I: Collective Preference*. Ann Arbor: University of Michigan Press.

Austen-Smith, D. and Banks, J. S. 2005. *Positive Political Theory II: Strategy and Structure*. Ann Arbor: University of Michigan Press.

Aziz, H. 2013. Stable Marriage and Roommate Problems with Individual-Based stability. In *Proceedings of the 12th International Conference on Autonomous Agents and Multiagent Systems* (AAMAS), 287–294. Richland, SC: IFAAMAS.

Aziz, H. 2014. A Note on the Undercut Procedure. In *Proceedings of the 13th International Conference on Autonomous Agents and Multiagent Systems* (AAMAS), 1361–1362. Richland, SC: IFAAMAS.

Aziz, H. and Brandl, F. 2012. Existence of Stability in Hedonic Coalition Formation Games. In *Proceedings of the 11th International Conference on Autonomous Agents and Multiagent Systems* (AAMAS), 763–770. Richland, SC: IFAAMAS.

Aziz, H. and de Keijzer, B. 2011. Complexity of Coalition Structure Generation. In *Proceedings of the 10th International Conference on Autonomous Agents and Multiagent Systems* (AAMAS), 191–198. Richland, SC: IFAAMAS.

Aziz, H. and Mestre, J. 2014. Parametrized Algorithms for Random Serial Dictatorship. *Mathematical Social Sciences*, **72**, 1–6.

Aziz, H. and Stursberg, P. 2014. A Generalization of Probabilistic Serial to Randomized Social Choice. In *Proceedings of the 28th AAAI Conference on Artificial Intelligence*, 559–565. Palo Alto, CA: AAAI.

Aziz, H. and Ye, C. 2014. Cake Cutting Algorithms for Piecewise Constant and Piecewise Uniform Valuations. In *Proceedings of the 10th International Conference on Web and Internet Economics* (WINE), 1–14. New York: Springer.

Aziz, H., Bachrach, Y., Elkind, E., and Paterson, M. S. 2011. False-Name Manipulations in Weighted Voting Games. *Journal of Artificial Intelligence Research (JAIR)*, **40**, 57–93.

Aziz, H., Harrenstein, P., and Pyrga, E. 2012a. Individual-Based Stability in Hedonic Games Depending on the Best or Worst Players. In *Proceedings of the 11th International Conference on Autonomous Agents and Multiagent Systems* (AAMAS), 1311–1312. Richland, SC: IFAAMAS.

Aziz, H., Brill, M., Fischer, F., Harrenstein, P., Lang, J., and Seedig, H. G. 2012b. Possible and Necessary Winners of Partial Tournaments. In *Proceedings of the 11th International Conference on Autonomous Agents and Multiagent Systems* (AAMAS), 585–592. Richland, SC: IFAAMAS.

Aziz, H., Brandt, F., and Brill, M. 2013a. The Computational Complexity of Random Serial Dictatorship. *Economics Letters*, **121**(3), 341–345.

Aziz, H., Brandt, F., and Seedig, H. G. 2013b. Computing Desirable Partitions in Additively Separable Hedonic Games. *Artificial Intelligence*, **195**, 316–334.

Aziz, H., Brandt, F., and Stursberg, P. 2013c. On Popular Random Assignments. In *Proceedings of the 6th International Symposium on Algorithmic Game Theory* (SAGT), 183–194. New York: Springer.

Aziz, H., Brandt, F., and Brill, M. 2013d. On the Tradeoff between Economic Efficiency and Strategyproofness in Randomized Social Choice. In *Proceedings of the 12th International Conference on Autonomous Agents and Multiagent Systems* (AAMAS), 455–462. Richland, SC: IFAAMAS.

Aziz, H., Brandt, F., and Harrenstein, P. 2013e. Pareto Optimality in Coalition Formation. *Games and Economic Behavior*, **82**, 562–581.

Aziz, H., Gaspers, S., Mattei, N., Narodytska, N., and Walsh, T. 2013f. Ties Matter: Complexity of Manipulation when Tie-breaking with a Random Vote. In *Proceedings of the 27th AAAI Conference on Artificial Intelligence*, 74–80. New York: AAAI.

Aziz, H., Harrenstein, P., Lang, J., and Wooldridge, M. 2014a. Boolean Hedonic Games. In *Proceedings of the 11th Conference of Logic and the Foundations of Game and Decision Theory* (LOFT).

Aziz, H., Brandt, F., and Harrenstein, P. 2014b. Fractional Hedonic Games. In *Proceedings of the 13th International Conference on Autonomous Agents and Multiagent Systems* (AAMAS), 5–12. Richland, SC: IFAAMAS.

Aziz, H., Brandl, F., and Brandt, F. 2014c. On the Incompatibility of Efficiency and Strategyproofness in Randomized Social Choice. In *Proceedings of the 28th AAAI Conference on Artificial Intelligence*, 545–551. New York: AAAI.

Aziz, H., Gaspers, S., Mackenzie, S., and Walsh, T. 2014d. Fair Assignment of Indivisible Objects Under Ordinal Preferences. In *Proceedings of the 13th International Conference on Autonomous Agents and Multiagent Systems* (AAMAS), 1305–1312. Richland, SC: IFAAMAS.

Aziz, H., Gaspers, S., Mackenzie, S., and Mattei, N. 2014e. Fixing a Balanced Knockout Tournament. In *Proceedings of the 28th AAAI Conference on Artificial Intelligence* (AAAI), 552–558. Palo Alto, CA: AAAI.

Babaioff, M., Dobzinski, S., Oren, S., and Zohar, A. 2012. On Bitcoin and Red Balloons. In *Proceedings of the 13th ACM Conference on Electronic Commerce* (EC), 56–73. New York: ACM.

Bacchus, F. and Grove, A. 1995. Graphical Models for Preference and Utility. In *Proceedings of the Conference on Uncertainty in Artificial Intelligence* (UAI), 3–10. New York: Morgan Kaufmann.

Bachmeier, G., Brandt, F., Geist, C., Harrenstein, P., Kardel, K., and Seedig, H. G. 2014. *k*-Majority Digraphs and the Hardness of Voting with a Constant Number of Voters. Working paper.

Bachrach, Y. and Shah, N. 2013. Reliability Weighted Voting Games. In *Proceedings of the 6th International Symposium on Algorithmic Game Theory* (SAGT), 38–49. New York: Springer.

Bachrach, Y., Markakis, E., Resnick, E., Procaccia, A. D., Rosenschein, J. S., and Saberi, A. 2010a. Approximating Power Indices: Theoretical and Empirical Analysis. *Autonomous Agents and Multi-Agent Systems*, **20**(2), 105–122.

Bachrach, Y., Betzler, N., and Faliszewski, P. 2010b. Probabilistic Possible Winner Determination. In *Proceedings of the AAAI Conference on Artificial Intelligence*, 697–702. Palo Alto, CA: AAAI.

Bachrach, Y., Elkind, E., and Faliszewski, P. 2011. Coalitional Voting Manipulation: A Game-Theoretic Perspective. In *Proceedings of the 22nd International Joint Conference on Artificial Intelligence* (IJCAI), 49–54. Palo Alto, CA: AAAI.

Baharad, E., Koppel, M., Goldberger, J., and Nitzan, S. 2011. Distilling the Wisdom of Crowds: Weighted Aggregation of Decisions on Multiple Issues. *Journal of Autonomous Agents and Multi-Agent Systems*, **22**, 31–42.

Baharad, E., Koppel, M., Goldberger, J., and Nitzan, S. 2012. Beyond Condorcet: Optimal Judgment Aggregation Using Voting Records. *Theory and Decision*, **72**, 113–130.

Baigent, N. 1987. Metric Rationalisation of Social Choice Functions According to Principles of Social Choice. *Mathematical Social Sciences*, **13**(1), 59–65.

Baïou, M. and Balinski, M. 2000. Many-To-Many Matching: Stable Polyandrous Polygamy (or Polygamous Polyandry). *Discrete Applied Mathematics*, **101**, 1–12.

Bakos, Y. and Dellarocas, C. N. 2003. Cooperation without Enforcement? A Comparative Analysis of Litigation and Online Reputation as Quality Assurance Mechanisms. MIT Sloan School of Management Working Paper No. 4295-03.

Baldiga, K. A. and Green, J. R. 2013. Assent-Maximizing Social Choice. *Social Choice and Welfare*, **40**(2), 439–460.

Baldwin, J. M. 1926. The Technique of the Nanson Preferential Majority System of Election. *Transactions and Proceedings of the Royal Society of Victoria*, **39**, 42–52.

Balinski, M. L. and Demange, G. 1989. Algorithms for Proportional Matrices in Reals and Integers. *Mathematical Programming*, **45**(1–3), 193–210.

Balinski, M. L. and Laraki, R. 2010. *Majority Judgment: Measuring, Ranking, and Electing.* Cambridge, MA: MIT Press.

Balinski, M. L. and Sönmez, T. 1999. A Tale of Two Mechanisms: Student Placement. *Journal of Economic Theory*, **84**(1), 73–94.

Balkanski, E., Brânzei, S., Kurokawa, D., and Procaccia, A. D. 2014. Simultaneous Cake Cutting. In *Proceedings of the 28th AAAI Conference on Artificial Intelligence*, 566–572. Palo Alto, CA: AAAI.

Ballester, C. 2004. NP-Completeness in Hedonic Games. *Games and Economic Behavior*, **49**(1), 1–30.

Banerjee, S., Konishi, H., and Sönmez, T. 2001. Core in a Simple Coalition Formation Game. *Social Choice and Welfare*, **18**, 135–153.

Banks, J. S. 1985. Sophisticated Voting Outcomes and Agenda Control. *Social Choice and Welfare*, **1**(4), 295–306.

Banks, J. S. and Bordes, G. A. 1988. Voting Games, Indifference, and Consistent Sequential Choice Rules. *Social Choice and Welfare*, **5**, 31–44.

Banks, J. S., Duggan, J., and Le Breton, M. 2006. Social Choice and Electoral Competition in the General Spatial Model. *Journal of Economic Theory*, **126**, 194–234.

Bansal, N. and Sviridenko, M. 2006. The Santa Claus problem. In *Proceedings of the 38th ACM Symposium on Theory of Computing* (STOC), 31–40. New York: ACM.

Bansal, V., Agrawal, A., and Malhotra, V. S. 2007. Polynomial Time Algorithm for an Optimal Stable Assignment with Multiple Partners. *Theoretical Computer Science*, **379**(3), 317–328.

Banzhaf, J. F. 1965. Weighted Voting Doesn't Work: A Mathematical Analysis. *Rutgers Law Review*, **19**, 317–343.

Baral, C., Kraus, S., Minker, J., and Subrahmanian, V. S. 1992. Combining Knowledge Bases Consisting of First-Order Theories. *Computational Intelligence*, **8**(1), 45–71.

Barbanel, J. B. 2005. *The Geometry of Efficient Fair Division*. New York: Cambridge University Press.

Barberà, S. 1979. Majority and Positional Voting in a Probabilistic Framework. *Review of Economic Studies*, **46**(2), 379–389.

Barberà, S. 2011. Strategyproof Social Choice. *Handbook of Social Choice and Welfare*, **2**, 731–831.

Barberà, S. and Gerber, A. 2007. A Note on the Impossibility of a Satisfactory Concept of Stability for Coalition Formation Games. *Economic Letters*, **95**, 85–90.

Barberà, S. and Peleg, B. 1990. Strategy-Proof Voting Schemes with Continuous Preferences. *Social Choice and Welfare*, **7**, 31–38.

Barberà, S., Sonnenschein, H., and Zhou, L. 1991. Voting by Committees. *Econometrica*, **59**(3), 595–609.

Barberà, S., Gul, F., and Stacchetti, E. 1993. Generalized Median Voter Schemes and Committees. *Journal of Economic Theory*, **61**(2), 262–289.

Barberà, S., Dutta, B., and Sen, A. 2001. Strategy-Proof Social Choice Correspondences. *Journal of Economic Theory*, **101**(2), 374–394.

Barberà, S., Bossert, W., and Pattanaik, P. K. 2004. Ranking Sets of Objects. In *Handbook of Utility Theory, Vol. II: Extensions*, 893–977. New York: Kluwer Academic.

Barthelemy, J. P. and Monjardet, B. 1981. The Median Procedure in Cluster Analysis and Social Choice Theory. *Mathematical Social Sciences*, **1**, 235–267.

Bartholdi, J. and Orlin, J. B. 1991. Single Transferable Vote Resists Strategic Voting. *Social Choice and Welfare*, **8**(4), 341–354.

Bartholdi, J., Tovey, C., and Trick, M. 1989a. The Computational Difficulty of Manipulating an Election. *Social Choice Welfare*, **6**, 227–241.

Bartholdi, J., Tovey, C., and Trick, M. 1989b. Voting Schemes for Which it Can Be Difficult to Tell Who Won the Election. *Social Choice and Welfare*, **6**(2), 157–165.

Bartholdi, J., Tovey, C., and Trick, M. 1992. How Hard Is It to Control an Election? *Mathematical and Computer Modeling*, **16**(8/9), 27–40.

Bauer, E. and Kohavi, R. 1999. An Empirical Comparison of Voting Classification Algorithms: Bagging, Boosting, and Variants. *Machine Learning*, **36**(1–2), 105–139.

Baumeister, D. and Rothe, J. 2010. Taking the Final Step to a Full Dichotomy of the Possible Winner Problem in Pure Scoring Rules. In *Proceedings of the 19th European Conference on Artificial Intelligence* (ECAI), 1019–1020. Amsterdam: IOS.

Baumeister, D. and Rothe, J. 2012. Taking the Final Step to a Full Dichotomy of the Possible Winner Problem in Pure Scoring Rules. *Information Processing Letters*, **112**(5), 186–190.

Baumeister, D. and Rothe, J. 2015. Preference Aggregation by Voting. In *Economics and Computation: An Introduction to Algorithmic Game Theory, Computational Social Choice, and Fair Division*, ed. Rothe, J., Chapter 4, 197–325. New York: Springer.

Baumeister, D., Erdélyi, G., Hemaspaandra, E., Hemaspaandra, L., and Rothe, J. 2010. Computational Aspects of Approval Voting. In *Handbook on Approval Voting*, ed. Laslier, J.-F., and Sanver, M. R., 199–251. New York: Springer.

Baumeister, D., Erdélyi, G., and Rothe, J. 2011. How Hard Is It to Bribe the Judges? A Study of the Complexity of Bribery in Judgment Aggregation. In *Proceedings of the 2nd International Conference on Algorithmic Decision Theory* (ADT), 1–15. New York: Springer.

Baumeister, D., Faliszewski, P., Lang, J., and Rothe, J. 2012a. Campaigns for Lazy Voters: Truncated Ballots. In *Proceedings of the 11th International Conference on Autonomous Agents and Multiagent Systems* (AAMAS), 577–584. Richland, SC: IFAAMAS.

Baumeister, D., Erdélyi, G., Erdélyi, O., and Rothe, J. 2012b. Control in Judgment Aggregation. In *Proceedings of the 6th European Starting AI Researcher Symposium* (STAIRS), 23–34. Amsterdam: IOS Press.

Baumeister, D., Roos, M., Rothe, J., Schend, L., and Xia, L. 2012c. The Possible Winner Problem with Uncertain Weights. In *Proceedings of the 20th European Conference on Artificial Intelligence* (ECAI), 133–138. Amsterdam: IOS Press.

Baumeister, D., Brandt, F., Fischer, F., Hoffmann, J., and Rothe, J. 2013a. The Complexity of Computing Minimal Unidirectional Covering Sets. *Theory of Computing Systems*, **53**(3), 467–502.

Baumeister, D., Erdélyi, G., Erdélyi, O., and Rothe, J. 2013b. Computational Aspects of Manipulation and Control in Judgment Aggregation. In *Proceedings of the 3rd International Conference on Algorithmic Decision Theory* (ADT), 71–85. New York: Springer.

Baumeister, D., Erdélyi, G., and Rothe, J. 2015. Judgment Aggregation. In *Economics and Computation: An Introduction to Algorithmic Game Theory, Computational Social Choice, and Fair Division*, ed. Rothe, J., Chapter 6, 361–391. New York: Springer.

Beaujard, A., Igersheim, H., Lebon, I., Gavrel, F., and Laslier, J.-F. 2014. Evaluative Voting: An Experiment During the 2012 French Presidential Election. *Electoral Studies*, **34**, 131–145.

Bei, X., Chen, N., Hua, X., Tao, B., and Yang, E. 2012. Optimal Proportional Cake Cutting with Connected Pieces. In *Proceedings of the 26th AAAI Conference on Artificial Intelligence*, 1263–1269. Palo Alto, CA: AAAI.

Ben-Yashar, R. C. and Nitzan, S. 1997. The Optimal Decision Rule for Fixed-Size Committees in Dichotomous Choice Situations: The General Result. *International Economic Review*, **38**(1), 175–186.

Ben-Yashar, R. C. and Paroush, J. 2001. Optimal Decision Rules for Fixed-Size Committees in Polychotomous Choice Situations. *Social Choice and Welfare*, **18**(4), 737–746.

Benoît, J.-P. and Kornhauser, L. A. 1991. Voting Simply in the Election of Assemblies. Technical report 91–32. C.V. Starr Center for Applied Economics.

Benoît, J.-P. and Kornhauser, L. A. 2010. Only a Dictatorship is Efficient. *Games and Economic Behavior*, **70**(2), 261–270.

Berg, S. 1985. Paradox of Voting Under an Urn Model: The Effect of Homogeneity. *Public Choice*, **47**, 377–387.

Berg, S. 1993a. Condorcet's Jury Theorem, Dependency Among Jurors. *Social Choice and Welfare*, **10**(1), 87–95.

Berg, S. 1993b. Condorcet's Jury Theorem Revisited. *European Journal of Political Economy*, **9**(3), 437–446.

Berghammer, R. 2014. Computing Minimal Extending Sets by Relation-algebraic Modeling and Development. *Journal on Logic and Algebraic Programming*, **83**(2), 103–119.

Berghammer, R., Rusinowska, A., and de Swart, H. 2013. Computing Tournament Solutions Using Relation Algebra and RelView. *European Journal of Operational Research*, **226**(3), 636–645.

Bertsimas, D., Farias, V. F., and Trichakis, N. 2011. The Price of Fairness. *Operations Research*, **59**(1), 17–31.

Bervoets, S., Merlin, V., and Woeginger, G. J. 2015. Vote Trading and Subset Sums. *Operations Research Letters*, **43**(1), 99–102.

Betzler, N. and Dorn, B. 2010. Towards a Dichotomy for the Possible Winner Problem in Elections Based on Scoring Rules. *Journal of Computer and System Sciences*, **76**(8), 812–836.

Betzler, N. and Uhlmann, J. 2009. Parameterized Complexity of Candidate Control in Elections and Related Digraph Problems. *Theoretical Computer Science*, **410**(52), 5425–5442.

Betzler, N., Fellows, M. R., Guo, J., Niedermeier, R., and Rosamond, F. A. 2009. Fixed-Parameter Algorithms for Kemeny Rankings. *Theoretical Computer Science*, **410**(45), 4554–4570.

Betzler, N., Guo, J., and Niedermeier, R. 2010. Parameterized Computational Complexity of Dodgson and Young Elections. *Information and Computation*, **208**(2), 165–177.

Betzler, N., Niedermeier, R., and Woeginger, G. J. 2011. Unweighted Coalitional Manipulation Under the Borda Rule Is NP-Hard. In *Proceedings of the 22nd International Joint Conference on Artificial Intelligence* (IJCAI), 55–60. Palo Alto, CA: AAAI.

Betzler, N., Bredereck, R., Chen, J., and Niedermeier, R. 2012. Studies in Computational Aspects of Voting—A Parameterized Complexity Perspective. In *The Multivariate Algorithmic Revolution and Beyond*, 318–363. New York: Springer.

Betzler, N., Slinko, A., and Uhlmann, J. 2013. On the Computation of Fully Proportional Representation. *Journal of Artificial Intelligence Research (JAIR)*, **47**, 475–519.

Betzler, N., Bredereck, R., and Niedermeier, R. 2014. Theoretical and Empirical Evaluation of Data Reduction for Exact Kemeny Rank Aggregation. *Autonomous Agents and Multi-Agent Systems*, **28**(5), 721–748.

Beviá, C. 1998. Fair Allocation in a General Model with Indivisible Goods. *Review of Economic Design*, **3**, 195–213.

Bezáková, I. and Dani, V. 2005. Allocating Indivisible Goods. *SIGecom Exchanges*, **5**(3), 11–18.

Bhalgat, A., Chakraborty, T., and Khanna, S. 2010. Approximating Pure Nash Equilibrium in Cut, Party Affiliation, and Satisfiability Games. In *Proceedings of the 11th ACM Conference on Electronic Commerce* (EC), 73–82. New York: ACM.

Biedl, T., Brandenburg, F. J., and Deng, X. 2009. On the Complexity of Crossings in Permutations. *Discrete Mathematics*, **309**(7), 1813–1823.

Bilbao, J. M., Fernández, J. R., Jiminéz, N., and López, J. J. 2002. Voting Power in the European Union Enlargement. *European Journal of Operational Research*, **143**, 181–196.

Bilò, V., Fanelli, A., Flammini, M., Monaco, G., and Moscardelli, L. 2014. Nash Stability in Fractional Hedonic Games. In *Proceedings of the 10th International Conference on Web and Internet Economics* (WINE), 486–491. New York: Springer.

Binkele-Raible, D., Erdélyi, G., Fernau, H., Goldsmith, J., Mattei, N., and Rothe, J. 2014. The Complexity of Probabilistic Lobbying. *Discrete Optimization*, **11**(1), 1–21.

Biró, P. and Klijn, F. 2013. Matching with Couples: A Multidisciplinary Survey. *International Game Theory Review*, **15**, 1–18.

Biró, P., Irving, R. W., and Schlotter, I. 2011. Stable Matching with Couples: An Empirical Study. *ACM Journal of Experimental Algorithmics*, **16**, 1–27.

Birrell, E. and Pass, R. 2011. Approximately Strategy-Proof Voting. In *Proceedings of the 22nd International Joint Conference on Artificial Intelligence* (IJCAI), 67–72. Palo Alto, CA: AAAI.

Bistarelli, S., Fargier, H., Montanari, U., Rossi, F., Schiex, T., and Verfaillie, G. 1999. Semiring-Based CSPs and Valued CSPs: Frameworks, Properties and Comparison. *Constraints*, **4**(3), 199–240.

Björklund, A., Husfeldt, T., Kaski, P., and Koivisto, M. 2007. Fourier Meets Möbius: Fast Subset Convolution. In *Proceedings of the ACM Symposium on Theory of Computing* (STOC), 67–74. New York: ACM.

Black, D. 1948. On the Rationale of Group Decision-Making. *Journal of Political Economy*, **56**(1), 23–34.

Black, D. 1958. *The Theory of Committees and Elections*. New York: Cambridge University Press.

Blais, A., Massicotte, L., and Dobrzynska, A. 1997. Direct Presidential Elections: A World Summary. *Electoral Studies*, **16**, 441–455.

Bogomolnaia, A. and Jackson, M. O. 2002. The Stability of Hedonic Coalition Structures. *Games and Economic Behavior*, **38**(2), 201–230.

Bogomolnaia, A. and Moulin, H. 2001. A New Solution to the Random Assignment Problem. *Journal of Economic Theory*, **100**, 295–328.

Bogomolnaia, A., Moulin, H., and Stong, R. 2005. Collective Choice Under Dichotomous Preferences. *Journal of Economic Theory*, **122**(2), 165–184.

Booth, R., Chevaleyre, Y., Lang, J., Mengin, J., and Sombattheera, C. 2010. Learning Conditionally Lexicographic Preference Relations. In *Proceedings of the European Conference on Artificial Intelligence* (ECAI), 269–274. Amsterdam: IOS Press.

Borda, J.-C. Chevalier de. 1781. *Mémoire sur les Élections au Scrutin*. Paris: Histoire de l'Académie Royale des Sciences.

Bordes, G. 1976. Consistency, Rationality and Collective Choice. *Review of Economic Studies*, **43**(3), 451–457.

Bordes, G. 1979. Some More Results on Consistency, Rationality and Collective Choice. In *Aggregation and Revelation of Preferences*, ed. Laffont, J. J., 175–197. Amsterdam: North-Holland.

Bossert, W. and Suzumura, K. 2010. *Consistency, Choice, and Rationality*. Cambridge, MA: Harvard University Press.

Boutilier, C. 2013. Computational Decision Support: Regret-based Models for Optimization and Preference Elicitation. In *Comparative Decision Making: Analysis and Support across Disciplines and Applications*, ed. Crowley, P. H., and Zentall, T. R., 423–453. Oxford: Oxford University Press.

Boutilier, C. and Procaccia, A. D. 2012. A Dynamic Rationalization of Distance Rationalizability. In *Proceedings of the 26th AAAI Conference on Artificial Intelligence*, 1278–1284. Palo Alto, CA: AAAI.

Boutilier, C., Brafman, R. I., Hoos, H. H., and Poole, D. 1999. Reasoning with Conditional Ceteris Paribus Preference Statements. In *Proceedings of the 15th Conference on Uncertainty in Artificial Intelligence* (UAI), 71–80. New York: Morgan Kaufmann.

Boutilier, C., Bacchus, F., and Brafman, R. I. 2001. UCP-Networks: A Directed Graphical Representation of Conditional Utilities. In *Proceedings of the 17th Conference on Uncertainty in Artificial Intelligence* (UAI), 56–64. New York: Morgan Kaufmann.

Boutilier, C., Brafman, R., Domshlak, C., Hoos, H., and Poole, D. 2004. CP-Nets: A Tool for Representing and Reasoning with Conditional Ceteris Paribus Statements. *Journal of Artificial Intelligence Research (JAIR)*, **21**, 135–191.

Boutilier, C., Caragiannis, I., Haber, S., Lu, T., Procaccia, A. D., and Sheffet, Or. 2012. Optimal Social Choice Functions: A Utilitarian View. In *Proceedings of the ACM Conference on Electronic Commerce* (EC), 194–214. New York: ACM.

Boutilier, C., Lang, J., Oren, J., and Palacios, H. 2014. Robust Winners and Winner Determination Policies Under Candidate Uncertainty. In *Proceedings of the 28th AAAI Conference on Artificial Intelligence*, 1391–1397. Palo Alto, CA: AAAI.

Bouveret, S. and Lang, J. 2008. Efficiency and Envy-Freeness in Fair Division of Indivisible Goods: Logical Representation and Complexity. *Journal of Artificial Intelligence Research (JAIR)*, **32**, 525–564.

Bouveret, S. and Lang, J. 2011. A General Elicitation-Free Protocol for Allocating Indivisible Goods. In *Proceedings of the 22nd International Joint Conference on Artificial Intelligence* (IJCAI), 73–78. Palo Alto, CA: AAAI.

Bouveret, S. and Lemaître, M. 2014. Characterizing Conflicts in Fair Division of Indivisible Goods Using a Scale of Criteria. In *Proceedings of the 13th International Conference on Autonomous Agents and Multiagent Systems* (AAMAS), 1321–1328. Richland, SC: IFAAMAS.

Bouveret, S., Fargier, H., Lang, J., and Lemaître, M. 2005. Allocation of Indivisible Goods: A General Model and some Complexity Results. In *Proceedings of the 4th International Conference on Autonomous Agents and Multiagent Systems* (AAMAS), 1309–1310. Richland, SC: IFAAMAS.

Bouveret, S., Endriss, U., and Lang, J. 2009. Conditional Importance Networks: A Graphical Language for Representing Ordinal, Monotonic Preferences over Sets of Goods. In *Proceedings of the 21st International Joint Conference on Artificial Intelligence* (IJCAI), 67–72. Palo Alto, CA: AAAI.

Bouveret, S., Endriss, U., and Lang, J. 2010. Fair Division Under Ordinal Preferences: Computing Envy-Free Allocations of Indivisible Goods. In *Proceedings of the 19th European Conference on Artificial Intelligence* (ECAI), 387–392. Amsterdam: IOS Press.

Bouyssou, D. 2004. Monotonicity of "ranking by choosing": A progress report. *Social Choice and Welfare*, **23**(2), 249–273.

Bouyssou, D., Marchant, T., Pirlot, M., Tsoukiàs, A., and Vincke, P. 2006. *Evaluation and Decision Models: Stepping Stones for the Analyst*. New York: Springer.

Bovet, D. and Crescenzi, P. 1993. *Introduction to the Theory of Complexity*. Mahwah, NJ: Prentice Hall.

Bowman, C., Hodge, J., and Yu, A. 2014. The Potential of Iterative Voting to Solve the Separability Problem in Referendum Elections. *Theory and Decision*, **77**(1), 111–124.

Bradley, W. J., Hodge, J. K., and Kilgour, D. 2005. Separable Discrete Preferences. *Mathematical Social Science*, **49**(3), 335–353.

Brafman, R. I., Domshlak, C., and Shimony, S. E. 2006. On Graphical Modeling of Preference and Importance. *Journal of Artificial Intelligence Research (JAIR)*, **25**, 389–424.

Brams, S. J. 2008. *Mathematics and Democracy*. Princeton, NJ: Princeton University Press.

Brams, S. J. and Fishburn, P. C. 1978. Approval Voting. *American Political Science Review*, **72**(3), 831–847.

Brams, S. J. and Fishburn, P. C. 2002. Voting Procedures. In *Handbook of Social Choice and Welfare*, vol. 1, ed. Arrow, K., Sen, A., and Suzumura, K., 173–236. New York: Elsevier.

Brams, S. J. and Fishburn, P. C. 2007. *Approval Voting*. Rev. ed. New York: Springer.

Brams, S. J. and King, D. 2005. Efficient Fair Division—Help the Worst off or Avoid Envy? *Rationality and Society*, **17**(4), 387–421.

Brams, S. J. and Potthoff, R. F. 1998. Proportional Representation: Broadening the Options. *Journal of Theoretical Politics*, **10**, 147–178.

Brams, S. J. and Sanver, M. R. 2006. Critical Strategies Under Approval Voting: Who Gets Ruled in and Ruled Out. *Electoral Studies*, **25**(2), 287–305.

Brams, S. J. and Sanver, M. R. 2009. Voting Systems That Combine Approval and Preference. In *The Mathematics of Preference, Choice, and Order: Essays in Honor of Peter C. Fishburn*, ed. Brams, S. J., Gehrlein, W. V., and Roberts, F., 215–237. New York: Springer.

Brams, S. J. and Taylor, A. D. 1995. An Envy-Free Cake Division Protocol. *American Mathematical Monthly*, **102**(1), 9–18.

Brams, S. J. and Taylor, A. D. 1996. *Fair Division: From Cake-Cutting to Dispute Resolution*. New York: Cambridge University Press.

Brams, S. J. and Taylor, A. D. 2000. *The Win-Win Solution: Guaranteeing Fair Shares to Everybody*. New York: W. W. Norton.

Brams, S. J., Kilgour, D., and Zwicker, W. S. 1997a. Voting on Referenda: The Separability Problem and Possible Solutions. *Electoral Studies*, **16**(3), 359–377.

Brams, S. J., Taylor, A. D., and Zwicker, W. S. 1997b. A Moving-Knife Solution to the Four-Person Envy-Free Cake-Division problem. *Proceedings of the American Mathematical Society*, **125**(2), 547–554.

Brams, S. J., Kilgour, D., and Zwicker, W. S. 1998. The Paradox of Multiple Elections. *Social Choice and Welfare*, **15**(2), 211–236.

Brams, S. J., Edelman, P. H., and Fishburn, P. C. 2004. Fair Division of Indivisible Items. *Theory and Decision*, **5**(2), 147–180.

Brams, S. J., Jones, M. A., and Klamler, C. 2006. Better Ways to Cut a Cake. *Notices of the AMS*, **53**(11), 1314–1321.

Brams, S. J., Kilgour, D., and Sanver, M. R. 2007. A Minimax Procedure for Electing Committees. *Public Choice*, **3–4**(132), 401–420.

Brams, S. J., Feldman, M., Morgenstern, J., Lai, J. K., and Procaccia, A. D. 2012a. On Maxsum Fair Cake Divisions. In *Proceedings of the 26th AAAI Conference on Artificial Intelligence*, 1285–1291. Palo Alto, CA: AAAI.

Brams, S. J, Kilgour, D. M., and Klamler, C. 2012b. The Undercut Procedure: An Algorithm for the Envy-Free Division of Indivisible Items. *Social Choice and Welfare*, **39**(2–3), 615–631.

Brams, S. J., Jones, M. A., and Klamler, C. 2013. N-Person Cake-Cutting: There May Be No Perfect Division. *American Mathematical Monthly*, **120**(1), 35–47.

Brams, S. J., Kilgour, M., and Klamler, C. 2014. Two-Person Fair Division of Indivisible Items: An Efficient, Envy-Free Algorithm. *Notices of the AMS*, **61**(2), 130–141.

Brandl, F., Brandt, F., and Hofbauer, J. 2015a. Incentives for Participation and Abstention in Probabilistic Social Choice. In *Proceedings of the 14th International Conference on Autonomous Agents and Multiagent Systems* (AAMAS), 1411–1419. Richland, SC: IFAAMAS.

Brandl, F., Brandt, F., Geist, C., and Hofbauer, J. 2015b. Strategic Abstention based on Preference Extensions: Positive Results and Computer-Generated Impossibilities. In *Proceedings of the 24th International Joint Conference on Artificial Intelligence* (IJCAI), 18–24. Palo Alto, CA: AAAI.

Brandt, F. 2009a. Some Remarks on Dodgson's Voting Rule. *Mathematical Logic Quarterly*, **55**(4), 460–463.

Brandt, F. 2009b. Tournament Solutions—Extensions of Maximality and Their Applications to Decision-Making. Habilitation Thesis, Faculty for Mathematics, Computer Science, and Statistics, University of Munich.

Brandt, F. 2009c. Some Remarks on Dodgson's Voting Rule. *Mathematical Logic Quarterly*, **55**(4), 460–463.

Brandt, F. 2011a. Minimal Stable Sets in Tournaments. *Journal of Economic Theory*, **146**(4), 1481–1499.

Brandt, F. 2011b. Group-Strategyproof Irresolute Social Choice Functions. In *Proceedings of the 22nd International Joint Conference on Artificial Intelligence* (IJCAI), 79–84. Palo Alto, CA: AAAI.

Brandt, F. 2015. Set-monotonicity implies Kelly-Strategyproofness. *Social Choice and Welfare*, **45**(4), 793–804.

Brandt, F. and Brill, M. 2011. Necessary and Sufficient Conditions for the Strategyproofness of Irresolute Social Choice Functions. In *Proceedings of the 13th Conference on Theoretical Aspects of Rationality and Knowledge* (TARK), 136–142. New York: ACM.

Brandt, F. and Brill, M. 2012. Computing Dominance-Based Solution Concepts. In *Proceedings of the 13th ACM Conference on Electronic Commerce* (EC), 233. New York: ACM.

Brandt, F. and Fischer, F. 2007. PageRank as a Weak Tournament Solution. In *Proceedings of the 3rd International Conference on Web and Internet Economics* (WINE), 300–305. New York: Springer.

Brandt, F. and Fischer, F. 2008a. Computing the Minimal Covering Set. *Mathematical Social Sciences*, **56**(2), 254–268.

Brandt, F. and Fischer, F. 2008b. On the Hardness and Existence of Quasi-Strict Equilibria. In *Proceedings of the 1st International Symposium on Algorithmic Game Theory* (SAGT), 291–302. New York: Springer.

Brandt, F. and Geist, C. 2014. Finding Strategyproof Social Choice Functions via SAT Solving. In *Proceedings of the 13th International Conference on Autonomous Agents and Multiagent Systems* (AAMAS), 1193–1200. Richland, SC: IFAAMAS.

Brandt, F. and Harrenstein, P. 2010. Characterization of Dominance Relations in Finite Coalitional Games. *Theory and Decision*, **69**(2), 233–256.

Brandt, F. and Harrenstein, P. 2011. Set-Rationalizable Choice and Self-Stability. *Journal of Economic Theory*, **146**(4), 1721–1731.

Brandt, F. and Seedig, H. G. 2013. A Tournament of Order 24 With Two Disjoint TEQ-Retentive Sets. Technical report.

Brandt, F. and Seedig, H. G. 2015. On the Discriminative Power of Tournament Solutions. In *Selected Papers of the International Conference on Operations Research* (OR2014). New York: Springer.

Brandt, F., Fischer, F., and Harrenstein, P. 2009. The Computational Complexity of Choice Sets. *Mathematical Logic Quarterly*, **55**(4), 444–459.

Brandt, F., Brill, M., Hemaspaandra, E., and Hemaspaandra, L. 2010a. Bypassing Combinatorial Protections: Polynomial-Time Algorithms for Single-Peaked Electorates. In *Proceedings of the 24th AAAI Conference on Artificial Intelligence*, 715–722. Palo Alto, CA: AAAI.

Brandt, F., Brill, M., Hemaspaandra, E., and Hemaspaandra, L. 2010b. Bypassing Combinatorial Protections: Polynomial-Time Algorithms for Single-Peaked Electorates. Technical report TR-955, Department of Computer Science, University of Rochester, Rochester, NY. Revised September 2013.

Brandt, F., Fischer, F., Harrenstein, P., and Mair, M. 2010c. A Computational Analysis of the Tournament Equilibrium Set. *Social Choice and Welfare*, **34**(4), 597–609.

Brandt, F., Brill, M., and Seedig, H. G. 2011. On the Fixed-Parameter Tractability of Composition-Consistent Tournament Solutions. In *Proceedings of the 22nd International Joint Conference on Artificial Intelligence* (IJCAI), 85–90. Palo Alto, CA: AAAI.

Brandt, F., Conitzer, V., and Endriss, U. 2013a. Computational Social Choice. In *Multiagent Systems*, 2nd ed. Weiss, G., 213–283. Cambridge, MA: MIT Press.

Brandt, F., Chudnovsky, M., Kim, I., Liu, G., Norin, S., Scott, A., Seymour, P., and Thomassé, S. 2013b. A Counterexample to a Conjecture of Schwartz. *Social Choice and Welfare*, **40**, 739–743.

Brandt, F., Brill, M., and Harrenstein, P. 2014a. Extending Tournament Solutions. In *Proceedings of the 28th AAAI Conference on Artificial Intelligence*, 580–586. Palo Alto, CA: AAAI.

Brandt, F., Geist, C., and Seedig, H. G. 2014b. Identifying *k*-Majority Digraphs via SAT Solving. In *Proceedings of the 1st AAMAS Workshop on Exploring Beyond the Worst Case in Computational Social Choice* (EXPLORE).

Brandt, F., Harrenstein, P., and Seedig, H. G. 2014c. Minimal Extending Sets in Tournaments. In *Proceedings of the 13th International Conference on Autonomous Agents and Multiagent Systems* (AAMAS), 1539–1540. Richland, SC: IFAAMAS.

Brandt, F., Brill, M., Fischer, F., and Harrenstein, P. 2014d. Minimal Retentive Sets in Tournaments. *Social Choice and Welfare*, **42**(3), 551–574.

Brandt, F., Brill, M., Seedig, H. G., and Suksompong, W. 2014e. On the Structure of Stable Tournament Solutions. Working paper.

Brandt, F., Geist, C., Harrenstein, P. 2015a. A Note on the McKelvey Uncovered Set and Pareto Optimality. *Social Choice and Welfare*, Online First.

Brandt, F., Dau, A., and Seedig, H. G. 2015b. Bounds on the Disparity and Separation of Tournament Solutions. *Discrete Applied Mathematics*, **187**, 41–49.

Brandt, F., Brill, M., Hemaspaandra, E., and Hemaspaandra, L. 2015c. Bypassing Combinatorial Protections: Polynomial-Time Algorithms for Single-Peaked Electorates. *Journal of Artificial Intelligence Research (JAIR)*, **53**, 439–496.

Branzei, S. and Larson, K. 2011. Social Distance Games. In *Proceedings of the 22nd International Joint Conference on Artificial Intelligence (IJCAI)*, 273–279. Palo Alto, CA: AAAI.

Brânzei, S. and Miltersen, P. B. 2013. Equilibrium Analysis in Cake Cutting. In *Proceedings of the 12th International Conference on Autonomous Agents and Multiagent Systems (AAMAS)*, 327–334. Richland, SC: IFAAMAS.

Brânzei, R., Dimitrov, D., and Tijs, S. 2005. *Models in Cooperative Game Theory*. Springer.

Brânzei, S., Procaccia, A. D., and Zhang, J. 2013a. Externalities in Cake Cutting. In *Proceedings of the 23rd International Joint Conference on Artificial Intelligence* (IJCAI), 55–61. Palo Alto, CA: AAAI.

Brânzei, S., Caragiannis, I., Morgenstern, J., and Procaccia, A. D. 2013b. How Bad Is Selfish Voting? In *Proceedings of the 27th AAAI Conference on Artificial Intelligence*, 138–144. Palo Alto, CA: AAAI.

Bredereck, R., Chen, J., and Woeginger, G. J. 2013a. Are There Any Nicely Structured Preference Profiles Nearby? In *Proceedings of the 23rd International Joint Conference on Artificial Intelligence* (IJCAI), 62–68. Palo Alto, CA: AAAI.

Bredereck, R., Chen, J., and Woeginger, G. J. 2013b. A Characterization of the Single-Crossing Domain. *Social Choice and Welfare*, **41**(4), 989–998.

Bredereck, R., Chen, J., Hartung, S., Kratsch, S., Niedermeier, R., Suchý, O., and Woeginger, G. J. 2014a. A Multivariate Complexity Analysis of Lobbying in Multiple Referenda. *Journal of Artificial Intelligence Research (JAIR)*, **50**, 409–446.

Bredereck, R., Chen, J., Faliszewski, P., Nichterlein, A., and Niedermeier, R. 2014b. Prices Matter for the Parameterized Complexity of Shift Bribery. In *Proceedings of the 28th AAAI Conference on Artificial Intelligence*, 1398–1404. Palo Alto, CA: AAAI.

Brelsford, E., Faliszewski, P., Hemaspaandra, E., Schnoor, H., and Schnoor, I. 2008. Approximability of Manipulating Elections. In *Proceedings of the 23rd AAAI Conference on Artificial Intelligence*, 44–49. Palo Alto, CA: AAAI.

Brightwell, G. and Winkler, P. 1991. Counting Linear Extensions is #P-Complete. In *Proceedings of the ACM Symposium on Theory of Computing* (STOC), 175–181. New York: ACM.

Brill, M. and Conitzer, V. 2015. Strategic Voting and Strategic Candidacy. In *Proceedings of the 29th AAAI Conference on Artificial Intelligence*, 819–826. Palo Alto, CA: AAAI.

Brill, M. and Fischer, F. 2012. The Price of Neutrality for the Ranked Pairs Method. In *Proceedings of the 26th AAAI Conference on Artificial Intelligence*, 1299–1305. Palo Alto, CA: AAAI.

Brin, S. and Page, L. 1998. The Anatomy of a Large-Scale Hypertextual Web Search Engine. *Computer Networks and ISDN Systems*, **30**(1–7), 107–117.

Buchanan, J. M. 1954. Social Choice, Democracy, and Free Markets. *Journal of Political Economy*, **62**, 114–123.

Budish, E. 2011. The Combinatorial Assignment Problem: Approximate Competitive Equilibrium from Equal Incomes. *Journal of Political Economy*, **119**(6), 1061–1103.

Caminada, M. and Pigozzi, G. 2011. On Judgment Aggregation in Abstract Argumentation. *Autonomous Agents and Multiagent Systems*, **22**(1), 64–102.

Campbell, D. E. and Kelly, J. S. 2003. Strategy-Proofness Characterization of Majority Rule. *Economic Theory*, **22**(3), 557–568.

Campbell, D. and Nitzan, S. 1986. Social Compromise and Social Metrics. *Social Choice and Welfare*, **3**(1), 1–16.

Camps, R., Mora, X., and Saumell, L. 2014. Social Choice Rules Driven by Propositional Logic. *Annals of Mathematics and Artificial Intelligence*, **70**(3), 279–312.

Caragiannis, I. and Procaccia, A. D. 2011. Voting Almost Maximizes Social Welfare Despite Limited Communication. *Artificial Intelligence*, **175**(9–10), 1655–1671.

Caragiannis, I., Kaklamanis, C., Kanellopoulos, P., and Kyropoulou, M. 2009. The Efficiency of Fair Division. In *Proceedings of the 5th International Conference on Web and Internet Economics* (WINE), 475–482. New York: Springer.

Caragiannis, I., Kalaitzis, D., and Markakis, E. 2010. Approximation Algorithms and Mechanism Design for Minimax Approval Voting. In *Proceedings of the AAAI Conference on Artificial Intelligence*, 737–742. Palo Alto, CA: AAAI.

Caragiannis, I., Lai, J. K., and Procaccia, A. D. 2011. Towards More Expressive Cake Cutting. In *Proceedings of the 22nd International Joint Conference on Artificial Intelligence* (IJCAI), 127–132. Palo Alto, CA: AAAI.

Caragiannis, I., Kaklamanis, C., Kanellopoulos, P., and Kyropoulou, M. 2012a. The Efficiency of Fair Division. *Theory of Computing Systems*, **50**(4), 589–610.

Caragiannis, I., Covey, J., Feldman, M., Homan, C., Kaklamanis, C., Karanikolas, N., Procaccia, A. D., and Rosenschein, J. S. 2012b. On the Approximability of Dodgson and Young Elections. *Artificial Intelligence*, **187–188**, 31–51.

Caragiannis, I., Procaccia, A. D., and Shah, N. 2013. When Do Noisy Votes Reveal the Truth? In *Proceedings of the 13th ACM Conference on Electronic Commerce* (EC), 143–160. New York: ACM.

Caragiannis, I., Procaccia, A. D., and Shah, N. 2014a. Modal Ranking: A Uniquely Robust Voting Rule. In *Proceedings of the 28th AAAI Conference on Artificial Intelligence*, 616–622. Palo Alto, CA: AAAI.

Caragiannis, I., Kaklamanis, C., Karanikolas, N., and Procaccia, A. D. 2014b. Socially Desirable Approximations for Dodgson's Voting Rule. *ACM Transactions on Algorithms*, **10**(2), Article 6.

Cary, D. 2011. Estimating the Margin of Victory for Instant-Runoff Voting. In *Proceedings of the Electronic Voting Technology Workshop and the Workshop on Trustworthy Elections* (EVT/WOTE). Berkeley, CA: USENIX.

Caspard, N., Leclerc, B., and Monjardet, B. 2012. *Finite Ordered Sets: Concepts, Results and Uses*. New York: Cambridge University Press.

Cavallo, R. 2012. Fairness and Welfare through Redistribution When Utility Is Transferable. In *Proceedings of the 26th AAAI Conference on Artificial Intelligence*, 1306–1312. Palo Alto, CA: AAAI.

Cechlárová, K. 2008. Stable Partition Problem. In *Encyclopedia of Algorithms*, 885–888. New York: Springer.

Cechlárová, K. and Hajduková, J. 2002. Computational Complexity of Stable Partitions With B-Preferences. *International Journal of Game Theory*, **31**(3), 353–354.

Cechlárová, K. and Hajduková, J. 2004a. Stability of Partitions Under BW-Preferences and WB-Preferences. *International Journal of Information Technology and Decision Making*, **3**(4), 605–618.

Cechlárová, K. and Hajduková, J. 2004b. Stable Partitions with W-Preferences. *Discrete Applied Mathematics*, **138**(3), 333–347.

Cechlárová, K. and Romero-Medina, A. 2001. Stability in Coalition Formation games. *International Journal of Game Theory*, **29**, 487–494.

Cervone, D., Gehrlein, W. V., and Zwicker, W. S. 2005. Which Scoring Rule Maximizes Condorcet Efficiency Under IAC? *Theory and Decision*, **58**, 145–185.

Chalkiadakis, G., Elkind, E., Markakis, E., and Jennings, N. R. 2010. Cooperative Games with Overlapping Coalitions. *Journal of Artificial Intelligence Research (JAIR)*, **39**, 179–216.

Chalkiadakis, G., Elkind, E., and Wooldridge, M. 2011. *Computational Aspects of Cooperative Game Theory*. San Rafael, CA: Morgan and Claypool.

Chamberlin, J. R. and Courant, P. N. 1983. Representative Deliberations and Representative Decisions: Proportional Representation and the Borda Rule. *American Political Science Review*, **77**(3), 718–733.

Chambers, C. P. and Thomson, W. 2002. Group Order Preservation and the Proportional Rule for the Adjudication of Conflicting Claims. *Mathematical Social Sciences*, **44**(3), 235–252.

Charbit, P., Thomassé, S., and Yeo, A. 2007. The Minimum Feedback Arc Set Problem Is NP-Hard for Tournaments. *Combinatorics, Probability and Computing*, **16**(1), 1–4.

Charon, I. and Hudry, O. 2006. A Branch-And-Bound Algorithm to Solve the Linear Ordering Problem for Weighted Tournaments. *Discrete Applied Mathematics*, **154**(15), 2097–2116.

Charon, I. and Hudry, O. 2007. A Survey on the Linear Ordering Problem for Weighted or Unweighted Tournaments. *4OR*, **5**(1), 5–60.

Charon, I. and Hudry, O. 2010. An Updated Survey on the Linear Ordering Problem for Weighted or Unweighted Tournaments. *Annals of Operations Research*, **175**(1), 107–158.

Chebotarev, P. Yu. and Shamis, E. 1998. Characterizations of Scoring Methods for Preference Aggregation. *Annals of Operations Research*, **80**, 299–332.

Chen, J., Faliszewski, P., Niedermeier, R., and Talmon, N. 2014. Combinatorial Voter Control in Elections. In *Proceedings of the 39th International Symposium on Mathematical Foundations of Computer Science*, 153–164. New York: Springer.

Chen, J., Faliszewski, P., Niedermeier, R., and Talmon, N. 2015. Elections with Few Voters: Candidate Control Can Be Easy. In *Proceedings of the 29th AAAI Conference on Artificial Intelligence*, 2045–2051. Palo Alto, CA: AAAI.

Chen, Y.-L., Cheng, L.-C., and Chuang, C.-N. 2008. A Group Recommendation System with Consideration of Interactions among Group Members. *Expert Systems with Applications*, **34**(3), 2082–2090.

Chen, Y., Lai, J. K., Parkes, D. C., and Procaccia, A. D. 2013. Truth, Justice, and Cake Cutting. *Games and Economic Behavior*, **77**, 284–297.

Chernoff, H. 1954. Rational Selection of Decision Functions. *Econometrica*, **22**, 422–443.

Chevaleyre, Y., Dunne, P. E., Endriss, U., Lang, J., Lemaître, M., Maudet, N., Padget, J., Phelps, S., Rodríguez-Aguilar, J. A., and Sousa, P. 2006. Issues in Multiagent Resource Allocation. *Informatica*, **30**, 3–31.

Chevaleyre, Y., Lang, J., Maudet, N., and Ravilly-Abadie, G. 2009. Compiling the votes of a subelectorate. In *Proceedings of the 21st International Joint Conference on Artificial Intelligence* (IJCAI), 97–102. Palo Alto, CA: AAAI.

Chevaleyre, Y., Endriss, U., and Maudet, N. 2010. Simple Negotiation Schemes for Agents with Simple Preferences: Sufficiency, Necessity and Maximality. *Journal of Autonomous Agents and Multi-Agent Systems*, **20**(2), 234–259.

Chevaleyre, Y., Lang, J., Maudet, N., and Monnot, J. 2011. Compilation/Communication Protocols for Voting Rules with a Dynamic Set of Candidates. In *Proceedings of the 13th Conference on Theoretical Aspects of Rationality and Knowledge* (TARK), 153–160. New York: ACM.

Chevaleyre, Y., Lang, J., Maudet, N., Monnot, J., and Xia, L. 2012. New Candidates Welcome! Possible Winners with Respect to the Addition of New Candidates. *Mathematical Social Sciences*, **64**(1), 74–88.

Chichilnisky, G. and Thomson, W. 1987. The Walrasian Mechanism from Equal Division is Not Monotonic with Respect to Variations in the Number of Consumers. *Journal of Public Economics*, **32**(1), 119–124.

Chopra, S., Pacuit, E., and Parikh, R. 2004. Knowledge-Theoretic Properties of Strategic Voting. In *Proceedings of the 9th European Conference on Logics in Artificial Intelligence* (JELIA), 18–30. New York: Springer.

Chou, J.-H. and Lu, C.-J. 2010. Communication Requirements for Stable Marriages. In *Proceedings of the 7th International Conference on Algorithms and Complexity* (CIAC), 371–382. New York: Springer.

Christian, R., Fellows, M. R., Rosamond, F., and Slinko, A. 2007. On Complexity of Lobbying in Multiple Referenda. *Review of Economic Design*, **11**(3), 217–224.

Chun, Y. and Thomson, W. 1988. Monotonicity Properties of Bargaining Solutions when Applied to Economics. *Mathematical Social Sciences*, **15**(1), 11–27.

CNN. 2012. Olympic Badminton Players Disqualified for Trying to Lose, August 22.

Cohen, S. and Zohar, A. 2015. An Axiomatic Approach to Link Prediction. In *Proceedings of the AAAI Conference on Artificial Intelligence*, 58–64. Palo Alto, CA: AAAI.

Cohen, W. W., Schapire, R. E., and Singer, Y. 1999. Learning to Order Things. *Journal of Artificial Intelligence Research (JAIR)*, **10**, 243–270.

Cohler, Y. J., Lai, J. K., Parkes, D. C., and Procaccia, A. D. 2011. Optimal Envy-Free Cake Cutting. In *Proceedings of the 25th AAAI Conference on Artificial Intelligence*, 626–631. Palo Alto, CA: AAAI.

Coleman, J. S. 1971. Control of Collectivities and the Power of a Collectivity to Act. In *Social Choice*, ed. Lieberman, B., 269–298. New York: Gordon and Breach.

Coleman, T. and Teague, V. 2007. On the Complexity of Manipulating Elections. In *Proceedings of the 13th Australasian Symposium on Theory of Computing* (CATS), 25–33. Darlinghurst: Australian Computer Society.

Condorcet, J.-A.-N. de Caritat, Marquis de. 1785. *Essai sur l' Application de L' Analyse à la Probabilité des Décisions Rendues à la Pluralité des Voix*. Facsimile reprint of original published in Paris, 1972, by the Imprimerie Royale.

Conitzer, V. 2006. Computing Slater Rankings Using Similarities among Candidates. In *Proceedings of the 21st AAAI Conference on Artificial Intelligence*, 613–619. Palo Alto, CA: AAAI.

Conitzer, V. 2008. Anonymity-Proof Voting Rules. In *Proceedings of the 4th International Conference on Web and Internet Economics* (WINE), 295–306. New York: Springer.

Conitzer, V. 2009. Eliciting Single-Peaked Preferences Using Comparison Queries. *Journal of Artificial Intelligence Research (JAIR)*, **35**, 161–191.

Conitzer, V. and Sandholm, T. 2002. Vote Elicitation: Complexity and Strategy-Proofness. In *Proceedings of the AAAI Conference on Artificial Intelligence*, 392–397. Palo Alto, CA: AAAI.

Conitzer, V. and Sandholm, T. 2003. Universal Voting Protocol Tweaks to Make Manipulation Hard. In *Proceedings of the 18th International Joint Conference on Artificial Intelligence* (IJCAI), 781–788. Palo Alto, CA: AAAI.

Conitzer, V. and Sandholm, T. 2004. Computational Criticisms of the Revelation Principle. In *Proceedings of the ACM Conference on Electronic Commerce* (EC), 262–263. New York: ACM.

Conitzer, V. and Sandholm, T. 2005a. Common Voting Rules as Maximum Likelihood Estimators. In *Proceedings of the Conference on Uncertainty in Artificial Intelligence* (UAI), 145–152. New York: Morgan Kaufmann.

Conitzer, V. and Sandholm, T. 2005b. Communication Complexity of Common Voting Rules. In *Proceedings of the ACM Conference on Electronic Commerce* (EC), 78–87. New York: ACM.

Conitzer, V. and Sandholm, T. 2006. Nonexistence of Voting Rules That Are Usually Hard to Manipulate. In *Proceedings of the AAAI Conference on Artificial Intelligence*, 627–634. Palo Alto, CA: AAAI.

Conitzer, V. and Xia, L. 2012. Paradoxes of Multiple Elections: An Approximation Approach. In *Proceedings of the International Conference on Principles of Knowledge Representation and Reasoning* (KR), 179–187. Palo Alto: AAAI.

Conitzer, V., Davenport, A., and Kalagnanam, J. 2006. Improved Bounds for Computing Kemeny Rankings. In *Proceedings of the 21st AAAI Conference on Artificial Intelligence*, 620–627. Palo Alto, CA: AAAI.

Conitzer, V., Sandholm, T., and Lang, J. 2007. When Are Elections with Few Candidates Hard to Manipulate? *Journal of the Association for Computing Machinery*, **54**(3), 1–33.

Conitzer, V., Lang, J., and Xia, L. 2009a. How Hard Is It to Control Sequential Elections via the Agenda? In *Proceedings of the 21st International Joint Conference on Artificial Intelligence* (IJCAI), 103–108. Palo Alto, CA: AAAI.

Conitzer, V., Rognlie, M., and Xia, L. 2009b. Preference Functions that Score Rankings and Maximum Likelihood Estimation. In *Proceedings of the 21st International Joint Conference on Artificial Intelligence* (IJCAI), 109–115. Palo Alto, CA: AAAI.

Conitzer, V., Walsh, T., and Xia, L. 2011a. Dominating Manipulations in Voting with Partial Information. In *Proceedings of the 25th AAAI Conference on Artificial Intelligence*, 638–643. Palo Alto, CA: AAAI.

Conitzer, V., Lang, J., and Xia, L. 2011b. Hypercubewise Preference Aggregation in Multi-issue Domains. In *Proceedings of the International Joint Conference on Artificial Intelligence* (IJCAI), 158–163. Palo Alto, CA: AAAI.

Connolly, R. A. and Rendleman, R. J. 2011. Tournament Qualification, Seeding and Selection Efficiency: An Analysis of the PGA TOUR's FedExCup. Working paper, Tuck School of Business.

Copeland, A. H. 1951. A "Reasonable" Social Welfare Function. Mimeo, University of Michigan Seminar on Applications of Mathematics to the Social Sciences.

Coppersmith, D., Fleischer, L., and Rudra, A. 2006. Ordering by Weighted Number of Wins Gives a Good Ranking for Weighted Tournaments. In *Proceedings of the 17th Annual ACM-SIAM Symposium on Discrete Algorithms*, 776–782. New York: ACM.

Coppersmith, D., Fleischer, L., and Rudra, A. 2010. Ordering by Weighted Number of Wins Gives a Good Ranking for Weighted Tournaments. *ACM Transactions on Algorithms*, **6**(3), 1–13.

Cornaz, D., Galand, L., and Spanjaard, O. 2012. Bounded Single-Peaked Width and Proportional Representation. In *Proceedings of the 20th European Conference on Artificial Intelligence* (ECAI), 270–275. Amsterdam: IOS Press.

Cornaz, D., Galand, L., and Spanjaard, O. 2013. Kemeny Elections with Bounded Single-Peaked or Single-Crossing Width. In *Proceedings of the 23rd International Joint Conference on Artificial Intelligence* (IJCAI), 76–82. Palo Alto, CA: AAAI.

Coste-Marquis, S., Lang, J., Liberatore, P., and Marquis, P. 2004. Expressive Power and Succinctness of Propositional Languages for Preference Representation. In *Proceedings of the 9th International Conference on Principles of Knowledge Representation and Reasoning* (KR), 203–212. New York: AAAI.

Coughlan, P. J. and Le Breton, M. 1999. A Social Choice Function Implementable via Backward Induction with Values in the Ultimate Uncovered Set. *Review of Economic Design*, **4**(2), 153–160.

Cox, G. 1997. *Making Votes Count: Strategic Coordination in the World's Electoral Systems*. New York: Cambridge University Press.

Cramton, P., Shoham, Y., and Steinberg, R, eds. 2006. *Combinatorial Auctions*. Cambridge, MA: MIT Press.

Cuhadaroğlu, T. and Lainé, J. 2012. Pareto efficiency in Multiple Referendum. *Theory and Decision*, **72**(4), 525–536.

Curiel, I. 1997. *Cooperative Game Theory and Applications*. Dordrecht: Kluwer Academic.

Dagan, N. 1996. A Note on Thomson's Characterizations of the Uniform Rule. *Journal of Economic Theory*, **69**(1), 255–261.

van Dalen, D. 2013. *Logic and Structure*. 5th ed. New York: Springer.

Dalla Pozza, G., Pini, M. S., Rossi, F., and Venable, K. B. 2011. Multi-Agent Soft Constraint Aggregation via Sequential Voting. In *Proceedings of the International Joint Conference on Artificial Intelligence* (IJCAI), 172–177. Palo Alto, CA: AAAI.

Dall'Aglio, M. and Hill, T. P. 2003. Maxmin Share and Minimax Envy in Fair Division Problems. *Journal of Mathematical Analysis and Applications*, **281**(1), 346–361.

Dall'Aglio, M. and Mosca, R. 2007. How to Allocate Hard Candies Fairly. *Mathematical Social Sciences*, **54**, 218–237.

Daniels, H. E. 1969. Round-Robin Tournament Scores. *Biometrika*, **56**(2), 295–299.

Darmann, A. 2013. Popular Spanning Trees. *International Journal of Foundations of Computer Science*, **24**(5), 655–678.

Darmann, A., Klamler, C., and Pferschy, U. 2009. Maximizing the Minimum Voter Satisfaction on Spanning Trees. *Mathematical Social Sciences*, **58**(2), 238–250.

Darmann, A., Kurz, E., Lang, J., Schauer, J., and Woeginger, G. J. 2012. Group Activity Selection Problem. In *Proceedings of the 8th International Conference on Web and Internet Economics* (WINE), 156–169. New York: Springer.

Dash, R., Ramchurn, S., and Jennings, N. R. 2004. Trust-Based Mechanism Design. In *Proceedings of the 3rd International Conference on Autonomous Agents and Multiagent Systems* (AAMAS), 748–755. Richland, SC: IFAAMAS.

Davenport, A. and Kalagnanam, J. 2004. A Computational Study of the Kemeny Rule for Preference Aggregation. In *Proceedings of the 19th AAAI Conference on Artificial Intelligence*, 697–702. Palo Alto, CA: AAAI.

Davey, B. A. and Priestley, H. A. 2002. *Introduction to Lattices and Order*. 2nd ed. New York: Cambridge University Press.

Davies, J., Katsirelos, G., Narodytska, N., and Walsh, T. 2011. Complexity of and Algorithms for Borda Manipulation. In *Proceedings of the 25th AAAI Conference on Artificial Intelligence*, 657–662. Palo Alto, CA: AAAI.

Davies, J., Narodytska, N., and Walsh, T. 2012. Eliminating the Weakest Link: Making Manipulation Intractable? In *Proceedings of the 26th AAAI Conference on Artificial Intelligence*, 1333–1339. Palo Alto, CA: AAAI.

Davies, J., Katsirelos, G., Narodytska, N., Walsh, T., and Xia, L. 2014. Complexity of and Algorithms for the Manipulation of Borda, Nanson's and Baldwin's voting rules. *Artificial Intelligence*, **217**, 20–42.

De Donder, P., Le Breton, M., and Truchon, M. 2000. Choosing from a Weighted Tournament. *Mathematical Social Sciences*, **40**, 85–109.

de Keijzer, B., Bouveret, S., Klos, T., and Zhang, Y. 2009. On the Complexity of Efficiency and Envy-Freeness in Fair Division of Indivisible Goods with Additive Preferences. In *Proceedings of the 1st International Conference on Algorithmic Decision Theory* (ADT), 98–110. New York: Springer.

Debord, B. 1987. Caractérisation des matrices des préférences nettes et méthodes d'agrégation associées. *Mathématiques et sciences humaines*, **97**, 5–17.

Debreu, G. 1954. Representation of a Preference Ordering by a Numerical Function. *Decision Processes*, **3**, 159–165.

Deegan, J. and Packel, E. W. 1978. A New Index of Power for Simple N-Person Games. *International Journal of Game Theory*, **7**, 113–123.

Deineko, V. G. and Woeginger, G. J. 2013. Two Hardness Results for Core Stability in Hedonic Coalition formation games. *Discrete Applied Mathematics*, **161**, 1837–1842.

Deineko, V. G. and Woeginger, G. J. 2014. Two Hardness Results for Gamson's Game. *Social Choice and Welfare*, **43**, 963–972.

Dekel, O., Fischer, F. A., and Procaccia, A. D. 2010. Incentive Compatible Regression Learning. *Journal of Computer and System Sciences*, **76**(8), 759–777.

Demange, G. 2009. The Strategy Structure of Some Coalition Formation Games. *Games and Economic Behavior*, **65**, 83–104.

Demko, S. and Hill, T. P. 1988. Equitable Distribution of Indivisible Items. *Mathematical Social Sciences*, **16**, 145–158.

Deng, X. and Fang, Z. 2008. Algorithmic Cooperative Game Theory. In *Pareto Optimality, Game Theory and Equilibria*, ed. Chinchuluun, A., Pardalos, P. M., Migdalas, A., and Pitsoulis, L. 158–185. New York: Springer.

Deng, X. and Papadimitriou, C. H. 1994. On the Complexity of Cooperative Solution Concepts. *Mathematics of Operations Research*, **19**(2), 257–266.

Deng, X., Papadimitriou, C. H., and Safra, S. 2003. On the Complexity of Equilibria. *Journal of Computer and System Sciences*, **67**(2), 311–324.

Deng, X., Qi, Q., and Saberi, A. 2012. Algorithmic Solutions for Envy-Free Cake Cutting. *Operations Research*, **60**(6), 1461–1476.

Dery, L. N., Kalech, M., Rokach, L., and Shapira, B. 2010. Iterative Voting Under Uncertainty for Group Recommender Systems. In *Proceedings of the 4th ACM Conference on Recommender Systems*, 265–268. New York: ACM.

Desmedt, Y. and Elkind, E. 2010. Equilibria of Plurality Voting with Abstentions. In *Proceedings of the ACM Conference on Electronic Commerce* (EC), 347–356. New York: ACM.

Diaconis, P. and Graham, R. L. 1977. Spearman's Footrule as a Measure of Disarray. *Journal of the Royal Statistical Society*, **39**(2), 262–268.

Dickerson, J. P., Procaccia, A. D., and Sandholm, T. 2013. Failure-Aware Kidney Exchange. In *Proceedings of the 14th ACM Conference on Electronic Commerce* (EC), 323–340. New York: ACM.

Dickerson, J. P., Goldman, J., Karp, J., Procaccia, A. D., and Sandholm, T. 2014. The Computational Rise and Fall of Fairness. In *Proceedings of the 28th AAAI Conference on Artificial Intelligence*, 1405–1411. Palo Alto, CA: AAAI.

Dietrich, F. 2007. A Generalised Model of Judgment Aggregation. *Social Choice and Welfare*, **28**(4), 529–565.

Dietrich, F. 2014. Scoring Rules for Judgment Aggregation. *Social Choice and Welfare*, **42**, 873–911.

Dietrich, F. and List, C. 2004. A Model of Jury Decision Where All the Jurors Have the Same Evidence. *Synthese*, **142**, 175–202.

Dietrich, F. and List, C. 2007a. Judgment Aggregation by Quota Rules: Majority Voting Generalized. *Journal of Theoretical Politics*, **19**(4), 391–424.

Dietrich, F. and List, C. 2007b. Arrow's Theorem in Judgment Aggregation. *Social Choice and Welfare*, **29**(1), 19–33.

Dietrich, F. and List, C. 2007c. Strategy-Proof Judgment Aggregation. *Economics and Philosophy*, **23**(3), 269–300.

Dietrich, F. and List, C. 2010. Majority Voting on Restricted Domains. *Journal of Economic Theory*, **145**(2), 512–543.

Dimitrov, D. and Sung, S. C. 2006. Top Responsiveness and Nash Stability in Coalition Formation Games. *Kybernetika*, **42**(4), 453–460.

Dimitrov, D. and Sung, S. C. 2007. On Top Responsiveness and Strict Core Stability. *Journal of Mathematical Economics*, **43**(2), 130–134.

Dimitrov, D., Borm, P., Hendrickx, R., and Sung, S. C. 2006. Simple Priorities and Core Stability in Hedonic Games. *Social Choice and Welfare*, **26**(2), 421–433.

Dimopoulos, Y., Michael, L., and Athienitou, F. 2009. Ceteris Paribus Preference Elicitation with Predictive Guarantees. In *Proceedings of the 21st International Joint Conference on Artificial Intelligence* (IJCAI), 1890–1895. Palo Alto, CA: AAAI.

Ding, N. and Lin, F. 2014. On Computing Optimal Strategies in Open List Proportional Representation: The Two Parties Case. In *Proceedings of the 28th AAAI Conference on Artificial Intelligence*, 1419–1425. Palo Alto, CA: AAAI.

Dobzinski, S. and Procaccia, A. D. 2008. Frequent Manipulability of Elections: The Case of Two Voters. In *Proceedings of the 4th International Conference on Web and Internet Economics* (WINE), 653–664. New York: Springer.

Dodgson, C. 1876. *A Method of Taking Votes on More Than Two Issues*. Reprinted in McLean and Urken (1995).

Doğan, O. 2015. Monotonicity Properties Fulfilled by Resolute Refinements of Social Choice Functions. Mimeo.

Doignon, J.-P. and Falmagne, J.-C. 1994. A Polynomial Time Algorithm for Unidimensional Unfolding Representations. *Journal of Algorithms*, **16**(2), 218–233.

Dokow, E. and Holzman, R. 2010. Aggregation of Binary Evaluations. *Journal of Economic Theory*, **145**(2), 495–511.

Dolev, D., Feitelson, D. G., Halpern, J. Y., Kupferman, R., and Linial, N. 2012. No Justified Complaints: On Fair Sharing of Multiple Resources. In *Proceedings of the 3rd Innovations in Theoretical Computer Science Conference* (ITCS), 68–75. New York: ACM.

Dorn, B. and Schlotter, I. 2012. Multivariate Complexity Analysis of Swap Bribery. *Algorithmica*, **64**(1), 126–151.

Douceur, J. R. and Moscibroda, T. 2007. Lottery Trees: Motivational Deployment of Networked Systems. *ACM SIGCOMM Computer Communication Review*, **37**(4), 121–132.

Dowding, K. and Hees, M. Van. 2008. In Praise of Manipulation. *British Journal of Political Science*, **38**(1), 1–15.

Downey, R. G. and Fellows, M. R. 1999. *Parameterized Complexity*. New York: Springer.

Downey, R. G. and Fellows, M. R. 2013. *Fundamentals of Parameterized Complexity*. New York: Springer.

Drèze, J. H. and Greenberg, J. 1980. Hedonic Coalitions: Optimality and Stability. *Econometrica*, **48**(4), 987–1003.

Driessen, T. S. H. 1988. *Cooperative Games, Solutions and Applications*. New York: Kluwer.

Drissi-Bakhkhat, M. and Truchon, M. 2004. Maximum Likelihood Approach to Vote Aggregation with Variable probabilities. *Social Choice and Welfare*, **23**(2), 161–185.

Drucker, F. A. and Fleischer, L. K. 2012. Simpler Sybil-Proof Mechanisms for Multi-Level Marketing. In *Proceedings of the 13th ACM Conference on Electronic Commerce* (EC), 441–458. New York: ACM.

Drummond, J. and Boutilier, C. 2013. Elicitation and Approximately Stable Matching with Partial Preferences. In *Proceedings of the 23rd International Joint Conference on Artificial Intelligence* (IJCAI), 97–105. Palo Alto, CA: AAAI.

Dubey, P. and Shapley, L. S. 1979. Mathematical Properties of the Banzhaf Power Index. *Mathematics of Operations Research*, **4**(2), 99–131.

Dubins, L. E. and Freedman, D. A. 1981. Machiavelli and the Gale-Shapley Algorithm. *American Mathematical Monthly*, **88**(7), 485–494.

Dubins, L. E. and Spanier, E. H. 1961. How To Cut a Cake Fairly. *American Mathematical Monthly*, **68**(1), 1–17.

Duddy, C., Piggins, A. and Zwicker, W. S. 2013. Social Dichotomy Functions. Preprint.

Duggan, J. 2013. Uncovered Sets. *Social Choice and Welfare*, **41**, 489–535.

Duggan, J. and Le Breton, M. 1996. Dutta's Minimal Covering Set and Shapley's Saddles. *Journal of Economic Theory*, **70**, 257–265.

Duggan, J. and Le Breton, M. 2001. Mixed Refinements of Shapley's Saddles and Weak Tournaments. *Social Choice and Welfare*, **18**(1), 65–78.

Duggan, J. and Schwartz, T. 2000. Strategic Manipulability Without Resoluteness or Shared Beliefs: Gibbard-Satterthwaite Generalized. *Social Choice and Welfare*, **17**, 85–93.

Dunne, P. E. 2005. Extremal Behaviour in Multiagent Contract Negotiation. *Journal of Artificial Intelligence Research (JAIR)*, **23**, 41–78.

Durán, E. A., Bilbao, J. M., García, J. R. F., and López, J. J. 2003. Computing Power Indices in Weighted Multiple Majority Games. *Mathematical Social Sciences*, **46**(1), 63–80.

Durant, E. 2010. Hearing Aids and Methods and Apparatus for Audio Fitting Thereof. U.S. patent **20100172524A1**.

Dutta, B. 1988. Covering Sets and a New Condorcet Choice Correspondence. *Journal of Economic Theory*, **44**, 63–80.

Dutta, B. and Laslier, J.-F. 1999. Comparison Functions and Choice Correspondences. *Social Choice and Welfare*, **16**(4), 513–532.

Dutta, B. and Pattanaik, P. K. 1978. On Nicely Consistent Voting Systems. *Econometrica*, **46**(1), 163–170.

Dutta, B., Jackson, M., and Le Breton, M. 2001. Strategic Candidacy and Voting Procedures. *Econometrica*, **69**(4), 1013–1037.

Dwork, C., Kumar, R., Naor, M., and Sivakumar, D. 2001. Rank Aggregation Methods for the Web. In *Proceedings of the 10th International Conference on the World Wide Web*, 613–622. New York: ACM.

Echenique, F. and Oviedo, J. 2006. A Theory of Stability in Many-To-Many Matching Markets. *Theoretical Economics*, **1**(2), 233–273.

Eckert, D. and Klamler, C. 2011. Distance-Based Aggregation Theory. In *Consensual Processes*, 3–22. New York: Springer.

Eckert, D. and Monjardet, B. 2010. Guilbaud's 1952 Theorem on the Logical Problem of Aggregation. *Mathematiques et Sciences Humaines*, **48**(189), 19–35.

Edmonds, J. and Pruhs, K. 2006a. Balanced Allocations of Cake. In *Proceedings of the 47th Annual Symposium on Foundations of Computer Science* (FOCS), 623–634. New York: IEEE.

Edmonds, J. and Pruhs, K. 2006b. Cake Cutting Really is Not a Piece of Cake. In *Proceedings of the 17th Annual ACM-SIAM Symposium on Discrete Algorithms*, 271–278. New York: ACM.

Eğeciouğlu, Ö. and Giritligil, A. E. 2013. The Impartial, Anonymous, and Neutral Culture Model: A Probability Model for Sampling Public Preference Structures. *Journal of Mathematical Sociology*, **37**(4), 203–222.

Eğeciouğlu, Ö. and Giritligil, A. E. 2014. Anonymous and Neutral Social Choice: Existence Results on Resoluteness. Working paper 201401, Murat Sertel Center for Advanced Economic Studies.

Ehlers, L. and Klaus, B. 2004. Resource-Monotonic House Allocation. *International Journal of Game Theory*, **32**, 545–560.

Ehlers, L. and Klaus, B. 2007. Consistent House Allocation. *Economic Theory*, **30**, 561–574.

Ehlers, L. and Klaus, B. 2011. Corrigendum to "Resource-Monotonicity for House Allocation Problems." *International Journal of Game Theory*, **40**, 281–287.

Ehlers, L. and Klaus, B. 2014. Strategy-Proofness Makes the Difference: Deferred-Acceptance with Responsive Priorities. *Mathematics of Operations Research*, **39**, 949–966.

Ehlers, L., Klaus, B., and Pápai, S. 2002. Strategy-Proofness and Population-Monotonicity for House Allocation Problems. *Journal of Mathematical Economics*, **38**(3), 329–339.

Eirinakis, P., Magos, D., Mourtos, I., and Miliotis, P. 2012. Finding All Stable Pairs and Solutions to the Many-To-Many Stable Matching Problem. *INFORMS Journal on Computing*, **24**(2), 245–259.

Eirinakis, P., Magos, D., Mourtos, I., and Miliotis, P. 2013. Finding a Minimum-Regret Many-To-Many Stable Matching. *Optimization*, **62**(8), 1007–1018.

Elkind, E. and Erdélyi, G. 2012. Manipulation Under Voting Rule Uncertainty. In *Proceedings of the 11th International Conference on Autonomous Agents and Multiagent Systems* (AAMAS), 627–634. Richland, SC: IFAAMAS.

Elkind, E. and Faliszewski, P. 2010. Approximation Algorithms for Campaign Management. In *Proceedings of the 6th International Conference on Web and Internet Economics* (WINE), 473–482. New York: Springer.

Elkind, E. and Faliszewski, P. 2014. Recognizing 1-Euclidean Preferences: An Alternative Approach. In *Proceedings of the 7th International Symposium on Algorithmic Game Theory* (SAGT), 146–157. New York: Springer.

Elkind, E. and Lackner, M. 2014. On Detecting Nearly Structured Preference Profiles. In *Proceedings of the 28th AAAI Conference on Artificial Intelligence*, 661–667. Palo Alto, CA: AAAI.

Elkind, E. and Lipmaa, H. 2005. Hybrid Voting Protocols and Hardness of Manipulation. In *Proceedings of the 16th International Symposium on Algorithms and Computation* (ISAAC), 206–215. New York: Springer.

Elkind, E. and Shah, N. 2014. Electing the Most Probable without Eliminating the Irrational: Voting over Intransitive Domains. In *Proceedings of the Conference on Uncertainty in Artificial Intelligence* (UAI), 182–191. New York: Morgan Kaufmann.

Elkind, E. and Wooldridge, M. 2009. Hedonic Coalition Nets. In *Proceedings of the 8th International Conference on Autonomous Agents and Multiagent Systems* (AAMAS), 417–424. Richland, SC: IFAAMAS.

Elkind, E., Faliszewski, P., and Slinko, A. 2009a. On Distance Rationalizability of Some Voting Rules. In *Proceedings of the Conference on Theoretical Aspects of Rationality and Knowledge* (TARK), 201–214. New York: ACM.

Elkind, E., Goldberg, L., Goldberg, P., and Wooldridge, M. 2009b. On the Computational Complexity of Weighted Voting Games. *Annals of Mathematics and Artificial Intelligence*, **56**(2), 109–131.

Elkind, E., Faliszewski, P., and Slinko, A. 2009c. Swap Bribery. In *Proceedings of the 2nd International Symposium on Algorithmic Game Theory* (SAGT), 299–310. New York: Springer.

Elkind, E., Faliszewski, P., and Slinko, A. 2010a. Good Rationalizations of Voting Rules. In *Proceedings of the AAAI Conference on Artificial Intelligence*, 774–779. Palo Alto, CA: AAAI.

Elkind, E., Faliszewski, P., and Slinko, A. 2010b. On the Role of Distances in Defining Voting Rules. In *Proceedings of the International Conference on Autonomous Agents and Multiagent Systems* (AAMAS), 375–382. Richland, SC: IFAAMAS.

Elkind, E., Faliszewski, P., and Slinko, A. 2011a. Cloning in Elections: Finding the Possible Winners. *Journal of Artificial Intelligence Research (JAIR)*, **42**, 529–573.

Elkind, E., Faliszewski, P., and Slinko, A. 2011b. Homogeneity and Monotonicity of Distance-Rationalizable Voting Rules. In *Proceedings of the International Conference on Autonomous Agents and Multiagent Systems* (AAMAS), 821–828. Richland, SC: IFAAMAS.

Elkind, E., Faliszewski, P., and Slinko, A. 2012a. Clone Structures in Voters' Preferences. In *Proceedings of the 13th ACM Conference on Electronic Commerce* (EC), 496–513. New York: ACM.

Elkind, E., Faliszewski, P., and Slinko, A. 2012b. Rationalizations of Condorcet-Consistent Rules via Distances of Hamming Type. *Social Choice and Welfare*, **4**(39), 891–905.

Elkind, E., Rahwan, T., and Jennings, N. R. 2013. Computational Coalition Formation. In *Multiagent Systems*, 329–380. Cambridge, MA: MIT Press.

Elkind, E., Faliszewski, P., Skowron, P., and Slinko, A. 2014a. Properties of Multiwinner Voting Rules. In *Proceedings of the 13th International Conference on Autonomous Agents and Multiagent Systems* (AAMAS), 53–60. Richland, SC: IFAAMAS.

Elkind, E., Grandi, U., Rossi, F., and Slinko, A. 2014b. Games Gibbard-Satterthwaite Manipulators Play. In *Proceedings of the 5th International Workshop on Computational Social Choice* (COMSOC).

Elkind, E., Lang, J., and Saffidine, A. 2015a. Condorcet Winning Sets. *Social Choice and Welfare*, **44**(3), 493–517.

Elkind, E., Faliszewski, P., Lackner, M., and Obraztsova, S. 2015b. The Complexity of Recognizing Incomplete Single-Crossing Elections. In *Proceedings of the 29th AAAI Conference on Artificial Intelligence*, 865–871. Palo Alto, CA: AAAI.

Emek, Y., Karidi, R., Tennenholtz, M., and Zohar, A. 2011. Mechanisms for Multi-Level Marketing. In *Proceedings of the 12th ACM Conference on Electronic Commerce* (EC), 209–218. New York: ACM.

Endriss, U. 2011. Logic and Social Choice Theory. In *Logic and Philosophy Today*, vol. 2, ed. Gupta, A., and van Benthem, J., 333–377. London: College Publications.

Endriss, U. 2013. Reduction of Economic Inequality in Combinatorial Domains. In *Proceedings of the 12th International Conference on Autonomous Agents and Multiagent Systems* (AAMAS), 175–182. Richland, SC: IFAAMAS.

Endriss, U. and Fernández, R. 2013. Collective Annotation of Linguistic Resources: Basic Principles and a Formal Model. In *Proceedings of the 51st Annual Meeting of the Association for Computational Linguistics* (ACL), 539–549. Stroudsburg, PA: ACL.

Endriss, U. and Grandi, U. 2014. Binary Aggregation by Selection of the Most Representative Voter. In *Proceedings of the 28th AAAI Conference on Artificial Intelligence*, Palo Alto, CA: AAAI.

Endriss, U. and Maudet, N. 2005. On the Communication Complexity of Multilateral Trading: Extended Report. *Journal of Autonomous Agents and Multi-Agent Systems*, **11**(1), 91–107.

Endriss, U., Maudet, N., Sadri, F., and Toni, F. 2006. Negotiating Socially Optimal Allocations of Resources. *Journal of Artificial Intelligence Research (JAIR)*, **25**, 315–348.

Endriss, U., Pini, M. S., Rossi, F., and Venable, K. B. 2009. Preference Aggregation over Restricted Ballot Languages: Sincerity and Strategy-Proofness. In *Proceedings of the 21st International Joint Conference on Artificial Intelligence* (IJCAI), 122–127. Palo Alto, CA: AAAI.

Endriss, U., Grandi, U., and Porello, D. 2012. Complexity of Judgment Aggregation. *Journal of Artificial Intelligence Research (JAIR)*, **45**, 481–514.

Ephrati, E. and Rosenschein, J. S. 1993. Multi-Agent Planning as a Dynamic Search for Social Consensus. In *Proceedings of the 13th International Joint Conference on Artificial Intelligence* (IJCAI), 423–429. Palo Alto, CA: AAAI.

Erdélyi, G. and Rothe, J. 2010. Control Complexity in Fallback Voting. In *Proceedings of Computing: The 16th Australasian Theory Symposium*, 39–48. Darlinghurst: ACS.

Erdélyi, G., Nowak, M., and Rothe, J. 2009. Sincere-Strategy Preference-Based Approval Voting Fully Resists Constructive Control and Broadly Resists Destructive Control. *Mathematical Logic Quarterly*, **55**(4), 425–443.

Erdélyi, G., Piras, L., and Rothe, J. 2011. The Complexity of Voter Partition in Bucklin and Fallback Voting: Solving Three Open Problems. In *Proceedings of the 10th International Conference on Autonomous Agents and Multiagent Systems* (AAMAS), 837–844. Richland, SC: IFAAMAS.

Erdélyi, G., Fellows, M. R., Rothe, J., and Schend, L. 2015a. Control Complexity in Bucklin and Fallback Voting: A Theoretical Analysis. *Journal of Computer and System Sciences*, **81**(4), 632–660.

Erdélyi, G., Fellows, M. R., Rothe, J., and Schend, L. 2015b. Control Complexity in Bucklin and Fallback Voting: An Experimental Analysis. *Journal of Computer and System Sciences*, **81**(4), 661–670.

Erdős, P. and Moser, L. 1964. On the Representation of Directed Graphs as Unions of Orderings. *Publications of the Mathematical Institute of the Hungarian Academy of Science*, **9**, 125–132.

Ergin, H. 2000. Consistency in House Allocation Problems. *Journal of Mathematical Economics*, **34**(1), 77–97.

Escoffier, B., Lang, J., and Öztürk, M. 2008. Single-Peaked Consistency and Its Complexity. In *Proceedings of the 8th European Conference on Artificial Intelligence* (ECAI), 366–370. Amsterdam: IOS Press.

Escoffier, B., Gourvès, L., and Monnot, J. 2013. Fair Solutions for Some Multiagent Optimization Problems. *Autonomous Agents and Multi-Agent Systems*, **26**(2), 184–201.

Even, S. and Paz, A. 1984. A Note on Cake-Cutting. *Discrete Applied Mathematics*, **7**, 285–296.

Everaere, P., Konieczny, S., and Marquis, P. 2014. Counting Votes for Aggregating Judgments. In *Proceedings of the 13th International Conference on Autonomous Agents and Multiagent Systems* (AAMAS), 1177–1184. Richland, SC: IFAAMAS.

Fabrikant, A., Papadimitriou, C. H., and Talwar, K. 2004. The Complexity of Pure Nash Equilibria. In *Proceedings of the 36th ACM Symposium on Theory of Computing* (STOC), 504–612. New York: ACM.

Fagin, R., Kumar, R., and Sivakumar, D. 2003. Efficient Similarity Search and Classification via Rank Aggregation. In *Proceedings of the 2003 ACM SIGMOD International Conference on Management of Data*, 301–312. New York: ACM.

Faliszewski, P. 2008. Nonuniform Bribery. In *Proceedings of the 7th International Conference on Autonomous Agents and Multiagent Systems* (AAMAS), 1569–1572. Richland, SC: IFAAMAS.

Faliszewski, P. and Hemaspaandra, L. 2009. The Complexity of Power-Index Comparison. *Theoretical Computer Science*, **410**(1), 101–107.

Faliszewski, P. and Procaccia, A. D. 2010. AI's War on Manipulation: Are We Winning? *AI Magazine*, **31**(4), 53–64.

Faliszewski, P., Hemaspaandra, E., and Schnoor, H. 2008. Copeland Voting: Ties Matter. In *Proceedings of the 7th International Conference on Autonomous Agents and Multiagent Systems* (AAMAS), 983–990. Richland, SC: IFAAMAS.

Faliszewski, P., Elkind, E., and Wooldridge, M. 2009a. Boolean Combinations of Weighted Voting Games. In *Proceedings of the 8th International Conference on Autonomous Agents and Multiagent Systems* (AAMAS), 185–192. Richland, SC: IFAAMAS.

Faliszewski, P., Hemaspaandra, E., and Hemaspaandra, L. 2009b. How Hard Is Bribery in Elections? *Journal of Artificial Intelligence Research (JAIR)*, **35**, 485–532.

Faliszewski, P., Hemaspaandra, E., Hemaspaandra, L., and Rothe, J. 2009c. Llull and Copeland Voting Computationally Resist Bribery and Constructive Control. *Journal of Artificial Intelligence Research (JAIR)*, **35**, 275–341.

Faliszewski, P., Hemaspaandra, E., Hemaspaandra, L., and Rothe, J. 2009d. A Richer Understanding of the Complexity of Election Systems. In *Fundamental Problems in Computing: Essays in Honor of Professor Daniel J. Rosenkrantz*, ed. Ravi, S., and Shukla, S., 375–406. New York: Springer.

Faliszewski, P., Hemaspaandra, E., Hemaspaandra, L. A., and Rothe, J. 2009e. The Shield that Never Was: Societies with Single-Peaked Preferences are More Open to Manipulation and Control. In *Proceedings of the Conference on Theoretical Aspects of Rationality and Knowledge* (TARK), 118–127. New York: ACM.

Faliszewski, P., Hemaspaandra, E., and Hemaspaandra, L. 2010. Using Complexity to Protect Elections. *Communications of the ACM*, **53**(11), 74–82.

Faliszewski, P., Hemaspaandra, E., and Hemaspaandra, L. 2011a. The Complexity of Manipulative Attacks in Nearly Single-Peaked Electorates. In *Proceedings of the 13th Conference on Theoretical Aspects of Rationality and Knowledge* (TARK), 228–237. New York: ACM.

Faliszewski, P., Hemaspaandra, E., and Hemaspaandra, L. 2011b. Multimode Control Attacks on Elections. *Journal of Artificial Intelligence Research (JAIR)*, **40**, 305–351.

Faliszewski, P., Hemaspaandra, E., Hemaspaandra, L., and Rothe, J. 2011c. The Shield that Never Was: Societies with Single-Peaked Preferences are More Open to Manipulation and Control. *Information and Computation*, **209**(2), 89–107.

Faliszewski, P., Hemaspaandra, E., and Hemaspaandra, L. 2013. Weighted Electoral Control. In *Proceedings of the 12th International Conference on Autonomous Agents and Multiagent Systems* (AAMAS), 367–374. Richland, SC: IFAAMAS.

Faliszewski, P., Hemaspaandra, E., and Hemaspaandra, L. A. 2014. The complexity of Manipulative Attacks in Nearly Single-Peaked Electorates. *Artificial Intelligence*, **207**, 69–99.

Faliszewski, P., Reisch, Y., Rothe, J., and Schend, L. 2015. Complexity of Manipulation, Bribery, and Campaign Management in Bucklin and Fallback Voting. *Journal of Autonomous Agents and Multi-Agent Systems*, **29**(6), 1091–1124.

Farkas, D. and Nitzan, S. 1979. The Borda Rule and Pareto Stability: A Comment. *Econometrica*, **47**(5), 1305–1306.

Farquharson, R. 1969. *Theory of Voting*. New Haven, CT: Yale University Press.

Fatima, S. S., Wooldridge, M., and Jennings, N. R. 2008. A Linear Approximation Method for the Shapley Value. *Artificial Intelligence Journal*, **172**(14), 1673–1699.

Favardin, P. and Lepelley, D. 2006. Some Further Results on the Manipulability of Social Choice Rules. *Social Choice and Welfare*, **26**(3), 485–509.

Favardin, P., Lepelley, D., and Serais, J. 2002. Borda Rule, Copeland Method and Strategic Manipulation. *Review of Economic Design*, **7**(2), 213–228.

Feige, U. 1998. A Threshold of $\ln n$ for Approximating Set Cover. *Journal of the ACM*, **45**(4), 643–652.

Fekete, S. P., Skutella, M., and Woeginger, G. J. 2003. The Complexity of Economic Equilibria for House Allocation Markets. *Information Processing Letters*, **88**, 219–223.

Fellows, M. R., Jansen, B., Lokshtanov, D., Rosamond, F., and Saurabh, S. 2010. Determining the Winner of a Dodgson Election is Hard. In *Proceedings of the 29th Conference on Foundations of Software Technology and Theoretical Computer Science*, 459–469. Dagstuhl: LIPICS.

Felsenthal, D. and Machover, M. 1998. *The Measurement of Voting Power*. Cheltenham, UK: Edward Elgar.

Fey, M. 2008. Choosing from a Large Tournament. *Social Choice and Welfare*, **31**(2), 301–309.

Fischer, F. and Klimm, M. 2014. Optimal Impartial Selection. In *Proceedings of the 15th ACM Conference on Economics and Computation* (EC), 803–820. New York: ACM.

Fischer, F., Procaccia, A. D., and Samorodnitsky, A. 2011. A New Perspective on Implementation by Voting Trees. *Random Structures and Algorithms*, **39**(1), 59–82.

Fishburn, P. C. 1970. *Utility Theory for Decision-Making*. New York: John Wiley.

Fishburn, P. C. 1972. Even-Chance Lotteries in Social Choice Theory. *Theory and Decision*, **3**, 18–40.

Fishburn, P. C. 1977. Condorcet Social Choice Functions. *SIAM Journal on Applied Mathematics*, **33**(3), 469–489.

Fishburn, P. C. 1982. Monotonicity Paradoxes in the Theory of Elections. *Discrete Applied Mathematics*, **4**(2), 119–134.

Fishburn, P. C. 1984. Probabilistic Social Choice Based on Simple Voting Comparisons. *Review of Economic Studies*, **51**(167), 683–692.

Fishburn, P. C. 1985. *Interval Orders and Interval Graphs: A Study of Partially Ordered Sets*. Hoboken, NJ: Wiley.

Fisher, D. C. and Reeves, R. B. 1995. Optimal Strategies for Random Tournament Games. *Linear Algebra and Its Applications*, **217**, 83–85.

Fisher, D. C. and Ryan, J. 1995. Tournament Games and Positive Tournaments. *Journal of Graph Theory*, **19**(2), 217–236.

Fitzsimmons, Z., Hemaspaandra, E., and Hemaspaandra, L. 2013. Control in the Presence of Manipulators: Cooperative and Competitive Cases. In *Proceedings of the 23rd International Joint Conference on Artificial Intelligence* (IJCAI), 113–119. Palo Alto, CA: AAAI.

Fleiner, T. 2003. On the Stable *b*-Matching Polytope. *Mathematical Social Sciences*, **46**(2), 149–158.

Fleurbaey, M. and Maniquet, F. 2011. *A Theory of Fairness and Social Welfare*. New York: Cambridge University Press.

Foley, D. K. 1967. Resource Allocation and the Public Sector. *Yale Economic Essays*, **7**(1), 45–98.

Fomin, F. V. and Kratsch, D. 2010. *Exact Exponential Algorithms*. New York: Springer.

Fomin, F. V., Lokshtanov, D., Raman, V., and Saurabh, S. 2010. Fast Local Search Algorithm for Weighted Feedback Arc Set in Tournaments. In *Proceedings of the 24th AAAI Conference on Artificial Intelligence*, 65–70. Palo Alto, CA: AAAI.

Frances, M. and Litman, A. 1997. On Covering Problems of Codes. *Theory of Computing Systems*, **30**, 113–119.

Freeman, R., Brill, M., and Conitzer, V. 2014. On the Axiomatic Characterization of Runoff Voting Rules. In *Proceedings of the 28th AAAI Conference on Artificial Intelligence*, 675–681. Palo Alto, CA: AAAI.

Freeman, R., Brill, M., and Conitzer, V. 2015. General Tiebreaking Schemes for Computational Social Choice. In *Proceedings of the 14th International Conference on Autonomous Agents and Multiagent Systems* (AAMAS), 1401–1409. Richland, SC: IFAAMAS.

Freixas, J. and Zwicker, W. S. 2009. Anonymous Yes-No Voting with Abstention and Multiple Levels of Approval. *Games and Economic Behavior*, **67**, 428–444.

Friedgut, E., Kalai, G., and Nisan, N. 2008. Elections Can Be Manipulated Often. In *Proceedings of the Annual Symposium on Foundations of Computer Science* (FOCS), 243–249. New York: IEEE.

Gaertner, W. 2006. *A Primer in Social Choice Theory*. New York: Oxford University Press.

Gairing, M. and Savani, R. 2010. Computing Stable Outcomes in Hedonic Games. In *Proceedings of the 3rd International Symposium on Algorithmic Game Theory* (SAGT), 174–185. New York: Springer.

Gairing, M. and Savani, R. 2011. Computing Stable Outcomes in Hedonic Games with Voting-Based Deviations. In *Proceedings of the 10th International Conference on Autonomous Agents and Multiagent Systems* (AAMAS), 559–566. Richland, SC: IFAAMAS.

Gale, D. and Shapley, L. S. 1962. College Admissions and the Stability of Marriage. *American Mathematical Monthly*, **69**, 9–15.

Gale, D. and Sotomayor, M. 1985. Some Remarks on the Stable Matching Problem. *Discrete Applied Mathematics*, **11**, 223–232.

Gamson, W. A. 1961. A Theory of Coalition Formation. *American Sociological Review*, **26**, 373–382.

Gärdenfors, P. 1975. Match Making: Assignments Based on Bilateral Preferences. *Behavioural Science*, **20**, 166–173.

Gärdenfors, P. 1976. Manipulation of Social Choice Functions. *Journal of Economic Theory*, **13**, 217–228.

Gärdenfors, P. 1979. On Definitions of Manipulation of Social Choice Functions. In *Aggregation and Revelation of Preferences*, ed. Laffont, J. J., 29–36. Amsterdam: North-Holland.

Gärdenfors, P. 2006. A Representation Theorem for Voting with Logical Consequences. *Economics and Philosophy*, **22**(2), 181–190.

Garey, M. R. and Johnson, D. S. 1979. *Computers and Intractability: A Guide to the Theory of NP-Completeness*. New York: W. H. Freeman.

Garman, M. B. and Kamien, M. I. 1968. The Paradox of Voting: Probability Calculations. *Behavioral Science*, **13**(4), 306–316.

Gaspers, S., Kalinowski, T., Narodytska, N., and Walsh, T. 2013. Coalitional Manipulation for Schulze's Rule. In *Proceedings of the International Conference on Autonomous Agents and Multiagent Systems* (AAMAS), 431–438. Richland, SC: IFAAMAS.

Gehrlein, W. V. 2002. Condorcet's Paradox and the Likelihood of Its Occurrence: Different Perspectives on Balanced Preferences. *Theory and Decision*, **52**, 171–199.

Gehrlein, W. V. 2006. *Condorcet's Paradox*. New York: Springer.

Gehrlein, W. V. and Fishburn, P. C. 1976. Condorcet's Paradox and Anonymous Preference Profiles. *Public Choice*, **26**(1), 1–18.

Gehrlein, W. V. and Fishburn, P. C. 1978. Coincidence Probabilities for Simple Majority and Positional Voting Rules. *Social Science Research*, **7**(3), 272–283.

Geist, C. and Endriss, U. 2011. Automated Search for Impossibility Theorems in Social Choice Theory: Ranking Sets of Objects. *Journal of Artificial Intelligence Research (JAIR)*, **40**, 143–174.

Gelain, M., Pini, M. S., Rossi, F., Venable, K. B., and Walsh, T. 2010. Elicitation Strategies for Soft Constraint Problems with Missing Preferences: Properties, Algorithms and Experimental Studies. *Artificial Intelligence*, **174**(3–4), 270–294.

Gelain, M., Pini, M. S., Rossi, F., Venable, K. B., and Walsh, T. 2013. Local Search Approaches in Stable Matching Problems. *Algorithms*, **6**(4), 591–617.

Ghodsi, A., Zaharia, M., Hindman, B., Konwinski, A., Shenker, S., and Stoica, I. 2011. Dominant Resource Fairness: Fair Allocation of Multiple Resource Types. In *Proceedings of the 8th USENIX Conference on Networked Systems Design and Implementation* (NSDI), 24–37. Berkeley: USENIX.

Gibbard, A. 1973. Manipulation of Voting Schemes: A General Result. *Econometrica*, **41**, 587–601.

Gibbard, A. 1977. Manipulation of Schemes that Mix Voting with Chance. *Econometrica*, **45**, 665–681.

Gillies, D. B. 1959. Solutions to General Non-zero-sum Games. In *Contributions to the Theory of Games IV*, ed. Tucker, A. W., and Luce, R. D., 47–85. Princeton, NJ: Princeton University Press.

Glorie, K. M., van de Klundert, J. J., and Wagelmans, A. P. M. 2014. Kidney Exchange with Long Chains: An Efficient Pricing Algorithm for Clearing Barter Exchanges with Branch-and-Price. *Manufacturing & Service Operations Management*, **16**(4), 498–512.

Goel, A. and Lee, D. 2012. Triadic Consensus: A Randomized Algorithm for Voting in a Crowd. In *Proceedings of the 8th International Conference on Web and Internet Economics* (WINE), 434–477. New York: Springer.

Golovin, D. 2005. *Max-Min Fair Allocation of Indivisible Goods*. Technical Report CMU-CS-05-144, School of Computer Science, Carnegie Mellon University.

Gonzales, C. and Perny, P. 2004. GAI Networks for Utility Elicitation. In *Proceedings of the 9th International Conference on Principles of Knowledge Representation and Reasoning* (KR), 224–234. Pal Alto, CA: AAAI Press.

Gonzales, C., Perny, P., and Queiroz, S. 2008. Preference Aggregation with Graphical Utility Models. In *Proceedings of the AAAI Conference on Artificial Intelligence*, 1037–1042. Palo Alto, CA: AAAI.

Good, I. J. 1971. A Note on Condorcet Sets. *Public Choice*, **10**, 97–101.

Gordon, S. and Truchon, M. 2008. Social Choice, Optimal Inference and Figure Skating. *Social Choice and Welfare*, **30**(2), 265–284.

Gourvès, L., Monnot, J., and Tlilane, L. 2013. A Matroid Approach to the Worst Case Allocation of Indivisible Goods. In *Proceedings of the 23rd International Joint Conference on Artificial Intelligence* (IJCAI), 136–142. Palo Alto, CA: AAAI.

Grabisch, M. 1997. k-order Additive Discrete Fuzzy Measure and Their Representation. *Fuzzy Sets and Systems*, **92**, 167–189.

Graham, R. L. 1969. Bounds on Multiprocessing Timing Anomalies. *SIAM Journal of Applied Mathematics*, **17**, 416–429.

Grandi, U. and Endriss, U. 2011. Binary Aggregation with Integrity Constraints. In *Proceedings of the International Joint Conference on Artificial Intelligence* (IJCAI), 204–209. Palo Alto, CA: AAAI.

Grandi, U. and Endriss, U. 2013. Lifting Integrity Constraints in Binary Aggregation. *Artificial Intelligence*, **199–200**, 45–66.

Grandi, U., Loreggia, A., Rossi, F., Venable, K. B., and Walsh, T. 2013. Restricted Manipulation in Iterative Voting: Condorcet Efficiency and Borda Score. In *Proceedings of the 3rd International Conference on Algorithmic Decision Theory* (ADT), 181–192. New York: Springer.

Groh, C., Moldovanu, B., Sela, A., and Sunde, U. 2012. Optimal Seedings in Elimination Tournaments. *Economic Theory*, **49**(1), 59–80.

Grossi, D. and Pigozzi, G. 2014. *Judgment Aggregation: A Primer*. San Rafael, CA: Morgan and Claypool.

Guha, R., Kumar, R., Raghavan, P., and Tomkins, A. 2004. Propagation of Trust and Distrust. In *Proceedings of the 13th International Conference on the World Wide Web*, 403–412. New York: ACM.

Guilbaud, G.-T. 1952. Les Théories de l'Intérêt Général et le Problème Logique de l'Agrégation. *Économie Appliquée*, **5**(4), 501–584. English translation appears in *Journal Électronique d'Histoire des Probabilités et de la Statistique*, **44**(1), 57, 2008.

Guo, J. and Niedermeier, R. 2007. Invitation to Data Reduction and Problem Kernelization. *ACM SIGACT News*, **38**(1), 31–45.

Gusfield, D. and Irving, R. W. 1989. *The Stable Marriage Problem: Structure and Algorithms*. Cambridge, MA: MIT Press.

Gutman, A. and Nisan, N. 2012. Fair Allocation without Trade. In *Proceedings of the 11th International Conference on Autonomous Agents and Multiagent Systems* (AAMAS), 719–728. Richland, SC: IFAAMAS.

Hajduková, J. 2006. Coalition Formation Games: A Survey. *International Game Theory Review*, **8**(4), 613–641.

Hammond, P. 1991. Interpersonal Comparisons of Utility: Why and How They Are and Should Be Made. In *Interpersonal Comparisons of Well-Being*, ed. Elster, J., and Roemer, J., 200–254. New York: Cambridge University Press.

Hare, T. 1859. *Treatise on the Election of Representatives, Parliamentary and Municipal*. London: Longman, Green, Reader, and Dyer.

Hartvigsen, D. 2006. Vote Trading in Public Elections. *Mathematical Social Sciences*, **52**(1), 31–48.

Hazon, N. and Elkind, E. 2010. Complexity of Safe Strategic Voting. In *Proceedings of the 3rd International Symposium on Algorithmic Game Theory* (SAGT), 210–221. New York: Springer.

Hazon, N., Dunne, P. E., Kraus, S., and Wooldridge, M. 2008. How to Rig Elections and Competitions. In *Proceedings of the 2nd International Workshop on Computational Social Choice* (COMSOC).

Hazon, N., Aumann, Y., Kraus, S., and Wooldridge, M. 2012. On the Evaluation of Election Outcomes Under Uncertainty. *Artificial Intelligence*, **189**, 1–18.

Hazon, N., Lin, R., and Kraus, S. 2013. How to Change a Group's Collective Decision? In *Proceedings of the 23rd AAAI Conference on Artificial Intelligence*, 198–205. Palo Alto, CA: AAAI.

Hemachandra, L. 1989. The Strong Exponential Hierarchy Collapses. *Journal of Computer and System Sciences*, **39**(3), 299–322.

Hemaspaandra, E. and Hemaspaandra, L. 2007. Dichotomy for Voting Systems. *Journal of Computer and System Sciences*, **73**(1), 73–83.

Hemaspaandra, L. and Ogihara, M. 2002. *The Complexity Theory Companion*. New York: Springer.

Hemaspaandra, L. and Williams, R. 2012. An Atypical Survey of Typical-Case Heuristic Algorithms. *SIGACT News*, **43**(4), 71–89.

Hemaspaandra, E. and Rothe, J. 1998. Recognizing When Greed Can Approximate Maximum Independent Sets Is Complete for Parallel Access to NP. *Information Processing Letters*, **65**(3), 151–156.

Hemachandra, L. and Wechsung, G. 1991. Kolmogorov Characterizations of Complexity Classes. *Theoretical Computer Science*, **83**, 313–322.

Hemaspaandra, E., Hemaspaandra, L., and Rothe, J. 1997a. Exact Analysis of Dodgson Elections: Lewis Carroll's 1876 Voting System is Complete for Parallel Access to NP. *Journal of the ACM*, **44**(6), 806–825.

Hemaspaandra, E., Hemaspaandra, L., and Rothe, J. 1997b. Raising NP Lower Bounds to Parallel NP Lower Bounds. *SIGACT News*, **28**(2), 2–13.

Hemaspaandra, E., Spakowski, H., and Vogel, J. 2005. The Complexity of Kemeny Elections. *Theoretical Computer Science*, **349**(3), 382–391.

Hemaspaandra, E., Hemaspaandra, L., and Rothe, J. 2007. Anyone But Him: The Complexity of Precluding an Alternative. *Artificial Intelligence*, **171**(5–6), 255–285.

Hemaspaandra, E., Hemaspaandra, L., and Rothe, J. 2009. Hybrid Elections Broaden Complexity-Theoretic Resistance to Control. *Mathematical Logic Quarterly*, **55**(4), 397–424.

Hemaspaandra, E., Hemaspaandra, L., and Rothe, J. 2012a. Controlling Candidate-Sequential Elections. In *Proceedings of the 20th European Conference on Artificial Intelligence* (ECAI), 905–906. Amsterdam: IOS Press.

Hemaspaandra, E., Hemaspaandra, L., and Rothe, J. 2012b. Online Voter Control in Sequential Elections. In *Proceedings of the 20th European Conference on Artificial Intelligence* (ECAI), 396–401. Amsterdam: IOS Press.

Hemaspaandra, E., Hemaspaandra, L., and Menton, C. 2013a. Search versus Decision for Election Manipulation Problems. In *Proceedings of the 30th Annual Symposium on Theoretical Aspects of Computer Science*, 377–388. Dagstuhl: LIPICS.

Hemaspaandra, L., Lavaee, R., and Menton, C. 2013b. Schulze and Ranked-Pairs Voting Are Fixed-Parameter Tractable to Bribe, Manipulate, and Control. In *Proceedings of the 12th International Conference on Autonomous Agents and Multiagent Systems* (AAMAS), 1345–1346. Richland, SC: IFAAMAS.

Hemaspaandra, E., Hemaspaandra, L., and Rothe, J. 2014a. The Complexity of Online Manipulation of Sequential Elections. *Journal of Computer and System Sciences*, **80**(4), 697–710.

Hemaspaandra, E., Hemaspaandra, L., and Schnoor, H. 2014b. A Control Dichotomy for Pure Scoring Rules. In *Proceedings of the 28th AAAI Conference on Artificial Intelligence*, 712–720. Palo Alto, CA: AAAI.

Hemaspaandra, L. A., Lavaee, R., and Menton, C. 2014c. Schulze and Ranked-Pairs Voting Are Fixed-Parameter Tractable to Bribe, Manipulate, and Control. *CoRR*, **abs/1210.6963**.

Hemaspaandra, E., Hemaspaandra, L., and Rothe, J. 2015. The Complexity of Manipulative Actions in Single-Peaked Societies. In *Economics and Computation: An Introduction to Algorithmic Game Theory, Computational Social Choice, and Fair Division*, ed. Rothe, J., Chapter 5, 327–360. New York: Springer.

Henriet, D. 1985. The Copeland Choice Function: An Axiomatic Characterization. *Social Choice and Welfare*, **2**(1), 49–63.

Herreiner, D. K. and Puppe, C. D. 2002. A Simple Procedure for Finding Equitable Allocations of Indivisible Goods. *Social Choice and Welfare*, **19**, 415–430.

Herreiner, D. K. and Puppe, C. D. 2009. Envy Freeness in Experimental Fair Division Problems. *Theory and Decision*, **67**(1), 65–100.

Hillinger, C. 2005. *The Case for Utilitarian Voting*. Discussion Papers in Economics No. 653, University of Munich.

Hoag, C. G. and Hallett, G. H., eds. 1926. *Proportional Representation*. New York: Macmillan.

Hojati, M. 1996. Optimal Political Districting. *Computers & OR*, **23**(12), 1147–1161.

Holler, M. J. 1982. Forming Coalitions and Measuring Voting Power. *Political Studies*, **30**, 262–271.

Homan, C. and Hemaspaandra, L. 2009. Guarantees for the Success Frequency of an Algorithm for Finding Dodgson-Election Winners. *Journal of Heuristics*, **15**(4), 403–423.

Homeshaw, J. 2001. Inventing Hare-Clark: The Model Arithmetocracy. In *Elections: Full, Free and Fair*, ed. Sawer, M., 96–114. Annandale: The Federation Press.

Horen, J. and Riezman, R. 1985. Comparing Draws for Single Elimination Tournaments. *Op. Research*, **33**(2), 1401–1409.

Horan, S. 2013. Implementation of Majority Voting Rules. Working paper.

Houy, N. 2009a. A Few New Results on TEQ. Mimeo.

Houy, N. 2009b. Still More on the Tournament Equilibrium Set. *Social Choice and Welfare*, **32**, 93–99.

Howard, R. A. and Matheson, J. E. 1984. Influence Diagrams. In *Readings on the Principles and Applications of Decision Analysis*, vol. 2, ed. Howard, R. A., and Matheson, J. E., 720–761. Menlo Park, CA: Strategic Decision Group.

Huang, C. C. and Kavitha, T. 2012. Weight-Maximal Matchings. In *Proceedings of MATCH-UP '12: The 2nd International Workshop on Matching Under Preferences*, 87–98.

Huang, J. and Guestrin, C. 2009. Riffled Independence for Ranked Data. In *Advances in Neural Information Processing Systems 21*, 799–807. Cambridge, MA: MIT.

Hudry, O. 1989. Recherche d'ordres Médians: Complexité, Algorithmique et Problèmes Combinatoires. PhD thesis, Telecom Paris Tech.

Hudry, O. 2004. A Note on "Banks Winners in Tournaments are Difficult to Recognize" by G. J. Woeginger. *Social Choice and Welfare*, **23**, 113–114.

Hudry, O. 2008. NP-Hardness Results for the Aggregation of Linear Orders into Median Orders. *Annals of Operations Research*, **163**(1), 63–88.

Hudry, O. 2009. A Survey on the Complexity of Tournament Solutions. *Mathematical Social Sciences*, **57**(3), 292–303.

Hudry, O. 2010. On the Complexity of Slater's Problems. *European Journal of Operational Research*, **203**(1), 216–221.

Hudry, O. 2012. On the Computation of Median Linear Orders, of Median Complete Preorders and of Median Weak Orders. *Mathematical Social Sciences*, **64**, 2–10.

Hylland, A. and Zeckhauser, R. 1979. The Efficient Allocation of Individuals to Positions. *Journal of Political Economy*, **87**(2), 293–314.

Ianovski, E., Yu, L., Elkind, E., and Wilson, M. C. 2011. The Complexity of Safe Manipulation Under Scoring Rules. In *Proceedings of the 22nd International Joint Conference on Artificial Intelligence* (IJCAI), 246–251. Palo Alto, CA: AAAI.

Ibaraki, T. and Katoh, N. 1983. On-Line Computation of Transitive Closures of Graphs. *Information Processing Letters*, **16**, 95–97.

Ieong, S. and Shoham, Y. 2005. Marginal Contribution Nets: A Compact Representation Scheme for Coalitional Games. In *Proceedings of the 6th ACM Conference on Electronic Commerce* (EC), 193–202. New York: ACM.

Immorlica, N. and Mahdian, M. 2005. Marriage, Honesty and Stability. In *Proceedings of the 16th Annual ACM-SIAM Symposium on Discrete Algorithms* (SODA), 53–62. New York: ACM-SIAM.

Irving, R. W. 1985. An Efficient Algorithm for the "Stable Roommates" Problem. *Journal of Algorithms*, **6**(4), 577–595.

Irving, R. W. 1994. Stable Marriage and Indifference. *Discrete Applied Mathematics*, **48**(3), 261–272.

Irving, R. W. 2008. Stable Marriage. In *Encyclopedia of Algorithms*, ed. Kao, M. Y., 877–879. New York: Springer.

Irving, R. W. and Leather, P. 1986. The Complexity of Counting Stable Marriages. *SIAM Journal on Computing*, **15**(3), 655–667.

Irving, R. W., Manlove, D. F., and Scott, S. 2000. The Hospitals/Residents Problem with Ties. In *Proceedings of the 7th Scandinavian Workshop on Algorithm Theory* (SWAT), 259–271. New York: Springer.

Irving, R. W., Manlove, D. F., and Scott, S. 2003. Strong Stability in the Hospitals/Residents Problem. In *Proceedings of the 20th Annual Symposium on Theoretical Aspects of Computer Science* (STACS), 439–450. New York: Springer.

Irving, R. W., Kavitha, T., Mehlhorn, K., Michail, D., and Paluch, K. 2006. Rank-Maximal Matchings. *ACM Transactions on Algorithms*, **2**(4), 602–610.

Isaksson, M., Kindler, G., and Mossel, E. 2012. The Geometry of Manipulation: A Quantitative Proof of the Gibbard-Satterthwaite Theorem. *Combinatorica*, **32**(2), 221–250.

Iwama, K., Manlove, D., Miyazaki, S., and Morita, Y. 1999. Stable Marriage with Incomplete Lists and Ties. In *Proceedings of the 26th International Colloquium on Automata, Languages, and Programming* (ICALP), 443–452. New York: Springer.

Jackson, B. N., Schnable, P. S., and Aluru, S. 2008. Consensus Genetic Maps as Median Orders from Inconsistent Sources. *IEEE/ACM Transactions on Computational Biology and Bioinformatics*, **5**(2), 161–171.

Johnson, D. S., Papadimitriou, C. H., and Yannakakis, M. 1988. How Easy Is Local Search? *Journal of Computer and System Sciences*, **37**, 79–100.

Johnson, R. J., Allen, J. E., Fuggle, S. V., Bradley, J. A., and Rudge, C. J. 2008. Early Experience of Paired Living Kidney Donation in the United Kingdom. *Transplantation*, **86**, 1672–1677.

Ju, B.-G. 2003. A Characterization of Strategy-Proof Voting Rules for Separable Weak Orderings. *Social Choice and Welfare*, **21**(3), 469–499.

Kadane, J. 1972. On Division of the Question. *Public Choice*, **13**, 47–54.

Kadin, J. 1989. $P^{NP[\log n]}$ and Sparse Turing-Complete Sets for NP. *Journal of Computer and System Sciences*, **39**(3), 282–298.

Kalech, M., Kraus, S., Kaminka, G. A., and Goldman, C. V. 2011. Practical Voting Rules with Partial Information. *Journal of Autonomous Agents and Multi-Agent Systems*, **22**(1), 151–182.

Kalinowski, T., Narodytska, N., and Walsh, T. 2013. A Social Welfare Optimal Sequential Allocation Procedure. In *Proceedings of the 23rd International Joint Conference on Artificial Intelligence* (IJCAI), 227–233. Palo Alto, CA: AAAI.

Kann, V. 1992. On the Approximability of NP-complete Optimization Problems. PhD thesis, Royal Institute of Technology, Stockholm.

Karakaya, M. 2011. Hedonic Coalition Formation Games: A New Stability Notion. *Mathematical Social Sciences*, **61**(3), 157–165.

Karpinski, M. and Schudy, W. 2010. Faster Algorithms for Feedback Arc Set Tournament, Kemeny Rank Aggregation and Betweenness Tournament. In *Proceedings of the 21st International Symposium on Algorithms and Computation* (ISAAC), 3–14. New York: Springer.

Kash, I., Procaccia, A. D., and Shah, N. 2014. No Agent Left Behind: Dynamic Fair Division of Multiple Resources. *Journal of Artificial Intelligence Research (JAIR)*, **51**, 579–603.

Kavitha, T., Mehlhorn, K., Michail, D., and Paluch, K. E. 2007. Strongly Stable Matchings in Time $O(nm)$ and Extension to the Hospitals-Residents Problem. *ACM Transactions on Algorithms*, **3**(2), Article 15.

Kavitha, T., Mestre, J., and Nasre, M. 2011. Popular Mixed Matchings. *Theoretical Computer Science*, **412**(24), 2679–2690.

Keeney, R. and Raiffa, H. 1976. *Decision with Multiple Objectives: Preferences and Value Tradeoffs*. Hoboken, NJ: John Wiley.

Keizer, K. M., de Klerk, M., Haase-Kromwijk, B. J., and Weimar, W. 2005. The Dutch Algorithm for Allocation in Living Donor Kidney Exchange. *Transplantation Proceedings*, **37**, 589–591.

Kelly, J. S. 1977. Strategy-Proofness and Social Choice Functions without Single-Valuedness. *Econometrica*, **45**(2), 439–446.

Kelly, J. S. 1993. Almost All Social Choice Rules are Manipulable, But a Few Aren't. *Social Choice and Welfare*, **10**(2), 161–175.

Kelso, A. S. and Crawford, V. P. 1982. Job Matching, Coalition Formation and Gross Substitutes. *Econometrica*, **50**, 1483–1504.

Kemeny, J. 1959. Mathematics Without Numbers. *Daedalus*, **88**(4), 577–591.

Kemeny, J. and Snell, L. 1960. *Mathematical Models in the Social Sciences*. Cambridge, MA: MIT Press.

Kendall, M. 1938. A New Measure of Rank Correlation. *Biometrika*, **30**, 81–89.

Kendall, M. 1962. *Rank Correlation Methods*. 3rd ed. Royal Oak, MI: Hafner.

Kendall, M. and Gibbons, J. 1990. *Rank Correlation Methods*. New York: Oxford University Press.

Kendall, M. and Smith, B. B. 1939. The Problem of m Rankings. *Annals of Mathematical Statistics*, **10**, 239–251.

Kenyon-Mathieu, C. and Schudy, W. 2007. How to Rank with Few Errors. In *Proceedings of the 39th ACM Symposium on Theory of Computing* (STOC), 95–103. New York: ACM.

Kesten, O. 2009. Coalitional Strategy-Proofness and Resource Monotonicity for House Allocation Problems. *International Journal of Game Theory*, **38**, 17–21.

Kesten, O. 2010. School Choice with Consent. *Quarterly Journal of Economics*, **125**, 1297–1348.

Kfir-Dahav, N. E. and Tennenholtz, M. 1996. Multi-Agent Belief Revision. In *Proceedings of the Conference on Theoretical Aspects of Rationality and Knowledge* (TARK), 175–194. New York: ACM.

Kim, H. 2004. Population Monotonic Rules for Fair Allocation Problems. *Social Choice and Welfare*, **23**(1), 59–70.

Kim, M. 2014. Kings that Win Single-Elimination Tournaments. Unpublished manuscript.

Kintali, S., Poplawski, L. J., Rajaraman, R., Sundaram, R., and Teng, S.-H. 2009. Reducibility among Fractional Stability Problems. In *Proceedings of the 50th Annual Symposium on Foundations of Computer Science* (FOCS), 283–292.

Király, Z. 2013. Linear Time Local Approximation Algorithm for Maximum Stable Marriage. *Algorithms*, **6**(3), 471–484.

Kirman, A. P. and Sondermann, D. 1972. Arrow's Theorem, Many Agents, and Invisible Dictators. *Journal of Economic Theory*, **5**(3), 267–277.

Klamler, C. and Pferschy, U. 2007. The Traveling Group Problem. *Social Choice and Welfare*, **29**(3), 429–452.

Klaus, B. and Klijn, F. 2006. Median Stable Matching for College Admissions. *International Journal of Game Theory*, **34**(1), 1–11.

Klaus, B. and Walzl, M. 2009. Stable Many-To-Many Matchings with Contracts. *Journal of Mathematical Economics*, **45**, 422–434.

Kleinberg, J. M. 1999. Authoritative Sources in a Hyperlinked Environment. *Journal of the ACM*, **46**(5), 604–632.

Kleinberg, J. M. and Raghavan, P. 2005. Query Incentive Networks. In *Proceedings of the Annual Symposium on Foundations of Computer Science* (FOCS), 132–141. New York: IEEE Press.

Kleinberg, J. M., Papadimitriou, C. H., and Raghavan, P. 2004. Segmentation Problems. *Journal of the ACM*, **51**(2).

Klijn, F. and Yazıcı, A. 2014. A Many-To-Many Rural Hospital Theorem. *Journal of Mathematical Economics*, **54**, 63–73.

Knuth, D. E. 1973. Selected Topics in Computer Science. Lecture Notes Series, Institute of Mathematics, University of Oslo.

Knuth, D. E. 1976. *Mariages stables*. Montreal: Les Presses de L'Université de Montréal.

Kojima, F. and Pathak, P. A. 2009. Incentives and Stability in Large Two-Sided Matching Markets. *American Economic Review*, **99**, 608–627.

Kojima, F. and Ünver, M. U. 2008. Random Paths to Pairwise Stability in Many-To-Many Matching Problems: A Study on Market Equilibration. *International Journal of Game Theory*, **36**, 473–488.

Kolm, S.-C. 1972. *Justice et équité*. Éd. du Centre National de la Recherche Scientifique.

Komusiewicz, C. and Niedermeier, R. 2012. New Races in Parameterized Algorithmics. In *Proceedings of the 37th International Symposium on Mathematical Foundations of Computer Science*, 19–30. New York: Springer.

Konczak, K. and Lang, J. 2005. Voting Procedures with Incomplete Preferences. Pages 124–129 of: Proceedings of the Multidisciplinary IJCAI-05 Workshop on Advances in Preference Handling.

Konieczny, S. and Pino Pérez, R. 2002. Merging Information Under Constraints: A Logical Framework. *Journal of Logic and Computation*, **12**(5), 773–808.

Konieczny, S. and Pino Pérez, R. 2011. Logic Based Merging. *Journal of Philosophical Logic*, **40**(2), 239–270.

Konieczny, S., Lang, J., and Marquis, P. 2004. DA^2 Merging Operators. *Artificial Intelligence*, **157**(1–2), 49–79.

Konishi, H. and Ünver, M. U. 2006. Credible Group Stability in Many-To-Many Matching Problems. *Journal of Economic Theory*, **129**, 57–80.

Koriche, F. and Zanuttini, B. 2010. Learning Conditional Preference Networks. *Artificial Intelligence*, **174**(11), 685–703.

Kornhauser, L. A. and Sager, L. G. 1993. The One and the Many: Adjudication in Collegial Courts. *California Law Review*, **81**(1), 1–59.

Kräkel, M. 2014. Optimal Seedings in Elimination Tournaments Revisited. *Economic Theory Bulletin*, **2**(1), 77–91.

Kreweras, G. 1965. Aggregation of Preference Orderings. In *Mathematics and Social Sciences I: Proceedings of the Seminars of Menthon-Saint-Bernard, France (1–27 July 1960) and of Gösing, Austria (3–27 July 1962)*, 73–79.

Krysta, P., Manlove, D., Rastegari, B., and Zhang, J. 2014. Size Versus Truthfulness in the House Allocation Problem. In *Proceedings of the 15th ACM Conference on Economics and Computation* (EC), 453–470. New York: ACM.

Kurokawa, D., Lai, J. K., and Procaccia, A. D. 2013. How to Cut a Cake Before the Party Ends. In *Proceedings of the 27th AAAI Conference on Artificial Intelligence*, 555–561. Palo Alto, CA: AAAI.

Kushilevitz, E. and Nisan, N. 1996. *Communication Complexity*. Cambridge: Cambridge University Press.

Lacey, M. 2010. Republican Runs Street People on Green Ticket. *New York Times*.

Lacy, D. and Niou, E. 2000. A Problem with Referenda. *Journal of Theoretical Politics*, **12**(1), 5–31.

Lackner, M. 2014. Incomplete Preferences in Single-Peaked Electorates. In *Proceedings of the 28th AAAI Conference on Artificial Intelligence*, 742–748. Palo Alto, CA: AAAI.

Ladha, K. K. 1992. The Condorcet Jury Theorem, Free Speech and Correlated Votes. *American Political Science Review*, **36**(3), 617–634.

Ladha, K. K. 1993. Condorcet's Jury Theorem in the Light of de Finetti's Theorem: Majority-Voting with Correlated Votes. *Social Choice and Welfare*, **10**(1), 69–85.

Ladha, K. K. 1995. Information Pooling Through Majority Rule: Condorcet's Jury Theorem with Correlated Votes. *Journal of Economic Behavior and Organization*, **26**(3), 353–372.

Lafage, C. and Lang, J. 2000. Logical Representation of Preferences for Group Decision Making. In *Proceedings of the International Conference on Principles of Knowledge Representation and Reasoning* (KR), 457–468. Burlington, MA: Morgan Kaufmann.

Laffond, G. and Lainé, J.-F. 2009. Condorcet Choice and the Ostrogorski paradox. *Social Choice and Welfare*, **32**(2), 317–333.

Laffond, G., Laslier, J.-F., and Le Breton, M. 1993a. The Bipartisan Set of a Tournament Game. *Games and Economic Behavior*, **5**, 182–201.

Laffond, G., Laslier, J.-F., and Le Breton, M. 1993b. More on the Tournament Equilibrium Set. *Mathématiques et sciences humaines*, **31**(123), 37–44.

Laffond, G., Laslier, J.-F., and Le Breton, M. 1994. Social-Choice Mediators. *American Economic Review*, **84**(2), 448–453.

Lang, J. 2004. Logical Preference Representation and Combinatorial Vote. *Annals of Mathematics and Artificial Intelligence*, **42**(1), 37–71.

Lang, J. and Slavkovik, M. 2013. Judgment Aggregation Rules and Voting Rules. In *Proceedings of the 3rd International Conference on Algorithmic Decision Theory* (ADT), 230–243. New York: Springer.

Lang, J. and Xia, L. 2009. Sequential Composition of Voting Rules in Multi-Issue Domains. *Mathematical Social Sciences*, **57**(3), 304–324.

Lang, J., Pini, M. S., Rossi, F., Venable, K. B., and Walsh, T. 2007. Winner Determination in Sequential Majority Voting. In *Proceedings of the International Joint Conference on Artificial Intelligence* (IJCAI), 1372–1377. Palo Alto, CA: AAAI.

Lang, J., Pigozzi, G., Slavkovik, M., and van der Torre, L. 2011. Judgment Aggregation Rules Based on Minimization. In *Proceedings of the Conference on Theoretical Aspects of Rationality and Knowledge* (TARK), 238–246. New York: ACM.

Lang, J., Mengin, J., and Xia, L. 2012a. Aggregating Conditionally Lexicographic Preferences on Multi-issue Domains. In *Proceedings of the International Conference on Principles and Practice of Constraint Programming*, 973–987. New York: Springer.

Lang, J., Pini, M. S., Rossi, F., Salvagnin, D., Venable, K. B., and Walsh, T. 2012b. Winner Determination in Voting Trees with Incomplete Preferences and Weighted Votes. *Autonomous Agents and Multi-Agent Systems*, **25**(1), 130–157.

Lang, J., Maudet, N., and Polukarov, M. 2013. New Results on Equilibria in Strategic Candidacy. In *Proceedings of the 6th International Symposium on Algorithmic Game Theory* (SAGT), 13–25. New York: Springer.

Lari, I., Ricca, F., and Scozzari, A. 2014. Bidimensional Allocation of Seats via Zero-One Matrices with Given Line Sums. *Annals of Operations Research*, **215**(1), 165–181.

Laruelle, A. and Valenciano, F. 2005. A Critical Reappraisal of Some Voting Power Paradoxes. *Public Choice*, **125**, 17–41.

Laslier, J.-F. 1997. *Tournament Solutions and Majority Voting*. New York: Springer.

Laslier, J.-F. 2000. Interpretation of electoral mixed strategies. *Social Choice and Welfare*, **17**, 283–292.

Laslier, J.-F. 2009. The Leader Rule: A Model of Strategic Approval Voting in a Large Electorate. *Journal of Theoretical Politics*, **21**, 113–136.

Laslier, J.-F. 2012. And the Loser is ... Plurality Voting. In *Electoral Systems: Paradoxes, Assumptions, and Procedures*, ed. Felsenthal, D. S., and Machover, M., 327–352. New York: Springer.

Laslier, J.-F. and Sanver, M. R., eds. 2010. *Handbook on Approval Voting*. New York: Springer.

Lazear, E. and Rosen, S. 1981. Rank Order Tournaments as Optimum Labor Contracts. *Journal of Political Economy*, **89**, 841–864.

Le Breton, M. 2005. On the Uniqueness of Equilibrium in Symmetric Two-Player Zero-Sum Games with Integer Payoffs. *Économie publique*, **17**(2), 187–195.

Le Breton, M. and Sen, A. 1999. Separable Preferences, Strategyproofness, and Decomposability. *Econometrica*, **67**(3), 605–628.

Le Breton, M., Ortuno-Ortin, I., and Weber, S. 2008. Gamson's Law and Hedonic Games. *Social Choice and Welfare*, **30**(1), 57–67.

Lebanon, G. and Mao, Y. 2008. Non-Parametric Modeling of Partially Ranked Data. *Journal of Machine Learning Research*, **9**, 2401–2429.

Lee, S. 2014. Incentive Compatibility of Large Centralized Matching Markets. Working paper.

Leech, D. 2003. Computing Power Indices for Large Voting Games. *Journal of Management Science*, **49**(6), 831–837.

LeGrand, R., Markakis, E., and Mehta, A. 2007. Some Results on Approximating the Minimax Solution in Approval Voting. In *Proceedings of the International Conference on Autonomous Agents and Multiagent Systems* (AAMAS), 1185–1187. Richland, SC: IFAAMAS.

Lehrer, E. 1988. An Axiomatization of the Banzhaf Value. *International Journal of Game Theory*, **17**(2), 89–99.

Lemaître, M., Verfaillie, G., and Bataille, N. 1999. Exploiting a Common Property Resource Under a Fairness Constraint: A Case Study. In *Proceedings of the 16th International Joint Conference on Artificial Intelligence* (IJCAI), 206–211. Palo Alto, CA: AAAI.

Lenstra, H. W. Jr. 1983. Integer Programming with a Fixed Number of Variables. *Mathematics of Operations Research*, **8**(4), 538–548.

Lenstra, H. W., Jr., Shmoys, D. B., and Tardos, E. 1990. Approximation Algorithms for Scheduling Unrelated Parallel Machines. *Mathematical Programming*, **46**, 259–271.

Lerer, E. and Nitzan, S. 1985. Some General Results on the Metric Rationalization for Social Decision Rules. *Journal of Economic Theory*, **37**(1), 191–201.

Lesca, J. and Perny, P. 2010. LP Solvable Models for Multiagent Fair Allocation problems. In *Proceedings of the 19th European Conference on Artificial Intelligence* (ECAI), 387–392. Amsterdam: IOS Press.

Lev, O. and Rosenschein, J. S. 2012. Convergence of Iterative Voting. In *Proceedings of the 11th International Conference on Autonomous Agents and Multiagent Systems* (AAMAS), 611–618. Richland, SC: IFAAMAS.

Li, M., Vo, Q. B., and Kowalczyk, R. 2010. An Efficient Majority-Rule-Based Approach for Collective Decision Making with CP-Nets. In *Proceedings of the International Conference on Principles of Knowledge Representation and Reasoning* (KR). Palo Alto, CA: AAAI.

Li, M., Vo, Q. B., and Kowalczyk, R. 2011. Majority-Rule-Based Preference Aggregation on Multi-Attribute Domains with CP-Nets. In *Proceedings of the International Conference on Autonomous Agents and Multiagent Systems* (AAMAS), 659–666. Richland, SC: IFAAMAS.

Liberatore, P. and Schaerf, M. 1998. Arbitration (or How to Merge Knowledge Bases). *IEEE Transactions on Knowledge and Data Engineering*, **10**(1), 76–90.

Lin, A. 2012. Solving Hard Problems in Election Systems. PhD thesis, Rochester Institute of Technology.

Lindner, C. and Rothe, J. 2009. Degrees of Guaranteed Envy-Freeness in Finite Bounded Cake-Cutting Protocols. In *Proceedings of the 5th International Conference on Web and Internet Economics* (WINE), 149–159. New York: Springer.

Lipton, R., Markakis, E., Mossel, E., and Saberi, A. 2004. On Approximately Fair Allocations of Indivisible Goods. In *Proceedings of the 5th ACM Conference on Electronic Commerce* (EC), 125–131. New York: ACM.

List, C. 2012. The Theory of Judgment Aggregation: An Introductory Review. *Synthese*, **187**(1), 179–207.

List, C. and Pettit, P. 2002. Aggregating Sets of Judgments: An Impossibility Result. *Economics and Philosophy*, **18**(1), 89–110.

List, C. and Puppe, C. 2009. Judgment Aggregation: A Survey. *Handbook of Rational and Social Choice*, ed. Anand, P., Pattanaik, P., and Puppe, C. New York: Oxford University Press.

Lita, D. 2008. Method and Apparatus for Managing Billiard Tournaments. US Patent **20080269925** (Oct).

Liu, H. and Zhu, D. 2010. Parameterized Complexity of Control Problems in Maximin Election. *Information Processing Letters*, **110**(10), 383–388.

Liu, H. and Zhu, D. 2013. Parameterized Complexity of Control by Voter Selection in Maximin, Copeland, Borda, Bucklin, and Approval Election Systems. *Theoretical Computer Science*, **498**, 115–123.

Liu, H., Feng, H., Zhu, D., and Luan, J. 2009. Parameterized Computational Complexity of Control Problems in Voting Systems. *Theoretical Computer Science*, **410**(27–29), 2746–2753.

Liu, Q., Mailath, G. J., Postewaite, A., and Samuelson, L. 2012. Matching with Incomplete Information. Working paper WP-12-032, Penn Institute for Economic Research.

Loreggia, A., Narodytska, N., Rossi, F., Venable, K. B., and Walsh, T. 2014. Controlling Elections by Replacing Candidates: Theoretical and Experimental Results. In *Proceedings of the 8th Multidisciplinary Workshop on Advances in Preference Handling*, 61–66. Palo Alto: AAAI Press.

Lu, T. and Boutilier, C. 2010. The Unavailable Candidate Model: A Decision-theoretic View of Social Choice. In *Proceedings of the ACM Conference on Electronic Commerce* (EC), 263–274. New York: ACM.

Lu, T. and Boutilier, C. 2011a. Budgeted Social Choice: From Consensus to Personalized Decision Making. In *Proceedings of the 22nd International Joint Conference on Artificial Intelligence* (IJCAI), 280–286. Palo Alto, CA: AAAI.

Lu, T. and Boutilier, C. 2011b. Learning Mallows Models with Pairwise Preferences. In *Proceedings of the 28th International Conference on Machine Learning* (ICML), 145–152. Madison, WI: Omnipress.

Lu, T. and Boutilier, C. 2011c. Robust Approximation and Incremental Elicitation in Voting Protocols. In *Proceedings of the 22nd International Joint Conference on Artificial Intelligence* (IJCAI), 287–293. Palo Alto, CA: AAAI.

Lu, T. and Boutilier, C. 2011d. Vote Elicitation with Probabilistic Preference Models: Empirical Estimation and Cost Tradeoffs. In *Proceedings of the 2nd International Conference on Algorithmic Decision Theory* (ADT), 135–149. New York: Springer.

Lu, T. and Boutilier, C. 2013. Multi-Winner Social Choice with Incomplete Preferences. In *Proceedings of the International Joint Conference on Artificial Intelligence* (IJCAI), 263–270. Palo Alto, CA: AAAI.

Lu, T., Tang, P., Procaccia, A. D., and Boutilier, C. 2012. Bayesian Vote Manipulation: Optimal Strategies and Impact on Welfare. In *Proceedings of the 28th Conference on Uncertainty in Artificial Intelligence* (UAI), 543–553. New York: Morgan Kaufmann.

Luce, R. Duncan. 1959. *Individual Choice Behavior: A Theoretical Analysis*. Hoboken, NJ: John Wiley.

Ma, J. 1994. Strategy-Proofness and the Strict Core in a Market with Indivisibilities. *International Journal of Game Theory*, **23**, 75–83.

Ma, J. 1996. On Randomized Matching Mechanisms. *Economic Theory*, **8**, 377–381.

Magdon-Ismail, M., Busch, C., and Krishnamoorthy, M. S. 2003. Cake Cutting is Not a Piece of Cake. In *Proceedings of the 20th International Symposium on Theoretical Aspects of Computer Science*, 596–607. New York: Springer.

Magiera, K. and Faliszewski, P. 2014. How Hard Is Control in Single-Crossing Elections? In *Proceedings of the 21st European Conference on Artificial Intelligence* (ECAI), 579–584. Amsterdam: IOS Press.

Magrino, T., Rivest, R., Shen, E., and Wagner, D. 2011. Computing the Margin of Victory in IRV Elections. In *Proceedings of the Electronic Voting Technology Workshop and the Workshop on Trustworthy Elections* (EVT/WOTE). Berkeley: USENIX.

Mahajan, M., Raman, V., and Sikdar, S. 2009. Parameterizing Above or Below Guaranteed Values. *Journal of Computer and System Sciences*, **75**, 137–153.

Majumdar, D. and Sen, A. 2004. Ordinally Bayesian Incentive Compatible Voting Rules. *Econometrica*, **72**(2), 523–540.

Mallows, C. L. 1957. Non-Null Ranking Models. *Biometrika*, **44**, 114–130.

Manjunath, V. 2013. *Stability and the Core of Probabilistic Marriage Problems*. Technical report 1809941. SSRN.

Manlove, D. F. 1999. *Stable Marriage with Ties and Unacceptable Partners*. Technical report TR-1999-29, Department of Computing Science, University of Glasgow.

Manlove, D. F. 2008. Hospitals/Residents problem. In *Encyclopedia of Algorithms*, ed. Kao, M. Y., 390–394. New York: Springer.

Manlove, D. F. 2013. *Algorithmics of Matching Under Preferences*. Singapore: World Scientific.

Manlove, D. F. and O'Malley, G. 2012. Paired and Altruistic Kidney Donation in the UK: Algorithms and Experimentation. In *Proceedings of the 11th International Symposium on Experimental Algorithms*, 271–282. New York: Springer.

Manlove, D. F., Irving, R. W., Iwama, K., Miyazaki, S., and Morita, Y. 2002. Hard Variants of Stable Marriage. *Theoretical Computer Science*, **276**(1–2), 261–279.

Mann, I. and Shapley, L. S. 1960. Values of Large Games, IV: Evaluating the Electoral College by Montecarlo Techniques. RAND Corporation.

Mann, I. and Shapley, L. S. 1962. Values of Large Games, VI: Evaluating the Electoral College Exactly. RAND Corporation.

Mao, A. Procaccia, A. D., and Chen, Y. 2013. Better Human Computation through Principled Voting. In *Proceedings of the 27th AAAI Conference on Artificial Intelligence*, 1142–1148. Palo Alto, CA: AAAI.

Marchand, E. 2002. On the Comparison between Standard and Random Knockout Tournaments. *The Statistician*, **51**, 169–178.

Marden, J. I. 1995. *Analyzing and Modeling Rank Data*. London: Chapman and Hall.

Markakis, E. and Psomas, C.-A. 2011. On Worst-Case Allocations in the Presence of Indivisible Goods. In *Proceedings of the 7th International Conference on Web and Internet Economics* (WINE), 278–289. New York: Springer.

Marple, A., Rey, A., and Rothe, J. 2014. Bribery in Multiple-Adversary Path-Disruption Games Is Hard for the Second Level of the Polynomial Hierarchy. In *Proceedings of the 13th International Conference on Autonomous Agents and Multiagent Systems* (AAMAS), 1375–1376. Richland, SC: IFAAMAS.

Martínez, R., Massó, J., Neme, A., and Oviedo, J. 2004. An Algorithm to Compute the Full Set of Many-To-Many Stable Matchings. *Mathematical Social Sciences*, **47**(2), 187–210.

Masatlioglu, Y., Nakajima, D., and Ozbay, E. Y. 2012. Revealed Attention. *American Economic Review*, **102**(5), 2183–2205.

Maschler, M., Solan, E., and Zamir, S. 2013. *Game Theory*. New York: Cambridge University Press.

Maskin, E. 1977. Nash Equilibrium and Welfare Optimality. Mimeo.

Maskin, E. 1987. On the Fair Allocation of Indivisible Goods. In *Arrow and the Foundations of the Theory of Economic Policy (Essays in Honor of Kenneth Arrow)* Vol. 2, ed. Feiwel, G., 341–349. New York: Macmillan.

Maskin, E. 1999. Nash Equilibrium and Welfare Optimality. *Review of Economic Studies*, **66**, 23–38.

Massa, P. and Avesani, P. 2005. Controversial Users Demand Local Trust Metrics: An Experimental Study on Epinions.com Community. In *Proceedings of the AAAI Conference on Artificial Intelligence*, 121–126. Palo Alto, CA: AAAI.

Matsui, T. and Matsui, Y. 2000. A Survey of Algorithms for Calculating Power Indices of Weighted Majority Games. *Journal of the Operations Research Society of Japan*, **43**(1), 71–86.

Matsui, Y. and Matsui, T. 2001. NP-Completeness for Calculating Power Indices of Weighted Majority Games. *Theoretical Computer Science*, **263**(1–2), 305–310.

Mattei, N. 2011. Empirical Evaluation of Voting Rules with Strictly Ordered Preference Data. In *Proceedings of the 2nd International Conference on Algorithmic Decision Theory* (ADT), 165–177. New York: Springer.

Mattei, N., Pini, M. S., Rossi, F., and Venable, K. B. 2012a. Bribery in Voting Over Combinatorial Domains Is Easy. In *Proceedings of the 11th International Conference on Autonomous Agents and Multiagent Systems* (AAMAS), 1407–1408. Richland, SC: IFAAMAS.

Mattei, N., Goldsmith, J., and Klapper, A. 2012b. On the Complexity of Bribery and Manipulation in Tournaments with Uncertain Information. In *Proceedings of the 25th AAAI Conference on Artificial Intelligence*, 549–554. Palo Alto, CA: AAAI.

May, K. 1952. A Set of Independent, Necessary and Sufficient Conditions for Simple Majority Decision. *Econometrica*, **20**(2–3), 680–684.

Maya, A. and Nisan, N. 2012. Incentive Compatible Two Player Cake Cutting. In *Proceedings of the 8th International Conference on Web and Internet Economics* (WINE), 170–183. New York: Springer.

McCabe-Dansted, J. 2006. Approximability and Computational Feasibility of Dodgson's Rule. MPhil thesis, University of Auckland.

McCabe-Dansted, J., Pritchard, G., and Slinko, A. 2008. Approximability of Dodgson's Rule. *Social Choice and Welfare*, **31**(2), 311–330.

McCutchen, R. M. 2008. The Least-Unpopularity-Factor and Least-Unpopularity-Margin Criteria for Matching Problems with One-Sided Preferences. In *Proceedings of the 8th Latin-American Theoretical Informatics Symposium*, 593–604. New York: Springer.

McDermid, E. J. 2009. A 3/2 Approximation Algorithm for General Stable Marriage. In *Proceedings of the 36th International Colloquium on Automata, Languages and Programming*, 689–700. New York: Springer.

McDermid, E. J. and Irving, R. W. 2011. Popular Matchings: Structure and Algorithms. *Journal of Combinatorial Optimization*, **22**(3), 339–358.

McDermid, E. J. and Manlove, D. F. 2010. Keeping Partners Together: Algorithmic Results for the Hospitals / Residents Problem with Couples. *Journal of Combinatorial Optimization*, **19**(3), 279–303.

McGarvey, D. C. 1953. A Theorem on the Construction of Voting Paradoxes. *Econometrica*, **21**(4), 608–610.

McKelvey, R. D. and Niemi, R. G. 1978. A Multistage Game Representation of Sophisticated Voting for Binary Procedures. *Journal of Economic Theory*, **18**, 1–22.

McLean, I. and Urken, A. 1995. *Classics of Social Choice*. Ann Arbor: University of Michigan Press.

McLennan, A. 1998. Consequences of the Condorcet Jury Theorem for Beneficial Information Aggregation by Rational Agents. *American Political Science Review*, **92**(2), 413–419.

McSweeney, P. J., Mehrotra, K., and Oh, J. C. 2014. Game-Theoretic Framework for Community Detection. In *Encyclopedia of Social Network Analysis and Mining*, 573–588. New York: Springer.

Meilă, M. and Chen, H. 2010. Dirichlet Process Mixtures of Generalized Mallows Models. In *Proceedings of the 26th Conference on Uncertainty in Artificial Intelligence* (UAI), 358–367. New York: Morgan Kaufmann.

Meir, R., Procaccia, A. D., Rosenschein, J. S., and Zohar, A. 2008. Complexity of Strategic Behavior in Multi-Winner Elections. *Journal of Artificial Intelligence Research (JAIR)*, **33**, 149–178.

Meir, R., Polukarov, M., Rosenschein, J. S., and Jennings, N. R. 2010. Convergence to Equilibria in Plurality Voting. In *Proceedings of the 24th AAAI Conference on Artificial Intelligence*, 823–828. Palo Alto, CA: AAAI.

Meir, R., Procaccia, A. D., and Rosenschein, J. S. 2012. Algorithms for Strategyproof Classification. *Artificial Intelligence*, **186**, 123–156.

Meir, R., Lev, O., and Rosenschein, J. S. 2014. A Local-Dominance Theory of Voting Equilibria. In *Proceedings of the 15th ACM Conference on Electronic Commerce* (EC), 313–330. New York: ACM.

Menton, C. 2013. Normalized Range Voting Broadly Resists Control. *Theory of Computing Systems*, **53**(4), 507–531.

Menton, C. and Singh, P. 2013. Control Complexity of Schulze Voting. In *Proceedings of the 23rd International Joint Conference on Artificial Intelligence* (IJCAI), 286–292. Palo Alto, CA: AAAI.

Merrill, S. 1982. Approximations to the Banzhaf Index. *American Mathematical Monthly*, **89**, 108–110.

Meskanen, T. and Nurmi, H. 2008. Closeness Counts in Social Choice. In *Power, Freedom, and Voting*, ed. Braham, M., and Steffen, F., 182–191. New York: Springer.

Messner, M. and Polborn, M. K. 2007. Strong and Coalition-Proof Political Equilibria Under Plurality and Runoff Rule. *International Journal of Game Theory*, **35**, 287–314.

Michalak, T., Sroka, J., Rahwan, T., McBurney, P., Wooldridge, M., and Jennings, N. R. 2010. A Distributed Algorithm for Anytime Coalition Structure Generation. In *Proceedings of the 9th International Conference on Autonomous Agents and Multiagent Systems* (AAMAS), 1007–1014. Richland, SC: IFAAMAS.

Milchtaich, I. 1996. Congestion Games with Player-Specific Payoff Functions. *Games and Economic Behavior*, **13**, 111–124.

Miller, M. K. and Osherson, D. 2009. Methods for Distance-Based Judgment Aggregation. *Social Choice and Welfare*, **32**(4), 575–601.

Miller, N. R. 1977. Graph-Theoretic Approaches to the Theory of Voting. *American Journal of Political Science*, **21**(4), 769–803.

Miller, N. R. 1980. A New Solution Set for Tournaments and Majority Voting: Further Graph-Theoretical Approaches to the Theory of Voting. *American Journal of Political Science*, **24**(1), 68–96.

Mossel, E. and Tamuz, O. 2010. Truthful Fair Division. In *Proceedings of the 3rd International Symposium on Algorithmic Game Theory* (SAGT), 288–299. New York: Springer.

Monjardet, B. 2008. Statement of Precedence and a Comment on IIA Terminology. *Games and Economic Behavior*, **62**, 736–738.

Monroe, B. L. 1995. Fully Proportional Representation. *American Political Science Review*, **89**, 925–940.

Montanari, U. 1974. Network of Constraints: Fundamental Properties and Applications to Picture Processing. *Information Sciences*, **7**, 95–132.

Moon, J. W. 1968. *Topics on Tournaments*. New York: Holt, Reinhard and Winston.

Moon, J. W. and Pullman, N. K. 1970. On Generalized Tournament Matrices. *SIAM Review*, **12**(3), 384–399.

Mossel, E. and Rácz, M. Z. 2012. A Quantitative Gibbard-Satterthwaite Theorem without Neutrality. In *Proceedings of the ACM Symposium on Theory of Computing* (STOC), 1041–1060. New York: ACM.

Mossel, E., Procaccia, A. D., and Rácz, M. Z. 2013. A Smooth Transition from Powerlessness to Absolute Power. *Journal of Artificial Intelligence Research (JAIR)*, **48**, 923–951.

Moulin, H. 1979. Dominance Solvable Voting Schemes. *Econometrica*, **47**, 1337–1351.

Moulin, H. 1983. *The Strategy of Social Choice*. Amsterdam: North Holland.

Moulin, H. 1986. Choosing from a Tournament. *Social Choice and Welfare*, **3**, 271–291.

Moulin, H. 1988a. *Axioms of Cooperative Decision Making*. New York: Cambridge University Press.

Moulin, H. 1988b. Condorcet's Principle Implies the No-Show Paradox. *Journal of Economic Theory*, **45**, 53–64.

Moulin, H. 1990. Uniform Externalities: Two Axioms for Fair Allocation. *Journal of Public Economics*, **43**(3), 305–326.

Moulin, H. 1995. *Cooperative Microeconomics: A Game-Theoretic Introduction*. Princeton, NJ: Princeton University Press.

Moulin, H. 2000. Priority Rules and Other Asymmetric Rationing Methods. *Econometrica*, **68**(3), 643–684.

Moulin, H. 2004. *Fair Division and Collective Welfare*. Cambridge, MA: MIT Press.

Moulin, H. and Thomson, W. 1988. Can Everyone Benefit from Growth?: Two Difficulties. *Journal of Mathematical Economics*, **17**(4), 339–345.

Muller, E. and Satterthwaite, M. A. 1977. The Equivalence of Strong Positive Association and Strategy-Proofness. *Journal of Economic Theory*, **14**(2), 412–418.

Munera, D., Diaz, D., Abreu, S., Rossi, F., Saraswat, V., and Codognet, P. 2015. Solving Hard Stable Matching Problems via Local Search and Cooperative Parallelization. In *Proceedings of the 29th AAAI Conference on Artificial Intelligence*, 1212–1218. Palo Alto, CA: AAAI.

Muroga, S. 1971. *Threshold Logic and Its Applications*. Hoboken, NJ: John Wiley.

Murphy, T. B. and Martin, D. 2003. Mixtures of Distance-Based Models for Ranking Data. *Computational Statistics and Data Analysis*, **41**, 645–655.

Myerson, R. B. 1991. *Game Theory*. Cambridge, MA: Harvard University Press.

Nanson, E. J. 1882. Methods of Election. *Transactions and Proceedings of the Royal Society of Victoria*, **19**, 197–240.

Narodytska, N. and Walsh, T. 2013. Manipulating Two Stage Voting Rules. In *Proceedings of the 13th International Conference on Autonomous Agents and Multiagent Systems* (AAMAS), 423–430. Richland, SC: IFAAMAS.

Narodytska, N., Walsh, T., and Xia, L. 2011. Manipulation of Nanson's and Baldwin's Rules. In *Proceedings of the 25th AAAI Conference on Artificial Intelligence*, 713–718. Palo Alto, CA: AAAI.

Narodytska, N., Walsh, T., and Xia, L. 2012. Combining Voting Rules Together. In *Proceedings of the 20th European Conference on Artificial Intelligence* (ECAI), 612–617. Amsterdam: IOS Press.

Nash, J. F. 1950. The Bargaining Problem. *Econometrica*, **18**(2), 155–162.

Nehama, I. 2013. Approximately Classic Judgement Aggregation. *Annals of Mathematics and Artificial Intelligence*, **68**(1–3), 91–134.

Nehring, K. and Puppe, C. 2007. The Structure of Strategy-Proof Social Choice. Part I: General Characterization and Possibility Results on Median Spaces. *Journal of Economic Theory*, **135**(1), 269–305.

Nemhauser, G. L. and Wolsey, L. A. 1999. *Integer and Combinatorial Optimization*. Hoboken, NJ: John Wiley.

Newman, M. E. J. 2008. The Mathematics of Networks. *The New Palgrave Encyclopedia of Economics*, **2**.

Ng, C. and Hirschberg, D. S. 1988. Complexity of the Stable Marriage and Stable Roommate Problems in Three Dimensions. Technical report UCI-ICS 88-28, Department of Information and Computer Science, University of California, Irvine.

Nguyen, N.-T., Nguyen, T. T., Roos, M., and Rothe, J. 2014. Computational Complexity and Approximability of Social Welfare Optimization in Multiagent Resource Allocation. *Journal of Autonomous Agents and Multi-Agent Systems*, **28**(2), 256–289.

Nguyen, T. T. and Rothe, J. 2015. Minimizing Envy and Maximizing Average Nash Social Welfare in the Allocation of Indivisible Goods. *Discrete Applied Mathematics*, **179**, 54–68.

Nguyen, T. T., Roos, M., and Rothe, J. 2013. A Survey of Approximability and Inapproximability Results for Social Welfare Optimization in Multiagent Resource Allocation. *Annals of Mathematics and Artificial Intelligence*, **68**(1–3), 65–90.

Nicolò, A. and Yu, Y. 2008. Strategic Divide and Choose. *Games and Economic Behavior*, **64**(1), 268–289.

Nicosia, G., Pacifici, A., and Pferschy, U. 2009. On Multi-agent Knapsack Problems. In *Proceedings of the 8th Cologne-Twente Workshop on Graphs and Combinatorial Optimization* (CTW), 44–47.

Niedermeier, R. 2006. *Invitation to Fixed-Parameter Algorithms*. New York: Oxford University Press.

Niou, E. M. S. 1987. A Note on Nanson's Rule. *Public Choice*, **54**, 191–193.

Nipkow, T. 2009. Social Choice Theory in HOL: Arrow and Gibbard-Satterthwaite. *Journal of Automated Reasoning*, **43**(3), 289–304.

Nisan, N. 2006. Bidding Languages for Combinatorial Auctions. In *Combinatorial Auctions*, ed. Cramton, P., Shoham, Y., and Steinberg, R., Chapter 9. Cambridge, MA: MIT Press.

Nisan, N. 2007. Introduction to Mechanism Design (for Computer Scientists). In *Algorithmic Game Theory*, 209–242. New York: Cambridge University Press.

Nitzan, S. 1981. Some Measures of Closeness to Unanimity and Their Implications. *Theory and Decision*, **13**(2), 129–138.

Nitzan, S. 2010. *Collective Preference and Choice*. New York: Cambridge University Press.

Nitzan, S. and Paroush, J. 1982. Optimal Decision Rules in Uncertain Dichotomous Choice Situations. *International Economic Review*, **23**, 289–297.

NRMP. 2014. National Resident Matching Program. http://www.nrmp.org.

Obraztsova, S. and Elkind, E. 2011. On the Complexity of Voting Manipulation Under Randomized Tie-Breaking. In *Proceedings of the 22nd International Joint Conference on Artificial Intelligence* (IJCAI), 319–324. Palo Alto, CA: AAAI.

Obraztsova, S., Elkind, E., and Hazon, N. 2011. Ties Matter: Complexity of Voting Manipulation Revisited. In *Proceedings of the 10th International Conference on Autonomous Agents and Multiagent Systems* (AAMAS), 71–78. Richland, SC: IFAAMAS.

Obraztsova, S., Markakis, E., and Thompson, D. R. M. 2013. Plurality Voting with Truth-Biased Agents. In *Proceedings of the 6th International Symposium on Algorithmic Game Theory* (SAGT), 26–37. New York: Springer.

Obraztsova, S., Rabinovich, Z., Lev, O., Markakis, E., and Rosenschein, J. S. 2015a. Analysis of Equilibria in Iterative Voting Schemes. In *Proceedings of the 29th AAAI Conference on Artificial Intelligence*, 1007–1013. Palo Alto, CA: AAAI.

Obraztsova, S., Markakis, E., Polukarov, M., Rabinovich, Z., and Jennings, N. R. 2015b. On the Convergence of Iterative Voting: How Restrictive Should Restricted Dynamics Be. In *Proceedings of the 29th AAAI Conference on Artificial Intelligence*, 993–999. Palo Alto, CA: AAAI.

Olsen, M. 2009. Nash Stability in Additively Separable Hedonic Games and Community Structures. *Theory of Computing Systems*, **45**, 917–925.

Olsen, M. 2013. A general view on computing communities. *Mathematical Social Sciences*, **66**(3), 331–336.

O'Neill, B. 1982. A Problem of Rights Arbitration from the Talmud. *Mathematical Social Sciences*, **2**(4), 345–371.

Oren, J., Filmus, Y., and Boutilier, C. 2013. Efficient Vote Elicitation Under Candidate Uncertainty. In *Proceedings of the 23rd International Joint Conference on Artificial Intelligence* (IJCAI), 309–316. Palo Alto, CA: AAAI.

Othman, A., Sandholm, T., and Budish, E. 2010. Finding Approximate Competitive Equilibria: Efficient and Fair Course Allocation. In *Proceedings of the 9th International Conference on Autonomous Agents and Multiagent Systems* (AAMAS), 873–880. Richland, SC: IFAAMAS.

Owen, G. 1975. Multilinear Extensions and the Banzhaf Value. *Naval Research Logistics Quarterly*, **22**(4), 741–750.

Özkal-Sanver, İ. and Sanver, M. R. 2006. Ensuring Pareto-Optimality by Referendum Voting. *Social Choice and Welfare*, **27**, 211–219.

Page, L., Brin, S., Motwani, R., and Winograd, T. 1998. The PageRank Citation Ranking: Bringing Order to the Web. Technical report, Stanford University.

Paluch, K. 2014. Faster and Simpler Approximation of Stable Matchings. *Algorithms*, **7**(2), 189–202.

Papadimitriou, C. H. 1994. *Computational Complexity*. Addison Wesley.

Papadimitriou, C. H. and Zachos, S. 1983. Two Remarks on the Power of Counting. In *Proceedings of the 6th GI Conference on Theoretical Computer Science*, 269–276. New York: Springer.

Pápai, S. 2004. Unique Stability in Simple Coalition Formation Games. *Games and Economic Behavior*, **48**, 337–354.

Pareto, V. 1919. *Manuale di Economia Politica con una Introduzione alla Scienza Sociale*. Società Editrice Libraria.

Parkes, D. C. and Procaccia, A. D. 2013. Dynamic Social Choice with Evolving Preferences. In *Proceedings of the 27th AAAI Conference on Artificial Intelligence*, 767–773. Palo Alto, CA: AAAI.

Parkes, D. C. and Xia, L. 2012. A Complexity-of-Strategic-Behavior Comparison between Schulze's Rule and Ranked Pairs. In *Proceedings of the 26th AAAI Conference on Artificial Intelligence*, 1429–1435. Palo Alto, CA: AAAI.

Parkes, D. C., Procaccia, A. D., and Shah, N. 2014. Beyond Dominant Resource Fairness: Extensions, Limitations, and Indivisibilities. *ACM Transactions on Economics and Computation*, **3**(1).

Pathak, P. A. 2011. The Mechanism Design Approach to Student Assignment. *Annual Reviews of Economics*, **3**, 513–536.

Pauly, M. 2014. Can Strategizing in Round-Robin Subtournaments be Avoided? *Social Choice and Welfare*, **43**(1), 29–46.

Pauly, M. and van Hees, M. 2006. Logical Constraints on Judgement Aggregation. *Journal of Philosophical Logic*, **35**(6), 569–585.

Pazner, E. A. 1977. Pitfalls in the Theory of Fairness. *Journal of Economic Theory*, **14**(2), 458–466.

Pazner, E. A. and Schmeidler, D. 1978. Egalitarian Equivalent Allocations: A New Concept of Economic Equity. *Quarterly Journal of Economics*, **92**(4), 671–687.

Pearl, J. 1988. *Probabilistic Reasoning in Intelligent Systems: Networks of Plausible Inference*. San Francisco: Morgan Kaufmann.

Peleg, B. 1975. Consistent Voting Systems. *Research Memorandum No.9, Centre for Research in Mathematical Economics and Game Theory, The Hebrew University, Jerusalem*.

Peleg, B. 1981. Monotonicity Properties of Social Choice Correspondences. In *Game Theory and Mathematical Economics*, ed. Moeschlin, O., and Pallaschka, D., 97–101. Amsterdam: Elsevier.

Peleg, B. and Sudhölter, P. 2007. *Introduction to the Theory of Cooperative Games*. 2nd ed. New York: Springer.

Peleg, B. and Zamir, S. 2012. Extending the Condorcet Jury Theorem to a General Dependent Jury. *Social Choice and Welfare*, **1**(39), 91–125.

Pennock, D. M., Horvitz, E., and Giles, C. L. 2000a. Social Choice Theory and Recommender Systems: Analysis of the Axiomatic Foundations of Collaborative Filtering. In *Proceedings of the 17th AAAI Conference on Artificial Intelligence*, 729–734. Palo Alto, CA: AAAI.

Pettit, P. 2001. Deliberative Democracy and the Discursive Dilemma. *Philosophical Issues*, **11**(1), 268–299.

Pickard, G., Pan, W., Rahwan, I., Cebrian, M., Crane, R., Madan, A., and Pentland, A. 2011. Time-Critical Social Mobilization. *Science*, **334**(6055), 509–512.

Pigozzi, G. 2006. Belief Merging and the Discursive Dilemma: An Argument-Based Account of Paradoxes of Judgment Aggregation. *Synthese*, **152**(2), 285–298.

Pini, M. S., Rossi, F., Venable, K. B., and Walsh, T. 2009. Aggregating Partially Ordered Preferences. *Journal of Logic and Computation*, **19**, 475–502.

Pini, M. S., Rossi, F., Venable, K. B., and Walsh, T. 2011a. Manipulation Complexity and Gender Neutrality in Stable Marriage Procedures. *Autonomous Agents and Multi-Agent Systems*, **22**(1), 183–199.

Pini, M. S., Rossi, F., Venable, K. B., and Walsh, T. 2011b. Stability in Matching Problems with Weighted Preferences. In *Proceedings of the 3rd International Conference on Agents and Artificial Intelligence*. Setubal: SciTePress.

Pinski, G. and Narin, F. 1976. Citation Influence for Journal Aggregates of Scientific Publications: Theory, with Applications to the Literature of Physics. *Information Processing and Management*, 297–312.

Pivato, M. 2012. Voting Rules as Statistical Estimators. *Social Choice and Welfare*, 40(2), 581–630.

Porello, D. and Endriss, U. 2011. Ontology Merging as Social Choice. In *Proceedings of the 12th International Workshop on Computational Logic in Multiagent Systems*, 157–170. New York: Springer.

Prasad, K. and Kelly, J. S. 1990. NP-Completeness of Some Problems Concerning Voting Games. *International Journal of Game Theory*, **19**(1), 1–9.

Pritchard, G. and Wilson, M. C. 2009. Asymptotics of the Minimum Manipulating Coalition Size for Positional Voting Rules Under Impartial Culture Behaviour. *Mathematical Social Sciences*, **58**(1), 35–57.

Procaccia, A. D. 2008. A Note on the Query Complexity of the Condorcet Winner Problem. *Information Processing Letters*, **108**(6), 390–393.

Procaccia, A. D. 2009. Thou Shalt Covet Thy Neighbor's Cake. In *Proceedings of the 21st International Joint Conference on Artificial Intelligence* (IJCAI), 239–244. Palo Alto, CA: AAAI.

Procaccia, A. D. 2010. Can Approximation Circumvent Gibbard-Satterthwaite? In *Proceedings of the 24th AAAI Conference on Artificial Intelligence*, 836–841. Palo Alto, CA: AAAI.

Procaccia, A. D. and Rosenschein, J. S. 2006. The Distortion of Cardinal Preferences in Voting. In *Proceedings of the 10th International Workshop on Cooperative Information Agents*, 317–331. New York: Springer.

Procaccia, A. D. and Rosenschein, J. S. 2007a. Average-Case Tractability of Manipulation in Voting via the Fraction of Manipulators. In *Proceedings of the 6th International Conference on Autonomous Agents and Multiagent Systems* (AAMAS), 718–720. Richland, SC: IFAAMAS.

Procaccia, A. D. and Rosenschein, J. S. 2007b. Junta Distributions and the Average-Case Complexity of Manipulating Elections. *Journal of Artificial Intelligence Research (JAIR)*, **28**, 157–181.

Procaccia, A. D. and Tennenholtz, M. 2013. Approximate Mechanism Design without Money. *ACM Transactions on Economics and Computation*, **1**(4), 18.

Procaccia, A. D. and Wang, J. 2014. Fair Enough: Guaranteeing Approximate Maximin Shares. In *Proceedings of the 15th ACM Conference on Electronic Commerce* (EC), 675–692. New York: ACM.

Procaccia, A. D., Rosenschein, J. S., and Zohar, A. 2008. On the Complexity of Achieving Proportional Representation. *Social Choice and Welfare*, **30**(3), 353–362.

Procaccia, A. D., Zohar, A., Peleg, Y., and Rosenschein, J. S. 2009. The Learnability of Voting Rules. *Artificial Intelligence*, **173**(12–13), 1133–1149.

Procaccia, A. D., Reddi, S., and Shah, N. 2012. A Maximum Likelihood Approach for Selecting Sets of Alternatives. In *Proceedings of the Conference on Uncertainty in Artificial Intelligence* (UAI), 695–704. New York: Morgan Kaufmann.

Pukelsheim, F., Ricca, F., Simeone, B., Scozzari, A., and Serafini, P. 2012. Network Flow Methods for Electoral Systems. *Networks*, **59**(1), 73–88.

Qing, C., Endriss, U., Fernández, R., and Kruger, J. 2014. Empirical Analysis of Aggregation Methods for Collective Annotation. In *Proceedings of the 25th International Conference on Computational Linguistics*, 1533–1542. Stroudsburg, PA: ACL.

Rabinovich, Z., Obraztsova, S., Lev, O., Markakis, E., and Rosenschein, J. S. 2014. Analysis of Equilibria in Iterative Voting Schemes. In *Proceedings of the 5th International Workshop on Computational Social Choice* (COMSOC).

Rahwan, T., Ramchurn, S., and Jennings, N. R. 2009a. An Anytime Algorithm for Optimal Coalition Structure Generation. *Journal of Artificial Intelligence Research (JAIR)*, **34**, 521–567.

Rahwan, T., Michalak, T. P., Jennings, N. R., Wooldridge, M., and McBurney, P. 2009b. Coalition Structure Generation in Multi-Agent Systems with Positive and Negative Externalities. In *Proceedings of the 21st International Joint Conference on Artificial Intelligence* (IJCAI), 257–263. Palo Alto, CA: AAAI.

Rajagopalan, S. and Vazirani, V. 1999. Primal-Dual RNC Approximation Algorithms for Set Cover and Covering Integer programs. *SIAM Journal on Computing*, **28**, 526–541.

Raman, V. and Saurabh, S. 2007. Improved Fixed Parameter Tractable Algorithms for Two "Edge" Problems: MAXCUT and MAXDAG. *Information Processing Letters*, **104**(2), 65–72.

Rassenti, S., Smith, V. L., and Bulfin, R. L. 1982. A Combinatorial Auction Mechanisms for Airport Time Slot Allocation. *Bell Journal of Economics*, **13**(2), 402–417.

Rastegari, B., Condon, A., Leyton-Brown, K., and Immorlica, N. 2013. Two-Sided Matching with Partial Information. In *Proceedings of the 14th ACM Conference on Electronic Commerce* (EC), 733–750. New York: ACM.

Ratliff, T. C. 2001. A Comparison of Dodgson's Method and Kemeny's Rule. *Social Choice and Welfare*, **18**(1), 79–89.

Raz, R. and Safra, S. 1997. A Sub-Constant Error-Probability Low-Degree Test, and Sub-Constant Error-Probability PCP Characterization of NP. In *Proceedings of the 29th ACM Symposium on Theory of Computing*, 475–484. New York: ACM.

Regenwetter, M., Grofman, B., Marley, A. A. J., and Tsetlin, I. 2006. *Behavioral Social Choice: Probabilistic Models, Statistical Inference, and Applications*. Cambridge: Cambridge University Press.

Reid, K. B. 2004. Tournaments. In *Handbook of Graph Theory*, ed. Gross, J. L., and Yellen, J., 156–184. Boca Raton, FL: CRC Press.

Reid, K. B. and Beineke, L. W. 1978. Tournaments. In *Selected Topics in Graph Theory*, ed. Beineke, L. W., and Wilson, R. J., 169–204. New York: Academic Press.

Reijngoud, A. and Endriss, U. 2012. Voter Response to Iterated Poll Information. In *Proceedings of the 11th International Conference on Autonomous Agents and Multiagent Systems* (AAMAS), 635–644. Richland, SC: IFAAMAS.

Reisch, Y., Rothe, J., and Schend, L. 2014. The Margin of Victory in Schulze, Cup, and Copeland Elections: Complexity of the Regular and Exact Variants. In *Proceedings of the 7th European Starting AI Researcher Symposium*, 250–259. Amsterdam: IOS Press.

Resnick, P. and Zeckhauser, R. 2001. Trust among Strangers in Internet Transactions: Empirical Analysis of eBay's Reputation System. Working paper, NBER Workshop on Empirical Studies of Electronic Commerce.

Resnick, P., Zeckhauser, R., Friedman, R., and Kuwabara, E. 2000. Reputation Systems. *Communications of the ACM*, **43**(12), 45–48.

Revesz, P. Z. 1997. On the Semantics of Arbitration. *International Journal of Algebra and Computation*, **7**(2), 133–160.

Rey, A. and Rothe, J. 2011. Bribery in Path-Disruption Games. In *Proceedings of the 2nd International Conference on Algorithmic Decision Theory* (ADT), 247–261. New York: Springer.

Rey, A. and Rothe, J. 2014. False-Name Manipulation in Weighted Voting Games is Hard for Probabilistic Polynomial Time. *Journal of Artificial Intelligence Research (JAIR)*, **50**, 573–601.

Reyhani, R. and Wilson, M. C. 2012. Best Reply Dynamics for Scoring Rules. In *Proceedings of the 20th European Conference on Artificial Intelligence* (ECAI), 672–677. Amsterdam: IOS Press.

Ricca, F., Scozzari, A., and Simeone, B. 2007. Weighted Voronoi Region Algorithms for Political Districting. *Mathematical and Computer Modelling*, **48**(9–10), 1468–1477.

Ricca, F., Scozzari, A., and Simeone, B. 2011. The Give-Up Problem for Blocked Regional Lists with Multi-Winners. *Mathematical Social Sciences*, **62**(1), 14–24.

Ricca, F., Scozzari, A., and Simeone, B. 2013. Political Districting: From Classical Models to Recent Approaches. *Annals of Operations Research*, **204**(1), 271–299.

Robertson, J. M. and Webb, W. A. 1998. *Cake Cutting Algorithms: Be Fair If You Can.* Natick, MA: A. K. Peters.

Rodríguez-Álvarez, C. 2009. Strategy-Proof Coalition Formation. *International Journal of Game Theory*, **38**, 431—452.

Roemer, J. 1986. The Mismarriage of Bargaining Theory and Distributive Justice. *Ethics*, **97**(1), 88–110.

Ronn, E. 1990. NP-Complete Stable Matching Problems. *Journal of Algorithms*, **11**, 285–304.

Rosen, S. 1986. Prizes and Incentives in Elimination Tournaments. *American Economic Review*, **76**, 701–715.

Rossi, F., Venable, K. B., and Walsh, T. 2004. mCP Nets: Representing and Reasoning with Preferences of Multiple Agents. In *Proceedings of the AAAI Conference on Artificial Intelligence*, 729–734. Palo Alto, CA: AAAI.

Roth, A. E. 1982a. The Economics of Matching: Stability and Incentives. *Mathematics of Operations Research*, **7**(4), 617–628.

Roth, A. E. 1982b. Incentive Compatibility in a Market with Indivisible Goods. *Economics Letters*, **9**, 127–132.

Roth, A. E. 1984a. The Evolution of the Labor Market for Medical Interns and Residents: a case study in game theory. *Journal of Political Economy*, **92**(6), 991–1016.

Roth, A. E. 1984b. Stability and Polarization of Interests in Job Matching. *Econometrica*, **52**(1), 47–57.

Roth, A. E. 1985. The College Admissions Problem is not Equivalent to the Marriage Problem. *Journal of Economic Theory*, **36**, 277–288.

Roth, A. E. 1986. On the Allocation of Residents to Rural Hospitals: A General Property of Two-Sided Matching Markets. *Econometrica*, **54**, 425–427.

Roth, A. E. 2008. Deferred Acceptance Algorithms: History, Theory, Practice, and Open Questions. *International Journal of Game Theory*, **36**(3–4), 537–569.

Roth, A. E. and Peranson, E. 1997. The Effects of the Change in the NRMP Matching Algorithm. *Journal of the American Medical Association*, **278**(9), 729–732.

Roth, A. E. and Peranson, E. 1999. The Redesign of the Matching Market for American Physicians: Some Engineering Aspects of Economic Design. *American Economic Review*, **89**(4), 748–780.

Roth, A. E. and Postlewaite, A. 1977. Weak versus Strong Domination in a Market with Indivisible Goods. *Journal of Mathematical Economics*, **4**, 131–137.

Roth, A. E. and Sotomayor, M. A. O. 1990. *Two-Sided Matching: A Study in Game-Theoretic Modeling and Analysis.* New York: Cambridge University Press.

Roth, A. E. and Vande Vate, J. H. 1990. Random Paths to Stability in Two-Sided Matching. *Econometrica*, **58**(6), 1475–1480.

Roth, A. E. and Xing, X. 1994. Jumping the gun: Imperfections and Institutions Related to the Timing of Market Transactions. *American Economic Review*, **84**(4), 992–1044.

Roth, A. E., Sönmez, T., and Ünver, M. U. 2004. Kidney Exchange. *Quarterly Journal of Economics*, **119**(2), 457–488.

Roth, A. E., Sönmez, T., and Ünver, M. U. 2005. Pairwise Kidney Exchange. *Journal of Economic Theory*, **125**, 151–188.

Rothe, J. and Schend, L. 2012. Control Complexity in Bucklin, Fallback, and Plurality Voting: An Experimental Approach. In *Proceedings of the 11th International Symposium on Experimental Algorithms*, 356–368. New York: Springer.

Rothe, J. and Schend, L. 2013. Challenges to Complexity Shields That Are Supposed to Protect Elections against Manipulation and Control: A Survey. *Annals of Mathematics and Artificial Intelligence*, **68**(1–3), 161–193.

Rothe, J., Spakowski, H., and Vogel, J. 2003. Exact Complexity of the Winner Problem for Young Elections. *Theory of Computing Systems*, **36**(4), 375–386.

Rothe, J., Baumeister, D., Lindner, C., and Rothe, I. 2011. *Einführung in Computational Social Choice: Individuelle Strategien und kollektive Entscheidungen beim Spielen, Wählen und Teilen*. Heidelberg, Germany: Spektrum.

Rubinstein, A. and Fishburn, P. C. 1986. Algebraic Aggregation Theory. *Journal of Economic Theory*, **38**(1), 63–77.

Russel, N. 2007. Complexity of Control of Borda Count Elections. MPhil thesis, Rochester Institute of Technology.

Russell, T. 2010. A Computational Study of Problems in Sports. PhD dissertation, University of Waterloo.

Russell, T. and Walsh, T. 2009. Manipulating Tournaments in Cup and Round Robin Competitions. In *Proceedings of the International Conference on Algorithmic Decision Theory* (ADT), 26–37. New York: Springer.

Ryvkin, D. 2010. The Selection Efficiency of Tournaments. *European Journal of Operational Research*, **206**(3), 667–675.

Ryvkin, D. and Ortmann, A. 2008. The Predictive Power of Three Prominent Tournament Formats. *Management Science*, **54**(3), 492–504.

Saad, W., Han, Z., Basar, T., Debbah, M., and Hjorungnes, A. 2011. Hedonic Coalition Formation for Distributed Task Allocation among Wireless Agents. *IEEE Transactions on Mobile Computing*, **10**(9), 1327–1344.

Saari, D. 1995. *Basic Geometry of Voting*. New York: Springer.

Saari, D. 2009. Condorcet Domains: A Geometric Perspective. In *The Mathematics of Preference, Choice, and Order: Essays in Honor of Peter C. Fishburn*, ed. Brams, S. J., Gehrlein, W. V., and Roberts, F. S., 161–182. New York: Springer.

Saari, D. and Merlin, V. R. 2000. A Geometric Examination of Kemeny's Rule. *Social Choice and Welfare*, **17**, 403–438.

Saari, D. and Sieberg, K. 2001. The Sum of the Parts Can Violate the Whole. *American Political Science Review*, **95**(2), 415–433.

Saban, D. and Sethuraman, J. 2013. The Complexity of Computing the Random Priority Allocation Matrix. In *Proceedings of the 9th International Conference on Web and Internet Economics* (WINE), 421. New York: Springer.

Saberi, A. and Wang, Y. 2009. Cutting a Cake for Five People. In *Proceedings of the 5th International Conference on Algorithmic Aspects in Information and Management*, 292–300. New York: Springer.

Sandholm, T. 1998. Agents in Electronic Commerce: Component Technologies for Automated Negotiation and Coalition Formation. In *Cooperative Information Agents*, ed. Klusch, M., 113–134. New York: Springer.

Sandholm, T., Larson, K., Andersson, M., Shehory, O., and Tohmé, F. 1999. Coalition Structure Generation with Worst Case Guarantees. *Artificial Intelligence*, **111**(1–2), 209–238.

Sanver, M. R. 2010. Approval as an Intrinsic Part of Preference. In *Handbook on Approval Voting*, ed. Laslier, J.-F. and Sanver, M. R., 469–481. New York: Springer.

Sanver, M. R. and Zwicker, W. S. 2009. One-Way Monotonicity as a Form of Strategy-Proofness. *International Journal of Game Theory*, **38**, 553–574.

Sanver, M. R. and Zwicker, W. S. 2012. Monotonicity Properties and Their Adaptation to Irresolute Social Choice Rules. *Social Choice and Welfare*, **39**, 371–398.

Sasaki, H. and Toda, M. 1992. Consistency and Characterization of the Core of Two-Sided Matching Problems. *Journal of Economic Theory*, **56**, 218–227.

Sato, S. 2009. Informational Requirements of Social Choice Rules. *Mathematical Social Sciences*, **57**(2), 188–198.

Satterthwaite, M. A. 1975. Strategy Proofness and Arrow's Conditions: Existence and Correspondence Theorems for Voting Procedures and Social Welfare Functions. *Journal of Economic Theory*, **10**, 187–217.

Savage, L. J. 1951. The Theory of Statistical Decision. *Journal of the American Statistical Association*, **46**(253), 55–67.

Scarsini, M. 1998. A Strong Paradox of Multiple Elections. *Social Choice and Welfare*, **15**(2), 237–238.

Schalekamp, F. and van Zuylen, A. 2009. Rank Aggregation: Together We're Strong. In *Proceedings of the 11th Workshop on Algorithm Engineering and Experiments*, 38–51. Philadelphia: SIAM.

Schiex, T., Fargier, H., and Verfaillie, G. 1995. Valued Constraint Satisfaction Problems: Hard and Easy Problems. In *Proceedings of the 14th International Joint Conference on Artificial Intelligence* (IJCAI), 631–637. Palo Alto, CA: AAAI.

Schlotter, I., Faliszewski, P., and Elkind, E. 2011. Campaign Management Under Approval-Driven Voting Rules. In *Proceedings of the 25th AAAI Conference on Artificial Intelligence*, 726–731. Palo Alto, CA: AAAI.

Schmeidler, D. and Vind, K. 1972. Fair Net Trades. *Econometrica*, **40**(4), 637–642.

Schulze, M. 2003. A New Monotonic and Clone-Independent Single-Winner Election Method. *Voting Matters*, **17**, 9–19.

Schulze, M. 2011. A New Monotonic, Clone-Independent, Reversal Symmetric, and Condorcet-Consistent Single-Winner Election Method. *Social Choice and Welfare*, **36**(2), 267–303.

Schwartz, T. 1972. Rationality and the Myth of the Maximum. *Noûs*, **6**(2), 97–117.

Schwartz, T. 1986. *The Logic of Collective Choice*. New York: Columbia University Press.

Schwartz, T. 1990. Cyclic Tournaments and Cooperative Majority Voting: A Solution. *Social Choice and Welfare*, **7**(1), 19–29.

Scott, A. and Fey, M. 2012. The Minimal Covering Set in Large Tournaments. *Social Choice and Welfare*, **38**(1), 1–9.

Scott, S. 2005. A Study of Stable Marriage Problems with Ties. PhD thesis, University of Glasgow.

See, A., Bachrach, Y., and Kohli, P. 2014. The Cost of Principles: Analyzing Power in Compatibility Weighted Voting Games. In *Proceedings of the 13th International Conference on Autonomous Agents and Multiagent Systems* (AAMAS), 37–44. Richland, SC: IFAAMAS.

Seedig, H. G. 2014. Majority Relations and Tournament Solutions: A Computational Study. PhD thesis, Technische Universität München.

Sen, A. K. 1966. A Possibility Theorem on Majority Decisions. *Econometrica*, **34**, 491–499.

Sen, A. K. 1970. *Collective Choice and Social Welfare*. Amsterdam: North-Holland.

Sen, A. K. 1986. Social Choice Theory. In *Handbook of Mathematical Economics*, vol. 3, ed. Arrow, K. J., and Intriligator, M. D., 1073–1181. New York: Elsevier.

Serafini, P. and Simeone, B. 2012. Parametric Maximum Flow Methods for Minimax Approximation of Target Quotas in Biproportional Apportionment. *Networks*, **59**(2), 191–208.

Sertel, M. R. and Sanver, M. R. 2004. Strong Equilibrium Outcomes of Voting Games are the Generalized Condorcet Winners. *Social Choice and Welfare*, **22**(2), 331–347.

Service, T. C. and Adams, J. A. 2012a. Strategyproof Approximations of Distance Rationalizable Voting Rules. In *Proceedings of the 11th International Conference on Autonomous Agents and Multiagent Systems* (AAMAS), 569–576. Richland, SC: IFAAMAS.

Service, T. C. and Adams, J. A. 2012b. Communication Complexity of Approximating Voting Rules. In *Proceedings of the 11th International Conference on Autonomous Agents and Multiagent Systems* (AAMAS), 593–602. Richland, SC: IFAAMAS.

Shapley, L. S. 1953. A Value for *n*-Person Games. In *Contributions to the Theory of Games*, vol. 2, ed. Kuhn, H. W., and Tucker, A. W., 307–317. Princeton, NJ: Princeton University Press.

Shapley, L. S. and Grofman, B. 1984. Optimizing Group Judgmental Accuracy in the Presence of Interdependencies. *Public Choice*, **43**, 329–343.

Shapley, L. S. and Scarf, H. 1974. On Cores and Indivisibility. *Journal of Mathematical Economics*, **1**, 23–37.

Shepard, R. N. 1959. Stimulus and Response Generalization: A Stochastic Model Relating Generalization to Distance in Psychological Space. *Psychometrika*, **22**(4), 325–345.

Shepsle, K. A. and Weingast, B. R. 1984. Uncovered Sets and Sophisticated Outcomes with Implications for Agenda Institutions. *American Journal of Political Science*, **28**(1), 49–74.

Shoham, Y. and Leyton-Brown, K. 2009. *Multiagent Systems: Algorithmic, Game-Theoretic, and Logical Foundations*. New York: Cambridge University Press.

Simjour, N. 2009. Improved Parameterized Algorithms for the Kemeny Aggregation Problem. In *Proceedings of the 4th International Workshop on Parameterized and Exact Computation*, 312–323. New York: Springer.

Simjour, N. 2013. Parameterized Enumeration of Neighbour Strings and Kemeny Aggregations. PhD thesis, University of Waterloo.

Skowron, P., Faliszewski, P., and Slinko, A. 2013a. Achieving Fully Proportional Representation is Easy in Practice. In *Proceedings of the International Conference on Autonomous Agents and Multiagent Systems* (AAMAS), 399–406. Richland, SC: IFAAMAS.

Skowron, P., Yu, L., Faliszewski, P., and Elkind, E. 2013b. The Complexity of Fully Proportional Representation for Single-Crossing Electorates. In *Proceedings of the International Symposium on Algorithmic Game Theory* (SAGT), 1–12. New York: Springer.

Skowron, P., Faliszewski, P., and Slinko, A. 2013c. Fully Proportional Representation as Resource Allocation: Approximability Results. In *Proceedings of the International Joint Conference on Artificial Intelligence* (IJCAI), 353–359. Palo Alto, CA: AAAI.

Skowron, P., Faliszewski, P., and Lang, J. 2015. Finding a Collective Set of Items: From Proportional Multirepresentation to Group Recommendation. In *Proceedings of the AAAI Conference on Artificial Intelligence*, 2131–2137. Palo Alto, CA: AAAI.

Slater, P. 1961. Inconsistencies in a Schedule of Paired Comparisons. *Biometrika*, **48**(3–4), 303–312.

Slinko, A. 2004. How Large Should a Coalition be to Manipulate an Election? *Mathematical Social Sciences*, **47**(3), 289–293.

Slinko, A. and White, S. 2008. Non-Dictatorial Social Choice Rules are Safely Manipulable. In *Proceedings of the 2nd International Workshop on Computational Social Choice* (COMSOC), 403–413.

Smith, J. 1973. Aggregation of Preferences with Variable Electorate. *Econometrica*, **41**(6), 1027–1041.

Smith, R. G. 1980. The Contract Net Protocol: High-Level Communication and Control in a Distributed Problem Solver. *IEEE Transactions on Computers*, **C-29**(12), 1104–1113.

Smith, W. D. 2000. Range Voting. http://scorevoting.net/WarrenSmithPages/homepage/rangevote.pdf.

Sönmez, T. and Ünver, M. U. 2011. Matching, Allocation and Exchange of Discrete Resources. In *Handbook of Social Economics*, vol. 1A, ed. Benhabib, J., Bisin, A., and Jackson, M., 781–852. Amsterdam: North-Holland.

Sotomayor, M. 1999. Three Remarks on the Many-To-Many Stable Matching Problem. *Mathematical Social Sciences*, **38**(1), 55–70.

Sprumont, Y. 1991. The Division Problem with Single-Peaked Preferences: A Characterization of the Uniform Allocation Rule. *Econometrica*, **59**(2), 509–519.

Stanton, I. and Vassilevska Williams, V. 2011. Manipulating Stochastically Generated Single-Elimination Tournaments for Nearly All Players. In *Proceedings of the International Conference on Web and Internet Economics* (WINE), 326–337. New York: Springer.

Stanton, I. and Vassilevska Williams, V. 2013. The Structure, Efficacy, and Manipulation of Double-Elimination Tournaments. *Journal of Quantitative Analysis in Sports*, **9**(4), 319–335.

Stearns, R. 1959. The Voting Problem. *American Mathematical Monthly*, **66**(9), 761–763.

Steinhaus, H. 1948. The Problem of Fair Division. *Econometrica*, **16**(1), 101–104.

van der Straeten, K., Laslier, J.-F., and Blais, A. 2013. Vote au Pluriel: How People Vote when Offered to Vote Under Different Rules. *Political Science and Politics*, **4**(2), 324–328.

Stromquist, W. 2008. Envy-Free Cake Divisions Cannot be Found by Finite Protocols. *Electronic Journal of Combinatorics*, **15**, #R11.

Sui, X., Francois-Nienaber, A., and Boutilier, C. 2013. Multi-Dimensional Single-Peaked Consistency and Its Approximations. In *Proceedings of the 23rd International Joint Conference on Artificial Intelligence* (IJCAI), 375–382. Palo Alto, CA: AAAI.

Sung, S. C. and Dimitrov, D. 2007a. On Core Membership Testing for Hedonic Coalition Formation Games. *Operations Research Letters*, **35**(2), 155–158.

Sung, S. C. and Dimitrov, D. 2007b. On Myopic Stability Concepts for Hedonic Games. *Theory and Decision*, **62**(1), 31–45.

Sung, S. C. and Dimitrov, D. 2010. Computational Complexity in Additive Hedonic Games. *European Journal of Operational Research*, **203**(3), 635–639.

Svensson, L. G. 1999. Strategy-Proof Allocation of Indivisible Goods. *Social Choice and Welfare*, **16**, 557–567.

Takagi, S. and Serizawa, S. 2010. An Impossibility Theorem for Matching Problems. *Social Choice and Welfare*, **35**, 245–266.

Tamura, A. 1993. Transformation from Arbitrary Matchings to Stable Matchings. *Journal of Combinatorial Theory, Series A*, **62**, 310–323.

Tan, J. J. M. and Su, W. C. 1995. On the Divorce Digraph of the Stable Marriage Problem. *Proceedings of the National Science Council, Republic of China, Part A*, **19**(2), 342–354.

Tang, P. and Lin, F. 2009. Computer-Aided Proofs of Arrow's and Other Impossibility Theorems. *Artificial Intelligence*, **173**(11), 1041–1053.

Taylor, A. D. 1995. *Mathematics and Politics*. New York: Springer.

Taylor, A. D. 2005. *Social Choice and the Mathematics of Manipulation*. New York: Cambridge University Press.

Taylor, A. D. and Pacelli, A. M. 2006. *Mathematics and Politics: Strategy, Voting, Power and Proof*. 2nd ed. New York: Springer.

Taylor, A. D. and Zwicker, W. S. 1999. *Simple games: Desirability Relations, Trading, Pseudoweightings*. Princeton, NJ: Princeton University Press.

Tennenholtz, M. 2004. Reputation Systems: An Axiomatic Approach. In *Proceedings of the Conference on Uncertainty in Artificial Intelligence* (UAI), 544–551. New York: Morgan Kaufmann.

Thompson, D. R. M., Lev, O., Leyton-Brown, K., and Rosenschein, J. S. 2013. Empirical Analysis of Plurality Election Equilibria. In *Proceedings of the 12th International Conference on Autonomous Agents and Multiagent Systems* (AAMAS), 391–398. Richland, SC: IFAAMAS.

Thomson, W. 1983. The Fair Division of a Fixed Supply among a Growing Population. *Mathematics of Operations Research*, **8**(3), 319–326.

Thomson, W. 1994a. Consistent Solutions to the Problem of Fair Division when Preferences are Single-Peaked. *Journal of Economic Theory*, **63**(2), 219–245.

Thomson, W. 1994b. Notions of Equal, or Equivalent, Opportunities. *Social Choice and Welfare*, **11**(2), 137–156.

Thomson, W. 1999. Welfare-Domination Under Preference-Replacement: A Survey and Open Questions. *Social Choice and Welfare*, **16**(3), 373–394.

Thomson, W. 2003. Axiomatic and Game-Theoretic Analysis of Bankruptcy and Taxation Problems: A Survey. *Mathematical Social Sciences*, **45**(3), 249–297.

Thomson, W. 2011. Fair Allocation Rules. *Handbook of Social Choice and Welfare*, **2**, 393–506.

Thomson, W. 2012. On the Axiomatics of Resource Allocation: Interpreting the Consistency Principle. *Economics and Philosophy*, **28**(03), 385–421.

Thomson, W. 2014a. Axiomatic and Game-Theoretic Analysis of Bankruptcy and Taxation Problems: A Survey. Technical report, University of Rochester, Center for Economic Research (RCER).

Thomson, W. 2014b. Consistent Allocation Rules. Technical report, University of Rochester-Center for Economic Research (RCER).

Thomson, W. 2014c. Population-Monotonic Allocation Rules. Technical report, University of Rochester, Center for Economic Research (RCER).

Thomson, W. 2014d. The Theory of Fair Allocation. Unpublished manuscript.

Tideman, N. 1987. Independence of Clones as a Criterion for Voting Rules. *Social Choice and Welfare*, **4**(3), 185–206.

Tideman, N. 2006. *Collective Decisions and Voting: The Potential for Public Choice*. Farnham: Ashgate.

Toda, M. 2006. Monotonicity and Consistency in Matching Markets. *International Journal of Game Theory*, **34**, 13–31.

Todo, T., Iwasaki, A., and Yokoo, M. 2011. False-Name-Proof Mechanism Design without Money. In *Proceedings of the 10th International Conference on Autonomous Agents and Multiagent Systems* (AAMAS), 651–658. Richland, SC: IFAAMAS.

Trick, M. A. 1989. Recognizing Single-Peaked Preferences on a Tree. *Mathematical Social Sciences*, **17**(3), 329–334.

Truchon, M. 1998. An Extension of the Concordet Criterion and Kemeny Orders. Cahier 98-15, Centre de Recherche en Économie et Finance Appliquées, Université Laval, Québec, Canada.

Truchon, M. 2008. Borda and the Maximum Likelihood Approach to Vote Aggregation. *Mathematical Social Sciences*, **55**(1), 96–102.

Uckelman, J. 2009. More Than the Sum of Its Parts: Compact Preference Representation Over Combinatorial Domains. PhD thesis, University of Amsterdam.

Uckelman, S. L. and Uckelman, J. 2010. Strategy and Manipulation in Medieval Elections. In *Proceedings of the 3rd International Workshop on Computational Social Choice* (COMSOC), 15–16.

Vassilevska Williams, V. 2009. Fixing a Single-Elimination Tournament. Unpublished manuscript.

Vassilevska Williams, V. 2010. Fixing a Tournament. In *Proceedings of the AAAI Conference on Artificial Intelligence*, 895–900. Palo Alto, CA: AAAI.

Vazirani, V. 2001. *Approximation Algorithms*. New York: Springer.

Vazirani, V. 2007. Combinatorial Algorithms for Market Equilibria. In *Algorithmic Game Theory*, ed. Nisan, N., Roughgarden, T., Tardos, É., and Vazirani, V., Chapter 5. New York: Cambridge University Press.

Vetschera, R. 2010. A General Branch-And-Bound Algorithm for Fair Division Problems. *Computers and Operations Research*, **37**, 189–201.

Vu, T. and Shoham, Y. 2010a. Broadening the Scope of Optimal Seeding Analysis in Knockout Tournaments. Unpublished manuscript.

Vu, T. and Shoham, Y. 2010b. Optimal Seeding in Knockout Tournaments. In *Proceedings of the International Conference on Autonomous Agents and Multiagent Systems* (AAMAS), 1579–1580. Richland, SC: IFAAMAS.

Vu, T., Altman, A., and Shoham, Y. 2009a. On the Complexity of Schedule Control Problems for Knockout Tournaments. In *Proceedings of the International Conference on Autonomous Agents and Multiagent Systems* (AAMAS), 225–232. Richland, SC: IFAAMAS.

Vu, T., Hazon, N., Altman, A., Kraus, S., Shoham, Y., and Wooldridge, M. 2009b. On the Complexity of Schedule Control Problems for Knock-out Tournaments. Working paper.

Vulkan, N., Roth, A. E., and Neeman, Z., eds. 2013. *Handbook of Market Design*. Oxford: Oxford University Press.

Wagner, K. 1987. More Complicated Questions about Maxima and Minima, and Some Closures of NP. *Theoretical Computer Science*, **51**(1–2), 53–80.

Wagner, K. 1990. Bounded Query Classes. *SIAM Journal on Computing*, **19**(5), 833–846.

Wakabayashi, Y. 1986. Aggregation of Binary Relations: Algorithmic and Polyhedral Investigations. PhD thesis, Universität Augsburg.

Wakabayashi, Y. 1998. The Complexity of Computing Medians of Relations. *Resenhas*, **3**(3), 323–349.

Walsh, T. 2007. Uncertainty in Preference Elicitation and Aggregation. In *Proceedings of the AAAI Conference on Artificial Intelligence*, 3–8. Palo Alto, CA: AAAI.

Walsh, T. 2008. Complexity of Terminating Preference Elicitation. In *Proceedings of the 7th International Conference on Autonomous Agents and Multiagent Systems* (AAMAS), 967–974. Richland, SC: IFAAMAS.

Walsh, T. 2009. Where are the Really Hard Manipulation Problems? The Phase Transition in Manipulating the Veto Rule. In *Proceedings of the 21st International Joint Conference on Artificial Intelligence* (IJCAI), 324–329. Palo Alto, CA: AAAI.

Walsh, T. 2010. An Empirical Study of the Manipulability of Single Transferable Voting. In *Proceedings of the 19th European Conference on Artificial Intelligence* (ECAI), 257–262. Amsterdam: IOS Press.

Walsh, T. 2011a. Is Computational Complexity a Barrier to Manipulation? *Annals of Mathematics and Artificial Intelligence*, **62**(1–2), 7–26.

Walsh, T. 2011b. Where are the Hard Manipulation Problems? *Journal of Artificial Intelligence Research (JAIR)*, **42**, 1–39.

Walsh, T. and Xia, L. 2012. Lot-Based Voting Rules. In *Proceedings of the 12th International Conference on Autonomous Agents and Multiagent Systems* (AAMAS), 603–610. Richland, SC: IFAAMAS.

Wilson, N. 2004. Extending CP-Nets with Stronger Conditional Preference Statements. In *Proceedings of the 19th AAAI Conference on Artificial Intelligence*, 735–741. Palo Alto, CA: AAAI.

Wilson, R. 1975. On the Theory of Aggregation. *Journal of Economic Theory*, **10**(1), 89–99.

Woeginger, G. J. 2013. Core Stability in Hedonic Coalition Formation. In *Proceedings of the 39th International Conference on Current Trends in Theory and Practice of Computer Science*, 33–50. New York: Springer.

Woeginger, G. J. 2003. Banks Winners in Tournaments Are Difficult to Recognize. *Social Choice and Welfare*, **20**, 523–528.

Woeginger, G. J. and Sgall, J. 2007. On the Complexity of Cake Cutting. *Discrete Optimization*, **4**, 213–220.

Wojtas, K. and Faliszewski, P. 2012. Possible Winners in Noisy Elections. In *Proceedings of the 26th AAAI Conference on Artificial Intelligence*, 1499–1505. Palo Alto, CA: AAAI.

Wooldridge, M. 2009. *Multiagent Systems*. 2nd ed. New York: John Wiley.

Xia, L. 2012a. Computing the Margin of Victory for Various Voting Rules. In *Proceedings of the 13th ACM Conference on Electronic Commerce* (EC), 982–999. New York: ACM Press.

Xia, L. 2012b. How Many Vote Operations Are Needed to Manipulate a Voting System? In *Proceedings of the 4th International Workshop on Computational Social Choice* (COMSOC), 443–454.

Xia, L. 2013. Generalized Scoring Rules: A Framework that Reconciles Borda and Condorcet. *SIGecom Exchanges*, **12**, 42–48.

Xia, L. 2014a. Deciphering Young's Interpretation of Condorcet's Model. Unpublished manuscript.

Xia, L. 2014b. Statistical Properties of Social Choice Mechanisms. In *Proceedings of the 5th International Workshop on Computational Social Choice* (COMSOC).

Xia, L. and Conitzer, V. 2008a. Generalized Scoring Rules and the Frequency of Coalitional Manipulability. In *Proceedings of the ACM Conference on Electronic Commerce* (EC), 109–118. New York: ACM.

Xia, L. and Conitzer, V. 2008b. A Sufficient Condition for Voting Rules to be Frequently Manipulable. In *Proceedings of the 9th ACM Conference on Electronic Commerce* (EC), 99–108. New York: ACM.

Xia, L. and Conitzer, V. 2009. Finite Local Consistency Characterizes Generalized Scoring Rules. In *Proceedings of the 21st International Joint Conference on Artificial Intelligence* (IJCAI), 336–341. Palo Alto, CA: AAAI.

Xia, L. and Conitzer, V. 2010a. Strategy-Proof Voting Rules Over Multi-Issue Domains with Restricted Preferences. In *Proceedings of the International Conference on Web and Internet Economics* (WINE), 402–414. New York: Springer.

Xia, L. and Conitzer, V. 2010b. Compilation Complexity of Common Voting Rules. In *Proceedings of the AAAI Conference on Artificial Intelligence*, 915–920. Palo Alto, CA: AAAI.

Xia, L. and Conitzer, V. 2010c. Stackelberg Voting Games: Computational Aspects and Paradoxes. In *Proceedings of the AAAI Conference on Artificial Intelligence*, 921–926. Palo Alto, CA: AAAI.

Xia, L. and Conitzer, V. 2011a. Determining Possible and Necessary Winners Given Partial Orders. *Journal of Artificial Intelligence Research (JAIR)*, **41**, 25–67.

Xia, L. and Conitzer, V. 2011b. A Maximum Likelihood Approach Towards Aggregating Partial Orders. In *Proceedings of the International Joint Conference on Artificial Intelligence* (IJCAI), 446–451. Palo Alto, CA: AAAI.

Xia, L. and Lang, J. 2009. A Dichotomy Theorem on the Existence of Efficient or Neutral Sequential Voting Correspondences. In *Proceedings of the International Joint Conference on Artificial Intelligence* (IJCAI), 342–347. Palo Alto, CA: AAAI.

Xia, L., Conitzer, V., and Lang, J. 2008. Voting on Multiattribute Domains with Cyclic Preferential Dependencies. In *Proceedings of the AAAI Conference on Artificial Intelligence*, 202–207. Palo Alto, CA: AAAI.

Xia, L., Zuckerman, M., Procaccia, A. D., Conitzer, V., and Rosenschein, J. S. 2009. Complexity of Unweighted Coalitional Manipulation Under Some Common Voting Rules. In *Proceedings of the 21st International Joint Conference on Artificial Intelligence* (IJCAI), 348–353. Palo Alto, CA: AAAI.

Xia, L., Conitzer, V., and Lang, J. 2010a. Aggregating Preferences in Multi-Issue Domains by Using Maximum Likelihood Estimators. In *Proceedings of the International Conference on Autonomous Agents and Multiagent Systems* (AAMAS), 399–408. Richland, SC: IFAAMAS.

Xia, L., Conitzer, V., and Procaccia, A. D. 2010b. A Scheduling Approach to Coalitional Manipulation. In *Proceedings of the 11th ACM Conference on Electronic Commerce* (EC), 275–284. New York: ACM.

Xia, L., Conitzer, V., and Lang, J. 2011a. Strategic Sequential Voting in Multi-Issue Domains and Multiple-Election Paradoxes. In *Proceedings of the ACM Conference on Electronic Commerce* (EC), 179–188. New York: ACM.

Xia, L., Lang, J., and Monnot, J. 2011b. Possible Winners when New Alternatives Join: New Results Coming Up! In *Proceedings of the 10th International Conference on Autonomous Agents and Multiagent Systems* (AAMAS), 829–836. Richland, SC: IFAAMAS.

Yager, R. R. 1988. On Ordered Weighted Averaging Aggregation Operators in Multicriteria Decision Making. *IEEE Transactions on Systems, Man, and Cybernetics*, **18**, 183–190.

Yannakakis, M. 2008. Equilibria, Fixed Points, and Complexity Classes. In *Proceedings of the 25th International Symposium on Theoretical Aspects of Computer Science* (STACS), 19–38. New York: Springer.

Yao, A. C.-C. 1979. Some Complexity Questions Related to Distributive Computing (Preliminary Report). In *Proceedings of the 11th ACM Symposium on Theory of Computing* (STOC), 209–213. New York: ACM.

Yokoo, M., Sakurai, Y., and Matsubara, S. 2004. The Effect of False-Name Bids in Combinatorial Auctions: New Fraud in Internet Auctions. *Games and Economic Behavior*, **46**(1), 174–188.

Young, H. P. 1975. Social Choice Scoring Functions. *SIAM Journal on Applied Mathematics*, **28**(4), 824–838.

Young, H. P. 1977. Extending Condorcet's Rule. *Journal of Economic Theory*, **16**(2), 335–353.

Young, H. P. 1987. On Dividing an Amount According to Individual Claims or Liabilities. *Mathematics of Operations Research*, **12**(3), 398–414.

Young, H. P. 1988. Condorcet's Theory of Voting. *American Political Science Review*, **82**(4), 1231–1244.

Young, H. P. 1995a. Optimal Voting Rules. *Journal of Economic Perspectives*, **9**(1), 51–64.

Young, H. P. 1995b. *Equity: in theory and practice*. Princeton, NJ: Princeton University Press.

Young, H. P. 1998. *Individual Strategy and Social Structure: An Evolutionary Theory of Institutions*. Princeton, NJ: Princeton University Press.

Young, H. P. and Levenglick, A. 1978. A Consistent Extension of Condorcet's Election Principle. *SIAM Journal on Applied Mathematics*, **35**(2), 285–300.

Yu, L., Chan, H., and Elkind, E. 2013. Multiwinner Elections Under Preferences That Are Single-Peaked on a Tree. In *Proceedings of the International Joint Conference on Artificial Intelligence* (IJCAI), 425–431. Palo Alto, CA: AAAI.

Zavist, T. M. and Tideman, T. N. 1989. Complete Independence of Clones in the Ranked Pairs Rule. *Social Choice and Welfare*, **6**(2), 167–173.

Zhou, L. 1990. On a Conjecture by Gale About One-Sided Matching Problems. *Journal of Economic Theory*, **52**(1), 123–135.

Zhu, M. 2014. College Admissions in China: A Mechanism Design Perspective. *China Economic Review*, **30**, 618–631.

Zick, Y., Skopalik, A., and Elkind, E. 2011. The Shapley Value as a Function of the Quota in Weighted Voting Games. In *Proceedings of the 21st International Joint Conference on Artificial Intelligence* (IJCAI), 490–496. Palo Alto, CA: AAAI.

Zivan, R. 2011. Can Trust Increase the Efficiency of Cake Cutting Algorithms? In *Proceedings of the 10th International Conference on Autonomous Agents and Multiagent Systems* (AAMAS), 1145–1146. Richland, SC: IFAAMAS.

Zuckerman, M., Faliszewski, P., Bachrach, Y., and Elkind, E. 2008. Manipulating the Quota in Weighted Voting Games. In *Proceedings of the 23rd AAAI Conference on Artificial Intelligence*, 215–220. Palo Alto, CA: AAAI.

Zuckerman, M., Procaccia, A. D., and Rosenschein, J. S. 2009. Algorithms for the Coalitional Manipulation Problem. *Artificial Intelligence*, **173**(2), 392–412.

Zuckerman, M., Faliszewski, P., Conitzer, V., and Rosenschein, J. S. 2011. An NTU Cooperative Game Theoretic View of Manipulating Elections. In *Proceedings of the 7th International Conference on Web and Internet Economics* (WINE), 363–374. New York: Springer.

van Zuylen, A. and Williamson, D. P. 2009. Deterministic Pivoting Algorithms for Constrained Ranking and Clustering Problems. *Mathematics of Operations Research*, **34**, 594–620.

Zwicker, W. S. 1991. The Voters' Paradox, Spin, and the Borda Count. *Mathematical Social Sciences*, **22**, 187–227.

Zwicker, W. S. 2008. Consistency without Neutrality in Voting Rules: When is a Vote an Average? *Mathematical and Computer Modelling*, **48**, 1357–1373.

Index

solidarity, 273
sophisticated voting, 79
SP-AV, *see* approval voting, sincere-strategy
    preference-based
split proof reward mechanism, 448
Splitting Lemma, 6
stability, 279, 355
stability of a tournament solution, 61
Stable Marriage problem (SM), 337
Stable Marriage problem with Incomplete lists (SMI),
    337
standard seeding, 472
strategic sequential voting, 220
strategyproofness, 127, 355
    Fishburn-strategyproofness, 77
    Kelly-strategyproofness, 77
    of tournament solutions, 76
strict core, 360
strict strong Nash stability (SSNS), 360
strong individual stability (SIS), 360
strong superset property, 61
StrongYoung voting rule, 105
StrongYoung winner problem, 112
STV, *see* single transferable vote
subtournament, 59
summary of a tournament, 60
Summing Contributions property, 445
superking, 466, 471
Superseed Algorithm, 466
Support-Bribery, 166
Swap-Bribery, 161, 164
SWF, *see* social welfare function
sybil attacks, 446
    local split, 447
    split, 446
systematicity, 405

Θ_2^p, 107, 112, 125
TE, *see* ties eliminate
tentative acceptance rule, 270
Tideman's voting rule, 123
ties eliminate, 155
ties promote, 155
Top Covering Algorithm, 370
top cycle, 36, 71, 455, 457
top responsive preferences, 367
Top Trading Cycles (TTC) algorithm, 348, 349
top-k voting (query), 243
totally blocked agenda, 417
tournament, 28, 59
tournament equilibrium set, 74
tournament fixing problem, 463, 464
tournament graph, 456
tournament solution, 60
TP, *see* ties promote
trade robustness, 391
transferable utility cooperative game, 358
trivial tournament solution, 62
trust based recommendations, 435
trust systems, 452
truth-biased voters, 143

ultrafilter, 415
unanimity
    in judgment aggregation, 404
unavailable candidate model, 245
uncovered set, 67, 464
    of a weighted tournament, 102
undercut procedure, 306
uniform quota rule, 408
uniform rule, 270
unique-winner model, 112, 160
upper bound on welfare, 271
utilitarian optimality, 295
utility function, cardinal, 250

value density function, 312
    piecewise constant, 312
    piecewise uniform, 312
variable electorate, 29
vector weighted voting games, 393
veto, 147, 163
veto player, 383
voter weight vs. voter power, 388
voting equilibrium, 256
voting network, 435
voting protocol, 236
voting rule, 147
    Borda, voting rule (Borda count), 191, 192
    Condorcet-consistent, 148
    continuity, 152
    distance rationalizable, 178
    immune to a control type, 151
    Kemeny's voting rule, 186, 192
    resistant to a control type, 152
    susceptible to a control type, 151
    Tideman's voting rule, 191
    vulnerable to a control type, 152
voting situation, 27
voting tree, 454, 472, 473

weak composition-consistency, 62
weak Condorcet winner, 103
weak tournament, 81
WeakDodgson voting rule, 104
WeakDodgson winner problem, 112
weight, 378
    total weight of a coalition, 379
weight vs. power, *see* voter weight vs. voter power
weighted tournament, 28, 85
weighted voting games, 377, 379
Weighted-Bribery, 161, 163, 164
Weighted-$Bribery, 161
Weighted-Manipulation, 164
welfare dominance under preference replacement,
    275
winning coalition, 405
worst-case vs. typical-case hardness, 139

yes/no voting systems, 378, 390
Young score, 104
Young winner problem, 112
Young's voting rule, 103, 104